THE ENCYCLOPEDIA
OF THE
ARAB-ISRAELI
CONFLICT

A Political, Social, and Military History

THE ENCYCLOPEDIA
OF THE
ARAB-ISRAELI
CONFLICT

A Political, Social, and Military History

VOLUME II: G-O

Dr. Spencer C. Tucker
Volume Editor

Dr. Priscilla Roberts
Editor, Documents Volume

Dr. Paul G. Pierpaoli Jr.
Associate Editor

Major General David Zabecki, USAR (retired)
Dr. Sherifa Zuhur
Assistant Editors

FOREWORD BY
General Anthony C. Zinni, USMC (retired)

A B C · C L I O

Santa Barbara, California   Denver, Colorado   Oxford, England

Cataloging-in-Publication Data is on file with the Library of Congress

ISBN 978-1-85109-841-5 (hard copy : alk. paper) — ISBN 978-1-85109-842-2 (ebook)

10 09 08 07 06 05   10 9 8 7 6 5 4 3 2 1

This book is also available on the World Wide Web as an ebook.
Visit abc-clio.com for details.

ABC-CLIO, Inc.
130 Cremona Drive, P.O. Box 1911
Santa Barbara, California 93116–1911

This book is printed on acid-free paper ∞ .
Manufactured in the United States of America

Contents

List of Entries

List of Maps

General Maps

MIDDLE EAST, 1920

Black Sea

30°E 40°E 50°E 40°N

☆ Constantinople

Ankara ☆ Erzerum Baku

TURKEY ARMENIA *Caspian Sea* **SOVIET UNION**

1918–20 Ashkhabad

Rhodes S.A. *Lake Urmia*

Cyprus Mosul Tehran ☆

Mediterranean Sea Beirut ☆ **SYRIA** *Russian Sphere of Influence 1907–21*

Haifa ● Damascus Baghdad ☆ **PERSIA**

PALESTINE

Jerusalem ☆ I R A Q

Alexandria ● **TRANS-** Basra 30°N

Cairo ☆ **JORDAN** **KUWAIT** Shiraz ●

EGYPT Neutral Zone Neutral Zone 1920

1922 Kingdom **BAHRAIN**

HEJAZ **QATAR** *Gulf of Oman*

1916 Kingdom, 1925–26 To Nejd **NEJD** Muscat ●

Aswan ● *1916 Emirate* **OMAN**

Medina ● Riyadh ●

Mecca ● **HEJAZ AND NEJD** 20°N

ANGLO-EGYPTIAN SUDAN *Red Sea* **ASIR** *Arabian Sea*

Khartoum ●

ERITREA **YEMEN** **HADHRAMAUT**

1919 Kingdom **ADEN PROT** *Socotra*

Gondar ● Aden ● 10°N

ABYSSINIA Djibouti ● *Gulf of Aden*

FRENCH SOMALILAND **BRITISH SOMALILAND** **ITALIAN SOMALILAND** *INDIAN OCEAN*

Nile R.

Blue Nile *White Nile*

Legend:

British possessions

Independent Arabian states under British protection

French possessions

Italian possessions

— — Boundary after Treaty of Sèvres, 1920

—— Boundary after Treaty of Lausanne, 1923

S.A. Sanjak of Alexandretta, 1920 Autonomous within French Mandate for Syria, 1938–1939 Independent Republic of Hatay

Territories placed by League of Nations under mandates in 1920

British mandate

French mandate

1858 Date of acquisition

1922 Date or period of autonomy

1919 Date of independence

0 150 300 mi

0 150 300 km

MIDDLE EAST, 1945 – 1990

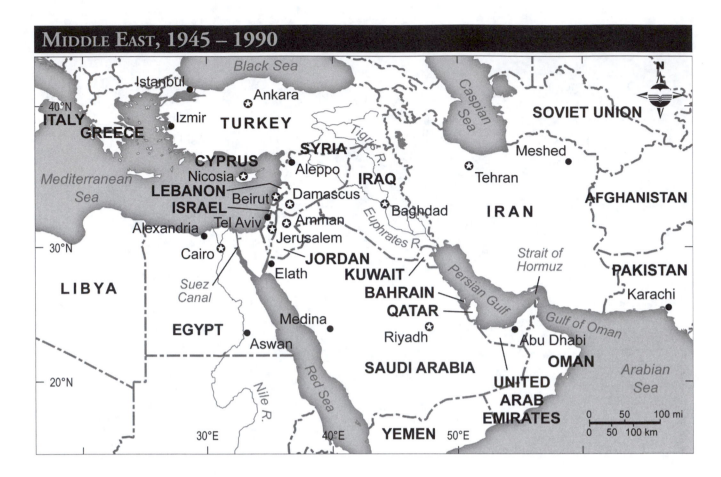

EUROPE, 1945 – 1990

ALLIANCES IN THE MIDDLE EAST, 1945 – 1990

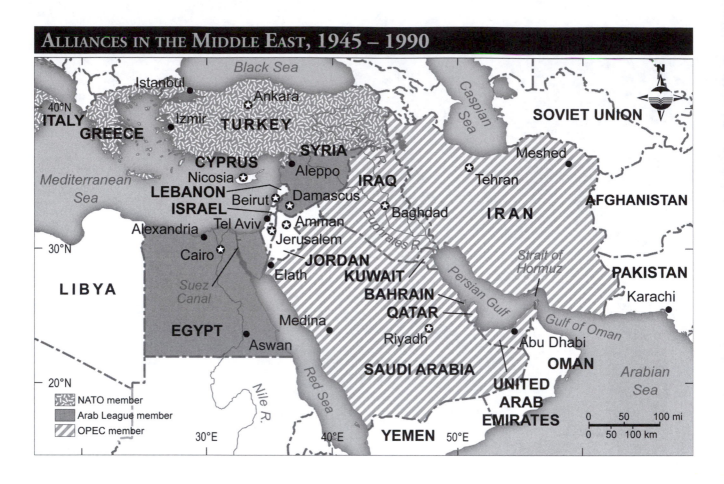

Legend:
- NATO member
- Arab League member
- OPEC member

Labels on map:

Black Sea, Istanbul, Ankara, Izmir, TURKEY, ITALY, GREECE, 40°N, CYPRUS, Nicosia, Mediterranean Sea, SYRIA, Aleppo, LEBANON, Beirut, Damascus, IRAQ, ISRAEL, Tel Aviv, Amman, Jerusalem, Alexandria, 30°N, Cairo, JORDAN, Elath, Suez Canal, LIBYA, EGYPT, Medina, Aswan, Nile R., Red Sea, 20°N, 30°E, 40°E, YEMEN, 50°E, Baghdad, Euphrates R., Caspian Sea, Meshed, Tehran, IRAN, SOVIET UNION, AFGHANISTAN, PAKISTAN, Karachi, Strait of Hormuz, Persian Gulf, Gulf of Oman, KUWAIT, BAHRAIN, QATAR, Riyadh, Abu Dhabi, SAUDI ARABIA, UNITED ARAB EMIRATES, OMAN, Arabian Sea

Scale: 0   50   100 mi / 0   50   100 km

G

Galilee

Region of northern Israel. Galilee has been traditionally subdivided into three geographic areas: Upper Galilee, Lower Galilee, and Western Galilee. Galilee encompasses more than one-third of present-day Israel's entire landmass. Upper Galilee runs from the Beit HaKerem Valley in the south to the Lebanese border in the north and borders the Sea of Galilee. Lower Galilee runs from Mount Carmel and the Gilboa Ridge in the south to the Beit HaKerem Valley in the north, and its eastern border is Jordan. Western Galilee covers the area from just north of Haifa to Rosh HaNikra. The region's principal towns include Nazareth, Tiberias, Akko, Nahariya, Karmel, and Safed. Although not technically part of Galilee, Haifa, on the Mediterranean coast, is the major commercial center for much of the region.

Galilee has a varied climate and an abundance of different geographical features. Mountain ranges traverse sections of it, and Mount Tabor and Mount Meron (3,950 feet high) are among them. In addition to mountains are valleys, streams, rivers, and plains. In the north, where rainfall is plentiful and the temperatures moderate, are expanses of green fields and indigenous flowers. Galilee is also home to a diverse range of fauna. The area's largest industries are agriculture and tourism.

Galilee has been inhabited for several thousand years. It is mentioned repeatedly in the Old Testament, and Jews inhabited the land for many years prior to the Diaspora. In the New Testament, Galilee takes center stage as the primary area of Jesus Christ's ministry. The area and places within it are frequently referenced in the New Testament. Nazareth and Capernaum—both in Galilee—were areas in which Jesus spent much time. Among other miracles, Jesus is said to have healed a blind man in Galilee.

After the Diaspora the region was ruled successively by large powers, some with few prior connections to the area. For almost 500 years, Galilee was controlled by the vast Ottoman Empire, whose power base was in Constantinople (present-day Istanbul). As the Ottoman Empire slowly imploded in the early years of the 20th century, the population of Galilee was made up chiefly of Arabs and Druze, with a small population of Jews. As Jewish immigration to the area accelerated, the Jewish population in Galilee swelled considerably. Israel took control of Galilee during the 1948–1949 Israeli War of Independence, and while many Palestinian Arabs fled, a relatively large number remained in Galilee.

Since 1948, Upper Galilee has been the scene of many Israeli military conflicts either with Syria, the Palestine Liberation Organization (PLO) operating in Lebanon, or Jordan. In the late 1990s, the militant group Hezbollah, based in Lebanon, launched frequent Katyusha rockets into Israeli towns in Upper Galilee. Since then, the area has seen numerous military confrontations. During the Israeli-Hezbollah war in the summer of 2006 and during Israeli operations against Lebanon, Hezbollah guerrillas launched a flurry of longer-ranged Katyusha rockets that hit targets throughout Galilee.

Galilee is unlike other parts of Israel in that it has a large Arab population. This is largely because many Palestinian Arabs chose to stay after the founding of Israel. And despite the best efforts of the Israeli government and the Jewish Agency before it, not many Jews have chosen to settle in Galilee. Roughly half of Galilee's population is Jewish, while the remainder includes Arabs, Christians, and Druze.

PAUL G. PIERPAOLI JR.

See also

Hezbollah; Israel; Katyusha Rocket; Lebanon; Lebanon, Israeli Operations against

The Sea of Galilee, also known as Lake Kinneret. (Corel)

References

Garfinkle, Adam A. *Politics and Society in Modern Israel.* Armonk, NY: M. E. Sharpe, 1997.

Horsley, Richard A. *Archaeology, History, and Society in Galilee.* New York: Continuum International Publishing Group, 1996.

Galilee, Sea of

See Lake Kinneret

Galut Nationalism

Galut nationalism, or Diaspora nationalism, is the idea that all Jewish individuals in the world, regardless of location, comprise a single, widely dispersed nation. *Galut* means "exile" or "exiled" in Hebrew and is a reference to the original dispersion of the Jewish population beginning in 70 CE, when Jerusalem fell under Roman rule. As Jewish populations spread throughout the world, they were always a minority within larger states and, in part for this reason, faced persecution at the hands of the majority. Many Jewish populations chose to assimilate into national populations, although some struggled to remain autonomous. Proponents of Galut nationalism argue that the Jewish Diaspora has maintained a unique identity through religious beliefs and cultural practices that set Jewish populations apart from the broader society.

By the mid-19th century, most Jewish populations in Central and Western Europe as well as the United States had rejected the idea of an overarching Jewish culture. They identified themselves as citizens of their home nations first, and as Jews second. However, in Eastern Europe the idea that Jewish people comprised a single, identifiable population remained strong. As Zionism became increasingly common, the notion of a Jewish national homeland drew particular interest from East European Jews, especially those who were nonreligious or even antireligious.

Chaim Zhitovsky and Simon Dubnow first propounded the idea of Galut nationalism. They argued that because all worldwide Jews constituted a national identity, they should be recognized as a separate nationality within their states of residence. Zhitovsky and Dubnow were not overtly religious, although neither was hostile to organized religion. Both defined Judaism as a cultural and biological phenomenon rather than a system of beliefs. As such, Zhitovsky argued that it was possible to be a Christian by faith and a Jew by nationality. Zhitovsky and Dubnow also believed that Jews, as a separate nation, deserved autonomy within their home countries.

In Eastern Europe, a sizable portion of the Jewish population argued that Jews should strive to assimilate completely into the national culture of their home countries rather than define themselves as different. They pointed to the Jewish populations of Western Europe, which had for the most part fully assimilated and had received the full rights of citizenship within their home countries. In contrast, East European Jews continued to struggle for equal rights.

Despite their assimilation, Western Jews demonstrated a certain degree of global solidarity by assisting the Jews of Eastern Europe. Groups such as the American Jewish Congress provided funding and advice to Jewish rights groups that sought identification as a national minority within the nations of Eastern Europe. Thus, to a certain extent the practitioners of Galut nationalism were those Jewish populations that had most closely integrated into larger national populations and rejected the ideology of the Jewish Diaspora.

PAUL J. SPRINGER

See also

Diaspora; Dubnow, Simon Meyervich; Zionism

References

Edelheit, Hershel, and Abraham J. Edelheit. *Israel and the Jewish World, 1948–1993: A Chronology.* Westport, CT: Greenwood, 1995.

Finkelstein, Norman G. *Image and Reality of the Israel-Palestine Conflict.* New York: Norton, 2003.

Patai, Raphael. *The Jewish Mind.* New York: Scribner, 1977.

Gamaat Islamiya

Gamaat Islamiya (al-Gamaa al-Islamiyya) is a loosely knit set of highly militant groups based in Egypt. The name was first used to describe a variety of student groups and other militant formations. The militant Gamaat should be distinguished from al-Jihad al-Islami (Egyptian Islamic Jihad), although the groups' ideologies are similar in that they oppose Israel's policies and support armed struggle for Palestine. Within an umbrella of organizations, the Gamaat Islamiya began to be described as a singular and cohesive group by outsiders.

Formed in the late 1970s, the Gamaat Islamiya is most noted for its involvement in the November 1990 assassination in New York of militant Zionist leader Rabbi Meir Kahane and the February 1993 bombing of New York's World Trade Center. Members of one group within the organization also claimed responsibility for the 1997 massacre of 58 foreign tourists in the southern Egyptian town of Luxor. The group's several hundred followers both in Egypt and in the United States desire the overthrow of the moderate Egyptian government in favor of a purely Islamic regime.

The Gamaat's adherents come from southern Egypt, Cairo, and the Nile Delta. Southern villages, including Assiut and Minya, became strongholds because of the vendetta system of family rivalries. The Gamaat is believed to be responsible for three attempts on the life of President Hosni Mubarak, including one aborted assassination attempt during one of his visits to the United Nations (UN) in 1993 and a highly organized ambush in Ethiopia in June 1995.

The Egyptian government holds the organization accountable for several fatal attacks on security forces, government officials, and tourists since 1992 and has executed several of its members after summary military trials. In February 1994, militants believed to belong to the Gamaat issued a public statement warning the 35,000 Americans and Europeans living and working in Egypt to leave the country or face injury or death. In early April 1994, police killed the leader of the group's military wing, Talat Yasin Hammam, and six other militants in a raid on an apartment in an eastern Cairo suburb. Egypt's most wanted Islamic militant, Hammam had received a death sentence in absentia in 1992 on charges of belonging to an illegal organization and attempting to overthrow the government.

The Gamaat's spiritual leader, Sheikh Omar Abdel-Rahman, fled Egypt in 1990 and legally entered the United States with a visa specifying him as a religious worker settling in New York. In late April 1994, a Cairo security court sentenced him in absentia to a seven-year prison term on charges of inciting riots and planning a failed assassination of two police officers in 1989. Abdel-Rahman's marriage to an American Muslim convert enabled him to avoid U.S. deportation despite Egypt's calls for his extradition and his status as a prominent figure on an official U.S. terrorist list. He was convicted in the United States in 1996 for his involvement in the 1993 World Trade Center bombing and sentenced to life in prison.

Egyptian security forces scored a number of notable successes in their fight against the organization in late 1994 and early 1995. In October 1994, security forces killed the group's regional commando leader, Atif abd al-Ghaffar Shahin, during a skirmish in the Nile River town of Mallawī. Shortly thereafter, the overall leader of the organization, Hassan abd al-Jalil, was also hunted down and killed. In January 1995, police shot al-Jalil's successor, Mohammad Sayyid Salim, in the southern city of Sohag and arrested some 40 members of the Gamaat, including a regional commander.

In November 1997 Gamaat militants opened fire on tourists visiting the popular Temple of Hatshepsut in Luxor, killing more than 60 people, including 58 foreigners. Several days later, members of the Gamaat faxed a statement to a foreign news agency claiming responsibility for the attack, saying that it was carried out in order to put pressure on the United States to release Abdel-Rahman. Subsequently, however, the Gamaat leaders as well as the main group of Jihad Islami announced a unilateral cease-fire and blamed the Luxor attack on an internal faction opposed to the renunciation of violence. The cease-fire went into effect in 1999, and some militants wrote of their misuse of violent tactics.

The Luxor massacre was the last large-scale terrorist attack aimed at Westerners in Egypt, although a violent attack in Kosheh in 2000 left 20 Copts (Christians) and a single Muslim dead, and in September 2003 Egyptian police arrested a group of 23 militants, including 19 Egyptians, who intended to join the resistance to the U.S. presence in Iraq. In 2004, bomb attacks on the Sinai Peninsula killed at least 33 people. The Gamaat denounced the attacks, calling them "unlawful under Islam" because they resulted in the deaths of Muslims, including women and children. However, the Gamaat remains divided, with one faction seeking to uphold the cease-fire and the other unofficial faction advocating a return to violent attacks. The latter is led by Rifa Taha Musa, a signer of Osama bin Laden's February 1998 fatwa (religious decree) ordering attacks against U.S. civilians and also the author of a book that justifies acts of terrorism that cause mass civilian casualties. The Gamaat's current strength is unknown, as is the number of members who are sympathetic to the cause of violent jihad.

SPENCER C. TUCKER

See also

Abdel-Rahman, Omar; Egypt; Kahane, Meir David; Mubarak, Hosni; Sadat, Anwar

References

Beattie, Kirk J. *Egypt during the Sadat Years.* New York: Palgrave, 2000.
Kepel, Giles. *Jihad: The Rise and Fall of Islamic Extremism.* London: Tauris, 2002.

Ganzouri, Kamal al-
Born: January 12, 1933

Egyptian economic planner, deputy prime minister, and prime minister (1996–1999). Kamal al-Ganzouri (known in Egypt as al-Ganzuri) was born in Minuf in 1933. He pursued his higher education first at Cairo University. Later he earned a doctorate in economics at Michigan State University in the United States. He taught at the Institute of National Planning and then served as an adviser to the Saudi government. In 1974 he returned to Egypt to serve as assistant minister for regional planning. He became the governor of New Valley and then Bani Suif in 1976.

Having established himself as a capable administrator, al-Ganzouri was appointed undersecretary of the Planning Ministry in 1975. In that capacity he served for a time as a planning and development consultant to the United Nations (UN). In 1982 he was appointed planning minister, a position he held until rising to the post of deputy prime minister in 1985, serving in the cabinet of Prime Minister Atif Sidqi.

On January 2, 1996, President Hosni Mubarak appointed al-Ganzouri to replace Sidqi in an apparent effort to calm public unrest over the National Democratic Party's allegedly fraudulent victory in the previous month's second-round legislative election. Al-Ganzouri's appointment as prime minister and his establishment of a new government were intended to revamp Egypt's image among its Arab neighbors and in the West, although this certainly failed. Al-Ganzouri proved more progressive than his predecessor, appointing a woman to the post of economy and foreign trade minister but prudently leaving the interior, defense, and foreign affairs portfolios untouched. He pursued policies of economic reform and liberalization: reducing tariffs, streamlining the Egyptian bureaucracy, and introducing legislation to encourage domestic and foreign investment in Egypt. His Partnership for Economic Growth and Development called for aggressive private-sector development following years of protectionism.

Kamal al-Ganzouri, prime minister of Egypt (1996–1999), prepares to meet his Israeli counterpart Ehud Barak at the Alexandria airport, July 9, 1999. (Mona Sharaf/Reuters)

Al-Ganzouri faced his first and perhaps most high-profile challenge in March 1996 when three Saudi Arabians hijacked a Libya-bound Egyptian airliner and held 152 passengers and crew hostage during a brief stopover in Luxor, Egypt. Libyan leader Muammar Qaddafi unexpectedly came to Egypt's assistance and persuaded the hijackers to release the passengers unharmed in Martubah, Libya.

Immediately after he was sworn in to serve a fourth six-year term as president in October 1999, Mubarak named Privatization Minister Atif Ubayd to replace al-Ganzouri as the country's new prime minister.

SPENCER C. TUCKER

See also

Egypt; Mubarak, Hosni; Sidqi, Atif

References

Kassem, Maye. *Egyptian Politics: The Dynamics of Authoritarian Rule.* Boulder, CO: Lynne Rienner, 2004.
Solecki, John. *Hosni Mubarak.* New York: Chelsea House, 1991.

García Granados, Jorgé
Born: 1900
Died: May 3, 1961

Guatemalan ambassador to the United Nations (UN) in 1947 when the British relinquished their mandate over Palestine and a sup-

Jorgé García Granados (left), Guatemalan ambassador to the United Nations (UN) and Zionist supporter, meeting with Israeli president Yitzhak Ben-Zvi in Jerusalem, July 11, 1955. (Israeli Government Press Office)

porter of the Zionist cause. Jorgé García Granados was born sometime in 1900 in Guatemala into a politically prominent, Liberal elite family. He studied law in Guatemala and supported the overthrow of dictator Manuel Estrada Cabrera in 1920.

From 1934 to 1944 García Granados lived with his family in exile in Mexico during the Jorgé Ubico dictatorship. García Granados participated in the 1944 October Revolution that ousted Ubico and was president of the Constitutional Convention in 1945 that brought democratically elected Juan José Arévalo to power. Arévalo first appointed García Granados to the ambassadorship to the United States and then chose him to be Guatemalan ambassador to the UN.

On May 13, 1947, García Granados was appointed to serve as his country's delegate on the UN Special Committee for Palestine (UNSCOP). Other members of the committee included Emil Sandstrom (Sweden), Enrique Rodriguez Fabregat (Uruguay), Nasrollah Entezan (Iran), Nicolaas Blom (Netherlands), Alberto Ulloa (Peru), Abdur Rahman (India), Kevel Lisicky (Czechoslovakia), Ivan Rand (Canada), John Hood (Australia), and Joshua Brilej (Yugoslavia). The committee was charged with finding a solution to the division of territory in Palestine between Arabs and Jews after the British announced that they were relinquishing control over the Palestinian Mandate. From the outset, García Granados and Rand favored

a division of the Palestinian Mandate that would result in the creation of an independent Jewish state.

By September 1, 1947, the deadline for the committee's recommendation to the General Assembly, the majority of the committee's members still preferred the creation of a single federated Palestinian state with an Arab majority and a Jewish minority. Rand and García Granados, however, were able to convince the representatives from Sweden, the Netherlands, Uruguay, Czechoslovakia, and Peru to vote for the partition of Palestine. India, Iran, and Yugoslavia voted against partition, while Australia abstained. On November 29, 1947, the General Assembly voted for UN Resolution 181, which recognized the Jewish claim to a portion of the Palestinian Mandate.

García Granados went on to serve as Guatemala's first ambassador to Israel beginning in 1948. Indeed, Guatemala's embassy in Jerusalem was the first embassy established in Israel. In 1950 García Granados ran unsuccessfully for president of Guatemala. Afterward, he served as Guatemala's ambassador to the United Kingdom and Chile. García Granados died in Santiago, Chile, on May 3, 1961.

MICHAEL R. HALL

See also

United Nations Special Commission on Palestine; Zionism

References

García Granados, Jorgé. *The Birth of Israel: The Drama ss I Saw It.* New York: Knopf, 1948.

———. *Cuaderno de Memorias, 1900–1922* [Notebook of Memories, 1900–1922]. Guatemala: Artemis y Edinter, 2000.

Gaza-Jericho Agreement

See Cairo Accord

Gaza Raid

Event Date: February 28, 1955

Israeli military raid of an Egyptian Army outpost in Gaza on February 28, 1955. The raid was undertaken by approximately 50 paratroopers of the Israel Defense Forces (IDF) and came as a complete surprise to the Egyptians. The Gaza Raid resulted in the deaths of 39 Egyptian soldiers and the wounding of another 30.

The attack was supposedly in retaliation for continuing fedayeen attacks on Israel, but Gaza appeared to be a strange target in that it had historically been the most quiet of the Israeli frontier borders. Yet there is more to the story than mere retaliation. Israeli prime minister David Ben-Gurion had come under increasing pressure from the political Right both in and out of the government to take a more proactive stance against fedayeen attacks. Thus, he somewhat reluctantly agreed to sanction the raid.

In retrospect, the Gaza Raid was a major Israeli miscalculation. In fact, before the February raid, the Egyptians—first under King Farouk I and then under President Gamal Abdel Nasser—had discouraged (or at the least had not officially blessed) raids on Israel from Egyptian soil, particularly raids by Palestinian fedayeen forces. Outraged by the audacity of the Israeli Gaza attack, Nasser now began to sanction commando and fedayeen raids against Israel. The Jordanians also began to encourage raids against the Israelis from their territory following the February attack. This marked the beginning of a trend of escalating violence among fedayeen forces, Israel's Arab neighbors, and Israel that would result in many hundreds of deaths.

The Gaza Raid proved to be a political hot potato for Nasser, who now believed that he had to take extraordinary measures to counter the growing threat of Israeli incursions into Egyptian territory. The raid also convinced Nasser and his military advisers that Israel was gaining strength militarily and that this buildup had to be counteracted by a commensurate Egyptian rearmament effort. Shortly thereafter, Nasser approached several Western nations, including the United States, about arms purchases. The Americans and British rebuffed the inquiry, citing the 1950 Tripartite Declaration that pledged no arms sales to Middle Eastern nations. In addition, Nasser's embrace of the Non-Aligned Movement did not sit well in Washington or London. For their part, the French would not sell arms to Nasser's government because of Egypt's support of Algerian rebels in the Algerian War (1954–1962), a colonial conflict in which the French were now deeply involved.

Having been turned down by the major powers in the West, Nasser naturally looked to the East, toward the Soviet Union, for his arms needs. Before the year was out, he had consummated a major arms deal with the Soviets. The 1955 arms deal delivered to the Egyptians some 200 tanks and other weapons and amounted to about $325 million (in 1955 dollars). This marked the start of a major Soviet effort to insert its influence in the Middle East. It was also the beginning of an Egyptian-Soviet alliance that would last until the mid-1970s and paved the way for similar Soviet arms deals with Syria and Iraq.

Clearly, the 1955 Gaza Raid set off a chain reaction of events that nobody might have imagined. The Egyptian-Soviet arms deal compelled the United States and Great Britain to pull their financial underwriting of Egypt's Aswan High Dam project. This in turn forced Nasser to nationalize the Suez Canal in 1956, which in turn precipitated the Suez Crisis of October–November 1956.

PAUL G. PIERPAOLI JR.

See also

Ben-Gurion, David; Egypt; Egyptian-Soviet Arms Deal; Fedayeen; Nasser, Gamal Abdel; Tripartite Declaration

References

Jabber, Paul. *Not by War Alone: Security and Arms Control in the Middle East.* Berkeley: University of California Press, 1981.

Leng, Russell J. *Bargaining and Learning in Recurrent Crises: The Soviet-American, Egyptian-Israeli, and Indo-Pakistani Rivalries.* Ann Arbor: University of Michigan Press, 2000.

Louis, William R., and Roger Owen, eds. *Suez, 1956: The Crisis and Its Consequences.* New York: Oxford University Press, 1989.

Gaza Strip

A 7-mile-wide, 25-mile-long, heavily populated strip of land along the Mediterranean Sea, adjacent to Egypt's Sinai Peninsula. The Gaza Strip takes its name from its principal city of Gaza. In biblical times the area that is today the Gaza Strip was the home of the Philistines, and the name Palestine is derived from Philistine.

The Gaza Strip has a border of approximately 31 miles with Israel on the northeast and east and 6.6 miles with Egypt on the southwest. It has been one of the main focal points of the Arab-Israeli conflict since 1967, when it became one of Israel's occupied territories. Although much of the strip is now under Palestinian Authority (PA) jurisdiction, borders and main roads are still controlled by Israel, and the entire area remains disputed. At the end of 2007 it had a population of some 1.5 million people.

According to a 1947 United Nations (UN) plan, which never took effect, the Gaza Strip and the West Bank were to form an independent Arab state following the dismantling of the British Mandate for Palestine. Arab leaders, however, rejected the plan and instead waged war. During the Israeli War of Independence (1948–1949), many of the Palestinian people who had lived in what had

Israel's Territorial Gains after the 1967 Six-Day War

Territory	Gained from	Approximate Area (sq. mi.)
Gaza Strip	Egypt	139
Golan Heights	Syria	775
Sinai Peninsula	Egypt	23,172
West Bank	Jordan	2,263
Total:		26,349

become Israel either fled or were forced into areas surrounding the new Jewish state, including Gaza. Although a Palestinian government began operation in the Gaza Strip, the 1949 armistice between Israel and Egypt that ended the war gave control of the area to Egypt, which suspended the government in 1959.

Despite the 1949 armistice, significant portions of the Israeli population believed that the Gaza Strip (along with the West Bank and parts of Lebanon and Syria) was part of biblical Eretz Israel, or land of Israel, and therefore should be part of the modern Jewish state. After a failed attempt to gain the strip in the 1956 Sinai Campaign, Israel launched the Six-Day War in 1967. In spite of fighting a war against Egypt, Syria, and Jordan, the Jewish state was nevertheless able to take control of Gaza from Egypt. UN Security Council Resolution 242 called for Israel to withdraw from territories captured in the war, but Israel instead began constructing Jewish settlements in the Gaza Strip.

At the beginning of the 21st century, there were 25 Israeli settlements in Gaza, although in 2005 the population of about 1.4 million included a mere 8,000 Israelis. In May 1994 the historic Declaration of Principles on Interim Self-Government Arrangements (also known as the Oslo Accords) transferred some governmental services of the strip to the PA, but its status remained in dispute.

A high birthrate has contributed to the Gaza Strip's ongoing poverty, unemployment, and low standard of living. Although control of the strip's finances was also transferred to the PA in 1994, government corruption and Israeli border closures severely hindered the economy until 1998, when Israel began taking measures to ensure that border closures resulting from terrorism threats would not so adversely affect cross-border trade. However, with the outbreak of the Second (al-Aqsa) Intifada in 2000, many of these measures were reversed, and the area witnessed another economic downturn.

In 2005, Israeli prime minister Ariel Sharon's government voted to begin disengagement from the Gaza Strip, a plan that met with mixed reactions in the international community. Although the European Union (EU) and the United States supported Sharon's plan to dismantle Israeli settlements in the area and withdraw Israeli forces from many areas, the EU said that the plan did not go far enough in establishing pre-1967 borders. Many Israelis opposed the plan and supported the settlers. Palestinians, while in favor of any move that increased PA jurisdiction, complained that the plan

was not comprehensive. Nonetheless, it was hoped that disengagement would mark a step in implementing the so-called Road Map to Peace in the Middle East, a peace plan brokered by the United States, the EU, Russia, and the UN.

The Israeli government began dismantling the settlements on August 15, 2005, as planned. Although contested by the nationalist Right within Israel, by some of the Jewish community abroad, and in some confrontational events, the Israel Defense Forces (IDF) completed the process on September 12, 2005. Israel retains offshore maritime control and control of airspace over the Gaza Strip, however. At the same time, Israel withdrew from the Philadelphi Route adjacent to the strip's border with Egypt, following a pledge by Egypt that it would secure its side of the border. Palestinian militants have, however, used the Gaza Strip to fire Qassam rockets into Israeli border settlements, and Israel carried out several military campaigns in 2006 against Palestinians in Gaza both prior to the war with Hezbollah in Lebanon and that November.

An optimistic attitude prevailed in Gaza in 2005 when Israel withdrew its troops, along with 9,000 Jewish settlers. These hopes were dashed by fighting among criminal gangs and clashes between Hamas and Fatah that soon escalated and ultimately killed an estimated 160 people and wounded 800 more. On June 14, 2007, Hamas took over Gaza entirely. This brought an end to the Palestinian unity government and also brought the declaration of a state of emergency by Palestinian president Mahmoud Abbas. The resulting emergency Palestinian government excluded Hamas and was limited to the West Bank.

On June 19, 2007, Abbas cut off all ties and dialogue with Hamas, pending the return of Gaza. This left Fatah, backed by the United States, the EU, and Israel, scrambling to consolidate its control in the West Bank, while Hamas tightened its own control of Gaza and increasingly imposed its brand of religious conservatism, especially as far as women were concerned.

With aid from the West largely cut off, Hamas soon found itself under siege along with the people of Gaza. As of the end of 2007, few of Gaza's 1.5 million people could leave Gaza for any reason. With the Egyptian border also closed, the economy was in a state of near collapse, with Gazans unable to export products and thus incapable of paying for imports. Gaza was more isolated than ever.

SPENCER C. TUCKER

See also

Gaza Strip Disengagement; Intifada, Second; Oslo Accords; Palestinian Authority; Qassam Rocket; Rafah Tunnels; Settlements, Israeli; Sharon, Ariel; Sinai Campaign; Six-Day War; United Nations Security Council Resolution 242

References

Oren, Michael B. *Six Days of War: June 1967 and the Making of the Modern Middle East.* Novato, CA: Presidio, 2003.

Said, Edward W. *The End of the Peace Process: Oslo and After.* New York: Vintage Books, 2001.

Smith, Charles D. *Palestine and the Arab-Israeli Conflict: A History with Documents.* 6th ed. New York: Bedford/St. Martin's, 2006.

Gaza Strip Disengagement
Start Date: August 15, 2005
End Date: September 12, 2005

A plan devised by Israeli prime minister Ariel Sharon to remove Israeli interests from the Gaza Strip. The Israeli government accepted and enacted the plan in August 2005. The Gaza Strip is a narrow slice of land on the east bank of the Mediterranean Sea just north of Egypt. The Israeli pullout also encompassed four Jewish settlements in the northern West Bank, on the western edge of the Jordan River.

Israel captured the Gaza Strip in 1967 during the Six-Day War and occupied the area until September 2005. The disengagement officially began on August 15, 2005, and was completed on September 12, 2005. Coupled with the November 2004 election of Palestinian leader Mahmoud Abbas, the Israeli disengagement gave rise to optimism among many in the region concerning the prospect of peace between the Palestinians and the Israelis.

Sharon first announced his plan for withdrawal on December 18, 2003, at the Fourth Herzliya Conference in Israel. The prime minister stated that he hoped to advance the implementation of the so-called Road Map to Peace, first advanced by the United States in June 2002. Sharon declared that the purpose of the pullout plan was "to reduce terror as much as possible, and grant Israeli citizens the maximum level of security." Sharon and supporters of the plan knew that Israel had to initiate the peace process and not rely on cooperation from the Palestinians.

Some analysts have suggested that the withdrawal was a shrewd strategic maneuver on Sharon's part designed to splinter the already fragile Palestinian unity. As they are geographically separated, there has long been a certain degree of friction and distrust between the Palestinians of the West Bank and those of Gaza. Prior to 1967, the former had spent almost 20 years under Jordanian occupation, while the latter spent the same period under Egyptian control. The Israeli withdrawal from Gaza also forced the Palestinian Authority (PA) to demonstrate for the first time that it was capable of governing and providing basic societal and governmental services to its people. In the year following the Israeli withdrawal, the PA generally failed that test. A different Arab and Palestinian perspective is that the withdrawal was meant to be the preface for an Israeli offensive on the West Bank.

Despite opposition from Sharon's own Likud Party, which believed that Sharon had betrayed his previous policies supporting the Gaza settlements, Sharon continued to press forward. On June 6, 2004, the Israeli cabinet approved the disengagement. Sharon's insistence on the plan upset many of his closest supporters, includ-

Security forces remove obstacles on their way to evacuate Gaza Strip disengagement opponents in the Chomesh settlement on August 23, 2005. (Mark Neyman/Israeli Government Press Office)

ing former Israeli prime minister Benjamin Netanyahu, who resigned his post as finance minister, accusing the Israeli government of destroying Jewish towns and villages while receiving nothing in return. However, Sharon garnered support from the leftist Labor Party and international policy makers such as the leaders of the European Union (EU), United Nations (UN) secretary-general Kofi Annan, and U.S. president George W. Bush.

Many Palestinians opposed the plan, as it did not call for Israel to withdraw militarily from the Gaza Strip and did not address any of the nearly intolerable conditions in the West Bank. Others simply did not trust Sharon to keep his word and believed that his support for the plan was nothing more than lip service. Despite opposition from many Palestinians, on August 8, 2005, Sheikh Jamal al-Bawatna, a senior Palestinian religious leader, issued an edict banning shooting attacks against Israeli security forces and settlements out of concern that such incidents would lead to a postponement of the pullout from the Gaza Strip. Prior to the pullout, demonstrators occupied allegedly empty buildings and attacked some Palestinian homes. Skepticism turned to joy when Israel pulled out of Gaza in August and September 2005. The militant Palestinian group Hamas, which had vociferously opposed Israel's presence in Palestine since the group's founding in 1987, claimed victory and celebrated along with thousands of Palestinian supporters worldwide.

Israelis who did not support the plan joined together in nonviolent protests, such as the July 25, 2004, demonstration in which tens of thousands of Israelis formed a human chain 50 miles long from the Nissanit settlement in Gaza to the Western Wall in Jerusalem. Other protests throughout the country occurred, including a symbolic war of flags (orange for those who opposed withdrawal and blue for those who favored withdrawal), until the disengagement was complete. Despite the protests, by July 2005 polls showed that a majority of Israelis supported Sharon and the withdrawal plan.

On August 15, 2005, the Gaza Strip was officially closed for Israeli entrance. Two days later, on August 17, the forced evacuation of those Israelis who refused to leave on their own began. Israeli civilians were removed from their homes, and their residences were demolished. While there was much less violence than expected, there were some scenes that witnessed Israeli troops dragging screaming Jews from their homes and synagogues in Gaza. In all, it took the Israel Defense Forces (IDF) and the Israeli police only four and a half days to forcibly evict some 5,000 settlers. Despite the stress on both the soldiers and the civilians, the process of removal was completed on September 12, 2005, when the last soldier left the Gaza Strip and the Kissufim Gate was closed.

Following the Israeli pullout, debate continued on all sides as to what role the disengagement would play in the Arab-Israeli peace process, particularly as Israeli forces bombed and shelled Gaza in the spring of 2006 and then reentered the Gaza Strip in the summer of 2006 in response to the kidnapping of an Israeli soldier.

GREGORY MORGAN

See also

Abbas, Mahmoud; Gaza Strip; Hamas; Labor Party; Likud Party; Sharon, Ariel

References

Efrat, Elisha. *The West Bank and Gaza Strip: A Geography of Occupation and Disengagement.* New York: Routledge, 2006.

Makovsky, David. *Making Peace with the PLO: The Rabin Government's Road to the Oslo Accord.* Boulder, CO: Westview, 1996.

General Intelligence Agency, Palestinian

Part of the Palestinian General Security Services (PGSS), or Palestinian Directorate of Police Force, the General Intelligence Agency (GIA), or Mukhabarrat al-Amma, is one of the two core intelligence agencies of the Palestinian Authority (PA). Formally established after the 1994 Cairo Agreement, which turned over most of the Gaza Strip and Jericho and its environs to the PA, the GIA is the primary civilian intelligence arm of the PA. Military Intelligence is the GIA's military counterpart. Both are part of the 10 official security or police agencies under PGSS direction, command, and control.

The GIA consists of an estimated 3,000 officers who engage in domestic and foreign intelligence gathering, counterespionage operations, and the prevention of domestic subversion. They also serve as the Palestinian intelligence liaison to foreign intelligence agencies. The PA maintains intelligence liaison capabilities with multiple countries, including the United States and Israel. The GIA's equivalent agency within the United States intelligence community structure is the U.S. Central Intelligence Agency (CIA). In Israel it is the Mossad.

The GIA, the Palestinian Special Security Force, and the Preventative Security Force have been credited with much of Prime Minister Yasser Arafat's ability to maintain control of the PA for nearly a decade. Indeed, they were central to the regular collection, analysis, and reporting of human intelligence information and contributed significantly to Arafat's ability to identify and proactively neutralize potential threats to his control of the PA. Their methods of human intelligence collection, although regarded by most as extreme, were successful both directly in the collection of key information and indirectly as a deterrent to potential opposition groups.

With the November 2004 death of Arafat and the resignation of its longtime head Amin al-Hindi, the GIA suffered a series of setbacks. In August 2005, interim head Tariq Abu Rajab was crippled in a bombing of his headquarters during an assassination attempt in the Gaza Strip. Key personnel issues such as corruption, exceptionally low pay, high-visibility human rights violations, and other factors dampened morale throughout the GIA. The loss of Arafat coupled with kidnappings, murders, and widespread violence led to universal calls for leadership change within the PA and the supporting intelligence infrastructure, including the GIA.

C. SCOTT BLANCHETTE

See also

Arafat, Yasser; Palestine Liberation Organization; Palestinian Authority; Palestinian Special Security Force

References

Hunter, Robert E., and Seth G. Jones. *Building a Successful Palestinian State: Security.* Santa Monica, CA: RAND, 2006.

RAND Palestinian State Study Team. *Building a Successful Palestinian State.* Santa Monica, CA: RAND, 2005.

Usher, Graham. "The Politics of Internal Security: The PA's New Intelligence Services." *Journal of Palestine Studies* 25(2) (Winter 1996): 21–34.

Genesis, Book of

The first book of the Bible, contained in the Old Testament. The book of Genesis tells the story of the creation of the universe and humanity in Chapters 1–11. In Chapters 12–25 it focuses on the life and descendants of Abraham (Ibrahim), the primogenitor of both the Hebrew people, first called Jews while exiled in Babylon in the fifth and sixth centuries BC, and the Arab peoples. God appeared to Abram (his name was later changed to Abraham as a sign of his covenant with God) and promised to make his descendants into a great nation. Abram, born circa 2166 BC, left his home in Ur of the Chaldeans, in present-day Iraq, and traveled at God's direction to the land of Canaan, or present-day Israel/Palestine, circa 2091 BC.

Islamic tradition and the book of Genesis agree that at the age of 86 Abraham fathered Ishmael, the ancestor from whom all Arab peoples are descended. Ishmael's mother was Hagar (Hajar), the Egyptian maidservant of Abraham's wife Sarai, who then changed her name to Sarah as a sign of the covenant agreement between her and God. She then bore the 99-year-old Abraham a son named Isaac, circa 2066 BC, whose second son Jacob (Israel) (born circa 2006 BC) is the progenitor through whom Jews trace their lineage back to Abraham (Genesis 21:1–7). Genesis asserts that it is the line through Isaac and Jacob that gives rise to the chosen people promised in God's original covenant with Abraham.

Islamic tradition asserts that although Abraham loved Ishmael and Hagar, Sarah's jealousy of them was so great that she demanded that Abraham banish them. Islamic tradition also asserts that Hagar was Abraham's second wife. It also adds to the Genesis record that Allah (God) instructed Abraham to take Ishmael and Hagar away. Thus, under Allah's guidance Abraham escorted them to the desert land of Mecca and there abandoned them at Allah's direction while Hagar was still nursing her young son. This abandonment taught Hagar to trust Allah and is commemorated as part of the obligatory

A Jew and a Muslim both pray at the Tomb of Abraham, also known as the Tomb of the Patriarchs, in Hebron. Jews, Christians, and Muslims all revere Abraham as a patriarch, November 1993. (Ricki Rosen/Corbis Saba)

hajj, the Islamic pilgrimage to Mecca. The Prophet Muhammad traced his lineage back to Ishmael.

Genesis asserts that enmity began to grow between Sarah and Hagar once both realized that Hagar was pregnant. It erupted years later when Sarah observed Ishmael mocking the newly weaned and much younger Isaac. Although the Genesis account differs from the Islamic tradition in that Ishmael is not a nursing youngster, they agree in their description of Abraham's distress over Sarah's demand that Hagar and Ishmael be sent away. God tells Abraham to follow Sarah's request, for it is through the offspring of Isaac that the promised great nation will arise. Genesis records, in disagreement with the Islamic tradition, that Abraham gave Hagar and Ishmael food and water and sent them away without escorting them to the land of Mecca. Genesis does record a promise to Hagar from God that God will also make Ishmael's descendants a great nation (Genesis 21:8–21).

The Genesis record never designates Hagar as a wife of Abraham but does note that a second wife, Keturah, bore him two sons, Sheba and Dedan, and that Abraham had other unnamed sons by his concubines, female cohabitants to whom Abraham was not married (Genesis 25:1–4). Before he died, Abraham gave gifts to all of his male descendants other than Ishmael and then sent them to the east away from Isaac. Before he died, Abraham deeded everything he still possessed to Isaac. Islamic tradition and Genesis agree that Ishmael returned to Canaan for Abraham's funeral and there, together with Isaac, buried their father in the Tomb of the Patriarchs near present-day Hebron.

Genesis 25:12–18 records that Ishmael fathered 12 sons whose descendants gave rise to 12 tribes from which contemporary Arab peoples trace their lineage back to Abraham. Isaac's story is found in Genesis 25:19–28:9 and traces the lineage of the Jews of the world through his second son Jacob and Jacob's two wives, Leah and Rachel, a story told in Genesis 28:10–36:43. Leah had 6 sons, and Rachel had 2. Two concubines each had 2 sons. These 12 sons are the progenitors of the Twelve Tribes of Israel (Jacob).

Rachel's sons, Joseph and Benjamin, were favored by Jacob, and in anger over this partiality Leah's sons sold Joseph (circa 1898 BC) to a caravan of Midianite merchants headed for Egypt. Joseph's story is told in Genesis 37:1–50:26 and relates how he rose to a position of power in Egypt second only to the pharaoh himself (circa 1885 BC). Joseph prepared Egypt for an extended famine, which drove all of Jacob's descendants to live in Egypt under Joseph's governance. Genesis ends with the death of Joseph (circa 1805 BC).

According to tradition, the Twelve Tribes of Israel increased in number and left Egypt in the Exodus led by Moses (circa 1446 BC). After 40 years of wandering in the Wilderness of the Sinai, the descendants of Jacob returned to Canaan, conquered the land, and parceled it out to each tribe. (There were 13 parcels because the tribe of Joseph was divided between his two sons.) This supposedly occurred around 1406 BC.

The 10 tribes descended from Leah and the concubines were later dispersed and lost in the Assyrian destruction of the Northern Kingdom (722 BC) following the division of the United Kingdom of Israel into the Northern Kingdom, Israel, and the Southern Kingdom, Judah (930 BC). The Southern Kingdom was conquered by the Babylonians in three waves during 605–586 BC, and these descendants of Abraham were taken to Babylon, where they are first called Jews because they are from the land of Judah.

Judaism and Christianity historically assert that Moses (ca. 1526–1406 BC) was the author of Genesis and the remaining four books of the Pentateuch (Exodus, Numbers, Leviticus, and Deuteronomy), called the Torah in Judaism. Muslims recognize Abraham and Moses as prophets. However, the Koran in Surah al-Saffat (37:100–110) tells the story of Abraham's readiness to sacrifice Ishmael, not Isaac. And Muslims believe that Hagar prayed for water in the hills near Mecca, finding it at the spring of Zamzam.

RICHARD EDWARDS

See also

Koran; Religious Sites in the Middle East, Christian; Religious Sites in the Middle East, Jewish; Religious Sites in the Middle East, Muslim; Tomb of the Patriarchs

References

Crown-Tamir, Hela. *How to Walk in the Footsteps of Jesus and the Prophets: A Scripture Reference Guide for Biblical Sites in Israel and Jordan.* Jerusalem: Gefen, 2000.

Feiler, Bruce. *Abraham: A Journey to the Heart of Three Faiths.* New York: HarperCollins, 2002.

Matthews, Kenneth A. *The New American Commentary: Genesis 11:27–50:26.* Nashville: B&H Publishing, 2005.

Peters, F. E. *The Children of Abraham: Judaism, Christianity, Islam: A New Edition.* Princeton Classic Editions. Princeton, NJ: Princeton University Press, 2006.

Walton, John H., and Victor H. Matthews. *The IVP Bible Background Commentary: Genesis-Deuteronomy.* Downers Grove, IL: InterVarsity, 2000.

Geneva Accord
Event Date: December 1, 2003

Peace agreement negotiated extragovernmentally between the Israelis and Palestinians designed to jump-start the ongoing Middle East peace process and address long-standing roadblocks to an Israeli-Palestinian rapprochement. The Geneva Accord was formally signed on December 1, 2003. It is considered an informal agreement because the negotiations that gave birth to it were not conducted through the official channels of the Israeli government or the Palestinian Authority (PA). While negotiators on both sides had held high-level posts in their respective governments, they were not acting at the specific behest of those governments.

On the Israeli side, the prime mover and negotiator of the Geneva Accord was Yossi Beilin, a leftist politician, former justice minister, and Labor Party member. Beilin had been one of the chief negotiators of the 1993 Oslo Accords and at the time had the backing of then Israeli foreign minister Shimon Peres. Beilin had been involved in the Palestinian-Israeli peace process for a number of

A Palestinian man reads a copy of the Geneva Accord on November 30, 2003, in Gaza City, one day before the formal signing of the accord in Geneva, Switzerland. (Getty Images)

years, although he had been recently defeated in elections. For the Palestinians, the principal architect of the agreement was Yasser Abed Rabbo, a member of the Palestine National Union and a minister in several PA cabinets. Most recently, he had served as minister of information. Seen as a moderate, propeace Palestinian, Rabbo took part in the failed Camp David Summit in 2000 and is thought to have had Chairman Yasser Arafat's implicit backing as he negotiated the Geneva Accord.

The accord agreed to the creation of a completely independent Palestinian nation to be located largely in the West Bank and the Gaza Strip. In return, the Palestinians were to officially recognize the State of Israel and Jewish claims to the lands that they would subsequently inhabit. All other land claims would be abandoned. The Palestinians would also have to agree to cease and desist from all forms of violence against Israel, including terrorist attacks. Furthermore, all armed groups with ties to the Palestinians that were not officially recognized would have to be disarmed and disbanded. Israel would be expected to submit to an International Commission that would oversee the settlement of Palestinian refugees within its boundaries. The commission would also establish a formula that would govern the number of refugees to be settled in Israel. Beyond that, Palestinians would waive the right of return for others of their refugees. On the perennially thorny issue of the disposition of Jerusalem, the accord called for the city to be divided, with much of East Jerusalem going to the Palestinians.

Under the terms of the Geneva Accord, the Palestinians would receive most of the territory captured by Israel in the 1967 Six-Day War. Israel would annex several areas, including Gush Etzion and Maale Adumim. Jewish settlers in Hebron and Ariel would be obliged to move into officially recognized Israeli territory.

The agreement was not particularly well received in Israel. The Israeli government, led by the Likud Party, refused to support any part of it. The Labor Party did not reject it but also would not support it. Indeed, Labor has remained officially silent on the issue, which is hardly a ringing endorsement. The accord received much play in the Israeli press, but it is believed that public support for it has never exceeded much more than 30 percent.

A number of Palestinian politicians and professionals embraced the basic tenets of the pact, for it went a considerable way in addressing long-standing Palestinian demands. However, the fact that it was informal and nonimplementable and was opposed in Israel limited any broad discussion or enthusiasm for the Geneva Accord among other Palestinians.

PAUL G. PIERPAOLI JR.

See also

Abed Rabbo, Yasser; Arafat, Yasser; Expellees and Refugees, Palestinian; Gaza Strip; Jerusalem; Labor Party; Likud Party; Oslo Accords; Palestinian Authority; West Bank

References

Lerner, Michael. *The Geneva Accord and Other Strategies for Healing the Israeli-Palestinian Conflict.* Berkeley, CA: North Atlantic Books, 2004.

Tilley, Virginia Q. *The One-State Solution: A Breakthrough for Peace in the Israeli-Palestinian Deadlock.* Ann Arbor: University of Michigan Press, 2005.

Watson, Geoffrey R. *The Oslo Accords: International Law and the Israeli-Palestinian Peace Agreements.* New York: Oxford University Press, 2000.

Geneva Peace Conference
Start Date: December 21, 1973
End Date: January 9, 1974

Meeting convened in Geneva, Switzerland, from December 21, 1973, to January 9, 1974, that was designed to foster peace negotiations between Israel and its Arab neighbors. Occurring in the immediate aftermath of the October 1973 Yom Kippur War, the Geneva Conference was officially sanctioned by the United Nations (UN) and was presided over by UN secretary-general Kurt Waldheim. More specifically, the Geneva Conference was designed to help implement UN Resolution 338 (passed in October 1973) and UN Resolution 242 (passed in November 1967). Indeed, in a closed-door session on December 15, 1973, UN Security Council members met to officially sanction the Geneva Conference, passing Resolution 344 that formally pledged UN support of the peace talks.

Participants included the foreign ministers of Egypt, Jordan, Israel, the United States, and the Soviet Union. Syria had been asked to join the conference but declined because the Palestine Liberation Organization (PLO) had not been invited. At the time the PLO's official position was the destruction of Israel, and therefore neither the Israelis nor the Americans would contemplate meeting with anyone representing the PLO. From the start the conference was rife with tension, and without any official representation from the Palestinians, the likelihood of reaching an agreement was dim indeed.

Throughout the talks, the Israeli and Arab ministers would not address one another directly, leaving Waldheim, the Americans, and Soviets in the awkward position of playing brokers among them. Be that as it may, it was the first time that high-level officials from the Soviet Union, the United States, Arab states, and Israel had gathered around the same table together. Almost no progress was made on any issue, and by early January the conferees were ready

View from the balcony at the conference room at the Palais des Nations in Geneva as the Geneva Peace Conference gets under way on December 21, 1973. The empty section was reserved for Syria, which boycotted the conference. (Bettmann/Corbis)

to depart. Interestingly, the 1973 Geneva Conference did produce the foundation of ongoing talks between the Egyptians and Americans, which culminated in the Camp David Accords of 1978 and the Israel-Egypt Peace Treaty of 1979.

PAUL G. PIERPAOLI JR.

See also

Camp David Accords; Israel-Egypt Peace Treaty; Palestine Liberation Organization; United Nations, Role of; United Nations Security Council Resolution 242; United Nations Security Council Resolution 338; Yom Kippur War

References

Allen, Peter. *The Kom Kippur War.* New York: Scribner, 1982.

Herzog, Chaim. *The Arab-Israeli Wars: War and Peace in the Middle East from the War of Independence to Lebanon.* Westminster, MD: Random House, 1984.

Geography of the Middle East

Although some scholars identify the Middle East in cultural terms to include those countries embracing Islam, the Middle East is generally delineated by geography and consists of those countries of Southwest Asia east of the Mediterranean and Red Seas and west of Afghanistan and Pakistan. In the past, Europeans had often designated the region between the eastern Mediterranean and the Persian Gulf as Asia Minor, the Orient, and the Levant. The first usage of the term "Middle East" can be traced to British maps of the 1850s for the purposes of differentiating the region from the Far East, which is defined as the areas east of India. In 1902, American naval strategist Alfred Thayer Mahan brought the term "Middle East" into prominence in his discussion of the geopolitical challenges of the early 20th century. After World War I, the British designated their forces in the regions of Mesopotamia and Egypt as the Middle Eastern Command, and during World War II the British General Headquarters in the Middle East included Egypt and North Africa. The generalization "Middle East and North Africa" has since been accepted in many works on geography.

There are no standard generalizations of what countries constitute the Middle East. The countries most associated with the Middle East are Bahrain, Egypt, Iran, Iraq, Israel (and the areas constituting the Palestinian Authority), Jordan, Kuwait, Lebanon, Oman, Qatar, Saudi Arabia, Syria, Turkey, the United Arab Emirates, and Yemen.

However, the Maghreb nations of Morocco, Algeria, and Tunisia as well as Libya, Sudan, and Somalia on the Horn of Africa, Cyprus on the Mediterranean, Afghanistan in Central Asia, and Pakistan in South Asia are sometimes included because of historical and cultural connections. While much of the Middle East is Arabic in language and ethnicity, Cyprus, Israel, Iran, and Turkey are not. Similarly, Cyprus and Israel are not Islamic. With the dissolution of the Soviet Union in 1991, the emergence of Armenia, Georgia, and Azerbaijan in the Caucasus and Kazakhstan, Kyrgyzstan, Tajikistan, Turkmenistan, and Uzbekistan in Central Asia has renewed

The Golan Heights near the Israeli-Jordanian border. (iStockPhoto.com)

the challenge of defining the Middle East. For the purposes herein required, the bulk of the discussion will focus on the first grouping of nations.

Contrary to popular belief, the Middle East and North Africa have a great deal of geographic diversity. The Middle East can be classified into two distinct geographical areas: a mountainous northern zone running through Turkey, Iran, and Afghanistan and a southern zone that consists of plains, dissected plateaus, and deserts.

It is mostly in the northern zone of the Middle East where the largest mountain ranges can be found. As a result of the convergence of the Turkish, African, Arabian, Iranian, and African plates, there are high mountain ranges in Turkey, Iran, and the Maghreb. The Taurus Mountains in southern Turkey rise to more than 13,000 feet. The Elburz Mountains stretch along northern Iran, and their highest peak, Mount Damavand, is nearly 18,400 feet high. The Zagros range stretches along western Iran and reaches a height of 13,000 feet.

The southern zone consists of the area along the Tigris-Euphrates River Valley, the Arabian Peninsula, the Red Sea, and the Nile River Valley. This area is marked by deserts such as the Rub-al-Khali in the Arabian Peninsula, the Libyan Desert in North Africa, and the

Negev Desert in Israel. Yet it contains very fertile areas along the Nile and the Tigris-Euphrates River Valley. This area can be divided further into an east-west axis along the Red Sea and the Suez Canal. These plateaus are also surrounded by elevated areas, such as the Red Sea Hills in eastern Egypt, the Asir Mountains in the southwestern corner of the Arabian Peninsula, and the uplands along the coast of the eastern Mediterranean Sea. The Yemen Highlands in the southern Arabian Peninsula average about 12,000 feet in height, while Mount Hermon in Syria is more than 9,800 feet in height. In North Africa, the Atlas Mountains rise to about 13,000 feet. This range straddles Morocco and Algeria.

Because much of the climate is arid, obtaining water is crucial to the survival of the Middle East. There are two types of rivers that provide water to the Middle East. One type of river that is common, particularly in Arabia and North Africa, is the wadi, a ravine that contains a watercourse. The wadi is dry for much of the year but fills with water during the rainy season. The more familiar rivers are the permanent ones that provide water on a continual basis. The major river systems such as the Nile and the Tigris and the Euphrates rivers provide irrigation and drinking water to many people in the Middle East. The rivers of the Middle East are fed by the snow that falls in the mountains during the winter months. The rivers of the Middle East are at their highest levels between November and Feb-ruary and at their lowest during the hot summer months. The Nile, however, is the only exception, as it floods during the late summer and early autumn after the heavy summer monsoon rains and again during the spring.

The first of the great rivers in the Middle East is the Nile. It is thus no understatement that the Greek historian Herodotus referred to Egypt as the "Gift of the Nile." The Nile stretches 4,132 miles from two sources, the White Nile in Burundi and the Blue Nile in Ethiopia, and flows out to the Mediterranean Sea. The Nile has made possible the flourishing of Egyptian civilization for millennia through its annual flooding, which serves to fertilize the soil with its alluvial deposits.

The Tigris and the Euphrates are other great rivers of the Middle East, and they too have figured prominently in the rise of civilization. Both rivers originate in Asia Minor. The Tigris flows for 1,150 miles, while the Euphrates is 1,700 miles long. Both rivers wind along an easterly course on the Anatolian Peninsula. The Euphrates heads southward through Syria and the Kurdish areas of northern Iraq before flowing on a southeasterly course toward the Persian Gulf and is fed by two tributaries, the Balikh and the Khabur, that flow southward from Turkey to Syria. The Tigris flows along the Zagros Mountains before moving southward toward the Persian Gulf. It is also fed by many lesser tributaries, such as the Great and

Mangrove and mountains in the Sinai, Nabq National Park, Egypt. (iStockPhoto.com)

Lesser Zab, the Diyala, and the Karun. Unlike the Nile's steady and predictable rate of flooding, the Tigris and the Euphrates are subject to fast-moving and destructive floods.

There are other smaller rivers across the Middle East that are no less crucial in providing water to the region. The Jordan River, for example, has several sources, such as the Yarmuk and the Zarqa, in southern Lebanon and Syria. The Jordan flows about 200 miles from north to south into Lake Tiberias, also known as the Sea of Galilee and Lake Kinneret. The Jordan descends about 65 miles into the Ghor Valley and then descends several thousand feet in elevation before ultimately flowing into the Dead Sea.

The Middle East has played a pivotal role in the events of the 20th and early 21st centuries. Key to the significance of the modern Middle East in world politics has been the role of oil. This development began in 1901 when William Knox D'Arcy gained a concession from Persia (Iran) to drill for oil. Throughout the 20th century, the Middle East has figured prominently in international diplomacy as the source of about 40 percent of the petroleum produced for the United States, Europe, and Japan, which account for about 70 percent of its consumers. As of 2002, Saudi Arabia leads the Middle East in producing approximately 9 million barrels of oil per day. Iran comes in second, producing nearly 4 million barrels of oil per day. The United Arab Emirates produces 2.5 million barrels of oil per day, while Kuwait comes close at 2.2 million barrels of oil per day. Algeria, Iran, Iraq, Kuwait, Libya, Qatar, Saudi Arabia, and the United Arab Emirates make up the majority of countries in the Organization of Petroleum Exporting Countries (OPEC).

It is hardly surprising that oil would be used as a political weapon by Middle Eastern countries. In 1973, OPEC imposed an embargo on the United States, the Netherlands, Portugal, South Africa, and Rhodesia because of their support for Israel during the Yom Kippur War. This embargo altered the economic arrangements of the post–World War II period. Indeed, it signaled the end of American independence over its energy policies, reminded the industrial world of its dependence on Middle Eastern oil, and triggered a drastic increase in oil prices. In 1979, the Islamic Revolution in Iran toppled the pro-Western Mohammad Reza Shah Pahlavi, who was a key ally in the Middle East. The resultant anti-American regime in Iran deprived the United States of the world's second-largest oil reserve.

When Iraq invaded Kuwait in August 1990, the United States and its European and Japanese allies forged an international coalition to prevent both Kuwait and Saudi Arabia from falling into the hands of Iraqi dictator Saddam Hussein. In the aftermath of the terrorist attacks on the United States on September 11, 2001, and the 2003 Iraq War, oil refineries in the Middle East have become vulnerable to sabotage, which would disrupt the regular flow of oil to the United States and Europe.

As with any region, the Middle East has a unique ecosystem that has been altered by the presence of humans. Throughout the 20th century, several species of large mammals, such as lions and tigers, have become extinct. In 1900 the crocodile became extinct, as did the ostrich in the 1930s. Only the ruggedness of the mountains in the northern Middle East and the aridity of the southern Middle East have protected species of gazelle, deer, mountain sheep and goats, wild boar, and the oryx. In the aftermath of the 1991 Persian Gulf War, the diverse plants and animals along the Persian Gulf were severely threatened because of the destruction of Kuwaiti oil fields by the retreating armies of Hussein. The Middle East in previous times had been subject to locust plagues, and only recently has the problem abated.

Water has also been an issue of national security for the nations of the Middle East. Nations that fall along large river systems such as the Nile, the Tigris, and the Euphrates have serious disputes over the allocation of water for irrigation and the pressures of exploding populations. For example, Egypt's Aswan High Dam, completed in 1971, provides hydroelectric power and generates 1.8 million kilowatts for Egypt. This output of energy, however, comes at a high price. As a result of the construction of the dam, the rich alluvial sediment that floods the Nile River Valley annually is trapped behind it, leaving the banks of the lower Nile less fertile than before. Additionally, Sudan and Ethiopia have plans for the development of dams farther upstream. This has raised tensions among the three countries because new dams would drastically threaten the flow of water to Egypt, the strongest power in the basin. The construction of dams along the Tigris and the Euphrates has caused tensions among Turkey, Syria, and Iraq for much the same reasons.

Even within the nations of the Middle East, the need for water has created stresses for the expanding needs of the people. Aside from rivers, aquifers are another source of drinking water. There are seven major groundwater basins in the Middle East. Three of them are found in the Arabian Peninsula, and four are in North Africa, including minor basins in Sinai and Jordan.

An exploding population and increasing water usage have exacerbated the general scarcity of water in the region, particularly in Egypt, Cyprus, Jordan, Palestine, Israel, and the Arabian Peninsula. As a whole, the Middle East devotes 70 percent of its water to agricultural production. In addition to human consumption, climactic changes have accelerated the evaporation rate of water in the region. For centuries, the peoples of the Middle East have improvised in devising methods to extract water through channels or wells. In recent times, water conservation and improved agricultural techniques have become important in addressing the balance between a growing population and a sustainable supply of water.

The geography and topography of the region in which the various Arab-Israeli wars have unfolded have clearly played a role in war strategy. The wide-open deserts, plains, and plateaus have left ground troops and equipment vulnerable to fire from the air and from high ground. By the same token, the level ground has also facilitated tank warfare and has given the advantage to the army with the best mobility (usually Israel's). The heat and aridity of the deserts have also shaped the way in which wars have been fought.

Dino Buenviaje

See also
Climate of the Middle East

References
Anderson, Ewan W. *The Middle East: Geography and Geopolitics.*
    London: Routledge, 2000.
Beck, John A. *The Land of Milk and Honey: An Introduction to the
    Geography of Israel.* St. Louis: Concordia, 2006.
Drysdale, Alasdair, and Gerald H. Blake. *The Middle East and North
    Africa: A Political Geography.* New York: Oxford University Press, 1985.
Fisher, W. B. *The Middle East: A Physical, Social, and Regional
    Geography.* 6th ed. London: Methuen, 1978.
Held, Colbert C. *Middle East Patterns: Places, Peoples, and Politics.*
    Boulder, CO: Westview, 1994.
Kemp, Geoffrey, and Robert E. Harkavy. *Strategic Geography and the
    Changing Middle East.* Washington, DC: Brookings Institution Press,
    1997.
Melamid, Alexander. *Oil and the Economic Geography of the Middle East
    and North Africa.* Princeton, NJ: Darwin, 1991.
Orni, Ephraim. *Geography of Israel.* Philadelphia: Jewish Publication
    Society of America, 1977.

Germany, Federal Republic of, Middle East Policy

Three major factors determined the Middle East policies of West Germany from its foundation in 1949 until German reunification in 1990. The first factor, one that led to what has often been called West Germany's special relationship with the State of Israel, was Schuldgefühl, or the sense of culpability for the destruction of Jewish life and property before and during World War II. During 1949–1950, the newly established West German government, under pressure from Israel and Western allies, held itself morally obligated to provide financial and material restitution to Israel.

The second factor lay in West Germany's solid placement in the Western sphere of influence during the Cold War, an alliance reinforced when the West German government received full sovereignty in 1955 and was declared a member of the North Atlantic Treaty Organization (NATO). In seeking to maintain amicable relations with the Arab states, thereby blocking the growth of Soviet influence in the area, West Germany's Middle East policy by and large reflected that of the Western allies and, from the 1970s onward, that of the European Economic Community (EEC), or the European Union (EU) as it was renamed in 1993. Since the end of the Cold War, however, the focus has shifted to preventing the spread of regional conflict, international terrorism, and an exacerbation of refugee crises.

The third factor lay in West Germany's rapid development as a major industrial nation, which made it increasingly dependent on Middle Eastern oil resources and eager to maintain bilateral trade. West German policy thus had to tread a fine line to fulfill its moral obligations to Israel without compromising relations with Arab oil producers.

Although a controversial issue in Israel, with the new state in economic crisis Israeli officials approached the West German government for reparations payments in September 1951. Eager to mark a decisive break with the Nazi German past, West German chancellor Konrad Adenauer saw in such reparations a chance to rehabilitate the international image of the new Germany. Negotiations led to the signing of the Luxembourg Reparations Agreement in September 1952 and its ratification in March 1953. West Germany thereby promised to pay the State of Israel 3 billion German marks (DM) in commodities and services over the next 12 years. Israel agreed to place orders with West German firms, which in turn would receive direct payment from the West German government. A provision allowed for about one-third of the payments to be made to British oil companies for shipments to Israel. Israel also promised to distribute about 450 million DM to the Conference on Jewish Material Claims against Germany, a body that represented almost two dozen Jewish organizations with headquarters outside Israel.

German technological assistance also strengthened the faltering Israeli economy. Five power plants quadrupled Israel's generating capacity from 1953 to 1956. Other assistance included oil supplements, installations of industrial plants, railroad tracks and cars, improved telegraph and telephone communications, irrigation pipelines for the Negev Desert project, and more than 60 ships.

The subsequent decade proved, however, the difficulty of maintaining good relations with both Israel and the Arab states. In 1955, moves to establish diplomatic relations between West Germany and Israel prompted Egyptian president Gamal Abdel Nasser to threaten to recognize East Germany. According to the West German Hallstein Doctrine, which was in effect from 1955 to 1969, West Germany claimed the exclusive right to represent the German nation. The West German government was also obligated to break off diplomatic relations with any state that recognized East Germany. Nevertheless, fear of antagonizing the Arab world and spurring the growth of Soviet influence in the Middle East forced West Germany to back down and delay recognition of Israel.

Other problems ensued when the United Nations (UN), the United States, and several Arab countries asked West Germany to withhold payments under the Luxembourg Agreement during Israel's advance on the Suez Canal in the Sinai Campaign of 1956. This time West Germany refused, holding fast to the initial treaty. Nevertheless, tension with Israel erupted with the disclosure that a number of scientists at a Stuttgart institute were involved in developing missiles for Egypt. Although the West German cabinet dismissed the scientists, it was unwilling to intercede when a number of the researchers relocated to Cairo. The conflict ended only when most of the scientists, fearful about their safety or lured by more profitable contracts, returned to West Germany.

A crisis with Egypt came to a head when it was revealed in 1964 that West Germany had secretly been training Israeli troops and supplying weapons to Israel. Although under public pressure the Bonn government soon stopped the shipments, it now made good its delayed decision to recognize Israel. No sooner had West Germany and Israel exchanged ambassadors in 1965 than Algeria, Lebanon,

Holocaust survivors demonstrate against German chancellor Helmut Kohl's visit to Israel near the Yad Vashem memorial on January 24, 1984. (Nati Harnik/Israeli Government Press Office)

Jordan, Syria, Saudi Arabia, Yemen, Iraq, Kuwait, Sudan, and Egypt broke diplomatic relations with Bonn.

In an attempt to mollify the Arab states at the end of 1965, Chancellor Ludwig Erhard promised neutrality in future Arab-Israeli disputes, a move reinforced by Chancellor Kurt Kiesinger's emphasis on the need for good relations with Arab countries during his inaugural address of 1966. Nevertheless, diplomatic ties with the Arab world were restored only after the new government of Chancellor Willy Brandt abandoned the Hallstein Doctrine after 1970 and adopted new foreign policies.

With West Germany's awareness of the Arab world's growing political and economic power in the 1970s, the Ostpolitik (Eastern Policy) launched by the government of Brandt sought to improve relations with the Arab nations and West European states. Thus, it announced that West German foreign policy would reflect that of the EEC. While stressing that West Germany would not forget its responsibilities to Israel in the light of the Nazi past, Brandt emphasized that West Germany's Middle East policy would address the legitimate rights of all states, Arab and Israeli alike.

Consequently, West Germany supported the EEC's call for Israel to withdraw from areas it had occupied during the June 1967 Six-Day War. Declaring itself neutral during the October 1973 Yom Kippur War, West Germany protested against U.S. use of port facilities at Bremen to resupply Israel. These moves led to improved German-Arab relations, and by 1974 all the Arab states that had broken off diplomatic ties with West Germany in 1965 resumed relations with Bonn. Consequently, when the Organization of Petroleum Exporting Countries (OPEC) announced its oil embargo on October 17, 1973, West Germany faced only relatively light cutbacks of 5 percent per month.

Within five years, West Germany more than doubled its exports to Arab states, and an increasing flow of economic delegations and diplomatic visits ensued. Other marks of a shift in West Germany's Middle East policy occurred when Chancellor Helmut Schmidt publicly voiced criticism of Israel's settlement policy to Israeli premier Menachem Begin in June 1979. The following month, former chancellor Brandt and Austrian chancellor Bruno Kreisky met with Palestine Liberation Organization (PLO) leader Yasser Arafat. In June 1981, West German spokespersons expressed dismay at the Israeli bombing of Iraq's nuclear installations at Osiraq and a year later, upon Israel's invasion of Lebanon, joined other EEC members in short-term economic sanctions against Israel. Nevertheless, pressure from his cabinet and Israel forced Schmidt to abandon a tentative arms deal with Saudi Arabia in 1981.

Under Chancellor Helmut Kohl, who voiced a determination to improve German-Israeli relations, West German Middle East policy adopted a more subdued tone, even though unfortunate wording marred the chancellor's first visit to Israel in January 1984. He stated that as the first chancellor of the postwar generation, he enjoyed "the grace of late birth" and thus had not been involved in the crimes committed under the Third Reich. This faux pas laid him open to accusations that he was trying to escape responsibility for German actions between 1933 and 1945. Tensions rose again in 1987 when Israeli president Chaim Herzog expressed concern about West German weapons sales to Saudi Arabia. By and large, however, Middle Eastern policy during the mid to late 1980s played a relatively minor role in West Germany's Foreign Office, overshadowed by relations with the crumbling Soviet bloc in Central and Eastern Europe.

Reunified Germany faced its first major international crisis with Iraq's 1990 invasion of Kuwait and the subsequent wider Persian Gulf War early in 1991. Following the Iraqi seizure of several hundred hostages, many of whom were German, Chancellor Kohl's government came under intense public pressure to negotiate with Iraqi dictator Saddam Hussein, in spite of EEC resolutions to hold firm. Kohl therefore hesitantly backed Brandt's mission to Baghdad, which led to the release of 175 hostages from 11 countries on November 9, 1990, but faced criticism for Germany's unilateral action.

The German government found itself in a further difficult position in the face of a U.S. request to contribute troops to a UN-backed effort to drive Iraq from Kuwait. The German Grundgesetz (Basic Law) precluded German military involvement, as it limited the

German chancellor Angela Merkel shakes hands with acting Israeli prime minister Ehud Olmert after their joint press conference at the King David Hotel in Jerusalem on January 29, 2006. (Amos Ben Gershom/Israeli Government Press Office)

Bundeswehr (German armed forces) to defensive actions within the traditional area covered by NATO. Furthermore, massive public antiwar demonstrations and parliamentary opposition impeded Kohl's efforts to amend the constitution.

Nevertheless, the German government voiced full support for alliance efforts and, in place of military participation, resorted to checkbook diplomacy, contributing the equivalent of about $7 billion to the American-led intervention. In addition, Germany gave the United States full use of its territory for transport and resupply, contributed substantial amounts of military equipment, and deployed a minesweeping unit in the eastern Mediterranean. Also, Germany not only sent jet fighters and antiaircraft missile units to Turkey but also stationed more than 1,000 troops there to protect Turkish airfields.

In the wake of Hussein's threats of chemical warfare against Israel and the launching of Scud missile attacks on January 18, 1991, Germany reacted promptly, sending to Israel 250 million DM in humanitarian aid, armored vehicles for antichemical warfare, and air defense missiles. This reaction was prompted, at least in part,

by public exposure that German companies had earlier contributed to Iraq's store of missiles and chemical agents. After the end of the war, German minesweepers operated in the Persian Gulf from April through July 1991, and following the March 1991 Kurdish uprising, Bundeswehr personnel assisted in founding refugee camps in Iran and Iraq.

Germany's Middle East policy remained relatively passive for the remainder of Kohl's chancellorship, even though with the founding of the Palestinian Authority (PA) in 1994 in the wake of the Madrid Peace Process (1991) and the Oslo Accords (1993) Germany was the first country to establish a diplomatic mission, temporarily in Jericho and later in Ramallah. Germany soon became the most important European economic supporter of the PA, contributing about 23 percent of EU total funding.

Another significant development during the Kohl administration paved the way for a stronger German military role in the Middle East and other parts of the world. On July 12, 1994, Germany's Federal Constitutional Court declared that German troops could participate in UN peacekeeping missions and out-of-area NATO or Western European Union (WEU) undertakings backed by the UN, provided that a majority vote in the Bundestag approved such actions.

Even though Kohl's successor, Chancellor Gerhard Schröder, stated in his inaugural address of 1998 that Germany's historical responsibilities to Israel and peace in the Middle East would best be furthered by economic aid, bilateral trade, and infrastructural measures, Germany now began to assume a more active diplomatic role. This was largely prompted by the escalation of Palestinian-Israeli conflict after the failure of the U.S.-led negotiations at the 2000 Camp David Summit. After a Hamas suicide attack on March 27, 2002, that killed 29 people in Netanya, Israel, German foreign minister Joschka Fischer presented a paper titled "Ideas for Peace in the Middle East." In it he called for a road map laying out a timetable for Israelis and Palestinians to arrive at a two-state solution, overseen by a Quartet consisting of the United States, the EU, the UN, and Russia. Fischer's proposal evolved into the Road Map to Peace presented on April 30, 2003, to Israeli prime minister Ariel Sharon and newly elected Palestinian prime minister Mahmoud Abbas.

Further signs of a more involved German role included Arafat's visit to Berlin in the spring of 2000 and Schröder's return visit in the fall of that year. Several months later, following a suicide bombing outside of a Tel Aviv discotheque in June 2001, Fischer began a course of shuttle diplomacy, appealing to Arafat for a swift condemnation of the violence and urging Sharon against retaliation. The Second (al-Aqsa) Intifada of 2002, however, led to a significant cooling of relations with Israel when on April 9 Chancellor Schröder announced the suspension of arms sales, called for the early creation of a Palestinian state, and asked that Israel immediately withdraw from recently seized territory. Outspoken criticisms of Israel's role among German political figures, most notably from Jürgen Möllemann, deputy chairman of the Federal Democratic Party, further exacerbated tensions with Israel and were only defused by Möllemann's forced resignation.

After September 11, 2001, Germany's Middle East policy focused on international terrorism. Pledging unconditional political and military support for President George W. Bush's war on terror, Schröder made an initial commitment of 3,900 German troops to Afghanistan. Less than a year later, however, the German government refused to commit troops to the U.S.-led coalition against Iraq on the grounds that with 10,500 soldiers already serving in foreign countries, the Bundeswehr was already spread thin. In addition, the Schröder government objected to the absence of a UN mandate and the lack of a clear postvictory plan. This refusal cooled relations with Washington but aided Schröder's bid for reelection in the fall of 2002. Nevertheless, since the coalition takeover of Iraq, Germany has undertaken training programs for Iraqi military, police, security, technical, and medical personnel. In addition, Germany's financial contributions include $652,000 for program funding and airlift of Iraqi personnel, $155 million to the coalition and UN/World Bank Trust Fund, and $8 million toward Iraqi elections.

With Chancellor Angela Merkel's grand coalition government that took office on November 22, 2005, German foreign policy has undergone a pronounced shift, particularly by way of strengthened ties with Washington and Israel. Soon after her inauguration and shortly after the Islamic militant party Hamas won the Palestinian parliamentary elections on January 26, 2006, Merkel paid a state visit to Israel and met with acting prime minister Ehud Olmert and with Abbas, now the Palestinian president. At the time Merkel took a tough stand, emphasizing that no negotiation with Hamas should occur unless the organization recognized Israel and renounced terrorism. She also stated that Iran had "crossed a red line" in its nuclear policy and constituted a threat to Israel and all democratic countries. Subsequently, Germany supported the EU decision to suspend direct aid to the PA on April 10, 2006.

The 2006 Lebanese War prompted yet another major change in Germany's Middle East policy. On September 13, Merkel announced her cabinet's "historic decision" to send troops to the Middle East to enforce a truce between Lebanon and Israel. Continuing sensitivity about Germany's role in the Holocaust, however, limited the rules of engagement, which stipulated that German forces would not be placed in combat that could involve Israeli forces. Consequently, German naval forces were delegated to patrol the Lebanese coastline. As of November 18, 2006, Germany had deployed 1,021 troops in Lebanon.

ANNA M. WITTMANN

See also

Abbas, Mahmoud; Adenauer, Konrad; Arab Oil Embargo; Arafat, Yasser; Hamas; Intifada, Second; Lebanon, Israeli Invasion of; Madrid Conference; Olmert, Ehud; Organization of Petroleum Exporting Countries; Osiraq Raid; Oslo Accords; Persian Gulf War; Sharon, Ariel; Sinai Campaign; Six-Day War; United States Coordinating and Monitoring Mission; Yom Kippur War

References

Erlanger, Steven, et al. *German and American Perspectives on Israel, Palestine, and the Middle East Conflict.* AICGS German-American Issues 06. Washington, DC: American Institute for Contemporary German Studies, 2006.

Feldman, Lily Gardner. *The Special Relationship between West Germany and Israel.* Boston: Allen and Unwin, 1984.

Gray, William Glenn. *Germany's Cold War: The Global Campaign to Isolate East Germany, 1949–1969.* Chapel Hill: University of North Carolina Press, 2003.

Hacke, Christian. "The Foreign Policy of the Schröder/Fischer Administration in Historical Perspective." *American Foreign Policy Interests* 27(4) (August 2005): 289–294.

Lewan, Kenneth M. "How West Germany Helped to Build Israel." *Journal of Palestine Studies* 4(4) (Summer 1975): 41–64.

Müller, Harald. "German Foreign Policy after Unification." Pp. 126–173 in *The New Germany and the New Europe*, edited by Paul B. Stares. Washington, DC: Brookings Institution, 1992.

Noack, Paul. *Die Außenpolitik der Bundesrepublik Deutschland* [The Foreign Policy of the German Federal Republic]. 2nd ed. Stuttgart: Kohlhammer, 1981.

Overhaus, Marco, Hanns W. Maull, and Sebastian Harnisch, eds. "German Foreign Policy and the Middle East Conflict." Special issue of

German Foreign Policy in Dialogue: A Quarterly Newsletter on German Foreign Policy 3(7) (2002).

Giddi Pass

Strategic pass in the west-central Sinai Peninsula located at 30″13′ north and 33″04′ east. The Giddi (Jiddi) Pass lies approximately 25 miles east of the Suez Canal near the Little Bitter Lake. The Sinai is Egyptian territory.

The Sinai Peninsula features very rugged terrain. The southern portion is quite mountainous, confining most vehicle traffic to the coast. In the north, extensive sand dunes that extend in an arc from the Gulf of Suez to southwestern Israel also restrict travel. Transportation routes are somewhat better in Central Sinai, which is dominated by the Tih Plateau. The plateau is separated from the sand dunes by several limestone massifs including Giddi Mountain (Jabal al-Jiddi). This north-south oriented mountain, with peaks rising to 2,750 feet, poses a significant obstacle to east-west travel to and from the southern Suez Canal. Giddi Pass, which is located about 4.5 miles northwest of the highest peak, is one of the few routes between the Tih Plateau and the Suez Canal.

For centuries, people traveling east and west across the central Sinai Peninsula typically used the Darb al-Hajj (pilgrimage route) through the Mitla Pass. During the 1956 Suez Crisis and Sinai Campaign, Israeli forces ignored the Giddi Pass in favor of the Mitla Pass to the south and Bir Gifgafah to the north. In the 1960s, however, the Egyptian government embarked on a Sinai road-building program that included the construction of a paved road through the Giddi Pass. Consequently, it became a strategic objective during the 1967 Six-Day War and the 1973 Yom Kippur War.

On June 8, 1967, the fourth day of the Six-Day War, Israeli armored units defeated a force of some 30 Egyptian tanks and seized control of the Giddi Pass. By that time, Egyptian forces were withdrawing in disarray. Aside from one failed Egyptian counterattack, fighting ended at the Giddi Pass.

On October 6, 1973, Egyptian and Syria forces launched attacks against Israel to initiate the Yom Kippur War. Following a meticulous plan, Egyptian forces conducted a successful crossing of the Suez Canal and overran Israel's Bar-Lev Line. On October 14, however, the Egyptians launched a hastily planned offensive against Israeli forces near Giddi Mountain in hopes of diverting Israeli pressure from Syria. The Egyptian Third Army sent a blocking force against Israeli units at the Giddi Pass but made the Mitla Pass its primary objective. The Egyptian offensive, one of history's largest tank battles, was a failure, and the Israelis seized the opportunity to launch successful counterattacks that continued until the cease-fire on October 28, 1973.

A bus in Giddi Pass in the Sinai, July 3, 1975. (Sa'ar Ya'acov/Israeli Government Press Office)

The Giddi Pass figured prominently in subsequent Egyptian-Israeli peace negotiations. The January 18, 1974, Sinai I agreement involved the withdrawal of Israeli forces from the Suez Canal east to a defensive line that included the Giddi Pass. Israeli forces withdrew from the Giddi Pass as part of the September 4, 1975, Sinai II agreement. That agreement stipulated that electronic sensors as well as human monitors would provide Israel with early warning of Egyptian military movements in the region. Successful international monitoring of the Giddi Pass contributed to the signing of an Egyptian-Israeli peace treaty on March 26, 1979.

CHUCK FAHRER

See also

Bar-Lev Line; Egypt, Armed Forces; Israel Defense Forces; Israel-Egypt Peace Treaty; Mitla Pass; Sinai; Sinai Campaign; Sinai I and Sinai II Agreements; Six-Day War; Yom Kippur War

References

Greenwood, Ned H. *The Sinai: A Physical Geography.* Austin: University of Texas Press, 1997.

Herzog, Chaim. *The Arab-Israeli Wars: War and Peace in the Middle East from the War of Independence to Lebanon.* Westminster, MD: Random House, 1984.

Pollack, Kenneth M. *Arabs at War: Military Effectiveness, 1948–1991.* Lincoln: University of Nebraska Press, 2002.

Glubb, Sir John Bagot
Born: April 16, 1897
Died: March 17, 1986

British Army officer and commander of the Arab Legion in Transjordan (present-day Jordan) during 1939–1956. Born on April 16, 1897, in Preston, Lancashire, John Glubb was the son of a British Army officer. He was educated at Cheltenham College and the Royal Military Academy at Woolwich. In 1915 he entered the army as a second lieutenant in the Royal Engineers.

During World War I, Glubb served with the British Expeditionary Force (BEF) on the western front in France and was wounded three times, leaving him with a crooked jaw. He continued in British military service after the war and in 1920 was posted to Iraq, where he lived among Arab Bedouin and studied their culture. In the process, he gained a strong command of the Arabic language and earned the respect and friendship of many Arabs. He also studied the political and military strategy of the Turks, especially the rulers of the Seljuk dynasty. The knowledge of tactics he acquired, especially as it related to mobile partisan groups, proved to be of great benefit to his military operations in the Middle East.

The native police force that Glubb organized in the early 1920s played a large part in bringing order to Iraq. In 1926 he was seconded to Transjordan and became the administrative inspector for the Iraqi government. In 1930 he went to Transjordan to become second-in-command of the Arab Legion. Organized in 1920, the Arab Legion was initially a small police force led by British officer Frederick Peake, a major general in the Jordanian Army and known to Jordanians as Peake Pasha.

As second-in-command of the Arab Legion and a brigadier general in the Jordanian Army, Glubb became a close personal friend and trusted political adviser of Jordan's King Abdullah. Glubb organized an effective Bedouin desert patrol consisting of mobile detachments based at strategic desert forts and equipped with communications facilities. Within a few years he had managed to get the Bedouin to abandon their habit of raiding neighboring tribes.

When Peake retired in 1939, Glubb took command of the Arab Legion and made it the best-trained military force in the Arab world. During World War II he led attacks on pro-German leaders in Iraq as well as on the French Vichy regime in control of Lebanon and Syria. The Arab Legion's Mechanized Regiment provided notable service alongside British forces in the 1941 overthrow of Iraq's pro-Nazi Rashid Ali al-Gaylani regime. The British continued to subsidize the Arab Legion. Through World War II most of its officers were drawn from serving British officers.

For the duration of the war, the Arab Legion provided train guards for the railways from Damascus to Cairo. By 1945 the Arab Legion numbered more than 8,000 men, including 37 British officers. At the conclusion of the war the Arab Legion was downsized to 4,500 men, however.

During the 1948–1949 Israeli War of Independence, Lieutenant General Glubb commanded the Arab Legion against Israel. Although the Arab Legion was the best-equipped and best-trained Arab army, it was relatively small compared to the Israeli forces. The Israeli government, which had been engaged in secret negotiations with King Abdullah, hoped that the Arab Legion would stay out of the war completely. Abdullah, however, ultimately decided that not joining the other Arab states would render untenable his position in the Arab world. After Israeli independence was declared on May 14, 1948, the armies of Egypt, Syria, Iraq, Lebanon, and Jordan invaded Israel. Israeli forces eventually prevailed, and Jordan signed an armistice with Israel on April 3, 1949.

On March 2, 1956, Jordan's King Hussein, bowing to pressure from Arab nationalists, dismissed Glubb as commander of the Arab Legion, which had then grown to a force of 20,000 men. Although Hussein maintained a cordial relationship with Glubb during and after his dismissal, the Jordanian king sought to placate Arab nationalists who claimed that he was under British control.

Returning to Britain, Glubb was knighted. He retired as a British Army lieutenant general. In retirement he wrote numerous books, including *A Soldier with the Arabs* (1957), *Britain and the Arabs* (1959), and *A Short History of the Arab Peoples* (1969). Known as Glubb Pasha, he lectured widely on Arab affairs. Glubb died on March 17, 1986, in Mayfield, East Sussex.

MICHAEL R. HALL

See also

Abdullah I, King of Jordan; Arab Legion; Hussein, King of Jordan; Latrun, Battles of

General Sir John Bagot Glubb, British Army officer and commander of the Arab Legion in Transjordan (later Jordan) during 1939–1956, handling his Muslim prayer beads (misbaha) in October 1951. (Charles Hewitt/Picture Post/Getty Images)

References

Glubb, John Bagot. *Into Battle: A Soldier's Diary of the Great War.* London: Cassell, 1978.

———. *The Middle East Crisis: A Personal Interpretation.* London: Hodder and Stoughton, 1969.

———. *The Story of the Arab Legion.* London: Hodder and Stoughton, 1950.

Lunt, James D. *Glubb Pasha, a Biography: Lieutenant-General Sir John Bagot Glubb, Commander of the Arab Legion, 1939–1956.* London: W. Collins, 1984.

Royle, Trevor. *Glubb Pasha: The Life and Times of Sir John Bagot Glubb, Commander of the Arab Legion.* New York: Time-Warner Books, 1992.

Young, Peter. *The Arab Legion.* London: Osprey, 2002.

Gog and Magog

Apocalyptic term appearing in both the Hebrew Bible and the Christian New Testament as well as the Koran. Gog and Magog also appear in folklore. They are variously identified as supernatural beings, national groups, or even lands.

The first reference to Magog appears in the "Table of Nations" in Genesis 10:2, with Magog given as one of the sons of Japheth. The first reference to Gog and Magog together is in Ezekiel 38:2–3 where Yahweh (God) warns the prophet, "Son of man, set thy face against Gog the land of Magog, the chief prince of Meshech and Tubal, and prophesy against him. . . . Behold, I come against thee, O Gog, the chief prince of Meshech and Tubal." The same command is repeated at the beginning of Chapter 39, but there is no clear identification of either the ruler or his country. In Chapter 38:5–6, Gog is identified as being accompanied in his invasion of Israel by the nations of Persia, Ethiopia, Libya, and Gomer and the house of Thogorma.

Because of the sheer number of peoples identified by Ezekiel as taking part in the invasion of Israel, some have asserted that Gog is simply a generic figure for all of the enemies of Israel and that reference to it in the Apocalypse denotes the enemies of the Church. The book of Revelation 20:7–8 reads: "And when the thousand years are expired, Satan shall be loosed out of his prison, and shall go out to deceive the nations that are in the four quarters of the earth, Gog and Magog, to gather them to battle: the number of whom is as the sand of the sea." The Koran 21:96–97 makes reference to Gog and Magog being "let loose" and that, at that time, "the True Promise shall draw near."

Scholars have also endeavored to identify Gog historically. One possible source is the Lydian king known to the Greeks as Gyges or in Assyrian inscriptions as Gu-gu. Others say that Gog and Magog are two tribes and refer to the Khazar kingdom in the northern Caucasus or the Mongols. Apparently, Gog may also have been used in ancient Israel to identify any northern population. Throughout history there have been repeated claims that Gog and Magog represent particular peoples, including the Goths.

The phrase "Gog and Magog" has been used by some extremists in the Arab-Israeli conflict to justify the unjustifiable. Some have claimed that Ezekiel's prophecy of the invasion of Israel by a vast number of enemies refers to the present conflict in the Middle East in which the Islamic nations will all invade Israel, and that this great conflict will see the rise of the Antichrist and end with the destruction of Israel's enemies by God Himself. At the outbreak of World War II, Avraham Stern, founder of the terrorist group Lehi, declared that the war was a struggle between Gog and Magog and that this justified increased violent action against the British Mandate for Palestine.

SPENCER C. TUCKER

See also

Bible; Genesis, Book of; Koran; Stern, Avraham

References

Berner, Douglas. *The Silence Is Broken: God Hooks Ezekiel's Gog and Magog.* London: Lulu, 2006.
The Catholic Encyclopedia, Vol. 6. New York: Robert Appleton, 1909.

Golan Heights

Plateau located on the border between Israel, Lebanon, and Syria. Israel captured the Golan Heights from Syria during the 1967 Six-Day War and retook it during the 1973 Yom Kippur War. The Golan Heights is an area of great strategic importance for Israel, as it dominates the entire eastern Galilee. Any military force occupying the Golan Heights is well positioned to cut Israel in two. The Golan Heights is also within operational striking distance of Damascus, the Syrian capital, that lies directly to the northeast. Control of the Golan Heights also gives Israeli forces a geographic advantage over Hezbollah forces operating in southern Lebanon.

The Golan Heights forms part of the Holocene volcanic field that reaches almost to Damascus. The heights covers an area of some 775 square miles. To the west are steep rocky cliffs that fall 1,700 feet to the Jordan River and the Sea of Galilee. To the south is the Yarmouk River, to the north lies Lebanon, and to the east is a plain known as the Hawran.

Syria continues to insist on the return of the Golan Heights as a precondition for normalizing relations with Israel, and bilateral peace talks on the highly volatile issue have thus far been unsuccessful. Lebanon claims a small portion of the Golan Heights, known as the Shaba Farms, as part of its territory, a claim that Syria acknowledges.

Following World War I, the Golan Heights was included in the French Mandate for Syria, although in 1924 a small portion of the Golan Heights was designated as part of the British Mandate for Palestine. When Syria became independent in 1944 it secured control of the Golan Heights, which was known within that country as the Syrian Heights. A plateau and part of an ancient volcanic field, it was strategically important to Syria in part because of its water resources, a valuable and often rare commodity in the Middle East.

During 1944–1967, Syria maintained control of the Golan Heights. Following the Israeli War of Independence (1948–1949), Syria used the area as a staging base for attacks against Israeli farming settlements. These actions, along with Israel's retaliatory strikes, were in violation of the Israel-Syria Armistice Agreement that ended the war. Tensions between the two sides increased, and during the 1967 Six-Day War Israel successfully captured the Golan Heights on June 9–10. At the time, approximately 90 percent of the population (mostly Druze Syrians and Circassians) fled the area. They have not been permitted to return. Israel immediately began building Jewish settlements in the area, with the first settlement town of Merom established in July 1967.

Syria refused to make peace with Israel unless the Golan Heights was returned, and Israel continued building settlements in the area, with 12 towns already established there by 1970. Tensions escalated sharply with the surprise attack on Israel by Egypt and Syria that began the Yom Kippur War in 1973. Israel found itself having to fight on two fronts (the Sinai Peninsula and the Golan Heights) but decided to assume the operational defensive against Egypt while taking the offensive against the more serious threat to Israel itself posed by the Syrians in the north. Despite being severely outnumbered by Syrian armor (170 Israeli tanks faced 1,500 Syrian tanks), Israel was able to turn the tide of the war on the northern front on October 8. After Israeli forces pushed the Syrians back to the 1967 border, they continued to drive into Syria proper, reaching to within 25 miles of Damascus before they halted and shifted priority to the southern front against Egypt.

After the end of the war, more than 1,000 United Nations (UN)

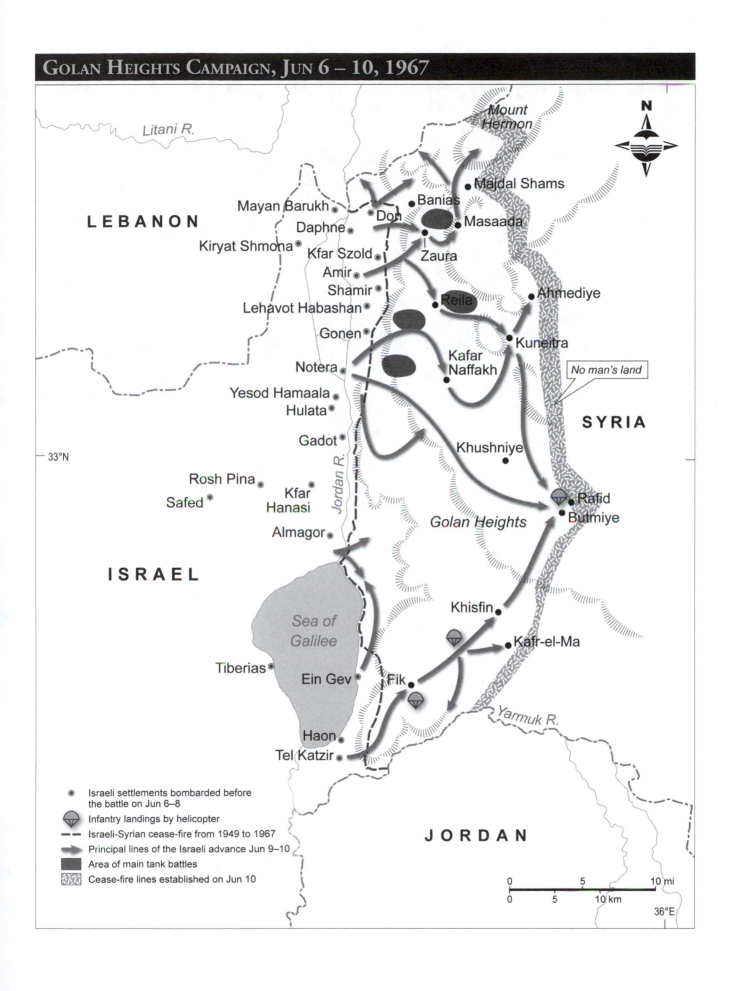

GOLAN HEIGHTS CAMPAIGN, JUN 6 – 10, 1967

Litani R.

Mount Hermon

N

LEBANON

Mayan Barukh
Daphne
Kiriyat Shmona
Kfar Szold
Amir
Shamir
Lehavot Habashan
Gonen
Notera
Yesod Hamaala
Hulata
Gadot

Don
Banias
Majdal Shams
Masaada
Zaura

Reila
Ahmediye

Kafar Naffakh
Kuneitra

No man's land

SYRIA

Khushniye

33°N

Rosh Pina
Kfar Hanasi
Safed
Almagor

Golan Heights

Rafid
Butmiye

ISRAEL

Sea of Galilee

Tiberias
Ein Gev

Khisfin

Kafir-el-Ma

Fik

Haon
Tel Katzir

Yarmuk R.

JORDAN

⊙ Israeli settlements bombarded before
    the battle on Jun 6–8
⬙ Infantry landings by helicopter
– ·– Israeli-Syrian cease-fire from 1949 to 1967
➤ Principal lines of the Israeli advance Jun 9–10
▮ Area of main tank battles
▨ Cease-fire lines established on Jun 10

| 0 | 5 | 10 mi |
| 0 | 5 | 10 km |

36°E

The Golan Heights overlooking Kibbutz En Gev, Israel, 1998. (Dave G. Houser/Corbis)

peacekeeping troops were stationed on the Golan Heights to monitor the cease-fire. The Golan Heights remained under Israeli military administration until 1981, when legislation was passed subjecting the area to Israeli law and granting citizenship privileges to people living there. Although Israel did not use the word "annexation" in the legislation, much of the international community saw the move as such. The UN responded with Security Council Resolution 497, which held that "the Israeli decision to impose its laws, jurisdiction and administration in the occupied Syrian Golan Heights is null and void and without international legal effect." However, the UN also avoided calling the move an annexation.

Possession of the Golan Heights remains central to the ongoing crisis in the Middle East, and Syria has repeatedly refused to normalize relations with the Jewish state until the Golan Heights is returned to Syria. Syria demands a withdrawal of Israel to the 1948 armistice line, which extends Syrian territory to the shores of the Sea of Galilee. Syria claims that its demands are in keeping with UN Security Council Resolution 242 and Resolution 338, which call for Israel to withdraw from the territories it occupied during the 1967 war. During the 1999–2000 peace negotiations, Israel proposed returning most of the Golan Heights to Syria. However, Syria refused the offer on the grounds that this would be less than a complete fulfillment of UN resolutions.

Some 38,900 people lived in the Golan Heights in 2005, including approximately 19,300 Druze, 16,500 Jews (in 34 settlements), and 2,100 Muslims. Israel maintains that the Golan Heights is a strategically important buffer between Israel and Syria and that it is essential for Israeli security. The Israeli government has refused to enter into direct peace negotiations with Syria (previous talks were brokered by the United States) unless Syria agrees to end Hezbollah attacks launched against Israel from Lebanon.

SPENCER C. TUCKER

See also

Hezbollah; Israel; Israeli War of Independence, Israeli-Syrian Front; Settlements, Israeli; Six-Day War; Syria; United Nations Peacekeeping Missions; United Nations Security Council Resolution 242; United Nations Security Council Resolution 338; Yom Kippur War

References

Asher, Jerry, and Eric Hammel. *Duel for the Golan: The 100-Hour Battle That Saved Israel.* Pacifica, CA: Pacifica Press, 1987.

Dunstan, Simon. *Campaign 118: The Yom Kippur War, 1973; The Golan Heights.* Oxford, UK: Osprey, 2003.

Lerman, Hallie. *Crying for Imma: Battling for the Soul on the Golan Heights.* San Francisco: Night Vision, 1998.

Maar'i, Tayseer, and Usama Halabi. "Life under Occupation in the Golan Heights." *Journal of Palestine Studies* 22 (1992): 78–93.

Moaz, Moshe. *Syria and Israel: From War to Peacemaking.* Oxford: Oxford University Press, 1995.

Rabil, Robert G. *Embattled Neighbors: Syria, Israel, Lebanon.* Boulder, CO: Lynn Rienner, 2003.

Goldmann, Nahum
Born: July 10, 1895
Died: August 29, 1982

Prominent Zionist leader and president of both the World Jewish Congress and World Zionist Organization. Born on July 10, 1895, in Vishnovo, Lithuania, then part of the Russian Empire, Nahum Goldmann immigrated with his parents to Germany in 1900 and grew up in Frankfurt-am-Main. He studied history, law, and philosophy at the Universities of Marburg, Heidelberg, and Berlin.

During World War I Goldmann headed the Jewish Division of the German Foreign Ministry. A Zionist from an early age, he joined with others in a vain attempt to enlist the support of Kaiser Wilhelm II for the establishment of a Jewish state in Palestine. Returning to Heidelberg after the war, Goldmann earned his doctorate in law in 1920. In 1919 he published a pamphlet, *The Three Demands of the Jewish People,* in which he spelled out the three demands as the right of Jews to Palestine, minority rights for Jews in the Diaspora, and civil equality for Jews.

During the 1920s Goldmann was involved in publishing a Jewish periodical and a German Jewish encyclopedia. Although the latter project was cut short by the rise to power of the Nazis in Germany, in the 1960s Goldmann was a key figure behind the English-language *Encyclopedia Judaica.* During the period of the British Mandate for Palestine, he was a staunch advocate for its partition into Jewish and Arab states.

Stripped of his citizenship and forced to leave Germany in 1935, he went first to Honduras and then to New York, where he was active in Zionist causes and became the representative of the Jewish Agency in New York for several years before going to Geneva to help assist in the escape of Jews from Nazi-controlled territory. He repeatedly pointed out the vital importance of the Jewish Diaspora to the Zionist cause, and in 1936 he helped organize the World Jewish Congress. The first chairman of its executive board, he then was its president in 1933 and held that post for many years. Between 1935 and 1939 he was the political representative of the World Zionist Organization (WZO) to the League of Nations in Geneva, where he busied himself with refugee issues. At the World Zionist Congress of 1937, he advocated the partition of Palestine and creation of a Jewish state.

Following World War II, Goldmann promoted the creation of a Jewish state in Palestine and actively negotiated toward that end with both the British and U.S. governments. But he also feared, correctly, that this would lead to a war between Jews and Arabs. He was subsequently a key figure in the negotiations with the West German government that led in 1952 to an agreement regarding reparations for the Holocaust, and he helped conclude a similar agreement in 1954 with Austria. He was also active in a variety of other causes, includ-

Dr. Nahum Goldmann, Zionist leader and president of both the World Jewish Congress and the World Zionist Organization (WZO), December 27, 1960. (Moshe Pridan/Israeli Government Press Office)

---

ing the plight of Jews in the Soviet Union, Jewish education, and Jewish culture. Strongly opposed to Jewish assimilation, he sought to create strong institutions among Jews in the Diaspora. Although he became an Israeli citizen in 1962, he never became a permanent resident, dividing his time between Israel and Switzerland.

Goldmann subsequently criticized Israel for what he believed was its excessive reliance on military force, and he was also sharply critical of what he thought to be lack of generosity on the part of Israel's leaders toward the Arab states following the 1967 Six-Day War. He tried but failed in efforts to talk with Egyptian president Gamal Abdel Nasser in 1970, while many Israelis regarded Goldmann's effort to meet with Palestine Liberation Organization (PLO) chairman Yasser Arafat in 1974 as nothing less than treason. Goldmann warned the Israeli government unsuccessfully against intervention in Lebanon in 1982, claiming that it would reignite anti-Semitism and anti-Israeli sentiment. He wanted Israel to be a moral beacon for the rest of the world and a neutral state like Switzerland, with its existence and borders recognized by its neighbors and perhaps guaranteed by a small international peacekeeping presence.

Goldmann died in Bad Reichenhall, Germany, on August 29, 1982. His body was returned to Israel for burial.

SPENCER C. TUCKER

See also

Arafat, Yasser; Assimilation; Diaspora; Holocaust; Nasser, Gamal Abdel; World Jewish Congress; World Zionist Organization; Zionism

References

Goldmann, Nahum. *The Autobiography of Nahum Goldmann: Sixty Years of Jewish Life.* New York: Holt, Rinehart and Winston, 1969.

———. *The Jewish Paradox.* New York: Grosset and Dunlap, 1978.

Laqueur, Walter. *A History of Zionism: From the French Revolution to the Establishment of the State of Israel.* Reprint ed. New York: Schocken, 2003.

Gonen, Shmuel

Born: 1930
Died: September 30, 1991

Israeli general. Shmuel Gonen was born in Lithuania sometime in 1930. At the age of 3, he moved with his family to Palestine. There at age 14 he joined the Haganah underground Jewish self-defense organization. In 1948 during the Israeli War for Independence, he was wounded on five separate occasions in the battles for Jerusalem.

Gonen then became part of the Israel Defense Forces (IDF). During the 1956 Sinai Campaign in the Suez Crisis he commanded a tank company with the rank of major. Following that conflict Israel acquired British Centurion tanks, and Gonen commanded the first IDF tank battalion to be equipped with this main battle tank (MBT). To do this, he had to accept a temporary reduction in rank. As a commander, he was generally unpopular with his men and was seen as something of a martinet.

In 1966 Gonen, now a colonel, commanded the 7th Armored Brigade. In the Six-Day War in 1967, he led his unit from Rafah to the Suez Canal. In 1968 he led an attack on the headquarters of Yasser Arafat in Lebanon, but the raid failed to inflict significant losses on the Palestine Liberation Organization (PLO).

In 1973 Gonen replaced Ariel Sharon as commander of the Southern Command, gaining the rank of major general. Despite recognizing the need to improve Israeli defensive positions along the Suez Canal, Gonen was unable to complete the upgrades in time to meet the Egyptian attack that began the Yom Kippur War in October 1973. He was forced to react to the initial Egyptian attacks and then launched a counterattack that proved unsuccessful. He was relieved of his command on October 10, 1973, by Lieutenant General Chaim Bar-Lev. Gonen's dismissal was more about the unpreparedness of IDF troops than about the failed counteroffensive.

Gonen's decisions came in for heavy criticism in the initial reports of the Agranat Commission's inquiry into the level of preparedness of Israeli forces prior to the Egyptian attack. Although

at first Gonen was removed from all command, late in 1973 he was given an appointment on the General Staff.

Gonen resigned from the IDF in 1974 to pursue a variety of business ventures in the Central African Republic. He died there on September 30, 1991. Shortly after his death, Israeli author Hillel Mittelpunkt wrote a play about his life titled *Gorodish*.

RALPH MARTIN BAKER

See also

Armored Warfare Doctrine; Israel Defense Forces; Sinai Campaign; Six-Day War; Tank Warfare; Yom Kippur War

References

Dunstan, Simon. *The Yom Kippur War, 1973.* 2 vols. Westport, CT: Praeger, 2005.

Rabinovich, Abraham. *The Yom Kippur War: The Epic Encounter That Transformed the Middle East.* New York: Schocken, 2005.

Great Britain, Middle East Policy

See United Kingdom, Middle East Policy

Great Palestinian Rebellion

See Arab Revolt of 1936–1939

Green Line

The border of Israel prior to the June 1967 Six-Day War delineated as a result of the truce agreements that followed the 1948–1949 Israeli War of Independence. The Green Line, so-named because it was drawn with green marker on the maps at the time, designated the area under Jewish control in Palestine.

The Green Line encompassed about 78 percent of Palestinian territory in 1947 before the Israeli War of Independence. Although it delineated a military boundary only, in effect the Green Line actually defined the de facto state borders between Israel and Egypt, Jordan, Syria, and Lebanon. The sole exception was the municipality of Jerusalem. Israel claimed as sovereign territory the parts of the city administered by Jordan until 1967.

Drawing of the Green Line was based almost exclusively on military considerations. As such, it wreaked havoc on a number of communities, dividing towns and villages and separating farmers from their fields. Jerusalem was especially impacted, being divided into West and East Jerusalem. The Jordanian city of Qalqilyah became virtually an enclave within Israel, while Kibbutz Ramat Rachel was left almost entirely outside of Israeli territory.

During the Six-Day War, Israel occupied sizable territories beyond the Green Line inhabited by perhaps 3 million Palestinians, including many displaced by the 1948–1949 war. The Green Line remains the administrative border for the West Bank territory acquired in the Six-Day War, with the exception of East Jerusalem, which was annexed by Israel. In 1981 the Israeli government extended Israeli law to the Golan Heights, which had been taken from Syria in the 1967 war.

SPENCER C. TUCKER

See also

Israeli War of Independence, Overview; Israeli War of Independence, Truce Agreements; Six-Day War

References

Bornstein, Avram. *Crossing the Green Line between the West Bank and Israel.* Philadelphia: University of Pennsylvania Press, 2002.

Cottrell, Robert Charles, et al. *The Green Line: The Division of Palestine.* New York: Chelsea House, 2004.

Grün, David

See Ben-Gurion, David

Gulf War

See Persian Gulf War

Gur, Mordechai
Born: May 6, 1930
Died: July 16, 1995

Israeli Army general and chief of staff of the Israel Defense Forces (IDF) during 1974–1978. Mordechai (Motta) Gur was born in Jerusalem on May 6, 1930. He joined the Haganah as a youth in April 1948 and fought in the 1948–1949 Israeli War for Independence. During 1951–1954 he attended Hebrew University in Tel Aviv, where he majored in Middle Eastern studies.

Gur then joined the newly formed IDF and served in its elite Parachute Brigade. By the 1950s he was a company commander under Colonel Ariel Sharon. In 1955 Gur was wounded in a counterterrorist raid in Khan Yunis. He played an important role in the 1956 Sinai Campaign, leading the reconnaissance in force into the Egyptian-held Mitla Pass. His troops walked into an ambush but were able to hold out until they were reinforced. Casualties were heavy, however.

From 1959 to 1960 Gur studied at the École Militaire in Paris. In 1961 Gur, now a colonel, received command of the Golani Brigade. In 1965 he headed the Operations Division of the General Staff and later had charge of the IDF Commander's School.

In 1966 Gur received command of the 55th Parachute Brigade. He led this formation in the Six-Day War the next year. At the start of the campaign his troops were in reserve, but they were soon committed to the attack on Jerusalem. In some of the hardest fighting in the war, much of it hand-to-hand with the Jordanians, Gur personally led the attack on the Lions' Gate. His men were the first

Lieutenant General Mordechai Gur, chief of staff of the Israel Defense Forces (1974–1978), in April 1974. (Israeli Government Press Office)

---

troops to reach the Western Wall and the Temple Mount. His signal to headquarters—"The Temple Mount is in our hands. Repeat. The Temple Mount is ours."—was the most memorable communication of the war.

Promoted to brigadier general in 1968, Gur then commanded IDF units in the Gaza Strip and the Sinai. In 1970 he commanded the northern front, where he waged a campaign against the Palestine Liberation Organization (PLO), which was launching attacks against Israel from Syria.

During 1972–1973 Gur was the Israeli military attaché in Washington, D.C. Following the Yom Kippur War in 1973, he returned to Israel to command the northern front. In April 1974 he was promoted to lieutenant general and succeeded Lieutenant General David Elazar as chief of staff of the IDF. In this post, Gur authorized the raid on Entebbe to release Israeli hostages as well as Operation LITANI.

Retiring from the IDF in 1978, Gur studied at the Harvard University School of Business, and the next year he became general manager of the Kur Mechanica Company. During 1981–1982 he served in the Knesset (Israeli parliament). Reelected to the Knesset in 1984, during 1984–1986 he was minister of health. From 1986 to

1988 he was chairman of the board of Solel Boneh Construction Company and also became a member of the Knesset Foreign Affairs and Defense Committee. Reelected to the Knesset in 1988, he became minister without portfolio. Reelected to the Knesset again in 1992, he was appointed deputy minister of defense. Diagnosed with terminal cancer, Gur committed suicide on July 16, 1995, at his home in Tel Aviv.

RALPH MARTIN BAKER

See also

Arab Legion; Entebbe Hostage Rescue; Mitla Pass; Six-Day War

References

Gur, Mordechai. *The Battle for Jerusalem.* New York: I Books, 2002.

Hammel, Eric. *Six Days in June: How Israel Won the 1967 Arab-Israeli War.* New York: Scribner, 1992.

Oren, Michael B. *Six Days of War: June 1967 and the Making of the Modern Middle East.* Novato, CA: Presidio, 2003.

Ha-Avara

Start Date: August 25, 1933
End Date: September 1939

A transfer agreement established jointly by the German Third Reich and the World Zionist Organization (WZO) on August 25, 1933, to allow German Jews to take some of their wealth with them when they emigrated for Palestine during the 1930s. Ironically, the greatest support for National Socialist ideas regarding the separation of races came from Zionists. Although the arrangement worked to the financial disadvantage of German Jews, it did allow them to escape with their lives and at least part of their wealth before World War II halted the operation and the Holocaust began.

The National Socialists came to power in Germany in 1933 determined to solve the so-called Jewish question. Nazi leader and new German chancellor Adolf Hitler believed that Jews differed from Christians not because of their religion but because they were a completely separate race. In contrast, most German Jews believed that Jews could be assimilated into German society. A minority of German Jews who were Zionists held similar opinions as the Nazis in that they believed Jews should not try to be assimilated into a larger society but should establish their own homeland. These Zionists believed that they could work with the Nazis to achieve their goal of creating a Jewish homeland. Representatives worked with members of the Nazi Party on ways to convince other Jews that they were Jews and not German citizens. During the 1930s, Zionist organizations received preferential treatment from Nazi leaders who hoped to create a Jewish identity among German Jews. Separate Jewish organizations were created, and the Zionist flag, the Star of David on a blue background, was allowed to be displayed by these groups.

Many Nazis and Zionists were in agreement that the best solution to the problem was for the Jews to leave Germany and settle in another country. Palestine was a natural choice, because Zionist settlements had already been created there and because Jews had emotional and spiritual connections to the land. To encourage emigration for Palestine, Germany allowed Zionists to establish training camps throughout the country. Potential settlers were oriented to the conditions in Palestine and trained in the work they would be asked to do there. Jewish emigration for Palestine was limited, however, because Palestine was under British control. Only a small quota of new settlers was allowed unless they could meet the capitalist qualification of proving that they had $5,000 in wealth. An unlimited number of those certified as capitalists could relocate to Palestine.

The shared goals of Zionists and Nazis led to the Ha-Avara, or Transfer Agreement. Shortly after the Nazis assumed power in Germany, most Jewish organizations around the world declared an embargo on German trade. As a result, the new government instituted strict currency laws to prevent the loss of capital to other countries.

Negotiations were held throughout the summer of 1933 between Chaim Arlosoroff, political secretary of the Jewish Agency, and Nazi officials. The Jewish Agency represented the WZO in Palestine. On August 25, 1933, the two groups signed an agreement establishing the Ha-Avara to promote Jewish emigration and to get around currency restrictions.

The terms of the agreement were relatively simple. Each Jew who decided to emigrate for Palestine deposited money into an account in Germany. The money was used to purchase German-made agricultural supplies including tools, building materials, pumps, and fertilizer. The supplies were then transported to Palestine, where

407

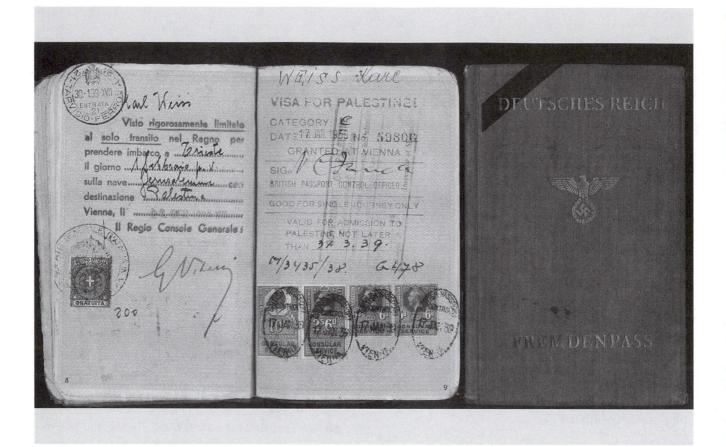

A German passport from 1939 with authorization to travel to Palestine. When World War II began in September 1939, all Jewish emigration under the Ha-Avara agreement was abruptly halted. (Israeli Government Press Office)

the Ha-Avara Company in Tel Aviv would sell them to Jewish settlers. The emigrant would receive the funds from the sale of goods that equaled the amount he deposited into the German account. Because of varying exchange rates and fees charged by the Germans, the emigrants lost about 30 percent of their funds in the transfer. A later addition set up a barter system whereby agricultural products from Palestine, such as oranges, were exchanged for goods manufactured in Germany. Other arrangements permitted Jewish leaders to pool funds so that emigrants could meet the $5,000 capitalist qualification. The German government organized a separate company called Intria to raise funds in other countries that could then be donated to Jewish organizations in Palestine.

Jewish organizations immediately debated whether the Ha-Avara was a proper action to undertake. It helped to undermine the embargo against the Nazis, but it allowed German Jews to escape from Nazi persecution. The 1933 Zionist Congress in Prague reluctantly approved the agreement after being assured by those involved that it would not help the Nazis.

Two years later, in 1935, the Zionist Congress meeting in Switzerland approved the Ha-Avara by a wide margin. In 1936 the Jewish Agency took direct control over the Ha-Avara. By 1937, members of the German government believed that the Ha-Avara

was harming German standing and trade with Arabs. Hitler himself reviewed the agreement before giving his approval to its continuance. Other countries, including Poland and Czechoslovakia, signed similar agreements so that their population could emigrate for Palestine. The Ha-Avara agreement remained in effect until war broke out in September 1939, making further emigration impossible.

The Ha-Avara made it possible for 60,000 German Jews, nearly 10 percent of that population, to emigrate for Palestine between 1933 and 1939. A further 10,000 were ready to leave in September 1939 when World War II began. These settlers brought much technical and financial knowledge to the Jewish population in Palestine. They also transferred considerable capital to Palestine. An estimated $100 million worth of goods flowed into Palestine between 1933 and 1939 because of the Ha-Avara. Ironically, Germany was the largest exporter of goods and capital to Palestine during the 1930s. Much of the infrastructure and industry that existed in 1948 was a result of Ha-Avara transfers, and the possibility of a Jewish state was indirectly tied to the Ha-Avara.

TIM J. WATTS

See also

Holocaust; Palestine, British Mandate for; World Zionist Organization

References

Amkraut, Brian. *Between Home and Homeland: Youth Aliyah from Nazi Germany.* Tuscaloosa: University of Alabama Press, 2006.

Black, Edwin. *The Transfer Agreement: The Untold Story of the Secret Agreement between the Third Reich and Jewish Palestine.* New York: Macmillan, 1984.

Kampe, Norbert. *Jewish Emigration from Germany, 1933–1942: A Documentary History.* Munich: K. G. Saur, 1992.

Nicosia, Francis R. *The Third Reich and the Palestine Question.* Austin: University of Texas Press, 1985.

Habash, George
Born: August 2, 1926
Died: January 26, 2008

Militant Palestinian politician and cofounder of the Popular Front for the Liberation of Palestine (PFLP). George (Jurj) Habash, sometimes known as al-Hakim (the doctor, or the sage) was born on August 2, 1926, in Lydda (Lod), Palestine, now Israel. Born into a family of Greek Orthodox merchants, he graduated with a degree in pediatric medicine from the American University in Beirut in 1951. In 1948 his family had been forcibly expelled from their home by Israeli forces, an incident that he never forgot. While a student, Habash, along with Hani al-Hindi, a Syrian, worked with a group of Egyptian terrorists aiming at Western targets in Damascus and Beirut. The group was caught when they were plotting to kill the Syrian president. Habash and al-Hindi returned to the university, intending to give up terrorism for mass struggle. They created a secret nationalist organization, the Arab Nationalist Movement (ANM), out of a campus committee. By 1951 the ANM moved off campus into activities in the Palestinian refugee camps in Lebanon. By 1953 the organization spread to Jordan. In 1954 the group protested against the Baghdad Pact on campus, and a student was killed in a confrontation with police. The students were expelled but were welcomed to Cairo University by order of President Gamal Abdel Nasser. The ANM cooperated with the Egyptian government until 1967 and developed its branches in different countries. Nayef Hawatmeh, who formed the DFLP (Democratic Front for the Liberation of Palestine), also emerged from a younger cohort of ANM activists. In 1957 he was accused of having been involved in a Palestinian-inspired plot to seize control of the Jordanian government. Forced into hiding after Jordan's King Hussein cracked down on political opposition and invoked martial law, Habash fled to Syria in 1958. Three years later when Syria pulled out of the United Arab Republic and the nation was returned to Baath rule, he went to Beirut.

In 1964 Habash organized the Palestinians within the Palestinian branch of the ANM into the National Front for the Liberation of Palestine (NFLP). The NFLP contained a military wing, the Shabab

George Habash, military leader of the Popular Front for the Liberation of Palestine (PFLP), shown here in Amman, Jordan, June 12, 1972. (Genevieve Chauvel/Corbis Sygma)

al-Tha'r, that conducted a raid against Israel over the border in the same year.

The Arab states' stinging loss in the June 1967 Six-Day War led Habash, like many Palestinians, to a fundamental reassessment of the philosophy undergirding the Palestinian struggle. Habash called for a unity appeal to other militant organizations, and the NFLP joined up with two other groups, the Palestine Liberation Front (Jabhat al-Tahrir al-Filastiniyya) and Heroes of the Return (Abtal al-Awda), to form the PFLP whose first statement promised revolutionary violence.

The PFLP took a harsh, uncompromising stance against Israel and those nations that aided it and had little use for conservative Arab regimes in the Middle East. At first, the PFLP argued with Fatah over the exclusivity of the PLO. Then Khalil al-Wazir of Fatah and Habash worked out a program to unify their activities. This agreement was disavowed after the Battle of Karameh in Jordan because the PFLP withdrew its fighters there.

Ideological friction after 1967 related to that defeat also divided the PFLP from within. Some members, led by Hawatmeh and Muhsin Ibrahim who had earlier idealized Nasser, criticized Nasser's government and ideology in radical socialist language, stating that its failures were due to its petit-bourgeois origins. Nasser cut off aid to the organization, although by then Habash was in jail in Syria following the PFLP's sabotage of the Trans-Arabia pipeline. Ahmad Jibril seceded from the main group into his PFLP General Command. Habash escaped from prison in 1968, but then the Hawatmeh group within the PFLP seceded from it. Habash became the group's secretary-general in 1969, and the group hoped to transfer its movement into a movement similar to Fidel Castro's and attract the working class. In the 1970s the General Union of Palestinian Workers (GUPW) was headquartered in Damascus, where the former ANM became the main force of the PFLP and of the GUPW.

By the early 1970s, the PFLP had become a well-recognized sponsor of international terrorism, including a series of airline hijackings. By 1972, however, Habash announced that he was against further hijackings. The PFLP continued to have friction with other Palestinian groups, and after the 1973 war this resulted in the resignation of the PFLP from the PLO Executive Committee to "avoid historical deviation." The PFLP and other groups formed the Rejection Front in that year in a meeting in Baghdad, Iraq. In 1975 the Rejection Front supporters were ambushed on a bus leaving a rally in West Beirut in the Ain al-Rummanah district. Twenty-seven of the passengers were killed, and that event marked the start of the civil war in Lebanon.

In 1980 Habash suffered a debilitating stroke. His influence within the PFLP predictably fell, and he relocated to Damascus, Syria, where he eventually worked with President Hafez al-Assad's protégés to oppose Yasser Arafat's seeming accommodation with moderate Palestinian forces. In 1992, in failing health, Habash returned to Amman, Jordan. Habash and the PFLP vociferously protested the 1993 Oslo Accords, accusing Arafat and the PLO of catering to pro-Zionist sentiments. Habash, like the Islamic Jihad,

opposed the PLO's tentative moves toward peace. He soon discovered, however, that his vehement anti-Arafat position had yielded no tangible results. As such, Habash then sought an awkward accommodation with Fatah, but by then the PFLP was losing ground, and its support among Palestinians was slackening. By the mid-1990s, it was evident that certain previous strongholds for the PFLP, such as Qalqilyah, had turned toward the Islamist parties, and the well-funded Fatah faction opposed the PFLP in other areas.

In 2000 Habash resigned as secretary-general of the PFLP because of poor health. He is nevertheless well respected by many Palestinians for his revolutionary fervor and dogged dedication to the Palestinian cause. Many outsiders, however, point to the PFLP's sponsorship of terrorism and accuse the intellectual Habash of being little more than a left-wing thug. In the 2006 Palestinian elections, the PLFP received less than 5 percent of the vote, mirroring the eclipsing fortunes of the organization. George Habash died in Amman, Jordan, on January 26, 2008.

PAUL G. PIERPAOLI JR. AND SHERIFA ZUHUR

See also

Arab Socialism; Arafat, Yasser; Black September; Fatah; Hamas; Islamic Jihad, Palestinian; Lebanon, Civil War in; Nasser, Gamal Abdel; Palestine Liberation Organization; Pan-Arabism; Six-Day War; Terrorism

References

Brand, Laurie. *Palestinians in the Arab World: Institution Building and the Search for State.* New York: Columbia University Press, 1988.

Cobban, Helena. *The Palestinian Liberation Organization: People, Power and Politics.* New York: Cambridge University Press, 1984.

Cubert, Harold M. *The PFLP's Changing Role in the Middle East.* London: Frank Cass, 1997.

Kazziha, Walid. *Revolutionary Transformation in the Arab World: Habash and His Comrades from Nationalism to Marxism.* New York: St. Martin's, 1975.

Habib, Philip
Born: February 25, 1920
Died: May 25, 1992

Noted U.S. diplomat, perhaps best known for his work in brokering a tenuous—and short-lived—peace in Lebanon in the early 1980s. Born in Brooklyn, New York, on February 25, 1920, to a Lebanese Meronite Christian family, Philip Habib grew up in a Jewish neighborhood. In his formative years he straddled cultural barriers. For a short while he worked as a shipping clerk in New York before enrolling in a forestry program at the University of Idaho. He earned his degree in 1942 and immediately joined the U.S. Army, where he served until his discharge as a captain in 1946.

Upon his return to civilian life, Habib enrolled at the University of California at Berkeley, where he studied agricultural economics. He earned his PhD there in 1952. In the meantime, in 1949 he joined the U.S. Foreign Service. He began a long and highly distinguished career with the U.S. State Department that included service in

U.S. special envoy Philip Habib (*right foreground*) meets with French, Italian, and U.S. ambassadors to greet the first U.S. marines to land as part of a multinational peacekeeping force in Lebanon in December 1982. (U.S. Department of Defense)

Canada, New Zealand, South Korea, Saigon, South Vietnam, and various other State Department posts. In 1968 he began serving on the U.S. delegation to the Vietnam Peace Talks.

Habib became the U.S. ambassador to South Korea in 1971, a post he held until 1974. During 1974–1976 he was assistant secretary of state for East Asian and Pacific affairs, and during 1976–1978 he served as undersecretary of state for political affairs. Following a heart attack, he retired from public service in 1978.

Just a year later, in 1979, Habib came out of retirement to serve as a special adviser to President Jimmy Carter on Middle East affairs. In the spring of 1981, newly elected president Ronald Reagan tapped Habib to serve as U.S. special envoy to the Middle East. Widely known for his tough but scrupulously fair negotiating prowess, Habib received the assignment of brokering a peace arrangement in the ongoing civil war in Lebanon.

During a series of tortuous negotiations and endless bouts of shuttle diplomacy, Habib managed to broker a cease-fire in Lebanon and resolved the mounting crisis over control of West Beirut. His efforts not only brought some semblance of order to Lebanon— albeit temporarily—but also served as a building block for the ongoing Arab-Israeli peace process. In September 1982 the Reagan administration awarded Habib with the Presidential Medal of Freedom for his diplomatic service. In 1986 Habib once again became a special envoy, this time to Central America. His task was to resolve the continuing conflict in Nicaragua. Realizing, perhaps, that U.S. policies in the region were a significant impediment to lasting peace

there, he resigned his post after just five months on the job. Habib died suddenly on May 25, 1992, while on vacation in Puligny-Montrachet, France.

PAUL G. PIERPAOLI JR.

See also

Lebanon; Lebanon, Civil War in; Lebanon, Israeli Invasion of

References

Boykin, John. *Cursed Is the Peacemaker: The American Diplomat versus the Israeli General, Beirut 1982.* Belmont, CA: Applegate, 2002.

Laffin, John. *The War of Desperation: Lebanon, 1982–1985.* London: Osprey, 1985.

Hadassah

Jewish advocacy and public service organization for women, the full name of which is the Women's Zionist Organization of America, Inc. A volunteer organization since its founding in New York City in 1912, the group uses the name Hadassah (meaning Esther in Hebrew). Esther was a Persian Jew and heroine whose story is told in the Old Testament book of Esther. Hadassah was founded by Henrietta Szold, a Jewish scholar and activist who sought to promote and integrate Judaism, Zionism, and American civic ideals in the form of a public service organization.

From the very beginning, Szold made health care a central part of Hadassah's mission. The group began its medical activities administering to Jews living in the British Mandate for Palestine, but over the decades it has greatly expanded its scope so that by the 21st century it has medical teams and facilities on five continents and administers to people of all races, religions, and ethnicities. In addition to its commitment to health care, Hadassah's overall mission is to promote Judaic unity, promote and protect the Israeli homeland, enhance the quality of life for U.S. Jews through youth programs and educational opportunities, and facilitate personal growth and enrichment for all of its members.

Perhaps the largest Zionist organization in the world, Hadassah currently has a paid membership of more than 300,000. Its headquarters are in New York City, although the group maintains a significant presence in Washington, D.C., for lobbying purposes with its Action Office. Hadassah has chapters and offices in all 50 states as well as Puerto Rico. Hadassah International, the global arm of the association, oversees the Hadassah Medical Organization, which is active in many areas of the world and, as Hadassah's mission statement claims, serves as a bridge to nations through medicine.

In 1912, Szold and Hadassah's charter members sought to foster Jewish institutions in Palestine and promote and spread the Zionist platform in America. In its early years, Hadassah was an allied group of the Federation of American Zionists. In the 1920s and 1930s, the group worked diligently to encourage the creation of a Jewish homeland in Palestine and shield as many Jews as possible from anti-Semitism and oppression in Europe, especially in Nazi Germany.

As early as 1913, Hadassah began dispatching medical workers to Palestine. That year the organization sent two American nurses

The opening ceremony of the Hadassah Medical Center on Mount Scopus in Jerusalem on May 9, 1939. Among the guests is Hadassah founder Henrietta Szold (*third from left*). (Zoltan Kluger/Israeli Government Press Office)

When many parts of Africa and Southern Asia became independent in the early and mid-1960s, Hadassah decided to expand its outreach programs and medical care to these fledgling nations. As such, by 1970 Hadassah's physicians, nurses, dentists, and other personnel were laboring in places such as Sierra Leone, Ethiopia, Liberia, and Tanzania.

Education is also part of Hadassah's public service commitment. In 1942 it set up its first vocational education program in Palestine. From there the effort expanded, including many parts of Palestine and encompassing Arab as well as Jewish students. In keeping with its commitment to youth activities, Hadassah has resettled and educated many thousands of young Jews from some 80 nations in Israel. It has accomplished its Youth Aliya programs with the help of the Jewish Agency for Israel. In the United States, Hadassah offers a plethora of educational, self-enrichment, and continuing education programs for its members. In addition, the American Affairs Program of Hadassah educates its membership on a wide array of issues—political, social, and economic—to help them understand and defend their rights as citizens of a free democracy.

In 2005 the Hadassah Medical Organization was recognized for its contributions with a nomination for the Nobel Peace Prize. Among other things, the nomination cited the organization's equal treatment of all patients, its commitment to maintaining a dedicated and cooperative staff comprised of people from all faiths, and its continuing commitment to attaining a sustainable peace, even through the Second (al-Aqsa) Intifada.

PAUL G. PIERPAOLI JR.

See also

Intifada, Second; Jewish Agency for Israel; Zionism

References

Diament, Carol. *Jewish Women Living the Challenge: A Hadassah Compendium.* New York: Hadassah, the Women's Zionist Organization of America, 1997.

Levin, Marlin. *It Takes a Dream: The Story of Hadassah.* Lynbrook, NY: Gefen, 1997.

Simmons, Erica B. *Hadassah and the Zionist Project.* New York: Rowman and Littlefield, 2006.

to set up a small clinic there. Before long, the contingent included several dozen physicians, nurses, and dentists. Small clinics sprang up throughout Palestine that served both Jews and Arabs. In addition, Hadassah built day care centers, playgrounds, and other such facilities, which the organization would turn over to local officials as soon as they were able to support and administer them on their own. In 1939 Hadassah built its first comprehensive hospital, which is still in operation today, on Mount Scopus in Jerusalem. From 1948 to 1967, however, this facility was closed as a result of the ongoing Arab-Israeli conflict. In 1961, Hadassah opened a second major medical center, affiliated with the Hebrew University, in En Karem. This too is still operational today. Over the years, Hadassah has established and funded hundreds of fellowships and advanced medical training programs to school Hadassah physicians in the United States and Western Europe.

Haddad, Nuhad

See Fayruz

Haganah

Haganah, Hebrew for "defense," was a Jewish underground self-defense and military organization during 1920–1948 that succeeded the Guild of Watchman (Hashomer) and was the precursor of the Israel Defense Forces (IDF). Hashomer was a small group of no more than 100 Jewish immigrants who began guarding Jewish settlements and kibbutzim in 1909. Haganah was organized to protect

Haganah soldiers in training, preparing for the battle for Jerusalem, January 6, 1948. (Israeli Government Press Office)

the Jewish community (Yishuv) following the Arab riots of 1920 and 1921.

After the demise of the Ottoman Empire in World War I, the League of Nations granted Britain temporary mandatory control of Palestine on July 24, 1922, to act on behalf of both the Jewish and non-Jewish populations. Although the British mandatory government (1922–1948) did not recognize Haganah, it did provide sufficient stability and security for the kibbutzim and the Yishuv to flourish. Nonetheless, the need for Jewish self-defense persisted and grew, as did Haganah.

During 1920–1929 Haganah was composed of localized and poorly armed units of Jewish farmers who took turns guarding one another's farms and kibbutzim. Haganah's structure and role changed radically after the Arab riots and ethnic cleansings of 1929. Haganah began to organize the rural and urban Jewish adult and youth populations throughout Palestine into a much larger, better-equipped, and better-trained but still primarily self-defense force. Although Haganah was able to acquire some foreign weapons, the British mandatory government's effective blockade of weapons to the Jews led Haganah to construct weapons fabrication workshops for ammunition, some small arms, and grenades.

Even as the British mandatory government slowly shifted its support to the Arab population of Palestine, the leadership of the Jewish Agency for Palestine continued to attempt to work closely with them to promote the interests of the Jewish population in Palestine. Haganah supported this position through its self-defense and military strategy of havlaga (self-restraint), but not all of Haganah's members agreed with a restrained response to what they perceived as the British mandatory government's pro-Arab bias. This political and policy disagreement and Haganah's prevailing socialist ideology led in 1931 to the formation of a minority splinter group headed by Avraham Tehomi known as Irgun Tsvai Leumi (National Military Organization). Irgun advocated harsh retaliation for Arab attacks and an active military campaign to end British mandatory governance of Palestine.

By 1936, the year that the Palestinian revolt known as the Great Uprising or Arab Revolt (1936–1939) began, Haganah had grown to 10,000 mobilized men and 40,000 reservists. Although the British mandatory government still failed to recognize Haganah, the strategy of havlaga seemed to bear fruit when the British Security Forces (BSF) cooperated in the establishment of the Jewish Settlement Police, Jewish Auxiliary Forces, and Special Night Squads as Jewish civilian militia. Additionally, the BSF and Haganah worked together to suppress the Arab Revolt and to protect British as well as Jewish interests.

Despite these perceived gains, in 1937 Haganah again split into right-wing and left-wing factions. The right-wing faction joined

Irgun, and some of the members of Irgun, including Tehomi, rejoined Haganah. Irgun had been nothing more than a small and ineffective irritant until this transition changed Irgun into an effective guerrilla force branded as terrorists by the British and some in Haganah.

The Great Uprising matured Haganah and taught it many lessons. Haganah improved its underground arms production capability, increased the acquisition of light arms from Europe, and established centralized arms depots and 50 strategically placed kibbutzim. Haganah also enhanced the training of its soldiers and officer corps and expanded its clandestine training of the general population.

The British White Paper of 1939 openly shifted British support away from the Jews to the Arabs. Jewish immigration, settlement, and land purchases in Palestine were severely restricted, and the British effectively retreated from any support for an independent Jewish homeland. This attempt on the threshold of World War II to appease the Arab world following the Great Uprising failed. Even with this betrayal, David Ben-Gurion asserted that the Zionists should stand against the change in policy while supporting the British during World War II. Haganah responded by organizing demonstrations against the British and by further facilitating illegal immigration through bases in Turkey and Switzerland under the auspices of Aliya Bet, the Organization for Illegal Immigration, created in 1938. Irgun's response was to begin bombing British installations and attacking British interests.

As World War II progressed, on May 19, 1941, Haganah created the Palmach to train young people in leadership and military skills and to help defend Palestine if the Germans invaded. The Palmach cooperated with the British during 1941–1943, fought behind the lines in Vichy-dominated Lebanon and Syria, worked with Irgun during 1945–1946 against British mandatory rule, and helped facilitate illegal Jewish immigration during 1946–1947 prior to being folded in 1948 into the IDF.

Fearing that the Germans would overrun all of North Africa, Britain negotiated a reciprocal support agreement with Haganah that provided intelligence and even commando assistance. The British retreated from the agreement following their victory at El Alamein (al-Alamayn) in November 1942, although in 1943 they did form the Jewish Brigade and deployed its 5,000 men in Italy in September 1944 before disbanding it in 1946. Although Palestinian Jews were not allowed to enlist in the British Army until 1940, more than 30,000 served in various units of the army during the war.

Haganah focused its operations after the war on the British mandatory government, attacking rail lines, bridges, and deportation ships and even freeing immigrants from the Atlit internment camp. Haganah also worked on preparations for partition. These clashes grew as Haganah facilitated illegal immigration from Jewish displaced person camps in Europe and secured its anticipated partitioned borders. Immediately after partition in 1947, Haganah concentrated on defending the Yishuv against attacks by Palestinian Arabs and the neighboring Arab states.

Haganah took the offensive in the Israeli War of Independence in April 1948. Haganah and Irgun took Tiberias, Haifa, and the Arab cities of Acre and Jaffa. In Operation NACHSHON they went on to open a road to West Jerusalem. On May 28, 1948, the provisional government of the newly declared State of Israel transformed Haganah into its national military, the IDF, and outlawed all other armed forces. In September 1948 the military activities of Irgun were folded into the IDF.

RICHARD EDWARDS

See also

Ben-Gurion, David; Irgun Tsvai Leumi; Israel Defense Forces; Israeli War of Independence, Overview; NACHSHON, Operation

References

Bauer, Yehuda. *From Diplomacy to Resistance: A History of Jewish Palestine, 1930–1945*. Translated by Alton M. Winters. Philadelphia: Jewish Publication Society of America, 1970.

Farris, Karl. *Growth and Change in the Israeli Defense Forces through Six Wars*. Carlisle Barracks, PA: U.S. Army War College, 1987.

Mardor, Munya M. *Haganah*. Edited by D. R. Elston. Foreword by David Ben-Gurion. Translated by H. A. G. Schmuckler. New York: New American Library, 1966.

Pentland, Pat Allen. *Zionist Military Preparations for Statehood: The Evolution of Haganah Organizations, Programs, and Strategies, 1920–1948*. Ann Arbor, MI: University Microfilms International, 1981.

Haifa

Major port and industrial city located in northern Israel. Haifa is situated along the Mediterranean coast and encompasses part of Mount Carmel, a small mountain range that is about 1,500 feet above sea level around Haifa. A portion of the city is built on the slopes of Mount Carmel, which offers a picturesque and commanding view of the city as it descends to the coast.

Haifa is a key city for Israel because of its locale on the sea, its modern port facilities, and the location of a large oil refinery nearby. As such, the city has developed a major petrochemical industry. One of just two Israeli refineries, the facilities at Haifa are capable of refining more than 68 million barrels of crude oil per year. Haifa's port serves as Israel's principal port for cargo as well as passengers. A number of technology-based firms are also located in Haifa. Although not technically a part of Galilee, Haifa's proximity to it has made the city the chief commercial city for Galilee's residents. Today Haifa has a population of some 275,000 people.

Haifa and its environs have a rich history. The area has been peopled by Jews, Muslims, and Christians over the past 2,000 years. Archaeological sites excavated just outside the city limits hint at a history that reaches even further back in time. Judaic Talmudic writings make mention of Haifa as early as the fourth century AD, although the main center of Jewish culture at the time was located in nearby Shikmona, which today is an active archaeological excavation site.

As with other areas in the region of Palestine, Haifa witnessed a parade of outside nations that attempted to control it. In the 600s

View from Mt. Carmel of Haifa and Haifa Bay, Israel. (Corel)

the Persians conquered the region from the Byzantine Empire, which in turn lost a power struggle with Arab leaders, who controlled the area for many years. Around 1100, Christian Crusaders wrested the city out of Muslim and Jewish hands. In 1265 the city fell to Muslim Mamluk invaders. Except for a few brief interludes, the Ottoman Empire ruled the area from the 1500s until 1918, when it fell to British forces during World War I.

Haifa became a place associated with great bloodshed on the eve of the Arab-Jewish Communal War (November 1947–May 1948). On December 30, 1947, several members of the radical Jewish organization Irgun Tsvai Leumi (National Military Organization) hurled bombs into a crowd of Palestinian Arabs seeking work at Haifa's oil refinery. In the melee, 6 Arabs died and 40 others were wounded. This prompted a spontaneous riot among Arab workers in the plant, the result of which was the wounding or deaths of some 60 Jews. If this had not been bad enough, on January 30, 1947, members of Haganah and Palmach sought retribution for the massacre in Haifa by attacking the nearby Arab village of Baldat al-Shaykh. When the raid was over, 60 Palestinian Arab civilians lay dead, many of them women, children, and the elderly. Realizing the vital strategic importance of Haifa, Jewish forces took the city in April 1948 just before the full-scale Israeli War of Independence (1948–1949) broke out. The city remained in Israeli hands thereafter.

Now home to the University of Haifa and several other colleges and vocational schools, Haifa also houses the Baha'i World Center and several important Baha'i shrines. A Carmelite monastery is located near the peak of Mount Carmel, with commanding views of the city below. Almost 90 percent of Haifa's population is Jewish, yet Haifa is often referred to as an example of a mixed Arab-Jewish city because it contains neighborhoods that are not strictly Arab or Jewish, resulting in a different type of municipal character. The University of Haifa has a sufficiently large population of Arab students to produce some identity-based friction. There is a small but vital Baha'i population as well. Until fairly recently, the industrial nature of the city made leftist labor parties quite popular among Haifa's population. In the past several elections, however, the power of laborites has been on the wane. In the summer of 2006, when Hezbollah guerrillas began launching Katyusha rockets from Lebanon into Israel, Haifa was one of the first targets. In one such attack, eight Israelis were killed. Subsequent rocket attacks caused considerable damage to several city sections.

Paul G. Pierpaoli Jr.

See also

Arab-Jewish Communal War; Baldat al-Shaykh Massacre; Galilee; Katyusha Rocket

References

Garfinkle, Adam A. *Politics and Society in Modern Israel.* Armonk, NY: M. E. Sharpe, 1997.

Wilson, Sir William Charles. *The Land of Galilee: Including Samaria, Haifa, and Esdraelon Valley.* Jerusalem: Ariel Publishing House, 1976.

Halperin, Isser

See Harel, Isser

Halukka

A charitable collection among Jews around the world to support fellow Jews living in Palestine. The Halukka commitment recognized a connection between the various Jewish communities and helped to reinforce the concept that Israel is the spiritual and cultural center of the Jewish people. The Halukka made it possible to maintain a Jewish presence in the region until it was replaced by a state-run welfare system administered by Israel.

The roots of the Halukka date back to the earliest Diaspora of the Jewish people. The concept probably had its roots in the religious tax annually paid by all Jews to maintain the Temple. The Temple prayers were offered up to Yahweh (God) for the benefit of all Jewish people, even if they were not present. After the destruction of the Temple, the remaining Jews in Palestine were regarded as continuing to represent the entire Jewish people. Most were members of religious communities who spent their time in prayer or study. All Jews accepted a responsibility to support them, even as they studied scriptures and offered prayers for the peace and welfare of their fellow Jews throughout the world.

During the Middle Ages, Jewish communities in Palestine sent messengers, or meshullahs, to Jewish groups in Europe and the Middle East. These meshullahs were often respected rabbis or scholars, who could speak about conditions in Palestine. They asked for charitable contributions for the poor Jewish scholars, widows, and orphans in Palestine. Many meshullahs concentrated on particular countries. The first meshullah to visit North America was Rabbi Moses Malki of Safed, who visited Newport, Rhode Island, in 1759. The success of the meshullahs varied. Some communities experienced frauds posing as meshullahs whose only goal was to enrich themselves. By the 19th century, most European and American Jewish communities agreed to collect the Halukka funds themselves. The most common method was the placement of charity boxes in synagogues and Jewish homes. They were named for Rabbi Meir Ba'al ha-Nes, a well-known Polish rabbi.

Once collected, the Halukka funds were distributed by rabbis in Jerusalem, Tiberias, Hebron, and Safed. Precedence was given to elderly men, the learned, the poor, and widows and orphans. As contributions became more nationalized during the 19th century, groups that identified with a particular country formed their own community, or kolel, so they would receive a larger portion of the Halukka funds. During the last half of the 19th century and the first half of the 20th century, the Halukka was widely criticized. The Jews in Palestine were sometimes portrayed as living an easy life, thanks to the contributions of European and American Jews. Critics believed that the Halukka encouraged pauperism and idleness. They also believed that it gave too much power to rabbis who controlled the distribution of funds. For many Zionists, such as the Hoveve Zion followers, the Halukka discouraged the development of real skills, such as knowledge of agricultural practices, that would allow Jews in Palestine to support themselves.

The Halukka did provide some real benefits, however. Funds from the Halukka encouraged and supported migration of Jews from around the world to Palestine. The Jewish population grew, due in part to Halukka funds. New housing was built, and immigrant groups were integrated into the existing population. The Halukka also provided an ongoing connection between Jews around the world and Palestine. Individual Jews recognized that they had a cultural and spiritual home in the Holy Land. For many, it led to the development of Zionist leanings. The Halukka dwindled in importance during the 20th century before being replaced by a state-run welfare system following the founding of Israel in 1948.

TIM J. WATTS

See also

Hoveve Zion; Israel; Palestine, Pre-1918 History of; Zionism

References

Barnai, Y. *The Jews in Palestine in the Eighteenth Century: Under the Patronage of the Istanbul Committee of Officials for Palestine.* Tuscaloosa: University of Alabama Press, 1992.

Baron, Salo Wittmayer. *Steeled by Adversity: Essays and Addresses on American Jewish Life.* Philadelphia: Jewish Publication Society of America, 1971.

Baron, Salo Wittmayer, and Jeannette Meisel Baron. *Palestinian Messengers in America, 1849–79: A Record of Four Journeys.* New York: Arno, 1977.

Hamas

Islamist Palestinian organization formally founded in 1987. The stated basis for Hamas (Harakat al-Muqawama al-Islamiyya, or Movement of Islamic Resistance) is the creation of an Islamic way of life and the liberation of Palestine through Islamic resistance. Essentially, Hamas combines Islamic fundamentalism with Palestinian nationalism. Hamas gained about 30–40 percent support in the Palestinian population within five years because of its mobilization successes and the general popular desperation experienced by the Palestinian population during the First Intifada. In January 2006 Hamas won a majority in the Palestinian Authority's (PA) general legislative elections, which brought condemnation from Israel and a power struggle with PA president Mahmoud Abbas and his Fatah Party.

The word "Hamas" means courage, bravery, or zeal. But it is also an Arabic acronym for the Movement of Islamic Resistance. Hamas is an Islamist movement, as are larger and longer-established groups such as the Muslim Brotherhood and the Palestinian Islamic Jihad. The growth of Islamist movements was delayed among Palestinians because of their status as a people without a state and the tight security controls imposed by Israel, which had strengthened the more secular nationalist expression of the Palestine Liberation Organization (PLO).

A Palestinian supporter of Hamas waves the party's flag during a protest in Gaza City, March 8, 2003. (AFP/Getty Images)

The Muslim Brotherhood, established in Egypt in 1928, had set up branches in Syria; Sudan; Libya; the Gulf states; Amman in Jordan, which influenced the West Bank; and Gaza. However, for two decades the Muslim Brotherhood focused on its religious, educational, and social missions and was quiescent politically. That changed with the First Intifada (1987). The Muslim Brotherhood advocated *dawah,* what may be called a re-Islamization of society and thought; *adala* (social justice); and an emphasis on *hakmiyya* (the sovereignty of God, as opposed to temporal rule). The Muslim Brotherhood turned to activism against Israel after Islamic Jihad had accelerated its operations during 1986 and 1987. Eventually Islamic Jihad split into three rival organizations. The new movement coming out of the Jordanian and Egyptian Muslim Brotherhood groups, unlike Islamic Jihad, retained its major programmatic emphasis on the Islamization or re-Islamization of society. As the new organization of Hamas emerged out of the Muslim Brotherhood, it was able to draw strength from the social work of Sheikh Ahmed Yassin, a physically disabled schoolteacher who had led the Islamic Assembly (al-Mujamma al-Islami), an organization influential in many mosques and at the Islamic University of Gaza.

In December 1987 Abd al-Aziz Rantisi, who was a physician at Islamic University, and former student leaders Salah Shihada and Yahya al-Sinuwwar, who had had charge of security for the Muslim Brotherhood, formed the first unit of Hamas. While Yassin gave his approval, as a cleric he was not directly connected to the new organization.

In February 1988 as a result of a key meeting in Amman involving Sheikh Abd al-Rahman al-Khalifa (the spiritual guide of the Jordanian Muslim Brotherhood), Ibrahiam Ghawsha (the Hamas spokesperson and Jordanian representative), Mahmud Zahar (a surgeon), Rantisi (acting as a West Bank representative), Jordanian parliament members, and the hospital director, the Brotherhood granted formal recognition to Hamas. In 1988 Hamas issued its charter. The charter condemns world Zionism and the efforts to isolate Palestine, defines the mission of the organization, and locates that mission within Palestinian, Arab, and Islamic elements. It does not condemn the West or non-Muslims but does condemn aggression against the Palestinian people, arguing for a defensive jihad. It also calls for fraternal relations with the other Palestinian nationalist groups.

Hamas is headed by a Political Bureau with representatives for military affairs, foreign affairs, finance, propaganda, and internal security. An Advisory Council, or Majlis al-Shura, is linked to the Political Bureau, which is also connected with all Palestinian communities; Hamas's social and charitable groups, elected members, and district committees; and the leadership in Israeli prisons.

Major attacks against Israel have been carried out by the Izz al-Din al-Qassam Brigades of Hamas. They also developed the Qassam rocket used to attack Israeli civilian settlements in the Negev Desert. However, much of Hamas's activity during the First Intifada consisted of its participation within more broadly based popular demonstrations and locally coordinated efforts at resistance, countering Israeli raids, enforcing opening of businesses, and the like.

Hamas greatly expanded by 1993 but decried the autonomy agreement between the Israelis and the PLO in Jericho and the Gaza Strip as too limited a gain. By the time of the first elections for the PA's Council in 1996, Hamas was caught in a dilemma. It had gained popularity as a resistance organization, but Oslo 1 and Oslo 2 (the Taba Accord of September 28, 1995) were meant to end the intifada. The elections would further strengthen the PLO, but if Hamas boycotted the elections and most people voted, then it would be even more isolated. Finally, Hamas's leadership rejected participation but without ruling it out in the future, and this gave the organization the ability to continue protesting Oslo.

When suicide attacks were launched to protest Israeli violence against Palestinians, Hamas was blamed for inspiring or organizing the suicide bombers, whether or not its operatives or those of the more radical Islamic Jihad were involved.

Hamas funds an extensive array of social services aimed at ameliorating the plight of the Palestinians. It provides funding for hospitals, schools, mosques, orphanages, food distribution, and aid to the families of Palestinian prisoners who, numbering more than

10,000 people, constituted an important political force. Given the PA's frequent inability to provide for such needs, Hamas stepped into the breach and in so doing endeared itself to a large number of Palestinians.

Until its electoral triumph in January 2006, Hamas received funding from a number of sources. Palestinians living abroad provided money, as did a number of private donors in the wealthy Arab oil states such as Saudi Arabia, Bahrain, and Kuwait and other states in the West. Iran has been a significant donor to Hamas. Much aid was directed to renovation of the Palestinian territories and was badly needed, and unfortunately a great deal of that rebuilding was destroyed in the Israeli campaign in the West Bank in 2002, which in turn was intended to combat the suicide bombings.

Over the years the Israel Defense Forces (IDF) has carried out targeted eliminations of a number of Hamas leaders. These include Shihada (July 23, 2002), Dr. Ibrahim Al-Makadma (August 3, 2003), Ismail Abu Shanab (August 21, 2003), Yassin (March 22, 2004), and Rantisi (April 17, 2004).

Hamas had two sets of leaders, those inside the West Bank and Gaza and those outside. The West Bank leadership is divided along the general structure into political, charitable, student, and military activities. The political leadership is usually targeted for arrests because its members can be located, unlike the secret military units. That leadership has organized very effectively before and since PLO leader Yasser Arafat's death and has become more popular than the PLO in the West Bank, an unexpected development. A current Hamas leader, Khalid Mishaal, is in Syria. Other senior Hamas leaders are there as well, and there is also some Hamas activity in refugee camps in Lebanon. Although Arafat was quickly succeeded by Abbas as the PLO leader, a sizable number of Palestinians had already begun to identify with Hamas, mainly because it was able to accomplish what the PA could not, namely, to provide for the everyday needs of the people.

Hamas won the legislative elections in January 2006. Locals had expected a victory in Gaza but not in the West Bank. Nonetheless, both Israel and the United States have steadfastly refused to recognize the Palestinian government now under the control of Hamas. The United States cut off $420 million and the European Union (EU) cut off $600 million in aid to the PA's Hamas-led government, which created difficulties for ordinary Palestinians. The loss of this aid halted the delivery of supplies to hospitals and ended other services in addition to stopping the payment of salaries. To prevent total collapse, the United States and the EU promised relief funds, but these were not allowed to go through the PA. The cutoff in funds was designed to discourage Palestinian support for Hamas.

On March 17, 2007, Abbas brokered a Palestinian unity government that included members of both Hamas and Fatah in which Hamas leader Ismail Haniyeh became prime minister. Yet in May armed clashes between Hamas and Fatah escalated, and on June 14 Hamas seized control of Gaza. Abbas promptly dissolved the Hamas-led unity government and declared a state of emergency. On June 18, having been assured of EU support, he dissolved the National

Security Council and swore in an emergency Palestinian government. That same day, the United States ended its 15-month embargo on the PA and resumed aid in an effort to strengthen Abbas's government, now limited to the West Bank. On June 19 Abbas cut off all ties and dialogue with Hamas, pending the return of Gaza. By the end of 2007, Hamas had imposed a more religiously conservative regime on Gaza, which was now largely cut off economically from the rest of the world and more than ever an economic basket case.

HARRY RAYMOND HUESTON II, PAUL G. PIERPAOLI JR.,
AND SHERIFA ZUHUR

See also

Abbas, Mahmoud; Arafat, Yasser; Intifada, First; Intifada, Second; Haniyeh, Ismail; Islamic Jihad, Palestinian; Israel; Israel Defense Forces; Jihad; Muslim Brotherhood; Palestine Liberation Organization; Palestinian Authority; Suicide Bombings; Terrorism; Yassin, Ahmed Ismail; Yusuf, Hasan

References

Legrain, Jean-François. "Hamas: Legitimate Heir of Palestinian Nationalism?" Pp. 159–178 in *Political Islam: Revolution, Radicalism, or Reform,* edited by John Esposito. Boulder, CO: Lynne Rienner, 1997.

Mishal, Shaul, and Avraham Sela. *The Palestinian Hamas: Vision, Violence, and Coexistence.* New York: Columbia University Press, 2000.

Nusse, Andrea. *Muslim Palestine: The Ideology of Hamas.* London: Routledge, 1999.

HaMiflagah HaQomonistit HaYisra'elit

See Communist Party of Israel

Hammarskjöld, Agne Carl Dag Hjalmar
Born: July 29, 1905
Died: September 18, 1961

Swedish economist, diplomat, and United Nations (UN) bureaucrat and secretary-general (1953–1961). Dag Hammarskjöld was born on July 29, 1905, in Jönköping, Sweden. His father, Hjalmar Hammarskjöld, had been prime minister of Sweden during 1914–1917. The younger Hammarskjöld studied law and economics at the universities of Uppsala and Stockholm (1933–1936), earning a doctorate from the latter institution.

Hammarskjöld was first employed by a Swedish commission on unemployment (1930–1934). In 1935 he became secretary of the Bank of Sweden, ultimately becoming the president of the board of the bank (1941–1948). He also served as undersecretary of the Swedish Ministry of Finance (1936–1945). He helped organize the European Recovery Program (1947) and then served as vice chairman of the executive committee of the Organization for European Economic Cooperation (1948–1949). During this time, he coined the term "planned economy" and, in consort with his eldest brother, Bo Hammarskjöld, then undersecretary in the Swedish Ministry of

Dag Hammarskjöld, Swedish economist, diplomat, and United Nations (UN) bureaucrat and secretary-general (1953–1961). (Corel)

Social Welfare, helped create the legal framework for the modern Swedish welfare state.

In 1951 Hammarskjöld became Sweden's deputy foreign minister and cabinet minister without portfolio. Later that same year he served as vice chairman of Sweden's delegation to the UN General Assembly. The next year he became its chairman.

On April 7, 1953, Hammarskjöld was elected the UN's second secretary-general. He was reelected to the post in September 1957, although increasingly in his second term he came under criticism from the Soviet bloc. Although Hammarskjöld practiced preventive diplomacy in an attempt to avert the breaking of the armistice agreements between Israel and the Arab states and in other potential conflicts, he did not flinch from committing UN forces to maintain or establish peace.

In 1955 Hammarskjöld traveled to Beijing and, through quiet diplomacy, secured the release of 15 U.S. prisoners held by the Chinese on espionage charges. He again employed personal diplomacy in negotiating with the governments of Israel, Britain, and France, which had intervened militarily in Egypt following President Gamal Abdel Nasser's nationalization of the Suez Canal in 1956. Securing their withdrawal from Egypt, Hammarskjöld then oversaw establishment of a UN Emergency Force (UNEF) to maintain the peace. His deft handling of the crisis resulted in new prestige for the UN.

Hammarskjöld shepherded UN interventions in 1958 in crises in Jordan and Lebanon that led to the founding of the UN Observation Group in Lebanon (UNOGIL), permitting the withdrawal of British and U.S. peacekeeping troops. He also established an office of the special representative of the UN secretary-general in Jordan, helped resolve a dispute between Thailand and Cambodia (1959), and strove to resolve internal strife in Laos.

Hammarskjöld's service as the secretary-general of the UN was not limited to conflict resolution. In 1955 and 1958 he organized the first and second UN-sponsored international conferences on the peaceful uses of atomic energy and planned a UN conference for 1962 that sought new ways to apply science and technology to the unique problems of the less-developed countries of the Third World.

Hammarskjöld sought to keep newly independent nations from being drawn into the Cold War. Increasingly absorbed by problems in the Congo, he was killed on September 18, 1961, in a plane crash near Ndola in northern Rhodesia (now Zambia) while on a peacekeeping mission to the Congo. In late 1961 he was awarded the Nobel Prize for Peace, the first person to be so honored posthumously. Hammarskjöld's personal moral and religious philosophy is evident in his book of meditations, *Markings* (1964).

RICHARD EDWARDS

See also
Nasser, Gamal Abdel; Suez Crisis; United Nations, Role of

References
Cordier, Andrew W., ed. *Public Papers of the Secretaries-General of the United Nations*, Vols. 2–5, *Dag Hammarskjöld*. New York: Columbia University Press, 1972–1975.

Gavshon, Arthur L. *The Last Days of Dag Hammarskjöld*. London: Barrie and Rockliff with Pall Mall Press, 1963.

Hammarskjöld, Dag. *Markings*. New York, Knopf, 1964.

Heller, Peter B. *The United Nations under Dag Hammarskjöld, 1953–1961*. Lanham, MD: Scarecrow, 2001.

Simon, Charlie May. *Dag Hammarskjöld*. New York: Dutton, 1967.

Urquhart, Brian. *Hammarskjöld*. New York: Knopf, 1972.

Van Dusen, Henry P. *Dag Hammarskjöld: The Statesman and His Faith*. New York: Harper and Row, 1967.

Hanit, Attack on the
Event Date: July 21, 2006

Hezbollah cruise missile attack on an Israeli Navy corvette off the coast of Lebanon. The missile attack occurred on July 21, 2006, during Operation CHANGE OF DIRECTION, the Israeli military operation against Hezbollah in Lebanon. The *Hanit,* an Israeli Navy corvette of some 1,275 tons built in the United States, was commissioned in 1995 as the last of three INS Saar V-class missile corvettes. On July 21 it was on duty about 10 miles off Beirut as part of an Israeli blockade designed to prevent Hezbollah from importing additional weapons by sea from neighboring Syria.

On the evening of July 21, two Chinese-manufactured C-802 (known in the west as Saccade) cruise missiles were fired from shore in the direction of the *Hanit,* probably from truck launchers. Indications suggest that the first missile was intentionally fired high to distract the *Hanit*'s defensive systems, while the second was sent low against the corvette. The first missile struck and sank a merchant ship steaming about 35 miles off the coast, a Cambodian flag vessel with an Egyptian crew. Twelve members of its crew were subsequently rescued. The second struck the *Hanit* at 8:45 p.m., heavily damaging it, starting a fire, and killing 4 of the 64-man crew.

The *Hanit* was able to return to port under its own steam. Repaired, it returned to duty three weeks later. Photographs of the ship after the attack show only a relatively small entrance hole and burn area under the helicopter platform at the stern of the ship, indicating that perhaps the C-802's warhead might not have exploded.

The radar-guided C-802 is a subsonic (0.9 Mach) missile powered by a turbojet engine. The missile weighs some 1,640 pounds and has a 363-pound warhead. Its range is roughly 740 miles. With only very small radar reflectivity, the missile flies at only about 15–20 feet above the surface of the water, making it difficult to detect

A fellow sergeant weeps as others lower the coffin of 21-year-old Staff Sergeant Tal Amgar, killed on July 21, 2006, when the Israeli warship *Hanit* was hit off the coast of Lebanon by a Hezbollah missile. (AFP/Getty Images)

and intercept. Hit probability is estimated at as high as 98 percent. Along with the U.S. Harpoon, the Saccade is considered to be among the best antiship missiles in the world.

The Israelis were well aware of the importance of massive decoys and jamming. Using such techniques, during the 1973 Yom Kippur War the Israelis had defeated 50 incoming Syrian and Egyptian antiship missiles while sinking 8 of their ships for only 1 Israeli missile boat damaged. The *Hanit* and its sisters mount impressive antimissile defensive systems: 64 Barak point-defense missiles, a 20-mm Phalanx rapid-fire cannon, and 20-mm and 7.62-mm machine guns as well as considerable chaff and decoy expendables and jamming equipment.

The attack succeeded for two reasons. First, unknown to Israeli intelligence, Hezbollah had acquired the C-802 cruise missiles, undoubtedly from Iran via Syria. Second, because of intense Israeli air activity in the area, the commander of the *Hanit* had turned off some of his ship's automated warning and defense systems. The Israel Defense Forces (IDF) remains convinced that Iranian advisers assisted with the missile firings.

SPENCER C. TUCKER

See also

Hezbollah; Lebanon, Israeli Operations against; Yom Kippur War

Reference

Polmar, Norman. "Hezbollah Attack: Lessons for the LCS?" *Naval Institute Proceedings* (September 2006): 88–89.

Ismail Haniyeh, senior Hamas official and prime minister of the Palestinian Authority (PA) during 2006–2007. (Ali Ali/epa/Corbis)

Haniyeh, Ismail
Born: January 1962

Palestinian Hamas official and prime minister of the Palestinian Authority (PA) during March 2006–June 2007. Ismail Haniyeh was born in January 1962 in the Palestinian refugee camp of Shati, located west of Gaza City. An excellent student, he studied at Islamic University in Gaza, from which he graduated in 1987 with a degree in Arabic literature. There he also became active in the Islamist movement.

Over the next several years as he became more involved in the Hamas resistance movement in Gaza, Haniyeh was repeatedly arrested and detained by Israeli officials. In 1989 he was sentenced to three years in prison for his part in the resistance effort. Upon his release in 1992, he was deported in a group of 400 individuals who were deposited on a hillside in Marj al-Zuhur in southern Lebanon. The Lebanese government refused to allow them out of their encampment, and this drew international attention. Subsequently returned in a prisoner exchange. Haniyeh was allowed back in Gaza, having been named dean of Islamic University.

Haniyeh's star within Hamas nevertheless continued to rise, and in 1997 he headed the office of Sheikh Ahmed Ismail Yassin, then the spiritual leader of Hamas. Yassin and Haniyeh enjoyed a close relationship, and it was soon clear that Yassin viewed him as

a valued protégé. By 1999 Haniyeh was acting as the Hamas liaison to the PA.

As a high-ranking political leader in Hamas, Haniyeh was the target of numerous Israeli assassination attempts. Indeed, in September 2003 Haniyeh and Yassin narrowly escaped death during an Israeli air strike in Gaza City. Just six months later, an Israeli helicopter attack killed Yassin. After Yassin's successor was assassinated by the Israelis in April 2004, Haniyeh became a member of Hamas's inner circle, or collective leadership. In the January 2006 Palestinian elections, Haniyeh headed Hamas's list of candidates, which included Christians. Hamas won 76 of the 132 seats in the Palestinian Legislative Council. Hamas's 2006 victory was a disappointment to PLO loyalists, who disputed the electoral victory.

As a result of the elections, Haniyeh became prime minister of the PA. He was sworn in on March 29, 2006. His political positions are actually more moderate than his Hamas pedigree might suggest. Haniyeh held out hope for the continuation of multilateral talks aimed at resolving the Palestinian-Israeli conflict, but he implored the United States and Western Europe not to cut funding to the PA. However, funding was indeed cut, as the George W. Bush administration made clear its unwillingness to work with the PA as long as it was controlled by Hamas. The European Union (EU) followed suit, despite talk of bringing in certain funds so as to permit hospitals and emergency services to continue functioning. Haniyeh did not rule out talks or negotiations with Israel, but he insisted that the Israelis must recognize Palestinian rights before any such dialogue takes place.

Escalating violence in May 2007 between Hamas and Fatah ended in the surprise Hamas takeover of Gaza on June 14. Abbas then immediately dissolved the Hamas-led unity government and declared a state of emergency. Shortly thereafter he dissolved the National Security Council and swore in an emergency Palestinian government. On June 19 he cut off all ties and dialogue with Hamas, pending the return of Gaza. By this point, Haniyeh's control was limited to the 1.5 million people of Gaza, although his hold there was anything but secure. And Gaza, isolated from the rest of the world, had become an economic basket case.

PAUL G. PIERPAOLI JR.

See also

Abbas, Mahmoud; Hamas; Palestinian Authority; Yassin, Ahmed Ismail

Reference

Mishal, Shaul, and Avraham Sela. *The Palestinian Hamas: Vision, Violence, and Coexistence.* New York: Columbia University Press, 2000.

Hapoel Hatzair

Jewish political party founded in Palestine in 1905. Hapoel Hatzair, which is Hebrew for "the Young Worker," was a socialist-oriented party that emphasized the value of labor for both the state and the individual but rejected the traditional Marxist notion of inevitable class struggle. In 1919, disaffected members of the party joined with a splinter group from Poalei Zion (Workers of Zion), a Marxist labor party. These dissidents formed Ahdut Ha'avodah (United Labor Party) that remained independent of Hapoel Hatzair until 1929.

In 1929, the Palestinian Labor Party (Mapai) was founded. After some initial hesitation, Hapoel Hatzair and Ahdut Ha'avodah reunited and incorporated the remnants of Poalei Zion. In 1930 the reunited factions joined the burgeoning Mapai, eventually emerging as the ruling party of the Yishuv, the Jewish community in Palestine. Some 85 percent of Hapoel Hatzair's membership voted in favor of the merger. In time, Mapai became the core of the modern Israeli Labor Party. After the proclamation of Israeli statehood on May 15, 1948, Mapai became the largest political party of the new Jewish state.

Hapoel Hatzair was founded in 1905 by 10 members, including 4 recent immigrants from Plonsk, Poland, who came to Palestine via the Second Aliya, a massive wave of immigration during 1904–1914. By February 1906 it had grown to 90 members and was centered in Jaffa. The following year it founded a newspaper, *Hapoel Hatzair,* that promoted the "practical Zionism" of the party's founders. In addition to promoting Jewish labor interests, the party also promoted the expansion and adoption of the Hebrew language.

In 1920 labor advocates founded Histadrut, or the General Federation of Labor, a nonpartisan labor organization. Of the 87 delegates to the initial meeting, 20 were members of Hapoel Hatzair. This made Hapoel Hatzair the second-largest group within the new umbrella organization.

The ideology of Hapoel Hatzair was primarily informed by Aharon David Gordon, a wealthy Orthodox farmer born in Russia. In 1903 Gordon decided to immigrate to Palestine, where he joined Kibbutz Degania in the Galilee region. He argued that the penultimate religious expression was agricultural labor and promoted what he termed the "religion of labor." He believed that the physical act of land cultivation redeemed the worker while working to restore the Jewish homeland. He also believed that the Jewish population of the world lacked a connection with the earth and that the only means to forge such a connection was through physical labor. His philosophy demanded a harsh lifestyle, as only through agricultural toil could the new Jewish homeland be forged. Despite coming from a background that involved no significant physical labor, he placed great emphasis on setting a personal example, working in the fields every day until his death in 1922. His physical example coupled with his ideological arguments provided inspiration for thousands of members of the new party.

Gordon was a pacifist and an antimilitarist, but these beliefs clashed with his desire that every tree and bush in the emerging Jewish homeland be planted by Jewish hands. An ardent socialist, he embraced the kibbutz movement as the ideal structure for the reconstruction of the Jewish nation. He was shocked to discover that the first Jewish pioneers were effectively plantation owners who purchased and managed their land but hired Arab laborers for the day-to-day operations of cultivation. In addition to Gordon, who supplied much of the ideological framework for Hapoel Hatzair, the founders included Yosef Ahronowitz and Yosef Sprinzak, who argued that new immigration to the region should be encouraged. They proposed active recruitment of Jewish laborers throughout Europe who could be encouraged to immigrate to Palestine to join collective farming efforts that were already in progress.

Hapoel Hatzair emphasized the physical act of labor, but by the 1920s most Jewish inhabitants of Palestine were moving away from physical toil. The organization preached toleration but ironically caused suspicion and separatism by insisting upon the necessity of Jewish labor to the exclusion of all other sources. The early organization of Hapoel Hatzair had little doctrine or ideology. Instead, it remained pragmatically focused on production. It always considered itself a political party, despite its tiny size and broad expectations. In reality, it served as a labor union, social club, and mutual aid society for its membership. From the founding membership of 10 workers in Jaffa, Hapoel Hatzair steadily grew, but its focus on agricultural labor led the party to ignore and marginalize urban laborers, severely limiting the potential membership of the party.

Hapoel Hatzair was heavily involved in encouraging young Jewish workers to immigrate to Palestine, helping to create a Jewish national homeland. Levi Eshkol served as a representative for

Hapoel Hatzair, traveling to Jaffa as part of a labor contingent. Although he began working as a common laborer and watchman, he soon became involved in a series of major infrastructure construction projects, bringing him notice from party leaders and beginning his political rise within the party. Eshkol's political career culminated in the office of prime minister, a position he held from 1963 until his death in 1969. Another major influential figure in the formation of Mapai was Golda Meir, who succeeded Eshkol as Israeli prime minister from 1969 until 1974.

One of the key ideas of Hapoel Hatzair was the creation of major agricultural outposts comprised entirely of Jewish laborers and their families. Rather than pushing existing inhabitants out of arable regions, the organization stressed the creation of new agricultural areas. In particular, Hapoel Hatzair workers strove to drain swamplands and irrigate deserts to create entirely new agricultural regions. When combined with the kibbutzim and moshavim, this created a powerful political and social force within the Jewish population of Palestine. Although the inhabitants of collective farming villages accounted for less than 10 percent of the population, they were heavily overrepresented in positions of political authority and in the military officer corps.

PAUL J. SPRINGER

See also

Aliya, Second; Eshkol, Levi; Hehalutz Movement; Histadrut; Kibbutz Movement; Labor Party; Labor Zionism; Moshavim; Zionism

References

Beilin, Yossi. *Israel: A Concise Political History.* New York: St. Martin's, 1992.

Laqueur, Walter. *A History of Zionism: From the French Revolution to the Establishment of the State of Israel.* Reprint ed. New York: Schocken, 2003.

Peretz, Don. *The Government and Politics of Israel.* Boulder, CO: Westview, 1979.

Reich, Bernard. *A Brief History of Israel.* New York: Facts on File, 2005.

Harakat al-Muqawama al-Islamiyya

See Hamas

Haram al-Sharif

A hotly contested religious site in the Old City of Jerusalem. Haram al-Sharif, also known as al-Haram al-Sharif, meaning the noble sacred space (what is haram is sacrosanct), is called the Temple Mount by Israelis and other Jews. It was built above the site of the first and second Jewish Temples in Jerusalem and according to Judaism is to be the site of the third and final Temple in the time of the Messiah. It is also a major Muslim religious complex, containing the Dome of the Rock and the al-Aqsa Mosque built in the seventh century as well as other historic features such as a fountain and Umayyad-era pillars and stairs.

The remains of the Temple are the holiest site in Judaism, and Haram al-Sharif is one of the three holiest sites in Islam, the other two being Mecca and Medina. Haram al-Sharif has special significance to Christianity as well. Israeli politician Ariel Sharon's September 2000 visit to Haram al-Sharif is credited for being a major contributor to the Second (al-Aqsa) Intifada.

A Muslim waqf (religious endowment) has encompassed the Temple Mount/Haram al-Sharif and adjacent land continuously since the Muslim reconquest of the Kingdom of Jerusalem beginning in the seventh century. Such endowments were taken over by the Israeli state within the Green Line and managed in some instances by local councils entirely composed of Israeli Jews with only token appointments of approved Muslim religious officials. Because of the historical renown of this particular site, it was handled differently. The legality of the waqf has been completely discounted by some Israelis, and as Sharon's comments made clear, Israel regards Haram al-Sharif, just like all parts of Jerusalem, as its territory. However, since the Oslo agreements, Palestinian security supervise entry to Haram al-Sharif. Under this arrangement Jews, like other non-Muslims, are generally permitted to visit the site in tour groups or as individuals but are not allowed to pray on the Temple Mount. Officials or Palestinian tour guides usually accompany such visitors to ensure that no prohibited Jewish prayer takes place. Palestinians of the West Bank or Gaza are never permitted to worship at Haram al-Sharif, a fact that Palestinians say shows that their fundamental religious rights of worship are being violated.

Few Israelis object to the continued Muslim presence on the Temple Mount, as the only remains of the actual Temple site are within the Western (Wailing) Wall, which is below and to the side of the entrance into Haram al-Sharif. One extremist group, the Temple Mount and Eretz Israel Faithful Movement, however, advocates the removal of the Dome of the Rock and the al-Aqsa Mosque. The group deems these as signs of Islamic conquest and domination, suggests that they be rebuilt in Mecca, and claims that God expects Israel to liberate the Temple Mount from the Arabs.

Sheikh Ikrima Sabri, chairman of the Palestinian Higher Islamic Commission and grand mufti of Jerusalem, claims that the Temple Mount and all its structures and walls, including the Western Wall at the base of the mount, are a sacred place only for Muslims. He bases this on the legality of the waqf.

Many Palestinians claim that Sharon's September 28, 2000, visit to the Temple Mount triggered the Second (al-Aqsa) Intifada. Others, however, have claimed that the uprising was a reaction to the derailment of the Camp David negotiations in July 2000.

MOSHE TERDIMAN AND SHERIFA ZUHUR

See also

Al-Aqsa Mosque; Dome of the Rock; Intifada, Second; Jerusalem, Old City of; Sharon, Ariel; Western Wall

References

Andrews, Richard. *Blood on the Mountain: A History of the Temple Mount from the Ark to the Third Millennium.* London: Weidenfeld and Nicolson, 1999.

Gonen, Rivka. *Contested Holiness: Jewish, Muslim, and Christian Perspectives on the Temple Mount in Jerusalem*. Jersey City, NJ: Ktav Publishing House, 2003.

Haredim

Jews commonly referred to as ultraorthodox Jews, or more colloquially as black hat orthodox. Within Orthodox Jewish communities, the name "Haredim," meaning "those who tremble" (i.e., before the Almighty), is preferred. Non-Haredi Israelis refer to the Haredim as the religious. The Haredim represent the most strictly religious and traditionalist wing of Judaism. Haredi Judaism is best distinguished from other forms of Judaism by its adherents' rejection of secular education and culture in favor of a lifestyle stringently devoted to the Tanakh (the Jewish Bible). The Haredim are easily recognized because of their distinctive dress (black suits and hats for men and ankle- and wrist-length attire for women), the high value they place on child rearing and extended family, and the prestige accorded to men in the Haredi community who dedicate their lives to religious study in the Yeshivot (religious schools).

Outsiders typically confuse Haredi Judaism with Hasidic Judaism. Hasidism is a pietistic or revivalist movement that emerged in traditional Jewish communities in Eastern and Central Europe during the 18th century. Initially, there was hostility between traditionalists and Hasidim, but today nearly all Hasidic groups are best classified as ultraorthodox, although not all ultraorthodox are Hasidic.

The Haredim are distinguished from modern orthodox religious Jews by a number of differences in outlook and practice, not least of which are their perspectives on Zionism and the State of Israel. The modern orthodox or Dati (meaning "the faithful") eagerly support the Jewish state with great enthusiasm and generally identify with the ideology currents of religious Zionism, which tend to see the emergence and survival of the modern State of Israel in redemptive terms. The Haredim, by contrast, remain to a great extent antipathetic to Zionism. Some Haredi communities have embraced religious Zionism, most notably the Chabad Lubavitch Hasidim whose late rebbe, Menachem Mendel Schneersohn, was a notable innovator in the area of religious outreach.

Religious Jews have long associated the return of Jewish exiles to Israel with the coming of the biblically foretold Messiah. This anointed one, an heir to King David, it is believed, will rule in Jerusalem over a restored Jewish state. In Orthodox Judaism, the idea of a personal Messiah who leads by divine mandate remains prevalent. As such, the emergence of a secular Jewish state represented a challenge to the traditionalists' worldview. They believed that the return of Jews to Zion was contingent upon Jews' strict Torah observance. In contrast, modern ideologies such as nationalism, socialism, liberalism, and democracy guided the secular Jews who founded Israel. For the ultraorthodox, then, the State of Israel was the product of a heretical movement. As a result, during the early decades of the 20th century, few orthodox rabbis were willing

An Israeli soldier prays beside a Haredi man at the Western Wall in Jerusalem's Old City, 1998. (Amos Ben Gershom/Israeli Government Press Office)

---

to lend support to Zionist efforts to create a Jewish state in Palestine. Today, while a few Haredi communities continue to reject the State of Israel entirely, most have come to an accommodationist position and indeed receive certain privileges in Israel. This was in large part due to concessions and considerations of the secular Zionists.

Led by David Ben-Gurion, the secular Zionists extended an exemption from military service to yeshiva students during the Israeli War of Independence (1948–1949), an exemption that has remained formal policy ever since. Ben-Gurion's motives for adopting this policy were in part political (to defuse religious opposition to the Zionist state) but also humanitarian, intended to allow for the survival of the traditional yeshiva culture.

Of all Jewish communities, the orthodox communities in Eastern Europe had been the most decimated by Stalinism, the Holocaust, and post–World War II pogroms. In contemporary Israeli politics, the military exemption is highly controversial. Many believe that it serves to marginalize the ultraorthodox because military service often serves as an avenue of professional and political advancement. Separate religious military units have been formed to accommodate ultraorthodox strictures in matters of social interaction between men and women, dietary rules, and maintaining an atmosphere of support for religious study and ritual observance. In one popular 2000 Israeli film, *Time of Favor,* the leader of an ultraorthodox army unit remains torn between his loyalty to the secular state and devotion to his best friend, a promising yeshiva scholar, as well as Rabbi Meltzer, the leader of a controversial movement that encourages prayer at the Temple Mount. Nonetheless, relatively few Haredi men of military service age participate.

The June 1967 Six-Day War had a transformative effect on the relationship between Orthodox Judaism and Zionism. In the initial phases of the war, it appeared that the very survival of the Jewish community in Israel might be at stake, but ultimately Israel's forces triumphed and gained control over areas of deep spiritual significance to religious Jews, most notably the Temple Mount and the adjoining Western Wall. The sole remaining physical structure connected to the Temples, the Western Wall, was built circa 19 BC during King Herod the Great's complete reconstruction of the Second Temple. Within the orthodox communities, the outcome of the war strengthened the position of those who supported Zionism and enhanced the movement toward religious Zionism.

Haredi communities in Israel were typically established by refugees from Central and Eastern Europe during the 1930s and 1940s or from Muslim countries after 1948. There are two significant Haredi political parties represented in the Knesset: United Torah Judaism and Shas. The latter has a constituency among secular Sephardic (Mediterranean and Middle Eastern) Jews, but its ideological orientation is ultraorthodox. These parties primarily focus on legislation of concern to the religious community such as state support for religious schools, maintenance of orthodox rabbinical control of Jewish marriage and divorce in Israel, and opposition to any recognition of nonorthodox Judaism. As to Israeli-Palestinian relations, however, the Haredi parties have expressed willingness to make territorial concessions for the sake of the peace and security of the Jewish people and have supported or participated in centrist or center-left governments that have pursued land for peace. Those religious Zionists who oppose territorial concessions over the biblical boundaries of the land of Israel, by contrast, are represented by the National Religious Party, which typically allies with the secular rightists, most notably the Likud Party.

DANIEL SKIDMORE-HESS AND CATHY SKIDMORE-HESS

See also

Ashkenazic Judaism; Hasidic Judaism; Mizrahic Judaism; Sephardic Judaism; Zionism

References

Efron, Noah J. *Real Jews: Secular vs. Ultra-Orthodox and the Struggle for Jewish Identity in Israel.* New York: Basic Books, 2003.

Fishkoff, Susan J. *The Rebbe's Army: Inside the World of Chabad-Lubavitch.* New York: Schocken, 2005.

Harel, Isser
Born: 1912
Died: February 19, 2003

Head of the Israeli Mossad intelligence organization (1952–1963). Born Isser Halperin in Vitebsk, Russia (now Belarus), in 1912, Harel's family owned a vinegar factory. Soviet authorities confiscated the factory, and the family fell on hard times financially, emigrating in 1922 from the Soviet Union to Dvinsk in Latvia, which was then independent. In Dvinsk, Harel completed secondary school and joined a Zionist youth organization.

In 1930 Harel immigrated to Palestine. He spent five years working on a kibbutz and then established his own orange-packing company. During World War II he joined the Haganah, the Jewish self-defense organization, and in 1942 he became head of the Tel Aviv branch of Shai, Haganah's intelligence organization. In 1948 Israeli prime minister David Ben-Gurion ordered Harel and his organization to sink the Irgun Tsvai Leumi (National Military Organization) ship *Atalanta* off Tel Aviv. From 1948 to 1952 Harel was director of Shin Bet (Shabak), and in 1952 he became head of Mossad, the foreign intelligence and security organization. In 1957 he became head of Israeli secret services. He held this post until 1963.

Isser Harel, head of the Israeli Mossad intelligence organization (1952–1963), shown here in 1969. (Israeli Government Press Office)

In 1957 Harel established the Trident intelligence network to gather intelligence against Egypt. He had a number of intelligence successes to his credit, including information gained from highly placed spies in both Egypt and Syria. He is best known, however, for shepherding the long hunt for Adolf Eichmann, who played a major role in the Holocaust. This search ended in May 1960 when Mossad agents tracked him down in Argentina and brought him to Israel to stand trial for his role in the Holocaust. Harel's agents were also responsible for the assassination of German scientists working on missile programs in Egypt. Protests by West Germany led Ben-Gurion to fear that Bonn might terminate the secret arms program between the two countries, and in March 1963 he ordered Harel to terminate all secret service activities against the scientists. Harel chose to resign instead.

Harel served as a special adviser to Prime Minister Levi Eshkol during 1965–1967 and also served one term in the Knesset (Israeli parliament) during 1969–1970. Harel died in Israel on February 19, 2003.

SPENCER C. TUCKER

See also

Altalena Incident; Ben-Gurion, David; Eichmann, Karl Adolf; Eshkol, Levi; Holocaust; Mossad

References

Black, Ian, and Benny Morris. *Israel's Secret Wars: A History of Israel's Intelligence Services.* New York: Grove, 1994.
Harel, Isser. *The House on Garibaldi Street: The Capture of Adolf Eichmann.* New York: Viking, 1975.
Steven, Stewart. *The Spymasters of Israel.* New York: Macmillan, 1980.

Rafik Hariri, Lebanese businessman and politician and premier of Lebanon (1992–1998, 2000–2004). (European Community/Breydel)

Hariri, Rafik
Born: November 1, 1944
Died: February 14, 2005

Lebanese businessman, politician, and premier of Lebanon (1992–1998, 2000–2004). Rafik Baha al-Din Hariri was born in Sidon, Lebanon, on November 1, 1944, the son of a Sunni Muslim farmer. He attended both elementary and secondary school in Sidon and then studied business administration at Beirut Arab University during 1965–1966. In 1966 he went to Saudi Arabia, where he became an auditor for an engineering firm.

In 1969 Hariri set up his own construction company, CICON-EST, which benefited greatly from the Saudi oil boom of the 1970s. He was involved in major construction projects, including offices, hotels, hospitals, and palaces in Lebanon and Saudi Arabia. He worked on both government and private contracts. His reasonable bids on construction work won him the respect of his clients, and he quickly built up businesses and amassed a fortune that made him one of the richest people in the world. In 1978 the Saudi Arabian royal family granted him Saudi citizenship, and he became Saudi Arabia's leading entrepreneur.

Hariri acquired control of the French construction company Oger in 1979 and established Oger International in Paris. His busi-ness interests included construction, banking, real estate, telecommunications, and oil.

Already known as a philanthropist, in 1979 Hariri founded the Hariri Foundation for Culture and Higher Education. In 1982 he donated $12 million to Lebanese victims of Israel's invasion of Lebanon, and in 1983 he built a hospital, school, and university in Kafr Falus, Lebanon. He also created a foundation that paid the university fees of at least 12,000 Lebanese students in Lebanon, Europe, and the United States. He reportedly donated about $90 million to charity every year.

In 1983 Hariri played a significant role in the talks that led to a cease-fire in the Lebanese civil war. He worked with U.S. special envoy Philip Habib to produce the Taif Accord of 1989 that ended the Lebanese Civil War. In 1992 Hariri was appointed prime minister of Lebanon in a move designed to attract foreign investors to help fund the massive rebuilding process required after years of civil war and to restore the confidence of the nation's own investors. He is associated with the Solidère project that rebuilt the historic downtown government district of Beirut, faithfully reproducing the French mandate architecture. In these years, Hariri, who owned property in Damascus, had excellent relations with the Syrian government, and Syrian president Hafez al-Assad consulted with him on occasion.

Considered the mastermind of Lebanon's postwar reconstruction program, Hariri was widely expected to retain his post after the extension of President Émile Lahoud's term of office, which occurred in November 1998 as a result of Syrian pressure. Hariri abruptly declined Lahoud's offer to form a new government, accusing the new president of acting unconstitutionally in his negotiations with the National Assembly. Hariri was replaced by former premier and veteran politician Salim al-Huss. In 2000 after less than two years in office, during which his administration was unable to stem economic and political crisis in the country, al-Huss resigned. Less than a week later, Hariri accepted Lahoud's offer to lead a new government as prime minister. On October 20, 2004, Hariri again resigned from the post.

Hariri became unpopular with some Syrian elements and pro-Syria factions in Lebanon when he called for a Syrian withdrawal from Lebanon and utilized his excellent relations with France to exert pressure in this regard. On February 14, 2005, Hariri, 6 of his bodyguards, and 15 other people died in a massive car bomb blast as his motorcade was passing the St. George Hotel in Beirut. An unknown Islamist terrorist group was blamed for the incident. The assassination brought an outpouring of anger from within Lebanon, the formation of an anti-Syrian Lebanese coalition and then a new government, Syria's military withdrawal from Lebanon under international pressure, and a call by the United Nations (UN) Security Council for a special international court to try suspects in the assassination.

Many Lebanese and international observers blamed Syrian officials for the assassination, suggesting that the plan must have been approved at a very high level of the Syrian government. Indeed, there was an eyewitness account that President Bashar al-Assad had threatened Hariri in August 2004. Although the Syrian government denied any knowledge of the deed, the UN investigation implicated Syrian officials along with members of the Lebanese security services. Hariri's violent end was not the last. The years after his death saw the assassination of other anti-Syrian Lebanese politicians.

SPENCER C. TUCKER

See also

Assad, Bashar al-; Habib, Philip; Hrawi, Elias; Lebanon; Syria

References

Fisk, Robert. *Pity the Nation: The Abduction of Lebanon.* 4th ed. New York: Nation Books, 2002.

Iskandar, Marwan. *Rafiq Hariri and the Fate of Lebanon.* London and Beirut: Saqi, 2006.

Hashemites

Hashemite is the Western name given to a modern dynasty based on the descendants of the Banu Hashim, or Clan of Hashim, within the larger Quraysh tribe. The Hashemites became the rulers of the Hejaz in the western portions of today's Saudi Arabia, Jordan, and Iraq.

The Banu Hashim were descendants of the Arab chieftain Quraysh, in turn a descendant of the Prophet Ismail, himself the son of the Prophet Ibrahim (Abraham). Quraysh first came to the holy city of Mecca during the second century AD. The first generation of Quraysh to rule the city came six generations later in the year 480.

The modern Hashemites trace their direct lineage from Hashim (died ca. 510), the great-grandfather of the Muslim prophet Muhammad. In the same clan line were the Abbasid caliphs who defeated the first imperial caliphal family, the Umayyads. The term "sharif" refers to descendents of the Prophet, who may be found all over the Muslim world because of the spread of the Banu Hashim through the Islamic conquests.

The holy cities of Mecca and Medina were traditionally protected by a leading sharif family. Hussein ibn Ali of the Hashemite Dhau-Awn clan was also a traditional leader in the western Arabian province of Hejaz. The Ottoman sultan Abdulhamid II kept him under house arrest in Constantinople until 1908. The sultan's enemies, the so-called Young Turks of the Committee of Union and Progress (CUP), at first allied with some of the Arab nationalist groups who, like Hussein, wanted self-rule or a new type of dual Arab-Turkish monarchy. The Young Turks had the sultan appoint Hussein as emir and sharif of Mecca in 1908, and he then returned to the Hejaz. His son, Abdullah, made discreet inquiries of the British about raising a rebellion against the Ottoman-CUP government, and when the CUP turned against the Arab nationalists, the stage was set for the Arab Revolt. Sharif Hussein's aim was to establish an Arab kingdom from the Hejaz to Syria and Iraq and including Palestine. Toward this end, he corresponded with British high commissioner for Egypt Sir A. Henry McMahon.

Hussein led the Great Arab Revolt beginning in 1916 to liberate the Arab lands. Between 1917 and 1924, with the collapse of the Ottoman Empire in World War I, Hussein and his son Ali ruled an independent Hejaz. However, the Arab kingdom they had sought was not realized, for the British had concluded the secret Sykes-Picot Agreement with the French during the war to secure much of the Middle East for themselves. In the postwar Treaty of Lausanne and Treaty of Sèvres with Turkey, the British and French secured as mandates under the League of Nations roughly the same areas spelled out in the Sykes-Picot Agreement. The territory conquered by Sharif Hussein's son Faisal, roughly comprising Syria and Lebanon, was to be returned to the French. Palestine, Iraq, and Transjordan went to the British.

Tribal leader Lord Abd al-Aziz ibn-Saud (known as Ibn Saud), who ruled most of central Arabia, aimed to take back the Hejaz. In 1924 his forces took Mecca, making it a part of the Kingdom of Saudi Arabia. Ibn Saud then annexed the Hejaz and set up his own son Faisal as governor.

These actions effectively ended the Hashemite claim to the Hejaz, but Hussein's two politically active sons, Abdullah and Faisal,

The three sons of Sharif of Mecca Hussein in Baghdad, 1923. Seated left to right are Faisal I, king of Iraq; Abdullah, emir of Transjordan (later king of Jordan); and Ali, who was briefly king of the Hejaz. (Bettmann/Corbis)

became the kings of Transjordan and Iraq, respectively. The Hashemite Kingdom of Iraq lasted from 1921 to 1958, and a line of Hashemite kings has been ruling Transjordan, now Jordan, since 1921.

JAMES H. WILLBANKS AND SHERIFA ZUHUR

See also

Abdullah I, King of Jordan; Faisal, King of Saudi Arabia; Faisal I, King of Iraq; Hussein, King of Jordan; Ibn Saud, King of Saudi Arabia; Palestine, Pre-1918 History of; Shia Islam; Sunni Islam; Sykes-Picot Agreement; Wahhabism; World War I, Impact of

References

Hourani, Albert. *A History of the Arab Peoples.* Cambridge: Harvard University Press, 1991.

Howarth, David A. *The Desert King: The Life of Ibn Saud.* Northampton, MA: Interlink, 1964.

Karsh, Efraim, and P. P. Kumaraswamy. *Israel, the Hashemites, and the Palestinians: The Fateful Triangle.* London: Frank Cass, 2003.

Milton-Edwards, Beverly, and Peter Hinchcliffe. *Jordan: A Hashemite Legacy.* London: Routledge, 2001.

Sabini, John. *Armies in the Sand: The Struggle for Mecca.* London: Thames and Hudson, 1981.

Teitelbaum, Joshua. *The Rise and Fall of the Hashemite Kingdom of Hejaz.* New York: New York University Press, 2001.

Hashomer

Jewish defense organization in Palestine, regarded as the forerunner of the Israel Defense Forces (IDF). The Hashomer (Hebrew for "guard") was first organized in 1909 by members of the Second Aliya (1904–1914) to provide security for the Jewish settlements in Palestine, especially the largely isolated kibbutzim. Hashomer was formed by members of Poalei Zion, a socialist Zionist group. Its founders were recent immigrants from Russia who had settled in Lower Galilee, and a number of them had participated in a self-defense organization of 1904–1906 known as Bar Giora. Among

Hashomer founders were Yitzhak Ben-Zvi, Israel Giladi, Rachel Yanait, Israel Shochat, and Manya Shochat.

Hashomer's stated aims were to protect Jewish lives and property, secure respect for the Jews from among the Arabs, and improve relations with the Arabs while learning their language and customs. Hashomer concluded agreements with a number of Jewish settlements in Lower Galilee in which its members would provide security services in return for a fixed fee. Hashomer achieved considerable success, and in 1911 it expanded its operations beyond Galilee. Hashomer did away with the need to employ Arab watchmen to warn against raids and provided security as well as prevented thefts.

Hashomer clashed with Arabs on a number of occasions and incurred casualties, but its activities also won the admiration of many Jews in Palestine and in the Diaspora. Members of Hashomer regarded themselves as the forerunners of a future Jewish national army. They refused to accept the authority of the Yishuv (Jewish community in Palestine) but nonetheless claimed the exclusive right to protect the Jewish settlements.

Shortly after the start of World War I, Hashomer proposed to Turkish authorities the establishment of a Jewish legion in the Turkish Army, an offer that was refused. Its pro-Turkish position, however, brought it into conflict with the pro-British Jewish intelligence network known as Nili.

In 1920 on the formation of the Jewish self-defense organization the Haganah, members of Hashomer were asked to turn over their arms to the Haganah and merge with it. This led to a considerable debate among Hashomer members, a number of whom claimed that their organization had the sole right to defend the Jews of Palestine. Not until the Arab riots of 1929 did the last Hashomer holdouts agree to turn over their arms to the Haganah, which itself gave way to the IDF during the Israeli War of Independence (1948–1949).

SPENCER C. TUCKER

See also

Aliya, Second; Galilee; Haganah

References

Mardor, Munya M. *Haganah.* Edited by D. R. Elston. Foreword by David Ben-Gurion. Translated by H. A. G. Schmuckler. New York: New American Library, 1966.

Pappe, Ilan. *A History of Modern Palestine: One Land, Two Peoples.* Cambridge: Cambridge University Press, 2003.

Hasidic Judaism

Hasidic (or Chasidic) Judaism is a branch of Judaism that originated in Eastern Europe (Belarus, Poland, and Ukraine) in the 18th century at a time when European Jews were being persecuted. The word "Hasidic" comes from the Hebrew word *Chasidut,* meaning "pious," which comes from the Hebrew root word *chesed,* meaning "loving kindness." Hasidic Judaism is also known as Hasidism (Pietism).

Religious persecution in Eastern Europe drove nearly half of European Jewry to emphasize an inner personal spirituality derived from intensive Talmudic study rather than academic and ethnic beliefs. This inner spirituality, or joy, is expressed outwardly in distinctive religious traditions and practices that allow the Hasidim to grow closer to God through everyday living as well as Torah study. This brings the Hasidim in constant communion (Devekut) with God.

Hasidism's founder, Rabbi Israel Baal Shem Tov (1699–1760), also known by the title "master of the good name" (the *a'al Shem Tov,* abbreviated as the *Besht*), was a scholar, mystic, and healer who taught that the Torah communicated God and the truths of God outwardly through revelation, the outer aspect of the Torah, and inwardly through devotion and piety, the hidden or inner aspect of the Torah. Hasidism asserts that Baal Shem Tov was a miracle worker and was infallible in his teaching and that these same defining attributes continue to be passed through a series of dynastic leaders known as rebbes (also spelled rebbi and rabbee), generally meaning "master" and "teacher" and less commonly "mentor."

This great elevation of Hasidic rebbes was one of the main reasons that European Jewry divided into Hasidic Judaism and Orthodox Judaism, called Mitnagdim (opponents) by the Hasidim. Another point of division is the Hasidic assertion that God permeates all that exists. The Mitnagdim understood this belief to be pantheism. But what the Hasidic philosophy actually asserts is the belief that although God does permeate all that exists, God is more than that. Hasidism also expands Judaism's traditional teaching that God implanted a divine spark in all humans by teaching that although the divine spark exists only in souls of humans, there is a divinely infused spark of goodness in all creation that can be redeemed to perfect the world. It is God's animation of all that exists that allows pious humans to commune with God. This belief in an interactive relationship between God and pious humans allowing God to influence the actions of pious humans and allowing pious humans to correlatively influence the will of God is a belief derived from the 16th-century rabbi Isaac Ben Solomon Luria's *Kabbalah* (Cabala).

The most common Hasidic prayer style (Nusach Sepharad) is based on Rabbi Luria's integration of Ashkenazic and Sephardic liturgies and is accompanied by melodies called *nigunim* (or nigguns) that are in themselves descriptive of the mood of the prayer. The *Amidah* (standing), the central prayer in all Jewish worship services, is generally recited while standing, and some particularly pious Hasidim concentrate for seven seconds on each of its words. Most Hasidim pray in a Yiddish-influenced, heavily accented Ashkenazic Hebrew and oppose the daily use of oral Hebrew. They believe it to be a holy language intended for prayer only, and they also believe that it is debased by common use.

The daily attire for Hasidic men is generally black trousers and coats with a white shirt and a black hat. A long black robe called a *bekishe* with a prayer belt called a *gartel* and a fur headdress are worn for Shabbat (Sabbath). Most Hasidic men wear long sideburns called *payoth,* following the biblical prohibition (Leviticus 19:27) not to shave the sides of one's face. White threads or fringes (*tzitzit* or *tsitsits*) are worn about the waist, either over or under the shirt, as directed by Numbers 15:38. Hasidic boys have their first haircut and are given their first fringed garment on their third birthday. Hasidic women generally wear long black skirts and sleeves past the elbow.

Immersion in a ritual pool of water (*mikvah*) is practiced as an outward manifestation of an inner or spiritual cleansing. Hasidic men generally practice this ritual cleansing prior to Jewish holidays, and many ritually wash daily prior to morning prayers. Female Hasidim generally immerse in a *mikvah* seven days after the end of their menstrual cycle.

The largest Hasidic fellowship, the Lubavitch (some 100,000 adherents), is based in Brooklyn, New York. There are also large populations residing in Israel along with other Hasidim such as the Gor (Gerer), Vizhnitz, and Bealz (Belzer). The Belzer, Bobov, Bostoner, Breslov, Gerer, Munkacz, Puppa, Rimnitz, Satmar, and Vizhnitz Hasidim are the largest of the remaining Hasidic groups.

RICHARD M. EDWARDS

See also

Ashkenazic Judaism; Mizrahic Judaism; Sephardic Judaism

References

Biale, David. *Cultures of the Jews: A New History.* New York: Schocken, 2002.

Dimont, Max. *Jews, God and History.* New York: Simon and Schuster, 1962.

Harris, Lis. *Holy Days: The World of the Hasidic Family.* New York: Touchstone, 1995.

Haumann, Heiko. *A History of East European Jews.* Budapest, Hungary: Central European University Press, 2001.

Robinson, George. *Essential Judaism: A Complete Guide to Beliefs, Customs & Rituals.* New York: Pocket Books/Simon and Schuster, 2001.

Seltzer, Robert. *Jewish People, Jewish Thought.* New York: Macmillan, 1980.

Shalomi, Zalman Schachter, and Nathaniel Miles-Yepez, eds. *Wrapped in a Holy Flame: Teachings and Tales of the Hasidic Masters.* San Francisco: Wiley, 2003.

Haskalah

The Haskalah, or Jewish Enlightenment, was an intellectual movement in Europe that lasted from the 1770s to the 1880s and called for Jews to become more acculturated to the societies in which they lived. Those who followed the Haskalah, known as *maskilim* in Hebrew, believed that Jews should become more involved with the secular world and should not separate themselves from it.

Moses Mendelssohn is regarded as the father of the Haskalah. Indeed, he epitomized the new Jew of the late 18th century. The son of a poor scribe, Mendelssohn learned German and became familiar with secular and non-Jewish learning. Eventually he became renowned as a philosopher and political thinker. He was placed under special protection by Frederick the Great and won a prize from the Prussian Academy of Sciences. *Maskilim* who followed Mendelssohn began to publish periodicals and write primers intended for Jews who wanted to learn more than the traditional rabbinic teachings.

Generally, those who belonged to the Haskalah movement supported education in science and other secular areas of knowledge. They wanted their children to receive an education comparable to that of non-Jewish children. The *maskilim* also wanted children to study Hebrew history and language. They believed that creating a Jewish consciousness among the young could help them take pride in their heritage even while they became more integrated into the surrounding society.

The Haskalah movement thrived in Germany and then spread eastward into the Russian Empire. Jewish leaders called for emancipation for Jews and equal rights for them comparable to those enjoyed by other groups. Like other Enlightenment thinkers, they saw a separation between religion and secular society and believed that Judaism should be considered a religious choice, not a racial identity. As a result of this broadening of thinking, numerous Jewish political movements and organizations were founded in the 19th century. When the Russian government sponsored pogroms against Jews in the 1870s and 1880s, many Jewish leaders lost faith in the Haskalah. They no longer believed that Jews would be accepted into broader European society, no matter what they did. As a result, Zionist organizations were born with a goal of creating a Jewish homeland.

TIM J. WATTS

See also

Pogroms; Zionism

References

Feiner, Shmuel. *The Jewish Enlightenment.* Philadelphia: University of Pennsylvania Press, 2004.

Lederhendler, Eli. *The Road to Modern Jewish Politics: Political Tradition and Political Reconstruction in the Jewish Community of Tsarist Russia.* New York: Oxford University Press, 1989.

Hasmonean Tunnel Incident
Start Date: September 23, 1996
End Date: September 28, 1996

Armed clash between Palestinians and Israeli border police and Israel Defense Forces (IDF) soldiers that began on September 23, 1996, in the Old City of Jerusalem on the Temple Mount (Haram al-Sharif). The Hasmonean Tunnel Incident is sometimes referred to as the Kotel Tunnel Incident. The Temple Mount is a holy site for Christians, Jews, and Muslims. For Jews, it is the site of the first and second Jewish Temples and is to be the site of the third and final Temple to be rebuilt upon the coming of the Messiah. For Muslims, it is the site of two very important religious shrines: the Dome of the Rock and the al-Aqsa Mosque.

Police officers restrain a Muslim protesting the opening of the Hasmonean Tunnel in Jerusalem on September 26, 1996. (Ricki Rosen/Corbis Saba)

Located in the Old City of eastern Jerusalem, the Temple Mount area remained under Jordanian control from 1948 to 1967, at which point the Israelis seized control of it as a result of the Six-Day War. A series of tunnels dating back to antiquity run beneath the site. After 1967, Israeli historians and archaeologists began excavations at the site. In an attempt to find and reconstruct lost portions of the Western Wall, the Israelis uncovered the Hasmonean Tunnel, which is along the northern edge of the wall, in 1987. It is actually a large aqueduct dating to the second century BC.

The Hasmonean Tunnel Incident was sparked when the Israeli government allowed archaeologists doing excavations near the Western Wall to open a new exit to the tunnel in the area. On the night of September 23, 1996, between 11:30 p.m. and 12:00 a.m. and under heavy police guard, a new exit was opened off the Hasmonean Tunnel. When the Palestinians realized what had happened, they were outraged because of the proximity of the tunnel to the Temple Mount, particularly the al-Aqsa Mosque. Some Muslim leaders in Jerusalem also claimed that the tunnel exit had damaged the al-Aqsa Mosque, under which part of the aqueduct ran.

Palestinian Authority (PA) president Yasser Arafat immediately denounced the tunnel as an act of Israeli aggression against the Islamic religion. He called for a general strike and demonstrations to be staged throughout the Palestinian territories. Even before Arafat's official condemnation of the Israeli move, protesters began to clash with Israeli forces, throwing rocks and bottles. Israeli worshipers at the Western Wall were also subjected to mob attacks.

What began as protests on September 24 quickly turned into fierce fighting between Palestinian militants and Israeli security forces. Indeed, many claim that this incident nearly turned into a full-fledged intifada against Israel. Although the worst of the fighting had died down by September 28, it was days after that before the riots in the Palestinian territories were entirely quelled. In the four days of heavy fighting, as many as 100 Palestinians and 15 Israeli soldiers and border policemen were killed.

The Hasmonean Tunnel Incident helped to convince right-wing Israeli prime minister Benjamin Netanyahu to sign the January 1997 Hebron Protocol with the PA under which Israel would withdraw from the West Bank city of Hebron as agreed to in the 1993 Oslo Accords. While the majority of the Israeli population supported the signing of this agreement, some hard-liners viewed it as an outrageous act of capitulation. Among the Palestinian population, the outcome of the protests over the Hasmonean Tunnel Incident was viewed as a victory.

DANIEL KUTHY AND PAUL G. PIERPAOLI JR.

See also

Al-Aqsa Mosque; Arafat, Yasser; Archaeological Sites and Projects; Haram al-Sharif; Hebron Protocol; Jerusalem, Old City of; Netanyahu, Benjamin; Oslo Accords; Palestinian Authority; Western Wall

References

Bickerton, Ian J., and Carla L. Klausner. *A Concise History of the Arab-Israeli Conflict.* 4th ed. Upper Saddle River, NJ: Prentice Hall, 2004.

Gorenberg, Gershom. *The End of Days: Fundamentalism and the Struggle for the Temple Mount.* New York: Oxford University Press, 2000.

Herzog, Chaim. *The Arab-Israeli Wars: War and Peace in the Middle East from the War of Independence to Lebanon.* Westminster, MD: Random House, 1984.

Hassan II, King of Morocco
Born: July 9, 1929
Died: July 23, 1999

King of Morocco from 1961 to 1999. Hassan II was born in Rabat, Morocco, on July 9, 1929. A direct descendant of the Prophet Muhammad's daughter Fatima, he was the 17th monarch of the Alawite dynasty, which has ruled Morocco since 1666. In January 1943, Hassan II accompanied his father, Muhammad V, to the Anfa (Casablanca) Conference, which was held in a suburb of Casablanca. At the conference, Morocco, the United States, the United Kingdom, and France agreed to the demand for the unconditional surrender of the Axis powers. In 1947 Hassan accompanied his father to Tangier, where Muhammad V first called for Moroccan independence from the French, who had established colonial rule over Morocco in 1912. In 1951 Hassan earned a law degree from the University of Bordeaux, France.

On August 20, 1953, French colonial authorities exiled Hassan and his father to Corsica. In 1954 they were moved to Madagascar. During their absence the call for Moroccan independence increased, and French political leaders reluctantly accepted the inevitable. On November 16, 1955, Muhammad V and Hassan returned to Morocco. Independence was declared in 1956, and Hassan was appointed chief of the Moroccan armed forces.

Following the death of his father, Hassan II became king on March 3, 1961. Surviving several assassination attempts, he ruled Morocco as a conservative theocracy. Although his human rights record was frequently criticized in the international press, he maintained friendly relations with the United States. Throughout his reign, he attempted to reestablish the territorial integrity of Morocco. Although the French had relinquished their claim over Morocco in 1956, Spain continued to hold the Spanish Sahara (also known as the Western Sahara or the Rio de Oro region), which Hassan II considered part of Morocco. The International Court of Justice, however, refused to recognize as valid claims by both Morocco and Mauritania on the Spanish Sahara and called on the people of the region to decide their future.

Hassan II launched the Green March in 1975. More than 300,000 unarmed Moroccans assembled on the frontier of the phosphate-

King Hassan II of Morocco during a visit to the United States in 1991. (U.S. Department of Defense)

rich Spanish Sahara, and a number of these crossed the border to demonstrate for the incorporation of the Spanish Sahara into Morocco. Their green banners and Korans symbolized Islam. After calling for a plebiscite there was an agreement to enter into bilateral negotiations with Morocco, also including Mauritania. By the terms of the secret Madrid Accords that November, these two nations split the Spanish Sahara between them, while Spain received economic concessions. The United Nations (UN), however, has yet to recognize this agreement, and the Western Saharans in the Polisario Party launched a resistance movement against it.

Hassan II also played an important behind-the-scenes role in the Middle East peace process. Throughout the 1970s, representatives of the Palestine Liberation Organization (PLO), Israel, the United States, and various Arab powers secretly met in Morocco. Although conducting diplomatic talks with Israel, Hassan II was nevertheless able to maintain credibility both at home and abroad because of his religious importance as a descendant of the Prophet Muhammad and because of Morocco's geographic distance from the controversy in Palestine. Hassan II is credited with being a key player in the 1979 peace treaty between Israel and Egypt.

During the 1970s and 1980s Hassan II ruled with a heavy hand. He governed directly, almost by decree; dissolved parliament for a time; and ordered dissidents jailed, exiled, or executed. These years have come to be known as the "years of lead." In 1991 he sent troops to join the UN forces that expelled Iraqi forces from Kuwait.

On July 23, 1999, Hassan II died in Rabat of a heart attack. He was succeeded by his son, who was crowned Muhammad VI on July 25, 1999.

MICHAEL R. HALL

See also
Camp David Accords; Morocco

References
Hassan II. *The Challenge: The Memoirs of King Hassan II of Morocco.* London: Macmillan, 1978.
Landau, Ron. *Hassan II, King of Morocco.* London: Allen and Unwin, 1962.

Havlaga

Term meaning "self-restraint" in Hebrew and referring to a policy of passive defense against Arab attacks in Palestine and later Israel. Havlaga was the official policy of the Yishuv (Jews in Palestine) until the outbreak of the Arab Revolt of 1936–1939. That conflict sparked a sharp debate among the Yishuv in terms of its response to Arab violence. Since the founding of the secret Jewish self-defense organization Haganah in 1920, Arab attacks were nearly always met not by retaliatory violence but rather by measured responses utilizing British law enforcement authorities. The official position was to prevent and repel Arab raids and, when possible, pursue the perpetrators and hand them over to British Mandate officials.

Jewish leaders in Palestine adopted havlaga as a way to influence public perception of Arabs and Jews. First, they feared that retaliation against the Arabs would compel the British to see the violence as a Jewish-Arab civil conflict instead of a one-sided, Arab-inspired affair. Second, many feared that retribution would raise the ire of the British public and diminish any chances of British support for a Jewish homeland. Also, some Yishuv leaders feared that retaliation against Arabs would only serve to radicalize moderate Arabs and embolden the extremists.

When the Arab Revolt began in 1936, the policy of havlaga came under great scrutiny. At first trying to maintain the policy as the violence became widespread, Jewish leaders including David Ben-Gurion, Vladimir Jabotinsky, and Chaim Weizmann urged calm and the continuation of self-restraint. Believing that the uprising would be short-lived, they figured to outlast the attacks. But the Arab Revolt endured, taking more and more Jewish lives and destroying much of their property. By mid-1937, many Jews in Palestine began to call for a more proactive response to Arab attacks. More and more Jews had come to the conclusion that havlaga was actually encouraging Arab violence and adversely affecting Jewish public opinion in the Yishuv and other parts of the world. Some made the argument that havlaga was undermining the morale of Jewish security forces and Haganah.

Soon, Haganah commanders began to carry out sporadic retaliatory strikes. When the radical Jewish paramilitary group Irgun

Tsvai Leumi (National Military Organization) organized in 1937, its members were not about to adhere to the havlaga policy. Instead, Irgun pressed for a firm policy of retribution and engaged in bombings against Arab interests in Jerusalem and Haifa. By 1939, even Haganah had deviated from havlaga in response to raids emanating from the Arab-Palestinian village of Baldat al-Shaykh, which it attacked in the summer of 1939. Then, on July 2, 1939, Haganah issued a statement declaring that while it would refrain from launching wholesale or random retaliatory actions against the Arabs, it reserved the right to pursue individuals responsible for violence against the Yishuv into their own villages. After the Arab Revolt ended, havlaga again became the official policy of Palestinian Jews, although there were certainly exceptions. By the mid-1940s, the policy once more came under great scrutiny. In Israel today, there are still those who adhere to havlaga, and the old debates about its effectiveness continue to reverberate throughout the nation.

PAUL G. PIERPAOLI JR.

See also
Arab Revolt of 1936–1939; Ben-Gurion, David; Haganah; Irgun Tsvai Leumi; Jabotinsky, Vladimir Yevgenyevich; Weizmann, Chaim

References
Bickerton, Ian J., and Carla L. Klausner. *A Concise History of the Arab-Israeli Conflict.* 4th ed. Upper Saddle River, NJ: Prentice Hall, 2004.
Levine, David. *The Birth of the Irgun Zvai Leumi: The Jewish Resistance Movement.* Jerusalem: Gefen, 1996.

Hawatmeh, Nayef
Born: ca. 1934–1937

Palestinian Arab leader. Born in Salt, Jordan, sometime between 1934 and 1937 to Greek Orthodox Christian Bedouin, Nayef Hawatmeh studied in Amman, Jordan, and then Cairo University in Egypt and the American University of Beirut, where he majored in philosophy and psychology. He joined the leftist Arab Nationalist Movement in 1954 and later was a member of George Habash's Popular Front for the Liberation of Palestine (PFLP) but seceded from that group because of arguments over ideology and tactics in the wake of the 1967 Yom Kippur War. Hawatmeh became known to some Palestinians as Abu al-Nouf.

In 1968 Hawatmeh cofounded with Yasser Abed Rabbo the Democratic Front for the Liberation of Palestine (DFLP), a leftist, Marxist group in Yasser Arafat's Palestine Liberation Organization (PLO). Hawatmeh was the secretary-general and head of the DFLP and its chief representative on the PLO Executive Committee. He initially supported negotiations to bring about a general peace settlement but opposed the Madrid Conference and was suspended from the PLO Executive Committee. Hawatmeh has written several books on Palestinian issues. He resides in Syria, where the DFLP receives Syrian government assistance.

SPENCER C. TUCKER

Palestinian leader Nayef Hawatmeh at the Twentieth National Palestinian Council in Algiers, September 23, 1991. (Bernard Bisson/Corbis Sygma)

See also

Abed Rabbo, Yasser; Arafat, Yasser; Democratic Front for the Liberation of Palestine; Madrid Conference; Palestine Liberation Organization

References

Nassar, Jamal R. *The Palestine Liberation Organization: From Armed Struggle to the Declaration of Independence.* New York: Praeger, 1991.

Rubin, Barry, and Judith Colp Rubin. *Yasir Arafat: A Political Biography.* New York: Oxford University Press, 2003.

Hawi, Khalil
Born: December 31, 1919
Died: June 6, 1982

Lebanese poet and scholar and a leader in the modernization of Arabic poetry. Khalil Hawi was born in modest circumstances on December 31, 1919, in al-Shwayr, an Arab village in Mount Lebanon. His family gives a birthdate in 1920 and the birthplace as Huwaya, where his father was then working. Hawi finished his elementary education in the village, but no secondary schooling was available.

Despite his lack of a formal education, Hawi's poetic talent manifested itself early when he began composing zajal, a type of lyric folk poetry or rhyming prized in Lebanon. Trained by his uncle in zajal, Hawi was pained when this beloved relative contracted tuberculosis and was forced to live in isolation. His father also fell ill, forcing Hawi to interrupt his education and seek work. Successive jobs as a shoemaker, wall plasterer, bricklayer, and restaurant manager were all difficult for Hawi, who yearned to complete his education.

In 1939 Hawi moved to Beirut, at first living on the outskirts and supporting himself as a laborer, reading poetry to console himself. Following World War II he was able to enroll in a prestigious prep school that qualified him to enter the American University of Beirut in 1947. Studying in the Arabic Department, he attained his bachelor's degree in 1951 and his master's degree in 1955, focusing his attention on Islamic philosophy. A scholarship enabled him to join the doctoral program at Cambridge University in England.

For decades Beirut had been an important intellectual center in the Arab world, and in the late 1940s its inhabitants were riveted by the events in Palestine and debated how to respond to the creation of the State of Israel. Hawi was also influenced by Antun Saada, the leader of the anticolonial Syrian Socialist National Party, whom he greatly admired. Saada's assassination in 1949 was a great emotional blow to Hawi, although he tended to remain aloof from political affiliations thereafter. He had, however, entered the university during the years when Arab radicals from all the countries of the Middle East were gathering at the American University of Beirut.

His commitment to Arab nationalism thus developed in association with poets and thinkers from many different Arab states.

By the time Hawi returned from Cambridge in the 1950s, Arab nationalism was at its height, buoyed by the accomplishments of Egyptian president Gamal Abdel Nasser. Hawi had written his doctoral dissertation on Gibran Khalil Gibran, a Lebanese writer whose origins were also in Mount Lebanon in a village near the one where Hawi had grown up.

Receiving a permanent teaching position at the American University of Beirut as a professor of Arabic, Hawi worked to reconcile the knowledge gained from the village society of his youth with the larger world of Arab nationalism that placed less emphasis on the particular state and more on the unity of all Arabs progressing under secular leadership. In 1957 Hawi wrote the poem for which he is best known, "The Bridge." It reveals the optimism of intellectuals such as Hawi during this period as they glimpsed the awakening of a new generation determined to resist occupation and all forms of colonization. "The Bridge" expressed Hawi's hope for his students and the young generation he hoped would take the ideas in which he believed and use them to strengthen the Arab world. His poem reached many people through the composition of Marcel Khalifa, a well-known Lebanese composer who set the words to music.

Hawi's optimism did not last very long, however, and his poetry came to express more sadness and grief. Heavy with symbolism, Hawi's poetry drew on images from Syrian and Greek mythology; Christian, Islamic, and Hindu mysticism; both the Old and New Testaments; and Arabic literature, history, and popular beliefs. His repeated insistence on such symbols as graves, caves, experience, vision, and ashes reflected not only his personal sorrows but also those of his nation and the Arab world. His poems expressed the agony of the Arabs' cultural duality between East and West and his grief over the conflicts between Arab states. Although he was a prolific literary critic and published his dissertation as *Gibran Khalil Gibran: His Background, Character, and Works* in 1982, Hawi's five volumes of poetry are his best-loved work. The first was *Nahr al-Ramad* (The River of Ashes), published in 1957, followed by *al-Nay wa al-Rih* (The Flute and the Wind), published in 1961; *Bayadir al-Jua* (The Threshing Floors of Hunger), published in 1965; and *al-Rad al Jarih* (The Wounded Thunder) and *Min Jahim al-Kumidiyya* (From the Hell of Comedy), both published in 1979.

The Arab defeat in the Six-Day War of 1967 had been difficult for all Arabs to accept, but even more difficult for Hawi was the arrival of the Palestine Liberation Organization (PLO) in Beirut in the early 1970s. He could not really identify with the leftist program of the PLO, nor did he believe in the Christian Maronites who resisted them. By 1975 the Lebanese Civil War raged in Beirut, and Hawi was forced to observe the ruin of his city and to fear for the destruction of his homeland. His previous faith in the power of language and the secular written word to carry the Arab people into the modern age was shattered. When the Israeli Army invaded Lebanon to strike at the PLO in June 1982, Hawi's despair was complete.

Lebanon, the Arab nation with the most diverse balance of population groups, was abandoned by the other Arab states and left to fight Israel alone. On the night of June 6, 1982, he shot himself to death on the balcony of his apartment. Hawi was viewed by many as the poetic interpreter of Arab politics, and his suicide in response to the Israeli invasion of Lebanon in 1982 was widely understood by his followers as a testament to the crisis of the Arab world.

SPENCER C. TUCKER

See also

Arab Nationalism; Lebanon; Lebanon, Civil War in; Lebanon, Israeli Invasion of; Nasser, Gamal Abdel; Palestine Liberation Organization

References

Ajami, Fouad. *The Dream Palace of the Arabs: A Generation's Odyssey.* New York: Vintage Books, 1999.

Hawi, Khalil, and Nadeem Naimy. *From the Vineyards of Lebanon: Poems by Khalil Hawi and Nadeem Naimy.* Syracuse, NY: Syracuse University Press, 1992.

Haydar, Adnon. *Naked in Exile: Khalil Hawi's Threshing Floors of Hunger.* Translated by Michael Beard. Boulder, CO: Paaseggiata, 1985.

Hebron

West Bank city in the mountains of southern Judea. Hebron is located some 23 miles south-southwest of Jerusalem and is about 3,050 feet above sea level. With a 2007 population of approximately 120,000 people, including some 600 Jewish settlers, Hebron has been the site of considerable violence between Arabs and Jews over the past century. The city is an important urban and agricultural center. With its narrow, winding streets, Hebron is known for its grapes, pottery making, leather tanning, and glass blowing, a craft that has been practiced there for 6,000 years.

One of the world's oldest cities and oldest continuously inhabited sites, Hebron was probably established around 3500 BC. Hebron is a holy site for Christianity, Islam, and Judaism. To Jews it is second only to Jerusalem, for Hebron is the location of the Tomb of the Patriarchs (also known as the Tomb of the Patriarchs and Matriarchs), known to the Arabs as the Cave of Machpelah. Here the prophets Abraham, Isaac, and Jacob and their wives Sarah, Rebecca, and Leah are believed to be buried. The Talmud also identifies Hebron as the resting place of Adam and Eve. Muslims venerate the site, as they also claim ancestry through Abraham.

Hebron played an important role in early Jewish history. It was the residence of the patriarchs, and King David was anointed king there and made it his capital. The city has also been identified as one of the locations to which Jews exiled to Babylon returned. A small Jewish community continued in Hebron thereafter. Herod the Great caused the construction of the wall around the Tomb of the Patriarchs. In the sixth century AD, Byzantine emperor Justinian I erected a Christian church over the Tomb of the Patriarchs. But in the seventh century, the Muslims built the al-Ibrahimi (Abraham) mosque over the tomb. Later the Jews were permitted to build a synagogue near the site.

Israeli soldiers in the West Bank city of Hebron, June 1968. (Pictorial Library of Bible Lands)

Leader of the First Crusade Godfrey de Bouillon, Duke of Lorraine, took Hebron in 1099 and converted the mosque and synagogue into a Christian church. The Crusaders also expelled the Jews from Hebron. The city changed hands a number of times thereafter. In 1266 under Mamluk rule, Christians and Jews were prohibited from visiting the Tomb of the Patriarchs. Following the imposition of Ottoman rule during 1516–1517 there was a pogrom in Hebron in which Jewish property was seized and Jews were murdered. Another pogrom occurred in Hebron in 1834.

In 1820 Habad Hasidim established the first Ashkenazic Jewish community in Hebron, and during the Arab riots of 1929 in Hebron, 68 Jews were killed and another 58 were wounded. British authorities evacuated the remaining Jews from the city. Some of the Jews returned to Hebron in 1931 but left again with the Arab Revolt of 1936.

The United Nations (UN) partition plan of 1947 assigned Hebron to the proposed Arab state. Forces of the Arab Legion held the area during the Israeli War of Independence (1948–1949). As a result, Jews could not access Hebron until the Six-Day War of June 1967, when Israel Defense Forces (IDF) captured the entire West Bank, including Hebron. It has been under Israeli control ever since. In 1968 Jewish settlers arrived in Hebron and reestablished the Jewish community there.

In May 1980, Palestinian terrorists killed 6 Jewish students and wounded another 20 as they returned from worship at the Tomb of the Patriarchs. Then, in February 1994, Jewish settler Baruch Goldstein opened fire on Muslims in the tomb, killing 29 Palestinians and wounding another 125 people. The UN subsequently established an unarmed international observer force in Hebron in an effort to keep the peace there.

According to the 1993 Oslo Accords, Israeli forces were to redeploy from the West Bank cities, but while this redeployment occurred in other cities in 1995, the Israeli Army did not leave Hebron, claiming that to do so would endanger the lives of the Jews living there. In 1997 the city was divided into two zones, H1 and H2, under the terms of the Hebron Protocol of January 15. H1 contains about 80 percent of the area and the bulk of the population, is exclusively Palestinian Arab, and came under the control of the Palestinian Authority (PA). H2 in the center of the city contains about 20 percent of the area and originally was home to some 30,000 Arabs and 500 Jews. The Arab population in H2 is believed to now number only about 10,000 people, the consequence of harassment from other Arabs and restrictions placed on them by the IDF. The maintenance of some sort of connection corridor between the two Jewish communities has been an ongoing flash point.

SPENCER C. TUCKER

See also
Arab Revolt of 1936–1939; Ashkenazic Judaism; Hebron Massacre;
Hebron Mosque Massacre; Pogroms; Six-Day War; Talmud

References
Lochery, Neill. *The Difficult Road to Peace: Netanyahu, Israel and the
Middle East Peace Process.* Reading, UK: Ithaca Press, 1999.
Murphy-O'Connor, Jerome. *The Holy Land: An Oxford Archeological
Guide from Earliest Times to 1700.* New York: Oxford University Press,
1998.
Shahin, Mariam. *Palestine: A Guide.* Northampton, MA: Interlink, 2005.

Hebron Massacre
Start Date: August 23, 1929
End Date: August 24, 1929

The West Bank town of Hebron (al-Khalil in Arabic) is one of the
most important geographic sites for all three of the world's major
monotheistic religions. Located in the town is the Tomb of the Patriarchs, the traditional burial place of Abraham, the biblical prophet
from whom the Jewish, Christian, and Muslim religions all trace
their origins. Hebron has also been one of the major flash points
between Arabs and Israelis in the past 100 years. Today, half of the
building containing the Tomb of the Patriarchs is a mosque, while
the other half is a synagogue.

For hundreds of years a Sephardic Jewish community lived in
Hebron in relatively peaceful coexistence with the Arab majority.
With the rise of Zionism in the early 20th century and the arrival of
Ashkenazic Jews from Europe and the United States, Hebron began
to experience the tensions that were growing elsewhere in Palestine.
By the middle of the 1920s, the Jewish community in Hebron
numbered about 800 people, with only a small percentage of that
number being relatively recent Ashkenazic arrivals.

In September 1928, tensions between Muslims and Jews flared
in Jerusalem when Haj Amin al-Husseini, the mufti of Jerusalem,
accused the Jews of carrying out unauthorized construction at the
Western Wall. The following year, in early August, Muslims and
Jews again clashed over Jewish demands for access to the Western
Wall and Muslim concerns about encroachment of the al-Aqsa
Mosque. A series of inflammatory sermons delivered by al-Husseini
preceded a wave of disturbances that built in intensity.

Concerned about the possibility of a major pogrom, leaders of
Haganah, the secret Jewish self-defense force, went to Hebron on
August 20 and proposed a defensive plan for the Jews in the town.
The leaders of the Sephardic community, who were largely anti-
Zionist, refused the offer and insisted that Haganah leave immedi-
ately. The Jews of Hebron were convinced that the local Arab leaders
would shield them from whatever violence might sweep the rest of
the country.

On August 23, false reports started to reach Hebron of Jews
desecrating Muslim holy places in Jerusalem. As tensions rose in
Hebron, an angry mob killed a student at the Ashkenazic Yeshiva. At
the time, the entire Hebron police force consisted of 34 men: a single
British officer, Raymond Cafferata, with 18 mounted policemen
and 15 on foot. One member of Cafferata's force was a Jew, and all
the others were Arabs.

After the killing on August 23, Cafferata managed to calm things
down temporarily, but the next morning things got out of hand.
Arab mobs in Hebron went on a rampage of murder and rape. The
Hebron police were powerless to stop the carnage. Almost all of
the Arab constables joined the mob. Cafferata later testified that he
came upon one Arab in the act of beheading a child and another
Arab nearby butchering a woman with a dagger. Cafferata shot both
of the Arabs, one of whom was one of his own constables.

Overwhelmed, Cafferata called for reinforcements, which did
not arrive until five hours later. The lack of timely response led to
bitter recriminations against the British Mandate government that
have reverberated ever since. The British at the time, however, had
only 292 policemen and fewer than 100 soldiers in all of Palestine.

By the time it was over, the Hebron Massacre had resulted in
the deaths of 68 of Hebron's Jews and the wounding of another 58.
Hebron's Arabs, however, did manage to shield some 435 Jews from
the carnage. At least 28 Arab families risked their lives to hide their
Jewish neighbors. Elsewhere in Palestine, another 65 Jews were
killed, including 18 in Safed. British police and soldiers killed 116
Arabs during the widespread violence.

Hebron's surviving Jews were evacuated to Jerusalem. In 1931
a handful of families returned to Hebron, but they again were evacuated by the British during the Arab Revolt of 1936. After that, no
Jews lived in Hebron until the entire West Bank was captured by
Israel during the Six-Day War in 1967. A few of the remaining massacre survivors attempted to reclaim their property, but they never
did succeed.

The large Jewish community in Hebron today is made up of
settlers who live on occupied or disputed land, although they claim
to be the representatives of the Jews murdered and evicted from
Hebron in 1929. The Tomb of the Patriarchs remains one of the flash
points between Muslim and Jew, heavily guarded by the Israel
Defense Forces (IDF) and surrounded by barbed wire and armored
personnel carriers. On February 25, 1994, Baruch Goldstein, an IDF
reserve physician, entered the mosque half of the building with his
military-issue automatic rifle, murdering 29 Muslim worshipers
and wounding 125 others.

DAVID T. ZABECKI

See also
Arab Revolt of 1936–1939; Ashkenazic Judaism; Haganah; Husseini, Haj
Amin al-; Palestine, British Mandate for; Sephardic Judaism; Six-Day
War; Zionism

References
Dershowitz, Alan M. *The Case for Israel.* New York: Wiley, 2004.
Morris, Benny. *Righteous Victims: A History of the Zionist-Arab Conflict,
1881–2001.* New York: Vintage Books, 2001.
Segev, Tom. *One Palestine, Complete: Jews and Arabs under the British
Mandate.* New York: Owl Books, 2001.

Hebron Mosque Massacre
Event Date: February 25, 1994

Mass killing of 29 Palestinian Muslims by a lone militant Israeli gunman at the Mosque of Abraham (Ibrahim) in Hebron, located in the Judean region of the West Bank, on February 25, 1994. Also known as the Cave of the Patriarchs or Tomb of the Patriarchs, the mosque site is held holy by both Muslims and Jews. The attack occurred during a period of religious holidays that saw both Jews and Muslims using the site for their observances. For Muslims, the event was Ramadan, the month-long period of prayer, fasting, charity, and self-introspection. The Jews were observing Purim, a remembrance of Jews in Persia who had escaped a scheme to murder them en masse as told in the book of Esther.

Divided into two sections—one Muslim and one Jewish—the Cave of the Patriarchs includes Isaac Hall, which is reserved for Muslims, and Jacob and Abraham Halls, used by Jews. On February 25, 1994, at 5:00 a.m., a group of some 750 Palestinian Muslims entered the complex to pray. Israeli security forces were supposed to be guarding the mosque, but that morning they were significantly understaffed. Shortly after the early morning prayers commenced, a lone gunman, Baruch Goldstein, dressed in an Israeli Army uniform and carrying an assault rifle, got past the security detail and entered Isaac Hall. As he placed himself in front of the lone exit and immediately in back of the Muslim worshipers, he began firing randomly into the crowd. Pandemonium ensued, and before the gunfire stopped, 29 Palestinians had died, many of gunshot wounds but some trampled to death as the crowd tried to flee the hall. An additional 125 Palestinians were injured in the attack.

Goldstein, who was wrestled to the floor and then killed by his would-be victims, was an American-born Orthodox Jew who had immigrated to Israel in the mid-1980s. He was also a member of the radical Jewish Defense League and was a follower of Rabbi Meir David Kahane, an extremist American-born Jew who advocated open warfare against all Arabs and who vehemently opposed the Israeli-Palestinian peace process.

The Hebron Mosque Massacre shocked Israelis and the world and cast dark shadows over the emergent Israeli-Palestinian peace process, which had gained momentum only during the previous year via the Oslo Accords. Not surprisingly, the event sparked protests in many Arab nations, and major rioting after the killings claimed the lives of another 26 Palestinians as well as 9 Jews in the West Bank and other occupied territories. Protests in Jordan turned particularly violent, and a British tourist in Amman died at the hands of an unruly mob.

Immediately following the carnage, the Israeli government and all the mainstream political parties roundly condemned Goldstein and his deed. The Israelis offered compensation to the victims of the massacre and stepped up efforts to disarm and detain would-be Jewish terrorists. Polls in early March showed that the vast majority of Israelis denounced the killings and considered them nothing less than a cowardly act of terrorism.

Within weeks, Israeli prime minister Yitzhak Shamir convened a formal inquiry into the Hebron Mosque Massacre headed by Judge Meir Shagmar, then head of the Israeli Supreme Court. Shagmar's committee determined that Goldstein had acted alone and had not shared his plans with anyone else, security forces had not appropriately interacted with other local officials or Israeli national forces such as the Israel Defense Forces (IDF), and gunfire alone had caused the deaths. (Many Palestinians charged that grenades had been used as well.) Few Palestinians were assuaged by the findings of the committee, however, and the entire episode clearly showed the continued precariousness of the peace process.

PAUL G. PIERPAOLI JR.

See also

Kahane, Meir David; Oslo Accords; Terrorism; Tomb of the Patriarchs

References

Crown-Tamir, Hela. *How to Walk in the Footsteps of Jesus and the Prophets: A Scripture Reference Guide for Biblical Sites in Israel and Jordan.* Jerusalem: Gefen, 2000.

Friedman, Robert I. *The False Prophet: Rabbi Meir Kahane, from FBI Informant to Knesset Member.* Westport, CT: Lawrence Hill, 1990.

Hebron Protocol
Event Date: January 15, 1997

The January 15, 1997, Hebron Protocol immediately redeployed 80 percent of the Israel Defense Forces (IDF) stationed in the West Bank city of Hebron since the 1967 Six-Day War. The protocol scheduled the redeployment in three additional phases of the IDF in the West Bank and Gaza by mid-1998 in accordance with the provisions of the 1995 Oslo II Israeli-Palestinian Interim Agreement on the West Bank and the Gaza Strip, allowed for sufficient IDF security forces to protect the established Jewish settlements in these areas and to maintain positions considered necessary for the external defense of Israel, mandated the removal of the call for the destruction of Israel from the Palestinian National Charter, limited the size of the Palestinian Authority (PA) police force, and committed the PA to more vigorously deter terrorism in the West Bank and Gaza.

Hebron is a major religious site. The Tomb (Cave) of the Patriarchs and Matriarchs in Hebron (ancient Judea and now the West Bank) is the second-holiest site in Judaism and the burial place of the great patriarchs and matriarchs buried as couples (Abraham and Sarah, Isaac and Rebecca, Jacob and Leah, and Adam and Eve) in two caves. Both a mosque (Sanctuary of Abraham) and a synagogue are built on top of the tomb. Jacob's second wife is buried in the Tomb of Rachel on the Jerusalem-Hebron Road near the Iron Gate of Israel's security fence at Bethlehem's northern entrance. Both tombs are holy to Jews and Muslims, who claim a common ancestry through Abraham. Hebron was the capital of the ancient

Following the signing of the Hebron Protocol, Palestinian policemen distribute small arms to Palestinian security forces in Hebron, January 17, 1997. (Avi Ohayon/Israeli Government Press Office)

Kingdom of Israel before Jerusalem and had a continuing Jewish presence until pogroms drove the Jewish inhabitants from the city in 1929.

A small number of Jews, numbering 450 by the time of the protocol, returned to the city after Hebron came under the control of Israel as a consequence of the 1967 Six-Day War. At the same time, Rabbi Moshe Levinger and 10 Jewish families began a settlement named Kiryat Arba just outside of Hebron that by the time of the Hebron Protocol had approximately 5,000 inhabitants. These settlers remained a flash point for the Israeli-Palestinian conflict until the protocol.

The Hebron Protocol, negotiated in 1996 by Israeli lieutenant general Dan Shomron, chief of staff of the IDF, and witnessed by U.S. secretary of state Warren Christopher, was signed on January 15, 1997, by Israeli prime minister Benjamin Netanyahu and Palestine Liberation Organization (PLO) president Yasser Arafat. The protocol was followed by the Agreement on the Temporary International Presence in Hebron (TIPH), signed on January 21, 1997. The TIPH established a Norwegian-coordinated 180-person monitoring force with members drawn from Italy, Denmark, Sweden, Switzerland, Turkey, and Norway.

The Hebron Protocol mandated the commencement of immediate negotiations to resolve the following issues: a Gaza airport, a Gaza maritime port, Palestinian and Israeli transit between the West Bank and Gaza, the status of the then 144 Jewish settlements in the West Bank and Gaza, and the resolution of the relationship between Israel and the PA, including permanent borders.

RICHARD M. EDWARDS

See also

Arafat, Yasser; Netanyahu, Benjamin; Oslo Accords; Palestine Liberation Organization; Religious Sites in the Middle East, Jewish; Shomron, Dan

References

Bauer, Yehuda. *From Diplomacy to Resistance: A History of Jewish Palestine, 1930–1945.* Translated by Alton M. Winters. Philadelphia: Jewish Publication Society of America, 1970.

Beilin, Yossi. *Touching Peace: From the Oslo Accord to a Final Agreement.* Translated by Philip Simpson. London: Weidenfeld and Nicolson, 1999.

Hoffman, Lawrence A. *Israel, a Spiritual Travel Guide: A Companion for the Modern Jewish Pilgrim.* 2nd ed. Woodstock, VT: Jewish Lights, 2005.

Lochery, Neill. *The Difficult Road to Peace: Netanyahu, Israel and the Middle East Peace Process.* Reading, UK: Ithaca Press, 1999.

Pappe, Ilan. *A History of Modern Palestine: One Land, Two Peoples.*
Cambridge: Cambridge University Press, 2003.

Rubin, Barry. *Revolution until Victory? The Politics and History of the PLO.* Reprint ed. Cambridge: Harvard University Press, 2003.

Hehalutz Movement

The Hehalutz (Pioneering) movement was motivated by the belief that immigrants to Palestine should be trained and prepared in their home countries prior to their transplantation to Palestine. It was first propounded by Joseph Trumpeldor in 1908, and by 1909 Halutzim (those Jews who had made the move to Palestine) had created the first communal kibbutz at Degania in the Jordan River Valley. The Halutzim at the Degania Kibbutz blended Zionism and socialism into a single functioning unit. They argued that the communal life presented by the kibbutz system offered the best hope for successful creation of a Jewish national homeland in Palestine. Members of the Hehalutz movement and the kibbutz system, although always a small percentage of the Jewish population, remained heavily overrepresented in Israeli society and politics and came to symbolize the Jewish state for many of the residents of the new nation.

Members of the Hehalutz movement typically lived together on farms in their home countries for a training period prior to emigration for Palestine. Other Halutzim created urban labor communities in European cities, also with the purpose of preparing members for emigration for Palestine. The primary emphasis of each commune was on preparation for a difficult life of manual labor in a harsh new land. As such, the Hehalutz movement appealed overwhelmingly to young workers, particularly those who had few prospects in their home countries. The Halutzim envisioned a massive commune system as the cornerstone of an independent Jewish state.

The first major Halutzim conference was held in Moscow in 1919, and participants elected Joseph Trumpeldor to serve as president of the organization. Trumpeldor soon moved to Palestine, where he was attacked and killed in 1920 by Arabs opposed to Jewish immigration. By that year, the newly formed Soviet Union had begun to adopt a distinctly anti-Zionist stance. This caused the headquarters of the Hehalutz movement to shift to Berlin in 1921. Within the Soviet Union, the organization split into two separate factions. One completely renounced all aspects of capitalism and as a result retained its legal status within the Soviet Union. The other remained true to its original goals but refused to embrace Leninist communism and was thus deemed counterrevolutionary. It was forced underground, and much of its membership was arrested. Although some members escaped to Palestine, many others were jailed or exiled to labor camps in Siberia by the new Bolshevik regime.

In 1921 the Twelfth Zionist Congress recognized the Hehalutz movement as an autonomous body within the World Zionist Organization (WZO). As the center of the movement gradually shifted to Poland, training centers were established in Germany, Lithuania, Poland, and Romania. From 1918 until 1939, more than 45,000 Halutzim moved to Palestine, provoking a great deal of unrest among the Arab population. Because most Halutzim were young laborers, the Jewish militia of interwar Palestine, the Haganah, sent representatives to the Hehalutz movement training centers in the 1930s. These representatives provided rudimentary military training to prospective immigrants. Such training proved invaluable during the Arab Revolt of 1936–1939 and during the Israeli War of Independence (1948–1949).

Throughout the 1920s the postwar German economy offered few opportunities for young laborers, and the prospects for young Jewish workers were even more bleak than for the population at large. As the German economy gradually improved, the heart of the movement shifted to Warsaw, and Polish Jews became the largest recruiting service for new members. In 1921, the Hehalutz movement held its first world conference in Karlsbad (Karlovy Vary), Czechoslovakia. Membership in the organization rose quickly, from 5,400 in 1923 to 33,000 in 1925. By 1933, more than 83,000 Halutzim lived in preparatory communes awaiting permission to move to Palestine. Approximately half of Halutzim lived in Germany and Poland in 1933, but the ascension to power of Adolf Hitler and the National Socialists soon began to curtail Hehalutz movement activities in Germany.

Farmers living near Hehalutz communes in the 1920s and 1930s saw a small but determined group of urban boys and girls arriving in rural communities in an attempt to learn the routines of farm life from scratch. The vast majority of Halutzim had no background in agricultural or manual labor, and many observers thus labeled their attempts as pathetic. Despite their pitiful preparation, a significant number of Halutzim succeeded in their attempts to prepare for emigration. In the 1930s, more than 34,000 Halutzim reached Palestine, half of them bearing workers' permits, half as permanent immigrants.

By 1935, British Mandate officials began to cut the total number of immigration certificates issued each year. Arab inhabitants of Palestine did not welcome the new arrivals and petitioned the British government to reduce or end Jewish immigration to the region. As the number of legal opportunities to reach Palestine declined, the preparatory period increased. Early Halutzim had trained for one or two years prior to emigration, but by the late 1930s the typical waiting period reached four years or more. The longer waiting period proved unacceptable to many members, who found it too difficult to maintain the Spartan lifestyle of the training communes while surrounded by plenty.

Although legal immigration certificates declined in the second half of the 1930s, the number of illegal immigrants, many of them Hehalutz movement members, rose in the same period. By 1939, more than 10,000 illegal Jewish immigrants reached Palestine on an annual basis. However, the influx of illegal immigrants quickly abated with the commencement of World War II in 1939. Both legal and illegal immigration virtually halted during the conflict, as British warships blockaded much of the European coastline and German officials closed European ports to emigrants. When the war ended, the British continued to resist allowing a massive wave of legal Jewish immigrants to travel to Palestine, but demand was great enough that thousands of illegal immigrants attempted to reach Palestine in spite of British naval patrols. From 1945 to 1948, more than 60 passenger ships attempted to slip past the British patrols and deliver illegal immigrants to the Palestinian coast. The vast majority were stopped, boarded, and rerouted to Cyprus, where the erstwhile occupants were placed into internment camps run by the British government.

The British anti-immigration policies proved to be a domestic and international public relations disaster in the post-Holocaust period. They also sparked a series of protests in the Jewish communities of Palestine. Soon after the proclamation of Israeli statehood on May 15, 1948, the new nation opened its borders to virtually every hopeful Jewish immigrant from around the globe, rapidly swelling the population of the state.

World War II virtually destroyed the Hehalutz movement. Members were prime targets of the Holocaust, because as young laborers they were immediately designated for transfer to labor camps established under the Nazi regime. Furthermore, by living in communes throughout Germany and Eastern Europe, Hehalutz movement members could be quickly rounded up and deported to the camps. Finally, as an organized movement, the commune members were perceived as an inherent threat to the government of the Third Reich. Those members who survived the Nazi labor camps faced a new threat when the Soviet military advanced into Eastern and Central Europe. The Soviet government maintained its hostility to the Hehalutz movement and prevented the reestablishment of the training communes.

As the Soviet occupation of Eastern Europe tightened in the post–World War II era and with British officials remaining hostile to the idea of increased Jewish immigration to Palestine, Halutzim began to strenuously advocate illegal immigration to Palestine. New training camps were soon established in Italy, which also provided a vital departure point for prospective immigrants. Soon a massive smuggling network, largely funded by Halutzim, began to operate in the Mediterranean Sea. Because the chartered transport vessels sailed under Italian flags, they were not subject to search and seizure by the British warships patrolling the coast until they left international waters for the final approach to deposit their charges.

Worldwide attempts to rebuild the Hehalutz movement after the foundation of Israel proved largely ineffective. With Israel's lenient immigration policies for worldwide Jews, the need to spend years in a preparatory commune, rather than emigrating directly, did not prove attractive to significant numbers of potential immigrants. Only in South America was the movement even moderately successful, and by the 1960s it was virtually defunct. However, the legacy of the movement lives on, particularly in the kibbutzim and moshavim of modern Israel, as well as in the socialist labor movement.

PAUL J. SPRINGER

See also

Aliya Bet; Arab Revolt of 1936–1939; Hapoel Hatzair; Holocaust; Kibbutz Movement; Labor Zionism; Moshavim; Tnuat Hamoshavim; Trumpeldor, Joseph; Zionism

References

Brenner, Lenni. *Zionism in the Age of the Dictators.* Westport, CT: Lawrence Hill, 1983.

Laqueur, Walter. *A History of Zionism: From the French Revolution to the Establishment of the State of Israel.* Reprint ed. New York: Schocken, 2003.

Peretz, Don. *The Government and Politics of Israel.* Boulder, CO: Westview, 1979.

Reich, Bernard. *A Brief History of Israel.* New York: Facts on File, 2005.

Sereni, Enzo, and R. E. Ashery. *Jews and Arabs in Palestine: Studies in a National and Colonial Problem.* Westport, CT: Hyperion, 1976.

Weintraub, D., M. Lissak, and Y. Azmon. *Moshava, Kibbutz, and Moshav: Patterns of Jewish Rural Settlement and Development in Palestine.* Ithaca, NY: Cornell University Press, 1969.

Herzl, Theodor
Born: May 2, 1860
Died: July 3, 1904

Founder of the Zionist movement. Theodor Herzl was born in Budapest, Hungary, on May 2, 1860. In 1878 his assimilated German-speaking Jewish family moved to Vienna, where he obtained a doctorate in law from the University of Vienna in 1884. He practiced law only briefly, drawn instead to a literary calling. He published numerous unremarkable dramas and established a reputation as a fashionable cosmopolitan journalist, notably as a Parisian correspondent for the Viennese *Neue Freie Presse* (New Free Press) during 1881–1895 and thereafter as its literary editor.

Herzl's *Der Judenstaat: Versuch einer modernen Lösung der Judenfrage* (*The Jewish State: An Attempt at a Modern Solution of the Jewish Question*), published in 1896, was not, as customarily thought, a simple reaction to the anti-Semitism of the Dreyfus Affair in France in which a Jewish French Army officer was falsely accused of treason. Rather, it was the culmination of evolving reflections. Herzl did not invent Zionism and claimed only to state the facts more clearly. Indeed, he believed that anti-Semitism persisted even in the face of emancipation because the so-called Jewish question was national rather than social. The normalization of the Jewish condition therefore required a Jewish state in any territory made available for mass migration.

The insistence on sovereignty distinguished Herzl's stance from the predominant practical or philanthropic Zionism, which was aimed at small-scale settlement in Palestine. Herzl's contribution was thus to view the Jewish question in Europe as a unitary thing requiring a unitary solution, both of which he redefined as political and international. By the force of his persona and above all through his leadership of the Zionist Congress, which he founded in Basel in 1897, he turned an idea into a driving force.

Theodor Herzl, principal founder of the Zionist movement. (Israeli Government Press Office)

Herzl devoted the ensuing years to sustaining the movement and seeking the international support he considered essential to success. After failing to win assistance from Germany and Turkey, he increasingly placed his hopes on Great Britain, although his willingness to accept Uganda even as a provisional substitute for Palestine nearly split the movement in 1903 on the eve of his death.

Herzl's character and policies abound in paradoxes and blend the realistic and the naive, accounting for his brilliant successes as well as his shortcomings. The combination of intellectual over-simplification and attention to minute but symbolic detail allowed the essentially aristocratic Westerner to cast himself in the role of charismatic leader whose dream of a reborn nation inspired the Eastern masses and bridged factional differences regarding its precise character. His ultimate vision of the new commonwealth was Eurocentric but not chauvinistic (or even particularly Jewish). What he envisioned was a nonmilitarized technologically advanced society dedicated to social justice in which Jews and Arabs lived together in prosperity. He declared that his next dream was to assist in the liberation of the Africans.

Herzl died at age 44 in Edlach near Vienna, Austria, on July 3, 1904.

JIM WALD

See also
Jewish Agency for Israel; Zionism; Zionist Conference

References
Elon, Amos. *Herzl.* New York: Holt, Rinehart and Winston, 1975.
Herzl, Theodor. *The Jewish State.* Mineola, NY: Dover, 1989.
Laqueur, Walter. *A History of Zionism: From the French Revolution to the Establishment of the State of Israel.* Reprint ed. New York: Schocken, 2003.
Pawel, Ernst. *The Labyrinth of Exile: A Life of Theodor Herzl.* New York: Farrar, Straus and Giroux, 1989.
Robertson, Ritchie, and Edward Timms, eds. *Theodor Herzl and the Origins of Zionism.* Edinburgh, UK: Edinburgh University Press, 1997.

Herzog, Chaim
Born: September 17, 1918
Died: April 17, 1997

Israeli chief of military intelligence during 1948–1950 and 1959–1962, ambassador to the United Nations (UN) during 1975–1978, and president of Israel during 1983–1993. Born in Belfast, Ireland, on September 17, 1918, Chaim Herzog was the son of the chief rabbi of Ireland. Herzog studied at Wesley College, Dublin, and in 1935 immigrated to the British Mandate for Palestine. He served in the Haganah Jewish self-defense force in Palestine during the Arab Revolt of 1936–1939. In 1939 he returned to England to enroll at Cambridge University and later would earn a doctorate of law at the University of London.

With the beginning of World War II in September 1939, Herzog enlisted in the British Army, rising by the end of the war to the rank of lieutenant colonel. He participated in the Normandy invasion of June 1944 and ended the war serving with British military intelligence in northern Germany.

With the establishment of the State of Israel in May 1948 and the beginning of the Israeli War of Independence (1948–1949), Herzog joined the Israel Defense Forces (IDF), fighting in the Battles for Latrun in 1948. During 1948–1950 and 1959–1960 he headed Israeli military intelligence. During 1950–1954 he was Israeli military attaché in Washington, D.C. During 1957–1959 he commanded the Jerusalem District, and during 1957–1959 he was chief of staff of the Southern Military Command. He retired from the IDF in 1962 as a major general. He then pursued opportunities in business and law. During the 1967 Six-Day War, Herzog was the leading military commentator on Israeli radio. He then was the first military governor of the West Bank territory. In 1972 Herzog, Michael Fox, and Yaakov Neeman formed the law firm of Herzog, Fox, and Neeman.

Appointed ambassador to the UN in 1975, Herzog held that post until 1978, during which time he argued forcefully but unsuccessfully against passage of UN General Assembly Resolution 3379 that equated Zionism with racism. Elected to the Knesset (Israeli parliament) on the Labor Party ticket in 1981, he served until 1983 when

Chaim Herzog, Israeli major general and chief of military intelligence (1948–1950, 1959–1962), ambassador to the United Nations (1975–1978), and president of Israel (1983–1993). (Israeli Government Press Office)

he was elected president of Israel. He served as president for two terms, until 1993, and while in office traveled widely abroad.

Herzog died in Tel Aviv on April 17, 1997. A prolific and accomplished writer and military historian, he wrote a half dozen books, including histories of the Six-Day War and Yom Kippur War as well as a history of battles in the Bible. His general survey, *The Arab-Israeli Wars* (1982), is regarded as a classic. Herzog also edited a book on Jewish law and ethics. His son, Michael Herzog, also became a general officer in the IDF.

SPENCER C. TUCKER

See also

Arab Revolt of 1936–1939; Israeli War of Independence, Overview; Latrun, Battles of

References

Gilbert, Martin. *Israel: A History.* New York: William Morrow, 1998.

Herzog, Chaim. *The Arab-Israeli Wars: War and Peace in the Middle East from the War of Independence to Lebanon.* Westminster, MD: Random House, 1984.

———. *Living History: A Memoir.* New York: Pantheon, 1996.

Hess, Moses
Born: June 21, 1812
Died: Apil 6, 1875

German Jewish philosopher, socialist, and proto-Zionist. Born in Bonn, Germany, on June 21, 1812, Moses Hess received instruction in Judaism early in life from his grandfather. However, Hess was not interested in Jewish problems until relatively late. He studied philosophy for a time at the University of Bonn and there became preoccupied with socialism. He founded a socialist newspaper and was for a time its Paris correspondent, although he fled that city for Brussels following reaction to the Revolution of February 1848 and again during the Franco-Prussian War of 1870–1871. He lived at various times in Germany, France, Belgium, and Switzerland.

Hess was a close associate of Karl Marx and Friedrich Engels, both of whom acknowledged their indebtedness to him. Reportedly Hess introduced Engels to Marx. Hess apparently coined a number of phrases later used by Marx. Hess broke with Marx over the concept of economics and class struggle as being the basis of history. Instead, Hess believed that history reflected the struggle of races or nationalities.

Hess wrote extensively, publishing both articles and books on philosophical and scientific subjects. He also wrote for a number of newspapers. While in Germany during 1861–1863, he protested against Jewish assimilation and became an advocate for Jewish nationalism, which he spelled out in his most important book, *Rome and Jerusalem: The Last National Question* (1862). He predicted that Germans would be not tolerant of nationalism in other peoples, and would be particularly hostile toward the Jews. Noting the rising nationalism in Europe, he said that Jews were also ready for such a movement and that they would be fulfilled as a people only when they were on their own soil and able to give free expression to their beliefs and traditions. That could only occur with the establishment of a Jewish national home in Palestine. Hess believed that this was not a utopian dream but would be possible with the establishment of Jewish settlements in Palestine, funded in part by France. Although *Rome and Jerusalem* passed largely unnoticed at the time, it later came to be seen as the first theoretical expression of Zionism in book form.

Hess died in Paris on April 6, 1875. On his request, his body was buried in the Jewish cemetery in Köln (Cologne). In 1961 his remains were reinterred in Israel. Hess was an important forerunner of political and cultural Zionism and particularly of socialist Zionism.

SPENCER C. TUCKER

See also

Zionism; Zionist/Israeli Socialism

References

Avineri, Shlomo. *The Making of Modern Zionism: The Intellectual Origins of the Jewish State.* New York: Basic Books, 1981.

———. *Moses Hess: Prophet of Communism and Zionism.* New York: New York University Press, 1985.

Hess, Moses. *The Revival of Israel: Rome and Jerusalem; The Last National Question.* Lincoln: University of Nebraska Press, 1995.

Hezbollah

Lebanese radical Shia Islamist organization. Founded in Lebanon in 1984, Hezbollah is a major political force in Lebanon and, along with the Amal movement, a principal political party representing the Shia community in Lebanon. There have been other smaller parties by the name of Hezbollah in eastern Saudi Arabia and Iraq, and their activities have been mistakenly or deliberately associated with the Lebanese party. The Lebanese Hezbollah also operates a number of social service programs, schools, hospitals, clinics, and housing assistance programs to Lebanese Shiites. (Some Christians also attended Hezbollah's schools and ran on their electoral lists.)

One of the core founding groups of Hezbollah, meaning the "Party of God," actually fled from Iraq when Saddam Hussein cracked down on the Shia Islamic movement in the shrine cities. Lebanese as well as Iranians and Iraqis studied in Najaf and Karbala, and some 100 of these students returned to Beirut and became disciples of Sayyid Muhammad Husayn Fadlallah, a Lebanese cleric who was also educated in Najaf.

Meanwhile, in the midst of the ongoing civil war in Lebanon, a Shia resistance movement developed in response to Israel's invasion in 1982. Israel's first invasion of southern Lebanon had occurred in 1978, but the invasion of 1982 was more devastating to the region, with huge numbers of casualties and prisoners taken and peasants displaced.

The earliest political movement of Lebanese Shia was established under the cleric Musa al-Sadr and known as the Movement of the Dispossessed. The Shia were the largest but poorest sect in Lebanon and suffered from discrimination, underrepresentation, and a dearth of government programs or services that, despite some efforts by President Fuad Shihab, persist to this day. After al-Sadr's disappearance on a trip to Libya, his nonmilitaristic movement was subsumed by the Amal Party, which had a military wing and fought in the civil war. However, a wing of Amal, Islamic Amal led by Husayn al-Musawi, split off after it accused Amal of not resisting the Israeli invasion.

On the grounds of resistance to Israel (and its Lebanese proxies), Islamic Amal made contact with Iran's ambassador to Damascus, Akbar Muhtashimi, who had once found refuge as an Iranian dissident in the Palestinian camps in Lebanon. Iran sent between 1,000 and 1,200 Revolutionary Guards to the Bekáa Valley to aid an Islamic resistance to Israel. At a Lebanese Army barracks near Baalbek, the Revolutionary Guards began training Shia fighters identifying with the resistance, or Islamic Amal.

Fadlallah's followers now included displaced Beiruti Shia and displaced southerners, and some coordination between his group and the others began to emerge in 1984. The other strand of Hezbollah came from the Islamic Resistance in southern Lebanon led by Sheikh Raghib Harb, the imam of the village of Jibshit who was killed by the Israelis in 1984. In February 1985, Harb's supporters met and announced the formation of Hezbollah, led by Sheikh Subhi Tufayli.

Another militant Shia group was the Organization of the Islamic Jihad, led by Imad Mughniya. It was responsible for the 1983 bombings of the U.S. and French peacekeeping forces' barracks and the U.S. embassy and its annex in Beirut. This group received some support from the elements in Baalbek. Hezbollah, however, is to this day accused of bombings committed by Mughniya's group. While it had not yet officially formed, the degree of coordination or sympathy between the various militant groups operative in 1982 can only be ascertained on the level of individuals. Hezbollah stated officially that it did not commit the bombing of U.S. and French forces, but it also did not condemn those who did. Regardless, Hezbollah's continuing resistance in the south earned it great popularity with the Lebanese, whose army had split and had failed to defend the country against the Israelis.

With the Taif Agreement the Lebanese Civil War should have ended, but in 1990 fighting broke out, and the next year Syria mounted a major campaign in Lebanon. The Taif Agreement did not end sectarianism or solve the problem of Muslim underrepresentation in government. Militias other than Hezbollah disbanded, but because the Lebanese government did not assent to the Israeli occupation of southern Lebanon, Hezbollah's militia remained in being.

The leadership of Hezbollah changed over time and adapted to Lebanon's realities. The multiplicity of sects in Lebanon meant that an Islamic republic there was impractical, and as a result Hezbollah ceased trying to impose the strictest Islamic rules and focused more on gaining the trust of the Lebanese community. The party's Shura Council was made up of 7 clerics until 1989, from 1989 to 1991 it included 3 laypersons and 4 clerics, and since 2001 it has been entirely composed of clerics. An advisory Politburo has from 11 to 14 members. Secretary-General Abbas Musawi took over from Tufayli in 1991. Soon after the Israelis assassinated Musawi, Hassan Nasrallah, who had studied in Najaf and briefly in Qum, took over as secretary-general.

In 1985, as a consequence of armed resistance in southern Lebanon, Israel withdrew into the so-called security zone. Just as resistance from Hezbollah provided Israel with the ready excuse to attack Lebanon, Israel's continued presence in the south funded Lebanese resentment of Israel and support for Hezbollah's armed actions. In 1996 the Israelis mounted Operation GRAPES OF WRATH against Hezbollah in south Lebanon, pounding the entire region from the air for a two-week period.

Subhi Tufayli, the former Hezbollah secretary-general, opposed the party's decision to participate in the elections of 1992 and 1996. He launched the Revolt of the Hungry, demanding food and jobs for the impoverished people of the upper Bekáa, and was expelled from Hezbollah. He then began armed resistance, and the Lebanese Army was called in to defeat his faction.

Hezbollah members and supporters parade through the city of Tyre en route to a demonstration in Beirut, September 21, 2006. (Lynsey Addario/Corbis)

In May 2000 after suffering repeated attacks and numerous casualties, Israel withdrew its forces from southern Lebanon, a move that was widely interpreted as a victory for Hezbollah and boosted its popularity hugely in Lebanon and throughout the Arab world. Hezbollah disarmed in some areas of the country but refused to do so in the border area because it contests the Jewish state's control of the Shaba Farms region.

Sheikh Fadlallah survived an assassination attempt in 1985 allegedly arranged by the United States. He illustrates Lebanonization of the Shia Islamist movement. He had moved away from Ayatollah Khomeini's doctrine of government by cleric (*wilaya al-faqih*), believing that it is not suitable in the Lebanese context, and called for dialogue with Christians. Fadlallah's stance is similar to that of Ayatollah Sistani in Iraq. He, like some of the Iraqi clerics, called for the restoration of Friday communal prayer for the Shia. He has also issued numerous reforming views, for example, decrying the abuse of women by men. Fadlallah is not, however, closely associated with Hezbollah's day-to-day policies.

Some Israeli and American sources charge that Iran directly conducts the affairs of Hezbollah and provides it with essential funding. While at one time Iranian support was crucial to Hezbollah, the Revolutionary Guards were withdrawn from Lebanon for some time. The party's social and charitable services claimed independence in the late 1990s. They are supported by a volunteer service, provided by medical personnel and other professionals, and by local and external donations. Iran has certainly provided weapons to Hezbollah. Some, apparently through the Iran-Contra deal, found their way to Lebanon, and Syria has also provided freedom of movement across its common border with Lebanon as well as supply routes for weapons.

Since 2000 Hezbollah has disputed Israeli control over the Shaba Farms area, which Israel claims belongs to Syria but Syria says belongs to Lebanon. Meanwhile, pressure began to build against Syrian influence in Lebanon with the constitutional amendment to allow Émile Lahoud (a Christian and pro-Syrian) an additional term. Assassinations of anti-Syrian, mainly Christian, figures had also periodically occurred. The turning point was the assassination of Prime Minister Rafik Hariri in February 2005. This led to significant international pressure on Syria to withdraw from Lebanon, although pro-Syrian elements remained throughout the country.

Hezbollah now found itself threatened by a new coalition of Christians and Hariri-supporting Sunnis who sought to deny its aim of greater power for the Shia in government. The two sides in this struggle were known as the March 14th Alliance, for the date of a large anti-Syrian rally, and the March 8th Alliance, for a prior and even larger rally consisting of Hezbollah and anti-Syrian Christian general Michel Aoun. These factions have been sparring since 2005 and in some ways since the civil war.

Demanding a response to the Israeli campaign against Gaza in the early summer of 2006, Hezbollah forces killed three Israeli soldiers and kidnapped two others, planning to hold them for a prisoner exchange as has occurred in the past. The Israel Defense Forces (IDF) responded with a massive campaign of air strikes throughout Lebanon, and not just on Hezbollah positions. Hezbollah responded by launching missiles into Israel, forcing much of that country's northern population into shelters. In this open warfare, the United States backed Israel. At the conflict's end, Sheikh Nasrallah's popularity surged in Lebanon and in the Arab world, and even members of the March 14th Alliance were furious over the destruction of the fragile peace in post–civil war Lebanon. Hezbollah offered cash assistance to the people of southern Lebanon displaced by the fighting and those in the southern districts of Beirut who had been struck there by the Israelis. They disbursed this aid immediately. The government offered assistance to other Lebanese, but this assistance was delayed.

In September 2006 Hezbollah and its ally Aoun began calling for a new national unity government. The existing government, dominated by the March 14th Alliance forces, has refused to budge, however. Five Shia members and one Christian member of the Lebanese cabinet also resigned in response to disagreements over the proposed tribunal to investigate Syrian culpability in the Hariri assassination. At the same time, Hezbollah and Aoun argue for the ability of a sizable opposition group in the cabinet to veto government decisions. Hezbollah and Aoun called for public protests, which began as gigantic sit-ins and demonstrations in the downtown district of Beirut in December 2006. There was one violent clash in December and another in January of 2007 between the supporters of the two March alliances. Meanwhile, the United Nations Interim Force in Lebanon (UNIFIL) has taken up position in southern Lebanon. Its mission, however, is not to disarm Hezbollah but only to prevent armed clashes between it and Israel.

HARRY RAYMOND HUESTON II AND SHERIFA ZUHUR

See also

Iran; Israel Defense Forces; *Hanit,* Attack on the; Hariri, Rafik; Jihad; Lebanon; Lebanon, Armed Forces; Lebanon, Civil War in; Lebanon, Israeli Invasion of; Shia Islam; Suicide Bombings; Terrorism

References

Hajjar, Sami G. *Hezbollah: Terrorism, National Liberation, or Menace?* Carlilse Barracks, PA: Strategic Studies Institute, U.S. Army War College, 2002.

Harik, Judith Palmer. *Hezbollah: The Changing Face of Terrorism.* London: Taurus, 2005.

Jaber, Hala. *Hezbollah: Born with a Vengeance.* New York: Columbia University Press, 1997.

Lebanese Political Parties: Hizbullah. Arabic documentary. Farid Assaf, Lebanese National Broadcasting Company, 2003.

Zuhur, Sherifa. "Hasan Nasrallah and the Strategy of Steadfastness." *Terrorism Monitor* 4(19) (October 5, 2006).

Histadrut

Israeli labor union. Founded in Haifa in 1920, Histadrut (General Federation of Laborers in the Land of Israel) became one of the largest and most powerful institutions in Israel. Before the founding of Israel in 1948, Histadrut was a practically indispensable part of life for Jews living and working in Palestine (Yishuv). Almost immediately, Histadrut attracted a large membership representing laborers from many different walks of life. Just two years after it began, the labor union represented 50 percent of the entire Palestinian-Jewish workforce (Arabs were not permitted to join at this time). Records also show that 75 percent of newly arriving Jewish immigrants were joining Histadrut.

Unlike many trade unions, Histadrut is both an employer and a worker's advocate organization. As such, it wielded extraordinary economic clout that gave it the ability to establish—virtually unimpeded—wage policies, working conditions, worker benefits, and the like. In its early years, the union created a Bureau of Public Works that hired thousands of workers to construct schools, hospitals, administrative and government offices, apartment buildings, private homes, etc. Histadrut was also instrumental in the establishment of many moshavim and kibbutzim throughout Palestine. That so powerful a group became involved in areas besides employment comes as no great surprise. For example, Histadrut has engaged in many public service endeavors, including education, medical and indigent care, aid to immigrants, promotion of the arts and cultural outlets, and political advocacy. Prior to 1949, in fact, Histadrut acted as a sort of de facto government entity for Palestinian Jews. During the late 1930s and early 1940s, Histadrut was also actively involved in underground resistance activities against British authorities and the Arab population, and the union's facilities were used extensively (if clandestinely) by the Haganah.

Although Histadrut encompasses members from many segments of the political spectrum, it has most often been associated with the Left, including socialism and communism. It was the Third Aliya (1919–1923) that prompted the formation of Histadrut. Prior efforts to form an inclusive labor federation had failed, but it was mainly the outlook and politics of Jews from the Second Aliya (1904–1919), many of whom had fled czarist Russia, that lent their imprimatur to Histadrut.

In the early 1920s, Histadrut sought to build bridges with Jewish labor unions in America in hopes of gaining financial support. In this it was somewhat successful. Much of its capital, however, came from private donations among Jews of the Diaspora (mostly in the United States and Western Europe). To cater to the specific needs of female workers, Histadrut formed a number of splinter organizations for this purpose. And to bring together working women in the cities as well as the countryside, the Working Women's Council was created within Histadrut.

One of Histadrut's major goals was the attainment of full employment. This was a challenging endeavor in times of economic hardship that periodically swept through Palestine, as they do all nations. To accomplish this, Histadrut worked closely with the World Zionist Organization (WZO) to increase the number of Jewish workers in well-established settlements as well as kibbutzim and moshavim. Many of these had traditionally employed Arab

A Histadrut rally outside the Vaad Hapoel (Zionist General Council) building in Tel Aviv, June 15, 1977. (Moshe Milner/Israeli Government Press Office)

workers. When Arabs began to be turned away, however, this produced much enmity in the Arab community.

The formation of Israel in 1948 presented unique challenges to Histadrut. Accustomed to acting as a de facto government, it now had to share power—and responsibility—with the de jure government. Not surprisingly, debates and arguments ensued over wage policies, the place of politics within the union, and overlapping areas of interest and jurisdiction. In 1956, Israeli prime minister David Ben-Gurion outlined the nature of the relationship between the Israeli government and Histadrut at the federation's convention. Ben-Gurion was blunt. He told the group that it must not engage in cultural, political, or social programs that fall within the purview of the government. This was a tall order for an organization that had been functioning as a de facto government for more than 30 years. Since then, Histadrut has been split over its role and relationship to the Israeli government. In 1959, and for the first time, Histadrut began admitting Arab members.

There can be little doubt that Histadrut has played a major role in the lives of almost every Israeli citizen. Its central role in all aspects of society and its great economic influence are impossible to ignore. Some have argued (and continue to argue) that the trade union has too much power. At its peak in 1983, the organization had nearly 1.5 million members (and dependents) and represented an astounding 83 percent of all Israeli wage earners. Because it was able to set most wages and dictate working conditions, Histadrut for years acted like a ministry of labor and commerce combined. Its wide-ranging health care network also came to dominate the medical scene in most of Israel. The number of those employed by Histadrut or its subsidiaries has plummeted in the last 25 years, however. Still, though, Histadrut's policies engendered much inefficiency. For many years it was virtually impossible to terminate poor employees or those with seniority. And preset wage formulas obligated businesses to hike wages and salaries even during times of economic contraction.

Since the late 1970s, the rise of the Likud Party and the gradual move toward the political Right in Israel have reduced Histadrut's power and effectiveness. Today, paid membership in Histadrut is about 650,000. Despite its diminution in power, however, Histadrut remains a potent force in Israel.

Paul G. Pierpaoli Jr.

See also

Aliya, Third; Aliya, Fourth; Kibbutz Movement; Labor Zionism; Moshavim

References

Bernstein, Deborah S. *Constructing Boundaries: Jewish and Arab Workers in Mandatory Palestine.* Albany, NY: SUNY Press, 2000.

Kraus, Vered. *Secondary Breadwinners: Israeli Women in the Labor Force.* New York: Praeger, 2002.

Sachar, Howard M. *A History of Israel: From the Rise of Zionism to Our Time.* 3rd ed. New York: Knopf, 2007.

Hod, Mordechai
Born: September 28, 1926
Died: June 30, 2003

Israeli Air Force (IAF) major general who commanded the IAF during the Six-Day War in June 1967. Born on September 28, 1926, at Kibbutz Degania on the Sea of Galilee in British-administered Palestine, Mordechai Hod was a career soldier. He served initially with the British Army (1944–1947) and later joined the IAF as one of its first fighter pilots. Earning his pilot's wings early in 1949, he rose quickly through the ranks, holding positions both as squadron commander (1955–1956) and base commander (1957–1959) before his promotion to deputy air commander (1962–1966). In the latter post he served under Ezer Weizman, a tireless advocate of the expansion and modernization of the air force. As Weizman's successor in April 1966, Hod (promoted to major general in April 1967) continued that process during his seven years (1966–1973) in command of the IAF.

Hod brought a new spirit and sense of direction to the IAF when he assumed command. Less hesitant than Weizman about engaging in conflict, Hod allowed his fighters to seek out and engage in dogfights with Arab aircraft. Within mere months of taking control of the IAF, he oversaw the Israeli downing of several Syrian MiGs as well as aerial combat with Jordanian aircraft over the West Bank. In August 1966 he also benefitted from the carefully planned, yet fortuitous, defection to Israel of an Iraqi Christian pilot who flew his MiG-21 to an IAF airfield. This event allowed the Israelis to learn the weaknesses and strengths of the frontline fighter of their Arab enemies, an advantage that would help IAF pilots secure victory in the air.

IAF domination of the Middle Eastern skies was further bolstered in 1969 by the delivery of U.S. F-4 Phantoms. The new planes provided the Israelis with so potent a strategic capability that it unbalanced the regional power dynamics and led the Soviet Union to send hundreds of pilots and antiaircraft personnel to help defend Egypt. Under Hod the capabilities of the IAF were therefore revolutionized much as they were a decade earlier by the acquisition of French-made Mirage fighters when Weizman commanded the air force.

The high point of Hod's lengthy military career was undoubtedly the stunning success achieved by the IAF during the 1967 Six-Day War. In a bold and daring operation, largely masterminded by Israeli chief of staff Lieutenant General Yitzhak Rabin, and the product of more than a decade of intensive training and drilling of pilots and ground crews, the IAF launched a series of coordinated surprise attacks on Egyptian airfields on the morning of June 5,

Israeli Air Force major general Mordechai Hod in a Mirage fighter, June 1967. (Israeli Government Press Office)

1967. Within hours more than 300 Egyptian planes were destroyed, most of them on the ground, effectively eliminating the Egyptian Air Force as a factor in the conflict. Over the course of the day, the IAF delivered similarly devastating attacks against Syria, Jordan, and Iraq, securing for Israel complete mastery of the skies and providing its ground forces the tactical advantage needed to win a spectacular victory on all fronts. However, Hod would later note that the great success achieved on the battlefield was indeed a mixed blessing, as the expansion of Israel's borders planted the seeds for decades of further conflict.

Retiring from the military in 1973, Hod founded Kal, a company specializing in the transportation of agricultural products by air. Later in the 1970s he served as the chief executive officer of El Al, the Israeli national airline, and during 1987–1993 he chaired the country's aerial industrial board. In 1995, at the age of almost 70, he earned a PhD in business management from Pacific Western University in Los Angeles, California. Hod died in Tel Aviv, Israel, on June 30, 2003.

JONAS KAUFFELDT

See also

Egypt, Armed Forces; Israeli Air Strikes Beginning the Six-Day War; Rabin, Yitzhak; Six-Day War; Syria; Weizman, Ezer

References

Braverman, Libbie L., and Samuel M. Silver. *The Six-Day Warriors*. New York: Bloch, 1969.

Hammel, Eric. *Six Days in June: How Israel Won the 1967 Arab-Israeli War*. New York: Scribner, 1992.

Neff, Donald. *Warriors for Jerusalem: The Six Days That Changed the Middle East*. New York: Linden, 1984.

Weizman, Ezer. *On Eagles' Wings: The Personal Story of the Leading Command of the Israeli Air Force*. New York: Macmillan 1977.

Hofi, Yitzhak
Born: January 25, 1927

Israeli military officer and head of Mossad, Israel's chief civilian intelligence agency, from 1974 to 1982. Yitzhak Hofi was born in Tel Aviv, then in the British Mandate for Palestine, on January 25, 1927. As a young man he joined the Haganah, the Zionist paramilitary self-defense organization in Palestine and the primary basis for the Israel Defense Forces (IDF). During the Israeli War of Independence (1948–1949) he commanded a company at the rank of captain. A career officer, he held numerous commands and staff positions

Israeli major general Yitzhak Hofi, head of the Mossad intelligence agency from 1974 to 1982, shown in 1972. (Israeli Government Press Office)

while steadily rising through the ranks. In the 1973 Yom Kippur War, Hofi—now a major general—had charge of Israel's Northern Command. His excellent performance in that war earned him considerable respect and admiration.

In early 1974, Hofi was tapped to assume the post of acting chief of staff for the IDF. He held this position for a very short period before deciding to retire from active military duty. Remaining a reserve major general, he became director of Mossad later that year. During the June–July 1976 Entebbe Hostage Crisis in which terrorists hijacked Air France Flight 139 from Tel Aviv to Paris and threatened to kill scores of Israelis on the aircraft, Hofi urged the government to mount a daring rescue mission at the Entebbe Airport in Uganda. Finally overcoming the considerable reluctance to undertake such a risky venture, he played a key role in devising the rescue plan, including working covertly with Kenya's intelligence service to facilitate the refueling of Israeli planes in Nairobi. The Entebbe hostage rescue mission was a stunning success and continues as a model of such small, covert missions. Of the remaining 103 hostages being held at the airport, only 3 died. Only 1 of the IDF raiders was killed. Hofi resigned his post in 1982 and continues to reside in Israel.

PAUL G. PIERPAOLI JR.

See also

Entebbe Hostage Rescue; Mossad

References

Black, Ian, and Benny Morris. *Israel's Secret Wars: A History of Israel's Intelligence Services*. New York: Grove, 1994.

Gordon, Thomas. *Gideon's Spies: The Secret History of the Mossad*. New York: St. Martin's, 1999.

Holocaust
Start Date: 1941
End Date: 1945

The purposeful and systematic murder of some 6 million European Jews by the Nazi German regime during World War II. The Holocaust, also known by the Nazis as the Final Solution (Endlösung) and in Hebrew as Shoah, represented German dictator Adolf Hitler's efforts to exterminate the Jews of Europe, which, he bizarrely claimed, would solve many of the problems of European societies. He came close to succeeding in this grisly endeavor and also targeted for extermination Roma peoples (also referred to as Gypsies), persons with mental and physical limitations, homosexuals, and political and religious dissenters. The mass killings occurred in numerous concentration camps in Eastern Europe. Initially, the world viewed the situation with indifference. Indeed, many nations, including the United States, turned away Jewish refugees. Partially in response to such indifference and once the war was over, Jewish leaders—with backing from key world politicians—were determined to establish a Jewish state to provide a haven for Jews and defend them against any future persecution.

Entrance gate to Auschwitz, Nazi Germany's largest concentration camp during World War II. Auschwitz was a large complex in Poland that played a central role in Adolf Hitler's so-called Final Solution, the extermination of millions of Jews. (Corel)

The Holocaust was once thought to have begun with the Wannsee Conference held at a villa of that name outside of Berlin on January 1942, but most scholars now see it as having begun with the German invasion of the Soviet Union in the summer of 1941. The Wannsee meeting instead formalized a process that was, in effect, already under way. The very nature of the Holocaust also remains open to debate. Scholars have disagreed about whether the circumstances of the war merely permitted the evolution of the Final Solution as a crime of opportunity or whether the Nazi regime had planned the horrific extermination from the beginning. Finally, in the 1980s and 1990s, a small but vociferous group of so-called historians on the fringe of popular culture asserted that the Holocaust had never occurred or had at the very least not been the work of Adolf Hitler. Among these was British historian David Irving. Such an assertion is utterly preposterous, of course, as the historical record is replete with thousands of photographs and many thousands of documents detailing the Holocaust and those responsible for its execution. Having had both their day in court and exposure to criticism by the academic community, the complete falsehood of these claims has been clearly established.

Coming to power in 1933, the Hitler regime initiated over the next six years a number of actions and policies, most notably the Nuremberg Laws, designed to force Jews to leave Germany. Boycotts, expulsions from government positions, laws criminalizing Jewish-Gentile intermarriage, prohibitions against Jews owning land, nullification of citizenship, restrictions on professional activity, registration regulations, and the wearing of yellow stars and public identification all were aimed at encouraging Germany's 600,000 Jews to leave. Almost half did flee, largely bereft of their possessions, but few countries welcomed them. Many chose to leave for Austria because of existing cultural affinities with Germany. Thus, after the German annexation of Austria (Anschluss) in 1938, Germany's Jewish population exceeded that of 1933, owing to the return of the refugees and the native Austrian Jews.

The Nazis resorted to violence against the Jews in November 1938 in what has come to be known as Kristallnacht (Crystal Night) for the numerable panes of glass shattered in Jewish shops. More than 7,000 Jewish businesses were destroyed along with more than 500 synagogues. Some 100 Jews were killed, and 30,000 were seized and sent to concentration camps. The closing of borders when the war began in September 1939 halted any further Jewish exodus, however.

The acquisition of western Poland opened a new phase in the persecution of Jews. Those areas of Poland that had belonged to

Germany centuries earlier were annexed, while much of eastern Poland was taken by the Soviet Union. But the Germans made the remainder of Poland, centered on Warsaw, the destination for dispossessed Jews. Deportations were carried out with extreme brutality. Jews were usually transported east in railroad boxcars, under appalling conditions, to ghettos in Warsaw, Lodz, Kraków, and Lublin. That many died en route was a welcome by-product of the process to the Nazis rather than cause for concern. Little or no advance warning was provided, and Jews went away carrying but one suitcase of clothing. Within the ghettos, conditions were dreadful. The Nazis moved the Jews first from Germany, then the western countries, and then Eastern Europe, and for the most part, deportations continued throughout the war. When the Nazis began to exterminate the Jews, deportations bypassed the ghetto cities, and Jews went straight to the death camps.

Following the German armies into Poland in 1939 was a Schutzstaffel (SS) unit known as the Einsatzgruppe (Special Task Force), charged with eliminating likely resistance to military occupation. Polish government officials, professionals, teachers, professors, and business executives, among them many Jews, perished. When German forces invaded the Soviet Union in 1941 on three fronts, behind each was an Einsatzgruppe. SS leader Reinhard Tristan Eugen Heydrich charged these groups with eliminating the same categories of so-called undesirables in addition to Bolshevik (communist) functionaries. A fourth Einsatzgruppe was committed where needed. The scope and ferocity of the fighting in the east, to say nothing of the fact that it soon became apparent that the campaign would not be short, ruled out moving Russian Jews to city ghettos. The Einsatzgruppen simply killed large numbers of Jews rather than attempting to move them, and in some areas, particularly the Baltic region, locals participated in settling old scores and securing Jewish property. As the Germans moved east and acquired control over more and more Jews, it became clear that deportation to Poland would not be sufficient, for the ghettos were full, and transportation was not available.

An exasperated Hermann Göring, effectively second-in-command under Hitler, told Heydrich at the end of July 1941 to provide some plan for the Final Solution of the Jewish question.

Thousands of wedding rings removed by the Germans from Holocaust victims, photographed in May 1945. (National Archives and Records Administration)

HOLOCAUST DEATHS, 1941 – 1945

Bergen-Belsen
Neuengamme
Stutthof
Ravensbrück
Sachsenhausen
Treblinka
Vught
Chelmno
Sobibor
Mittelbaudora
Majdanek
Belzec
Buchenwald
Auschwitz
Flossenbürg
Terezin
Gross-Rosen
Dachau
Mauthausen

ATLANTIC
OCEAN

IRELAND

UNITED
KINGDOM

NORWAY

SWEDEN

FINLAND

SOVIET
UNION

DENMARK
6,000
100

ESTONIA

LATVIA
100,000
70,000

LITHUANIA
140,000
104,000

NETHERLANDS
140,000
106,000

GERMANY
250,000
180,000

POLAND
3,000,000
2,600,000

GERMAN-
OCCUPIED
SOVIET UNION
2,500,000
750,0000

BELGIUM
85,000
28,000

CZECHOSLOVAKIA
281,000
277,000

LUXEMBOURG

FRANCE
300,000
83,000

AUSTRIA
70,000
65,000

HUNGARY
710,000
402,000

ROMANIA
1,000,000
750,000

SWITZERLAND

YUGOSLAVIA
70,000
60,000

Black
Sea

PORTUGAL

SPAIN

ITALY
120,000
9,000

ALBANIA

BULGARIA
48,000
40,000

GREECE
67,000
65,000

TURKEY

Mediterranean
Sea

AFRICA

Germany in 1937
Under German control 1941 – 1944
■ Major concentration camps

LATVIA —— Country
100,000 —— Jewish population in 1941
70,000 —— Jewish population killed
by 1945
(conservative estimate)

0   200   400 mi
0   200   400 km

Jewish children, Buchenwald concentration camp survivors, on their way to Palestine on June 5, 1945. The girl on the left is from Poland, the boy is from Latvia, and the girl on the right is from Hungary. (National Archives and Records Administration)

Heydrich complied, presenting a plan in the January 20, 1942, meeting of senior SS and government officials at the Wannsee villa in a Berlin suburb. The plan was twofold. First, Jews in the Soviet Union would be worked to death or killed on the spot, because sending them west would be a poor use of transportation. Second, Jews remaining in Germany and elsewhere would be transported to new killing camps. These were termed annihilation camps (*Vernichtungslager*). Auschwitz, Treblinka, Sobibor, Majdanek, and Chelmno were the principal death camps, and all were located in Poland. The existing ghettos in Poland would be emptied, and the inmates would be moved to the killing camps for eventual extermination.

Upon arrival in the railroad freight cars (some Jews from Western Europe were sent east in passenger cars), selection took place at the railhead. SS medical personnel—among the most notorious, Josef Mengele at Auschwitz—made a hasty but final determination of who initially survived and who did not. Guidelines called for eliminating any persons who seemed unfit for the brutal labor that awaited. Thus, the elderly, the unhealthy or disabled, and very young children went straight to the gas chambers. Realizing that mothers would not easily be separated from their children, they too were gassed. Those selected went into the annihilation camps to be worked to death. Almost none would ever come out. Food rations were less than 900 calories per day, a level that leads to a slow and sure death from malnutrition and exhaustion.

Theresienstadt (Terczin), located in Czechoslovakia, was the model concentration camp, the showplace where Jews who had international reputations were sent so that friends and colleagues in the West could ascertain that they were alive. In late 1943 the Nazis tired of this charade, however, and sent the Terczin inmates to Auschwitz as well.

Much has been made of the lack of Jewish resistance, although there was some both in Warsaw and in a few of the camps. At first, deportations did not seem terribly sinister. In the Nazi racial hierarchy, Poles were barely ahead of Jews, and thus sending the Jews to Poland seemed to fit with Nazi logic. Once moved east, those who wanted to resist faced even greater obstacles. Means of resistance, such as weapons, were not available. And the Polish Underground Army was not about to help the Jews. Anti-Semitism was certainly one reason. Another reason was the fact that the Poles refused to hand over any weapons to what they perceived as a lost cause. Escape was almost as hopeless. Where could one go? Poland itself had seen considerable anti-Semitism, and most local inhabitants near the camps were in any case terrified of the Nazis and would not risk harboring escapees. The nearest neutral nations were hundreds of miles distant, and the Nazis punished with death anyone who assisted escapees.

The Nazi destruction of the killing camps as the war ended, the fact that most summary executions took place on the spot with imperfect record keeping, the postwar realignments of political and administrative boundaries, and the trauma of the heavy fighting in and around the massacre sites in the east all conspire to make any tally of Holocaust victims at best an estimate. Most scholars accept a figure of at least 6 million for the number of Jewish victims. This figure does not include perhaps millions of Roma, up to 2 million non-Jewish Poles, political prisoners, opponents of the regime, and homosexuals let alone Red Army prisoners of war, many of whom were simply starved to death. Jews tend to define the Holocaust as an event unique to them because their religion/race was the source of persecution. Non-Jews include all the victims, for indeed the Nazi persecutions had the same end.

After the Allies liberated the camps in 1945, there were two questions: Who was responsible for the incredible massacre, and how could the rest of society have allowed it? Blame fell initially on the SS personnel who had run the camps, but the Waffen-SS (Fighting SS) brazenly denied its role, instead blaming the specialized Death's Head–SS (Totenkopfverbaende). To a certain extent, members of the Waffen-SS succeeded in deflecting blame, claiming that they were merely soldiers like all of the others, and in truth both soldiers and policemen did participate in the process. German Army (Wehrmacht) veterans denied complicity in the extermination of the Jews, asserting that it was purely the work of the SS, but the army was well aware of what was transpiring. When the Hamburg Institute for Social Research organized a photographic exhibit in 1995 that revealed the Wehrmacht participating in atrocities, a firestorm of controversy followed. Tarnishing the Wehrmacht's good-soldier image amounted to iconoclasm of the first instance, and the sensation was enormous. The issue is controversial to this day, for it countered a half century of effective self-denial on the part of rank-and-file Germans.

The churches would be found to share the blame as well, but especially troublesome were the accusations concerning the role of the Pope. What the Pope knew and why he did not condemn the killings became the framing issues in the debate. Eugenio Pacelli, who became Pope as Pius XII, was a Germanophile, known as the "German Pope." In 1959, Swiss playwright Rolf Hochhuth wrote *The Deputy: A Christian Tragedy,* accusing Pius XII of being Hitler's accessory. A more recent biography of Pius, titled *Hitler's Pope* (1999), draws the same conclusion. Papal defenders make a pragmatic argument: by speaking out against the killings, Pius would not have saved a single Jew, but his actions might have turned the wrath of Hitler on Catholics as well, and millions more innocent victims might have perished. The German Evangelical-Lutheran Church also stood accused of failing to repudiate the killings. It, too, had its heroes, but overall its record in acting against the Holocaust does not appear to be a proud one.

Even the Allies came under fire for failing to aid the Jews before and during the war. The Nazis made no attempt to hide their treatment of the Jews prior to 1939. Jewish organizations in the United States entreated President Franklin D. Roosevelt to admit more Jews, but indifference and anti-Semitism triumphed. As increasing evidence of the Holocaust came to light during the war, Jewish agencies again urged the United States to do more, even to bomb the death camps and the rail lines leading to them. Two Czech Jews (Rudolf Virba and Alfred Weztler) escaped to Switzerland, described in detail the killing camps, and gave the U.S. embassy a map of the sprawling Birkenau subcamp of Auschwitz, but it was hand-drawn and rejected as insufficient. At first, the U.S. military could argue that the camps lay beyond the range of its bombers, but this changed by the summer of 1944. Then it was a matter that military targets had priority, although Auschwitz inmates worked the Buna plant, the world's largest synthetic rubber plant. And in August 1944 the Eighth Air Force did strike the plant, but the official line was that winning the war, best done by hitting military targets, would simultaneously end the persecution.

In the early 1970s, a number of self-professed historians at the fringes of popular culture began to question the very existence of the Holocaust as a historical event. Not denying that large numbers of Jews died or that Nazis treated Jews brutally and that large numbers perished miserably, they deny instead the existence of a coherent plan and set of tools and processes used to exterminate the Jewish race. Called Holocaust Revisionists, they argue that the Germans moved Jews to the east for labor reasons, that the camps existed to provide labor pools, that the Nazis were brutal, and that the number who died in these camps was very high. This argument has made little headway, and courts as well as prominent academics and historians have rejected it out of hand.

A more intriguing debate that emerged in the 1990s was the question of intention: whether Hitler had planned all along (Intentionalists) to kill the Jews or whether through the war he and his fellow Nazis simply encountered an irresistible opportunity and the functional means (hence the moniker Functionalists) to carry out the extermination. The debate has sparked strong emotions. The guilt of the Germans appears to some to be mitigated to some extent if Hitler was merely a functionalist who took advantage of contingencies and circumstances, while the burden of guilt is much greater if Hitler had planned from the start to kill the Jews and the German population acted in complicity to this desire. The debate was reignited in 1996 when American Daniel Goldhagen published a book provocatively titled *Hitler's Willing Executioners.* There was nothing new to be found among the charges, but the book punctured some 40 years of denial and reawakened the question of who in Germany had known what and when.

In the end, the Nazi-inspired Holocaust stands as one of the largest mass exterminations of human beings in modern history. It was, at its core, a genocide perpetrated across a large swath of Europe. There can be no doubt that the world's Jews, after having suffered through or witnessed such horrific persecutions, were determined to establish a Jewish state at the end of World War II. Indeed, the Holocaust gave new meaning and new urgency to Zionism. And many world leaders, perhaps out of guilt, perhaps out of outrage, helped to bring the Zionist vision to reality in 1948.

MICHAEL B. BARRETT

See also

Pius XII, Pope; Yad Vashem Holocaust Memorial; Yom HaShoah ve ha-Gevurah; Zionism; Zionist Conference

References

Bartov, Omer. *The Eastern Front 1941–45: German Troops and the Barbarization of Warfare.* 2nd ed. Palgrave/St. Martin's, 2001.

———. *Hitler's Army: Soldiers, Nazis, and War in the Third Reich.* Oxford: Oxford University Press, 1991.

Browning, Christopher R. *Ordinary Men: Reserve Police Battalion 101 and the Origins of the Final Solution in Poland.* New York: HarperCollins, 1992.

———. *The Origins of the Final Solution: The Evolution of Nazi Jewish Policy, September 1939–March 1942.* Lincoln: University of Nebraska Press, 2004.

Cornwell, John. *Hitler's Pope: The Secret History of Pius XII.* New York: Viking, 1999.

Dawidowicz, Lucy S. *The War against the Jews, 1933–1945.* New York: Holt, Rinehart, and Winston, 1975.

Gilbert, Martin. *The Holocaust: The History of Jews of Europe during the Second World War.* New York: Henry Holt, 1987.

Goldhagen, Daniel Jonah. *Hitler's Willing Executioners: Ordinary Germans and the Holocaust.* New York: Knopf, 1996.

Holocaust Martyrs' Remembrance Day

See Yom HaShoah ve ha-Gevurah

Hope-Simpson Report
Event Date: October 31, 1930

British government report on economic conditions in Palestine that was produced after the Arab Revolt of 1929–1930 and formed the basis of the Passfield White Paper. As a consequence of the Shaw Commission recommendation, the British government appointed Sir John Hope-Simpson, a retired civil servant in India and member of the League of Nations Commission charged with the resettlement of Greek refugees, to investigate Arab complaints that had sparked the violence of 1929–1930. The Hope-Simpson Report was published simultaneously with the Passfield White Paper on October 31, 1930.

Hope-Simpson traveled to Palestine but spent only two months there. He submitted his report to the British government in August 1930, and it became the basis for the subsequent and more pro-Arab British government decisions aimed at restricting land sales to Jews and Jewish immigration to Palestine, which were contained in the Passfield White Paper.

Hope-Simpson concentrated his inquiries on the effects of Jewish immigration on the Palestinian economy and the impact of this and land sales to Jews by Arabs on the general Arab population. He concluded that Palestine was basically agricultural and discounted the possibility of future significant industrial development there. He also concluded that there was insufficient agricultural land in Palestine to sustain future immigration.

Hope-Simpson calculated that there were about 6.544 million dunams of arable land (the dunam is the basic surface measurement used for land in Israel and is equivalent to 1,000 square meters or about a quarter acre) in Palestine. This figure was about 60 percent of the figure determined by Jewish experts. Calculating 130 dunams as the minimum to sustain an Arab family in a reasonable standard of living, Hope-Simpson concluded that there was a serious shortage of land for the Arab population. He also pointed out that Arab farmers were plagued by high rents and taxes and poor crop yields. Hope-Simpson blamed the Jewish practice of purchasing Arab lands to hold for future immigrants and the policy of hiring only Jews as the major factors in the high rates of Arab unemployment. His report called for greater development with an emphasis on irrigation. He also urged partition of land, the introduction of new crops, and improvements in education. Once these reforms were implemented, he believed it would be possible to permit the immigration to Palestine of only 20,000 additional families.

Jewish experts criticized his figures not only on the amount of agricultural land available but also regarding its negative assessment of the possibilities for industrial development. Nonetheless, Hope-Simpson's conclusions were the basis of the Passfield White Paper that sought to limit both land sales by Arabs to Jews and future Jewish immigration.

Spencer C. Tucker

See also
Balfour Declaration; Palestine, British Mandate for; Shaw Commission; United Kingdom, Middle East Policy; White Paper (1930)

References
Sachar, Howard M. *A History of Israel: From the Rise of Zionism to Our Time.* 3rd ed. New York: Knopf, 2007.
Shepherd, Naomi. *Ploughing Sand: British Rule in Palestine, 1917–1948.* New Brunswick, NJ: Rutgers University Press, 1999.

Hoveve Zion

Pioneering Jewish organization created in 1884 that founded modern Zionism. Spurred by the official pogroms in Russia, the founders of Hoveve Zion (Lovers of Zion), also known as Hibbat Zion, believed that Jews would never find true freedom in other countries. Instead, they believed that a Jewish homeland was the only answer. This stand was a reversal of the Haskalah movement, which had prevailed throughout the 19th century and had preached Jewish integration into larger societies. Zion originally referred to Mount Zion near Jerusalem, with a Jebusite fortress captured by King David. The term "Zion" then was applied to the section of Jerusalem where the fortress stood. Following construction of Solomon's Temple, the term referred to the temple grounds and the temple itself. Today the word "Zion" is often used metaphorically for Jerusalem and the Promised Land.

The driving force behind Hoveve Zion was Leon Pinsker, a Russian physician. He was one of the first Jews to attend Odessa University, where he studied law. He soon realized that Russian prejudice would prevent him from practicing law, so he transferred to the University of Moscow, where he earned a medical degree. Pinsker returned home to Odessa in 1849, where he established a medical practice.

Pinsker had been influenced by Haskalah, a movement established during the Enlightenment. He and like-minded individuals believed that Jews could be assimilated into European culture. Pinsker founded a Russian-language newspaper for Jews and encouraged his readers to adopt Russian culture. Assimilation was defeated, however, by a growing belief in Russia that being Jewish was not a question of religion and culture but rather of race. For those who believed this teaching, Jewishness could not be changed by baptism or assimilation. Instead, the Jews were seen as the ultimate outsiders who threatened a nation's power. As a result, pogroms broke out in Odessa in 1871, severely shaking Pinsker's faith that Jews could become an accepted part of Russian society. After a hiatus of several years, Pinsker resumed his activities in favor of assimilation, but another wave of pogroms swept Russia in 1881. The czarist government was suspected of sponsoring much of the violence.

The pogroms completely reversed Pinsker's opinions. He now began to discuss Jewish immigration with other Jewish leaders. In 1882, Pinsker published "Autoemancipation," an analysis of anti-

Semitism that called for the establishment of a Jewish homeland in Palestine or elsewhere. He believed that Jews could only be safe and free in a homeland in another part of the world. He did not necessarily believe that a separate Jewish state was desirable or possible.

Other Jews in Eastern Europe agreed with Pinsker's position. A number of local organizations were founded in Russia in 1881 and afterward to promote the idea of Jewish immigration. These groups were informally known as Hoveve Zion or Hibbat Zion. They were informal and autonomous organizations of varying sizes and held different stances on religious issues.

In 1882, one such Russian group founded Rishon le Zion southeast of Jaffa. This settlement was the first permanent Jewish community founded in Palestine in modern times. The settlement had 2,000 acres and 500 settlers and was devoted to agricultural production. The most important product was mulberry trees, used to feed silkworms. Thanks to funds from wealthy philanthropists, the group was able to purchase the land from the Arab landowners. The poor Arab farmers who worked the land expected that they would be allowed to remain and continue to farm. Instead, the Arab farmers were displaced, and only Jews were allowed to live and work in Rishon le Zion.

In 1884, 36 delegates from various Jewish groups met in Kattowitz, Germany (now Katowice, Poland), to discuss the idea of Jewish immigration. They were all from different parts of the Russian Empire, especially western Russia and Poland. Pinsker was named chairman of a new organization titled Hoveve Zion. It was the first international organization devoted to Jewish immigration. The group solicited financial support from wealthy Jews across Europe. Baron Edmond de Rothschild, for example, underwrote the cost of several settlements in Palestine. Sir Moses Montefiore, a British financier, was another early supporter of Hoveve Zion. In the end, however, Pinsker's attempts to establish chapters of Hoveve Zion outside of Russia were unsuccessful. Jewish leaders in other countries were less anxious to immigrate, as they were more fully integrated into their nations' societies.

Pinsker was in failing health by the late 1880s. He resigned from his leadership role in Hoveve Zion, but divisions within the organization forced him to return. The divisions were deep and followed religious lines. Orthodox and religious Jews were more interested in a return to Jewish values but were not so supportive of actual immigration. They insisted that Hoveve Zion offer financial support to settlers in Palestine only if they observed Jewish traditions and teachings. More practical groups believed that immigration was necessary, even if a return to traditional values was not. Most supported a return to the land and believed that settlers should establish socialist, agricultural settlements.

Members of Hoveve Zion hoped to establish a formal structure for the organization in Russia. The Russian government refused to recognize the society unless it was set up as a charity. After extensive negotiations, Hoveve Zion was recognized by the czarist government in early 1890. The formal name was The Society for the Support of Jewish Farmers and Artisans in Syria and Eretz-Israel.

It was headquartered in Odessa, and the leadership became known as the Odessa Committee. Pinsker died in 1891, upset over the lack of progress in establishing a Jewish homeland. He had considered the possibility of instead establishing settlements in more remote locations, such as Argentina.

By 1892, Hoveve Zion had approximately 14,000 members. It was overtaken by other international Zionist organizations, especially the World Zionist Organization (WZO), founded by Theodor Herzl. By the beginning of the 20th century, the chapters of Hoveve Zion had been absorbed into the WZO. Hoveve Zion thus ceased to exist as an independent organization. As the first attempt at a Zionist organization, however, Hoveve Zion had played an important role in promoting the idea of establishing a Jewish homeland where Jews would be free to practice their faith without penalties or persecution.

TIM J. WATTS

See also

Anti-Semitism; Haskalah; Herzl, Theodor; Montefiore, Sir Moses; Pogroms; Rothschild, Edmond de; World Zionist Organization; Zionism

References

Friedman, Isiah. *The Rise of Israel: From Precursors of Zionism to Herzl.* New York: Garland, 1987.

Luz, Ehud. *Parallels Meet: Religion and Nationalism in the Early Zionist Movement (1882–1904).* Philadelphia: Jewish Publication Society, 1988.

Schweid, Eliezer. *The Land of Israel: National Home or Land of Destiny.* Rutherford, NJ: Fairleigh Dickinson University Press, 1985.

Vital, David. *The Origins of Zionism.* Oxford, UK: Clarendon, 1975.

Hrawi, Elias

Born: September 4, 1925
Died: July 7, 2006

Lebanese political leader and president of Lebanon (1989–1998). A Maronite Catholic, Elias (Ilyas) Hrawi was born on September 4, 1925, in Hawsj Al-Umara near the town of Zahla in the Bekáa Valley. The son of a wealthy landowner, Hrawi graduated with a degree in business from Saint Joseph University in Beirut. He became wealthy from a vegetable export business and food processing factory in the Bekáa Valley and from heading agricultural cooperatives. When the export business was halted by the civil war in Lebanon during 1975–1990, he began oil importation and operated a gas station chain in Beirut.

Hrawi followed his two brothers into politics and was elected to the Lebanese National Assembly in 1972. In the 1980s, he began to play an increasing role in the nation's political life. A member of the National Assembly from 1972 until 1989 and a member of the chamber's independent Maronite bloc, he worked to maintain good relations with both Christian and Muslim groups, partly due to the growing Muslim population in his constituency.

On November 24, 1989, two days after the assassination of President René Mouawad, Hrawi was elected president of Lebanon dur-

Elias Hrawi, Lebanese political leader and president of Lebanon (1989–1998). (Reuters/Bettmann/Corbis)

ing an emergency National Assembly session. He was the first Lebanese president to come from outside the Maronite area of Mount Lebanon. The election occurred amid an ongoing civil war between Syrian-supported Muslim militias and Christian army forces. Hrawi formed a civilian government rival to the military government headed by General Michel Aoun, former Christian commander in chief of the Lebanese Army, whose aim was to expel all Syrian forces from Lebanon. Hrawi's task was to implement the Taif Agreement, a national charter of reconciliation designed to transfer executive power from the presidency to a cabinet composed equally of Christian and Muslim ministers and to expand the legislature to allow for equal representation there as well. Aoun rejected the agreement, however, because it allowed Syria to participate in the implementation of the plan over a two-year period. Indeed, Hrawi's critics claimed that he too closely supported Syrian interests in Lebanon.

Backed by the Syrian Army, Hrawi campaigned to remove Aoun but soon withdrew the effort out of concern that he would alienate

the Christian community, which had divided into factions supporting and opposing the Taif Agreement. In May 1990, battling Christian forces signed a truce, paving the way for the approval of constitutional changes to implement the agreement, which Hrawi signed into law on September 21, 1990. Hrawi continued his efforts to oust Aoun, and forces loyal to Hrawi attacked Aoun's headquarters on October 13, 1990, forcing him to flee. Hrawi then moved to restore national government control to the whole of Lebanon. In October 1995, under Syrian pressure, the National Assembly amended the constitution to allow Hrawi to remain in office for an additional three years without benefit of election. His critics charged that this action subverted democracy and undermined the delicate political balance in Lebanon.

During almost a decade as president, Hrawi came to be seen as an old-school leader who had been manipulated by the Syrian government. He was often overshadowed by the far more dynamic Lebanese political leader, Prime Minister Rafik Hariri, with whom Hrawi often differed on political and economic reform issues. Émile

Lahoud succeeded Hrawi in November 1998. Hrawi died of cancer at the American University Hospital in Beirut on July 7, 2006.

SPENCER C. TUCKER

See also

Hariri, Rafik; Lebanon; Syria

Reference

Fisk, Robert. *Pity the Nation: The Abduction of Lebanon.* 4th ed. New York: Nation Books, 2002.

Hula Valley

The Hula Valley is located in northeastern Galilee. Before the founding of Israel, the Hula Valley was home to both Arab and Jewish settlements. Between 1948 and 1967, it was part of the border between Israel and Syria. Control over the valley was an important political objective for both sides because it was the site of potentially rich agricultural lands and water supplies.

The Hula Valley is situated along the ancient route between Egypt and Damascus and has been inhabited for thousands of years. The Jordan River originates in the northern part of the valley from streams flowing out of the nearby mountains. During the 19th century Bedouin inhabited most of the valley, surviving by producing products made of local reeds. Most of the valley was taken up by a shallow lake and marshy ground.

Mortality rates were very high among the Arabs because the marshes were breeding grounds for mosquitoes. The Ottoman government became interested in draining the lake and marshes and in 1908 sold a concession to do so to a French firm. The concession was sold two more times to Lebanese businessmen before World War I.

In the late 19th century, Zionists became interested in the Hula Valley as a place for agricultural settlements. In 1883 during the First Aliya of European Jewish settlers, Yesod Hamaala was founded. During the 1920s and 1930s other Zionist settlements followed, and by 1948 there were 12 Jewish and 23 Arab settlements in the valley.

In 1934 the Palestine Land Development Corporation purchased the concession to drain the Hula Valley. Zionist leaders believed that up to 15,000 acres of prime agricultural land could be gained from draining the lake and marshes. Digging canals that would improve the flow of the Jordan River was also part of the plan, as it would increase the supply of water farther downstream. World War II and uncertainty over the division of Palestine prevented any activities toward this before 1950, however.

The United Nations (UN) partition plan of November 1947 called for the border between Israel and Syria to follow the Jordan River in the Hula Valley, with a narrow strip of land on the eastern bank to go to Israel. The Arab settlements in the valley would have been included in Israel. As tensions grew between Jews and Arabs,

Dredging canals into the Hula swamps in May 1954, part of a controversial Israeli drainage project begun in 1951. (Israeli Government Press Office)

Jewish forces entered the Hula Valley in March 1948. They forcibly removed the Arabs from most of the settlements and forced them into Syria.

During the 1948–1949 Israeli War of Independence, the Syrians captured parts of the southern valley on the west side of the Jordan. Between April and July 1949, a series of UN-sponsored talks led to a General Armistice Agreement between Israel and Syria that included the Hula Valley. The Syrians evacuated the Hula Valley and established their lines east of the Jordan on the Golan Heights. Much of the Hula Valley was declared a demilitarized zone, and the original Arab settlers were given Syrian identity cards and allowed to return.

In 1951 Israel began to drain the lake and marshes. The locations of drainage canals were chosen to force the Arabs, who had recently returned, from their homes. Although Syrians sporadically fired on Israeli machinery, the drainage was largely complete by 1958. Additional Israeli settlements were placed in the valley. By 1963, however, the Israeli government gave in to environmentalists and restored part of the lake and marshes as Israel's first nature preserve. When war with Syria broke out during the June 1967 Six-Day War, Israeli forces took the Golan Heights, partially to protect Israelis living in the Hula Valley from being attacked.

TIM J. WATTS

See also

Bedouin; Galilee; Golan Heights; Israel; Jordan River; Syria

References

Amery, Hussein A., and Aaron T. Wolf, eds. *Water in the Middle East: A Geography of Peace.* Austin: University of Texas Press, 2000.

Muslih, Muhammad Y. *The Golan: The Road to Occupation.* Washington, DC: Institute for Palestine Studies, 1999.

Youth and Hechalutz Department (World Zionist Organization). *The Huleh and the Upper Jordan Region.* Jerusalem: The Organization, 1954.

Hussein, King of Jordan

Born: November 14, 1935
Died: February 7, 1999

King of Jordan (1953–1999). Born in Amman on November 14, 1935, into the Hashemite family that claims direct descent from the Prophet Muhammad's clan, Hussein ibn Talal was the son of Prince Talal ibn Abdullah. Hussein was educated in Jordan and then at Victoria College in Alexandria, Egypt, before transferring to the prestigious Harrow School in Britain. He was with his grandfather, King Abdullah, when the king was assassinated in 1951.

Hussein's father was crowned king but was forced to abdicate the throne on August 11, 1952, because of mental illness. Hussein was proclaimed king as Hussein I and returned from Britain to take up the throne at age 17. He formally ascended the throne on May 2, 1953.

Hussein's policies tended to be contradictory but also realistic, a useful combination that got him through the early years of his

King Hussein of Jordan, who ruled during 1953–1999, shown here in 1987. (AFP/Getty Images)

reign. The nation's stability was threatened by a large influx of Palestinian refugees on the West Bank, which had been recently annexed by Jordan in a move that was not popular with the Israelis, the Palestinians, or other Arab states. In addition, Jordan still enjoyed considerable financial and military support from Britain, which also displeased Arab leaders who were working to build Arab nationalism and alliances. Hussein continued the close ties with Britain until 1956. At that time, he was pressured to dismiss General John Bagot Glubb, the British head of the Arab Legion that had been formed in 1939 to fight in World War II.

The dismissal of Glubb was a popular move among Jordanians, but Hussein delayed another year before terminating the Anglo-Jordanian Treaty and signing the Arab Solidarity Agreement that pledged Egypt, Syria, and Saudi Arabia to provide Jordan with an annual subsidy of $36 million. When Hussein accepted U.S. aid in 1958, however, Egyptian and Syrian leaders began to campaign against him.

By the mid-1960s, Hussein was making attempts to alleviate the increasing isolation that separated Jordan from neighboring Arab states. After some hesitation, he linked his country with Egypt and Syria in war against Israel, permitting Jordanian long-range artillery fire against Jewish areas of Jerusalem and the suburbs of

Tel Aviv in the 1967 Six-Day War. The Israelis had hoped that Jordan would remain neutral, but Hussein's steps brought retaliatory Israeli air strikes. Hussein later said that he made the decision because he feared that Israel was about to invade. The war was a disaster for Jordan, which lost the entire West Bank and its air force and suffered some 15,000 casualties. After the war, Hussein helped draft United Nations (UN) Resolution 242, which urged Israel to give up its occupied territories in exchange for peace.

In the early 1970s, Hussein was forced to challenge the presence of the Palestine Liberation Organization (PLO) in his country because the PLO had turned the region into a war zone and challenged Hussein's authority over his own territory. After an assassination attempt on Hussein and the hijacking of four British airliners by the Popular Front for the Liberation of Palestine and their destruction in Jordan, the king decided that Palestinian militants were threatening the very survival of Jordan and that he must take action. In 1970, in what became known as Black September, Hussein began a controversial military campaign against the PLO, forcing it from Jordanian territory. Although he achieved his goal and the PLO moved its headquarters to Lebanon, the unrest lasted until July 1971, and his action undermined his position as the principal spokesperson for the Palestinian people.

Hussein regained favor in the Arab world when he rejected the 1979 Israel-Egypt Peace Treaty. He received considerable international criticism for his neutrality regarding Iraqi leader Saddam Hussein's invasion of Kuwait and for not joining the coalition against Iraq in the 1991 Persian Gulf War. Jordan had to remain faithful to its own policy toward Iraq, which had resulted from their initial emergence as Hashemite kingdoms and was reflected in their close economic ties. King Hussein nonetheless continued to play a significant role in the ongoing Middle East peace talks. In July 1994 he signed a peace agreement with Israeli prime minister Yitzhak Rabin.

On the domestic front, Hussein was a popular but autocratic leader who guided his nation to relative prosperity. He saw to it that more Jordanians had access to running water, proper sanitation, and electricity. He also actively promoted education and dramatically increased the literacy rate. In the late 1960s he oversaw construction of a modern highway system in the kingdom.

In 1992 Hussein began to take some steps toward the liberalization of the political system and the development of a multiparty system. That same year he was diagnosed with pancreatic cancer. He underwent treatment several times in the United States, each time designating his brother Hasan as regent during his absence. Less than two weeks before his death in 1999, Hussein surprised the world by naming his eldest son Abdullah as crown prince and designated heir, publicly denouncing Hasan's performance as regent and ensuring his own immediate family's control of the throne. Abdullah became King Abdullah II upon Hussein's death in Amman on February 7, 1999. Beloved by Jordanians for his attention to their welfare, Hussein had strengthened Jordan's position in the Arab world and contributed to the foundations of peace in the region.

SPENCER C. TUCKER

See also

Abdullah I, King of Jordan; Abdullah II, King of Jordan; Camp David Accords; Israel-Jordan Peace Treaty; Jordan; Palestine Liberation Organization; Rabin, Yitzhak; Six-Day War

References

Dallas, Roland. *King Hussein: A Life on the Edge*. New York: Fromm International, 1999.

Dann, Uriel. *King Hussein and the Challenge of Arab Radicalism: Jordan, 1955–1967*. Oxford: Oxford University Press, 1997.

Hussein, King of Jordan. *Uneasy Lies the Head: The Autobiography of His Majesty King Hussein I of the Hashemite Kingdom of Jordan*. New York: B. Geis, 1962.

Matusky, Gregory, and John P. Hayes. *King Hussein*. New York: Chelsea House, 1987.

Robins, Philip. *A History of Jordan*. Cambridge: Cambridge University Press, 2004.

Satloff, Robert B. *From Abdullah to Hussein: Jordan in Transition*. New York: Oxford University Press, 1993.

Hussein, Saddam
Born: April 28, 1937
Died: December 30, 2006

Iraqi president (1979–2003). Saddam Hussein was born on April 28, 1937, in Al Awjy, near Tikrit. He experienced a difficult childhood, his father dying when Hussein was an infant. At age 20 he joined the Pan-Arab Baath Party. When General Abdul Karim Qassem overthrew Iraq's King Faisal II in 1958, one wing of the Baath Party opposed the new government.

In 1959 Hussein participated in an assassination attempt on the new prime minister. Slightly wounded, Hussein fled to Syria and later Egypt. Tried and sentenced to death in absentia, he attended the faculty of law at the University of Cairo while in exile.

In 1963 army officers came to power in a coup. Although a number of them were loyal to the Baathists, the majority were Arab nationalists. The new military government soon crumbled. Returning to Iraq, Hussein was imprisoned in 1964 by anti-Baathists then in power. Three years later, upon his escape from prison, he became a leading member of the Baath Party, in charge of internal party security. In July 1968, in another coup, the Baath Party took power under General Ahmad Hasan al-Bakr, a relative of Hussein and a fellow Tikriti. Hussein became vice president and vice chairman of the Iraqi Revolutionary Command Council and assumed control of foreign affairs. In 1976 he traveled to France and there met with both politicians and businessmen. This trip led to the building of an Iraqi nuclear reactor in Osiraq with French assistance.

In 1970 Hussein negotiated an agreement with Kurdish rebel leaders in Iraq giving the Kurds limited autonomy. When the agreement broke down, the Iraqi Army attacked Kurdish villages, killing thousands and leading to a deterioration in relations with Iran. In 1975 Hussein negotiated a treaty with Mohammad Reza Shah Pahlavi of Iran in which Iran withdrew its support for the Kurds in Iraq and made border concessions. Further improving relations,

Saddam Hussein, president and dictator of Iraq from 1979 until he was overthrown by a U.S.-led coalition in the Iraq War of 2003, shown here in October 1995. (AFP/Getty Images)

Hussein agreed in 1978 to expel Ayatollah Ruhollah Khomeini from Iraq. Khomeini then fled to France. These events ensured bitter enmity between Hussein and Khomeini, one cause of the Iran-Iraq War (1980–1988).

Hussein built and later maintained his base of political power through intimidation, relying on relatives and fellow Tikritis for support. His de facto rule dates from 1976. In 1979 when President al-Bakr planned to unite Iraq with Syria, also under Baathist rule, Hussein rightly feared for his power. That July, however, al-Bakr resigned allegedly for reasons of health, leading directly to the Hussein presidency. On July 22 of the same year, Hussein ordered the executions of scores of Baath Party members accused of disloyalty.

After he had consolidated his rule, Hussein worked for social modernization. He created a secular legal framework, adopted a system of social benefits, and granted rights to women. A new health care system, probably the most comprehensive and modern in the Middle East, earned him an award from the United Nations (UN). Iraqi oil reserves and a growing demand for skilled labor brought an influx of foreigners from other Arab countries and Europe to Iraq.

Hussein was an Iraqi nationalist who also supported Pan-Arabism and the Palestinian cause, but many of his social accomplishments were undermined by the long and costly war with Iran, which he instigated and which was fought over territorial, ethnic, and religious issues, but also because he sought to play the central role in the Arab world. As part of the process of enhancing Iraqi power and influence, he initiated programs to develop weapons of mass destruction (WMDs). But with the Osiraq Tammuz I nuclear

reactor nearing completion, the Israel Air Force carried out a raid in June 1981 that destroyed the facility. Not deterred, Hussein established a chemical weapons program with the assistance of foreign firms, including those in West Germany. Hussein employed these chemical weapons in the war with Iran and also against the Iraqi Kurdish minority in the north.

During the long war with Iran, Hussein turned to other Arab states and to the West for both financial and diplomatic support. The U.S. government, which was not anxious to see fundamentalist Iran triumph, provided military intelligence to Hussein's regime in the form of satellite reconnaissance. Washington also did not take action against Iraq when, on May 17, 1987, an Iraqi Mirage aircraft fired two Exocet missiles at and disabled the USS *Stark*. The attack killed 37 crewmen and injured another 21 on board the Oliver Hazard Perry–class frigate. The *Stark* was one of the U.S. warships sent to the Persian Gulf by President Ronald Reagan to keep open the Persian Gulf during the so-called Tanker War.

Hussein's authoritarian government fostered a cult of personality around the leader. The country was filled with his opulent palaces and with statues and posters of him trumpeting his alleged achievements. To thwart assassination, he employed dozens of doubles. Meanwhile, his secret police, intelligence services, and military security maintained a thoroughly oppressive rule with little respect for human rights.

Hussein further consolidated his power during the withering Iran-Iraq War, using the conflict as an excuse to eliminate potential rivals and suspected radicals and also to attack the Kurds. Aware of the fact that as a Sunni he ruled over a majority of Shiites, he sought to intimidate the latter. The so-called Marsh Arab Shiites in the southern provinces were driven from their land, and vast swampy areas were artificially laid dry. He firmly repressed the Islamic revival among the Shia in the holy cities and in Baghdad. In the north, the Kurds, while Sunnis, were non-Arabs. Opposed to Hussein's Pan-Arab tendencies, they were also brutally oppressed with mass arrests and wanton killings. Hussein also resettled Arabs in Kurdish areas in an effort to weaken Kurdish nationalism.

Even though Iraq did not share a border with Israel, Iraqi forces participated in each of the wars fought by the Arab community against that country. In 1948, 1967, and 1973, Iraq supported Syria and Jordan militarily.

Hussein was a firm believer in Pan-Arab nationalism and an ardent admirer of Egypt's president Gamal Abdel Nasser, especially following the 1956 Suez Crisis. Hussein was in the forefront of efforts to punish the West by means of an oil embargo for its support of Israel in the 1973 Yom Kippur War. Although Syria was also run by the Baath Party, relations between Iraq and Syria became antagonistic. There were, however, wings of the Baath Party in each country that had supported a union of the two countries, but relations soured so thoroughly that Syria created an alliance with and supported Iran throughout the Iran-Iraq war.

In August 1990 Hussein miscalculated both U.S. resolve and Arab opinion and invaded neighboring Kuwait with the intention of incorporating that oil-rich state and using the revenues to pay off massive debts accumulated during the war with Iran. This act led to the formation of a U.S.-led coalition against Hussein. During the resulting Persian Gulf War (1991), he sought to entangle Israel in the war and unhinge the support of Arab states such as Syria and Egypt for the coalition by firing Scud surface-to-surface missiles against Israel. While this step gained him support from the Palestine Liberation Organization (PLO) as well as many Palestinians, heavy U.S. pressure on Israel prevented him from realizing his plan of drawing the Jewish state into the war.

Hussein managed to maintain his hold on power despite the crushing defeat of his forces in the war. He took immediate revenge on the Shiites who had risen in the south, killing tens of thousands. The war and its aftermath brought a decade of international isolation and crippling economic sanctions against Iraq.

During 2002–2003, Hussein's belligerence and missteps once again brought intense international scrutiny and allegations by President George W. Bush that Hussein had WMDs. Although this proved not to be the case, in the 2003 Operation IRAQI FREEDOM, a smaller U.S.-led coalition without any Arab troops invaded Iraq, this time with the intention of overthrowing the regime. Although Baghdad fell on April 9, Hussein eluded capture until December 13, when he was found hiding at the bottom of a narrow pit dug beneath a mud shack on a sheep farm. He was subsequently brought to trial before an Iraqi Special Tribunal, established by the interim Iraqi government.

On November 5, 2006, the Iraqi Special Tribunal found Hussein guilty in the 1982 deaths of 148 Shiite Muslims, whose murders he had ordered. That same day he was sentenced to hang. Meanwhile, on August 21, 2006, a second trial had begun on charges that he had committed genocide and other atrocities by ordering the systematic extermination of northern Iraqi Kurds during 1987–1988, resulting in as many as 180,000 deaths. Before the second trial moved into high gear, however, Hussein's attorneys filed an appeal, which was rejected by the Iraqi court on December 26, 2006. Four days later, on December 30, 2006, on the Muslim holiday of 'Id al-Adha, Hussein was executed by hanging in Baghdad.

THOMAS J. WEILER

See also

Arab Oil Embargo; Chemical Weapons and Warfare; Iran-Iraq War; Iraq; Khomeini, Ruhollah; Lebanon, Israeli Invasion of; Nasser, Gamal Abdel; Nuclear Weapons; Organization of Petroleum Exporting Countries; Pan-Arabism; Yom Kippur War

References

Aburish, Said. *Saddam Hussein: The Politics of Revenge*. London: Bloomsbury, 2001.

Cockburn, Andrew, and Patrick Cockburn. *Out of the Ashes: The Resurrection of Saddam Hussein*. London: Harper Perennial, 2000.

Coughlin, Con. *Saddam: His Rise and Fall*. New York: HarperCollins, 2002.

Karsh, Efraim, et al. *Saddam Hussein: A Political Biography*. New York: Grove, 2003.

Munthe, Turi. *The Saddam Hussein Reader*. Berkeley, CA: Thunder's Mouth, 2002.

Hussein ibn Ali, Sharif of Mecca
Born: ca. 1854–1856
Died: June 4, 1931

Sharif of Mecca and king of the Hejaz. Born at Constantinople sometime around 1856 into the Hashemite, traditionally held as descendants of Mohammed and therefore referred to with the honorific title of sharif, Hussein ibn Ali studied in Mecca from age eight. In 1893 Sultan Abdulhamid II required Hussein to travel to Constantinople and, although placing him on the Council of State, held him in virtual captivity until 1908 when Hussein was appointed sharif of Mecca on the death of his uncle Abdullah. By 1908 the Committee of Union and Progress (CUP) had come to control the government and initially promoted the Arabs as allies against the sultan. Hussein had long hoped for an independent Arab kingdom under his own rule. World War I provided that opportunity. In 1909 the counterrevolution against the CUP leaders in Constantinople caused them to turn against Arab nationalists in the Levant and leaders such as Hussein.

As early as February 1914, Hussein was in communication through his son Abdullah with British authorities in Cairo. Abdullah met with then British high commissioner in Egypt Lord Kitchener and told him that the Arabs were prepared to revolt against

Hussein ibn Ali, king of the Hejaz and sharif of Mecca, leaving his palace in Amman in the Hejaz Kingdom on April 3, 1924. Ibn Ali proclaimed the independence of all Arabs from the Ottoman Empire in the Arab Revolt in 1916. (Bettmann/Corbis)

Constantinople if the British would pledge their support for such a move. The British remained skeptical until the Ottoman Empire's entrance into the war in October 1914. Kitchener was then secretary of state for war in London, and on his advice Sir Harold Wingate, British governor-general of the Sudan, and Sir Henry McMahon, high commissioner in Egypt, kept in touch with Hussein.

Meanwhile, in the spring of 1915 Hussein sent his third son, Emir Faisal, to Damascus to reassure Turkish authorities there of his loyalty but also to sound out Arab opinion. Faisal was moved by the profound discontent of the Arab population there and completely changed his views.

Hussein then entered into active negotiations with McMahon. Hussein promised to declare war on the Ottoman Empire and raise an Arab army to assist the British in return for British support for him as king of a postwar Pan-Arab state. On June 5, 1916, Hussein initiated the Arab Revolt, and on November 2 he proclaimed himself king of Arab lands, which caused the British government embarrassment with the French because of private negotiations then ongoing with the French and Russians about the disposition of the Middle East after the war. Finally, the Allies worked out a compromise by which they addressed Hussein as king of the Hejaz.

Hussein was the official leader of the Arab Revolt, and his four sons were in command of its forces that included rebels from the Turkish Army along with Bedouin fighters. Throughout the revolt, Hussein worried about the ambitions of Ibn Saud, a tribal ruler from Najd, today in the central portion of Saudi Arabia. McMahon's pledge to Hussein preceded by just six months the Sykes-Picot Agreement (1916) among the British, French, and Russian governments that represented a breach of the promises made to the Arabs. Hussein was profoundly upset when he learned of the Sykes-Picot Agreement in December 1917, exposed by the new Bolshevik government of Russia. He refused to sign the peace agreements at the end of the war in protest against the mandate system created by the Paris Peace Conference.

Hussein's son Faisal had led the revolt to the liberation of Syria, where he established a government and was generally well received by the Syrian people, but he was deposed by the French in August 1920. He then became king of Iraq under British protection. Son Abdullah became king of the newly created Transjordan. Hussein abdicated as king of the Hejaz to his son Ali when Ibn Saud conquered most of the Hejaz. Hussein went into exile in Cyprus and died in Amman, Transjordan, on June 4, 1931.

SPENCER C. TUCKER

See also

Abdullah I, King of Jordan; Ibn Saud, King of Saudi Arabia; McMahon-Hussein Correspondence; Ottoman Empire; Sykes-Picot Agreement; World War I, Impact of

References

Adelson, Roger. *London and the Invention of the Middle East: Money, Power, and War, 1902–1922.* New Haven, CT: Yale University Press, 1995.

Fromkin, David. *A Peace to End All Peace: The Fall of the Ottoman Empire and the Creation of the Modern Middle East.* New York: Avon, 1989.

Glubb, Sir John. *A Short History of the Arab Peoples.* New York: Dorset, 1969.

Hourani, Albert. *A History of the Arab Peoples.* Cambridge: Harvard University Press, 1991.

Kedourie, Elie. *In the Anglo-Arab Labyrinth: The McMahon-Husayn Correspondence and Its Interpretations.* Cambridge: Cambridge University Press, 1976.

Nevakivi, Jukka. *Britain, France and the Arab Middle East, 1914–1920.* London: Athlone, 1969.

Tauber, Eliezer. *The Arab Movements in World War I.* London: Frank Cass, 1993.

Husseini, Haj Amin al-
Born: ca. 1895
Died: July 4, 1974

Palestinian Arab nationalist, Muslim religious leader and scholar, and mufti of Jerusalem from 1921 to 1948 who vehemently opposed the creation of an Israeli state in Palestine. Haj Mohammad Amin al-Husseini was born in Jerusalem to an aristocratic family, probably in 1895, and studied religious law for a year at the al-Azhar University in Cairo. In 1913 he made the requisite pilgrimage to Mecca, which earned him the honorific title of haj. In 1919, he attended the

Haj Amin al-Husseini, Palestinian Arab nationalist, Muslim religious leader and scholar, and mufti of Jerusalem from 1921 to 1948. (Hulton Archive/Keystone/Getty Images)

Pan-Syrian Congress in Damascus, where he supported Emir Faisal's bid to be king of Greater Syria, which was to include Syria, Lebanon, Jordan, and Palestine.

The 1916 Sykes-Picot Agreement, however, precluded the establishment of a Greater Syria. Thus, al-Husseini abandoned Pan-Arabism centered around Damascus. Instead, he adhered to a Palestinian ideology that centered on the creation of a Palestinian entity revolving around Jerusalem.

In 1920, al-Husseini instigated an Arab attack against Jews in Jerusalem and was jailed by the British authorities who still held a mandate there. In 1921 when the existing mufti (a Muslim scholar who interprets Islamic holy law, the Sharia) died, Sir Herbert Samuel, Britain's first high commissioner in Palestine, pardoned al-Husseini and appointed him the new mufti. Al-Husseini also became president of the newly created Supreme Muslim Council, making him the most important religious and political leader of the Palestinian Arabs.

In 1937 al-Husseini expressed his solidarity with Nazi Germany, asking Berlin to oppose the establishment of an Israeli state, help stop Jewish immigration to Palestine, and provide arms to the Arabs. That same year, German SS officer Adolf Eichmann visited al-Husseini in Jerusalem. In response, the British government removed al-Husseini from the Supreme Muslim Council and sent him into exile in Syria.

Just before the start of World War II, al-Husseini went to Iraq, where in 1941 he supported the anti-British regime of Rashid Ali al-Gaylani. After the British removed al-Gaylani from power, al-Husseini fled to Germany disguised as a woman, which was a violation of Islamic law. He spent the remainder of the war organizing and recruiting Muslims in the Balkans, especially through radio broadcasts.

In 1946 al-Husseini escaped house arrest in Paris and fled to Egypt, where he lived until the 1960s. In 1948, Jordan's King Abdullah gave the title of mufti of Jerusalem to Hussam al-Din Jarallah. This allegedly angered al-Husseini. In 1948 he was proclaimed president of the All Palestine Government in Gaza. Recognized only by Egypt, Syria, Iraq, Lebanon, Saudi Arabia, and Lebanon, his government was completely dependent on Egyptian support, which was eventually withdrawn in 1959. He retired from public life after serving as president of the 1962 World Islamic Congress, which he had founded in 1931. Al-Husseini died in Lebanon on July 4, 1974.

MICHAEL R. HALL

See also

All Palestine Government; Israel; Jerusalem; Sykes-Picot Agreement; United Kingdom, Middle East Policy

References

Jbara, Taysir. *Palestinian Leader Hajj Amin Al-Husayni, Mufti of Jerusalem.* New York: Kingston Press, 1985.

Mattar, Philip. *The Mufti of Jerusalem.* New York: Columbia University Press, 1988.

I

Ibn Saud, King of Saudi Arabia
Born: November 26, 1880 (disputed)
Died: November 9, 1953

Founder and first king of the present-day Kingdom of Saudi Arabia (1932–1953). Abd al-Aziz ibn Abd al-Rahman al-Saud, more commonly known as Ibn Saud, was born in Riyadh, capital of the central Saudi Arabian emirate of Najd, probably on November 26, 1880, although birth dates given vary widely from 1875 to 1880. He was the son of Abd al-Rahman ibn Faisal al-Saud (1850–1928) and Sara bint Ahmad al-Sudairi, the daughter of a powerful clan leader from Central Arabia. Ibn Saud received a traditional religious Islamic education and was trained in martial arts and traditional skills such as riding, tracking, shooting, and fencing.

The al-Saud family was ousted from power in 1891 by the al-Rashid clan of the northern emirate of Hail. Between 1891 and 1902 the deposed Emir Abd al-Rahman and his family lived in exile in Kuwait. Leading a daring expedition, young Ibn Saud succeeded in recapturing Riyadh in January 1902. When his father Abd al-Rahman declined to reassume the position of emir, Ibn Saud became the dynasty's new ruler.

The first decade of Ibn Saud's reign required that he reestablish authority over Najd, which had come under the control of the rival al-Rashid clan during the al-Saud family's years in exile. Ibn Saud accomplished this through a mixed policy of armed force, negotiations, and forging marriage alliances with important nomadic Bedouin tribes and settled clans. By 1913 he was in a position to shift his attention to the Persian Gulf coast, which was then controlled by the Ottoman Empire. He succeeded in ousting the Ottomans from Al-Hasa Province and established regular contacts with the British. For their part, the British maintained permanent diplomatic representations in Kuwait and other Gulf emirates.

In the run-up to the fighting and during World War I, Ibn Saud sought to establish himself as the leading ally of the British on the Arabian Peninsula. The British wanted this also in order to secure the neutrality of the leader of the Najd during their own military operations in Mesopotamia. In the subsequent friendship treaty of December 26, 1915, the British recognized Ibn Saud as ruler of the Najd and its dependencies, agreed to protect him against his external enemies, and granted him an annual subsidy. In return, Ibn Saud agreed to maintain friendly relations with Britain, not to alienate any part of his kingdom to a foreign power, and to refrain from attacking British-supported Gulf coast sheikdoms.

Although Ibn Saud did not take arms against the Turks, he also did not respond to the Sultan's call for a jihad (holy war). As a consequence, the Turks were not able to receive supplies by sea from the Persian Gulf coast. He was also free to fight his archenemies, the pro-Ottoman al-Rashid clan.

By the end of World War I, Ibn Saud's policies had yielded considerable dividends. He consolidated his control over the tribes and settlements in central Arabia and ousted the Ottomans from their positions along the Persian Gulf. He also outmaneuvered the al-Rashid clan, reducing their authority to their northern capital of Hail. When this last stronghold of the al-Rashid clan fell in 1921, Ibn Saud turned against the newly established Hashemite Kingdom of Hejaz. After taking the holy cities of Mecca and Medina, he was proclaimed king of the Hejaz in 1926. By the 1930s the new king had also extended his authority over the Asir and Najran regions adjacent to Yemen.

During 1928–1930 the king's authority was challenged by revolting Bedouin irregulars known as the Ikhwan. They had been

Abd al-Aziz ibn Abd al-Rahman al-Saud, founder and first king of the present-day Kingdom of Saudi Arabia (1932–1953). (Library of Congress)

instrumental to Saudi conquests but were effectively disbanded to secure peaceful relations with neighboring countries. Following the capture or execution of the Bedouin ringleaders, Ibn Saud became the unchallenged king of the unified Kingdom of Saudi Arabia in 1932.

Oil was discovered in the country's Eastern Province in 1938, but the full exploitation of this new resource was interrupted by World War II. In the course of the war, Ibn Saud joined the Allied cause for pragmatic rather than principled reasons because Britain and, since the start of oil exploration, the United States as well had been bankrolling him for decades. As a result of his rapidly declining health and inexperience with the growing complexities of international relations and state finances, Ibn Saud became an increasingly passive ruler while also not passing the necessary authority to others.

On February 14, 1945, Ibn Saud met with President Franklin D. Roosevelt on board the heavy cruiser USS *Quincy*, and this marked the symbolic beginning of the postwar strategic partnership between the United States and Saudi Arabia. With respect to its alleged immediate purpose of obtaining Ibn Saud's agreement to a huge increase in the settlement of Jewish refugees in Palestine, the meeting was a failure.

Ibn Saud consistently held to the position that the Palestinians should not be made to pay the price for the sufferings inflicted on the Jews by others. Although he withdrew more and more from daily politics in the last decade of his reign, his position did not waver from the unreserved support given to Arab interests. With the aging king withdrawing further into the background, it was Prince Faisal (1906–1975) who became the architect of Saudi foreign policy. While the Saudis were upset by the American endorsement of the State of Israel, which in their view was a violation of Roosevelt's pledge not to act contrary to Arab interests, they took care to preserve their relationship with the United States. With oil production being mainly conducted by American companies, the United States took over Britain's position as the paymaster of Saudi Arabia's treasury.

Ibn Saud died in Taif on November 9, 1953, leaving 48 sons and an unknown number of daughters. His oldest surviving son, Saud, succeeded him.

CAROOL KERSTEN

See also

Ottoman Empire; Roosevelt, Franklin Delano; Saudi Arabia

References

Al-Sa'ud, Abdul Aziz al-Saud. *The Holy Quran and the Sword: Selected Addresses, Speeches, Memoranda and Interviews.* 4th ed. Edited by Mohydin al-Qabesi. Riyadh: Saudi Desert House for Publications and Distribution, 2002.

Armstrong, H. C. *Lord of Arabia.* London: Arthur Barker, 1934.

De Gaury, Gerald. *Arabia Felix.* London: George Harrap, 1947.

Lacey, Robert. *The Kingdom.* London: Hutchinson, 1981.

Philby, H. St. J. B. *Arabian Jubilee.* London: Robert Hale, 1952.

Van der Meulen, Daniel. *The Wells of Ibn Saud.* New York: Praeger, 1957.

Vassiliev, Alexei. *The History of Saudi Arabia.* London: Saqi, 1998.

Imam

The term "imam" has multiple meanings, including "leader" or "leader of prayer" and the "ultimate leader" of the Muslim community. The use of the term also differs between Shia Islam and Sunni Islam. Early texts referred to the imam of the Muslims as the person who had inherited the Prophet Muhammad's spiritual authority, although his leadership and political authority passed on to a caliph (khalifa). As the theology of Shia Islam developed, the doctrine of the imamate (a'ima) developed, namely that an infallible spiritual knowledge ('ilm) resided in the imam, designated by his predecessor going back to Ali ibn Abu Talib, which he passed on to the next imam. These individuals are therefore the absolute religious authority and, when on Earth, are superior to the temporal authority (which was held by caliphs and later emirs and sultans). The Twelver Shia, found in Iran, Lebanon, and Iraq, believe that a line of 12 imams existed, although the last imam disappeared and is in occultation, neither dead nor alive, and will appear on the Day of Judgment. Other branches of Shiism (the Zaydis and Ismailis) hold to a different number and personage of the imams.

Sunni Muslims do not accept the doctrine of the imamate. For Sunnis today, the term "imam" may refer simply to the person who leads prayers in any group. Sometimes a particular imam is appointed to a mosque and carries the title. "Imam" is also an honorific title, which for Shia may be applied to a cleric, scholar, or jurist. Sunni figures may also be referred to with such an honorific, for instance, one associated with the four Sunni schools of Islamic jurisprudence.

PAUL G. PIERPAOLI JR. AND SHERIFA ZUHUR

See also
Shia Islam; Sunni Islam

References

Halm, Heinz. *Shi'a Islam: From Religion to Revolution.* Princeton, NJ: Markus Wiener, 1997.
Nasr, Seyyed Hossein. *Islam: Religion, History, and Civilization.* New York: HarperCollins, 2003.

Immigration to Palestine/Israel

Jewish immigration to Palestine was central to the ideology of the Zionist movement from its official inception in 1897. Israel represents an interesting case in immigration because the return of Diaspora Jews began long before the establishment of an independent state (in 1948), which was able to regulate immigration on the basis of its own laws. Since the early days of the Zionist movement, immigration of Jews to Palestine—later Israel—was conceived of in the ideological terms of aliya, literally meaning "going up." Of course, Jewish immigration to Palestine (and later Israel) also created monumental problems for Palestinian Arabs, who believed, with justification, that the land belonged to them as well.

By 1922, early ideological immigration to Palestine by mainly European pioneers accounted for the presence of 83,704 Jews in British-mandated Palestine, which, at the time, was populated by almost 700,000 Palestinian Arabs. The census taken on March 31, 1947, a year before the creation of the Jewish state, showed that Jews had gone from making up 11.1 percent of the population in 1922 to 31.1 percent, or 649,500 of 1.95 million inhabitants. This situation had been brought about by five successive waves of Jewish immigration between 1882 and 1936. Until 1932, these immigrants consisted mainly of ideological Zionists originating in Eastern Europe, in particular Russia, Romania, and Poland. These early waves of immigration were accompanied largely by a settling of the land by means of collective agricultural settlement, even in the form of kibbutzim or moshavim. Those who arrived after 1932 tended to focus on building the area's urban centers.

The period from 1933 to 1939 brought about a sizable inflow of Central European and German Jews, who were fleeing Nazi persecution. After 1933, however, this immigration was officially constrained under the British Mandate. Clandestine or illegal immigration took place, especially after 1936, as a result of Zionist activity to bring German Jews to Palestine. An underground military organization, the Haganah (1920–1948), and the Af-al-pi (Despite) project operated in spite of British restrictions and official opposition to clandestine immigration under the Jewish Agency (the prestate Jewish leadership). The Jewish Agency itself refused to violate British Mandate regulations regarding visas and certificates for entry into Palestine out of fear of jeopardizing official channels.

Its control over entry into Palestine was opposed by a number of organizations, including Irgun Tsvai Leumi (National Military Organization) leader Vladimir Jabotinsky, who advocated illegal entry toward the aim of what he called free immigration.

The period of immigration between 1939 and 1948, known as Aliya Bet (Immigration B), was characterized by illegal immigration organized covertly by activists in Palestine, mainly those in the Yishuv (settlement), together with partisans and Zionist youth groups in Europe and the Middle East. A small number of visas were also issued under the 1939 British White Paper quota. From 1945 to 1948 the British quotas were extremely restrictive, and many boats carrying Jewish immigrants were sent back and their passengers interned on Cyprus.

Following the founding of the State of Israel in May 1948, a period of mass migration took place through 1951. The arrival of nearly 700,000 Jews during this time period doubled the total Jewish population in the nascent state, bringing it to 1.4 million. However, this ran concurrently with a nearly equal Palestinian Arab immigration, brought about by the expulsion of some 760,000 Palestinian Arabs, most of whom became refugees in neighboring Arab countries, and the destruction of many of their villages. This lasted for almost two years and took place in two waves, from December 1947 to March 1948 and from April to June 1948.

The period 1948–1951 was also characterized by a shift in the demography of the Jewish population. Until 1948, 90 percent of the Jewish immigrants to Palestine originated in Europe. Although many of those immigrating after May 15, 1948, were European Holocaust survivors, by 1951 the percentage of Mizrahim (Oriental) Jews from Asia and Africa had increased from 12 percent to 33 percent, or by some 300,000 individuals. The very mission of the new state was based on the principle of Jewish immigration, or what was referred to as the ingathering of exiles. The fact that many new arrivals at this time came without capital or property added to the ideological nature of immigration as conceived by the state's founders. Absorption is a key Zionist concept, and a Ministry for Absorption aimed to provide Jewish immigrants with housing, Hebrew-language training, and a panoply of financial measures to ease their integration.

The principle of free Jewish immigration at the core of Zionist ideology was institutionalized by the 1950 Law of Return. The law stated that every Jew had the right to settle in Israel and that all Jews had an automatic right to citizenship. Jews are defined as those born to a Jewish mother or who have converted to Judaism. Some in Israel do not recognize conversions to Reform or Conservative Judaism, but, regardless, all Jews might claim Israeli citizenship.

The Law of Return continues to be a source of contention to the present day. It has come under attack mainly from those arguing for a Palestinian right of return that would recognize the dispossession of the Palestinian people following 1948 and accord the same right to Palestinians as that currently held only by Jews to return to their land. It has also been critiqued in recent times by those arguing for a multicultural Israeli state no longer exclusively based on Jewish citizenship.

Jewish immigrants arriving at Haifa in 1929. (Hulton-Deutsch Collection/Corbis)

Following the foundational period of Israeli nation-building (1948–1951) and the institutionalization of the Law of Return as the basis for Israeli citizenship, immigration to the state was characterized by several distinct periods. The first of these stretched from 1952 to 1966. During this time, immigration declined. The period was characterized by significant demographic changes brought about by the arrival of North African Jews, mainly Moroccans, who helped bring about an ethnic transformation of the Jewish state.

The immigration of the Mizrahim has proven to be the most problematic in Israel's history because it sharply highlighted the extent to which the state's public political culture was defined by an elite Ashkenazi (European Jewish) vision. The mainly Moroccan-born arrivals added to the Jewish populations originating from Yemen, Bulgaria, and Iraq that had come to Israel during the previous period of mass immigration. The 1950s and 1960s saw rising numbers of Mizrahim, with a younger population and a higher birthrate, and the proportion of Mizrahim equaled that of Ashkenazim by the early 1970s. Mizrahi Jews, however, and in particular

the North Africans, were frequently stigmatized in Israeli society. Housed in transit camps upon their arrival, they were subsequently sent to so-called development towns often far from the urban centers on confiscated Palestinian lands. Here they generally worked in unskilled labor for low pay and at constant risk of unemployment. Culturally, they were seen as inferior by the Ashkenazi elite, and attempts were made to strip them of their Arabic cultural heritage and impose upon them a European vision of modernized Israeli Jewry.

It was in relation to Mizrahim that the sentiment was publicly expressed in Israel for the second time that immigration may not always constitute a good in itself. Mizrahim reactions to this subjugation began with uprisings against unequal housing conditions in Wadi Salib, a formerly Arab district of Haifa that had become an overpopulated slum inhabited mainly by Moroccans. By the end of the 1960s, Mizrahic discontent was solidified in an outgrowth of the Black Panther organization, the so-called Black Jews, who spoke out against Ashkenazi domination and the idea, expressed, for

Yemeni immigrants traveling by train to the Atlit reception camp, March 1943. (Zoltan Kluger/Israeli Government Press Office)

example, by Israel's first prime minister, David Ben-Gurion, that non-European Jews were devoid of culture and education.

After 1967, the character of immigration changed once more. Economic development made Israel much less a haven for Jews fleeing persecution and more a destination for economic improvement. Furthermore, following Israel's victory in the 1967 Six-Day War, some 200,000 Jews from North America, South Africa, Australia, Latin America, and Western Europe were ideologically motivated to immigrate to the country. The occupation of the West Bank and the Gaza Strip and the annexation of the Golan Heights in 1967 created more Palestinian refugees, and the ideological immigrants, many of whom held right-wing religious beliefs, established settlements there. It was only in later years, as these expanded, that the occupied territories came to be populated also by groups that were not ideologically motivated but instead encouraged mainly by cheap housing and other subsidies. The individuals who made up this wave of immigrants often left property and family in their countries of origin, preferring to come to Israel on tourist visas or as temporary residents with a view to returning should their aliya fail. As a result, 50 percent of those arriving in the period between June 1969 and October 1970 returned to their countries of origin. Thus, a gradual normalization of immigration occurred in the Israeli context as unemployment or housing concerns began to figure more prominently in immigration decisions.

The ideological commitment to immigration was once again fulfilled by the arrival of Soviet Jews in the 1970s. The Soviet Union, pressured by the United Nations (UN) Committee on Human Rights, permitted 150,000 Jews to leave for Israel. The Soviet Jews arriving in the early 1970s were met with great enthusiasm. The post-1967 Ashkenazi immigration began a trend, lasting until the present day, in which the number of first- and second-generation Mizrahis declined and the number of their Ashkenazi counterparts stabilized. Furthermore, 16 percent of the population was defined as of Israeli origin, that is, born to Israeli-born fathers, by 1983.

Ethiopian Jews formed another minority in Jewish immigration to Israel in the post-1967 period. They arrived in two airlift operations in 1984 and 1991. Numbering approximately 80,000 people, the Ethiopian Jews were mainly housed in absorption centers in development towns upon their arrival. Several thousand now live in settlement towns in the occupied territories, although they face racism and discrimination.

The most well-known and numerically significant of the recent immigration waves to Israel is that of the Jews of the former Soviet Union. Between 1990 and 1998, 879,486 immigrants, many of them from the former Soviet Union, entered the country, representing an Israeli population growth rate of 19.3 percent. The majority of these arrived before 1993, making a significant impact on the Israeli society and economy. The Israeli approach toward this new immigration differed significantly from that adopted in the past. The state implemented a policy of direct absorption that eliminated state intervention in housing, education, and employment matters. This mass immigration triggered economic growth especially, for example, in the construction industry, pulling the country out of recession. Although unemployment decreased by 1996, immigrants were not always employed according to their qualifications. Soviet immigrants were generally highly educated, many of them holding professional qualifications, and the demand for their skills was not high.

The Soviet immigrants of the 1990s, unlike their predecessors who emigrated from the Soviet Union in the 1970s, were not, for the most part, motivated by ideology but rather by the promise of a better standard of living. Moreover, a significant proportion were not Jewish themselves but were admitted under the Law of Return because they had Jewish relatives. This has led to a significant backlash against them, in particular by the religious right-wing, elements of which even call for their repatriation. Other elements of Israeli society mock Soviet immigrants and their customs and habits. In reaction, or because of their relatively recent immigration, many Soviet immigrants have not wholeheartedly adopted an Israeli identity but have retained their own customs and, most important, continue to speak Russian. Russian has thus unofficially become the country's third language after Hebrew and Arabic. In the south of the country, it is far more prevalent than English, and immigration programs, social services, and even medical care are either designed for Russian-speakers or can serve them. The immigrants of the former Soviet Union are also very well organized politically.

Soviet immigration was accompanied by one other development in the history of Israeli immigration: the arrival of foreign migrant workers in the early 1990s. Migrants from Thailand, the Philippines, Romania, China, and Bulgaria, among others, started to arrive following Israel's decision to seal the border with the West Bank and the Gaza Strip occupied territories in 1993. Once this was done, Palestinian blue-collar workers were no longer able to freely access their workplaces in Israel. Although it was hoped for a time that Soviet immigrants would fill the place of Palestinian workers, it soon became apparent that the mostly overqualified Russians, with some exceptions, did not want menial labor. Recent figures show that there are an estimated 300,000 migrant workers in Israel, representing 13 percent of the workforce. Of these, at least two-thirds (Africans, Asians, and Latin Americans, in particular) are illegally residing in Israel, having entered the country as tourists, or have expired work permits. The Knesset has passed a resolution that by 2008, Palestinians from the occupied territories may not come into Israel for work; hence an anticipated labor shortage may well prolong a trend of foreign workers.

PAUL G. PIERPAOLI JR.

See also

Aliya Bet; Ashkenazic Judaism; Expellees and Refugees, Palestinian; Holocaust; Kibbutz Movement; Law of Return; Mizrahic Judaism; Moshavim; Right of Return, Palestinian; Soviet Jews, Immigration to Israel; Zionism

References

Cohen, Yinon. "From Haven to Hell: Changing Patterns of Immigration to Israel." Pp. 36–53 in *Challenging Ethnic Citizenship: German and Israeli Perspectives on Immigration,* edited by Daniel Levy and Yfaat Weiss. Oxford: Berghahn, 2002.

Morris, Benny. *The Birth of the Palestinian Refugee Problem Revisited.* 2nd ed. Cambridge: Cambridge University Press, 2004.

Zertal, Idith. *From Catastrophe to Power: Holocaust Survivors and the Emergence of Israel.* Berkeley: University of California Press, 1998.

Improvised Explosive Devices

Improvised explosive devices (IEDs) have been employed in warfare almost since the introduction of gunpowder. They remain the weapon of choice for insurgent and resistance groups that lack the numerical strength and firepower to conduct conventional operations against an opponent. IEDs are the contemporary form of booby traps employed in World War II and the Vietnam War. Traditionally they are used primarily against enemy armor and thin-skinned vehicles.

A water cart filled with explosives was employed in a futile effort to assassinate Napoleon Bonaparte in Paris as he traveled to the opera on Christmas Eve 1800. The emperor escaped injury, but the blast killed the little girl the conspirators paid to hold the horse's bridle and killed or maimed a dozen other people. In more recent times, IEDs have been employed against civilian targets by Basque separatists and the Irish Republican Army. Molotov cocktails, or gasoline bombs, are one form of IED. The largest, most deadly IEDs

in history were the U.S. jetliners hijacked by Al Qaeda on September 11, 2001, and used to attack the World Trade Center in New York City and the Pentagon in Washington, D.C.

IEDs became one of the chief weapons employed by insurgents and terrorists against Israel as well as the chief weapon used by insurgents during the Iraq War (2003) and its aftermath to attack U.S. forces and Iraqi police to carry out sectarian violence. The simplest type of IED was a hand grenade, rigged artillery shell, or bomb triggered by a trip-wire or simple movement. It might be as simple as a grenade with its pin pulled and handle held down by the weight of a corpse. When the corpse was raised, the grenade exploded. Bombs and artillery shells are also used as IEDs. Such weapons may be exploded remotely by wireless detonators in the form of garage door openers and two-way radios or infrared motion sensors. More powerful explosives and even shaped charges can be used to attack armored vehicles. Casualty totals are one way to judge the effectiveness of a military operation, and growing casualties from IEDs in the 1980s and 1990s induced the Israeli Army to withdraw from southern Lebanon.

SPENCER C. TUCKER

See also

Antitank Weapons; Molotov Cocktail

References

Crippen, James B. *Improvised Explosive Devices (IED).* New York: CRC Press, 2007.

DeForest, M. J. *Principles of Improvised Explosive Devices.* Boulder, CO: Paladin, 1984.

Tucker, Stephen. *Terrorist Explosive Sourcebook: Countering Terrorist Use of Improvised Explosive Devices.* Boulder, CO: Paladin, 2005.

Intermediate-Range Ballistic Missiles

See Missiles, Intermediate-Range Ballistic

International Red Cross

An organization devoted to the prevention and alleviation of human suffering and the promotion of humanitarian law. The International Red Cross is a private institution governed by Swiss law, but acts in the international field as the International Committee of the Red Cross (ICRC) or through its National Societies of the Red Cross.

In 1859 a young Swiss philanthropist, Henri Dunant (1828–1910), was horrified by the aftermath of a bloody battle in Solferino, Italy, in which 40,000 men lay dead or dying. He resolved to create national relief societies to assist those wounded in war. In 1863 he and 4 other citizens of Geneva created the International and Permanent Committee for Relief to Wounded Military Personnel. This organization was designed to be a universal movement that would operate through a series of national relief committees in individual countries. The International Geneva Conference, held on August 22, 1863, created these national committees.

The International Red Cross, as founder of the International Red Cross Movement, holds the authority to recognize Red Cross National Societies. The ICRC recognizes the National Society of any country on condition that its government has first recognized it and signed the Geneva Conventions. The organization expanded rapidly from its original 7 National Societies in 1864 to 21 in 1869, 37 in 1899, and 62 in 1939.

The 1864 Geneva Convention for the amelioration of the condition of the wounded in armies in the field authorized care for the wounded and defined medical services offered on the battlefield as neutral. This convention was initially adopted by 12 governments and created a precedent in international humanitarian law. Dunant was awarded the first Nobel Peace Prize in 1901 for his efforts, and the International Red Cross has won this prize on two additional occasions.

This new organization adopted a symbol that was designed to place the wounded and those caring for them under a protective sign. This symbol, an inversion of the Swiss flag, is used to mark the neutrality of medical and relief personnel, sick and wounded military personnel, and locations that house the sick and wounded, such as hospitals and ambulances.

In 1867 the first International Conference of the Red Cross was held, and the organization became formally known as the International Committee of the Red Cross. With the Hague Conventions of 1899 and the creation of bodies to administer relief to the sick, the wounded, and prisoners of war, the ICRC also underwent changes. The ICRC drafted its first statutes in 1915 and revised them four times before 1945 (in 1921, 1928, 1930, and 1939). Initially, the founding members of the ICRC acted as the assembly responsible for the general conduct of affairs, the administrative infrastructure, and the delegates in the field. Gradually, however, three separate levels of decision making were formed as the organization grew in size and scope.

The ICRC has played an active role in most of the major crises of the past 140 years, and its work falls into three broad categories: maintaining a presence in a theater of conflict to provide care and aid to the sick and wounded, the transmission and delivery of aid, and visitations to prisoners of war and other detainees. Although the ICRC originally adopted no mandate to act directly in theaters of conflict, preferring that this work be carried out by its National Societies, it progressively became involved in areas of protection and assistance to victims of war. The ICRC first sent its delegates into the field during the Balkan War of 1912. During World War I, it became involved in the delivery of aid to sick and wounded military personnel and civilians alike. The scale of the humanitarian disaster caused by war required the mobilization of the entire Red Cross Movement, which was repeated during World War II.

The need for close cooperation between National Societies during World War I led American Red Cross president Henry Davidson to suggest a federation of Red Cross National Societies. The League of Red Cross Societies was thus created in 1919. This league enabled the National Societies to improve communication and coordination and to retain the volunteer and knowledge base that they had accumulated during wartime. The goals of its founding member societies of Britain, France, Italy, Japan, and the United States were to strengthen and unite the already-existing Red Cross Societies in the area of public health and to promote the creation of new societies.

In October 1983 the league was renamed the League of Red Cross and Red Crescent Societies, which became the International Federation of Red Cross and Red Crescent Societies in 1991. The Red Crescent is the name for the organization in Muslim states. There are 183 recognized National Societies, and the federation mounts on average more than 80 relief operations yearly.

In addition to reacting to situations of need, the Red Cross has acted to limit the destructive capabilities of states. The ICRC agitated against the use of chemical weapons during World War I, and the Geneva Protocol of June 17, 1925, prohibited the use in war of asphyxiating toxic and similar gases and of bacteriological means. Since the end of the Cold War, the ICRC has passed protocols and conventions relating to the rights of individuals, the prohibition of various types of weapons, and the Rome Statute of the International Criminal Court, among others.

The complexity of modern warfare and the humanitarian disasters it has wrought have led to the recognition that the ICRC needs to freely act in many countries around the globe. To this end, the Diplomatic Conference 2005 adopted the Third Additional Protocol to create an additional emblem alongside the red cross and red crescent. The red crystal, formally adopted in December 2006, appears as a red frame in the shape of a square on edge on a white background. The adoption of this emblem was intended to provide a lasting solution to the religious and political symbolism inherent in the red cross and red crescent. The red crystal was adopted to represent no other principles but those put forward in the 1965 Proclamation of the Fundamental Principles of the Red Cross: humanity, impartiality, neutrality, independence, and voluntary service.

Throughout the various Arab-Israeli wars since 1948, the International Red Cross maintained a constant presence in the Middle East. When not responding to shooting wars, it administered aid to millions of expellees, refugees, prisoners of war, and homeless and displaced civilians. It has maintained effective operations designed to mitigate the suffering of Palestinians for decades.

TRISTA GRANT

See also

Al-Mawasi; Bernadotte, Folke; Deir Yassin Massacre; Israeli Security Fence; Marshall, George Catlett; NACHSHON, Operation; Sabra and Shatila Massacre; Star of David; United Nations, Role of; World Jewish Congress

References

Hutchison, John F. *Champions of Charity: War and the Rise of the Red Cross.* Boulder, CO: Westview, 1996.

Moorehead, Caroline. *Dunant's Dream: War, Switzerland and the History of the Red Cross.* New York: Carroll and Graf, 1998.

Willemin, Georges, and Roger Heacock. *The International Committee of the Red Cross.* Boston: M. Nijhoff, 1984.

Intifada, First
Start Date: December 1987
End Date: September 1993

A spontaneous protest movement by Palestinians against Israeli rule and an effort to establish a Palestinian homeland through a series of demonstrations, improvised attacks, and riots. The First Intifada (literally, "shaking off") began in December 1987 and ended in 1993 with the signing of the Oslo Accords and the creation of the Palestinian Authority (PA).

The founding of Israel in 1948 created a situation in which Palestinians and citizens of the new Israeli state suddenly found themselves occupying a single body of land but under Israeli control. This basic reality would remain the most contentious issue in the region for decades to come. It also led to an emerging Palestinian national consciousness calling for Israel's destruction. Such anti-Israeli sentiment was generally shared by other Arab nations and by the Arab world at large, and material and military support often followed suit. While the Palestinians had not resisted under the repressive measures of the 1950s and 1960s, their treatment became even worse later, especially with the ascendance of the Likud Party in Israel. Many Palestinians, and especially the young, became

more convinced of the need for resistance from 1968 to the early 1970s; then just as Palestinians experienced even poorer treatment, more property encroachment, and more difficulties, their leadership moved toward negotiation as a strategy. By the time of the intifada, most Palestinians had experienced or knew those who had experienced Israel's de jure or de facto draconian civil and criminal enforcement practices including torture, summary executions, mass detentions, and the destruction of property and homes.

In 1987 strained relations between Palestinians and Israelis were pushed to the limit when, on October 1, Israeli soldiers ambushed and killed seven Palestinian men from Gaza alleged to have been members of the Palestinian terrorist organization Islamic Jihad. Days later, an Israeli settler shot a Palestinian schoolgirl in the back. With violence against Israelis by Palestinians also on the increase, a wider conflict may have been inevitable.

The tension only mounted as the year drew to a close. On December 4, an Israeli salesman was found murdered in Gaza. On December 6, a truck driven by the Israel Defense Forces (IDF) struck a van, killing its four Palestinian occupants. That same day, sustained and heavy violence involving several hundred Palestinians took place in the Jabalya refugee camp, where the four Palestinians who died in the traffic accident had lived. The unrest spread quickly and eventually involved other refugee camps. By the end of Decem-

Palestinian women demonstrating during a protest on February 27, 1988, in Ramallah, West Bank, during the First Intifada. (Patrick Robert/Sygma/Corbis)

FIRST INTIFADA, 1987 – 1991

● Principal Arab towns
○ Arab villages
— The "Green" Line, the Israel-Jordan border, 1949–1967
■ Main prisons in which, at different times during the Intifada, 80,000 Arabs were detained at least 48 hours

ber, the violence had made its way to Jerusalem. The Israelis reacted with a heavy hand, which did nothing but fan the fires of Palestinian outrage. On December 22, 1987, the United Nations (UN) Security Council officially denounced the Israeli reaction to the unrest, which had taken the lives of scores of Palestinians.

The result of the escalating spiral of violence was the intifada, a series of Palestinian protests, demonstrations, and ad hoc attacks whose manifestations ranged from youths throwing rocks at Israeli troops to demonstrations by women's organizations. While quite spontaneous at first, a shadowy organization, the Unified Leadership of the Intifada, emerged, issuing directives via numbered statements. Along with a series of general strikes and boycotts, the demonstrations caused such disruption to the Israeli state that the government responded with military force. Heated tensions proved a hotbed for further violence, which led to increasingly violent reprisals on both sides. While the Palestinians had begun by relying on rocks and superior numbers under the auspices of the Unified Leadership, they were soon throwing Molotov cocktails and grenades as well as simply burning tires and using spray paint to write graffiti of the intifada. Israeli rules were such that the Palestinian flag and its colors were banned, so these were displayed by the demonstrators. In the meantime, Israeli defense minister Yitzhak Rabin exhorted the IDF to "break the bones" of demonstrators. Rabin's tactics resulted in more international condemnation and a worsening relationship with Washington, which had

already been on the skids. Moshe Arens, who succeeded Rabin in the Ministry of Defense in 1990, seemed better able to understand both the root of the uprising and the best ways of subduing it. Indeed, the number of Palestinians and Israelis killed declined during the period from 1990 to 1993. However, the intifada itself seemed to be running out of steam after 1990, perhaps because so many Palestinian men were in prison by then.

Despite continued violence on the part of Hamas (Islamic Resistance Movement), on September 13, 1993, Rabin, now prime minister, and Palestine Liberation Organization (PLO) chairman Yasser Arafat signed the historic Oslo Accords on the White House lawn. The accords, which brought both Rabin and Arafat the Nobel Peace Prize, called for a five-year transition period during which the Gaza Strip and the West Bank would be jointly controlled by Israel and the PA, with power eventually meant to be turned over to the Palestinian people.

The First Intifada caused both civil destruction and humanitarian suffering, but it also produced gains for the Palestinian people before it was brought to an end. First, it solidified and brought into focus a clear national consciousness for the Palestinian people and made statehood a clear national objective. Second, it cast Israeli policy toward Palestine in a very negative light on the world stage, especially the killing of Palestinian children. Third, it was seen by some Israelis to indicate that their primary struggle was with Palestinians and not all Arabs. Thus, it rekindled public and political dialogue on the Arab-Israeli conflict across Europe, in the United States, and in other Middle Eastern states. Fourth, the First Intifada threatened the leadership role of the PLO in Tunis, illustrating the self-mobilization of the population in the territories, leading eventually to friction between the Tunis old guard and younger leadership. Finally, it cost Israel hundreds of millions of dollars in lost imports and tourism.

At the time the Oslo Accords were signed in September 1993, the six-year-long intifada had resulted in well over 1,000 deaths, most of them Palestinian. It is believed that approximately 1,160 Palestinians died in the uprising, of which 241 were children. On the Israeli side, 160 died, 5 of whom were children. Clearly, the IDF's inexperience in widespread riot control had contributed to the high death toll, for in the first 13 months of the intifada alone, more than 330 Palestinians were killed. Indeed, the policies and performance of the IDF split Israeli public opinion on the handling of the intifada and also invited international scrutiny.

In more recent years, continued terrorist attacks by pro-Palestinian interests and Israeli control of the Palestinian territories long beyond the time line set by the Oslo Accords and the failure of the accords to proceed have caused unrest both in the international community and in Palestinian-Israeli relations. In 2000, a new wave of violent Palestinian protest broke out and would eventually become known as the Second (al-Aqsa) Intifada.

PAUL G. PIERPAOLI JR.

See also

Arafat, Yasser; Hamas; Intifada, Second; Islamic Jihad, Palestinian; Israel; Israel Defense Forces; Oslo Accords; Palestine Liberation Organization; Palestinian Authority; Palestinian Refugee Camps; Rabin, Yitzhak

References

Brynen, Rex, ed. *Echoes of the Intifada: Regional Repercussions of the Palestinian-Israeli Conflict.* Boulder, CO: Westview, 1991.

Farsoum, Samih K., and Naseer H. Aruri. *Palestine and the Palestinians: A Social and Political History.* 2nd ed. Jackson, TN: Westview, 2006.

Hudson, Michael C. *The Palestinians: New Directions.* Washington, DC: Center for Contemporary Arab Studies, Georgetown University, 1990.

Hunter, F. Robert. *The Palestinian Uprising: A War by Other Means.* Berkeley: University of California Press, 1991.

Peretz, Don. *Intifada: The Palestinian Uprising.* Boulder, CO: Westview, 1990.

Pines, Ayala M. "The Palestinian Intifada and Israelis' Burnout." *Journal of Cross-Cultural Psychology* 25(4) (December 1994): 414–438.

Said, W. Edward. *Intifada: The Palestinian Uprising against Israeli Occupation.* Boston: South End, 1989.

Schiff, Ze'ev, and Ehud Ya'ari. *Intifada: The Palestinian Uprising— Israel's Third Front.* New York: Simon and Schuster, 1990.

Intifada, Second

Start Date: September 28, 2000
End Date: 2004

A popular Palestinian uprising and period of enhanced Israeli-Palestinian hostilities that broke out in 2000 following the collapse of the Camp David peace talks that summer. The Second Intifada is also called the al-Aqsa Intifada because it began at the al-Aqsa Mosque in the Old City of Jerusalem. On September 28, 2000, Likud Party leader Ariel Sharon, accompanied by a Likud Party delegation and 1,500 police and security forces, entered and moved through the Haram al-Sharif complex, the area of Jerusalem's Old City also called the Temple Mount. There the al-Aqsa Mosque and the Dome of the Rock are located. The enclave is one of Islam's three most holy sites and is sacred to Jews as well. Many observant Jews will not walk on the Temple Mount for fear of desecrating the remnants of the Temple underneath it. Some Jewish and Christian organizations have called for the destruction of the Dome of the Rock or its transferal to an Arab country so that Jews can reclaim the site.

Sharon said that he was investigating Israeli complaints that Muslims were damaging archeological remains below the surface of the Temple Mount. By agreement, at that time the area was then supervised by Palestinian rather than Israeli security, with Israeli tour guides handing over their charges to their Arab counterparts during the times when the area was open to non-Muslims.

Palestinians believed that Sharon's actions demonstrated Israeli contempt for limited Palestinian sovereignty and for Muslims in general. Anger began to build as a result, and soon riots and demonstrations erupted. Israeli troops launched attacks in Gaza, and on September 30, 2000, television footage showed the shooting of an unarmed 12-year-old boy, Muhammad Durrah, hiding behind his father as Israeli forces attacked. Protests now grew more violent, involving Israeli Arabs as well as Palestinians. For the first time, stores and banks were burned in Arab communities. Thousands of Israelis also attacked Arabs and destroyed Arab property in Tel Aviv and Nazareth during the Jewish holiday of Yom Kippur. On October 12, two Israeli reservists were lynched by a mob at the Ramallah police station, further inflaming Israeli public opinion. In retaliation, Israel launched a series of air strikes against Palestinians.

On October 17 Israeli and Palestinian officials signed the Sharm al-Sheikh agreement to end the violence, but it continued nevertheless. Sharon's election as prime minister in February 2001 heightened Israel's hard-line tactics toward the Palestinians, such as the use of F-16 aircraft for the first time. Both Palestinians and Israelis admitted that the Oslo period was now over. Some Palestinians characterized their response as the warranted resistance of an embittered population that had received no positive assurances of sovereignty from years of negotiations. Others began or encouraged suicide attacks, also new to the situation, as in the June 1, 2001, attack on Israelis waiting to enter a Tel Aviv discotheque and another attack on a Jerusalem restaurant on August 9, 2001. While some attacks were claimed by various Palestinian organizations, the degree of organizational control over the bombers and issues such as payments made to the so-called martyrs' families remain disputed.

These attacks in public places terrified Israelis. Those in modest economic circumstances had to use public transportation, but most malls, movie theaters, stores, and day care centers hired secu-

Palestinian youths run for cover as Israeli tanks open fire during Palestinian clashes with Israeli soldiers during the Second (al-Aqsa) Intifada. The clash occurred in the southern Gaza village of al-Moghraqa near the Israeli Jewish settlement of Netzarim in the Gaza Strip on June 27, 2003. (Abid Katib/Getty Images)

rity guards. Israeli authorities soon began a heightened campaign of targeted killings, or assassinations, of Palestinian leaders. Some political figures began to call for complete segregation of Arabs and Israelis, even within the Green Line (the 1967 border). This would be enforced by a security wall and even population transfers, which would involve evicting Arab villagers and urban residents from Israel in some areas and forcing them to move to the West Bank.

A virulent campaign against Palestine Liberation Organization (PLO) chairman and Palestinian Authority (PA) president Yasser Arafat's leadership began in Israel with American assent, complicating any negotiations between the two sides. Arafat was charged with corruption and with supporting the intifada. Israelis argued that he had actually planned it, a less than credible idea to most professional observers. However, when the Israel Defense Forces (IDF) captured the ship *Santorini* filled with weapons purchased by Ahmad Jibril, head of the Popular Front for the Liberation of Palestine (PFLP) General Command (a PLO faction that did not accept the Oslo Accords), in May of 2001 and with the January 2002 capture of the *Karine-A,* a vessel carrying weapons allegedly from Iran, the anti-Arafat campaign increased.

The regional response to the al-Aqsa Intifada consisted of cautious condemnation by Egypt and Jordan, which had concluded

peace agreements with Israel, and calls of outrage from other more hard-line states such as Syria. In February 2002, Crown Prince Abdullah called for Arabs to fully normalize relations with Israel in return for Israeli withdrawal from the occupied territories. This plan was formally endorsed at an Arab League Summit in Beirut in March, although Israeli authorities prohibited Arafat from attending the summit. The proposal was never acknowledged by Israel.

Instead, in response to a suicide bomber's attack on the Netanya Hotel on March 28, 2002, in which 30 Israeli civilians died, the Israeli military began a major military assault on the West Bank. The PA headquarters were targeted, and international negotiations became necessary when militants took refuge in the Church of the Nativity in Bethlehem. Charges of a massacre in the IDF's onslaught on Jenin were investigated, showing a smaller death count of 55.

The Israeli military response to the intifada did not successfully convince Palestinians to relinquish their aims of sovereignty and seemed to spark more suicide attacks rather than discouraging them. In contrast, political measures and diplomacy produced some short interruptions in the violence, which gradually lengthened on the part of some Palestinian organizations and actors. In March 2003 Mahmoud Abbas, under pressure from Israel and the United States, became the first Palestinian prime minister of the PA because the

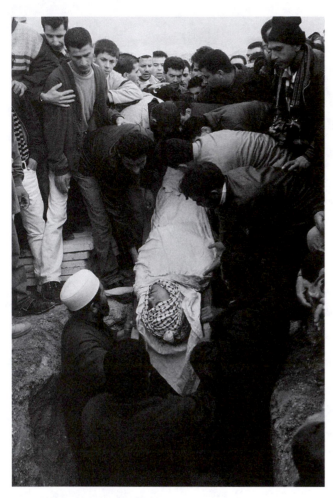

Family and friends mourn the death of 16-year-old Amar Mahnies, who was killed during clashes between the Israeli Army and Palestinians outside the al-Aqsa Mosque on December 8, 2000. The funeral took place at Beit Aoor on the West Bank. (Touhig Sion/Corbis Sygma)

United States refused to recognize or deal with Arafat. On April 30, 2003, the European Union (EU), the United States, Russia, and the United Nations (UN) announced the so-called Road Map to Peace that was to culminate in an independent Palestinian state.

The plan did not unfold as designed, however, and in response to an Israeli air strike intended to kill Abd al-Aziz Rantisi, the leader of Hamas, militants launched a bus bombing in Jerusalem. At the end of June 2003, Palestinian militants agreed to a *hudna* (truce), which lasted for seven weeks and longer on the part of certain groups. There was no formal declaration that the intifada had ceased, and additional Israeli assassinations of Palestinian leaders as well as suicide attacks continued. Nevertheless, since 2004 Hamas has respected the cease-fire, and the issues of Israeli withdrawal from Gaza, Arafat's November 2004 death, Palestinian elections, and the Israeli response to their outcome took the spotlight in late 2004 and throughout 2005.

Casualty numbers for the al-Aqsa Intifada are disputed. Approximately 1,000 Israelis had died, and 6,700 more were wounded by September 2004. By 2003 the Israelis reported that 2,124 Palestini-ans had been killed, but a U.S. source reported 4,099 Palestinians killed, 30,527 wounded by 2005. Israel's tourism sector has suffered a considerable decline at a time in which inflation and unemployment were already problematic.

An outcome of the al-Aqsa Intifada in the global context of the September 11, 2001, terror attacks on the United States was that Israeli officials have tended to brand all Palestinian resistance, indeed all activity on behalf of Palestinians, as being terrorism. This discourse and the heightened violence have lent credence to those who call for separation rather than integration of Israelis with Arabs. Therefore, the building of the security barrier known as the Israeli Security Fence, which effectively cuts thousands of Palestinians off from their daily routes to work or school, was widely supported by Israelis. Similarly, Sharon's idea of withdrawal from Gaza was essentially funded by this idea, but his government had to confront those who were unwilling to relinquish settlements in that area.

The intifada resulted in crisis and despair among some Israeli peace activists and discouraged many independent efforts by Israelis and Palestinians to engage the other. A 2004 survey showed that the numbers of Israelis in general who believed that the 1993 Oslo Peace Accords would lead to settlements declined during the intifada, and greater numbers believed that Israel should impose a military solution on the Palestinians. Such opinions may well have shifted, however, following Israeli attacks on Lebanon in the summer of 2006.

The intifada also had deleterious effects on Palestinians who had hoped for the blossoming of normalcy in the West Bank, particularly as 85 percent of those in Gaza and 58 percent in the West Bank live in poverty. Since the outbreak of the intifada, the IDF demolished 628 housing units in which 3,983 people had lived. Less than 10 percent of these individuals were implicated in any violence or illegal activity.

Another outcome of the intifada was its highlighting of intra-Palestinian conflict. This includes that between the Tunis PLO elements of the PA and the younger leaders who emerged within the occupied territories, between Fatah and Hamas, and between Fatah and the al-Aqsa Martyrs Brigades. Also evident were the difficulties of responding to Israeli demands for security when security for Palestinian citizens was not in force. Some Palestinian Israeli citizens have asserted their Palestinian identity for the very first time as a result of the intifada. The conflict most certainly caused discord in the Arab world as well.

SHERIFA ZUHUR

See also

Abbas, Mahmoud; Al-Aqsa Martyrs Brigades; Al-Aqsa Mosque; Arafat, Yasser; Church of the Nativity; Fatah; Gaza Strip; Hamas; Haram al-Sharif; Intifada, First; Jerusalem, Old City of; Oslo Accords; Palestine Liberation Organization; Palestinian Authority; Rantisi, Abd al-Aziz; Sharon, Ariel; Suicide Bombings; Terrorism; United States Coordinating and Monitoring Mission; West Bank

References

Baroud, Ramzy, et al. *The Second Palestinian Intifada: A Chronicle of a People's Struggle.* London: Pluto, 2006.

Bucaille, Laetitia. *Growing Up Palestinian: Israeli Occupation and the Intifada Generation.* Princeton, NJ: Princeton University Press, 2004.

Khalidi, Walid. "The Prospects of Peace in the Middle East." *Journal of Palestine Studies* 32 (Winter 2003): 50–63.

Reinhart, Tanya. *The Road Map to Nowhere: Israel/Palestine since 2003.* London: Verso, 2006.

Shulz, Helena Lindholm. "The al-Aqsa Intifada as a Result of Politics of Transition." *Arab Studies Quarterly* 24 (Fall 2002): 21–47.

Stork, Joe. "Erased in a Moment: Suicide Bombing Attacks against Israeli Civilians." *Human Rights Watch* (2002): 1–160.

Iran

Middle Eastern nation of 636,293 square miles, slightly larger than the U.S. state of Alaska. Iran is bordered by the Persian Gulf and the Gulf of Oman to the south; Turkey, Azerbaijan, the Caspian Sea, and Armenia to the north; Afghanistan and Pakistan to the east; and Iraq to the west. Iran has long been important because of its strategic location at the geographic nexus of the Middle East, Europe, and Southwest Asia. Its location captured the attention of both Britain and Russia in the 19th century, with each nation seeking to control the area. Rivalry over Iran continued in the early years of the Cold War as both the United States and the Soviet Union sought to control its oil resources.

Iran is predominantly a Shia Islam nation. However, Shiism did not become identified with the state until the Safavid Empire formed. The Shia were found in a variety of locations in the Middle East and South Asia, having originated in the Arabian Peninsula before the sect actually coalesced as such. Sunni Muslims comprise the great majority of Muslims in the Middle East and around the world, and Shia Iranians have periodically viewed the actions of Sunni-dominated governments as a direct threat to their economic, political, religious, and social well-being and independence.

In 1921 the Pahlavi dynasty was established in Iran by Shah Reza Pahlavi I, a military officer known first as Reza Khan, who led a coup against the last Qajar shah. A reformer and modernizer, Reza Shah instituted agricultural, economic, and educational reforms and began the modernization of the country's transportation system. In the end, these and other reforms threatened the status of the Shia clerics in Iran, who began to oppose the shah and his reforms. Desiring to stress the country's lengthy and imperial pre-Islamic tradition and so as to include Iranians who were not from Fars (the central province), Reza Pahlavi changed the country's name from Persia to Iran in 1935.

Reza Pahlavi's lack of cooperation with the Allies during World War II led to his forced abdication in 1941 in favor of his son, Mohammad Reza Pahlavi. During the war, Iran was occupied by

View of Tehran, the capital and largest city of Iran. (iStockphoto.com)

An antishah, anti–United States demonstration in January 1979, shortly after Mohammad Reza Shah Pahlavi left the country. (Patrick Chauvel/Sygma/Corbis)

Soviet and British forces in the north and south of the country, respectively, and was a key conduit for Lend-Lease supplies. The shah's strong ties to the West over the next four decades often meant economic difficulty for Iran. For example, during World War II the British-controlled Anglo Iranian Oil Company (AIOC) artificially deflated the price of oil to reduce the cost of the war to the British economy. Certainly, the shah's popularity declined because of his ties to the West.

Mohammad Mosaddeq, a member of the National Front Party (NFP), became prime minister in 1951 and soon became the shah's most prominent critic. Mosaddeq's persistent criticism of the regime's weak position vis-à-vis Britain led him to nationalize the British-owned AIOC in 1951, which Washington chose to see as a clear example of his communist tendencies. Britain responded by imposing an embargo on Iranian oil and blocking the export of products from the formerly British properties. Because Britain was Iran's primary oil consumer, this had a considerable impact on Iran. Mosaddeq then asked the shah to grant him emergency powers

that included direct control of the military. The shah refused, precipitating a domestic political crisis.

Mosaddeq understood the power of his popularity. He promptly resigned, causing widespread protests and demands that he be returned to power. Unnerved, in 1952 the shah reappointed Mosaddeq, who then took steps to consolidate his power. This included the implementation of land reforms and other measures, which to the West seemed socialist. Although Mosaddeq had not had any direct contact with the Soviets, the events in Iran were nevertheless of great concern to the United States, which feared a Soviet takeover (based on Soviet efforts to annex northern Iran at the end of World War II).

The United States refused Mosaddeq's repeated requests for financial aid because he refused to reverse the nationalization of the AIOC. By the summer of 1953, Mosaddeq's intransigence and his legalization of the leftist Tudeh Party led the United States to join Britain and the temporarily exiled shah in a covert August 1953 plot to overthrow Mosaddeq. Known as Operation AJAX, the coup against Mosaddeq was successful, and the shah was back in power by the end of August 1953. While the British were correct in viewing Mosaddeq as a threat to their position in Iran, the United States was incorrect in presuming that he was a communist. Rather, he was an Iranian nationalist who saw the income of Iranian farmers drop to $110 a year and witnessed many Iranians fall into abject poverty. He sought to ameliorate these conditions and establish a more independent foreign policy.

The decade that followed was marked by the creation in 1957 of the Sazeman-e Ettelaat va Amniyat-e Keshvar (SAVAK, National Information and Security Organization), the shah's dreaded secret police, and a number of failed economic reforms. Iranian economic policy was similar to that of many other developing nations, which showed preference to large state projects over a true free-market economy. Predictably, the largely state-run economy failed to perform as promised. This and pressure by the West finally led the shah to propose the White Revolution, which called for land reform, privatization of government-owned firms, electoral reform, women's suffrage, the nationalization of forests, rural literacy programs, and profit sharing for industrial workers. The shah hoped that such ambitious measures would spark economic growth and mitigate growing criticism of his regime. The White Revolution proved far less than revolutionary. That same year also witnessed a brutal crackdown on Iranian dissidents and fundamentalist clerics, which did nothing to endear the shah to his own people.

Ayatollah Ruhollah Khomeini, a conservative Muslim cleric, became the shah's most prominent opponent in the early 1960s, berating the regime for its secular focus and the shah for his elaborate and regal Western lifestyle. Khomeini was especially critical of Iran's close relationship to the United States and Israel. From Khomeini's perspective, the Americans provided arms, training, and technical assistance to their key anticommunist ally in the Middle East. And Israel provided training to SAVAK, which included intelligence-gathering, interrogation, and counterterrorism techniques. Thus, when SAVAK arrested, tortured, and killed anti-regime activists, the United States and Israel were blamed along with the shah.

Khomeini's popularity prevented the shah from eliminating him but did not prevent the shah from exiling the cleric. Forced to leave Iran in 1964, Khomeini set himself apart from other Iranian clerics by refusing to compromise with the shah. While in exile Khomeini continued to denounce the shah, Zionism, and the United States in his many sermons.

As the shah's reforms failed to bring about the desired effects, leftist groups such as the Mujahideen-e Khalq and Fedayeen-e Islami Khalq joined the National Front Party and religious conservatives in unified opposition. The increase in oil revenue after the 1973–1974 oil crisis was insufficient to compensate for an Iranian economy teetering on insolvency and lacking clear private property rights.

During the 1970s opposition to the regime often took the form of overt acts of defiance, such as the wearing of the *hijab* by Iranian women or the attendance of mosques whose imams openly criticized the shah. When an article critical of Khomeini ran in a Tehran newspaper in January 1978, the city's streets filled with Khomeini supports and regime opponents. The shah's failure to quell the riots that followed only emboldened his opponents.

U.S. president Jimmy Carter's administration was repeatedly given false information by SAVAK, which misrepresented the level of civil unrest in Iran. In the end, after massive general strikes in the fall of 1978, the shah lost control of the country in January 1979 and fled. This was followed by the triumphal return of Khomeini from exile on February 1, 1979, and the establishment of a transitional government composed of the various opposition groups.

Relative moderates such as Mehdi Bazargan and Abolhasan Bani-Sadr, the first prime minister and president, respectively, after the Pahlavi collapse, were soon forced out of power by Khomeini's supporters, who firmly held the reins of power by 1980. Iran was transformed into a fundamentalist Islamic theocracy, with Khomeini as supreme faqih, the de facto national leader. It was with the support of the Revolutionary Guards—and the tacit support of Khomeini himself—that Iranian students were able to seize the U.S. embassy in Tehran on November 4, 1979, and take the Americans there hostage. The crisis endured for 444 days, paralyzing the Carter administration.

The incoming Ronald Reagan administration (1981–1989) viewed the fundamentalist regime as a threat to American interests in the Middle East and to its closest ally, Israel. This led the United States to support Iraqi dictator Saddam Hussein's September 22, 1980, invasion of Iran. Initially, the Iraqi Army had great success against the poorly led, disorganized, and surprised Iranians. However, Iranian zeal led to counteroffensives in 1982 that pushed the Iraqis back. The war then settled into a bloody stalemate during which the Iraqis for the most part fought from prepared defensive positions in the fashion of World War I and the Iranians endured huge casualties while staging unsophisticated human wave attacks

against prepared Iraqi positions. Khomeini viewed the war as a jihad, or holy war, and rejected any end to the fighting before the destruction of Hussein's secular government. After almost a decade of war and more than a million casualties, the Iran-Iraq War ended in 1988 with no clear victor.

Khomeini died in 1989, but a movement promoting reform did not begin until the late 1990s. Following Khomeini's death, his Islamic Religious Party continued to dominate the government bureaucracy and the policy-making apparatus. The ongoing conflict with Iraq did not limit the regime from becoming the single most important state sponsor of terrorism in the 1980s. Hezbollah traces one of its roots directly to Iran's support. Nearly two decades later, a policy of eradicating Israel and forcing the United States out of the Middle East continues to dominate Iranian foreign and military policy. This has influenced other groups, not only Hezbollah but also the secular Amal group and many other smaller militias that do not want Western intervention in the Middle East.

Israel's superior military and presumed nuclear weapons would make a direct Iranian strike against the Jewish state suicidal, but Israel has accused Iran of waging a proxy war in Gaza and Lebanon, a strategic blow to Israel well within Iran's capabilities. When Israel finally withdrew from southern Lebanon in May 2000, Iran continued, verbally at least, to support Hezbollah's struggle against Israeli encroachment of Lebanon.

The Islamic Republic of Iran has also strongly supported the Palestinian struggle against Israel and criticized the United States for its blind support of Israel. One reason for that stance is to differentiate itself from the former shah, who was an ally of Israel and an even stronger ally of the United States.

During the 1990s, U.S. president Bill Clinton attempted to pursue détente with Iran and sought to restore economic relations. Instead of accepting the American offer, Saudi Shia terrorists detonated a car bomb outside the Khobar Towers housing complex at Dharan Air Base (Saudi Arabia) in 1996. More than a dozen Americans were killed. The United States blamed Iran, but the Saudi Arabian government urged restraint and achieved a détente of sorts with Iran at that time.

More recently, Iran has been accused of being a key supporter of the insurgency in Iraq following the Anglo-American invasion of that nation in 2003. Ties between Iran and insurgents are widely reported, with the regime providing weapons, training, and safe passage into Iraq. These ties go back to the Islamist opposition to Saddam Hussein, and so it is difficult to separate the Iraqi militia's self-ambitions and those of Tehran, but they are distinct. This is in addition to Iran's support for Hezbollah, which waged a bloody month-long war against Israel during July–August 2006.

In the near future, Iran is unlikely to end nearly two decades of anti-American and anti-Israeli foreign policy. The U.S. government claimed that Iran was moving toward the development of nuclear weapons and long-range missile technology needed to deliver nuclear warheads to Israel and Europe. Some of the Iranian clerics, however, showed signs of increasing disapproval of the confrontational course taken by Khomeini and President Mahmoud Ahmadinejad toward the United States and Israel. A student-led reform movement that seemed to argue for the rise of moderation has not been broadly supported.

ADAM LOWTHER, LOUIS A. DiMARCO, AND PAUL G. PIERPAOLI JR.

See also

Hamas; Hezbollah; Hussein, Saddam; Iran, Armed Forces; Iran-Iraq War; Iraq; Israel; Jihad; Katyusha Rocket; Khomeini, Ruhollah; Reza Pahlavi, Mohammad, Shah of Iran; Shia Islam; Sunni Islam; Terrorism; United States, Middle East Policy

References

Ansari, Ali. *Confronting Iran.* New York: Basic Books, 2006.

———. *A History of Modern Iran since 1921: The Pahlavis and After.* Boston: Longman, 2003.

Daniel, Elton. *The History of Iran.* Westport, CT: Greenwood, 2001.

Keddie, Nikki. *Modern Iran.* New Haven, CT: Yale University Press, 2003.

Kinzer, Stephen. *All the Shah's Men: An American Coup and the Roots of Middle East Terror.* Hoboken, NJ: Wiley, 2003.

Pappas, Theodore, ed. *Iran.* New York: Wiley, 2006.

Pollack, Kenneth. *The Persian Puzzle.* New York: Random House, 2006.

Shirazi, Saeed. *A Concise History of Iran.* Baltimore: Publish America, 2004.

Iran, Armed Forces

Iran's armed forces, which during much of the Cold War were heavily equipped with U.S. weaponry and hardware, served as a symbol of modernism until the 1979 Iranian Revolution, which overthrew Mohammad Reza Shah Pahlavi. After that, Iranian armed forces tended to reflect the new Islamic regime's inability—and even unwillingness—to maintain and upgrade technical capabilities as well as the state's emphasis on the personal zeal of military personnel rather than their training and leadership abilities.

From the earliest days of the shah's reign, indeed as early as 1941, Iran's armed forces were vitally important to his rule. Iran's strategic geographical position and the shah's constitutional authority that gave him direct control over the armed forces (but not over other matters of state) made military expansion and modernization his single most important program. After the 1953 coup led by the U.S. Central Intelligence Agency (CIA) that solidified his position, the shah increasingly turned to the United States for matériel and technical support.

Although the shah was a much-welcomed customer, U.S. officials up until 1969 expressed concerns that he should channel more efforts toward internal reforms, including land and economic restructuring. Washington often did not have complete confidence in the shah's ability to retain control over his nation, and his placing of military objectives above other national interests did not ease this apprehension.

There were caps on both the quantity and types of weapons systems available to Iran, but that changed during Richard Nixon's presidency, which began in January 1969. By 1972, the shah could order virtually any type of military technology in whatever quanti-

ties he wished. This set a significant new precedent, as both the U.S. Defense and State departments had previously sought to limit Iranian weapons purchases. The Nixon administration, in an attempt to pull back from worldwide military and defense commitments, hoped to use the shah as a bulwark against communist and Pan-Arab advances in the Middle East.

The results were immediate and dramatic. Iranian military purchases from the United States skyrocketed from $500 million per year in 1972 to $2.5 billion in 1973. By 1976, Iran had purchased $11 billion in new weaponry from American suppliers. Weapons acquisitions included helicopters, jet fighters, antiaircraft missiles, submarines, and destroyers. These acquisitions continued until 1977, when President Jimmy Carter reimposed limits on such sales.

The 1970s also brought significant importations of Western technical assistance. Large numbers of military advisers, technicians, and logistics and maintenance personnel arrived in Iran, primarily from the United States. As long as military matériel and spare parts arrived from the West, to be used by nonnative technicians, the military functioned smoothly. If that flow of goods and expertise were to be halted, as it was after 1979, the Iranian military's ability to function would be seriously compromised.

In early 1979 the shah was forced to abdicate and depart the country, the place of the monarchy taken over by the conservative Islamic Republic. Less than two years later, in September 1980, Iraq attacked Iran, sparking the Iran-Iraq War (1980–1988). The Iraqis faced a diminished military, augmented by and sometimes competing with nonprofessional Revolutionary Guard units that met the first assaults and performed poorly.

When the Islamic Republic of Iran was created, the officer corps of all three Iranian armed services had been purged, followed by a rash of desertions. One estimate holds that 60 percent of the army deserted in 1979 alone. The numbers of qualified pilots and technicians in the air force plummeted, as did the number of naval personnel. One significant exception was an increase in the number of marines, at least up until the mid-1980s.

In August 1980 just prior to the Iraqi attack, the Iranian Air Force numbered 447 first-line combat aircraft, including 66 U.S.-built Grumman F-14 Tomcats. The Iranian Navy had 7 guided-missile combatants (destroyers and frigates) and 7 guided-missile corvettes. The Iranian Army stood at 150,000 men equipped with 1,700 tanks and 1,000 artillery pieces, many of them self-propelled. The country also reportedly had more than 100,000 Revolutionary Guards, or Pasadran. Armed primarily with light infantry weapons, they were a highly motivated but very poorly trained combat force.

The departure from Iran of foreign advisers and technicians who had serviced aircraft, radar, missile, and ground systems had a dramatic effect on the Iranian armed forces. One example of the dangers of relying on technology created and supported by outsiders was the air force's computer-based logistics system. Without the proper technical support, the system was unusable. Procuring spare parts, which grew increasingly scarce, was a slow and laborious process. As the war progressed, the multinational boycott on

Iranian forces on the Ahvaz front (west of Ahvaz, Iran) during the Iran-Iraq War, 1982. (Françoise de Mulder/Corbis)

Iranian oil, which depleted government funds, forced the Iranians to continually cannibalize their own equipment. This took a heavy toll on effectiveness and readiness.

The Iraqi invasion caught the Iranian military divided and decimated. Iraqi aircraft roamed over the battlefield almost unchallenged, as the Iranian air defense system was overwhelmed and lay in disarray. Iraqi armored units were able to engage and defeat individual Iranian armored and mechanized infantry units in detail. However, at the tactical level, Iranian units enjoyed superior combat cohesion and tactical direction. Moreover, the Revolutionary Guard units proved fanatical in their defense of cities and fixed positions, and the Iraqi offensive bogged down within two weeks. Iranian Air Force units struck back at targets in Iraq and along the battlefield, and individual Iranian pilots proved superior to their Iraqi counterparts, but shortages of spare parts inhibited aircraft availability, which declined rapidly over time.

The war entered a period of stalemate after October 1980 as the Iraqis shifted to the defensive. Heavy losses in seizing Khorramshahr forced the Iraqis to reconsider assaulting the oil center of Abadan, and they settled on a siege instead. The Iranians used the period of relative calm to reorganize and restructure their forces. Armored and artillery units were concentrated, and the infantry reorganized into combat brigades. A working relationship was established with the Revolutionary Guards. Combined arms tactics with specialized units (engineers, armor, and artillery) were practiced with the units designated to conduct an attack. Revolutionary Guards were to provide the initial shock and exploitation force in any offensive.

These new tactics were first employed in a series of small-scale offensives near Susangerd and then Abadan. By the fall of 1981 the tactics began to prove effective, slowly driving back the Iraqi forces. By early 1982 the Iraqis had been driven completely from Iran. The tactics were then expanded to follow a repetitive pattern. Short, sharp artillery barrages were directed at Iraqi trenches, which were then subjected to massive human wave attacks by Revolutionary Guard units. Iranian Army mechanized units followed.

This was a costly approach to ground operations. The Iraqis, lacking the combat cohesion of their Iranian counterparts, resorted to using chemical weapons and massive artillery barrages to destroy Iranian forces' concentrations. Over time, the losses began to take a horrific toll. Some analysts estimate that Iran sacrificed more than 1 million men in the eight-year-long war. Certainly, the Iranians suffered at the very least several hundred thousand wounded, killed, and missing. By 1988, even Revolutionary Guard units began to suffer morale breakdowns. Ultimately, that is what drove Iran to reach a peace agreement with the Iraqis.

Iran's second Kilo-class Russian-built diesel-powered submarine under way from the Baltic Sea to Iran, photographed in July 1993. (U.S. Department of Defense)

During the 1980–1988 war with Iraq, Iran was forced to seek weapons from sources other than the United States and Western Europe. Thus, Iran received war matériel from the People's Republic of China (PRC), Brazil, North Korea, and Israel. It also secured some Soviet equipment, usually purchased through third parties. Reflecting the reliance on Chinese weapons, the Iranian armed forces possessed Silkworm antiship cruise missiles and Chinese-built armored personnel carriers. Most bizarre was the supply of some American equipment, especially air-to-surface and antitank missiles. These weapons systems were furnished by the United States in return for cash used to finance U.S. government actions against the Sandinistas in Nicaragua in what came to be known as the Iran-Contra Affair.

Following the Iran-Iraq War the Iranians moved to improve their military, which meant procuring matériel from abroad. By 2000, increased oil revenues and Russian frustration with U.S. policies in the Middle East had enabled Iran to purchase limited numbers of weapons and equipment from Russia. It remains to be seen if Iran can successfully develop indigenous missile and other weapons systems. But there is widespread belief that Iran is pursuing weapons of mass destruction (WMDs), including nuclear weapons. Indeed, the Iranians' efforts at enriching uranium that began in 2006 have brought much international concern over Iranian intentions. Only the future will tell for certain the direction of the Iranian military establishment, but as of 2007 the efficiency and effectiveness of the armed forces continues to be inhibited by political interference in the leadership-selection process, a lack of modern arms and equipment, and limited access to high-tech weapons systems and training opportunities.

ROBERT N. STACY AND CARL O. SCHUSTER

See also

Arms Sales, International; Iran; Iran-Iraq War; Iraq, Armed Forces; Khomeini, Ruhollah; Reza Pahlavi, Mohammad, Shah of Iran

References

Hickman, William F. *Ravaged and Reborn: The Iranian Army 1982.* Washington, DC: Brookings Institute Press, 1983.

Karsh, Efraim. *The Iran-Iraq War, 1980–1988.* London: Osprey, 2002.

Krosney, Herbert. *Deadly Business: Legal Deals and Outlaw Weapons; The Arming of Iran and Iraq, 1975 to the Present.* New York: Four Walls Eight Windows, 1993.

Rubin, Barry, and Thomas A. Keaney, eds. *Armed Forces in the Middle East: Politics and Strategy.* Portland, OR: Frank Cass, 2002.

Schahgaldian, Nikola. *The Iranian Military under the Islamic Republic.* Santa Monica, CA: RAND, 1987.

Iran-Iraq War
Start Date: September 22, 1980
End Date: August 20, 1988

A protracted military conflict that began in September 1980 when Iraq invaded western Iran along their common border and ended in August 1988 after both sides accepted a cease-fire supported by the United Nations (UN). The Iran-Iraq War can be seen as another phase of the ancient Persian-Arab rivalry that was fueled by 20th-century border disputes and political competition, complicated by the Islamic Revolution in Iran.

The border between Iraq and Iran had been contested diplomatically and sometimes militarily for several centuries. The dispute centered chiefly around control over the Shatt al Arab, a waterway that provided Iraq's only outlet to the Persian Gulf. In 1937 the two sides came to an agreement establishing a boundary that gave Iraq control of the Shatt al Arab. Despite the border agreement, relations between Iraq and Iran remained problematic, and a bitter rivalry continued between the two neighboring countries.

There were several contributing factors to this rivalry. First, the border cut across political loyalties. In the north, a large Kurdish population (who are neither Arab nor Persian) straddled both sides of the border. On the southern part of the border, an Arab minority inhabited the oil-rich Iranian province of Khuzestan among a Persian majority. Second, Iraq and Iran were both politically unstable. When either Iraq or Iran experienced a revolution or coup, the other country would exploit the troubled country's political weakness to gain a diplomatic advantage.

In 1975 after a Kurdish rebellion, a militarily weaker Iraq had agreed to a treaty that placed the boundary between Iraq and Iran on a line running down the middle of the Shatt al Arab in exchange for an Iranian agreement to stop supporting Kurdish rebels in Iraq. However, after the fall of Mohammad Reza Shah Pahlavi to Ayatollah Ruhollah Khomeini's Islamic fundamentalist regime in 1979, the shah's army was disbanded, and Iran lost its military supplier and close ally in the United States. Iraq's Saddam Hussein saw the unstable situation in Iran as an opportunity to reclaim both banks of the Shatt al Arab as well as Khuzestan and punish Iran for its support of Kurdish and Shia opposition in Iraq.

On September 22, 1980, Hussein, using an accusation against Iran of backing an assassination aimed at Foreign Minister Tariq Aziz as a pretext, launched a full-scale surprise attack on Iran that initiated eight years of warfare. Attacking across a 300-mile front, Iraqi troops were initially successful against the disorganized Iranian defenders, advancing into southwestern Iran, securing the far side of the Shatt al Arab, and capturing the port city of Khorramshahr and Ahvaz in Khuzestan Province. However, the Iranians reacted decisively and established a very effective blockade with their navy. Additionally, the Iranian Air Force conducted retaliatory raids that checked the Iraqi advance on the ground. In January 1981 the Iranians launched a counteroffensive, but the Iraqi forces defeated the attackers, and the war devolved into a protracted stalemate with neither side willing to back down.

Later in 1981, Iraq expressed some willingness to enter into negotiations, but Iranian leader Khomeini declared that Iran would never negotiate with the Iraqi government and would not cease fighting until Hussein's regime was toppled. Iran mobilized irregular forces, including the ill-trained but fanatical fighters of the

Revolutionary Guard. Iran now began a series of offensives, which regained Khorramshahr, pushed most of the Iraqi forces out of Iran, and brought the fighting into Iraqi territory. Throughout the summer and fall of 1982, the Iranian attack along the border focused on splitting the south of Iraq, where the majority of the Shiites lived, from the north and capturing the southern city of Basra. The pattern for the fighting of 1982 was that the Revolutionary Guard, supported by the Iranian Army, usually outnumbered the Iraqi defenders, who inflicted heavy casualties on the attackers before falling back.

The Iranian leaders were willing to suffer enormous casualties in sending unsophisticated human wave attacks against Iraq's better-equipped forces. In February 1984, Khomeini's troops captured oil-rich Majnun Island, strategically situated on the southern front, some 40 miles north of Basra. The Iraqis became more desperate and ultimately resorted to the use of chemical weapons, a tactic reviled by the international community.

In February 1986, the Iranians managed to breach the Iraqi lines and captured the al-Faw (Fao) Peninsula at the southeastern tip of Iraq. In response, Hussein widened the war to civilian targets, launching missiles against Iranian cities, bombing Iranian oil installations, and attacking Iranian shipping in the Persian Gulf. This drew severe reprisals from Iran against Iraqi oil production and shipping, including attacks against ships from countries that had allied themselves with Iraq, such as Kuwait. The attacks on Kuwaiti oil tankers in 1987 led the United States and several West European nations to send naval forces to station warships in the Persian Gulf to ensure oil flow to the rest of the world.

Later, in 1987, the Iranians prepared for what they hoped would be the last round of offensives to end the war and topple the Iraqi government. Tensions mounted as the situation grew critical. In July, the UN Security Council passed Resolution 598 calling for both sides to stop fighting, withdraw to prewar borders, and submit to an international body to determine responsibility for the war. Iraq was ready to negotiate, but Iran, sensing that victory was near, continued its attacks but failed to achieve the victory for which it had hoped.

In 1988 a resurgent Iraq drove the Iranians from the al-Faw Peninsula and several other border areas. As the pendulum swung in Iraq's favor on the battlefield and Iran's economy faltered, Iranian leaders worked to persuade Khomeini to accept UN Resolution 598. Khomeini endorsed the cease-fire in July, and on August 20, 1988, both sides ceased fighting in accordance with the terms of the resolution.

The Iran-Iraq War lasted eight years and resulted in catastrophic destruction in both countries. There are no reliable casualty figures, although estimates hold that the Iraqis suffered an estimated 200,000 casualties. Another 70,000 were taken prisoner by the Iranians. The war probably claimed at least 200,000 Iranian lives and wounded more than 500,000. Estimates suggest that there were more than a million war and war-related casualties on both sides. Some estimates put this figure at close to 2 million. This includes some 100,000 Kurds who were killed by Iraqi forces during the final months of fighting.

The war was also extremely destructive to each country's economy. Estimates vary, but the war's cost, including military supplies and civilian damage, probably exceeds $500 billion for each side. Both Iran and Iraq sacrificed their oil wealth to the war for nearly a decade, and Iraq was forced to borrow heavily, especially from its allies on the Arabian Peninsula.

Negotiations between Iraq and Iran remained deadlocked for two years after the cease-fire went into effect, but in 1990, concerned with securing its forcible annexation of Kuwait, Iraq restored diplomatic relations with Iran and agreed to Iranian terms for the settlement of the war. This included the withdrawal of Iraqi troops from occupied Iranian territory, division of sovereignty over the Shatt al Arab waterway, and a prisoner-of-war exchange.

In the end, virtually none of the issues that started the war were resolved, and the conflict brought no tremendous political change in either country. Hussein, despite having led his nation into a disastrous war, emerged from the war stronger than ever and claimed that Iran's failure to unseat him represented a great Iraqi victory. In Iran, the years of fighting served to consolidate support for the Islamic Revolution.

The Iran-Iraq War contributed to the outbreak of the Persian Gulf War in 1991 because it left Iraq with a strong army and staggering debts to Arab nations, including Kuwait. Indeed, Iraq cited Kuwait's refusal to forgive Iraq's war debt as one reason for invading its oil-rich neighbor.

JAMES H. WILLBANKS

See also

Chemical Weapons and Warfare; Hussein, Saddam; Iran; Iran, Armed Forces; Iraq; Iraq, Armed Forces; Khomeini, Ruhollah; Persian Gulf War; Reza Pahlavi, Mohammad, Shah of Iran

References

Bulloch, John, and Harvey Morris. *The Gulf War: Its Origins, History and Consequences.* London: Pergamon, 1988.

Hiro, Dilip. *The Longest War: The Iran-Iraq Military Conflict.* London: Routledge, 1991.

Karsh, Efraim. *The Iran-Iraq War: A Military Analysis.* London: William Heinemann, 1991.

———. *The Iran-Iraq War, 1980–1988.* London: Osprey, 2002.

O'Ballance, Edgar. *The Gulf War.* London: Brassey's, 1988.

Workman, W. Thom. *The Social Origins of the Iran-Iraq War.* Boulder, CO: Lynne Rienner, 1994.

Iraq

Middle Eastern nation covering 168,753 square miles, slightly smaller than the U.S. state of California. Iraq borders Saudi Arabia to the west and south, Kuwait and the Persian Gulf to the south, Iran to the east, and Syria and Turkey to the north. Most important to a modern understanding of Iraq is the Arab conquest of the region (AD 633–644), which was responsible for making Iraq the culturally, ethnically, linguistically, and religiously diverse country it is today. As the capital of the Muslim Abbasid Empire shifted from Damascus to Baghdad, Iraq rose to renewed prominence with a new culture and religion. The synthesis of this empire and subsequent Muslim states with the influence of Iraq's numerous tribes remains a powerful historical aspect of life in Iraq.

The Ottoman defeat in World War I left Great Britain the new master of the former Ottoman provinces of Mosul, Baghdad, and Basra, which now form the modern state of Iraq. Independence in 1932, however, was far less than the salvation many Iraqis assumed it would be. Iraq was split between Sunni and Shia, among Arab, Kurd, and Turcoman, and between urban and rural, and deep cleavages tore at the fabric of Iraqi society.

While it lasted, the Hashemite monarchy (1921–1958) attempted to build a unified sense of identity in Iraq. Following the 1958 coup that toppled the monarchy and brought General Abdul Karim Qassem to power, Iraqi governments fell in rapid succession.

In 1940, Prime Minister Rashid Ali al-Gaylani offered to support Britain in World War II if Palestine were to be established as a state. Winston Churchill's refusal caused a split between the nationalists, who thought that Axis support would help them, and moderates such as former prime minister Nuri al-Said. The crisis led to a British and Arab Legion occupation of Baghdad and the flight of al-Gaylani and his allies from Iraq and lent support to the later Baathist anti-imperialist stance.

When Israel declared its independence on May 14, 1948, a new dimension was added to an already unstable regional situation. In the Israeli War of Independence (1948–1949), Iraq provided 3,000 troops in May 1948, adding 15,000 troops during the months that followed. Iraqi forces successfully held the Jenin-Nablus-Tulkaram triangle but singularly failed to launch an attack on Jewish forces. The failure of the allied Arab forces to succeed on the battlefield left Arab leaders with little choice but to negotiate the 1948 cease-fire.

Arab failure, as in the past, led to the persecution of Iraqi Jews, whose loyalty was suspect. The focus on internal deficiencies of the regime was replaced by charges that the small number of Iraqi Jews had spied for Israel and were responsible for Iraq's military failure. This pattern of behavior repeated itself during the 1967 Six-Day War and the 1973 Yom Kippur War. Later, Iraqi dictator Saddam Hussein would perfect this ploy and use it on a number of occasions against other enemies to deflect attention away from his own economic, military, and political failures.

In 1955 Iraq joined the pro-Western Baghdad Pact, allying itself with Turkey, Iran, and Pakistan in a mutual defense agreement sponsored by the United States. The pact was a direct affront to the long-simmering nationalist sentiments within the Iraqi Army officer corps. Indeed, the pact became the catalyst that ignited the 1958 revolution, the first in a string of coups and countercoups that would plague Iraq until the Baathists finally consolidated power in 1968. The 1958 coup was led by a secret nationalist organization known as the Free Officers Movement. On July 14, 1958, its members seized control of Baghdad and executed King Faisal II and Prime Minister al-Said. The revolutionaries then abolished the

The skyline of Baghdad, Iraq's capital and largest city. (U.S. Department of Defense)

monarchy, proclaimed Iraq a republic, and sought closer ties to the Soviet Union. Colonel Qassem had led the coup, but his policies ultimately created a great many internal and external enemies.

The republican period of Iraqi history (1958–1968) was marked as one of internal conflict in which the antimonarchist factions fought among themselves. Qassem's rule of Iraq was short-lived, and he was overthrown in 1963 by a coalition of anticommunist military officers and secular Arab nationalists and Baathists who installed Colonel Abd al-Salam Arif as president and Hasan al-Bakr as prime minister. Allies in the National Council of the Revolutionary Command that took the reigns of government in February 1963 soon turned against one another, as it became clear that the military and the Baath Party fundamentally disagreed on the path that Iraq should pursue. President Arif's tenure in office ended abruptly when he was killed in a helicopter crash in 1966. His more pliable brother, Abdal-Rahman Arif, took over and served as president until 1968.

Iraq's failure to support fellow Arab states in the Six-Day War led to massive riots in Baghdad, which the regime was ineffective in suppressing. On July 17, 1968, the Baathists seized radio stations, the Ministry of Defense, and the headquarters of the Republican Guard. The Baath Party thus came to power with Hasan al-Bakr taking the posts of president, prime minister, and secretary-general of the party. His cousin, Saddam Hussein, worked in the background to eliminate adversaries of the new regime.

Over time, Hussein proved to be a ruthless operator whose patronage system broke down the historic bonds in Iraqi society. His network of security organizations so thoroughly penetrated government, the military, and society that he was able to remove al-Bakr from power without a challenge. Security operatives also settled old scores with the communists and Free Officers on Hussein's behalf.

The Baath regime did, however, pursue numerous needed reforms. These included land reform, agricultural investment, the renegotiation of oil contracts, hospital and school construction, and a number of other reforms in a continuing effort to bring the society into the regime's broader network of patronage. This task was also accomplished through the activities of the large Baath Party itself. Iraqi society was dependent on a patronage network in which association with party, military, or government officials was necessary and in which bribes were used. For this and other reasons such as rural-urban migration, economic reforms did not succeed, and from 1973 onward Iraq was largely dependent on oil revenues.

When the Yom Kippur War began in October 1973, a recently attempted coup by the brutal head of state security services, Nadhim Kzar, was still at the forefront of government efforts to purge

Iraqi leaders Deputy Premier and Defense Minister Lieutenant General Hardan Tikriti, President Ahmed Hasan al-Bakr, and Chief of Staff Lieutenant General Hammad Chehab take the salute on the reviewing stand during a military parade at Baghdad on July 17, 1969. (Bettmann/Corbis)

the Baath Party. This led to Iraq playing only a minor role in the war in the form of an armored division sent to Syria. The Iraqis fought alongside the Syrians as they sought to retake the Golan Heights. The effort failed.

Defeat in the war was the third consecutive defeat for the Arabs at the hands of Israel, and it led the Iraqi regime to turn inward. This meant that the Kurds, Shiites, and communists suffered the brunt of the regime's onslaught throughout the 1970s. Survival became the focus of existence for these three groups. With the establishment of the Islamic Republic of Iran in 1979, the Iraqi regime saw a looming threat in Ayatollah Ruhollah Khomeini's Shiite-fundamentalist regime.

After Hussein assumed the presidency in 1979, his consolidation of power was complete. He launched an offensive against the southern Iranian city of Khorramshahr on September 17, 1980, sparking the Iran-Iraq War that would drag on until 1988 and would witness more than 1 million combined casualties. Neither side achieved a clear victory, and both countries saw their economies dramatically decline during the war. For Israel, however, the Iran-Iraq War was a respite that reduced foreign threats.

Exhausted, Iran and Iraq reached a cease-fire agreement in July 1988. In the aftermath of the war, Hussein turned to Saudi Arabia and Kuwait for financial assistance but was rebuffed. Under Ottoman rule, Kuwait had been part of Basra Province and only became an independent emirate during the British Mandate. This historical quirk provided Hussein with an excuse to invade Kuwait.

But Hussein had other reasons to attack Kuwait. He accused the Kuwaitis of manipulating the price of oil to the detriment of Iraq and asserted that Kuwait was illegally tapping Iraqi oil reserves by slant-drilling into Iraqi oil fields. The dictator also fumed that the Kuwaitis would not accede to debt reduction to help a struggling Iraqi economy. To Hussein's way of thinking, if the Kuwaiti emir would not provide financial relief to Iraq, then the Iraqi Army would simply conquer Kuwait.

In the days leading up to the 1990 Iraqi invasion of Kuwait, the United States failed to clearly communicate its disapproval of an Iraqi invasion but instead led the Iraqis to believe that they were free to invade Kuwait. After the invasion began on August 2, 1990, the United Nations (UN) quickly condemned Iraq, and U.S. president George H. W. Bush began deploying American troops to Saudi

Arabia. Although the Iraqi regime was convinced that the United States would not attack, the Iraqi high command began planning for such a contingency. Part of the plan called for a massive air strike that would see Israel's major cities hit by devastating chemical weapons attacks designed to bring Israel into the war and cause other Arab nations to terminate their support of the U.S.-led coalition. The attack never materialized, but Iraq did manage to strike Israel with approximately two dozen Scud missiles in January 1991. The United States responded rapidly and deployed two Patriot missile batteries to Israel.

In the wake of a resounding coalition victory in February 1991, Iraq was reduced economically and politically by the sanctions placed on Hussein's regime and the presence of UN weapons inspectors who scoured the country for weapons of mass destruction (WMDs). Average Iraqis suffered intensely under the sanctions. The UN's Oil for Food Program was designed to bring needed medicine and food to Iraq while preventing the regime from rebuilding its WMD capabilities. Instead, Hussein built lavish palaces and exported the medical supplies and food intended for Iraqis to foreign countries. He also ruthlessly suppressed uprisings by both the Kurds and Shiites.

Iraq's link to international terrorism had begun as early as the 1980s. It was in fact the Iraqi regime that provided Abu Abbas, mastermind of the *Achille Lauro* ocean liner hijacking, safe haven in 1985. In the years that followed the Persian Gulf War, Hussein dramatically stepped up his support for terrorist organizations. Ramzi Yusef, mastermind of the 1993 World Trade Center bombing, received support from regime elements prior to traveling to the United States on a valid Iraqi passport. In addition, Abu Nidal, Abu Musab al-Zarqawi, the Popular Front for the Liberation of Palestine (PFLP), and Hamas all received financial support, training, and/or military assistance from Iraq prior to 2003. Perhaps most notoriously, Hussein allegedly sent checks for $25,000 to the families of Palestinian suicide bombers.

It was not until President George W. Bush launched Operation IRAQI FREEDOM in March 2003, with a thin multinational coalition, that direct action was taken against the Iraqi regime. Bush offered three reasons for the invasion. First, tyranny in Iraq was no longer acceptable. Second, Iraq's WMD capability was a threat to the United States and its allies. Third, Iraqi support of terrorism presented an unacceptable danger to free nations.

The vaunted Iraqi military proved to be a shell of its former self. Within three weeks, the regime collapsed. In the months that followed, however, Fedayeen Saddam as well as Iraqi Sunnis, foreign Islamists, and former members of the Baathist army began an insurgency that continues to plague Iraq and the ongoing U.S. occupation to the present.

In order to assist in the rebuilding of civil society in Iraq, the Bush administration initiated an effort to train a new Iraqi military and police force capable of taking over security operations throughout the country. This process proved far more difficult than the administration had anticipated. What became evident, however, is that some of the reasons Bush cited for going to war with Iraq were exceedingly dubious. After more than four years in Iraq, no WMDs were found. And despite Bush administration claims that Hussein had links to the terrorist organization Al Qaeda, no such relationship was established. Indeed, Hussein would have had little reason to support an Islamic extremist group, as he had ruthlessly suppressed Iraqi Islamist groups whose philosophy countered that of the Baath Party and, according to him, threatened Iraqi unity.

Iraq's relationship with Israel in the coming years is unlikely to see Iraqi state-sponsored terrorism visited upon the Jewish state, but neither is Iraq likely to become Israel's greatest ally. Among Israelis, the hope is that Iraq will focus on its domestic affairs and the rebuilding of its shattered economy, leaving Israel with one less adversary. If Iraq can quell its civil war, which is highly questionable at this point, it may emerge with a prosperous economy and a stable civil society. There is also a distinct possibility that Iraq might spiral into greater violence, which would provide fertile ground for Al Qaeda and other terrorist organizations. As of this writing the future of Iraq is highly uncertain.

ADAM LOWTHER, LOUIS A. DiMARCO, AND PAUL G. PIERPAOLI JR.

See also

Abbas, Abu; *Achille Lauro* Hijacking; Baathism; Baghdad Pact; Bush, George Herbert Walker; Bush, George Walker; Hussein, Saddam; Iran-Iraq War; Iraq, Armed Forces; Israeli War of Independence, Israeli-Iraqi Front; Israeli War of Independence, Overview; Persian Gulf War; Said, Nuri al-; Six-Day War; Terrorism; Yom Kippur War

References

Abdullah, Thabit. *A Short History of Iraq*. London: Pearson, 2003.
Dodge, Toby. *Inventing Iraq*. New York: Columbia University Press, 2003.
Karsh, Efraim. *Islamic Imperialism*. New Haven, CT: Yale University Press, 2006.
Keegan, John. *The Iraq War*. New York: Vintage Books, 2005.
Makiya, Kanan. *Republic of Fear: The Politics of Modern Iraq*. Berkeley: University of California Press, 1998.
Murray, Williamson, and Robert H. Scales Jr. *The Iraq War: A Military History*. Cambridge: Harvard University Press, 2003.
Oren, Michael B. *Six Days of War: June 1967 and the Making of the Modern Middle East*. Novato, CA: Presidio, 2003.
Pelletiere, Stephen. *The Iran-Iraq War: Chaos in a Vacuum*. New York: Praeger, 1992.
Polk, William R. *Understanding Iraq*. New York: Harper Perennial, 2005.
Tripp, Charles. *A History of Iraq*. Cambridge: Cambridge University Press, 2002.

Iraq, Armed Forces

The armed forces of Iraq have an extremely long history, as the area has been continually fought over for millennia. Indeed, some of the earliest recorded battles in human history occurred in Mesopotamia. Today the armed forces of Iraq include the Iraqi Army, the Iraqi Air Force, and the Iraqi Coastal Defense Force. All three branches were reconstituted after the March 2003 U.S.-led invasion of Iraq, during which the military commanded by Iraqi dictator Saddam Hussein was disbanded and disarmed.

Iraqi soldiers give the "V" for victory sign at Ahvaz, Iran, during the Iran-Iraq War, September 25, 1980. (Henri Bureau/Sygma/Corbis)

Iraq was one of five Arab nations that attacked Israel after the proclamation of the independent Jewish state in May 1948. As the only Arab belligerent that did not share a border with Israel, Iraq sent its troops through Transjordan. At the beginning of the conflict, the entire Iraqi Army consisted of 21,000 men organized in 12 brigades and supported by 100 aircraft. The initial Iraqi deployment in the war was 5,000 men, including 4 infantry brigades and an armored battalion. This commitment, under the command of General Nur ad-Din Mahmud, eventually grew to more than 20,000 troops by the end of the conflict. Iraqi deployments in the Israeli War of Independence (1948–1949) remained primarily limited to commitments on the central front. Although Iraqi units generally held numerical superiority in their areas of operations, they performed poorly against the Israelis.

During the 1956 Suez Crisis, Iraqi and Syrian troops took up supporting positions in Jordan. In 1961 when Kuwait obtained its independence from Britain, Iraq immediately attempted to claim sovereignty over disputed territory in Kuwait. Britain deployed troops to Kuwait to prevent an Iraqi takeover.

During the 1967 Six-Day War, the Israeli Air Force mauled the Iraqi Air Force on the first day of the fighting. Nonetheless, by the fifth day of the war Iraqi bombers managed to hit air bases inside

Israel, and Iraqi fighters shot down two Israeli aircraft. The Iraqi Army committed almost no units to the fighting, although a few ground units were sent to Jordan. Iraqis protested this lack of commitment to Palestine in massive riots in Baghdad.

On October 6, 1973, the Yom Kippur War started with a series of surprise attacks by Egyptian, Jordanian, and Syrian forces against Israeli positions. The Iraqi Air Force conducted some of the first air strikes against Israeli bases in the Sinai and managed to shoot down 12 Israeli aircraft in air-to-air combat. Prewar Iraqi-Syrian tensions, however, prevented a larger-scale Iraqi participation, although Iraqi tanks saw limited action on the Golan Heights front during the first week of the war. On October 13, the Iraqi 3rd Armored Division advanced into an Israeli ambush and was badly mauled, losing 80 tanks without destroying a single Israeli armored vehicle. It was the first major armored battle fought by the Iraqi Army. Within one hour, almost an entire armored brigade had been destroyed.

Iraqi performance for the remainder of the war was poor. The Iraqis, Jordanians, and Syrians were unable to coordinate their forces and actually inflicted significant casualties upon one another through a series of friendly fire blunders. Although Iraqi battlefield performance was generally substandard, the Iraqis nevertheless pressed their attacks with a grim determination. Iraq emerged from the war territorially intact but with a badly beaten military, greatly demoralized and in need of foreign reconstitution.

The disastrous results of the Yom Kippur War had some positive technological effects for Iraq. Receiving new equipment from the Soviet Union, Iraq between 1973 and 1980 steadily rebuilt and modernized its military forces, purchasing hundreds of tanks and aircraft and beginning a domestic armament program that focused on unconventional weapons.

In 1979, Saddam Hussein assumed power in a military coup and immediately began to threaten neighboring nations while increasing Iraqi research efforts into chemical, biological, and nuclear weapons development. It was clear that he believed he had assumed the leadership of the Pan-Arab cause championed by the late Egyptian president Gamal Abdel Nasser. Indeed, with Iran then in the midst of a wrenching Islamic fundamentalist revolution and Egypt officially on peaceful terms with Israel, Hussein envisioned Iraq as the predominant power in the Middle East. A powerful Iraqi military was a vital aspect of his policy.

On September 22, 1980, Iraq invaded Iran, beginning the long and sanguinary Iran-Iraq War (1980–1988), the latest in the centuries-old hostilities between Sunni and Shia Muslims and Persians and Arabs. Although the Iraqis initially made advances into Iran, the mountainous terrain, fanatical Iranian resistance, and Iranian human wave tactics stopped the Iraqi thrust. Iraq eventually resorted

to chemical weapons, killing perhaps as many as 250,000 Iranian troops and civilians but doing little to alter the course of the war. Meanwhile, Israeli Air Force fighter-bombers penetrated Iraqi airspace on June 7, 1981, and destroyed the Osiraq nuclear reactor, effectively ending Iraq's nuclear program before it could produce weapons-grade matériel. Despite having a four-to-one advantage over Iran in tanks and other armored vehicles and a two-to-one advantage in field and antiaircraft artillery, Iraq failed to achieve anything significant in the war.

Iraq nonetheless emerged from the Iran-Iraq War with the largest military in the Middle East as well as one of the most technologically advanced. The Iraqi Army then consisted of 70 divisions, the most capable of which were armed with Soviet-built T-72 tanks and armored personnel carriers, and artillery units armed with multiple rocket launchers, FROG-7 and Scud-B surface-to-surface missiles, and self-propelled guns. The Iraqi Air Force numbered 700 aircraft, including French Dassault Mirage and Soviet Mikoyan-Gurevich MiG-29 fighters. The Iraqi air defense network was the most sophisticated in the Arab world, including antiaircraft artillery and surface-to-air missiles. Iraq was by far the most well-armed Arab nation, with the world's fifth-largest military.

Iraq soon renewed its claims to sovereignty over Kuwait, and on August 2, 1990, Iraqi forces invaded Kuwait on a massive scale, quickly overwhelming the tiny military forces of the small Persian

Rusted Iraqi military vehicles sit abandoned in a junkyard in Kuwait, photographed in 1999. (Adrian Arbib/Corbis)

Gulf nation. International condemnation was immediate. The United States organized a broad coalition to prevent Iraqi attacks against Saudi Arabia and to persuade the Iraqis to withdraw from Kuwait. The coalition operation, named DESERT SHIELD, operated under United Nations (UN) mandate. Coalition forces included many of Iraq's Arabic neighbors. When economic sanctions and deadlines did not force Iraq to withdraw from Kuwait, coalition forces launched Operation DESERT STORM, starting with a massive air offensive in January 1991.

Despite heavy Iraqi air defenses, particularly around Baghdad, coalition forces quickly moved from aerial superiority to aerial supremacy over Iraq, striking Iraqi command and control centers as well as armor and infantry concentrations and eviscerating the Iraqi military. On the first night of the war, however, an Iraqi MiG-25 managed to shoot down an American F/A-18. Many Iraqi pilots flew to Iran, which never returned the aircraft to Iraq. The follow-on four-day ground campaign in February forced the Iraqis out of Kuwait. Iraq lost thousands of military vehicles and hundreds of aircraft and suffered some 20,000 military deaths and perhaps as many as 110,000 civilian deaths.

From 1991 until 2003, Iraq remained under international economic sanctions, limiting Hussein's ability to rebuild his armed forces. UN weapons inspectors repeatedly searched suspected Iraqi sites in an attempt to destroy the entire Iraqi chemical and biological weapons arsenal. Although Iraq could not account for its entire stockpile of unconventional weapons, it is likely that virtually all were destroyed during the period of sanctions.

During the same period, Iraqi military aircraft were banned from two no-fly zones, one north and one south of Baghdad. Hussein periodically tested Western resolve by defying the no-fly zones and by firing on Western aircraft, but the result was almost always swift retaliation. The Iraqis lost a number of their aircraft in probing the no-fly zones.

Prior to 2003, the Iraqi military was still a formidable force even if diminished from its 1990 capabilities. The army had 23 divisions, including 3 armored and 3 mechanized. The Iraqi main armament was still Soviet, with 700 T-72, 500 T-62, and 500 T-54/55 main battle tanks, 1,200 BMP armored infantry fighting vehicles, and 1,800 armored personnel carriers. The Iraqi Air Force had a little more than 300 operational aircraft, including MiG-21, MiG-23, MiG-25, and MiG-29 fighters and Su-22 ground-attack aircraft. The regular army was augmented by some 80,000 to 100,000 troops of the Republican Guard, organized into 3 armored and 2 mechanized divisions, 1 motorized infantry division, and 1 special forces division. The Special Republican Guard, a separate unit of 12,000 troops all drawn from clans loyal to Hussein, had two armored brigades. Most of the Republican Guard units maintained the immediate defenses of Baghdad, while the regular army was deployed primarily in eastern Iraq. According to estimates from 2000, Iraq had more than 5 million men of military age (18–49 years old), of whom more than 3 million were fit for service.

On March 20, 2003, another coalition led by the United States invaded Iraq. Smaller and far less cohesive than the first coalition, it did not include any of the Arab state participants from the 1990–1991 war. The pretense for the 2003 invasion was to rid Iraq of suspected chemical and possibly nuclear weapons, collectively known as weapons of mass destruction (WMDs). In a little more than three weeks, the U.S.-led coalition conquered the entire nation and deposed Hussein. The expected stockpiles of chemical and biological agents, however, were never found, although a series of hidden research facilities for the production of such weapons were discovered, and small numbers of chemical artillery rounds were located. The evidence seems to support the conclusion that the only reason for the invasion was that the United States wanted to force a regime change in Iraq as part of the so-called global war on terror.

In the post-Hussein era, the coalition leadership decided to dismantle the Iraqi Army and rebuild it from the ground up. The Iraqi armed forces have been slow to take over security responsibilities from U.S. and coalition troops and, as of 2007, the Iraqi armed forces still lad large inventories of obsolete Soviet equipment. The new Iraqi Army consists of 10 divisions, including a single mechanized division. The Iraqi Air Force still has a few aircraft from the period of the Persian Gulf War but has great difficulty in maintaining combat readiness because of a lack of spare parts and trained personnel. The air force consists of five squadrons. The 800-man Coastal Defense Force has two patrol boat squadrons and a handful of marine platoons.

PAUL J. SPRINGER

See also

Hussein, Saddam; Iran; Iran, Armed Forces; Iran-Iraq War; Iraq; Israeli War of Independence, Israeli-Iraqi Front; Kuwait; Kuwait, Armed Forces; Persian Gulf War; Six-Day War; Suez Crisis; Yom Kippur War

References

Butler, Richard. *The Greatest Threat: Iraq, Weapons of Mass Destruction, and the Crisis of Global Security.* New York: PublicAffairs, 2000.

Finnie, David H. *Shifting Lines in the Sand: Kuwait's Elusive Frontier with Iraq.* Cambridge: Harvard University Press, 1992.

Herzog, Chaim. *The Arab-Israeli Wars: War and Peace in the Middle East from the War of Independence to Lebanon.* Westminster, MD: Random House, 1984.

Hiro, Dilip. *The Longest War: The Iran-Iraq Military Conflict.* London: Routledge, 1991.

Murray, Williamson, and Robert H. Scales Jr. *The Iraq War: A Military History.* Cambridge: Harvard University Press, 2003.

Rubin, Barry, and Thomas A. Keaney, eds. *Armed Forces in the Middle East: Politics and Strategy.* Portland, OR: Frank Cass, 2002.

Iraq War
Start Date: March 2003
End Date: Ongoing

U.S.-led invasion of Iraq in March 2003 that resulted in the fall of Iraqi dictator Saddam Hussein and the occupation of the country

U.S. secretary of defense Donald H. Rumsfeld (*left*) and chairman of the Joint Chiefs of Staff General Richard B. Myers (*right*) brief reporters on the first actions of Operation IRAQI FREEDOM at the Pentagon on March 20, 2003. (U.S. Department of Defense)

by coalition troops. The achievement of rapid military victory in April 2003 was followed by a prolonged and bloody insurgency that continues to the present.

The September 11, 2001, terrorist attacks against the United States forced Americans to respond by invading Afghanistan less than one month later. Code-named Operation ENDURING FREEDOM, the intention of the offensive was to oust the Taliban regime that had given refuge to Osama bin Laden and Al Qaeda, the perpetrators of the attacks. That objective was largely accomplished by the end of 2001. After that, it soon became clear that President George W. Bush regarded Iraq as the next target in the so-called war on terror.

Bush and his defense advisers regarded Hussein, whom they suspected of having weapons of mass destruction (WMDs), as a significant long-term threat to American security. Bush identified Iraq as one of the members of an anti-American "axis of evil" in a speech to the American public on January 29, 2003. The two other rogue states were identified as Iran and North Korea. Unlike North Korea and Iran, however, Iraq was seen as a country that could not effectively defend itself against a U.S. invasion force. Bush and his advisers hoped that toppling the Hussein regime would allow Iraq to emerge as a market-based, Western-style democracy, thereby reshaping the dynamic of politics in the Middle East. An American

presence in Iraq, it was hoped, would also put pressure on Syria and Iran, both of which were aiding terrorists and extremists. Indeed, Syria and Iran had often been accused of sponsoring terrorism in the Middle East and beyond.

The pending invasion of Iraq also coincided with two new currents of thinking in Washington. First, Bush had already enunciated a doctrine of preemption (the Bush Doctrine), under which the United States would strike first at any potential security threats. Second, since becoming secretary of defense in 2001, Donald Rumsfeld had consistently argued in favor of reshaping the American military, which he regarded as top-heavy and slow moving. The post–September 11 security environment required a smaller and more responsive and highly mobile military that could strike with precision and lethality by taking advantage of the new technologies offered by the information revolution. The spectacularly successful American invasion of Afghanistan seemed to bear out Rumsfeld's thinking.

Rumsfeld overrode objections from planners and insisted that the attack be mounted with minimum troop strength and with as much rapidity as possible. Secretary of State Colin Powell expressed serious reservations about the planning for the invasion, suggesting that the postwar situation might be far more difficult than Pentagon

Explosion of a second car bomb aimed at U.S. and Iraqi forces arriving to inspect the site of another car bomb detonated an hour earlier, southern Baghdad, April 14, 2005. (U.S. Department of Defense)

planners envisaged and that the United States needed to gain more international support for its case against Iraq. Powell was largely ignored. As the leader of the major U.S. ally in the forthcoming campaign, British prime minister Tony Blair also emphasized the need for international support.

Accordingly, on November 9, 2002, the United Nations (UN) Security Council adopted Resolution 1441, which called on Iraq to fully disclose details of its WMD program and to comply with earlier, similar UN resolutions. Resolution 1441 threatened "serious consequences" if Iraq did not comply. While Iraq did provide a report on its weapons holdings, the United States claimed that the Iraqis were lying. The United States and Britain attempted to pass a resolution in the UN authorizing the use of force, but the proposal did not gain sufficient support and was abandoned. In the meantime, the Bush administration continued to argue—with no real proof—that Hussein had had a role in the September 11, 2001, disaster by cooperating with Al Qaeda.

Following the disastrous 1991 Persian Gulf War with the United States, Hussein believed that the major threat to the survival of his regime came from within his country, including possible uprisings by the Shia in the south and the Kurds in the north. The Shia uprising in southern Iraq after the 1991 war had been savagely repressed by Hussein. Reprisals had also been carried out against the Kurds,

but they had recovered a degree of autonomy by 2003, a reflection of Hussein's weakness. Externally, Hussein thought that the major threat was Iran, against which he had fought a bloody and inconclusive war from 1980 to 1988. He feared that Iran might take advantage of Iraqi vulnerability after 1991.

Iraq remained evasive about its alleged WMD programs throughout the 1990s because it thought that uncertainty about its WMD capability might serve as a deterrent against an Iranian attack. Hussein apparently never seriously considered that the United States might launch another invasion since it had stopped short of attacking Baghdad in 1991 and had withdrawn from Somalia in 1993 after suffering just a few casualties.

By 2003, the Iraqi military was only a shadow of what it had been in 1991. The rank and file of the army were deeply demoralized and showed little inclination to fight, and the officer corps lived in terror of the consequences of Hussein's legendary paranoia. The Iraqi regular army in 2003 consisted of 17 understrength divisions numbering perhaps 150,000 to 200,000 soldiers, although estimates of Iraqi troop strength vary greatly. The elite Republican Guard added another 6 understrength divisions, possibly an additional 60,000 soldiers. Equipment in all formations of the Iraqi Army was antiquated and poorly maintained, and the severely degraded Iraqi Air Force was never a serious factor in the war. Hussein had also created a number of irregular units collectively known as fedayeen to provide additional security for his regime in the event of another internal uprising.

Because Turkey opposed the 2003 invasion of Iraq, it refused to allow American or British troops on its territory. Thus, the flimsy allied coalition was restricted to attacking from bases in Kuwait, with logistical and air support from bases in neighboring Persian Gulf states. The Americans made up the overwhelming mass of the coalition forces, committing approximately 214,000 armed forces personnel. The British contributed another 45,000. Australia sent naval vessels and aircraft, while Poland contributed some Special Forces personnel. Other nations provided token troop deployments and logistical support. To be sure, the coalition in 2003 paled in comparison to the truly international coalition arrayed against Iraq in 1991.

Operation IRAQI FREEDOM began without UN approval on March 20, 2003, with massive air strikes against targets in Baghdad. They included places where Hussein was thought to be hiding as well as communications, transportation, and electrical-generating facilities. On the right of the allied advance, British and U.S. marines quickly seized the Iraqi port of Umm Qasr before moving on to surround Basra, Iraq's second-largest city, finally taken on April 6 after careful reconnaissance of Iraqi defenses. On the left, the U.S. 3rd Infantry Division swept rapidly through Iraq's western desert, seizing Najaf on April 1 and Karbala two days later, which provided jump-off points for the attack on Baghdad. In the center, the 1st U.S. Marine Division overran the strategic Rumaila oil fields before fighting a stiff battle to cross the Euphrates River at Nasiriya.

Denied the option of inserting forces into Iraq from the north through Turkey, the Italy-based U.S. 173rd Airborne Brigade made a combat jump on the night of March 26 to seize critical airfields in northern Iraq and then coordinate action with Kurdish forces there. It was the largest airborne operation since the Vietnam War. Once the paratroopers consolidated their positions on the ground, U.S. Air Force C-17s brought in a company of M-1A2 Abrams main battle tanks from Germany to provide heavy support. It was history's first combat air-landing of main battle tanks.

Gridlock at Nasiriya, meanwhile, temporarily slowed the American advance, as did a major sandstorm on March 27 and 28. Iraqi regular army divisions that had been bypassed by fast-moving American units simply disintegrated as the officers abandoned their troops and the rank and file deserted and returned to their homes. Republican Guard divisions occasionally offered more determined resistance but were ultimately overwhelmed by American firepower. Quite ominously, the most ferocious resistance was offered by the fedayeen, although they were invariably overwhelmed as well. The percentage of American ordinance that could be considered precision guided was far greater than had been the case in 1991, with devastating results.

After a brief pause to reconnoiter Iraqi defenses around and inside Baghdad, including two dramatic thunder runs by American armor through sections of Baghdad, the Americans made their move, and by April 9 the city had been overrun. Hussein fled the capital and went into hiding. The rest of the country was occupied by American troops in succeeding days. President Bush declared an end to combat operations on May 1, 2003, although the fighting for Iraq has continued to the present day. The growing Iraqi insurgency has resulted in many more deaths since April 2003 and threatens to plunge Iraq into a full-scale civil war. Hussein's sons Uday and Qusay, major figures in the regime, were killed in action with American Special Forces on July 22, 2003. Hussein himself was not captured until December 13, 2003.

Casualty figures—especially on the Iraq side—are difficult to determine precisely. One estimate suggests that approximately 10,800 Iraqi soldiers and 4,300 Iraqi civilians died during the invasion, with an additional 10,000 Iraqi militant and 69,100 Iraqi civilian deaths between June 2003 and June 2007. The United States lost 117 soldiers during the invasion and an additional 2,820 during June 2003–June 2007. Coalition forces report 32 killed during the invasion and 183 additional military deaths during June 2003–June 2007.

Operation IRAQI FREEDOM was a rapid success in its initial phase of offensive operations because the soldiers and equipment of the coalition forces were vastly superior to their Iraqi opponents, who were poorly trained, poorly motivated, poorly equipped, and even more poorly led. The coalition also had complete air supremacy from the start. Once the initial combat operations were complete, however, the occupation and rebuilding of Iraq turned into a quagmire because the coalition had far too few troops on the ground to provide even minimal levels of internal security.

Once Baghdad fell, it also became painfully obvious that the United States had gone in without anything resembling a viable plan for what came next. During congressional hearings held before the invasion, the U.S. Army's highly respected chief of staff, General Eric Shinseki, had testified that in his opinion it would take "several hundred thousand" troops to secure postwar Iraq. Almost immediately, top Pentagon officials roundly condemned Shinseki, his assessment was dismissed as being "widely off the mark," and the army chief was subjected to shabby treatment for his remaining year in office. Shinseki, of course, had been completely right.

Another reason for the American failure was the Pentagon's blind adherence to Rumsfeld's untested and dubious theories about military transformation, the center of gravity of which was the supremacy of modern technology to the human factor in warfare. Military history is one long series of cycles that repeatedly demonstrate the failure of that dogma. By abandoning the historically proven Powell Doctrine of the necessity of going in with overmatching force, Operation IRAQI FREEDOM was designed for failure.

PAUL W. DOERR

See also

Al Qaeda; Bush, George Walker; Chemical Weapons and Warfare; Hussein, Saddam; Iran; Iran, Armed Forces; Iraq; Iraq, Armed Forces; Nuclear Weapons; Persian Gulf War; Terrorism; United States, Middle East Policy

References

Gordon, Michael R., and Bernard E. Trainor. *Cobra II: The Inside Story of the Invasion and Occupation of Iraq.* New York: Pantheon, 2006.

Kagan, Frederick. *Finding the Target: The Transformation of American Military Policy.* New York: Encounter Books, 2006.

Tripp, Charles. *A History of Iraq.* Cambridge: Cambridge University Press, 2002.

Woodward, Bob. *Plan of Attack.* New York: Simon and Schuster, 2004.

Irgun Tsvai Leumi

The Irgun Tsvai Leumi (National Military Organization) was a right-wing paramilitary Zionist underground movement in Palestine from 1931 to 1948. It was better known later as Etzel for its contracted Hebrew initials. Irgun became renowned for launching immediate and harsh retaliatory attacks on persons or organizations that had initiated violence against the Jewish community in Palestine (Yishuv). It was also known for its advocacy of military action against the British, who held a mandate over Palestine until May 1948. The British categorized Irgun as a terrorist organization, and the Jewish Agency for Palestine, Haganah, and Histadrut declared many of its operations to be acts of terrorism.

Even as the British slowly shifted their support to the Palestine's Arab population in the 1930s, the leadership of the Jewish Agency for Palestine, in particular David Ben-Gurion, continued to work closely with the British to promote the interests of the Jewish population in Palestine. Haganah supported this position through its self-defense and military strategy of havlaga, or self-restraint. But not all of the Haganah membership agreed with a restrained response to the perceived British pro-Arab bias. This political and policy disagreement, coupled with Haganah's prevailing socialist ideology, caused a minority of its members, led by Avraham Tehomi, to leave Haganah in 1931 and form Irgun. Irgun was based on premises formulated by Vladimir Jabotinsky, who had led the Jewish Legion when it had fought with the British to remove the Ottoman Turks from Palestine in World War I. He believed strongly that swift, retaliatory action would forestall Arab attacks on the Yishuv.

By 1936 Irgun was little more than a pawn of the extreme nationalist Revisionist Zionists (Revisionist Party), led by Jabotinsky. The Revisionists had seceded from the World Zionist Organization (WZO) and were advocating the creation by force of a Jewish homeland, spanning both banks of the Jordan River. In 1937 Haganah again split into right-wing and left-wing factions. The right-wing faction joined Irgun, and some of the members of Irgun, including Tehomi, rejoined Haganah. Until this time, Irgun had been little more than a small and ineffective irritant in the region.

When Arab attacks during the Arab Revolt of 1936–1939 killed some 400 Jews, Irgun began launching retaliatory attacks against Arabs, utilizing car bombs in areas of high Arab congregation. These endured until the beginning of World War II and killed as many as 250 Arab civilians. Irgun, which considered the British mandatory government to be illegal under international law, also directed acts

The ruins of Jerusalem's King David Hotel, blown up by the Jewish terrorist group Irgun Tsvai Leumi. The bombing on July 22, 1946, caused the deaths of 91 people. (Hugo Mendelson/Israeli Government Press Office)

of terrorism and assassination against the British. When the British White Paper of 1939 openly shifted British support away from the Jews to the Arabs by severely restricting Jewish immigration, settlement, and land purchases in Palestine, Irgun focused on attacking British military installations and interests. Irgun's rationale for the attacks was that the new, more severe British restrictions on Jewish immigration from Europe were contributing to Nazi Germany's genocide against Jews that soon became known as the Holocaust. Indeed, Irgun demonstrated that immigration to Palestine had saved approximately 18,000 European Jews prior to the shift in British policy, which began in earnest in early 1940.

During 1941–1943, Irgun suspended its attacks on British interests and supported the Allies against Germany and its Arab allies in the Middle East. However, a small group of men known as the Stern Gang, the Fighters for the Freedom of Israel, or Lehi and led by Avraham Stern separated from Irgun in 1941 and continued to attack the British in Palestine during this period. When Irgun was under the command of Menachem Begin (1943–1948), the organization declared war against the British in February 1944 and resumed attacks on Arab villages and British interests.

On November 6, 1944, in Cairo, Lehi assassinated Walter Edward Guinness, Lord Moyne, heir to the Guinness beer fortune and the British minister resident in the Middle East. The murder was allegedly in retaliation for the 1939 White Paper's restrictions on Jewish immigration that were contributing to the deaths of Jews in the Holocaust. At that point, Haganah and the Jewish Agency for Palestine launched a campaign against Irgun and Lehi named Sezon ("Hunting Season"), which turned over to the British a number of the members and leaders of Irgun. The British, with more than 100,000 soldiers in Palestine alone, ultimately arrested and jailed about 1,000 Irgun and Lehi members.

In an attempt to fight more effectively against the continuing British restrictions on Jewish immigration, Irgun, Lehi, and Haganah allied during October 1944–July 1945 as the Jewish Resistance Movement. This alliance ended in August 1945 after Irgun killed 91 soldiers and British, Arab, and Jewish civilians on July 22, 1946, when it bombed the British military, police, and civil headquarters at the King David Hotel in Jerusalem. Begin and Irgun claimed to have issued three warnings in an attempt to limit casualties. Nevertheless, the British arrested, tried, convicted, and hanged several members of Irgun. When Irgun responded by hanging two British sergeants, the executions stopped, although British arrests of Irgun members continued. On May 5, 1947, Haganah and Irgun combined forces to breach the wall of the supposedly secure British prison at Akko (Acre), thereby freeing 251 prisoners.

In anticipation of and following the United Nations (UN) partition of Palestine in 1947, from July 1947 to June 1948 Irgun and Haganah increasingly coordinated their forces. Irgun's greatest victory and largest operation was the capture of the Arab city of Jaffa. On May 28, 1948, the provisional government of the newly declared State of Israel transformed Haganah into its national military, the Israel Defense Forces (IDF). In doing so, it outlawed all other armed forces. In September 1948 the military activities of the Irgun were folded into the IDF. Begin, meanwhile, adapted what remained of the movement into a political party that was the precursor of the Herut (Freedom) Party, which merged in 1965 with the Liberal Party to form the Gahal Party. Gahal served as the foundation for the present-day Likud Party.

RICHARD EDWARDS

See also

Begin, Menachem; Ben-Gurion, David; Haganah; Holocaust; Israel Defense Forces; Jewish Agency for Israel; Likud Party; Palestine, British Mandate for; United Kingdom, Middle East Policy

References

Begin, Menachem. *The Revolt*. Los Angeles: Nash Publishing, 1972.

Bell, J. Bowyer. *Terror out of Zion: Irgun Zvai Leumi, Lehi and the Palestine Underground, 1929–1949*. New York: St. Martin's, 1979.

Ben Ami, Yitshaq. *Years of Wrath, Days of Glory: Memoirs from the Irgun*. New York: R. Speller, 1982.

Levine, David. *The Birth of the Irgun Zvai Leumi: The Jewish Resistance Movement*. Jerusalem: Gefen, 1996.

Islamic Jihad, Palestinian

Militant nationalist Palestinian group. Harakat al-Jihad al-Islami fi Filastin, known as the Palestinian Islamic Jihad (PIJ), was established by Fathi Shiqaqi, Sheikh Abd al-Aziz al-Awda, and others in the Gaza Strip during the 1970s. Several different factions identified with the name Islamic Jihad, including the Usrat al-Jihad (founded in 1948); the Detachment of Islamic Jihad, identified with the Abu Jihad contingent of Fatah; the Islamic Jihad Organization al-Aqsa Battalions, founded by Sheikh Asad Bayyud al-Tamimi in Jordan in 1982; Tanzim al-Jihad al-Islami, led by Ahmad Muhanna; and several non-Palestinian groups. This has caused much confusion over the years. Also, the PIJ movement portrayed itself as being a part of a jihadi continuum rather than a distinct entity.

While in Egypt in the 1970s, Shiqaqi, al-Awda, and the current director-general of the PIJ Ramadan Abdullah Shallah embraced an Islamist vision similar to the Egyptian Muslim Brotherhood. But they rejected the moderation forced on that organization by the Egyptian government's aim of political participation in tandem with *dawa* (proselytizing and education). The Palestinian group distinguished itself from secular nationalists and antinationalist Islamists in calling for grassroots organization and armed struggle to liberate Palestine as part of the Islamic solution.

Shiqaqi returned to Palestinian territory, and the PIJ began to express its intent to wage jihad (holy war) against Israel. Israeli sources claim that the PIJ developed the military apparatus known as the Jerusalem Brigades (Saraya al-Quds) by 1985, and this organization carried out attacks against the Israeli military, including an attack known as Operation GATE OF MOORS at an induction ceremony in 1986. The PIJ also claimed responsibility for the suicide bombing in Beit Led, near Netanya, Israel, on January 22, 1994. In the attack, 19 Israelis were killed and another 60 injured.

Shiqaqi spent a year in jail in the early 1980s and then in 1986 was jailed for two more years. He was deported to Lebanon along with al-Awda in April 1988. The PIJ established an office in Damascus, Syria, and began support and services in Palestinian refugee camps in Lebanon.

Shallah had meanwhile completed a doctorate at the University of Durham, served as the editor of a journal of the World and Islam Studies Enterprise, and taught briefly at the University of South Florida. When Shiqaqi was assassinated by unidentified agents (allegedly Mossad) in Malta in 1995, Shallah returned to lead the PIJ. His Florida associations led to the trials of Dr. Sami Al-Arian and Imam Fawaz Damra and others who allegedly supported the PIJ in the United States.

The PIJ emerged prior to Hamas. The two organizations were rivals despite the commonality of their nationalist perspectives, but Hamas gained a much larger popular following than the PIJ, whose estimated support is only 4–5 percent of the Palestinian population in the territories. The PIJ has a following among university students at the Islamic University in Gaza and other colleges and became very active in the Second (al-Aqsa) Intifada, which began in September 2000.

In Lebanon, the organization competes with Fatah, the primary and largest political faction in the Palestine Liberation Organization (PLO). Like Hamas and secular nationalist groups known as the Palestinian National Alliance, the PIJ rejected the 1993 Oslo Accords and demanded a full Israeli withdrawal from Palestinian lands. The group has a following among Palestinian refugees and at Ain Hilweh but also suffers from the political fragmentation of Palestinian and Islamist organizations there.

The Palestinian Authority (PA) closed down a publication sympathetic to the PIJ but eventually allowed it to reopen. In June 2003, under significant international pressure, Syria closed PIJ and Hamas offices in Damascus, and Shallah left for Lebanon. Khalid Mishaal went to Qatar, but both later returned to Syria.

In the Palestinian territories, the PIJ continues to differ with Hamas. Hamas ceased attacks against Israel beginning in 2004 and successfully captured a majority in the Palestinian elections of January 2006. Hamas moderates are also considering the recognition of Israel and a two-state solution. The PIJ, in contrast, had called for Palestinians to boycott the 2006 elections and refused any accommodation with Israel. It continued to sponsor suicide attacks after 2004 in retaliation for Israel's military offensives and targeted killings of PIJ leaders, including Louay Saadi in October 2005. The PIJ claimed responsibility for two suicide attacks in that year.

Israeli authorities continue to highlight Iranian-PIJ links. They cite Shiqaqi's early publication of a pamphlet that praised Ayatollah Ruhollah Khomeini for the 1979 Islamic revolution based on Sharia (Islamic law) and for recognizing the Palestinian cause. And an intercepted PA security briefing has led the Israelis to assert that the PIJ continues to rely on Syrian support and Iranian funding.

SHERIFA ZUHUR

See also

Fatah; Hamas; Intifada, Second; Jihad; Muslim Brotherhood; Oslo Accords; Palestine Liberation Organization; Palestinian Authority; Palestinian Elections of 2006

References

Abu-Amr, Ziad. *Islamic Fundamentalisms in the West Bank and Gaza: Muslim Brotherhood and Islamic Jihad.* Bloomington: Indiana University Press, 1994.
Journal of Palestine Studies. "The Movement of Islamic Jihad and the Oslo Process: An Interview with Ramadan Abdullah Shallah." *Journal of Palestine Studies* 28 (1999): 61–73.
Knudsen, Are. "Islamism in the Diaspora: Palestinian Refugees in Lebanon." *Journal of Refugee Studies* 18(2) (2005): 216–234.

Islamic Movement in Israel

The Islamic Movement in Israel has encompassed both specific Islamic revivalist and activist efforts and Muslim efforts to gain more control over their own institutions. Because the Israeli government feared that any autonomous Arab body (such as the pre-1948 Supreme Muslim Council) would support Arab nationalism, it exerted strict control over education, *awqaf* (endowments), Islamic courts, and judges.

The Islamic Movement in Israel dates to the 1970s. The Usrat al-Jihad movement, founded by Farid Ibrahim Abu Muh in 1979, burned down a theater in Umm al-Fahm and carried out other attacks. Members of that group along with the spiritual leader of the broader Islamic movement, Abdallah Nimr Darwish, were imprisoned and then released in 1985 in a prisoner exchange. Darwish subsequently rejected jihad as a tactic, and the Islamic Movement established educational and health services and constructed mosques. In 1993, its candidates won in mayoral elections in Kafr Qasim, Darwish's hometown.

Among the grievances addressed by the Islamic Movement have been the corruption and irregularities surrounding the sale of waqf (religiously endowed) land. Once administered by the Supreme Muslim Council, these were later handled by Israeli-appointed waqf boards of trustees. Disputes over Muslim graveyards, lack or closures of mosques, and the depressed economic circumstances of the Arab sector also concerned the Islamic Movement. Waqf land in the Old City of Jerusalem has been a key political issue, as has been the closure of newer mosques closed for political reasons. Because of waqf land adjacent to the Basilica of the Annunciation, demand for a mosque there intensified. And media attention prior to Pope John Paul II's 2000 visit illustrated the transformation of Nazareth to a majority Muslim town.

Arab students in Israel are enrolled in a separate educational system, by all accounts inferior to that for Jewish students. According to the curriculum requirements in the late 1960s, Arab students studied 256 hours per year about Jewish topics, but only 30 hours were dedicated to Islamic issues. Meanwhile, in the Jewish schools no hours of instruction were devoted to Islamic issues. Reforms occurred by the 1990s, but many concerns remained regarding the minority curriculum. The Islamic Movement protested the curriculum and addressed the resulting gaps in knowledge through mosques and study groups.

The Islamic Movement's political success grew in each subsequent election, and it soon spread to Kafr Bara, Kafr Kanna, Nazareth, and many other towns. An unacknowledged split occurred in 1996 between Darwish's faction, which favored running for parliamentary elections as well as dawa (proselytizing and education) activities, and the more separatist Sheikh Raid Salah, mayor of Umm al-Fahm, and Khamal Khatib of Kafr Kana. The Islamic Movement began to publish *Al-Sirat* in 1986 and distributed more than 10,000 copies by 1989, when the Islamic Movement began to publish the journal *Sawt al-Haqq wa-l-Huriyya*. Later, the more pragmatic faction published *al-Mithaq*. The movement also became involved in Islamic art festivals in the late 1980s and early 1990s. The movement also evolved in the Negev Desert, where Sheikh Juma al-Qassassi, a Bedouin, was an early leader. In recent elections, the Bedouin supported Islamic Movement candidates for the Knesset (Israeli parliament).

Three terrorist attacks were blamed on the Islamic Movement in 1992 and 1999. The government has condemned the movement because of the emergence of Islamic Jihad inside Israel and because of the movement's expressed sympathy with Hamas and support for the Second (al-Aqsa) Intifada. The Israeli government typically blames the Islamic Movement's preachers for inciting violence against Israel. During 2003–2004, Salah and other Islamic Movement members were held in detention for more than a year and put on trial by direct order of Prime Minister Ariel Sharon for providing humanitarian assistance to Palestinians in the occupied territories.

SHERIFA ZUHUR

See also

Bedouin; Hamas; Intifada, Second; Islamic Jihad, Palestinian; Israel; Israel, Arab Population in; Jihad; Waqf

References

Aburaiya, Issam. "The 1996 Split of the Islamic Movement in Israel: Between the Holy Text and Israeli-Palestinian Context." *International Journal of Politics, Culture, and Society* 17(3) (March 2004): 439–455.

Bitterlemons International. "Faith, Freedom, and Democracy: Interview with Abdallah Nimr Darwish." *Middle East Roundtable* 9(2) (March 4, 2004): 4–6.

Israeli, Raphael. *Muslim Fundamentalism in Israel.* London: Brassey's, 1993.

Peled, Alisa Rubin. *Debating Islam in the Jewish State: The Development of Policy toward Islamic Institutions in Israel.* Albany, NY: SUNY Press, 2001.

———. "Towards Autonomy? The Islamist Movement Quest for Control of Islamic Institutions in Israel." *Middle East Journal* 55(3) (Summer 2001): 378–398.

Zimmerman, Cheryl. "The Politicization of Umm al-Fahem." Unpublished PhD dissertation, University of Utah, Salt Lake City, 1993.

Ismail Ali, Ahmad
Born: October 14, 1917
Died: December 25, 1974

Egyptian military officer. Ahmad Ismail Ali was born on October 14, 1917, in Cairo, Egypt, and graduated from the Cairo Military Academy in 1938. During World War II he saw action in the Western Desert. In the Israeli War of Independence (1948–1949) he fought as a brigade commander in the Egyptian Army. From 1950 to 1953 he taught at the Cairo Military Academy. He also fought with Egyptian forces in the Sinai, opposing the Franco-British-Israeli intervention to secure the Suez Canal in 1956. He served as commander of forces at Port Said from 1957 to 1960.

After a brief tour in the Congo on a peacekeeping operation, Ismail served from 1961 to 1967 as a military adviser to the Egyptian government. During the 1967 Six-Day War, he was a divisional commander. In March 1969, President Gamal Abdel Nasser appointed Ismail chief of military operations, but he was later fired after a successful Israeli raid into Egypt caused embarrassment. He then served as head of the Egyptian Intelligence Service.

In 1972 Ismail was appointed commander in chief of the Egyptian Army. On January 21, 1973, he assumed the post of commander in chief of the Combined Armed Forces of Egypt, Libya, and Syria, and a week later, on January 28, he assumed the title of commander in chief of the Arab Fronts.

During the 1973 Yom Kippur War, Ismail was serving as the Egyptian minister of defense. Prior to the conflict, he had been actively involved in preparations for a preemptive attack on Israel. In February 1972 in his capacity as defense minister, he traveled to Moscow to secure both aircraft and missiles for offensive and defensive purposes. His goal was to build a missile wall around Egypt as protection against the Israeli Air Force, which had all but destroyed the Egyptian Air Force on the ground in the 1967 Six-Day War.

Ismail spearheaded an Egyptian disinformation campaign to confuse Israeli intelligence about the forthcoming Egyptian and Syrian attack. While visiting Romania, he let it slip that the Egyptians were inept at handling their Soviet military hardware, including the missiles. Before the 1973 war, he prepared war plans with General Saad el-Shazly, Egyptian chief of staff, that called for a massive surprise attack against Israel.

El-Shazly was opposed to Ismail's plans and refused to obey his orders. On October 14, 1973, el-Shazly reluctantly obeyed a direct order from President Anwar Sadat to advance against Israel. In a great tank battle designed to relieve pressure on the Syrians on the Golan Heights, the Egyptians were defeated. On October 16 Ismail was still at odds with el-Shazly, who wanted to withdraw west of Suez. By the morning of October 20, el-Shazly had been relieved of command. General Abd al-Ghani Gamasi (Jamasi) replaced him.

In November 1973, Ismail was promoted to the rank of field marshal. He died of cancer in London on December 25, 1974.

ANDREW J. WASKEY

See also

Egypt; Egypt, Armed Forces; Six-Day War; Yom Kippur War

References

Herzog, Chaim. *The Arab-Israeli Wars: War and Peace in the Middle East from the War of Independence to Lebanon.* Westminster, MD: Random House, 1984.

Rabinovich, Abraham. *The Yom Kippur War: The Epic Encounter That Transformed the Middle East.* New York: Schocken, 2005.

Israel

Israel, the only Jewish nation in the world, has an area of some 8,019 square miles (slightly larger than the U.S. state of Massachusetts) and a current population of about 7 million people. It is bordered by the eastern Mediterranean to the west, Lebanon to the north, Jordan and Syria to the east, and Egypt to the southwest. Its government is a parliamentary democracy, and the country boasts an advanced Western-style economy.

According to the Jewish Bible, the Tanakh (known as the Old Testament to Christians), Jews trace their origins to some 4,000

Israel's Mediterranean coastline. (Corel)

years ago to the prophet Abraham and his son Isaac. A series of Jewish kingdoms and states intermittently ruled Palestine or Israel for more than a millennium thereafter. Jews were the majority of the inhabitants of Palestine or, as the Jews called it, Israel (Land of God), for many centuries until the first century AD. After suppressing a series of Jewish revolts in the first century, the Romans expelled most Jews from Palestine. Over the next thousand years, Jews migrated to Western and Eastern Europe and then to the United States. Beginning at the end of the 19th century, however, a strong movement, known as Zionism, developed whereby Jews sought to return to and take up residence in Palestine.

During World War I in order to secure Jewish support for the war, the British government in 1917 issued the Balfour Declaration. Named for Foreign Secretary Arthur Balfour, it announced British support for the "establishment in Palestine of a national home for the Jewish people." At the same time, however, in order to secure Arab support against the Turks, the British government was promising support for establishment of an Arab state.

After the war, in 1920 Britain and France divided up the Middle Eastern possessions of the Ottoman Empire as League of Nations mandates. Britain secured Palestine and Iraq, while France was granted mandates in Syria and Lebanon. In 1922 Britain split Palestine into Transjordan, east of the Jordan River, and Palestine to the west.

Already a number of Jews had arrived in Palestine and settled there, purchasing Arab lands. Following World War I these numbers grew substantially, something that Palestinian Arabs viewed with alarm. The Arabs saw themselves becoming a marginalized minority in their own land. In response to continuing Jewish immigration, sporadic Arab attacks against Jews as well as British officials in Palestine occurred, escalating into the Arab Revolt of 1936–1939.

At the same time, militant Jewish groups began to agitate against what they saw as restrictive British immigration policies for Jews in Palestine. Armed militant Zionist groups such as the Lohamei Herut Israel (Stern Gang) and the Irgun Tsvai Leumi (National Military Organization) carried out actions against the British administration in Palestine, and in the 1930s a three-way struggle emerged that pitted the British against militant Arabs and Jews. Amid sharply increased violence, the British government attempted a delicate balancing act, made more difficult by the need to secure Arab (and also Jewish) support against Germany and Italy in World War II.

The Holocaust, the demonic Nazi scheme to exterminate the Jews during World War II, resulted in the deaths of some 6 million

Jews in Europe. During the war and immediately afterward, many of the survivors sought to immigrate to Israel. For Jews, the great lesson of the war was that they could not rely on national governments or international agencies to protect them. In order to be protected, they would require their own independent state. The Holocaust also created in the West, which did little to try to save the Jews during the war, a sense of moral obligation for the creation of a Jewish state and brought pressure on the British government to relax the prewar restrictive policies it had instituted regarding Jewish immigration into Palestine. At the same time, however, the Arabs of Palestine were adamantly opposed to any sharp increase in the number of Jews in Palestine or the creation there of a Jewish state.

Following World War II, as Jewish refugees sought to gain access to Palestine, many were forcibly turned away by British warships sent to patrol the Mediterranean coast for this very purpose. At the same time, British authorities wrestled with partitioning Palestine into Arab and Jewish states. Jews and Arabs proved intransigent, and in February 1947 after both rejected a final proposal for partition, Britain turned the problem over to the United Nations (UN).

In August 1947 the UN recommended granting Palestine its independence. The UN also developed a plan for partitioning Palestine into separate Arab and Jewish states. Jerusalem was to be classified as an international area under the UN in order to preclude conflict over its status. Although the Arab population in Palestine was then 1.2 million people and the Jews numbered just 600,000, the UN plan granted the proposed Jewish state some 55 percent of the land and the Arab state only 45 percent. The Arab states rejected the partition plan, which included an economic union. The Jews generally accepted it. The UN General Assembly approved the plan in November 1947, and the British government announced that it would accept the UN recommendation and declared that the British Mandate for Palestine would end on May 15, 1948.

The Council of the Arab League announced that it was prepared to prevent the creation of a Jewish state by force if necessary, and immediately following the UN vote militant Palestinian Arabs and foreign Arab fighters began attacks against Jewish communities in Palestine, beginning the Arab-Jewish Communal War (November 30, 1947–May 14, 1948). The United States, with the world's largest Jewish population, became the chief champion and most reliable ally of a Jewish state, a position that cost it dearly in its relations

The Jewish Gat settlement, founded in 1941 near ancient Gath, east of Gaza Road. (Library of Congress)

with the Arab world and greatly impacted subsequent geopolitics in the Middle East and throughout the world.

The British completed their pullout on May 14, 1948, and that same day David Ben-Gurion, executive chairman and defense minister of the Jewish Agency, immediately declared the independent Jewish State of Israel. Ben-Gurion, from Mapai (Worker's Party), became the new state's first prime minister, a post he held during 1948–1953 and 1955–1963.

At first, the interests of the United States and those of the Soviet Union regarding the Jewish state converged. U.S. recognition of Israel came only shortly before that of the Soviet Union. Moscow found common ground with the Jews in their suffering at the hands of the Nazis in World War II and also identified with the socialism espoused by the early Jewish settlers in Palestine as well as their anti-British stance. The Cold War, the reemergence of official anti-Semitism in the Soviet Union, and Moscow's desire to court the Arab states by supporting Arab nationalism against the West soon changed all that.

Immediately following Ben-Gurion's declaration of independence, the Arab armies of Egypt, Lebanon, Transjordan, Syria, and Iraq invaded Palestine, thus sparking the Israeli War of Independence (1948–1949). In the war, the Jews successfully defended their new state and defeated the Arab armies. A series of armistices in 1949 ended the war, with Israel left in control of an additional 26 percent of the land of Mandate Palestine west of the Jordan River. Transjordan, however, controlled large portions of Judea and Samaria, later known as the West Bank. The establishment of Israel and subsequent wars created some 600,000–700,000 Palestinian Arab refugees. Why these refugees fled their homes is hotly disputed. Arabs blame the Jews for expelling the Palestinian Arabs by causing mass panic and fear through warfare, terrorism, and massacres. Jews, on the other hand, insist that Arabs fled on their own or at the urging of Arab states, which incited fear and panic among Palestinian Arabs by warning darkly of imminent Jewish attacks and massacres.

Meanwhile, the Israelis set up the machinery of statehood. Mapai and its successor parties would govern Israel for the next 30 years. These were social democratic parties with strong roots in Zionism. As such, they were hawkish on defense but inclined toward moderate socialism in the socioeconomic sphere. The provisional government governed until February 14, 1949, following democratic elections on January 25, 1949, that established a unicameral parliament, later known as the Knesset, that consisted of 120 members. The executive (cabinet) was selected by the Knesset and was subject to it. Israel also adopted a system of proportional representation in which seats in the Knesset were based on the percentage of votes received. Even parties receiving relatively few votes had representatives in the Knesset. Such parties included those representing the Arab population, those espousing various degrees of Jewish orthodoxy, the communists, and Revisionist Zionist groups.

On May 11, 1949, Israel was admitted as the 59th member of the UN. Mapai remained the dominant political party after the second Knesset elections on July 30, 1951, in which a coalition government with religious parties was formed.

In 1950 Israel promulgated the so-called right of return law, which stipulated the right of any Jew to settle in Israel. In 1951 alone 687,000 Jews arrived in Israel, some 300,000 from the Arab states. Ben-Gurion remained prime minister until 1953 and returned to that position in October 1955, remaining in office until 1963.

Israel's early years were dominated by the great challenge of absorbing and integrating into society hundreds of thousands of Jewish immigrants from different parts of the world, including Ashkenazi Jews from Eastern and Central Europe; Sephardic Jews who had fled from Spain in 1492 and settled in Muslim or Ottoman lands, including what is today Bulgaria, parts of Romania, Turkey, and the Middle East; other Middle Eastern or Oriental Jews; and those from such places as Iran, India, and Afghanistan. In addition to money raised from Jewish communities overseas, especially in the United States, and the U.S. government, financial assistance came from an unlikely source. Chancellor Konrad Adenauer of West Germany secured passage of legislation to provide billions of dollars in assistance to Israel over a 12-year period. Federal indemnification laws provided for payments to individual victims of the Holocaust.

Israel's formative years also witnessed the creation of a mixed socialist-capitalist economy. Included in the expansion and maturation of the economy were agricultural incentives and cultivating more land. The differences in terms of cultural background and socioeconomic status among these various groups of Jews initially proved a challenge for the Israeli government.

The 1949 cease-fires that ended the 1948–1949 war were not followed by peace agreements. The Arab states not only refused to recognize the existence of Israel but also refused to concede defeat in the war. By 1950 they had imposed an economic and political boycott on Israel. Throughout most of the 1950s, Israel suffered from repeated attacks and raids from neighboring Arab states as well as Palestinian Arab paramilitary and terrorist groups. Aggressive Israeli retaliation failed to stop them. The 1952 coup and revolution in Egypt led by the Free Officers further increased tension between Israel and Egypt. Indeed, Egyptian president Gamal Abdel Nasser proved to be an outspoken opponent of Israel and the West and a champion of Arab nationalism and unity. He increased the power of the Egyptian military, supported cross-border raids into Israeli territory by fedayeen (guerrilla fighters) from the Gaza Strip, and formed alliances with other Arab states. He also cultivated close ties with the Soviet Union.

In 1956 Nasser nationalized the Suez Canal, which provided the pretext for the French, British, and Israeli governments to collaborate to attack Egypt. The British sought to retake control of the canal, while the French sought to end Nasser's support of the Algerian independence movement. At the same time, Israel also saw the Suez Crisis as an opportunity to cooperate with Britain and France to check Nasser's power and influence if not overthrow him. On October 29, 1956, Israeli forces invaded the Sinai and headed for the

Suez Canal. This provided the excuse for the British and the French to intervene. The U.S. government applied considerable pressure, and all three states agreed to withdraw. Israel secured the right to free navigation through the Suez Canal and on the waterways through the Straits of Tiran and the Gulf of Aqaba. The UN deployed a peacekeeping force between Egypt and Israel until 1967, when Egypt secured its departure just before the June 1967 Six-Day War.

During 1957–1967, Israel was primarily preoccupied with domestic politics, including continued agricultural and industrial development. Its border with Egypt generally remained calm, although incidents with Syria in particular increased, especially over water rights as Israel diverted water from the Jordan River to irrigate its land. This led Syria and Lebanon to divert water upstream from the Jordan River. In response to this so-called water war, Israel destroyed Lebanese and Syrian projects designed to reduce water flow downstream.

Ben-Gurion resigned as prime minister in 1963 and two years later defected from Mapai, creating a new party, the Rafi Party (Israeli Labor List). Upon Ben-Gurion's resignation, Levi Eshkol of Mapai served as prime minister until his death in 1969, when Foreign Minister Golda Meir replaced him as Israel's fourth prime minister.

On May 23, 1960, in Buenos Aires, Argentina, Israeli agents captured the fugitive Nazi official Adolf Eichmann, who had official charge of the deportation of Jews to the death camps during World War II. Spiriting Eichmann out of Argentina, Israeli agents brought him to Israel. The Israeli government then placed him on trial for crimes against humanity and the Jewish people. Convicted, he was hanged on May 31, 1962, the only time the death penalty was imposed according to Israeli law. In 1965, however, after much internal debate and controversy, Israel established formal diplomatic relations with West Germany.

On February 22, 1966, a coup brought a military government to power in Syria, committed to the Palestinian cause and the liberation of Palestine. Incidents along Israel's border with Syria increased significantly. Throughout the spring of 1967, Israel faced increasing attacks along its borders from Syria and the Palestine Liberation Organization (PLO), an organization created in 1964 to represent the Palestinian Arabs and coordinate efforts with Arab states to liberate Palestine. The PLO began mounting cross-border attacks from Jordan. By May war seemed imminent with Syria, as Egypt and Jordan announced that they had mobilized their armies. This was in reaction to what they claimed was an Israeli mobilization, and other Arab countries such as Iraq pledged to join in any war against Israel. On May 23, Egypt closed the Straits of Tiran and blockaded the Gulf of Aqaba, thereby blockading the Israeli port of Eilat.

Fearing an imminent Arab attack and invasion, Israel launched a preemptive attack on June 5, 1967, crippling the air forces of Egypt, Syria, Jordan, and Iraq. Having achieved air supremacy, Israel then easily defeated the armies of Egypt, Jordan, and Syria as well as Iraqi units. Five days later, Israel occupied the Sinai and the Gaza Strip from Egypt, the West Bank and East Jerusalem from Jordan, and the Golan Heights from Syria, doubling the amount of territory under the control of the Jewish state and providing buffer zones in the new territories. In the wake of its military victory, Israel announced that it would not withdraw from these captured territories until negotiations with the Arab states took place leading to recognition of Israel's right to exist.

Israel's military victory did not, however, lead to peace with its Arab neighbors. Humiliated by their defeat, the Arab states refused to negotiate with, recognize, or make peace with Israel, which was spelled out in the Khartoum Arab Summit Communiqué of September 1, 1967. The war united much of Israeli society and muted, if not silenced, most political disputes for several years. On January 21, 1968, the Mapai Party merged with two other socialist political parties to form the Labor Party.

In 1969 the War of Attrition began, with Egypt shelling Israeli targets in the Sinai along the Suez Canal. Israel responded by launching retaliatory raids and air strikes. Israel also constructed the Bar-Lev Line, an elaborate series of defensive fortifications to shield Israeli forces from Egyptian artillery attacks. Nasser sought Soviet military aid and support, including surface-to-air missiles (SAMs). By 1969, the euphoria from Israel's decisive 1967 victory had turned into disillusionment over rising Israeli casualties and the fact that peace still seemed elusive.

During this time, Israel also experienced increasing incidents along its border with Jordan as the PLO launched raids and attacks into Israel from Jordan, leading to retaliatory Israeli attacks. This ultimately provoked a civil war between the PLO and the Jordanian government in 1970, which culminated in the so-called Black September that brought heavy fighting involving the Jordanian Army and the expulsion of the PLO from Jordan to Lebanon. During Black September, Syria sought to intervene on the side of the PLO but was deterred from doing so by Israel, which dispatched a military force to the Jordanian border as a deterrence at the request of the United States.

Beginning in 1970 with American support, UN-sponsored peace talks between Egypt and Israel resulted in a cease-fire and a temporary end to the War of Attrition. But no lasting peace settlement was reached over the question of Israel's occupation of Arab territories since the 1967 war. President Nasser died in September 1970. His successor, Anwar Sadat, sought an end to the war with Israel so as to focus on Egypt's many internal problems. Frustrated at the lack of the peace process, on October 6, 1973, on the Jewish high holy day of Yom Kippur, Egypt and Syria launched a surprise attack on Israel. Although both attacking powers enjoyed initial success and inflicted heavy casualties on Israeli forces, Israel, after regrouping its forces and being resupplied by the United States, repulsed the Egyptian and Syrian offensives and retained control of the Sinai and Golan Heights. Israel won the war but only after early and heavy losses. Nevertheless, the military balance between Israel and its Arab foes had shifted, and the notion of Israeli invincibility had ended.

The Yom Kippur War shook Israel's confidence and morale and proved costly in terms of lives. It also made Israel more economically dependent on the United States. In the December 1973 Knesset elections the Labor Party lost seats, and the newly formed right-wing Likud Party gained strength. Public and political fallout from the war led Prime Minister Meir to resign on April 10, 1974. She was succeeded by Yitzhak Rabin, also of the Labor Party.

A series of cease-fire talks between Israel and Egypt and between Israel and Syria now occurred, followed up by intensive shuttle diplomacy by U.S. secretary of state Henry Kissinger in 1974 to turn the cease-fire agreements into the basis for peace talks. By this time, international opinion was growing increasingly anti-Israeli as the propaganda war turned in favor of the Arabs, especially given the latter's hold over much of the world's oil supply. Israel's refusal to withdraw from occupied Arab territories seized during the Six-Day War led to the loss of much world support and sympathy especially in Africa, which viewed Israel's occupation as but another form of colonialism.

During this time, Arab states along with the PLO proved much more effective in publicizing the plight of the Palestinians. Increasing acts of terrorism by the PLO during 1970–1972 also focused world attention on the Arab-Israeli conflict and the Palestinian cause. On October 14, 1974, the UN General Assembly authorized the PLO to participate in a series of debates. Included was PLO chairman Yasser Arafat, considered a terrorist in Israel. He addressed the body, and on November 10, 1975, the General Assembly declared Zionism as racist. Rabin refused to negotiate with the PLO because it refused to recognize Israel and had proclaimed as its goal the destruction of the Jewish state.

With little loss of life, on July 4, 1976, Israeli commandos rescued Israeli airline passengers who had been kidnapped by Palestinian hijackers and taken to Entebbe, Uganda, under the protection of Ugandan dictator Idi Amin. The hijackers threatened to kill the passengers unless Palestinian terrorists in Israeli and West European prisons were released. The successful rescue of the 103 jetliner passengers proved a major morale boost for Israel and its military.

In May 1977 the Likud Party ended the Labor Party's 29-year political reign, and Menachem Begin became prime minister. Now seeking to jump-start the peace process, Sadat shocked the world by announcing on November 9, 1977, his willingness to go to Jerusalem and meet with the Israelis face-to-face to negotiate peace. Accepting an invitation by Begin to visit, Sadat arrived in Israel on November 19, the first Arab head of state to do so, effectively recognizing Israel's right to exist. During his visit, Sadat met with Begin and addressed the Knesset. Although every other Arab state refused to negotiate with Israel, after two years of negotiations mediated by U.S. president Jimmy Carter, Egypt and Israel made peace on March 26, 1979. Per the Camp David Accords, Israel withdrew from the Sinai in exchange for Egypt recognizing Israel. Discussions about the status of the Palestinians took place but the two states never achieved any common ground on this issue. Sadat's assassination

on October 6, 1981, effectively ended the talks. The Arab world condemned the peace treaty with Israel, and Egypt was suspended from the Arab League.

On July 7, 1981, the Israeli Air Force bombed the Iraqi nuclear reactor at Osiraq, thwarting Iraqi efforts to acquire nuclear weapons. The next year Israel invaded Lebanon, which had been experiencing a civil war since 1975, ostensibly to defend its northern border from terrorist attacks but also to expel the PLO from Lebanon, which it did by capturing the capital of Beirut and forcing the PLO to relocate to Tunisia. This came at a terrible human cost and material destruction to Lebanese civilians, however, and Israel failed to achieve its broad policy objectives of creating a stable pro-Israeli government in Lebanon. In 1983 Begin resigned and was replaced by fellow Likud member Yitzhak Shamir. Israel withdrew from most of Lebanon in 1986 but maintained a security zone there until May 2000, when it surrendered that territory as well.

A major Palestinian uprising—the First Intifada—erupted in 1987 in the Israeli occupied territories of the West Bank and the Gaza Strip and consumed much of Israel's military resources. The images of armed Israeli soldiers battling Palestinian children and teenagers, mostly throwing rocks, led to considerable international criticism of Israel. In 1991 following Iraq's 1990 invasion of Kuwait, Iraq targeted Israel with missiles in an ultimately unsuccessful attempt to provoke Israel to attack Iraq and cause the Arab states to withdraw from the multinational U.S.-led coalition force.

The collapse of the Soviet Union in December 1991 and the end of the Cold War brought an influx into Israel of hundreds of thousands of Jews from the Soviet Union. It also left many Arab states, previously allied with Moscow, isolated and gave the United States much more influence and leverage in the region. Accordingly, peace talks were held in 1991 and 1992 among Israel, Syria, Lebanon, Jordan, and the Palestinians. Those talks paved the way for the 1993 Oslo Accords between Israel and the PLO, stipulating the beginning of Palestinian self-rule in the West Bank and the Gaza Strip, and peace between Israel and Jordan in 1994.

Initial Israeli support for the Oslo Accords waned following a series of terrorist attacks by Hamas, a Palestinian terrorist group founded in 1987 at the beginning of the First Intifada that opposed the Oslo Accords. On November 4, 1995, a right-wing Jewish nationalist assassinated Rabin for his peace efforts with the Palestinians and willingness to cede occupied territory in the West Bank to the Palestinians. Continued Hamas terrorism led to the election as prime minister of hard-liner Benjamin Netanyahu of Likud. Netanyahu refused to pursue the land-for-peace dialogue with the Palestinians. Thus, the peace process stalled. In 1999 Labor's Ehud Barak defeated Netanyahu, and in 2000 talks between Barak and Arafat, mediated by U.S. president Bill Clinton, failed to produce agreement on a Palestinian state. The collapse of these talks and the visit of Likud's Ariel Sharon to the contested religious site known to Jews as the Temple Mount and to Muslims as the Noble Sanctuary sparked the Second (al-Aqsa) Intifada. Relations between the Israelis and Palestinians tumbled downward.

Sharon was elected prime minister of Israel in March 2001 and reelected in 2003. In the face of stalled peace talks with the Palestinians, by September 2005 Israel had withdrawn from the Gaza Strip, although it controlled its borders, coast, and airspace. Under Sharon, the Israeli government also began building a series of walls, or barriers, to separate Israel from most of the West Bank. These barriers are designed to defend Israel from repeated Palestinian terrorist attacks, but their construction has been criticized as a violation of international law and as an impediment to the establishment of any viable, independent Palestinian state. After Sharon suffered a massive stroke on January 4, 2006, Ehud Olmert became acting prime minister. He was formally elected to the post following the victory of his only recently formed Kadima Party in the legislative elections of April 14, 2006.

In June 2006 after a Hamas raid killed two Israeli soldiers and led to the capture of another, Israel launched a series of attacks on Hamas targets and infrastructure in the Gaza Strip. The next month, the Olmert government opted to become involved in a month-long conflict in Lebanon following an attack by Hezbollah on Israel that killed three Israeli soldiers and captured two others. Hezbollah is a large political party with a social and charitable wing but also has a militia that has received Iranian backing in the past and Syrian logistical support. This month-long conflict, which devastated southern and central Lebanon and parts of its eastern region and ruined its infrastructure, seemed to many observers a repeat of 1982, with Israel having failed to achieve its broad policy objectives and leaving Hezbollah stronger than ever.

Israeli voters remained keenly interested in such issues as the role of the Orthodox minority, the rights of Israeli Arabs, the fate of Israeli settlements in the West Bank, and the ups and downs of the economy. As the first decade of the 21st century draws to a close, the two nearest and direct threats to Israel remain violence from Hezbollah and from Palestinians in the territories that are able to move into Israel. Israel also regards Iran's desire to acquire nuclear weapons—a charge denied by Iran—as a palpable threat. Iranian president Mahmoud Ahmadinejad has repeatedly attacked Israel's policies, denied the Holocaust, and called for the destruction of Israel, which has also greatly concerned the Israelis. With respect to peace with the Palestinians, the presence of several hundred thousand Israeli settlers in the West Bank, the continuance of violent attacks by Palestinians, and disputes over the precise borders of any future Palestinian state remain the principal outstanding issues of contention. In addition, the surprising victory of Hamas in the January 2006 legislative elections for the Palestinian government was regarded by Israelis as a major setback for the cause of peace. At the end of 2007, despite a pledge by the opposing sides, a general peace settlement seemed as elusive as ever.

STEFAN BROOKS, DANIEL E. SPECTOR, AND SPENCER C. TUCKER

See also

Arab-Jewish Communal War; Attrition, War of; Begin, Menachem; Ben-Gurion, David; Eichmann, Karl Adolf; Israel, Arab Population in; Israel Defense Forces; Israeli Security Fence; Israeli War of Independence, Overview; Lebanon, Israeli Invasion of; Lebanon, Israeli Operations against; Meir, Golda; Olmert, Ehud; Sharon, Ariel; Sinai Campaign; Six-Day War; Suez Crisis; Yom Kippur War

References

Dershowitz, Alan M. *The Case for Israel*. New York: Wiley, 2004.
Dowty, Alan. *Israel/Palestine*. Malden, MA: Polity, 2005.
Gilbert, Martin. *Israel: A History*. New York: William Morrow, 1998.
Reich, Bernard. *A Brief History of Israel*. New York: Facts on File, 2005.
Sachar, Howard M. *A History of Israel: From the Rise of Zionism to Our Time*. 3rd ed. New York: Knopf, 2007.

Israel, Arab Population in

Arabs constitute roughly 16 percent of Israel's current population. If Arabs residing in East Jerusalem are counted, the percentage rises to nearly 20 percent. The great majority of Arabs living in Israel are Israeli citizens, although Arabs inhabiting East Jerusalem are generally not citizens. Many Israeli Palestinians have familial, social, and economic ties with Palestinians living in the West Bank, the Gaza Strip, and elsewhere in the Middle East.

One aspect of Israeli policy has been to separate Israeli Arabs from other Palestinians. Indeed, the government will not allow Arabs to refer to themselves as Palestinians. They study Hebrew literature and Jewish history in schools, while students in the West Bank and Gaza are exposed to different historical materials and the study of Arabic literature (not as a foreign language). If permitted to travel, Israeli Arabs cannot travel on their Israeli passports to most Arab countries. Their assertion of a Palestinian identity emerged nonetheless, and demonstrations during the Second (al-Aqsa) Intifada and Israeli Arab suicide bombers caused Israelis to begin discussions of expulsion.

The Arab population in Israel has risen steadily since 1948, when the total number was estimated at about 180,000. By 2000 that figure had grown to nearly 1.2 million, which included about 160,000 Palestinians living in Israel illegally. The vast majority of Israeli Arabs are Muslims. Included among the aggregate Arab population are approximately 170,000 Bedouin, descended from nomadic agricultural tribes. There are also some 180,000 Christian Arabs and an estimated 120,000 Druze as well as a Circassian population, who are Muslims. Statistically, roughly 82 percent of the Arab population in Israel is Muslim, and the remainder are either Christian or Druze.

Arabs in Israel are confronted with a number of socioeconomic hurdles. Many had their property taken from them by the state, and when resettled after 1948 they could not own or purchase land in the same legal manner as Israeli Jews. Israeli Arabs are not allowed to build or construct without permits, which may be used to restrict doing so in Jewish municipalities. Ironically, home ownership is relatively high among Arabs and as a whole is higher than it is for Jews and other groups in Israel, perhaps because Israeli Arabs are not provided housing benefits by the state. Arabs have faced—and continue to experience—varying amounts of discrimination. This

Arab and Jewish Populations of Israel, 1950–2000

	Jewish Population		Arab Population	
Year	Number	Percentage of Total	Number	Percentage of Total
1950	1,203,000	50.7%	1,172,100	49.3%
1960	1,911,300	58.8%	1,340,100	41.2%
1970	2,582,000	71.2%	1,045,000	28.8%
1980	3,282,700	61.0%	2,100,000	39.0%
1990	3,946,700	57.5%	2,919,000	42.5%
2000	4,955,400	53.6%	4,281,900	46.4%

is especially the case for Muslim Arabs. The unemployment rate for Israeli Arabs is consistently higher than it is for other ethnic groups. On average, Arabs earn 69 percent of what Jews earn. Arab Muslims have the highest infant mortality rate of all the Arab groups, which exceeds that of Jewish infant mortality. In recent years, the Israeli government has taken efforts to reduce infant mortality and to ameliorate health care delivery systems for Israeli Arabs.

Although the level of education among Arabs has increased exponentially since 1960 (from 1.2 to 10.8 years), it remains below that of Jewish citizens, which in part explains the disparity in income between Arabs and Jews. Jews and Arabs attend different schools, and the standards and resources are dissimilar. Israeli government spending on Arab schoolchildren is just 60 percent of that spent on Jewish students. The quality of education among Israeli Arabs continues to be a major concern.

Under Israeli law, Arab citizens of Israel are to be afforded full rights and privileges, including due process, just like any Israeli citizen. However, Muslims who are not Circassians are not bound by the mandatory military conscription laws and do not serve in the Israeli military unless they volunteer to do so. The Israeli government developed a policy to categorize the Druze differently than other Muslim Arabs, recognizing them as a separate sect (included on identity documents), and some of the Druze leadership asked that Druze be included in mandatory military service. However, they are excluded from sensitive units and assignments.

Despite their alleged equal rights under Israeli law, institutional and social discrimination is a way of life for most Israeli Arabs. Arabs tend to receive longer, harsher prison terms than non-Arabs and are less likely to be granted bail. Government poverty-mitigation efforts for Arab Israelis have also fallen short. This institutional discrimination is often mirrored in and amplified by social discrimination.

Despite the problems facing most Israeli Arabs, a few of them have made modest inroads into the mainstream of Israeli society. In 2006 Arabs held 12 of the 120 seats in the Knesset (Israeli parliament), and an Arab Israeli has a permanent appointment to the Supreme Court of Israel. There have also been a small handful of Arabs in various Israeli cabinets.

Approximately 70 percent of the Israeli Arab population lives in 116 urbanized localities scattered throughout Israel where the Arab majority is most prevalent. Other Arab enclaves are administered by a local authority or are in rural areas. Some 40 percent (about 400,000) of Muslims live in northern Israel, where Nazareth is the largest of the predominantly Arab cities. About 25 percent of Arabs live in areas with a Jewish majority (so-called mixed cities). Only about 4 percent live in remote rural locales such as the Negev Desert, which is home to a sizable number of Bedouin who were forcibly settled by Israel in seven townships. Many others live in illegal settlements outside the townships.

PAUL G. PIERPAOLI JR.

See also

Bedouin; Israel

References

Al-Haj, Majid. *Education, Empowerment, and Control: The Case of the Arabs in Israel.* Albany, NY: SUNY Press, 1995.

Jiryis, Sabri. *The Arabs in Israel.* Translated by Inea Bushnaq. New York: Monthly Review Press, 1976.

Kretzmer, David. *The Legal Status of Arabs in Israel.* Boulder, CO: Westview, 1990.

Stendel, Ori. *The Arabs in Israel.* New York: Sussex Academic, 1996.

Israel, Defense Industry

Israel's defense industry had its genesis in the 1920s, when Jewish community leaders sought arms to defend Palestine's Jewish community from increasing Arab violence. This clandestine arms industry, opposed by the British authorities in Palestine, provided the foundation for a diverse Israeli arms industry that grew steadily in the 1950s and 1960s and achieved international recognition in the 1970s and 1980s. Since 1980, in fact, Israel has been listed among the world's 20 largest arms exporters, and by 2000 its 5 largest defense-related companies were among the 100 largest defense firms in the world.

In 1929, the Jewish Agency's secret military organization, Haganah, formed Taas to produce weapons within Palestine and Rekesh to procure weapons overseas and smuggle them into Palestine. Taas's secret arms facilities expanded dramatically during World War II, and by 1948 it was producing hand grenades, submachine guns, light mortars, and small arms ammunition. In the immediate aftermath of World War II, Haganah agents proved able to purchase discarded weapons as scrap along with machine tools and other specialized manufacturing equipment. Following Israel's declaration of independence in May 1948, these agents increased their efforts, smuggling a variety of weapons and equipment into Israel. Israel's armed forces fought the Israeli War of Independence (1948–1949) with a mixture of locally produced small arms, mortars, and armored cars and a number of imported weapons. Many of the latter had arrived in poor condition and were refurbished in Israeli factories.

Following the 1948–1949 war, Prime Minister David Ben-Gurion reorganized Israel's arms industry, establishing characteristics that

Former German defense minister Franz Joseph Strauss (*right*) with Uzi Gal, the inventor of the Uzi submachine gun, in 1963. (Moshe Pridan/Israeli Government Press Office)

remain today. Israel soon had numerous independent defense companies, but several of its largest defense firms were—and still are—either government-owned corporations, such as Israeli Aircraft Industries (IAI) and Israel Shipyards, or were directly controlled by Israel's Defense Ministry, such as Rafael (Armament Development Authority) and Israel Military Industries (IMI), formerly Taas. In addition to the companies it directly controlled, the Israeli government also encouraged (and sometimes funded) the creation of private companies to manufacture vital products. These included Tadiran, which manufactures batteries and transistors, and Soltam, which assembled mortars, artillery, and ammunition.

Because the major Western powers refused to sell Israel weapons—an arms boycott reaffirmed by the 1951 Tripartite Declaration by Britain, France, and the United States—Ben-Gurion made achieving arms independence a national priority and funded both government and private arms firms. Several of these specialized in refurbishing and upgrading the obsolete weapons that Israel managed to buy from a variety of sources. In 1953, the government founded Bedek (Institute for the Reconditioning of Planes) to repair and upgrade older aircraft, and it won several maintenance contracts with foreign airlines including Trans World Airlines (TWA)

and Air France. Bedek changed its name to Israeli Aircraft Industries in 1960, but upgrading commercial aircraft remains an important part of its business.

Israeli firms continued to produce small arms, and in 1952 IMI produced its first successful export product, the Uzi submachine gun, that was soon used to equip the armies of both the Netherlands and West Germany. In 1953 Burma purchased Uzis and reconditioned rifles from Israel, and in 1954 Israel sold Burma reconditioned British Supermarine Spitfire aircraft. These sales established another lasting trend for Israel's defense industry: the sale of older reconditioned weapons to raise funds to purchase new weapons.

In 1956, Israel signed agreements with France for the purchase of advanced weapons including AMX-13 tanks and Mystère jet fighters. As a result, the two nations formed a close partnership. Israeli engineers participated in the development of several French weapons systems, and France sold Israel its latest weapons, including the Mirage jet fighter, and shared technology with Israel. This spurred Israeli defense firms, which began work on missiles and other sophisticated weapons. These firms built French-designed weapons under license, such as France's Fouga Magister jet trainer

An Israel Military Industries Python 4 air-to-air missile on display in the Israeli pavilion at the Le Bourget air show outside Paris, June 18, 1997. (Amos Ben Gershom/Israeli Government Press Office)

(built by IAI), and laid the foundation to produce sophisticated weapons of their own design.

This close relationship between Israel and France ended with the 1967 Six-Day War, however, when French president Charles de Gaulle banned further weapons sales to Israel, including the newest version of its Mirage jet fighter. Two years later Britain, which had previously sold Centurion tanks to Israel, refused to sell Israel its new Chieftain tank. Both French and British arms embargoes resulted from Arab pressure and came despite Israeli participation in the development of both the Mirage 5 and the Chieftain. While the United States displaced France as Israel's primary foreign arms supplier, American presidents regularly halted or delayed arms shipments to pressure Israel diplomatically and denied Israel access to its most sophisticated weapons systems. Now convinced that they could not rely on foreign arms, Israel's leaders committed the nation to achieving complete arms independence. Israeli military research and development funding therefore quadrupled between 1966 and 1972, and by 1973 local firms produced about 60 percent of Israel's defense needs (95 percent in small arms and ammunition).

In the 1970s, Israeli companies produced a host of new weapons that marked the emergence of Israel as a major arms producer. IAI produced the Arava (a short takeoff-and-landing transport) and the Westwind executive jet, both available in military and commercial versions. IAI produced a copy of France's Mirage fighter, the Nesher, and followed it with the Kfir, an Israeli-designed fighter that used an American jet engine. IAI also developed the Gabriel antiship missile, and its Ramta division manufactured Dabur and Dvora fast patrol boats. Israel Shipyards produced the Reshef-class missile boat that carried IAI's Gabriel missiles and employed them with devastating effect in the October 1973 Yom Kippur War. IMI built on its success with the Uzi to produce the Galil assault rifle and leveraged its experience in upgrading foreign armored vehicles to produce the Merkava main battle tank (MBT). Rafael developed the Shafrir and Python air-to-air missiles, the Popeye air-to-surface missile, and a variety of armor and defensive systems for tanks and personnel. Soltam built on its experience in manufacturing mortars and upgrading older Soviet and American artillery pieces to manufacture a variety of artillery pieces, including self-propelled 155-mm howitzers. Tadiran and Elbit Systems (which later acquired a controlling interest of Tadiran) produced a variety of avionics, radar, electronic warfare, communications, and other specialized defense electronics.

Escalating costs and American resistance forced the cancellation of the Lavi, Israel's next-generation jet fighter, in 1987. As this cancellation rippled through the Israeli defense industry, the number of workers it employed dropped from 60,000 to 40,000. The Lavi project demonstrated the inability of a small state such as Israel to achieve arms independence in an era of rapidly increasing technological sophistication and rising costs. Forced to reassess their policy, Israeli leaders refocused their priorities. Israel continued to produce small arms, newer versions of the Merkava MBT, missiles, small warships, satellites, and specialized electronics but would purchase modern aircraft and larger warships from the United States. Spiraling costs also encouraged the development of unmanned aerial vehicles (UAVs) by IAI and Tadiran.

Military success certainly helped sell Israeli-made or refurbished and upgraded weapons and weapons systems. By 1990, Israeli companies had sold weapons or weapon systems to more than 50 nations. They achieved their greatest success in Central and South America, selling weapons to most countries in the region. These ranged from small arms and reconditioned older weapons to Kfir fighters (purchased by Colombia, Ecuador, Guatemala, Honduras, and Venezuela), Reshef missile boats (purchased by Chile), and Gabriel and Shafrir missiles (purchased by Argentina, Brazil, Chile, Colombia, and Venezuela). Israeli firms also sold weapons to the nations of sub-Saharan Africa, with particularly large sales to South Africa. They also achieved some sales in Asia, particularly to Iran, Taiwan, and Thailand. Britain, the United States, and other nations purchased Israeli UAVs after their successful debut in the 1982 Lebanon intervention. Sales of the Kfir proved problematic because its American engine required the U.S. government's approval to sell. President Jimmy Carter, for example, blocked a 1977 sale of Kfirs to Ecuador. The Ronald Reagan administration proved more pliant, however, and even arranged for the U.S. Navy to lease 12 Kfirs to simulate Soviet MiGs in training exercises, but U.S. firms complained that Israel's Kfirs competed for customers against American-made aircraft.

In the 1990s, Israeli firms emerged as leaders in missile defense, armor, missiles, fire control, electronic countermeasures and other defense electronics, and communications systems. Several East European nations contracted with Israeli firms to upgrade their Soviet-era military equipment, and Israeli firms negotiated similar contracts with India and the People's Republic of China (PRC), although American objections have limited Israel's sales of sophisticated electronics to the Chinese. Several Western nations contracted with IAI to upgrade their American-made McDonnell Douglas F-4 Phantom jets with IAI's Phantom 2000 package. Israeli companies increasingly partnered or subcontracted on large projects with American defense firms, particularly on aviation and missile defense projects. Rafael recently partnered with the American firm Raytheon to develop missile defense systems. In 2003, IAI partnered with U.S.-held Boeing to manufacture the IAI-designed Arrow 2 anti-tactical ballistic missile system. While sales to developing nations remain an important part of their business, Israeli defense firms increasingly sell cutting-edge systems to developed nations, successfully competing against the products of larger and better-known American and European counterparts.

STEPHEN K. STEIN

See also

Aircraft, Fighters; Aircraft, Kfir Fighter; Aircraft, Lavi Fighter-Bomber; Arms Sales, International; Haganah; Israel Defense Forces; Machine Guns; Merkava Tank; Missiles, Air-to-Air; Reshef-Class Guided-Missile Boat; Rifles; Unmanned Aerial Vehicles

References

Klieman, Aaron S. *Israel's Global Reach: Arms Sales as Diplomacy.* Washington, DC: Pergamon-Brassey's, 1985.

Lissak, Moshe, ed. *Israeli Society and Its Defense Establishment: The Social and Political Impact of a Protracted Violent Conflict.* London: Frank Cass, 1984.

Peres, Shimon. *David's Sling.* New York: Random House, 1970.

Reiser, Steward. *The Israeli Arms Industry: Foreign Policy, Arms Transfers, and Military Doctrine of a Small State.* New York: Homes and Meier, 1989.

Israel Defense Forces

Tzava Haganah L-Yisra'il is the official name of the State of Israel's military establishment known as the Israel Defense Forces (IDF). In the relatively short period of its existence, the IDF has become one of the most battle-tested, effective, and simultaneously respected and reviled military forces in the world. Israel claims to have no territorial ambitions. Its strategy is defensive, supported by offensive tactics. The IDF consists of a regular tactical air force, a regular coastal navy, and a small standing army with a large and well-trained reserve, an early warning capability, and efficient mobilization and transportation systems.

The IDF's approach to fighting wars is based on the premise that Israel cannot afford to lose a single war. Given the State of Israel's experience and the long-stated intentions of some of its more hostile neighbors, there can be little doubt of the validity of that assumption. Israel tries to avoid war through a combination of political means and the maintenance of a very credible military deterrent.

Once fighting starts, Israel's lack of territorial depth makes it imperative that the IDF take the war to the enemy's territory and determine the outcome as quickly and decisively as possible. In seven major wars beginning with the Israeli War of Independence (1948–1949) and continuing through the seemingly never-ending occupation duty and counterterrorism actions into 2006, 22,100 Israeli military personnel have been killed in the line of duty. During that same time period, the IDF, usually fighting outnumbered, has inflicted many times more that number of casualties on its enemies. The IDF continually strives to maintain a broad, qualitative advantage in advanced weapons systems, many of which are now developed and manufactured in Israel. The IDF's major strategic

Female Israel Defense Forces (IDF) soldier Rachel Weizel, shown here on June 18, 1955. (Israeli Government Press Office)

advantage, however, has always been the high quality, motivation, and discipline of its soldiers.

The IDF is the backbone of Israel. With the exception of most Muslim Israelis, all Israeli citizens are required to serve in it for some length of time, and that experience forms the most fundamental common denominator of Israeli society. For most new immigrants to Israel, the IDF is the primary social integrator, providing educational opportunities and Hebrew-language training that might not have been available to immigrants in their countries of origin.

Most Israelis are inducted into the IDF at age 18. Unmarried women serve for two years, and men serve for three years. Following initial service, the men remain in the reserves until age 51 and single women until age 24. Reservists with direct combat experience may qualify for discharge at age 45. Most reservists serve for 39 days a year, although that period can be extended during emergencies. Because older reservists in particular may have considerable mismatch between their military ranks and their positions in the civilian world, the IDF pays a reservist on active duty what he

was making in his civilian position. The IDF is one of the very few militaries in the world with such an expensive policy. Indeed, more than 9 percent of Israel's gross domestic product (GDP) goes to military expenditures.

There are some exceptions to IDF service. Older immigrants may serve shorter periods or be deferred completely. Most religiously Orthodox women receive deferments, as do ultraorthodox men who pursue Torah studies or are enrolled in other religious studies programs. Although Bedouin Arabs, Christian Arabs, Druze, Circassians, and some other Arab Israelis are permitted to serve in the IDF, most Arab Israelis are not, and this constitutes one of the principal fault lines of Israeli society.

Conscripts who have performed their initial IDF service successfully may apply to become career noncommissioned officers (NCOs) or officers. The recruitment process is highly selective, and the training is rigorous. There is no Israeli military academy or reserve officers' training corps (ROTC). Once an officer completes initial training, the IDF provides him or her with multiple opportunities to pursue advanced civilian education at IDF expense. IDF officers who retire or otherwise leave active duty retain reserve commissions and are subject to recall in time of war. The most famous example is Ariel Sharon, who commanded a division in the 1967 Six-Day War, retired as a major general in 1973, and was recalled only a few months later and placed in command of a division in the Yom Kippur War.

IDF general officers are a major force in Israeli society. Many go into politics when they leave active duty. In fact, many Israeli prime ministers have been IDF generals, as have most Israeli defense ministers. Lieutenant general (*rav aluf*) is the highest rank in the Israeli military, only held by the IDF chief of staff. Until recently, all the IDF chiefs of staff had come from the army. In 2005, Lieutenant General Dan Halutz became the first air officer to head the IDF. He

Israel Defense Forces (IDF) Chiefs of Staff (1947–Present)

Name	Term
Yaakov Dori	1947–1949
Yigael Yadin	1949–1952
Mordechai Maklef	1952–1953
Moshe Dayan	1953–1958
Chaim Laskov	1958–1961
Tzvi Tzur	1961–1964
Yitzhak Rabin	1964–1968
Chaim Bar-Lev	1968–1972
David Elazar	1972–1974
Mordechai Gur	1974–1978
Rafael Eitan	1978–1983
Moshe Levi	1983–1987
Dan Shomron	1987–1991
Ehud Barak	1991–1995
Amnon Lipkin-Shahak	1995–1998
Shaul Mofaz	1998–2002
Moshe Ya'alon	2002–2005
Dan Halutz	2005–2007
Gabi Ashkenazi	2007–Present

Israeli Air Force Kfir fighter-bomber displayed behind a variety of the armament it is capable of carrying, July 20, 1976. (Sa'ar Ya'acov/Israeli Government Press Office)

resigned in January 2007 after coming under widespread criticism for his handling of the 2006 war in Lebanon.

Although Israel has never formally admitted to having nuclear weapons, Mordecai Vanunu revealed the program to the world, becoming an enemy of the state as a result. The Jewish experience in the Holocaust is often cited as the justification for Israel to take any measures necessary, including nuclear weapons, to ensure its survival. With French support, Israel constructed its first nuclear reactor at Dimona in 1960. The IDF most probably acquired a nuclear weapons capability in the late 1960s. Most estimates today place Israel's nuclear stockpile at between 100 and 200 weapons, including warheads for the Jericho-1 and Jericho-2 mobile missiles and bombs for longer-range delivery by Israeli aircraft.

The IDF is the direct successor of the Haganah, the secret Jewish self-defense organization whose roots go back to the 1907 formation of the Bar Giora organization, established to protect Jewish towns and settlements in Palestine. During World War I, many Jews acquired military training and experience in the British Army, which formed the Zion Mule Corps in 1915 and the all-Jewish 38th, 39th, and 40th King's Fusiliers near the end of the war.

With Palestine becoming a British mandate following World War I, Haganah was formed in 1920 as a local self-defense force, although the British considered it an illegal militia. In 1931 a group of Haganah members broke away to form the far more aggressive Irgun Tsvai Leumi (National Military Organization). During the Great Arab Revolt of 1936–1939, the British cooperated unofficially with Haganah, with Captain Orde C. Wingate forming and training the Special Night Squads, one of Israel's first special operating forces.

In 1941 Haganah formed the Palmach as its strike force. The same year, an even more radical group broke away from Irgun to form the Lohamei Herut Israel (Lehi), also called the Stern Gang. During the course of World War II, more than 30,000 Palestinian Jews served in the British Army. The Jewish Brigade served with distinction against the Germans in northern Italy during the final stages of World War II.

Following World War II, Haganah defied British rule in Palestine by smuggling in Holocaust survivors and other Jewish refugees, all the while conducting clandestine military training and defending Jewish settlements. Irgun and Lehi, which many considered little more than terrorist organizations, launched an all-out armed rebellion against the British. Under the orders of future prime minister Menachem Begin, Irgun on July 22, 1946, bombed the King David Hotel, Britain's military headquarters in Jerusalem.

Outgoing Israel Defense Forces (IDF) chief of staff Lieutenant General Dan Halutz (*right*) shakes hands with his successor, Lieutenant General Gabi (Gabriel) Ashkenazi, as Prime Minister Ehud Olmert looks on, February 14, 2007. (Avi Ohayon/Israeli Government Press Office)

Immediately following the establishment of the State of Israel, the provisional government on May 28, 1948, issued Defense Army of Israel Ordinance No. 4 establishing the IDF and merging all Jewish fighting organizations under it. Immediately thereafter David Marcus, a U.S. Army Reserve colonel and World War II veteran, received a commission as Israel's first general (*aluf*), making him the first Jewish soldier to hold that rank since Judas Maccabeus 2,100 years earlier. Marcus was killed near Jerusalem less than two weeks later.

Although the IDF essentially absorbed the General Staff and combat units of Haganah, the integration of the other units was difficult and protracted. Lehi dissolved itself, and its members joined the IDF individually. Some battalions of Irgun joined the IDF, while others fought on independently. The turning point came when Prime Minister David Ben-Gurion ordered the IDF to sink Irgun's arms ship *Altalena* as it approached Tel Aviv in June 1948. It was a defining moment for the new State of Israel and established the authority of the central government. The remaining Irgun battalions finally disbanded on September 20, 1948.

The IDF is organized administratively into traditional branches of service, with the army, navy, and air force all having their own career tracks and distinctive uniforms. Operationally, the IDF is organized into four joint regional commands. The Northern Command is responsible for the occupation of the Golan Heights and the security of Israel's northern border with Lebanon and Syria. The Southern Command is responsible for the occupation of Gaza and for securing the porous southern border through the trackless Negev Desert. The Central Command is responsible for the occupation of the West Bank and the security of the Israeli settlements there. The Home Front Command's main role is to provide security to civilians during wars and mass disasters.

The Israeli standing ground force consists of four infantry brigades (Givati, Nahal, Golani, and Paratroopers) plus several mixed-unit battalions and several special forces and counterterrorism units, including Sayeret. The armor force has three brigades: the Barak Armored Brigade (the 188th Brigade), the Ga'ash Brigade (the 7th Brigade), and the Ikvot Habarzel Brigade (the 401st Brigade). The artillery also has three brigades, the engineers have one brigade, and each infantry brigade has an engineer company.

The Israeli Air Force (IAF) is one of the strongest air forces in the Middle East, and with much justification its pilots are considered the best in the world. Since the IAF began in 1948, its pilots have shot down 687 enemy aircraft in air-to-air combat. Only 23 Israeli aircraft have been shot down in air-to-air combat, giving the IAF an incredible 30-to-1 victory ratio. Thirty-nine IAF pilots have achieved ace status by shooting down 5 or more enemy aircraft. The leading Israeli ace is Major General Giora Epstein with 17 kills, all against jet aircraft, making him the world's record holder for number of jets shot down.

The Israeli Navy was also formed in 1948. Its predecessor was Haganah's Palyam (Sea Company). The Palyam's primary mission had been smuggling Jewish refugees from Europe to Palestine. The Israeli Navy today operates in two unconnected bodies of water. Its main base on the Mediterranean is at Haifa, and its main base on the Red Sea is at Eilat. The three principal operating units of the Israeli Navy are the Missile Boats Flotilla, the Submarine Flotilla, and Shayetet 13, a naval special operations force similar to the U.S. Navy's SEALs.

The IDF's Directorate of Main Intelligence (Aman) is a separate branch of service on the same level as the army, navy, and air force. The head of Aman is also a coequal to the heads of Shin Bet (internal security and counterintelligence) and Mossad (foreign intelligence), and together they direct all Israeli intelligence operations. The army itself has an Intelligence Corps (Ha-Aman) that is responsible for tactical-level intelligence but also comes under the overall jurisdiction of Aman.

The IDF recognizes six major wars for which it awards campaign ribbons. (Campaign ribbons have not yet been announced for the 2006 Gaza and Lebanon conflicts.) The 1948–1949 Israeli War of Independence began immediately after the declaration of statehood, as Egypt attacked from the south, Syria and Lebanon attacked from the north, and Jordan backed by Iraqi and Saudi troops attacked from the east. Outnumbered almost 60 to 1 in population, the new Jewish state's prospects for survival looked bleak. By the time of the cease-fire on July 20, 1949, however, the IDF had managed to secure all of its major objectives, with the exceptions of East Jerusalem and the Arab Legion fortress at Latrun.

Immediately following the war, the sectors of Palestine not under Israeli control were occupied by the other Arab states, with Jordan occupying the West Bank and Egypt occupying Gaza. Plagued throughout the early 1950s by continual Palestinian infiltration and terror raids, the IDF in 1953 formed Unit 101. Under the command of Sharon, the special operations unit carried out retaliatory strikes into Jordanian territory. Criticized for its ruthless tactics, Unit 101 was disbanded in late 1955.

The 1956 Sinai Campaign, the second of Israel's major wars, commenced after Egypt nationalized the Suez Canal. Simultaneously, the IDF launched a full-scale attack into the Sinai to eliminate an Egyptian and Palestinian irregular forces known as the fedayeen that had been conducting terror attacks against Israeli civilians in the south. The IDF captured Gaza and the entire Sinai Peninsula as well as the canal but later withdrew under international pressure.

In 1967, Egypt massed 100,000 troops in the Sinai and closed the Straits of Tiran to Israeli ships. In response, the IDF launched a massive preemptive strike on the morning of June 5, virtually destroying the Egyptian Air Force on the ground. By noon that day the IAF had also annihilated the Syrian and Jordanian Air Forces. During the Six-Day War, the IDF again captured the Sinai and Gaza and came within striking distance of Alexandria. The Egyptians lost some 15,000 soldiers killed, while only 338 Israelis died. The IDF also captured the strategic Golan Heights from Syria and captured East Jerusalem and the rest of the West Bank from Jordan. Following the Six-Day War, the War of Attrition ground on with the Egyptians along the Suez Canal and with the Syrians along the northern borders, only ending in 1970.

The Yom Kippur War began on October 6, 1973, when Egypt and Syria launched a surprise attack on the holiest Jewish holiday of the year. Initially the IDF took heavy losses, but after U.S. airlifted weapons and supplies began to arrive on October 14, the tide turned, and the IDF pushed the Egyptians and Syrians back to their original lines. On the Golan Heights, some 177 Israeli tanks stopped more than 1,500 Syrian tanks. In the critical Valley of Tears Pass, 8 tanks from the 77th Tank Battalion launched a counterattack against hundreds of Syrian tanks and armored personnel carriers and won. In the Sinai, an Israeli armored division started to cross the Suez Canal on October 15 and was only some 65 miles away from Cairo by October 24. By the time the war ended under international pressure, the IDF had suffered 2,700 dead while inflicting more than 15,000 deaths on its enemies.

The IDF's most famous special operation came during July 3–4, 1976, when the elite Sayeret Matkal (also known as General Staff Reconnaissance Unit 269) rescued Israeli passengers held hostage at the Entebbe airport in Uganda after their plane was hijacked by Palestinian terrorists. The complex operation managed to save 80 of the 83 passengers. The only IDF casualty was the operational commander, Colonel Jonathan Netanyahu, brother of future prime minister Benjamin Netanyahu.

On June 7, 1981, IAF F-15s and F-16s destroyed Iraq's Osiraq nuclear reactor. Although almost universally condemned in international circles at the time, the preemptive strike almost certainly neutralized Saddam Hussein's nuclear weapons program.

During Operation PEACE FOR GALILEE, the IDF invaded southern Lebanon on June 6, 1982, in retaliation for Palestinian terrorist and rocket attacks launched from Lebanon's territory against Israeli civilian targets in the north. Although the IDF neutralized the Palestinian threat, it became bogged down in a long and grinding occupation of southern Lebanon that only ended in September 2000. The reputation of the IDF also suffered severely from the September 16, 1982, massacre at the Sabra and Shatila refugee camps, with many international figures branding then-defense minister Sharon as a war criminal.

The IDF performed stability operations during the First Intifada in the Palestinian territories, which lasted from 1987 to 1993. The Second (al-Aqsa) Intifada, which began in September 2000, was far more violent than the first, and the resulting security demands have placed a heavy and seemingly endless burden on the IDF, with most reservists having to perform far more than the standard annual duty. The constant strain of occupation duty in the territories has resulted in morale and discipline problems.

Following Israel's withdrawal from its settlements in Gaza in the summer of 2005, Palestinian militant groups continued to conduct cross-border raids and they even increased the rate of Qassam rocket attacks. On June 28, 2006, the IDF mounted a major incursion into Gaza under the justification of rescuing a recently captured Israeli soldier. Hezbollah protested the campaign in Gaza, as did many Arab states. On July 12, Hezbollah crossed the border and killed 3 IDF soldiers and captured 2. In response, Israel launched a series of massive air attacks against not only Hezbollah installations but also Lebanese infrastructure nodes in Beirut and elsewhere in the country. Hezbollah responded with Katyusha rocket attacks and even longer-range missile attacks. Wary of getting drawn into another quagmire on the ground in Lebanon, the Israeli strategy was apparently to drive a wedge between Hezbollah and the rest of the Lebanese population. The air campaign did not work, however, and IDF ground forces started crossing the border on July 23. By the time a UN-brokered cease-fire went into effect on August 14, the IDF had lost 119 killed and more than 400 wounded. Israel finally lifted its blockade of Lebanon on September 8.

The 2006 Lebanon conflict was different in many ways from any of Israel's previous wars. For the first time, Israel suffered a large number of civilian casualties on its own soil as Hezbollah rockets slammed into Haifa, Tiberias, Nazareth, and other major cities in the north. Forty-four Israeli civilians were killed, and more than 1,350 were injured. For the first time, too, the IDF inflicted many more civilian than military casualties on its enemy. Only 250–600 Hezbollah fighters were killed, while 1,187 Lebanese civilians died, some 3,600 were injured, and more than 250,000 were internally displaced. The IDF reported 119 Israeli soldiers killed, 400–450 wounded, and 2 taken prisoner. IDF chief of staff Halutz came under severe criticism for the failure of the initial air campaign as well as for the halting and poorly organized ground campaign that followed. Rather than undermining its popular support among the Lebanese people, Hezbollah appeared to increase its support. Many observers proclaimed that by merely surviving the Israeli pounding, Hezbollah emerged the victor of the conflict. The myth of the IDF's invincibility had been shattered once and for all. That claim, however, has been made before, especially following the Yom Kippur War.

DAVID T. ZABECKI

See also

Altalena Incident; Arab Legion; Begin, Menachem; Ben-Gurion, David; Conscription Policies; Entebbe Hostage Rescue; Haganah; Hezbollah; Intifada, First; Intifada, Second; Irgun Tsvai Leumi; Israel; Israeli War of Independence, Overview; Latrun, Battles of; Lebanon, Israeli Invasion of; Lohamei Herut Israel; Marcus, David; Mossad; Netanyahu, Benjamin; Nuclear Weapons; Osiraq Raid; Palmach; Sayeret Matkal; Sharon, Ariel; Sinai Campaign; Six-Day War; Suez Crisis; Wingate, Orde Charles; Yom Kippur War

References

Heller, Charles E. *Economy of Force: A Total Army, the Israel Defense Force Model.* Carlisle, PA: Strategic Studies Institute, 1992.

Hersh, Seymour. *The Sampson Option: Israel's Nuclear Arsenal and American Foreign Policy.* New York: Random House, 1991.

Kahalani, Avigdor. *The Heights of Courage: A Tank Leader's War on the Golan.* Westport, CT: Praeger, 1992.

Van Creveld, Martin. *The Sword and the Olive: A Critical History of the Israeli Defense Force.* New York: PublicAffairs, 2002.

Williams, Louis. *The Israel Defense Forces: A People's Army.* Lincoln, NE: Authors Choice, 2000.

Israel-Egypt Peace Treaty
Event Date: March 26, 1979

Peace accord signed between Egypt and the State of Israel on March 26, 1979, in Washington, D.C. The Israel-Egypt Peace Treaty was the culmination of an ongoing peace process between the Israelis and Egyptians that dated to November 1977. It was also the result of the Camp David Accords, signed by Egyptian president Anwar Sadat and Israeli prime minister Menachem Begin on September 17, 1978.

The peace treaty stipulated that the two nations would officially recognize the sovereignty of the other and end the state of war that had existed between them since 1948. It also stipulated that Israel would withdraw from the Sinai Peninsula. Finally, it guaranteed Israel the right of passage through the Suez Canal and recognized that both the Straits of Tiran and the Gulf of Aqaba were international waterways subject to international law and maritime guidelines. The Israel-Egypt Peace Treaty was the first such treaty between an Arab state and Israel.

The Camp David Accords of 1978 had emerged from 13 days of intensive negotiations at the U.S. presidential retreat at Camp David. President Jimmy Carter had mediated the talks between Sadat and Begin. But it was President Sadat's unprecedented move in November 1977 that had made the historic Israeli-Egyptian peace process possible. On November 19, 1977, Sadat became the first Arab leader in history to visit Israel in an official capacity. He went at the invitation of Prime Minister Begin and addressed the Knesset (Israeli parliament). Sadat's speech offered conciliatory words and a genuine desire to end the conflict between Israel and Egypt, and laid out specific steps that might be taken to broker an enduring peace. Specifically, he called for the implementation of United Nations (UN) Resolutions 242 and 338, which among other things called for the withdrawal of Israeli forces from land captured in the 1967 Six-Day War. Sadat's visit stunned many Israelis as well as much of the world.

Most Arab nations, however, were outraged that Sadat would choose to negotiate with the Israelis. Not only did this go against the prevailing Arab philosophy that viewed Israel as a threat and a tool of Western hegemony, but it also meant that Sadat was essentially

Anwar Sadat, Jimmy Carter, and Menachem Begin sign the Israel-Egypt Peace Treaty at the White House in Washington, D.C., on March 26, 1979. (Sa'ar Ya'acov/Israeli Government Press Office)

recognizing the legitimacy of the State of Israel, something that no Arab state had been willing to do. Equally troubling to Arab states was that this peace overture was coming from Egypt, at the time the most powerful Arab state in the region and the birthplace of modern Arab nationalism under Gamal Abdel Nasser.

When the Camp David Accords were signed, there was no clear consensus or binding agreement that a formal, comprehensive peace treaty would be signed. Indeed, between September 1978 and March 1979, both parties to the accords had considerable hesitations about signing a formal treaty. Sadat had come under intense pressure from other Arab leaders not to sign a peace agreement. He also encountered resistance within his own country. For his part, Begin was under enormous pressure not to allow the issue of Palestinian independence to enter into any formal discussions or accords with the Egyptians. Indeed, Begin's refusal to do so nearly torpedoed the peace settlement.

Although Sadat lost the support of most Arab leaders (and Egypt was expelled from the Arab League after the treaty was signed), his government did gain the support of the United States, both diplomatically and economically. In fact, the United States gave Egypt and Israel subsidies worth billion of dollars as a result of the rapprochement. These subsidies continue to the present day. From the

Israeli perspective, the peace treaty was a coup because Egypt had now been separated from its Arab neighbors. Yet from a geopolitical perspective, the Israeli-Egyptian peace process led to the breakdown of the united Arab front against Israel, creating a power vacuum of sorts once Egypt fell out of that orbit. This allowed nations such as Iran and Iraq to fill in the gap, with disastrous consequences. Only months after the Israel-Egypt Peace Treaty was signed the Iran-Iraq War (1980–1988) broke out, which demonstrated Iraqi president Saddam Hussein's ambitions to become the undisputed Arab leader of the Middle East.

On the other hand, the Camp David process and the resultant peace treaty demonstrated that fruitful negotiations between Arabs and Israelis are indeed possible. Furthermore, it showed that progress toward peace can come only with meaningful dialogue, mutual cooperation, and strong leadership. Nevertheless, it would take another 15 years for a second Arab-Israeli peace treaty to come about, this time between the Jordanians and Israelis. Currently, only Egypt and Jordan have concluded such agreements.

PAUL G. PIERPAOLI JR.

See also

Aqaba, Gulf of; Arab League; Arab Nationalism; Begin, Menachem; Camp David Accords; Egypt; Israel; Israel-Jordan Peace Treaty; Nasser,

Gamal Abdel; Sadat, Anwar; Straits of Tiran; Suez Crisis; United Nations Security Council Resolution 242; United Nations Security Council Resolution 338

References

Carter, James E. *Keeping Faith: Memoirs of the President.* New York: Bantam, 1982.

Kamel, Mohamed Ibrahim. *The Camp David Accords: A Testimony.* London: Kegan Paul International, 1986.

Lenczowski, George. *The Middle East in World Affairs.* 4th ed. Ithaca, NY: Cornell University Press, 1980.

Quandt, William. *Camp David: Peacemaking and Politics.* Washington, DC: Brookings Institution, 1986.

Israel, Islamic Movement in

See Islamic Movement in Israel

Israel-Jordan Peace Treaty
Event Date: October 26, 1994

Comprehensive peace accord between Israel and Jordan signed on October 26, 1994, at the border settlement of Wadi Arabah. Officially titled the "Treaty of Peace between the State of Israel and the Hashemite Kingdom of Jordan," the agreement settled long-standing territorial conflicts and fully normalized diplomatic and economic relations between the two states. It was intended as part of the larger Arab-Israeli peace process that had begun in 1991 at the Madrid Conference and had continued in the Oslo Accords, agreed to and signed by the Israelis and Palestinians the previous summer. The treaty was only the second one of its kind signed between the Israelis and an Arab nation, the first one having been that negotiated with Egypt in 1979.

Over the years, relations between Jordan and Israel had been complex and sometimes hostile. Be that as it may, Israel's relations with Jordan were generally not as difficult as those with the other Arab states. Jordan's King Hussein, while cleaving to anti-Israeli stances alongside his Arab neighbors because a large proportion of Jordan's population was Palestinian, was also a pragmatist. Thus, his actions did not always match his anti-Zionist rhetoric. He was also reliably pro-Western in orientation, which surely tempered his anti-Israeli policies. Also, his relatively modest territorial demands and Jordan's proximity to Israel worked as a moderating force in the Israeli-Jordanian relationship.

This does not mean, however, that Jordanian-Israeli relations were not without serious tensions. Indeed, in the run-up to the 1967 Six-Day War, Israeli leaders implored King Hussein not to join the Egyptian-led coalition arrayed against Israel. King Hussein ignored the forewarning, and Jordan suffered the consequences. By war's end, the Israelis had seized control of East Jerusalem and the strategically and economically crucial West Bank, which had been an economic lifeline to the Kingdom of Jordan. The Israeli occupation of the West Bank would also significantly complicate future peace

negotiations with the Palestinians, who believe that the West Bank must be at the heart of any future Palestinian state. Indeed, the Jordanians conferred their claim to the West Bank to the Palestine Liberation Organization (PLO) in 1988.

In 1970 as the Jordanians prepared to expel the PLO from their country in what came to be called Black September, Israel tacitly aided them in the struggle by dispatching fighter jets to menace Syrian forces that had begun to intervene in Jordan on the side of the PLO.

In 1973, although King Hussein was caught off guard by the Egyptian and Syrian attack on Israel in the Yom Kippur War, he was soon under pressure from these two Arab states to join the conflict. He tried to keep out of the conflict but was nevertheless drawn in, ironically to stave off a crushing Syrian defeat. He did not commit his air force, realizing that this would bring a crushing Israeli retaliation as in 1967, but on October 13 he sent the crack 40th Armored Brigade, equipped with British-made Centurion tanks, into Syria, ironically to save that nation from the threat posed by the Israeli invasion to Damascus and the survival of the Syrian Army. The 40th Brigade came into battle with the Israelis on October 16 and fought bravely, holding until the Syrians were told by their Soviet advisers to withdraw.

In 1987 Israeli foreign minister Shimon Peres undertook a tentative attempt to arrive at a Jordanian-Israeli peace settlement. In secret deliberations, he and King Hussein agreed that the West Bank would be ceded back to Jordan in exchange for mutual peace and security guarantees. The deal was never consummated because internal Israeli politics prevented such a sweeping move. Be that as it may, the peace attempt did strengthen relations between the two nations, and a year later Jordan abandoned its claim to the West Bank and agreed to help settle the Palestinian-Israeli impasse without violence.

It was really the 1993 Oslo Accords that set the stage for the Israel-Jordan Peace Treaty. In light of what appeared at the time to be a historic period in Arab-Israeli peacemaking, King Hussein was more receptive to a peace deal with Israel. U.S. president Bill Clinton and secretary of state Warren Christopher had also begun to nudge King Hussein toward a peace agreement, even promising to reduce or eliminate Jordan's foreign aid debts to the United States. Perhaps what clinched the deal for the king was Egyptian president Hosni Mubarak's support of an Israeli-Jordanian peace accord, although Syrian president Hafez al-Assad opposed the agreement. The diplomacy worked, and King Hussein, ever the pragmatist, agreed to a nonbelligerency treaty with the Israelis. The Washington Declaration, signed in Washington, D.C., on July 25, 1994, ultimately led to the signing of the formal peace treaty on October 26, 1994.

The provisions of the treaty included the establishment of the Jordan River as the boundary between the two nations, the full normalization of diplomatic and economic relations, cooperation in antiterrorism, respect for each other's territory, a more equitable distribution of Jordan River water and other joint water supplies, and a joint effort at alleviating the Palestinian refugee problem. Soon thereafter, the Israeli-Jordanian border became an open one, and Israelis and Jordanians embarked on tourist and business excursions in each other's countries. Unfortunately, the Israeli-Jordanian peace settlement did not lead to a wider peace in the region.

PAUL G. PIERPAOLI JR.

See also

Assad, Hafez al-; Black September; Clinton, William Jefferson; Hussein, King of Jordan; Israel; Israel-Egypt Peace Treaty; Jordan; Jordan River; Mubarak, Hosni; Oslo Accords; Palestine Liberation Organization; Peres, Shimon; Six-Day War; Water Rights and Resources; West Bank; Yom Kippur War

References

Freedman, Robert Owen, ed. *The Middle East and the Peace Process: The Impact of the Oslo Accords.* Gainesville: University Press of Florida, 1998.

Majali, Abdul Salam, et al. *Peacemaking: An Inside Story of the 1994 Jordanian-Israeli Treaty.* Norman: University of Oklahoma Press, 2006.

Peres, Shimon. *The New Middle East.* New York: Henry Holt, 1993.

Weinberger, Peter. *Co-opting the PLO: A Critical Reconstruction of the Oslo Accords, 1993–1995.* New York: Rowman and Littlefield, 2006.

Israeli Air Strike on Presumed Syrian Nuclear Facility
Event Date: September 6, 2007

On September 6, 2007, Israeli aircraft struck and destroyed an unidentified facility in Syria, believed by Israeli and U.S. intelligence sources to be a partially constructed nuclear reactor. Reportedly the attack was carried out by four Israeli F-16 aircraft dropping six 1,000-pound precision-guided bombs. Apparently the facility was identified by satellite photography as closely resembling the Yongbyon nuclear facility in North Korea used to reprocess nuclear fuel into bomb-grade material. The attack was roundly condemned by both Syria and North Korea, which had been known to be providing assistance to the Syrian ballistics missile program.

Unlike criticism by President Ronald Reagan's administration of the Israeli strike on Iraq's Osiraq nuclear reactor in 1981, there was no such negative reaction from President George W. Bush's administration, strongly suggesting that Bush administration officials were briefed by the government of Prime Minister Ehud Olmert ahead of time and gave tacit approval to the strike. Unlike the Osiraq facility, which was believed to be close to operational status, the Syrian facility was apparently only in the early stages of development and was presumed to be years away from being able to produce weapons-grade plutonium. Although Syria is a signatory of the Nuclear Non-Proliferation Treaty, this does not bind it to report a nuclear reactor in the early stages of construction as long as its purpose is the generation of electricity. In his only comment on the strike, Syrian president Bashar al-Assad acknowledged that Israeli aircraft had struck a military building, which was not in use.

Some analysts interpreted the strike as a clear warning by Israel and, for that matter, by the United States to Iran not to proceed with

its own nuclear ambitions. Although Israel is itself widely believed to possess a stockpile of nuclear weapons, it has long said that it will not permit hostile powers on its borders to have nuclear weapons or even develop them. Given the small size of Israel, one atomic bomb could for all practical purposes wipe out the Jewish state. Interestingly, no other Arab government apart from Syria criticized the Israeli raid, suggesting that there was general opposition among Middle East governments to a nuclear-armed Syria.

SPENCER C. TUCKER

See also

Assad, Bashar al-; Nuclear Weapons; Olmert, Ehud; Osiraq Raid

References

Erlanger, Stephen. "Israel Silent on Reports of Bombing within Syria." *New York Times,* October 15, 2007.

Kessler, Glenn, and Robin Wright. "Israel, US Shared Data on Suspected Nuclear Site." *Washington Post,* September 21, 2007.

Israeli Air Strikes Beginning the Six-Day War
Event Date: June 5, 1967

The Six-Day War began on the morning of June 5, 1967, and was, for all intents and purposes, over by noon on the first day, the result of the preemptive attack by the Israeli Air Force (IAF). This aerial offensive remains one of the most stunning successes in modern warfare. In a mere three hours, the Israelis achieved air supremacy by destroying much of the Egyptian Air Force on the ground. Attacks against Egypt were followed by sorties against targets in Syria, Jordan, and western Iraq, thus ensuring that Israeli ground operations could go forward unimpeded.

The Israel Defense Forces (IDF) was heavily outnumbered in terms of men and equipment. Figures vary widely, but one estimate is as follows: manpower (mobilized strength of 230,000 for Israel versus 409,000 for Egypt, Syria, Jordan, and Iraq), tanks (1,100 versus 2,437), artillery (260 versus 649), naval vessels (22 versus 90), and aircraft, all types (354 versus 969).

Minister of Defense Moshe Dayan, chief of staff of the IDF Lieutenant General Yitzhak Rabin, and Premier Levi Eshkol determined that war was inevitable and decided that Israel should launch a preemptive attack. Defense against an Arab air attack would be difficult because Israel was too small for early warning systems to provide sufficient time for Israeli fighters to scramble. Tel Aviv was 25 minutes' flying time from Cairo but only 4.5 minutes from the nearest Egyptian air base at El Arish. For whatever reason, Egyptian leader Gamal Abdel Nasser did not believe that the Israelis would strike first, despite his own announced eagerness for battle.

The Israeli air attack relied on accurate, timely, and precise intelligence information. The plan called for a first strike against Egypt, the most formidable of Israel's opponents. IDF fighters would take off from airfields all over Israel, fly under radio silence and at low altitude west over the Mediterranean to avoid radar, and then turn

Israeli soldiers examine the wreckage of an Egyptian MiG-15 aircraft near El Arish Airport in Egypt during the Six-Day War, June 9, 1967. (Hulton-Deutsch Collection/Corbis)

south to strike Egyptian airfields as simultaneously as possible. Rather than attacking at dawn, the IAF strikes were timed to coincide with the return of Egyptian pilots to base from their morning patrols, when most Egyptian pilots would be having breakfast.

One of the best-trained air forces in the world, the IAF was well prepared for its mission. Air crews had been thoroughly briefed as to objectives and procedures. Ground crews were also highly trained and able to reduce turnaround time between missions to a minimum. The operation was quite daring in that it would employ almost all Israeli fighter and fighter-bomber aircraft, leaving only a dozen fighters behind to fly combat air patrols in defense of Israel.

The IAF achieved complete tactical surprise. It went into action at 7:45 a.m. (8:45 a.m. Cairo time). One unexpected development was that Field Marshal Abdel Hakim Amer, the United Arab Republic (UAR) commander in chief, and his deputy, General Mamud Sidqi, were in the air flying from Cairo to inspect units in the Sinai when the attacks occurred. Unable to land in the Sinai, they returned to Cairo. Thus, for 90 minutes two key UAR commanders were out of touch with their units and unable to give orders.

The first wave struck 10 Egyptian airfields, hitting all of them within 15 minutes of the scheduled time. On the final approach to

the targets, Israeli aircraft climbed to make themselves suddenly visible on radar in order to induce Egyptian pilots to attempt to scramble in the hopes of catching the pilots in their aircraft on the ground. Only four Egyptian aircraft, all trainers, were in the air at the time of the first strikes, and all were shot down. Subsequent waves of Israeli attacking aircraft, about 40 per flight, arrived at 10-minute intervals. These met increased Egyptian opposition, mostly antiaircraft fire. Only 8 Egyptian MiGs managed to take off during the strikes, and all were shot down.

In all, the IAF struck 17 major Egyptian airfields with some 500 sorties in just under three hours, destroying half of the Egyptian Air Force's strength. Most of the Egyptian aircraft were destroyed by accurate Israeli cannon fire, but the Israelis also dropped 250-, 500-, and 1,000-pound bombs. Special bombs with 365-pound warheads, developed to crack the concrete runways, were dropped on Egyptian airfields west of the Suez Canal, but none of these were employed against the Sinai airfields, which the Israelis planned for subsequent use by their own aircraft. During the war, Egypt lost a total of 286 aircraft: 30 Tupolev Tu-16 heavy bombers, 27 Ilyushin medium bombers, 12 Sukhoi Su-7 fighter-bombers, 90 MiG-21 fighters, 20 MiG-19 fighters, 75 MiG-17/15 fighters, and 32 transport planes and helicopters.

Later that same day, June 5, Israeli aircraft struck Syria and Jordan. Israeli leaders urged King Hussein of Jordan to stay out of the war. He desired to do so but was under heavy pressure to act and hoped to satisfy his allies with minimum military action short of all-out war. Jordanian 155-mm Long Tom guns went into action against Tel Aviv, and Jordanian aircraft attempted to strafe a small airfield near Kfar Sirkin. The Israeli government then declared war on Jordan. Following an Iraqi air strike on Israel, IAF aircraft also struck Iraqi air units based in the Mosul area. In all during the war, the Arabs lost 390 aircraft of their prewar strength of 969 aircraft of all types (Egypt, 286 of 580; Jordan, 28 of 56; Syria, 54 of 172; Iraq, 21 of 149; and Lebanon, 1 of 12). Israeli losses numbered 32 aircraft shot down of 354 before the war, only two of these to aerial combat.

With its opposing air forces largely neutralized, the IAF could turn to close air support and other missions in support of Israeli mechanized ground forces, which had begun operations in the Sinai simultaneous with the initial air attacks.

Spencer C. Tucker

See also

Amer, Abdel Hakim; Dayan, Moshe; Egypt, Armed Forces; Eshkol, Levi; Hussein, King of Jordan; Israel Defense Forces; Nasser, Gamal Abdel; Rabin, Yitzhak; Six-Day War

References

Hammel, Eric. *Six Days in June: How Israel Won the 1967 Arab-Israeli War*. New York: Scribner, 1992.

Oren, Michael B. *Six Days of War: June 1967 and the Making of the Modern Middle East*. Novato, CA: Presidio, 2003.

Rubenstein, Murray, and Richard Goldman. *Shield of David: An Illustrated History of the Israeli Air Force*. Englewood Cliffs, NJ: Prentice Hall, 1978.

Van Creveld, Martin. *The Sword and the Olive: A Critical History of the Israeli Defense Force*. New York: PublicAffairs, 2002.

Weizman, Ezer. *On Eagles' Wings: The Personal Story of the Leading Command of the Israeli Air Force*. New York: Macmillan, 1977.

Israeli Security Fence

A combined barrier wall and fortified fence separating Israel from the Palestinian-controlled West Bank. When completed, the barrier (also known as the separation fence or the segregation wall) will be approximately 415 miles in length as it meanders a rather circuitous route in and around the West Bank. The Israelis insist that the construction of the security fence was an absolute necessity given the number of terrorist attacks unleashed on Israel by militant Palestinians, particularly after the beginning of the Second (al-Aqsa) Intifada, which began in September 2001 and ended in 2004. The barrier is meant to foil would-be car and truck bombers as well as individual suicide bombers.

As early as 1992, Israeli politicians had begun to talk about pursuing a separation policy with the Palestinians. That is, they sought to separate Israelis from Palestinians by way of imposing physical barriers between the two populations. Indeed, in 1994 Israeli prime minister Yitzhak Rabin approved the erection of a barrier separating Israel from the Gaza Strip after militants had unleashed a number of violent attacks against Israel from that area.

In 2000 even prior to his failed summit with Palestine Liberation Organization (PLO) chairman Yasser Arafat, Israeli prime minister Ehud Barak spoke of building a more comprehensive barrier between Israelis and Palestinians. Barriers erected along the border between South Korea and North Korea and along parts of India's border with Pakistan have been widely recognized as effective means of preventing unwanted infiltration.

It was not until mid-2001, however, after the start of the Second Intifada and after the bombing of a Tel Aviv discotheque that killed 21 people that the Israeli public began clamoring for the erection of a security fence along the West Bank. In July 2001 the Israeli Defense Cabinet approved the building of the fence. The first phase of the barrier began in late 2002, under the government of Ariel Sharon, and was completed in late July 2003. When the fence is finally completed, the cost of construction alone will have topped $2 billion, and an estimated 400,000 Palestinians could be separated from the remaining Palestinian population on the West Bank.

The security fence along the border of the West Bank is not a wall per se, at least not along much of the route. Some 90 percent of it will be a high-tech fence, outfitted with surveillance cameras at regular intervals. For much of its length, a (usually) gravel road will run parallel to the fence for the purposes of patrol, interdiction, and maintenance. In some spots where infiltration has been especially troublesome, the fence will be augmented by trenches and even armored vehicles. Underground sensors, land mines, and unmanned aerial vehicles will also help secure the chain-link–type fence. On average, the barrier is roughly 160 feet wide. The Israelis claim that the fence portion of the barrier will comprise roughly 90 percent of the security fence. The remaining 10 percent will be high concrete walls—some as high as 30 feet—built around areas that have been hotbeds of past terrorist activities.

The initial route proposed for the barrier was projected to be at least three-and-a-half times longer than Israel's internationally recognized border with the West Bank and would annex large areas of Palestinian farmland, scores of Palestinian villages, and sections of several Palestinian urban areas. For example, the wall cuts right through the middle of the Palestinian towns of Abu Dis and al-Izariyyah (Bethany), just east of Jerusalem. This separates thousands of residents from their relatives, jobs, schools, churches, mosques, and health care facilities.

Critics of this strategy raised concerns that depending on the final route chosen for the incomplete sections, the wall would reduce Palestinian areas of the West Bank by as much as one-third. These remaining Palestinian areas would be subdivided into a series of noncontiguous cantons, each of which would be surrounded by the barrier and by land that would be unilaterally annexed by Israel. For example, by 2004 the Palestinian city of Qalqilya was surrounded on all sides by the security fence, making it impossible for anyone

A section of the Israeli-built security fence near Baka al-Garbiya, March 2, 2004. (Moshe Milner/Israeli Government Press Office)

to come into or go out of the city without permission from Israeli occupation authorities.

While the Israeli government claims that the security fence is the only reasonable way to protect its citizens from terrorist attacks, others—including some Israelis and most Palestinians, who deplored the fence—argue that there are ulterior motives for the barrier. The wall's detractors claim that Israel is illegally annexing Palestinian territory by gerrymandering the course of the fence. They also claim that Israel is able to force Palestinians to sell their land near the fence in the name of defense and national security. The barrier, of course, also makes it more burdensome for Palestinians to access jobs and resources on the other side of the wall, translating into economic dislocation. And in addition to preventing terrorist attacks, Israeli security personnel can and do use the fence as a way to screen all those who enter Israel from the West Bank. In this way, they can keep out anyone they consider undesirable.

The security wall has created unintended consequences, however. In Jerusalem, for example, Palestinians who had been living beyond where the barrier was erected have been compelled to move back into the city. The result has been serious housing shortages as well as higher rents and real estate values. And recently, Palestinians have begun to move into traditionally Jewish parts of the city to find housing. For Palestinian subsistence farmers, the security fence has proven to be a heavy burden. Because the barrier's route

includes some of the most fertile land in the region, farming there has always been a mainstay. But the presence of the barrier has made it difficult for farmers to reach their fields and bring their produce to market. The results of this have been devastating to a group that was already economically disadvantaged.

Not surprisingly, the Israeli decision to build this mammoth barrier—many times longer than the infamous Berlin Wall of the Cold War—has been highly controversial. The Palestinians, who refer to the barrier as the "racist segregation law," argue that Israel is doing nothing more than creating an apartheid-like system in Palestine that separates people based on ethnicity and religion. Palestinians have repeatedly challenged the construction of the wall and its proposed path, and on two separate occasions the Israeli Supreme Court has forced the government to change the path of the project to better protect Palestinian rights.

Both the United Nations (UN) and the International Court of Justice (ICJ) have issued nonbinding resolutions calling for the dismantlement of the barrier wall. The ICJ has deemed the wall to be a violation of international law. The George W. Bush administration waffled on the building of the wall, but all in all Israel has enjoyed U.S. government approval. Indeed, it publicly rejected the ICJ's judgment on the wall's construction. In 2004 the International Committee of the Red Cross claimed that the security fence posed "serious humanitarian and legal problems." The World Council of

A Palestinian climbs over the security fence separating the village of Abu Dis from East Jerusalem, January 25, 2004. (Moshe Milner/Israeli Government Press Office)

Churches, meanwhile, deemed the barrier a violation of basic human rights.

Despite the difficulties, border disputes, and negative international reaction that the security fence has engendered, many Israelis insist that the barrier is the only way to prevent attacks on Israeli civilians without resorting to a permanent wartime situation in which both Israeli and Palestinian civilians would be targeted. The Israelis continue to cite impressive statistics showing that the security fence has had the desired effect. Indeed, since construction commenced the number of terrorist attacks on Israeli citizens is down by more than 90 percent. The number of Israelis killed in such attacks has declined by better than 70 percent, while the number of those wounded has dropped by more than 85 percent.

Not all Israelis agree with the decision to erect the fence, however. Some have argued that constructing the barrier inside occupied territory actually increases the risks to Israeli security. Such critics include a number of prominent military and security officers who formed groups such as the Council for Peace and Security, which challenged the barrier's route. Avraham Shalom, former head of Israel's security service Shin Bet, has said that the wall "creates hatred, . . . expropriates land, and annexes hundreds of thousands of Palestinians to the state of Israel. The result is that the fence achieves the exact opposite of what was intended."

PAUL G. PIERPAOLI JR. AND STEPHEN ZUNES

See also

Arab Economic Boycott of Israel; Barak, Ehud; Gaza Strip; Intifada, Second; Israel; Jerusalem; Oil as an Economic Weapon; Palestinian Authority; Settlements, Israeli; Sharon, Ariel; Suicide Bombings; West Bank

References

Bickerton, Ian J., and Carla L. Klausner. *A Concise History of the Arab-Israeli Conflict.* 4th ed. Upper Saddle River, NJ: Prentice Hall, 2004.

Dowty, Alan. *Israel/Palestine.* Malden, MA: Polity, 2005.

Hall, John G. *Palestinian Authority: Creation of the Modern Middle East.* Langhorne, PA: Chelsea House, 2002.

Lagerquist, Peter. "Fencing the Last Sky: Excavating Palestine after Israel's 'Separation Wall.'" *Journal of Palestine Studies* 33(2) (Winter 2004): 5–15.

Zunes, Stephen. "Implications of the U.S. Reaction to the World Court Ruling against Israel's 'Separation Barrier.'" *Middle East Policy* 11(4) (Winter 2004): 72–85.

Israeli War of Independence, Israeli-Egyptian Front

Start Date: May 14, 1948
End Date: January 7, 1949

On May 14, 1948, Israel declared its independence, basing its boundaries on the 1947 United Nations (UN) partition plan for the former

Aerial view of a Jewish outpost near the Egyptian border, January 1948. Note the trenches, gun emplacements, and barbed wire perimeter. (Time & Life Pictures/Getty Images)

British Mandate for Palestine. None of the Arab nations in the region recognized Israel's right to statehood, and all had rejected the UN plan. That same day, Egyptian forces along with armies from Jordan, Syria, Lebanon, and Iraq launched an invasion against the new Jewish state. The Egyptian-Israeli phase of the war lasted eight months. Ultimately, the defeat of the Egyptian Army in southern Israel marked a crucial turning point in the war, which the Arabs would refer to as the Nakba, or the Catastrophe.

Contrary to popular perceptions, the newly created Israel Defense Forces (IDF) of 1948 had an advantage in numbers compared to the combined attacking Arab armies. The Israelis mobilized about 30,000 troops, while the Arabs committed approximately 23,500 troops in the opening stages of the war. While the Israelis had sufficient light weapons, they lacked heavy artillery, tanks, and aircraft. However, the Israelis benefitted from high morale, a unified command, a central position on interior lines, and a network of fortified settlements, the kibbutzim.

Estimates vary, but the Egyptians initially committed about 10,000 troops to the invasion of Israel. They deployed a battalion of British-built Mark VI and Matilda tanks, sixteen 25-pounder guns, eight 6-pounder guns, and a machine-gun battalion. The Egyptian Air Force, which suffered from poorly trained pilots and other per-

sonnel as well as substandard maintenance, consisted of 30 Supermarine Spitfires, 4 Hawker Hurricanes, and a small number of transport aircraft converted into bombers. None of the invading Arab armies had made any effort to coordinate their moves, and all were overconfident, expecting a rapid Israeli collapse.

Major General Ahmad Ali al-Mwawi had overall field command of Egyptian forces. The Egyptians planned two separate advances. One column would proceed along the Mediterranean coast with the objective of capturing Tel Aviv. A second and smaller column, located farther inland and composed of a number of irregular volunteers, would move through Beersheba and Hebron before capturing Jerusalem.

The Egyptian column advancing along the coast had considerable difficulty dealing with several Israeli kibbutzim, but by May 29 the Egyptians had reached the town of Ashdod, about 19 miles south of Tel Aviv. Here the Egyptians were held up by a determined Israeli defense. The Egyptian column advancing in the interior made rapid progress but was stalled on May 21 by the Israelis at the village of Ramat Rachel, just south of Jerusalem. The two Egyptian columns then cleared a corridor along the road from Ashqelon near the coast to Hebron in the interior, establishing lateral communications. Nevertheless, the Israelis still controlled about 24 kibbutzim in the northern Negev Desert. Although technically surrounded by the Egyptians, the Israelis had little difficulty infiltrating across Egyptian lines and harassing Egyptian communications. The UN then negotiated a cease-fire, which took effect on June 11.

The Egyptians used the truce period to augment their troop strength to a total of 18,000 men. But the stubborn Israeli defenses had persuaded the Egyptians to abandon any hope of future advance. Instead, their troops now hunkered down into strung-out static defensive positions with vulnerable communications. The Egyptians had effectively surrendered the initiative to the Israelis, who were rapidly expanding their army and overcoming the early deficiencies in artillery, armor, and aircraft. Aware of Israeli preparations, al-Mwawi launched preemptive attacks on Israeli positions on July 8, just before the cease-fire expired. The Egyptian attacks were beaten off, but Israeli counterattacks proved equally inconclusive. A second UN cease-fire went into effect on July 18.

Further reinforcements brought Egyptian numbers up to more than 20,000 men, supported by a total of 135 armored vehicles of all types. Yet al-Mwawi knew that his forces were badly overextended and vulnerable. He subsequently asked permission from Cairo to pull back and consolidate, but his request was denied.

The Israeli counteroffensive, code-named Operation YOAV, began on October 15, 1948. By this time, the Israelis had won aerial parity. An Israeli offensive from the Negev pocket moving toward the Mediterranean came very close to cutting off a large portion of the Egyptian Army north of Gaza. Desperate Egyptian resistance and a skillful retreat ensured an Egyptian escape, but all the territory held by the Egyptians north of Gaza was lost to the Israelis. The Israelis then cut the Ashqelon-Hebron corridor, although not without considerable difficulty. The Israelis reestablished links with the Negev settlements and isolated the two prongs of the Egyptian force from each other. Further Israeli attacks isolated a pocket of 4,000–5,000 Egyptians at the Negev town of Fallujah. The Fallujah pocket succeeded in holding off Israeli attacks until the end of the war. In the meantime, Jordanian forces operating nearby stood aside and did nothing to help their Egyptian allies. The Israeli capture of Beersheba on October 21 prompted the dismissal of al-Mwawi, who became a scapegoat for the Egyptian defeat. Major General Sadiq replaced him.

The final stage of fighting on the Israeli-Egyptian front came with Israel's Operation HOREV, launched on December 22, 1948. A diversionary Israeli attack on Gaza masked the main Israeli attack, which was aimed at the last remaining Egyptian positions in the southern Negev. Here the Egyptian positions formed a salient with the base at al-Aujah, near the Egyptian border, and the tip at Asluj, south of Beersheba. Employing rapid maneuver and mobile forces, the Israelis defeated the Egyptians in the southern Negev and forced them to withdraw. The Israelis then swept onto the Sinai itself, approaching the outskirts of the Egyptian town of El Arish. Although the Israelis quickly determined that they did not have the strength to capture the town, their advance threatened to encircle Egyptian troops positioned in Gaza.

The Israeli advance into the Sinai brought Israel into a confrontation with Britain, which still had a treaty of alliance with Egypt. Now under British pressure, the Israelis began to withdraw from the Sinai, but not before Israeli aircraft shot down five unarmed British reconnaissance aircraft on January 7, 1949.

Egypt and Israel agreed to a cease-fire on January 7, 1949, and an armistice was signed in Rhodes on February 24. The Israelis had defeated the Egyptian invasion force and driven it from all the territory that it had occupied in Israel during the early phase of the war. The Egyptian government admitted to losses of 1,400 dead and 3,731 seriously wounded in the fighting.

PAUL W. DOERR

See also

Egypt, Armed Forces; Israel Defense Forces; Israeli War of Independence, Overview; Mwawi, Ahmad Ali al-

References

Bregman, Ahron. *Israel's Wars, 1947–93*. London: Routledge, 2000.
Dupuy, Trevor N. *Elusive Victory: The Arab-Israeli Wars, 1947–1974*. Garden City, NY: Military Book Club, 2002.
Morris, Benny. *Righteous Victims: A History of the Zionist-Arab Conflict, 1881–2001*. New York: Vintage Books, 2001.
Pollack, Kenneth M. *Arabs at War: Military Effectiveness, 1948–1991*. Lincoln: University of Nebraska Press, 2002.

Israeli War of Independence, Israeli-Iraqi Front
Start Date: May 14, 1948
End Date: October 15, 1949

When the independent State of Israel was declared on May 14, 1948, the new nation was immediately attacked by five Arab nations fighting as a loose coalition, supplemented by Palestinian militia forces and volunteers from other Muslim nations. Iraq, which became independent of British colonial rule in 1946, was then ruled by King Faisal II, half brother of King Abdullah of Transjordan. Both states belonged to the Arab League, a confederation of seven nations that coordinated external military and foreign relations policies.

Iraq was the only official Arab belligerent that did not share a border with Israel. As such, while Iraqi logistics required the movement of troops and supplies through Jordanian territory, at no time did Iraq face a threat to its own sovereign territory. The Arab allies held the advantage in airpower, artillery, and armored vehicles at the beginning of the war. The Israel Defense Forces (IDF) possessed virtually no heavy weaponry and no warplanes. Iraq had the second-largest military of the Arab forces in 1948, outgunned only by Egypt. At the beginning of the conflict, the Iraqi Army numbered more than 20,000 troops, and the Iraqi Air Force counted approximately 100 combat aircraft. The first Iraqi deployment against Israel included four infantry brigades and one armored battalion, totaling 5,000 combat personnel. By the end of the war, the number of Iraqi forces deployed against Israel had tripled in size, eventually including more than 15,000 troops.

With the impending end of the British Mandate for Palestine, King Faisal sent Iraqi troops into Jordan in April 1948. General Nur al-Din Mahmud commanded the Iraqi expeditionary force. On the first day of the war, the Iraqi forces constructed a pontoon bridge across the Jordan River. They operated between the sectors controlled by the Syrians on the northern front and the Jordanians on the central front. Early Iraqi advances met with some success, and one assault captured and held the Naharayim Power Station, while another moved into Judea and Samaria on the West Bank of the Jordan River. The Iraqi attacks were soon blunted by stiff Israeli resistance.

Iraqi forces then adopted a defensive posture in the vicinity of the Arabic settlement of Jenin. To relieve the pressure on the central front near Jerusalem, the IDF launched an attack against Jenin, directly into the heart of Iraqi defenses. The Iraqi positions held, albeit at a high cost, and drove the IDF troops completely out of the region. It was one of the heaviest defeats sustained by the IDF during the war but sufficiently damaged the Iraqi units involved to ensure that Iraq's military remained in defensive positions for the remainder of the war.

The Iraqi Air Force played a relatively minor role in the Israeli War of Independence. Its operations were poorly coordinated with the Iraqi Army, despite the fact that it was designed primarily to provide tactical air support. Iraqi warplanes periodically attacked Jewish settlements and IDF positions but did not play a decisive role in the conflict.

By early June 1948, Iraqi and Israeli forces were essentially in a stalemate. Although the Iraqi presence in Israel grew steadily, it served primarily to tie down IDF troops and prevent their transfer to other sectors of the conflict. It did not represent a major threat by the time of the first United Nations (UN) truce, which went into effect on June 11, 1948. The truce lasted until July 8, 1948, when Egyptian forces resumed fighting on the southern front. In July the IDF counterattacked in the northern and central sectors of the war, pushing Lebanese and Syrian troops completely out of Israel's declared borders and making smaller gains against Jordanian and Iraqi troops.

During the first truce, UN mediator Folke Bernadotte presented a plan to partition Palestine into two states, one Jewish and one Muslim. Both sides rejected the proposal out of hand, and each attempted to break the terms of the cease-fire by obtaining new munitions. In this objective Iraq failed almost completely, while Israel successfully purchased weapons from Czechoslovakia and resupplied the depleted IDF.

In the second phase of the fighting (July 8–18, 1948), the IDF concentrated most of its efforts on the Tel Aviv–Jerusalem corridor. As such, combat between Iraqi and Israeli forces consisted primarily of minor raids and reprisals without sustained offensive efforts by either belligerent. Iraq remained on the tactical defensive, and Iraqi commanders were content to cede the initiative to their Israeli counterparts.

During the second UN-mediated truce (July 18–October 15, 1948), Bernadotte proposed another plan to partition Palestine that was again rejected by Iraq and Israel as well as all of the other belligerents. After the cease-fire ended, Israel resumed the offensive in a final push to rid the nation of the invading Arab armies. The IDF attacked each enemy in turn, driving them from Israeli soil.

In 1949 Israel signed separate cease-fire agreements with Egypt, Lebanon, Syria, and Transjordan. Iraq and Israel did not conclude a formal armistice, but the lack of a common border prevented either side from continuing hostilities. Iraqi-Israeli enmity remained, although Iraq also had increasingly strained relations with Jordan. During the 1956 Suez Crisis, Iraqi troops occupied part of Jordan but did not engage Israeli forces. In the Six-Day War (1967), Iraq sent planes and troops to Jordan but did not enter the conflict. Not until the 1973 Yom Kippur War did Iraq and Israel openly resume their conflict from 1948.

PAUL J. SPRINGER

See also
Israel; Israel Defense Forces; Israeli War of Independence, Israeli-Jordanian Front; Israeli War of Independence, Overview; Iraq; Iraq, Armed Forces

References
Draper, Thomas. *Israel and the Middle East.* New York: H. W. Wilson, 1983.

Herzog, Chaim. *The Arab-Israeli Wars: War and Peace in the Middle East from the War of Independence to Lebanon.* Westminster, MD: Random House, 1984.

Lustick, Ian. *From War to War: Israel vs. the Arabs, 1948–1967.* New York: Garland, 1994.

Pollack, Kenneth M. *Arabs at War: Military Effectiveness, 1948–1991.* Lincoln: University of Nebraska Press, 2002.

Israeli War of Independence, Israeli-Jordanian Front
Start Date: May 14, 1948
End Date: April 3, 1949

The Arab Legion of Jordan was the most professional and capable of the Arab armies participating in the 1948–1949 Israeli War of Independence and the Arab military force most feared by the Israelis. The Jordanian Arab Legion overran the West Bank and East Jerusalem early in the war, then held on to the greater part of those gains against Israeli counterattacks.

The Arab Legion had been created in the early 1920s to assist the British in maintaining control of their Middle Eastern holdings. Modeled on the British Army, the legion was comparatively small in size but highly mobile. The rank and file consisted of long-service volunteers who received extensive training in individual skills such as marksmanship. By 1948 the legion numbered about 8,000 troops along with 120 armored cars—of which 70 carried 6-pounder guns—and a highly skilled artillery element. The officer corps of the legion was still dominated by several dozen British officers, either seconded from the British Army or working under contract directly with the legion itself. A British officer, Lieutenant

General John Bagot Glubb, known as Glubb Pasha, commanded the legion.

In 1948, however, Jordan had neither tanks nor aircraft to support the Arab Legion and no trained reserve for casualty replacement. The Jordanians were also plagued by ammunition shortages throughout the war. As one of the poorest Middle Eastern states, Jordan did not have the infrastructure necessary to sustain a long conflict.

Unlike other Arab states, the Jordanians apparently did not want to destroy Israel in 1948. Instead, Jordan's King Abdullah wanted to seize the areas of Palestine that had been allotted to Palestinian Arabs under the United Nations (UN) partition plan of 1947. Abdullah also wanted to take as much of the city of Jerusalem as possible.

The Israelis could muster 30,000 highly motivated troops for the defense of their new state in 1948, but the training and equipment of those troops varied greatly. This number doubled within a few months, with almost all the new troops having little or no military training. The Israelis also lacked heavy equipment and had to split their forces to fight the Egyptians in the south, the Jordanians in the east, plus Syrians, Lebanese, and later the Iraqis in the north and northeast.

Small units of the Arab Legion had already been operating on the West Bank, around Jerusalem, in cooperation with the British during the last phase of the UN Palestine mandate. When the Israelis proclaimed independence on May 14, 1948, the bulk of the legion crossed into the West Bank from Jordan the same day, while the Egyptians and Syrians attacked simultaneously.

Glubb organized the Arab Legion into two brigades for the invasion. The first occupied the hills of Samaria from Jenin to Ramallah, meeting minimal resistance. On May 20 units from this brigade captured the Latrun police fort, an imposing position on a hill that dominated the road from Tel Aviv to Jerusalem. Glubb's second brigade was deployed around Jerusalem, and on May 17 Abdullah ordered the legion to attack the city. Latrun and Jerusalem subsequently formed the focal points of the fighting on the Israeli-Jordanian front during 1948.

Glubb feared that fighting in Jerusalem would result in heavy casualties for the Arab Legion, which had been trained to fight in the open. His fears proved correct, and the Jordanian attack into the heart of Jerusalem was stopped by the outnumbered and outgunned Israelis at the Notre Dame de France monastery in the northeast corner of the Old City. Jordanian attacks to the north and south of Jerusalem aimed at pinching off the city were likewise halted by determined Israeli defenders. The Jordanians had more success taking the isolated Jewish quarter of Jerusalem, which capitulated on May 28.

The fighting at Latrun proved particularly vicious, as Jordanian possession of the fort threatened to cut the tenuous Israeli corridor connecting Tel Aviv to Jerusalem. Israeli attacks on Latrun during May 24–25 were thrown back with heavy losses. A second Israeli offensive on May 30 was also defeated, and the Israelis were forced to build a road farther south circumventing Latrun. A UN cease-fire then went into effect on June 11, 1948.

Both sides used the 10 days of the truce period to prepare for the next round of fighting. The Israelis were able to make up for their initial deficiencies in equipment, and their superiority in numbers alarmed Glubb. Some Arab Legion companies had suffered very heavy losses, and Glubb had difficulty finding replacements. The legion was also hard hit by the decision of the British government to recall all British officers, although those under direct contract to the legion, including Glubb, remained. But the sudden withdrawal of senior British officers, including both brigade commanders and three out of four battalion commanders, meant that Glubb had to scramble to rebuild his chain of command. The legion was bolstered, on the other hand, by the arrival of an Iraqi expeditionary force that took up positions in northern Samaria, allowing Glubb to concentrate at Latrun.

The UN cease-fire expired on July 9. The Israelis launched furious attacks in Jerusalem that failed to make major inroads other than the capture of Mount Herzl. The heaviest fighting was around Latrun. As part of his efforts to consolidate his defenses, Glubb had pulled back advance Arab Legion forces from the villages of Lod and Ramla, which were located only 10 miles from Tel Aviv. The defense of these villages was turned over to indigenous Palestinian militias, which succumbed to Israeli brigade-scale attacks during July 9–13.

The Israelis then launched attacks against the shoulders of the Latrun position during July 14–17, by which time they had come within two miles of surrounding the fort. A final Israeli attack on July 18 had more success against the exhausted Arab Legion, and had the fighting continued, the Israelis might have been able to starve the Latrun garrison into submission. However, a second UN cease-fire went into effect on the evening of July 18.

This second cease-fire marked the end of Jordanian participation in the 1948–1949 war. Abdullah knew that he could make no further gains and did not want to jeopardize what he had won. The Israeli-Jordanian front remained relatively quiet thereafter. Abdullah made sure that Jordan would have political control of northern Samaria and Judea when the war ended, and Iraqi and Egyptian troops withdrew from those areas, respectively. Abdullah signed a cease-fire with Israel on December 1, 1948, and annexed the West Bank to Jordan in 1950. Jordanian casualties in the war probably numbered several hundred dead.

PAUL W. DOERR

See also

Abdullah I, King of Jordan; Glubb, Sir John Bagot; Israel Defense Forces; Israeli War of Independence, Overview; Jordan, Armed Forces; Latrun, Battles of

References

Bregman, Ahron. *Israel's Wars, 1947–93*. London: Routledge, 2000.

Dupuy, Trevor N. *Elusive Victory: The Arab-Israeli Wars, 1947–1974*. Garden City, NY: Military Book Club, 2002.

Morris, Benny. *Righteous Victims: A History of the Zionist-Arab Conflict, 1881–2001*. New York: Vintage Books, 2001.

O'Ballance, Edgar. *The Arab-Israeli War, 1948*. London: Faber, 1956.

Pollack, Kenneth M. *Arabs at War: Military Effectiveness, 1948–1991.* Lincoln: University of Nebraska Press, 2002.

Israeli War of Independence, Israeli-Lebanese Front

Start Date: May 14, 1948
End Date: March 23, 1949

On May 14, 1948, Jewish leaders in the former British Mandate for Palestine proclaimed the independence of the State of Israel. This act was immediately followed by the invasion of the new nation by the five Arab nations of Egypt, Iraq, Lebanon, Syria, and Transjordan. The Arab armies heavily outnumbered their Israeli opponents and had a technological superiority, particularly in heavy weapons, for the duration of the war. However, the Arab military effort was poorly coordinated, and the Arabs never successfully unified their command structure, nominally headed by King Abdullah I of Transjordan. In comparison, the Israeli military, organized under the auspices of the Israel Defense Forces (IDF) on May 26, continually expanded its manpower base and used the advantages of interior lines and a clear chain of command.

Lebanon was the least populous nation among Israel's foes. When the war started, Lebanon's army numbered only some 3,500 men. The small Mediterranean nation committed to the conflict only a token force of 1,000 soldiers and virtually no heavy equipment. Their area of operations, the northern front, was primarily controlled by the Syrian Army, which could field more than 10,000 troops buttressed by a light armored battalion and 50 aircraft.

On the northern front the assault developed poorly. Moderate early Arab advances were quickly halted by Israeli militia forces. By June 1948 Lebanese forces, while occupying Israeli territory, had adopted a defensive posture. The IDF was content to accept a stalemate in the north while concentrating its primary efforts in the southern and central regions. The Lebanese Army directly supported the Arab Liberation Army (ALA), a multinational unit of volunteers that included a significant number of Lebanese recruits. None of the other Arab belligerents sought close cooperation with the ALA, although Syria and Iraq periodically donated equipment to it.

The United Nations (UN) brokered a truce between Israel and the Arab belligerents that went into effect on June 11, 1948. According to its terms, no belligerents were allowed to import munitions during the cease-fire, but all of the warring nations attempted this to varying degrees. Lebanon proved incapable of obtaining much-needed replacement weapons and ammunition and had virtually no domestic arms manufacturing capability. In comparison, Israel successfully smuggled in large quantities of weapons, particularly from Czechoslovakia, and quickly distributed the vehicles and armaments throughout the IDF on all fronts of the war.

When fighting resumed on July 8, the IDF seized the initiative in the war and embarked on a massive offensive. During the 10 days of fighting before another UN-mediated cease-fire, Israel made major gains, pushing Arab forces back on all fronts. On the Lebanese front, the ALA retreated from defensive positions in Galilee to an enclave in the northern theater where it could enjoy the direct tactical support of the Lebanese. Although this augmented the number of Arab troops in the region, it did little to arrest IDF advances. Only the renewed truce prevented the destruction of the ALA and the complete expulsion of Lebanese troops.

The second truce lasted until October 15, when fighting resumed between Israel and Egypt. The conflict soon spread to the other sectors of the war, and the IDF sought to push each Arab army out of Israel in succession. On the Israeli-Lebanese front, the major Israeli offensive was Operation HIRAM during October 29–31. It completely destroyed the ALA and drove the small Lebanese army from the war. IDF troops crossed the border into Lebanon and occupied the southern portion of that nation until the end of the war.

On March 23, 1949, Israel and Lebanon concluded an armistice that included the return of Lebanese territory and the withdrawal of IDF units.

PAUL J. SPRINGER

See also
Arab Liberation Army; Israel; Israel Defense Forces; Israeli War of Independence, Overview; Lebanon; Lebanon, Armed Forces

References
Friedman, Thomas. *From Beirut to Jerusalem.* New York: Anchor Books, 1995.
Herzog, Chaim. *The Arab-Israeli Wars: War and Peace in the Middle East from the War of Independence to Lebanon.* Westminster, MD: Random House, 1984.
Khalidi, Walid. *Conflict and Violence in Lebanon: Confrontation in the Middle East.* Cambridge: Harvard University Press, 1979.
Mackey, Sandra. *Lebanon: Death of a Nation.* New York: Congdon and Weed, 1989.
Rabil, Robert G. *Embattled Neighbors: Syria, Israel, and Lebanon.* Boulder, CO: Lynne Rienner, 2003.

Israeli War of Independence, Israeli-Syrian Front

Start Date: May 14, 1948
End Date: July 20, 1949

On May 14, 1948, when Israel proclaimed its independence, the new state was immediately attacked by armies from Egypt, Iraq, Lebanon, Syria, and Transjordan under the nominal command of Transjordan's King Abdullah I. Although unified in their intent to destroy Israel, the Arab states each pursued their individual objectives, and cooperation among the belligerent Arab states was virtually nonexistent. For its part, Syria had some territorial ambitions in Palestine and intended to establish itself as a major player in the region. The Syrian military commitment to the war, however, was much smaller than that of Egypt, Iraq, and Transjordan. Between 3,000 and 5,000 Syrian troops fought in the conflict.

Syria began the war with barely 12,000 soldiers, armed mostly with obsolete equipment. During the initial invasion of Israel, Syria committed an infantry brigade as well as a tank company and an artillery battalion in what was expected to be a quick, overwhelming assault. The Syrian troops were augmented by the Arab Liberation Army (ALA), commanded by Fawzi al-Qawuqji, a Syrian.

The ALA was a collection of international volunteers and Palestinians. Occasionally, the Syrian Army supplied the ALA with equipment and logistical support. At no time did ALA participation in a battle prove decisive, but the ALA did pin down some Israeli forces in the northern sector.

The Syrian military initially had several significant advantages. For one thing, it was relatively better equipped than the Israel Defense Forces (IDF). Although only 10 of Syria's 50 aircraft were of recent design, Israel began the war with no combat aircraft at all. And although most Syrian tanks were lesser-quality French export models, Israel started the war with no tanks and few artillery pieces. The Syrians also had the advantage of terrain, being able to initiate attacks into Israel from the high ground of the Golan Heights.

The Syrian assault against Zemach, on the southern edge of the Sea of Galilee, was supported by 30 armored vehicles and Renault tanks. The defenders had only two 20-mm guns to stop the Syrian armor. The Syrian commander, Brigadier General Husni al-Zaim, sent a flanking attack of infantry and armored vehicles to surround the village. This maneuver, combined with the loss of one of their antitank guns, forced the defenders to attempt a fighting withdrawal on May 18, 1948. Most of the defending forces were annihilated, opening the route for a Syrian advance into the Jordan Valley.

Only two villages, Degania A (Palestine's oldest kibbutz) and Degania B, stood in the way of the Syrian breakout. The 70 or so Israeli defenders were lightly armed settlers and militia. Their only heavy weapon was the remaining antitank gun from Zemach.

At dawn on May 20 the Syrian forces opened the attack on Degania with heavy artillery fire. Degania A was attacked by a Syrian infantry company supported by several tanks and an armored car platoon. The antitank gun destroyed one armored car and damaged a tank, but the defenders were soon driven from their prepared positions into a hastily dug system of communications trenches. From the trenches, the Israelis engaged the Syrian tanks with Molotov cocktails, neutralizing one tank and two more armored cars. The Syrian main effort then shifted to Degania B, where a pair of infantry companies supported by tanks, armored cars, and artillery attempted to overrun the defenders. Once again, the Israelis held.

While the Degania attacks were in progress, the first Israeli artillery pieces of the war entered the action. Arriving at Tel Aviv only a few days earlier, the guns had been rushed to the north and put into battery in the hills near Degania. The Israeli fire forced the Syrians to withdraw, abandoning all of their gains from the first week of the war. The Syrians abandoned their efforts to invade south of the Sea of Galilee and shifted their efforts to the north.

On June 6 Syria resumed the offensive, attacking Mishmar Hayarden in the northern Galilee region. The Syrian attack was preceded by a heavy preparatory bombardment, but the follow-on two-battalion attack failed. With the attack force strengthened to two brigades, the Syrians resumed the offensive on June 10, battering through the defenses of the settlement and killing almost the entire defensive force. The United Nations (UN) negotiated a cease-fire that went into effect the next day, leaving Syrian forces occupying Mishmar Hayarden, a position they held for the remainder of the war.

After the truce expired on July 8, Israeli forces launched Operation BROSH, attempting to encircle Mishmar Hayarden and cut off the Syrian lines of communication. The Israeli attack failed, and a Syrian counterattack on July 10 pushed the Israelis back to the western side of the Jordan River. Fighting in this sector was bloody but inconclusive. On July 15 another UN truce went into effect and lasted until October 15, allowing each side to resupply and reinforce its units in the Galilee region.

When fighting resumed in October, the Israelis on October 24 seized the initiative and launched Operation HIRAM. The objective of the operation was the complete expulsion of Arab forces from the Galilee region and the destruction of ALA units in the area. After seven days of intense fighting, Israeli troops annihilated the ALA and pushed the Lebanese completely from Israeli territory. The Syrian Army managed to retain its control over Mishmar Hayarden but remained on the defensive and made no significant attempt to expand its occupation of Israeli territory.

For all practical purposes, the war on the Syrian-Israeli border ended by November 1948, allowing the IDF to shift units to the central and southern sectors of the war. Syrian troops remained in and around Mishmar Hayarden until July 20, 1949, when Israel and Syria signed an armistice. The territory evacuated by Syria was designated as a demilitarized zone.

PAUL J. SPRINGER AND DAVID T. ZABECKI

See also

Arab Liberation Army; Israel; Israel Defense Forces; Israeli War of Independence, Overview; Qawuqji, Fawzi al-; Syria; Syria, Armed Forces

References

Herzog, Chaim. *The Arab-Israeli Wars: War and Peace in the Middle East from the War of Independence to Lebanon*. Westminster, MD: Random House, 1984.

Lustick, Ian. *From War to War: Israel vs. the Arabs, 1948–1967*. New York: Garland, 1994.

Pollack, Kenneth M. *Arabs at War: Military Effectiveness, 1948–1991*. Lincoln: University of Nebraska Press, 2002.

Rabil, Robert G. *Embattled Neighbors: Syria, Israel, and Lebanon*. Boulder, CO: Lynne Rienner, 2003.

Israeli War of Independence, Overview
Start Date: May 14, 1948
End Date: July, 20, 1949

Conflict between the newly created State of Israel and its Arab neighbors that occurred between May 1948 and May 1949. When the

Arab soldiers behind a barricade firing on Jewish Haganah fighters in the streets of Jerusalem, May 14, 1948. (AFP/Getty Images)

Ottoman Empire was dismantled in the wake of World War I, Great Britain received a mandate from the League of Nations over Palestine. Much of the British Mandate period (1920–1948) was spent maintaining peace among the Muslim, Jewish, and Christian populations in the region.

In the 1920s and 1930s the region received a large influx of Jewish immigrants, many of whom were fleeing persecution in Europe. The rising number of Jewish residents spawned a violent backlash from Palestinian Arabs. This often took the form of demonstrations against British policies, including a series of riots centered in Jerusalem. During the Arab Revolt of 1936–1939, Arab insurgents attacked Jewish settlements and businesses. They also boycotted British-owned businesses. Riots swept Palestine and were put down by British forces, which sometimes were augmented by Jewish auxiliary police.

Thousands of Palestinians were killed, wounded, or imprisoned during the revolt. After British forces successfully quelled the rebellion, the mandate administration adopted a decidedly pro-Jewish stance, turning a blind eye to Jewish militia forces such as Haganah, which were officially outlawed. These militia forces would prove vital when open fighting erupted between Arabs and Jews in 1948. At the same time, the British sought to enforce immigration quotas

that worked against Jews finding refuge in Palestine, even during World War II and the Holocaust. Increasingly, Jewish paramilitary forces such as the Irgun Tsvai Leumi (National Military Organization) battled the British occupiers, who arrested a number of them. The British seemed unable to please either side as the violence escalated.

World War II marked the end of colonialism in the Middle East and elsewhere. Lebanon became independent in 1943, although French troops did not leave that country until 1946, when they also departed from the French Mandate for Syria. British-controlled Transjordan and Iraq also gained independence in 1946, under King Abdullah and his half brother King Faisal, respectively. The British remained in Palestine until November 29, 1947, when the United Nations (UN) approved a partition plan that would have created two states, one Jewish and the other Arab. Jewish and Arab leaders each criticized aspects of the partition. However, the Jewish populace of Palestine mostly supported the UN resolution as the key to an independent Jewish state. The Arabs roundly rejected the plan.

On November 30, 1947, seven Jewish inhabitants of Palestine died in three separate attacks by Arabs. Jewish militia forces retaliated, and British authorities proved unable to halt the escalating violence in the region. The British became increasingly unwilling to

ISRAELI WAR OF INDEPENDENCE, 1948–1949

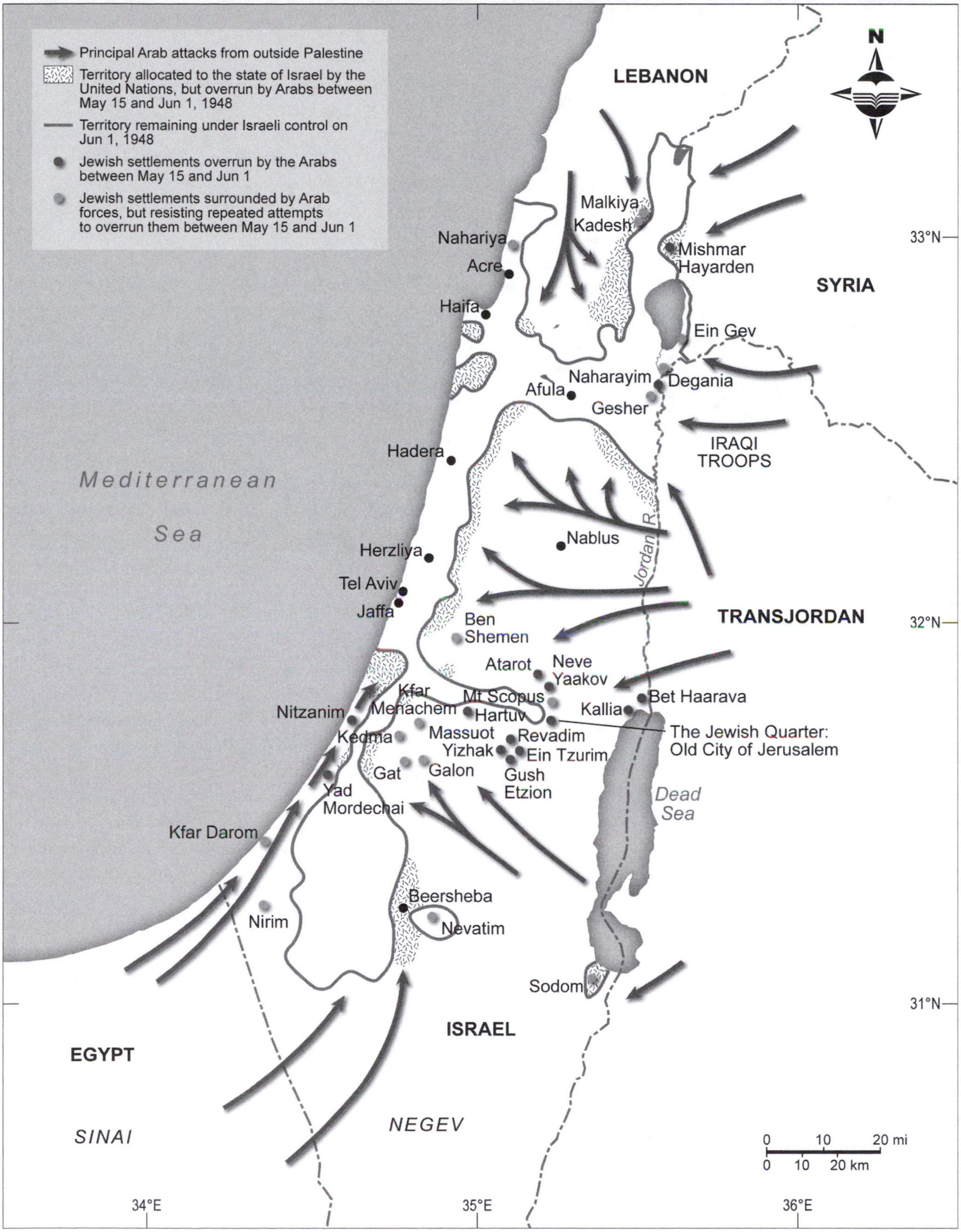

Legend

- ➤ Principal Arab attacks from outside Palestine
- Territory allocated to the state of Israel by the United Nations, but overrun by Arabs between May 15 and Jun 1, 1948
- Territory remaining under Israeli control on Jun 1, 1948
- ● Jewish settlements overrun by the Arabs between May 15 and Jun 1
- ● Jewish settlements surrounded by Arab forces, but resisting repeated attempts to overrun them between May 15 and Jun 1

N

LEBANON

SYRIA

Malkiya
Kadesh
Nahariya
Acre
Mishmar Hayarden
Haifa
Ein Gev
Naharayim
Degania
Afula
Gesher
IRAQI TROOPS

Mediterranean Sea

Hadera

Jordan R.

Nablus

Herzliya
Tel Aviv
Jaffa

TRANSJORDAN

Ben Shemen
Atarot
Neve Yaakov
Kfar Menachem
Mt Scopus
Kallia
Bet Haarava
Nitzanim
Hartuv
Kedma
Massuot Yizhak
Revadim
Ein Tzurim
The Jewish Quarter: Old City of Jerusalem
Gat
Galon
Gush Etzion
Yad Mordechai

Dead Sea

Kfar Darom

Beersheba
Nirim
Nevatim

Sodom

ISRAEL

EGYPT

SINAI

NEGEV

0   10   20 mi
0   10   20 km

Israeli soldiers employing a captured Egyptian antitank gun at Abu Ageila during Operation HOREV, December 15, 1948. (Israeli Government Press Office)

intervene in the growing conflict as the date of complete British withdrawal drew near. In December 1947 and January 1948, almost 1,000 Palestinian residents died in the fighting, which continued to escalate in early 1948.

Although Arabs outnumbered Jews in Palestine, Jewish forces proved better armed and organized. Arab military efforts focused on cutting communications between Jewish settlements and isolating the city of Jerusalem. Jewish counterattacks sought to control roads linking Jewish towns but could rarely open routes to Jerusalem.

With the British Mandate due to expire on May 15, 1948, and no agreement on partition, Jewish leaders declared the independence of the State of Israel on May 14, 1948. Israel promptly received diplomatic recognition from the United States and the Soviet Union but was also immediately invaded by troops from surrounding Arab nations. The Arab forces included regular units from Egypt, Iraq, Lebanon, Syria, and Transjordan, augmented by Libyan, Saudi Arabian, and Yemeni volunteers. Officially, the troops cooperated under the auspices of the Arab League, which had been formed in 1945. Nominally, King Abdullah of Transjordan was the commander in chief of the Arab armies, although cooperation among the Arab forces remained almost nonexistent throughout the war.

On May 15, 1948, the Arab League announced its intention to create the United State of Palestine, encompassing the Jewish and Arab regions created by the UN partition plan. Although the Arab invasion was denounced by the United States, the Soviet Union, and UN secretary-general Trygve Lie, it found support from the Republic of China (Taiwan) and other UN member states.

On May 26, 1948, the Israeli government created the Israel Defense Forces (IDF), primarily by incorporating the irregular Jewish militias that had existed under the British Mandate, including Haganah, the Palmach, and Irgun. Although the IDF numbered fewer than 30,000 troops at its formation, by mid-July 1948 it had more than doubled in size. It continued to grow exponentially, and by the end of 1948 Israel could place more than 100,000 troops in the field. The vast majority of those troops, however, were recently arrived immigrants from the concentration camps and displaced persons camps of Europe who had little or no military training. In comparison, the combined Arab armies, which began the conflict with approximately 23,500 troops, increased to only 40,000 by July 1948 and 55,000 that October.

Despite the rapid growth in the IDF's manpower, the Arab armies had a significant superiority in heavy weapons at the beginning of the conflict. Worldwide observers opined that the Jewish state would be quickly overrun because of its almost complete lack of armored vehicles, artillery, and warplanes. The new Israeli government quickly moved to purchase weapons, however, beginning with a shipment of 25 Czechoslovakian aircraft that arrived in late

May 1948. Czechoslovakia continued to provide weapons to the IDF for the remainder of the war, even during UN-mandated cease-fires that prohibited the sale of arms to any belligerent.

In the first phase of the fighting, Arab armies from Transjordan and Iraq advanced on Jerusalem with the aim of driving all Jewish inhabitants from the city. Abdullah ordered an assault on Jerusalem to begin on May 17, 1948. Two weeks of brutal house-to-house fighting followed, partially negating the Arab Legion's advantage in mobility and heavier weapons. Transjordanian troops succeeded in driving back IDF forces, but Iraqi attacks were ineffective, and soon the Iraqi force shifted to a defensive posture in the regions of Jenin and Nablus. A Syrian attack along the northern front of the war, supported by tanks and artillery, was defeated by Jewish settlers at Degania, the oldest kibbutz in Palestine. The settlers there had only light weapons, but they skillfully used terrain features and night attacks to halt the Syrian advance.

Only in the south did Arab forces make significant territorial gains. Egyptian forces captured several kibbutzim but took heavy losses in the process and bogged down near Ashdod. The first phase of the war ended when a UN-declared truce came into effect on June 11, 1948. Although the truce included an arms embargo for all belligerents, the Israelis successfully smuggled in munitions from Czechoslovakia while the four-week truce remained in effect. UN mediator Folke Bernadotte also proposed a new partition plan that was immediately rejected by both sides. When Egyptian forces resumed their attacks on July 8, the truce collapsed.

In the second phase of the war, the IDF assumed the offensive. Its primary objective was to restore Israeli command of the Tel Aviv–Jerusalem corridor. This it secured by a massive assault against Lod, which included the first Israeli use of bomber aircraft. The city, defended by Transjordanian troops augmented by Palestinian irregulars and the Arab Liberation Army (ALA), surrendered on July 11. The next day, the IDF captured Ramla, also in the vital corridor. The IDF, however, failed to take Latrun.

With the Jerusalem sector fairly stable, the IDF launched Operation DEKEL, a major push against Syrian and Lebanese troops in lower Galilee. The IDF captured Nazareth on July 16. Only against Egyptian forces in the south did the IDF fail to make any significant progress in the July fighting.

Another UN-brokered truce went into effect on July 18. Bernadotte presented yet another partition plan, this time calling for Transjordan to annex the Arab regions, the creation of an independent Jewish state, and the establishment of Jerusalem as an international city. All belligerents again rejected the plan, and the day after Bernadotte presented his latest solution to the conflict, he was assassinated by members of the Zionist militia Lehi. The truce remained in effect, however, until October 15, when Israel ended the cease-fire with a series of offensives designed to drive out the Arab armies completely.

In the third phase of the war, the Israelis began their offensives with an assault against Egyptian forces in the Negev Desert. Operation YOAV, commanded by Yigal Allon, sought to isolate Egyptian troops along the coast from those in the Negev. It was a tremendous success, forcing the Egyptian army to abandon its forward positions and evacuate the northern Negev. On October 24, Operation HIRAM commenced in the upper Galilee region, virtually destroying the remnants of the ALA and pushing several miles into Lebanon, driving Lebanese forces completely out of Israel. A renewed assault against the Egyptians started on December 22, when IDF troops encircled Egyptian units in the Gaza Strip and attacked their positions in the Sinai Peninsula. The Egyptians withdrew from and accepted a cease-fire effective January 7, 1949.

Once the truce went into effect, IDF troops withdrew from the Sinai and Gaza. In December 1948, the UN passed Resolution 194, which declared that refugees from the Arab-Israeli conflict should have the opportunity to return to their homes and live in peace. Those who chose not to return were to be offered compensation for their property by the government in control of that territory at the end of the conflict. The resolution never achieved its goals, and the huge population of Palestinian refugees became a lasting legal and diplomatic problem for the region.

International military observer forces occasionally were drawn into the conflict. One such clash between the British Royal Air Force and the Israeli Air Force occurred on January 7, 1949, when Royal Air Force observation aircraft overflew an Israeli convoy immediately after an attack by Egyptian aircraft. IDF troops opened fire upon the British aircraft, downing one. Three more British aircraft were shot down by Israeli interceptors. When more British planes entered the area they were attacked by Israeli warplanes, which destroyed an additional British plane and damaged another.

In 1949 Israel concluded separate armistices with each of the Arab belligerents with the exception of Iraq. On February 24 Egypt and Israel signed a cease-fire, which left Egyptian troops in occupation of the Gaza Strip. On March 23, Lebanon and Israel concluded an armistice, and the IDF withdrew from Lebanese territory. The Transjordan-Israel armistice, signed on April 3, left Transjordanian troops to remain in control of the West Bank. On July 20, Syria agreed to a cease-fire and the creation of a demilitarized zone along the Israeli-Syrian border.

The new State of Israel now covered three-fourths of the former British Mandate for Palestine and was 50 percent larger than the land area offered in Bernadotte's original partition proposal. Israel's independence cost 6,000 Israeli lives, one-third of which were civilian casualties. Arab losses were higher. Most estimates place the number of Arabs killed at approximately 10,000. In the aftermath of the war, Jewish residents of Arab nations were expelled. Hundreds of thousands traveled to Israel or immigrated to Europe. Likewise, thousands of Palestinians left the new Israeli nation. The surprising Israeli victory humiliated the Arabs, who had expected quick and easy success. This humiliation fueled hatred for Jews in Arab nations, and this enmity, coupled with rising Arab nationalism, virtually ensured that future conflict would erupt within the region before a lasting peace could be achieved.

PAUL J. SPRINGER

See also

Arab Liberation Army; Bernadotte, Folke; Egypt, Armed Forces; Haganah; Iraq, Armed Forces; Irgun Tsvai Leumi; Israel Defense Forces; Jordan, Armed Forces; Latrun, Battles of; Lebanon, Armed Forces; Palmach; Syria, Armed Forces; United Nations General Assembly Resolution 194

References

Draper, Thomas. *Israel and the Middle East.* New York: H. W. Wilson, 1983.

Herzog, Chaim. *The Arab-Israeli Wars: War and Peace in the Middle East from the War of Independence to Lebanon.* Westminster, MD: Random House, 1984.

Lustick, Ian. *From War to War: Israel vs. the Arabs, 1948–1967.* New York: Garland, 1994.

Pollack, Kenneth M. *Arabs at War: Military Effectiveness, 1948–1991.* Lincoln: University of Nebraska Press, 2002.

Rubin, Barry, and Thomas A. Keaney, eds. *Armed Forces in the Middle East: Politics and Strategy.* Portland, OR: Frank Cass, 2002.

Sachar, Howard Morley. *Egypt and Israel.* New York: R. Marek, 1981.

Israeli War of Independence, Truce Agreements

Start Date: February 24, 1949
End Date: July 20, 1949

The truce agreements, or General Armistice Agreements, ended the Israeli War of Independence (1948–1949) and secured Israel's independence. Israel signed four separate pacts, with Egypt (February 24, 1949, at Rhodes), Lebanon (March 23, 1949, at Ras en Naquora), Jordan (April 3, 1949, at Rhodes), and Syria (July 20, 1949, at Hill 232 near Mahanayim). The other major Arab participant in the conflict, Iraq, and those states that provided token help, Saudi Arabia and Yemen, refused to meet with the Israeli officials and did not sign truce agreements. The American diplomat Ralph Bunche, as a representative of the United Nations (UN), mediated the agreements.

The UN played a central role in bringing the parties together, particularly after the September 17, 1948, assassination of the original mediator, Count Folke Bernadotte. The November 16, 1948, UN Security Council Resolution (S-1080) even threatened military intervention to encourage an armistice.

All of these agreements created armistice demarcation lines. The lines set provisional boundaries that military forces and civilians were forbidden to cross. They also ensured the exchange of prisoners of war and made a preexisting unarmed observer peacekeeping mission, the UN Truce Supervision Organization (UNTSO), overseer of the armistices. Each agreement established Mixed Armistice Commissions, and UNTSO reported armistice violations directly to the Security Council.

The first armistice negotiations began on January 12, 1949, when Egyptian and Israeli representatives met under UN auspices on the Greek island of Rhodes. Throughout the talks, Egyptian forces remained besieged around Faluja in the Negev Desert. While nego-

tiations were carried out on the basis of equality and none of the Arab states had been decisively defeated, they all undertook armistice negotiations because of Israel's military success. The Israelis withdrew from land they captured in the Sinai Peninsula, but Egypt retained control of a thin coastal area of Palestine, which became known as the Gaza Strip.

Of the agreements, that between Israel and Lebanon functioned most smoothly, becoming the model for the Jordan and Syria agreements. Under this arrangement, Israel withdrew from villages it occupied near the Litani River, and the demarcation line conformed to the prewar international frontier.

The Israeli and Jordanian agreement encompassed the most change. Jordan's British-commanded Arab Legion occupied the West Bank, including East Jerusalem and the Old City. The Jordanians withdrew some of their forces in the Sharon Plain area, and the final agreement respected all earlier Jerusalem accords between the two sides.

Syria, the state most reluctant to meet with Israeli representatives, signed its agreement under Western pressure during the brief rule of Husni al-Zaim. To better correspond with the prewar international frontier, the Syrians withdrew from territory they occupied, creating three contentious demilitarized zones.

As a result of its military gains, largely enshrined in these accords, Israel controlled nearly 75 percent of mandatory Palestine, a much larger area than the Arab-rejected 1947 UN partition plan had granted the Jewish state. This territory denotes what is often referred to as Israel's pre-1967 borders.

The Arab states considered all of the truce talks to be purely military discussions, while the Israelis sought to establish more far-reaching political settlements. The Arab signatories were all military officers, while the Israelis included both soldiers and civilians among their representatives. During the negotiations, much to the frustration of the Israelis, the sides did not always meet face to face, often transmitting statements through UN officials. Most importantly, the Arab governments did not consider the agreements to have granted official recognition to Israel. Indeed, the Arab states deemed the truce agreements as temporary cessations of hostilities and continued to carry out belligerent acts against Israel, including economic boycotts. They also pledged to present a common front against Israel, believing that their opponent had benefited from negotiating with each country individually.

Significantly, until the 1970s Arab peace offers were based upon the UN partition plan or the 1948 Bernadotte proposals, not the 1949 truce agreements. In contrast, Israeli peace offers usually took the armistice agreements as their starting point. Deliberately vague in order to foster compromise and because both the UN and Israel considered them a first step toward peace, the 1949 truce agreements survived longer than anyone expected. Indeed, they still officially govern Syria's relations with Israel. All parties regularly violated the agreements throughout the 1950s and beyond, however, and the initial transition from armistice to peace came only

United Nations (UN) mediator Dr. Ralph Bunch presides over the Egyptian-Israeli cease-fire conference at Rhodes, 1949. The Israeli delegation is at the right. (Herman Chanania/Israeli Government Press Office)

after three additional wars and the signing of the 1979 Israel-Egypt Peace Treaty.

ANDREW THEOBALD

See also

Bernadotte, Folke; Bunche, Ralph Johnson; Israeli War of Independence, Overview; United Nations, Role of; United Nations Peacekeeping Missions

References

Bailey, Sydney D. *How Wars End,* Vol. 2, *The United Nations and the Termination of Armed Conflict, 1946–1964.* Oxford, UK: Clarendon, 1982.

Caplan, Neil. *Futile Diplomacy,* Vol. 3, *The United Nations, the Great Powers, and Middle East Peacemaking, 1948–1954.* London: Frank Cass, 1997.

Herzog, Chaim. *The Arab-Israeli Wars: War and Peace in the Middle East from the War of Independence to Lebanon.* Westminster, MD: Random House, 1984.

Institute for Palestinian Studies. *Arab-Israeli Armistice Agreements, February–July 1949: U.N. Texts.* Beirut: Institute for Palestinian Studies, 1967.

Rosenne, Shabtai. *Israel's Armistice Agreements with the Arab States: A Juridical Interpretation.* Tel Aviv: International Law Association, Israel Branch, 1951.

Izz al-Din al-Qassam Brigades

Armed paramilitary wing of the Palestinian group Hamas. The al-Qassam Brigades were formally established in 1991 by Yahya Ayyash, the key military strategist for Hamas. The al-Qassam Brigades, named for Izz al-Din al-Qassam, the militant Palestinian leader of the Black Hand organization in the 1920s, have mounted attacks and terror campaigns against Israelis. Ayyash claims to have established the brigades to facilitate Hamas's political goals, which in the early 1990s were meant to stymie any Palestinian compromise or accommodation with Israel. Specifically, Hamas was vehemently opposed to the 1993 Oslo Accords and competed with Fatah, its main rival within the Palestinian nationalist movement.

The al-Qassam Brigades have operated amid much secrecy and are not organized along typical military lines. Rather, they are small, largely independent cells directed by the head of the organization. It is not uncommon for the various cells to be completely unaware of other cells' goals or activities. Hamas and the brigades have been the strongest in the Gaza Strip, although they tried to maintain a significant presence in the West Bank as well. During 2004, however, retaliatory strikes by Israel Defense Forces (IDF) against brigade cells in the West Bank decimated the group there.

From 1992 to 2000, al-Qassam Brigades fought an on-again off-again guerrilla campaign against the IDF as well as Israeli civilians. Palestinian Authority (PA) president Yasser Arafat was unable to rein in the brigades. When the Second (al-Aqsa) Intifada began in September 2000, the brigades played a role in fomenting unrest and in arming and training militants to carry out terrorist attacks against Israel, but other attacks were organized by Islamic Jihad or carried out by individuals.

By 2003 the al-Qassam Brigades had developed in a different manner, not only focusing on terrorist attacks but also, with intra-Palestinian conflict on the rise, acting as a security force. Although multiple IDF attacks took a toll on the brigades' foot soldiers and leadership alike, the group continued to maintain its cohesion and attract many new recruits. Hamas accepted a truce in 2004 as part of an overall truce between the PA and Israel. The organization used the time to reconstitute and rearm itself.

After the Israelis pulled out of the Gaza Strip in August 2005, the al-Qassam Brigades sought to dominate the area in the ongoing effort by Hamas to supplant Fatah. Nevertheless, the brigades decreased their activity against the Israelis by generally honoring the truce that had begun in 2004 and was reiterated in 2005. Meanwhile, the PA was under heavy pressure to disarm Hamas. That attempt failed, however, when Hamas won the 2006 legislative elections.

Emboldened by their electoral success, Hamas leaders sought to assert control in Gaza. Indeed, the brigades formed a potent security source there beginning in May 2006, soon clashing with militias supported by Fatah. In June 2006, the al-Qassam Brigades allegedly supported Hezbollah's capture of an IDF soldier, Gilad Shalit, that precipitated the Israel-Gaza War that lasted for nearly a month. Brigade soldiers were heavily involved in the fighting. On July 12, 2006, Mohammed Dayf (Deif), leader of the al-Qassam Brigades, narrowly escaped an Israeli attack on a house in Gaza in which a Hamas official and his entire family were killed.

PAUL G. PIERPAOLI JR.

See also

Arafat, Yasser; Fatah; Gaza Strip; Hamas; Hezbollah; Intifada, Second; Oslo Accords; Palestine Liberation Organization; Palestinian Authority; West Bank

References

La Guardia, Anton. *War without End: Israelis, Palestinians, and the Struggle for a Promised Land.* New York: Thomas Dunne, 2002.

Mishal, Shaul, and Avraham Sela. *The Palestinian Hamas: Vision, Violence, and Coexistence.* New York: Columbia University Press, 2000.

Pappe, Ilan. *A History of Modern Palestine: One Land, Two Peoples.* Cambridge: Cambridge University Press, 2003.

Rubin, Barry. *Revolution until Victory? The Politics and History of the PLO.* Reprint ed. Cambridge: Harvard University Press, 2003.

J

Jabotinsky, Vladimir Yevgenyevich
Born: October 18, 1880
Died: August 4, 1940

Zionist leader, author, soldier, and founder of the Jewish Legion of World War I. Vladimir Yevgenyevich (Ze'ev Yina) Jabotinsky was born into a middle-class Jewish family in Odessa in Ukraine, Russia, on October 18, 1880. He left Russia in 1898 to study law in Italy and Switzerland and then became a highly acclaimed foreign correspondent whose articles appeared under the nom de plume of "Altalena" in several well-known Russian newspapers.

In 1903 when a pogrom seemed imminent in Odessa, Jabotinsky helped form the first Zionist self-defense group. As a consequence of a pogrom in Kishniew, Russia, that same year, he became active in Zionist work. He not only worked to organize self-defense units within the Jewish communities of Russia but also became an outspoken advocate of full civil rights for Russian Jews. Elected a delegate to the Sixth Zionist Congress in Basle in 1903, he opposed the scheme to establish a Jewish homeland in East Africa. Soon the most important Zionist speaker and journalist in Russia, he worked to promote Jewish culture in Russia, launching an effort in 1910 to make Hebrew the language in all Jewish schools, and he also helped establish the Hebrew University in Jerusalem. His Zionism, it should be noted, was political rather than cultural.

With the beginning of World War I, Jabotinsky became a war correspondent. He met Joseph Trumpeldor in Alexandria, Egypt, and the two men then worked to establish Jewish military units as part of the British Army. Jabotinsky believed that the Ottoman Empire was doomed and that Jewish support for the Allies in the war would help bring about creation of a Jewish state in Palestine. Their efforts began with the Zion Mule Corps of several hundred Jewish men that served with distinction in the Gallipoli Campaign.

From the beginning, Jabotinsky wanted the Jewish units to be frontline forces rather than auxiliaries. Later, the Jewish Legion (also known as the Jewish Battalions) served with distinction in other campaigns against the Ottomans. Enlisting in the 38th Battalion of Royal Fusiliers as a private, Jabotinsky was soon promoted to lieutenant and participated in the British crossing of the Jordan River and the liberation of Palestine from Ottoman rule. He was both decorated for bravery and mentioned in dispatches.

After the war, Jabotinsky joined the Zionist Committee and for a while headed its Political Department. The British authorities in Palestine denied his requests that he be allowed to arm a small number of Jews for self-defense purposes. Nonetheless, he was able to arm perhaps 600 men in secret self-defense groups.

The early April 1920 rioting by Arabs in Jerusalem led to the deaths of 6 people, the wounding of several hundred, and the destruction of Jewish property and torching of several synagogues. Jabotinsky had sought to create a legal Jewish police force for Jerusalem that would help to balance the Arab police there. During the riots he secured permission from the British military government to introduce 100 armed Jews into the city, but when he tried to do this he was promptly arrested along with 19 other Jews. The British then searched his residence and discovered arms there. Jabotinsky was tried and sentenced to 15 years at hard labor for weapons possession. Following a public outcry over the British conclusion that Jews were responsible for the riots and the outrageous verdicts handed out against the Jews, Jabotinsky served only a few months in Akko Prison before he was amnestied in July 1920. The April 1920 Arab riots, meanwhile, led to the establishment in Palestine of the Jewish self-defense organization, the Haganah.

In March 1921 Jabotinsky joined the Executive of the World Zionist Organization (WZO), headed by Chaim Weizmann. Disagreeing

Zionist leader Vladimir Jabotinsky, founder of the Jewish Legion of World War I. (Library of Congress)

sharply with British policies in Palestine and with what he considered the lack of Jewish resistance to them, Jabotinsky resigned from the Executive in January 1923. That same year he helped found and headed the youth movement Betar (Hebrew acronym for B'rit Trumpeldor, the League of Joseph Trumpeldor).

In 1925 Jabotinsky founded in Paris his own organization, the Union of Zionist Revisionists (B'rit Herut-Hatzohar), and became its president. It called for the immediate establishment in Palestine of a Jewish state. Jabotinsky argued that this state should occupy both sides of the Jordan River and also argued for continued immigration until Jews were a majority there and the establishment of a military organization to defend the new creation. He much admired the British form of government and wanted the future Jewish state to be similar to it as a liberal democracy.

From 1925 Jabotinsky made his home in Paris except during 1928–1929, when he lived in Jerusalem and was director of the Judea Insurance Company and edited the Hebrew daily newspaper *Doar Hayom.* In 1929 he left Palestine to attend the Sixteenth Zionist Congress, after which the British administration in Palestine denied him reentry. For the rest of his life, he lived abroad.

When the Seventeenth Zionist Congress of 1931 rejected Jabotinsky's demand that it announce that the aim of Zionism was the creation of a Jewish state, he resigned from the WZO and founded his own New Zionist Organization (NZO) at a congress held in Vienna in 1935. The NZO demanded free immigration of Jews into Palestine and establishment of a Jewish state. Supplementing the NZO were its military arm, the Irgun Tsvai Leumi (National Military Organization), established in 1937 and commanded by Jabotinsky, and the Betar youth movement. Jabotinsky hoped that Betar might train the young Jews of the Diaspora so that they could return to Palestine and fight for the establishment of a Jewish state. These organizations cooperated in abetting illegal immigration by ship to Palestine.

Fluent in a number of languages, Jabotinsky also continued to write poetry, short stories, novels, and articles. Deeply concerned in the 1930s about the plight of Jews in Poland, where there was rampant anti-Semitism, he called for the evacuation of the entire Jewish population of Poland and its relocation to Palestine. During 1939–1940 he traveled in Britain and the United States. He especially sought the establishment of a Jewish army that would fight on the Allied side against Nazi Germany. Jabotinsky suffered a massive heart attack while visiting the Betar camp near Hunter, New York, and died on August 4, 1940. In 1964 his remains and those of his wife were reinterred in Israel. The State of Israel also created in his honor a medal that is awarded for distinguished accomplishment.

SPENCER C. TUCKER

See also

Akko Prison; Arab Riots, Jerusalem; Haganah; Irgun Tsvai Leumi; Jewish Legion; Palestine, British Mandate for; Weizmann, Chaim; Zionism

References

Jabotinsky, Vladimir. *The Story of the Jewish Legion.* New York: Bernard Akerman, 1945.

Katz, Shmel. *Lone Wolf: A Biography of Vladimir Ze'ev Jabotinsky.* 2 vols. Fort Lee, NJ: Barricade Books, 1996.

Sachar, Howard M. *A History of Israel: From the Rise of Zionism to Our Time.* 3rd ed. New York: Knopf, 2007.

Shavit, Yaacov. *Jabotinsky and the Revisionist Movement, 1925–1948.* New York: Routledge, 1988.

Shepherd, Naomi. *Ploughing Sand: British Rule in Palestine, 1917–1948.* New Brunswick, NJ: Rutgers University Press, 1999.

Jackson-Vanik Amendment
Event Date: 1974

U.S. legislation designed to force the Soviet Union to allow the immigration of Jews. Introduced by Sen. Henry M. "Scoop" Jackson,

Democrat from Washington state, and Rep. Charles Vanik, Democrat from Cleveland, Ohio, the legislation was an amendment to the Foreign Trade Act of 1974, signed into law by President Gerald R. Ford. The Jackson-Vanik Amendment denies unconditional trade relations to nations with non-market economies and restrictive immigration practices. It requires semiannual reports but also empowers the president of the United States to grant yearly waivers.

This legislation was intended to force the Soviet Union to allow more Jews to emigrate. Soviet Jews already faced considerable official pressure when they sought to leave, but beginning in 1972 Soviet leader Leonid Brezhnev imposed a diploma tax on would-be emigrants who had earned higher education degrees in the Soviet Union. Although international pressure brought a revocation of this tax, the Kremlin then imposed other restrictions, including the blanket caveat of national security reasons. Such measures effectively ended emigration by Soviet Jews, including even family reunifications.

Emigration of Jews did increase in the years immediately after the passage of Jackson-Vanik. It then slowed dramatically in the 1980s, when it again became a major source of contention between the governments of the United States and the Soviet Union. Soviet leader Mikhail Gorbachev then eased these restrictions.

Between 1975 and 2001, an estimated 1 million Jews emigrated from the Soviet Union and its successor states for Israel. In that same period, 573,000 other refugees, many of them Jews, evangelical Christians, and Catholics, settled in the United States.

President George H. W. Bush waived Jackson-Vanik in 1990, a year before the collapse of the Soviet Union. It was again waived in the case of the People's Republic of China (PRC) when the latter sought to joint the World Trade Organization (WTO) and the legislation was held incompatible with WTO rules. The waiver has also been extended to Vietnam.

Since 1994 the U.S. government has found the Soviet Union to be in compliance with Jackson-Vanik, but the Soviet Union nonetheless continues to be subject to Jackson-Vanik's semiannual reviews. President Vladimir Putin of Russia has requested that the legislation be scrapped. There has also been a movement in Congress to do away with it as a relic of the Cold War, and President George W. Bush has expressed his support for such a step.

SPENCER C. TUCKER

See also

Brezhnev, Leonid Ilyich; Bush, George Herbert Walker; Bush, George Walker; Soviet Jews, Immigration to Israel

References

Gurevitz, Baruch. *Open Gates: The Story behind the Mass Immigration to Israel from the Soviet Union and Its Successor States.* Jerusalem: Jewish Agency for Israel, 1996.

Lazin, Fred. *The Struggle for Soviet Jewry in American Politics: Israel versus the American Jewish Establishment.* Lanham, MD: Lexington Books, 2005.

United States, Office of the Press Secretary of the President. *Jackson-Vanik and Russia Fact Sheet.* Pamphlet. November 13, 2001.

Jadid, Salah al-
Born: 1926
Died: August 19, 1993

Syrian military officer, prominent figure within the Syrian Baath Party, and de facto Syrian leader from 1966 to 1970. Salah al-Jadid was born in 1926 in a small village near Latakia (Ladhakiyya), Syria, a member of the minority Alawi community. He joined the military at a young age and ultimately rose to the rank of general.

Al-Jadid actively participated in the March 8, 1963, coup that brought the Baath Party to power in Syria. As a consequence of this event, he became Syrian Army chief of staff. Over the next three years he used his position as chief of staff to consolidate Baathist and sectarian control of the armed forces. In 1965 he assumed the position of deputy secretary-general of the Baath Party, a position with less power than he previously had.

In 1966, however, al-Jadid chose to wield his still-considerable influence in another coup that installed a more hard-line, neo-Baathist regime. This made him virtual ruler of Syria. Lacking widespread popular support, damaged by Syria's defeat in the Six-Day War (1967), and badly weakened by internal divisions, al-Jadid's government fell to another military coup only four years later. The coup de grace for al-Jadid's reign had been his ill-fated decision to send Syrian-backed Palestinian troops into Jordan during what came to be known as Black September. The pragmatists in the Baath Party, especially Minister of Defense Hafez al-Assad, decried al-Jadid's moves and launched the so-called Corrective Revolution on November 13, 1970. This coup ousted al-Jadid from power, and he was replaced by al-Assad. Al-Jadid spent the next 23 years in al-Mazzah Prison in Damascus, where he died on August 19, 1993.

JONAS KAUFFEDLT

See also

Assad, Hafez al-; Baathism; Black September; Syria; Syria, Armed Forces

References

Ma'oz, Moshe. *Syria and Israel: From War to Peacemaking.* Oxford, UK: Clarendon, 1995.

Van Dam, Nikolaos. *The Struggle for Power in Syria: Politics and Society under Asad and the Ba'th Party.* London: Croom Helm, 1996.

Jamal Pasha, Ahmad
Born: May 6, 1872
Died: July 21, 1922

Ottoman naval minister and military governor of Syria and member of the triumvirate governing the Ottoman Empire until the end of World War I. Born on May 6, 1872, in Mytilene, Lesbos, Ahmad Jamal graduated from the Kuleli Military High School in 1880 and from the Ottoman Military Academy in Istanbul in 1893. He held a

Ahmad Jamal Pasha, Ottoman naval minister, military governor of Syria, and member of the triumvirate governing the Ottoman Empire until the end of World War I. (Alexander Aaronsohn, *With the Turks in Palestine*, 1916)

succession of assignments and in 1898 was posted as a staff officer to the Third Army at Salonika.

Promoted to major in 1905, Jamal joined the Committee of Union and Progress (CUP), the Young Turk movement. Following the 1908 revolt of the Third Army and a brief civil war that led to the deposition of Sultan Abdulhamid II, Jamal became part of the new military administration. In 1911 he became military governor of Baghdad. In 1912, however, he resigned this post to participate with the army as a colonel in the First Balkan War. In the Second Balkan War he commanded a division.

Jamal participated in the coup d'état against Grand Vizier Mehmet (Muhammad) Kamil led by Ismail Enver Pasha on January 23, 1913. Jamal, then a lieutenant general, assumed emergency powers as military governor of Istanbul. He then became minister of public works, and in 1914 he was made naval minister. Jamal was by 1914 one of the most powerful figures in the Ottoman government. Unlike Enver, however, Jamal was disposed favorably toward the Entente and looked to both France and Great Britain for assistance to train and equip the badly neglected Ottoman Navy. His diplomatic approaches to the Entente powers met with no result, however, chiefly because the two Western allies were not prepared to jeopardize their cooperation with Russia, which harbored plans for substantial expansion at the expense of the Ottoman Empire.

Jamal eventually submitted to Enver's pro-German policy but remained opposed to a full-fledged alliance with Germany. Only under Enver's pressure and after Germany had offered substantial amounts of money to the Ottoman government did Jamal finally acquiesce and permit Vice Admiral Wilhelm Souchon, commander of the German Mediterranean Squadron and supreme commander of Ottoman Naval Forces, to launch a preemptive attack against the Russian Black Sea ports in October 1914. This decision brought a declaration of war by Russia against the Ottoman Empire.

Shortly thereafter, Jamal became military governor of Syria and commander of the Ottoman Fourth Army stationed in Damascus. In January 1915 he launched an ill-conceived offensive with his 80,000-man army across the Sinai Peninsula toward the Suez Canal. Following the collapse of the offensive, he confined himself to his governorship of Syria, where his harsh repression of Arab resistance and his persecution of the Armenian minority and of the Jews earned him the name "The Blood Shedder."

Jamal ordered all enemy aliens in Palestine to adopt Turkish citizenship or emigrate. Many Jewish leaders were obliged to depart Palestine as a result. In the spring of 1917, Jamal ordered the population of both Jaffa and Tel Aviv relocated to the interior of Palestine. With the discovery that same year of the Nili spy organization run by Jews to aid the British, he intensified his persecution of Jewish settlers.

With the disintegration of the Palestinian Front and the fall of Jerusalem in December 1917, Jamal returned to Istanbul as a cabinet member of the CUP administration. When the government was forced from office, he and other CUP leaders fled the Ottoman capital on board a German ship on November 1, 1918. Jamal thereafter served as a liaison officer in talks between the new communist government of Russia and the postwar Turkish government. He then served as a military adviser to Afghanistan. Tried in absentia by a military tribunal in Istanbul on war crimes charges, he was found guilty and sentenced to death. On July 21, 1922, Armenian assassins attacked and killed Jamal in Tbilisi, Georgia, in retribution for his role in the Armenian genocide.

Dirk Steffen and Spencer C. Tucker

See also

Aaronsohn, Aaron; Aaronsohn, Sarah; Ottoman Empire

References

Fromkin, David. *A Peace to End All Peace: The Fall of the Ottoman Empire and the Creation of the Modern Middle East.* New York: Avon, 1989.

Kent, Marian, ed. *The Great Powers and the End of the Ottoman Empire.* London: Routledge, 1996.

Palmer, Alan. *The Decline and Fall of the Ottoman Empire.* London: John Murray, 1992.

Jarring, Gunnar
Born: October 12, 1907
Died: May 28, 2002

Swedish diplomat, academic linguist, and specialist in Turkish studies, perhaps best known for his attempts to bring peace to the Middle East when he undertook a long series of negotiations underwritten by the United Nations (UN) known as the Jarring Mission (1967–1973).

Gunnar Jarring was born in Brunnby, Skane, in the southernmost part of Sweden. He studied at Lund University and ultimately earned his PhD in 1933 in Turkish linguistics. For the remainder of the decade, he taught Turkic languages at the university level. In 1940 he commenced his career in diplomacy as an attaché at the Swedish embassy in Ankara, Turkey.

Jarring served in a variety of important diplomatic postings. These included minister to India during 1948–1951, minister to Ceylon (Sri Lanka) during 1950–1951, and minister to Iraq, Iran, and Pakistan during 1951–1952. In 1956 he became Sweden's permanent representative and ambassador to the UN. His tenure there included time on the Security Council when Sweden became one of the rotating temporary members of that body. In 1958 he was named ambassador to the United States, a post he held until 1964. That same year he went to Moscow as Swedish ambassador to the Soviet Union.

In the wake of the 1967 Six-Day War, Jarring's considerable diplomatic expertise and his interest in the Middle East (he had continued to conduct research in Turkish linguistics) caught the attention of UN secretary-general U Thant, who hoped to engage the Swede in a special peace mission to the Middle East. When the UN Security Council passed Resolution 242 in November 1967, which created a blueprint for peace between the Arabs and Jews in the Middle East, both sides balked at its recommendations. Included in Resolution 242 was the critical land-for-peace formula calling for an Israeli withdrawal from occupied territories in return for Arab security guarantees to be extended to the State of Israel. The land-for-peace proposal became almost immediately controversial. As such, in late November 1967 U Thant appointed Jarring as a special UN envoy to the Middle East. His primary responsibility was to implement the various provisions of Resolution 242 and, ultimately, bring about a comprehensive and lasting peace in the Middle East.

Jarring's mandate was a difficult one. The language of the resolution had already been parsed by both sides in the conflict, with each putting a different spin to it. Beginning in the winter of 1968, Jarring embarked on a grueling program of shuttle diplomacy in the

Swedish diplomat Gunnar Jarring, 1970. (Bettmann/Corbis)

Middle East. While the Israelis, Jordanians, and Lebanese recognized him as a peacemaker, the Syrians flatly rejected Jarring and his mission, asserting that only a full and immediate Israeli withdrawal from all disputed territories could bring about negotiations. Several other Arab nations took this tack, as did the Soviets. Jarring made little progress in 1968, and when the War of Attrition (1968–1970) began, his job became harder still.

The Jarring Mission continued, despite the small progress made, until the outbreak of the Yom Kippur War in October 1973, when the mission was essentially defunct. Jarring continued to play a role in Middle East peace negotiations, and he stayed on as a special UN envoy until 1990. During this period, he held countless meetings and negotiations with both Arab and Israeli leaders. He also continued to conduct research and publish in the field of Turkic linguistics almost until his death on May 28, 2002, in Stockholm, Sweden.

PAUL G. PIERPAOLI JR.

See also

Jarring Mission; United Nations Security Council Resolution 242

References

Bailey, Sydney D. *Four Arab-Israeli Wars and the Peace Process.* New York: St. Martin's, 1982.

Dupuy, Trevor N. *Elusive Victory: The Arab-Israeli Wars, 1947–1974.* Garden City, NY: Military Book Club, 2002.

Toll, Christopher, and Ulla Ehrensvard. *Gunnar Jarring: Ein Bibliografi.* Stockholm: Sekr I Sv., 1977.

Jarring Mission
Start Date: December 9, 1967
End Date: October 1973

Diplomatic mission named for Swedish diplomat Dr. Gunnar Jarring that sought to implement a United Nations (UN) resolution calling for peace in the Middle East in the aftermath of the Six-Day War in June 1967. Jarring commenced the mission in December 1967, and sporadic negotiations continued until October 1973.

On November 22, 1967, the UN Security Council unanimously passed Resolution 242, which called for a lasting and comprehensive peace settlement in the Middle East. UN secretary-general U Thant duly appointed Jarring as his special representative to implement the resolution. Jarring had vast diplomatic experience as ambassador to the UN, the United States, and the Soviet Union. He was serving as Sweden's ambassador to the Soviet Union when he took up the Middle East assignment.

Given the complexity of circumstances and tensions in the region, Jarring had a very difficult job. He had to walk a diplomatic tightrope to maintain a balance between his ambassadorial duties and his UN mandate for peace in which the Soviets had a considerable interest. At the time, the Soviet Union did not maintain diplomatic relations with Israel.

Resolution 242 had called for the withdrawal of Israeli troops from the occupied territories (the West Bank, East Jerusalem, the Gaza Strip, the Sinai Peninsula, and the Golan Heights) in return for an end to the conflict. It also called for an end to the state of war that existed between Israel and Egypt, Jordan, and Syria. In addition, the resolution emphasized the sovereignty and territorial inviolability of all the countries of the Middle East and affirmed freedom of navigation in international waterways.

Jarring's mission became significantly more difficult because of the various interpretations of the resolution. The formula of land for peace, or the vacating of occupied territory in return for a peace guarantee, became immediately controversial. The definite article "the" was absent from the English version before the word "territories," which rendered a very wide meaning. The definite article was present in the French version, which suggested that the "territories" were those annexed by Israel. The omission of the word "Palestinians" before the word "refugees" also generated controversy.

United Nations (UN) special representative Gunnar Jarring arriving at Lod Airport, December 14, 1967. (Moshe Milner/Israeli Government Press Office)

Beginning in early 1968, Jarring shuttled among the capitals of the Middle East. Israel, Egypt, Jordan, and Lebanon recognized his role as peacemaker. Syria rejected the Jarring Mission, however, arguing that only a total Israeli withdrawal from occupied territories would suffice before peace negotiations could begin. Most Arabs as well as the Soviet Union took the position that there could be no direct talks with Israel without troop withdrawals. Jarring did not make much progress throughout much of 1968, and hostilities between warring parties continued in spite of a cease-fire. Indeed, the fighting became known as the War of Attrition. Toward the latter part of 1968, Palestinian and Israeli commandos became involved in attacks on each other, and the Israeli Air Force was striking targets in both Egypt and Jordan.

Although Jarring's efforts seemed futile in the face of continued violence, peace efforts continued. Both the United States and the Soviet Union put forth their own peace proposals, and Jarring continued his shuttle diplomacy.

U Thant submitted the first report on Jarring's efforts to the Security Council on January 4, 1971. The first phase of the report covered his activities from December 9, 1967, to November 27, 1968. The second phase covered the period from November 27, 1968, to June 1970 as well as correspondence until late 1970.

Jarring noted that the parties concerned had seemingly accepted Resolution 242. Another round of discussions began on August 16, 1968, in which differences became quite obvious. Israel regarded the resolution as a "statement of principles" from which negotiations would proceed. Egypt considered it as an already acceptable plan that was the basis for an agreement. By this time, it was generally agreed that the ambiguous withdrawal clause applied to all the territories occupied by Israel since June 5, 1967. Israel objected, however, arguing that it was applicable only when an agreement had been reached for a "secure and recognized" border.

The differences of opinion regarding interpretation of the resolution continued, however, as evident from the second phase of the report. Meetings between the parties did not take place. Jarring was also made aware of discussions in April 1969 among the United States, the Soviet Union, Britain, and France. From June 1970 to January 1971, he tried to hold discussions that would bring together the governments of Israel, Egypt, and Jordan as per an American proposal of June 1970. Negotiations continued under Jarring's supervision until the October 1973 Yom Kippur War. Despite his considerable efforts, he had been unable to forge anything close to a peace agreement.

PATIT PABAN MISHRA

See also

Jarring, Gunnar; Six-Day War; United Nations Security Council Resolution 242; Yom Kippur War

References

Bailey, Sydney D. *Four Arab-Israeli Wars and the Peace Process.* New York: St. Martin's, 1982.

Dupuy, Trevor N. *Elusive Victory: The Arab-Israeli Wars, 1947–1974.* Garden City, NY: Military Book Club, 2002.

Herzog, Chaim. *The Arab-Israeli Wars: War and Peace in the Middle East from the War of Independence to Lebanon.* Westminster, MD: Random House, 1984.

Pimlott, John. *The Middle East Conflicts from 1945 to the Present.* New York: Crescent, 1983.

Jaziernicki, Yitzhak

See Shamir, Yitzhak

Jenin

Town located in the northern West Bank with a present population of approximately 34,000 people. Jenin was the site of a fierce battle during April 3–11, 2002, between the Israel Defense Forces (IDF) and Palestinian terrorists. The Battle of Jenin gave rise to widespread but unfounded charges of a massacre by the IDF.

At the beginning of April 2002, in response to a wave of attacks on Israeli civilians, the IDF launched Operation DEFENSIVE SHIELD against what it called a terrorist infrastructure. In so doing, it reoccupied towns turned over to Palestinian control, including Jenin (which had reverted to Palestinian control in 1996) from which nearly half of the 28 suicide bombers of the preceding three months had originated. The operation was just one among several Israeli moves against the Second (al-Aqsa) Intifada, which began in earnest in 2000.

The Palestinian refugee camp at Jenin, in existence since 1953, was a formidable IDF objective. It was defended by 150–250 well-entrenched Islamic Jihad, Hamas, al-Aqsa, and Tanzim fighters whose arsenal included a large number of mines and booby traps. Fortunately, most of the camp's 14,000 or so inhabitants had already fled. Rather than destroying Jenin with air strikes and artillery, to minimize civilian casualties the IDF chose to commit some 1,000 ground troops, although this increased the risk of Israeli casualties. Thirteen infantry reservists died in a single ambush on April 9. Thereafter, the IDF made more extensive use of armored bulldozers and helicopter fire to demolish houses from which attacks emanated. The tactic speeded completion of the assault but fed growing rumors of atrocities.

Early in the battle, Palestinian officials accused the IDF of massacring up to 3,000 civilians (later a figure of 500 became more common). Authoritative Western (mainly European) newspapers adopted the discourse, noting with outrage alleged monstrous crimes in a devastated camp comparable to the September 11 terrorist attacks and the genocides of Cambodia and Bosnia.

The Israeli government vehemently denied atrocity charges. International nongovernmental organizations agreed that there had been no massacre or mass executions. They concluded, however, that some IDF actions needlessly endangered civilians or caused loss of life through excessive or disproportionate use of force, thus constituting war crimes. They also noted that Palestinian forces had deliberately violated the laws of war by fighting amid the civilian population.

The generally accepted death toll in the fighting at Jenin during April 3–11 is 23 Israeli soldiers and 52–56 Palestinians, including perhaps 22 civilians. The fighting leveled an area of perhaps 1.5 acres within a combat zone of 6 acres, or 6 percent of the camp.

The Israeli closure of the area during hostilities fueled the suspicions of journalists, who lacked experience in covering close combat, that something amiss was transpiring. Many were predisposed to believe Palestinian charges, recalling the Sabra and Shatila Massacre of Palestinians by Christian militia on Ariel Sharon's watch during the Israeli invasion of Lebanon in 1982. Because of the polarizing news coverage, subsequent literature on the battle remains largely partisan, and a definitive account is lacking. Among film treatments, Muhammad Bakri's *Jenin, Jenin* upholds the initial atrocity narrative, whereas Pierre Rehov's *The Road to Jenin* challenges it. Gil Mezuman's *Jenin Diary* documents the experiences of his IDF reserve unit.

Jenin was an object lesson in the practical and moral dilemmas of modern urban warfare, when irregular troops take refuge among noncombatants, regular forces are tasked with dislodging them, and journalists have to cover the struggle. It was a military victory for Israel, a propaganda victory for the Palestinians, and an unqualified defeat for the press.

JAMES WALD

See also

Al-Aqsa Martyrs Brigades; DEFENSIVE SHIELD, Operation; Fatah; Hamas; Intifada, Second; Islamic Jihad, Palestinian; Israel Defense Forces; Lebanon, Israeli Invasion of; Palestinian Authority; Palestinian Refugee Camps; Sharon, Ariel; Suicide Bombings; West Bank

References

Baroud, Ramzy, ed. *Searching Jenin: Eyewitness Accounts of the Israeli Invasion.* Seattle, WA: Cune, 2003.

Goldberg, Brett. *A Psalm in Jenin.* Tel Aviv: Modan, 2003.

Reporters without Borders, eds. *Israel/Palestine: The Black Book.* Sterling, VA: Pluto, 2003.

Jericho

West Bank city located in central Palestine between Mount Nebo to the east, the Central Mountains to the west, and the Dead Sea to the south. With natural defenses and being only four miles from the Jordan River to the west, Jericho was situated astride a major east-west trade route north of the Dead Sea. Jericho traces its history back more than 11,000 years and is thus one of the world's oldest continuously occupied cities. It is known in Arabic as al-Riha (aroma) for the scent of blossoms from the citrus trees in the area. Some 1,300 feet below sea level, Jericho has a current population of some 20,000 people.

In 1907 remains were discovered in Jericho of the Canaanite city of the Old Testament of the Bible. The book of Joshua describes how the Israelites, following 40 years of exile in the desert, moved against the city. God instructed Joshua to have the Israelites march around the city each day during a six-day period preceded by seven priests blowing rams' horns and walking beside the Ark of the Covenant containing the Ten Commandments. On the seventh day, according to the book of Joshua, the troops circled the city seven more times and shouted while the priests blew their horns, and the walls promptly collapsed. Modern archeologists believe that the walls did indeed fall down but most probably as the consequence of an earthquake rather than the miracle described in the Bible. This event probably occurred around 1550 BC.

The Babylonians subsequently captured Jericho, and it was rebuilt when the Jews returned from their exile. The Romans destroyed Jericho in the first century AD, but it was then rebuilt during the Byzantine Empire. Taken over by the Muslims, it became an important location when in 743 Caliph Hisham ibn Abd el-Malik ordered his winter palace to be built there. An earthquake destroyed much of the city in 747, however. Taken by the Crusaders, Jericho was recaptured by Saladin.

With the end of the British Mandate for Palestine in 1948, Jericho was assigned under the United Nations (UN) partition plan to the proposed Arab state, but at the end of the 1948–1949 Israeli War of Independence the Kingdom of Jordan held the West Bank. Many Palestinian Arabs who had fled land controlled by the new State of Israel then settled in Jericho, and a number of refugee camps were established in the area. Israel secured Jericho and the remainder of the West Bank as a consequence of the Six-Day War in June 1967.

According to the Declaration of Principles between Israel and the Palestinians on May 17, 1994, both Jericho and Gaza were made into Palestinian autonomous areas controlled by the Palestinian Authority (PA). Jericho was turned over to the PA on March 16, 2005. Palestinian leader Yasser Arafat maintained a residence there.

The chief tourist attraction in Jericho is the Tal al-Sultan, ruins that reportedly date back at least 7,000 years. Among other historic sites are Caliph Hisham's eighth-century palace; Mount Temptation, where Christians believe that Jesus fasted for 40 days and nights before his baptism; and the remains of a synagogue dating from the fifth or sixth century and discovered in 1936. Four miles east of the city is the Allenby Bridge, named for Lieutenant General Sir Edmund Allenby who led the British conquest of Palestine from the Turks in World War I. The bridge is one of two crossing points over the Jordan River. Perhaps the biggest attraction in the city, however, was the Oasis Casino, the region's only large gambling facility. Prior to the start of the Second (al-Aqsa) Intifada, the casino was a popular attraction for Israelis and a major source of income for the Palestinian economy. The thriving casino was one of the first victims of the intifada, and by 2003 it was an abandoned and rapidly deteriorating building.

SPENCER C. TUCKER

See also

Allenby, Sir Edmund Henry Hynman, 1st Viscount; Arafat, Yasser; Palestinian Authority; Six-Day War

References

Kenyon, Kathleen. *Digging Up Jericho.* Jerusalem: British School of Archeology in Jerusalem, 1965.

Miller, Edward B. "An Oasis or Just a Mirage: The Jericho Casino and the Future of the Israeli Palestinian Peace Process." *Richmond Journal of Global Law and Business* 2(1) (2001): 33–60.

Jericho Conference
Event Date: December 1, 1948

Meeting of Palestinian Arab leaders convened on December 1, 1948, in Jericho on the West Bank to settle Arab land claims as a result of the 1948–1949 Israeli War of Independence. The government of Palestine ceded control of Arab Palestinian territories (the West Bank and East Jerusalem)—apart from Gaza—to the Hashemite Kingdom of Jordan at the Jericho Conference. This was an attempt to assure Arab control over those territories not already lost to Israel in the fighting that followed the partition of Palestine by the United Nations (UN) on May 15, 1948. The common government of Palestine was formed in a meeting called by the High Arab Board and presided over by Ahmad Hilmy Pasha on September 30, 1948, following the perceived failure of the Arab forces in the war.

The failure of the Arab coalition to prevent the formation of the State of Israel in 1948 and the expansion of Israel's borders beyond those granted in the UN partition plan led to the dispersion of more than 1 million Palestinians who either fled of their own accord or were forced to flee by the Israelis throughout the Arab states. The upheaval threw both the Palestinian and Arab leadership into chaos. In an attempt to bring order, King Abdullah I of Jordan was authorized to represent and speak for the dispersed and displaced Palestinian people at an October 1, 1948, conference of refugee Palestinian leaders in Amman.

The Jericho Conference, also known as the Palestine or Jericho Congress, was a much larger conference of 2,000 to 3,000 prominent Palestinian Arabs primarily from west of the Jordan River. It was held on December 1, 1948, at the suggestion of King Abdullah and with the approval of British foreign secretary Ernest Bevin, who was concerned that Israel would take control of all of the territory partitioned to the Palestinians. Sheikh Muhammed Ali al-Ja'bari, the mayor of Hebron from 1948 to 1976, headed the conference. At the meeting, al-Ja'bari's proposal for the immediate annexation by Jordan of what remained of Arab Palestine land—roughly 80 percent—apart from Gaza was accepted. The Jericho Conference reconfirmed Abdullah as the official representative of the interests of the Palestinians until such time as the Palestinians could themselves regain and maintain control over the majority of the land of Arab Palestine. Abdullah was then crowned the king of Palestine, but his desire to have the West Bank, East Jerusalem, and the al-Aqsa environs named the Kingdom of Palestine never came to fruition.

Israel almost immediately recognized King Abdullah's leadership of Arab Palestine apart from Gaza. Yet the Jericho Conference was not met by universal acceptance in the Arab world. On December 10, 1948, King Farouk I of Egypt, who had favored the so-called All Palestine Government alternative, responded to the meeting's outcome by stigmatizing the Palestinians who had attended the Jericho Conference.

RICHARD EDWARDS

See also

Abdullah I, King of Jordan; All Palestine Government; Bevin, Ernest; Farouk I, King of Egypt; Jordan; Palestine, British Mandate for; West Bank

References

Nowar, Ma'an A., and Maon Abeu Neuwear. *The History of the Hashemite Kingdom of Jordan: The Creation & Development of Transjordan.* Reading, UK: Ithaca Press, 1989.

Robbins, Philip. *A History of Jordan.* Cambridge: Cambridge University Press, 2004.

Salibi, Kamal S. *The Modern History of Jordan.* London: Tauris, 1998.

Jerusalem

The ancient city of Jerusalem, located in present-day Israel, is considered the Israeli capital and Judaism's holiest city. Jerusalem is a diverse city sacred to Judaism, Christianity, and Islam, tracing its origins to King David's conquest in 1004 BC of a Jebusite citadel. David was the king of ancient Israel.

Jerusalem is built amid three valleys and four hills running east to west and is located near the border of the West Bank. It covers an area in excess of 42 square miles with a growing population exceeding 700,000 people, making it the largest city in Israel. Although the demography of the Old City's Armenian, Christian, Jewish, and Muslim quarters remains steady, the modern city has seen an ever-increasing Jewish population since Israel captured East Jerusalem in the 1967 Six-Day War. This has been especially true since the 1990s.

Jerusalem is sacred to Christians because it was the epicenter of the ministry, crucifixion, and believed resurrection of Jesus Christ. It is sacred to Muslims because it is the home of the third most sacred shrine in Islam, the al-Aqsa Mosque complex that includes the Dome of the Rock. The latter marks the spot from which Muslims believe Muhammad ascended to heaven during his Night Journey. Jerusalem is sacred to Judaism because it is the City of David and the Temple Mount on which three Temples were built.

Archeological studies indicate human habitation within present-day Jerusalem as far back as the 4th millennium BC, although the first written mention of the city dates from 1400 BC. According to biblical accounts, a Canaanite tribe known as the Jebusites lived in the city until the late 11th century BC. Around 1004 the Israelites under their king, David, defeated the Jebusites, capturing the city and making it the capital of the united kingdom of Israel and Judah.

Around 950 BC David's son, King Solomon, began construction of the first of what would be two principal temples within Jerusalem proper. Solomon's temple, known as the First Temple, was an

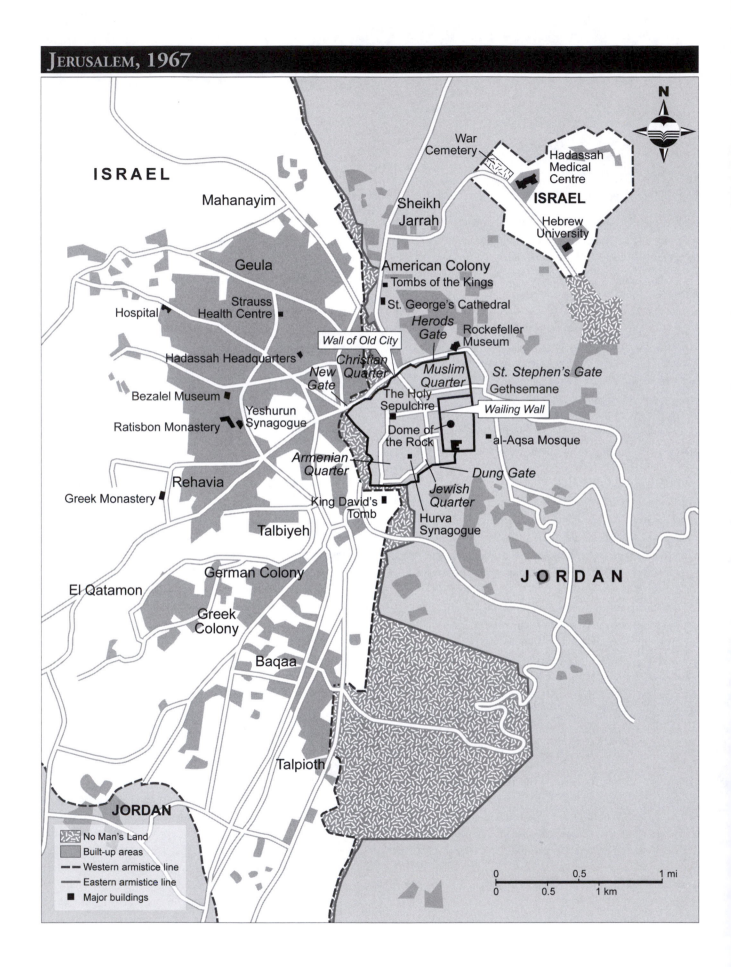

JERUSALEM, 1967

N

ISRAEL

Mahanayim

Geula

Strauss
Health Centre

Hospital

Hadassah Headquarters

Bezalel Museum

Yeshurun
Synagogue

Ratisbon Monastery

Rehavia

Greek Monastery

Talbiyeh

German Colony

El Qatamon

Greek
Colony

Baqaa

Talpioth

JORDAN

Sheikh
Jarrah

War
Cemetery

Hadassah
Medical
Centre

ISRAEL

Hebrew
University

American Colony
Tombs of the Kings

St. George's Cathedral

*Herods
Gate*

Rockefeller
Museum

Wall of Old City

*Christian
Quarter*

*New
Gate*

*Muslim
Quarter*

St. Stephen's Gate

Gethsemane

The Holy
Sepulchre

Wailing Wall

Dome of
the Rock

al-Aqsa Mosque

*Armenian
Quarter*

Dung Gate

*Jewish
Quarter*

King David's
Tomb

Hurva
Synagogue

JORDAN

No Man's Land
Built-up areas
Western armistice line
Eastern armistice line
Major buildings

0	0.5	1 mi
0	0.5	1 km

View of the city of Jerusalem from the top of the Mount of Olives. (Corel)

important place of worship for Jews and the last known location for the Ark of the Covenant. Following Solomon's death around 930 BC and the division of his kingdom, Jerusalem remained the capital of the southern kingdom of Judah. Around 930 BC, Egyptian pharaoh Sheshonk I (the biblical Shishak) mounted a military expedition into Palestine, entering Jerusalem and seizing the treasures of the temple and the royal palaces. In 597 BC Babylonian king Nebuchadnezzar laid siege to Jerusalem and took it. In response to the rebellion of King Zedekiah of Judah to Babylonian control, Jerusalem rose up against Babylonian rule in 587 BC but was starved into submission in 586 BC. Nebuchadnezzar ordered much of the city destroyed, including its temple. He then deported leading citizens, craftsmen, and troops to Babylon, beginning the period known in Jewish history as the Babylonian Captivity of the Jews. In 538 BC Persian king Cyrus the Great allowed the Jews to return to the city, and some 50,000 made the trek and began building what became known as the Second Temple.

In 332 BC Alexander the Great of Macedon captured Palestine from the Persians along with Jerusalem. In 320 BC the city fell to Ptolemy I and came under Egyptian rule. In 196 BC it passed under the Seleucid Empire of Syria. In 169 BC Seleucid king Antiochus IV Epiphanes outlawed Judaism and profaned the Temple, leading to the Maccabean Revolt of 166 BC and the capture of Jerusalem by Judas Maccabeus in 164 BC. In 63 BC the Roman general Pompey

captured Jerusalem and most of Palestine for Rome. In 18 BC King Herod began rebuilding the Temple, which was not completed until AD 63.

In AD 66 the Jews rose up against the Romans, who took Jerusalem in 70 and destroyed the Second Temple. In 135 following Bar Kokhba's Revolt against Rome, Emperor Hadrian totally destroyed Jerusalem, renamed the city Aelia Capitolina, and forbade Jews to live there. In 324 the city passed under control of the Byzantine Empire. In 326 Queen Helena, mother of Emperor Constantine the Great, visited the city and caused the construction of Christian churches there, including the Church of the Holy Sepulcher in 325. In 438 Empress Eudocia permitted Jews to live in the city. In 614 the Persians took Jerusalem from the Byzantines, destroying many churches and again expelling the Jews.

Although Jerusalem was recaptured by the Byzantines in 629, it passed under Muslim control in 638 when the Caliph Omar entered the city and permitted Jews to again return there. The Dome of the Rock was completed by Caliph Abd al-Maalik in 691, and construction of the al-Aqsa Mosque was completed under Caliph al-Walid in 701. In 1010 Caliph al-Hakim ordered the destruction of synagogues and churches in Jerusalem.

The failure of the Turks to allow Christian pilgrims access to Jerusalem was one of the factors behind the First Crusade, and in 1099 the Christian Crusaders, led by Geoffrey of Bouillon, captured

Jerusalem. The great Muslim general Saladin retook the city in 1187 but permitted Jews to settle there. In 1192, although he failed to retake Jerusalem from Saladin, King Richard I the Lionheart arranged a treaty with Saladin that permitted Christians to worship at the city's holy sites. In 1219 Sultan Malik al-Muattam ordered the city walls razed.

In 1244 the Mamluk sultans defeated the Ayyubid dynasty and ruled Jerusalem, but in 1260 the Mamluks of Egypt captured the city. Mamluk rule lasted until 1517, when the Ottoman Turks established control. The city had not been walled since 1219, but Sultan Suleiman caused them to be rebuilt during 1537–1541, including the present seven gates and the Tower of David.

The Ottoman Turks allowed some Jewish settlement in the latter part of the 19th and early 20th centuries but then exiled many of those who refused Turkish citizenship in 1915 during World War I (1914–1918). In 1917 British lieutenant general Sir Edmund Allenby's troops took Jerusalem as the Turks retreated. As a result of the peace treaties after World War I, on July 24, 1922, Britain secured a mandate over Palestine to include the city of Jerusalem in which it pledged to act on behalf of both the Jewish and non-Jewish populations in accordance with the 1917 Balfour Declaration.

Although there were numerous Arab-Jewish clashes during the period of British mandatory rule, most notably in 1920, 1929, and 1936–1939, the population of the city increased, and its economy grew. There were also military and terrorist actions launched against the British in Jerusalem as well, the most notable being the detonation on July 22, 1946, of a bomb by the Irgun Tsvai Leumi (National Military Organization) that destroyed a wing of the King David Hotel, killing 91 soldiers and civilians. On November 29, 1947, the United Nations (UN) partitioned British-ruled Palestine to allow for an independent Jewish state and an independent Arab state and declared Jerusalem to be an international city to be administered by the now-suspended UN Trusteeship Council.

Jerusalem was to be neither Jewish nor Arab, but neither the Arabs nor Jews accepted the internationalization of Jerusalem. Israel declared itself to be an independent state in 1948 and responded to the Arab rejection of the internationalization of Jerusalem by declaring Jerusalem as its capital.

The Israeli War of Independence (1948–1949) ended with Jerusalem divided between the Israelis (West Jerusalem) and the Jordanians (East Jerusalem and the entire Old City, including the al-Aqsa Mosque complex and the Temple Mount). In the June 1967 Six-Day War, the Israelis seized and annexed Jordanian-controlled East Jerusalem and occupied parts of the West Bank. Despite international protests, Israel declared the combined city its capital. The government offered Israeli citizenship to the residents of these annexed territories, but it was conditioned on the abdication of their Jordanian citizenship. Most rejected the offer. Some rejected the offer because they believed that acceptance of Israeli citizenship was a tacit acceptance of the legitimacy of Israel's annexation and absorption of East Jerusalem. These Palestinian residents maintain permanent resident status that permits their free movement within Israel proper. However, if they move out of Israel proper, even into the Palestinian territories, this status is terminated, and their reentry is denied.

Israel began constructing extensive Jewish satellite settlements around Jerusalem and the West Bank in the late 1970s and has continued the process despite repeated UN resolutions and international denunciations. The Knesset (Israeli parliament) attempted to legitimize these settlements and a "complete and united" Jerusalem as Israel's "eternal and indivisible capital" by passing in 1980 the Basic Law, which mandated Jerusalem as the capital of Israel. The UN Security Council responded with UN Resolution 478, declaring that the law was "null and void and must be rescinded forthwith" and instructing all UN member states to withdraw their diplomatic representation from Jerusalem. The vote was 14–0–1, with the United States abstaining.

Greece, Britain, and the United States maintain consulates in Jerusalem. The main American consulate is in West Jerusalem, with a satellite facility in East Jerusalem. Costa Rica and El Salvador maintain their embassies in the city, while Bolivia and Paraguay have their embassies in Mevasseret Zion, a suburb of Jerusalem. Rather than reporting to the American embassy in Tel Aviv, the consulate in Jerusalem is the only American consulate in the world that reports directly to the U.S. State Department. The office of the Israeli minister of defense and the headquarters of the Israel Defense Forces (IDF) are located in Tel Aviv. All other branches of the Israeli government have their primary offices and buildings located in Jerusalem, with the Knesset building being a well-known landmark.

In 1988 Jordan withdrew all claims to East Jerusalem and the West Bank in favor of the claims of the Palestinians. The Palestinian Authority (PA) and virtually all Palestinians remain adamant that East Jerusalem must be the capital of any future Palestinian state. They have expressed great concern over the Israeli policy of detaching and annexing property and encouraging settlements in East Jerusalem and the urbanized villages that surround the city. Furthermore, these areas are economically depressed and deprived of necessary funds, with frequent service cuts. The experience of East Jerusalem under Israeli control has been so dismal that the inhabitants are determined not to allow their current status to be formalized and made permanent. The status of Jerusalem continues to be a major stumbling block to any Palestinian-Israeli peace agreement.

After seizing East Jerusalem, the Temple Mount, and the al-Aqsa environs in 1967, the Israelis cleared the area in front of the Western Wall, creating a plaza used for prayer. Muslims have at times showered the plaza area with rocks from the al-Aqsa Mosque complex above. The Muslim holy sites also have been the target of Jewish extremists, most notably a fire started by a delusional Australian tourist in 1969. Ancient tunnels running underneath the Temple Mount were discovered in 1981, 1988, and 1996. In 1996 Israeli prime minister Benjamin Netanyahu and Jerusalem mayor Ehud Olmert opened an exit for the Western Wall tunnel, sparking three days of

Palestinian riots in which more than a dozen Israelis and some 100 Palestinians died.

When Israeli prime minister Ariel Sharon visited the Temple Mount (al-Aqsa Mosque complex) on September 28, 2000, all Palestinians saw it as deliberately provocative. This 34-minute visit and the ensuing civil violence, the worst in contemporary Israel's history, began the Second (al-Aqsa) Intifada.

RICHARD EDWARDS AND SPENCER C. TUCKER

See also

Al-Aqsa Mosque; Allenby, Sir Edmund Henry Hynman, 1st Viscount; Arafat, Yasser; Balfour Declaration; Dome of the Rock; Haganah; Intifada, First; Intifada, Second; Irgun Tsvai Leumi; Israel; Jordan; Netanyahu, Benjamin; Palestine Liberation Organization; Sharon, Ariel; West Bank; Western Wall

References

Armstrong, Karen. *Jerusalem: One City, Three Faiths.* Reprint ed. New York: Ballantine, 1997.

Cline, Eric H. *Jerusalem Besieged: From Ancient Canaan to Modern Israel.* Ann Arbor: University of Michigan Press, 2004.

Irving, Clifford. *The Battle of Jerusalem: The Six-Day War of June, 1967.* New York: Macmillan, 1970.

Lewis, David A., and Jim Fletcher. *The Last War: The Failure of the Peace Process and the Coming Battle for Jerusalem.* Green Forest, AZ: New Leaf, 2001.

Oren, Michael B. *Six Days of War: June 1967 and the Making of the Modern Middle East.* Novato, CA: Presidio, 2003.

Tamari, Salmi. *Jerusalem 1948: The Arab Neighbourhoods and Their Fate in the War.* Beirut, Lebanon: Institute of Palestine Studies, 1999.

Jerusalem, Old City of

Portion of Jerusalem, approximately 0.6 square mile in area, within the imposing walls constructed by Sultan Suleiman the Magnificent (1537–1541). The Old City is the site of the Church of the Holy Sepulcher, the Western (Wailing) Wall, and the adjoining Temple Mount or Haram al-Sharif, containing the Dome of the Rock and the al-Aqsa Mosque. The presence of sites sacred to Christians, Jews, and Muslims underlies the seemingly irreconcilable Israeli and Palestinian claims to the city as a capital. It also serves as the basis for persistent demands by outside powers (mainly Christian) for its internationalization. Under the Crusaders, the Dome of the Rock was converted to a church, and al-Aqsa became the Knights Templar headquarters. Salah al-Din al-Ayyubi (Saladin) restored these to to their original use. The Ayyubids and the Mamluks then invested in Jerusalem, building Sunni legal schools and Sufi khaniqas on the edges of the Haram al-Sharif.

As the focus of national as well as religious aspirations, the Old City has been the flashpoint of repeated conflicts. These included the Crusades, interethnic and communal strife under the British Mandate (1922–1948), open multinational warfare between the

The Old City of Jerusalem, including the Dome of the Rock and the Western (Wailing) Wall. (Corel)

1948 creation of Israel and the 1967 Six-Day War, and thereafter renewed interethnic clashes.

In 1947 Zionists reluctantly accepted the United Nations (UN) partition of Palestine and its recommendation for the internationalization of Jerusalem, whereas Arabs rejected both. Jordanian attacks in two wars produced conflicted results. In 1948 Jordan captured and annexed the Old City. Although both Jordan and Israel tacitly preferred division of Jerusalem to its internationalization, Jordan expelled the inhabitants of the Jewish Quarter, destroyed its synagogues, and, in violation of armistice agreements, denied Israelis access to its holy places. Israel's 1967 conquest of the Old City, which it took from Jordan, was thus for Israelis not just a return but a liberation. Indeed, Israelis employed this moral argument to buttress historical claims to their control over the city as heirs to the only state to have had its capital there.

Israeli rule in the Old City, as in united Jerusalem as a whole, remains controversial in areas ranging from municipal services to demographic and cultural policies. On the one hand, Israel left Christians and Muslims in control of their holy places and established a freedom of worship that was lacking under the previous Jordanian administration. On the other hand, Israelis viewed as rectification of past injustices what Arabs saw as unacceptable changes to the status quo. Notably, they pointed to the reconstruction and enlargement of the Jewish Quarter and to the more controversial return of a Jewish population to the Old City (only 8 percent of the 32,186 inhabitants, but many of them religious zealots and adherents of the political right-wing), including building seizures by settlers within the Muslim and Christian quarters. Arab politicians and Islamists, for their part, have used purported Israeli threats to the Temple Mount and its mosques as a rallying cry while dismissing Jewish claims to an ancient historical presence.

The city remained calm during the Yom Kippur (1973) and the Lebanese uprisings (early 1980s), but the First Intifada (1987–1993) revealed that Jews and Arabs were still worlds apart. Ironically, tensions over symbolic issues increased with the beginning of the Oslo peace process in 1993. Also, virtually all archaeological work in the Old City has been controversial. Prime Minister Ariel Sharon's visit to the Temple Mount in the wake of the failed Camp David meetings in 2000 served to trigger the Second (al-Aqsa) Intifada (2000–2004).

Nevertheless, the negotiations over Jerusalem have broken a taboo and narrowed the gap. Neither the habitual maximalist position of either side nor the old idea of internationalization is tenable in light of the realities on the ground. Likely solutions envision a completely shared city or, increasingly, one that is divided, but not in the former manner, with a hard international border. All assume, however, that Israel and Palestine will each exercise some form of sovereignty over the city and the holy sites of greatest national and religious relevance.

JAMES WALD

See also
Al-Aqsa Mosque; Arab-Jewish Communal War; Arab Legion; Arafat, Yasser; Church of the Holy Sepulcher; Dome of the Rock; Haganah; Haram al-Sharif; Hussein, King of Jordan; Intifada, First; Intifada, Second; Israel Defense Forces; Israeli War of Independence, Israeli-Jordanian Front; Israeli War of Independence, Overview; Israeli War of Independence, Truce Agreements; Jerusalem; Jordan; Jordan, Armed Forces; Latrun, Battles of; Lohamei Herut Israel; Likud Party; Mount Scopus; Oslo Accords; Palestinian Authority; Rabin, Yitzhak; Religious Sites in the Middle East, Christian; Religious Sites in the Middle East, Jewish; Religious Sites in the Middle East, Muslim; Sharon, Ariel; Six-Day War; United Nations, Role of; United Nations General Assembly Resolution 194; United Nations Security Council Resolution 242; Western Wall

References
Dumper, Michael. *The Politics of Sacred Space: The Old City of Jerusalem in the Middle East Conflict.* Boulder, CO: Lynne Rienner, 2002.

Golani, Motti. "Jerusalem's Hope Lies Only in Partition: Israeli Policy on Jerusalem." *International Journal of Middle East Studies* 31(4) (1999): 577–604.

Klein, Menachem. *Jerusalem: The Contested City.* Translated by Haim Watzman. New York: New York University Press, 2001.

New Outlook, ed. *Jerusalem: Perspectives towards a Political Settlement.* Washington, DC: United States Institute of Peace, 1993.

Oren, Michael B. *Six Days of War: June 1967 and the Making of the Modern Middle East.* Novato, CA: Presidio, 2003.

Jewish Agency for Israel

Zionist organization that promoted the formation of an Israeli state in Palestine. The Jewish Agency for Israel, also known simply as the Jewish Agency, was originally established in 1923 to speak on behalf of the Yishuv (Jewish community) in Palestine during the British Mandate for Palestine (1921–1948). It was officially recognized in 1929, and its first president was Chaim Weizmann. The Jewish Agency operated as the quasi government for the Yishuv until independence in 1948, developing the universal policies of the Zionist movement. The organization's goals were the promotion of Jewish immigration to Palestine, the purchase of land to be made a part of Jewish public property, the colonization of farmland to be supported by Jewish labor, the recovery of the Hebrew language, and a renewal of the Hebrew culture.

Members of the Jewish Agency were charged with leading the Zionist reconstruction effort in Palestine. Each department of the Jewish Agency had its own specialization, including colonization, health, immigration, labor, politics, and public works. For instance, the Department of Colonization promoted the establishment of new Jewish farming villages in Palestine. The Department of Immigration endeavored to find homes for newly arriving immigrants to Palestine. Meanwhile, the Department of Labor consulted with the British Mandate for Palestine on prospects for work and labor schedules. The Department of Politics maintained a close relationship with the British high commissioner in Jerusalem on all public policy issues. Finally, the Public Works Department either collaborated with the mandate authorities or, with its own resources, launched projects intended to absorb unemployed immigrants.

Following the Peel Commission Report, the Jewish Agency believed that an impending partition plan was in the works. The agency also thought that lines should be delimited according to evidence of Jewish occupation. Therefore, the Jewish Agency began to accelerate Jewish land purchases and colonization along the borders of Palestine, all prior to World War II.

The Jewish Agency responded to World War II by helping support the Haganah (Jewish Paramilitary Defense) and secretly conscripting young Jews, both men and women. The agency funded the Haganah, promoting military instruction and enabling the purchase of illegal weapons. During this period, the Jewish Agency also increased agricultural and industrial production. It assisted in the expansion of land under cultivation and helped build new factories aimed at satisfying the needs of the British military.

During World War II the British had adopted an essentially pro-Arab policy toward Palestine, especially in regard to the issue of immigration. Thus, after the war the Jewish Agency shifted its stance from accommodation with the British to physical resistance. The British responded by rounding up agency officials and jailing them.

Immigration became a point of contention in which the Jewish Agency was unwilling to back down in the face of German atrocities. The Jewish Agency sought to openly relocate Jewish refugees to Palestine regardless of British immigration quotas, believing that such a policy could take advantage of a horrible situation by demonstrating the insensitivity of British immigration policy in Palestine.

After the establishment of the State of Israel in May 1948, the newly formed Israeli government absorbed most of the Jewish Agency's departments. The Jewish Agency was made independent of the Israeli government, to continue its traditional work of absorbing and resettling Jewish refugees. The Jewish Agency also sought to market Israel abroad by promoting interest in Israel among the Diaspora and marketing Israeli accomplishments and ambitions for the future.

David Ben-Gurion, Israel's first prime minister, wanted to make sure that the Jewish Agency remained separate from the Israeli government for three reasons. First, he was unwilling to share authority with the Jewish Agency and did not want the agency involved in policymaking. Second, he believed that by endowing the Jewish Agency with the charitable task of assisting Jewish refugees, the agency could have the benefit of a tax-exempt status overseas. And third, Ben-Gurion realized that his government was not capable of handling the enormous undertaking of rescuing and resettling immigrants. By presenting the Jewish Agency with such a task, world Jewry would share this burden, not the Israeli government alone. The Jewish Agency had customarily taken on the responsibility of promoting and receiving the monetary support coming into Israel from Jews abroad.

During the Sephardic Aliya (immigration) of the 1950s, the Jewish Agency enacted a new ship-to-village program. The program sought to avoid the indeterminate state of the *ma'abarot* transit sites, instead resettling the fugitives in the moshavim. But the 1956 Suez Crisis exacerbated Arab xenophobia, accelerating the pace of immigrants flooding into Israel. The Jewish Agency was left with little choice but to place the newcomers in temporary facilities, whereupon they were enrolled in *ulpanim,* or Hebrew-language classes.

While the 1967 Six-Day War created an influx of Jewish refugees to Israel, it also provided the Jewish Agency with increased financial support from world Jewry. With such a financial windfall, the Jewish Agency was able to broaden its mission to encompass Diaspora fund-raising projects as well. Under the stewardship of Louis Pincus, the Jewish Agency spent much of its funds for education and to better assimilate immigrants into Israeli society. Teachers and sociologists convinced the Jewish Agency to abandon its old merging of the communities policy in support of cultural pluralism in an effort to better acculturate the Sephardim.

BRIAN PARKINSON

See also

Ashkenazic Judaism; Ben-Gurion, David; Haganah; Palestine, British Mandate for; Peel Commission; Sephardic Judaism; Six-Day War; Suez Crisis; Weizmann, Chaim; Zionism; Zionist Conference

References

Chinitz, Zelig. *A Common Agenda: The Reconsitution of the Jewish Agency for Israel.* Jerusalem: Jerusalem Center for Public Affairs, 1985.

Jewish Agency, The. *The Story of the Jewish Agency for Israel.* New York: The Jewish Agency, American Section, 1964.

Sachar, Howard M. *A History of Israel: From the Rise of Zionism to Our Time.* 3rd ed. New York: Knopf, 2007.

Stock, Ernest. *Chosen Instrument: The Jewish Agency in the First Decade of the State of Israel.* Jerusalem: Herzl, 1988.

Jewish Battalions

See Jewish Legion

Jewish Brigade

Jewish unit within the British Army during World War II. With the beginning of World War II in September 1939, Chaim Weizmann, head of the World Zionist Organization (WZO), offered the British government the full support of the Jewish community in Palestine and requested the right to form a Jewish military unit that would fight under a Jewish flag within the British Army. The government of Prime Minister Neville Chamberlain rejected the request. Many individual Jews joined the British forces, however, and a number fought in Greece in 1941.

In May 1940 the Chamberlain government fell and was replaced by one headed by Winston Churchill. The new prime minister did not share Chamberlain's misgivings about a Jewish military unit, if only because it would release British troops for service from Palestine elsewhere. Churchill broached the matter with U.S. president Franklin Roosevelt, who said that he had no objection. On September 6, 1940, during the height of the Battle of Britain, Churchill arranged a meeting with Weizmann and assured him of his full support for a Jewish military unit.

Churchill requested that a memorandum be drafted. It had three main points. First, it called for the recruitment of the largest possible number of Jews in Palestine, who would then be formed into battalions or larger formations. Second, it noted that the Colonial Office had insisted that equal numbers of Arabs and Jews be recruited, but because it was most likely that the number of Jews would be significantly higher than Arabs, any excess beyond an equal number must be trained in Egypt or some other Middle Eastern location. Third, officer cadres sufficient to staff a Jewish division were to be immediately selected in Palestine and trained in Egypt.

Within a week, Foreign Secretary Anthony Eden informed Weizmann of the approval of the draft memorandum and that plans were under way to form a Jewish army along the lines of the Czechoslovak and Polish forces in exile. The British initially planned for a force of about 10,000 men, 4,000 of whom were to come from Palestine. The force would be trained in Britain and then shipped back to the Middle East. Weizmann was ecstatic at the prospects, and in February 1941 he was introduced to Major General Leonard A. Hawes, designated as the new unit's commander. At this point, however, Colonial Secretary Lord Lloyd suddenly died. His replacement, Lord Moyne, strongly opposed the plans, pointing out to Churchill that the delicate political balance in the Middle East might be upset by such a step and also stressing supply shortages and logistical problems. Churchill reluctantly concurred and informed Weizmann that the matter was being deferred for six months because of "supply problems." At the end of the period, however, Moyne continued to delay.

In the meantime, smaller Palestinian units were created that consisted entirely of Jews and with Jewish officers. The British conceived of this procedure as one to produce mixed Arab-Jewish companies of so-called Pioneers who would serve as truck drivers, maintenance personnel, and the like. But because few Arabs signed up, the parity rule soon disappeared. In early 1940, some 500 Palestinian Jews were involved in maintenance work with the British Army in France. The defeat of France in July brought their temporary return to Palestine. They then became ground personnel with the Royal Air Force in North Africa. When Italy entered the war, another 400 Palestinian Jews were allowed to enlist to fill air force crew openings, and some were accepted for pilot training.

By early 1942, some 11,000 Jews were serving with the British forces in the Middle East. While their units were nominally of mixed Arab-Jewish composition, in reality they were almost all Jewish. The Zionists demanded that the scattered companies be organized into battalions. London gave way, and on August 6, 1942, some 18,000 Palestinian Jews were incorporated into purely Jewish battalions. By then, fully a quarter of them were in frontline assignments. Palestinian Jews distinguished themselves in fighting alongside the Free French at Bir Hacheim. Only some 45 of 1,000 who fought in that battle survived.

Following the Allied invasion of Italy and with the widespread revelations of the Holocaust, Churchill revived the matter of creating a Jewish army. It was an easier sell to the Arabs that Jewish forces would be fighting in Europe and not stationed in the Middle East. On July 12, 1944, Churchill drafted a memorandum calling for the establishment of a Jewish army group. In subsequent weeks, plans were coordinated with the Jewish Agency.

In October 1944 British brigadier Ernest Benjamin took command of the Jewish Brigade, which had its own colors. The unit's shoulder patch consisted of a Star of David on a background of one white vertical stripe between two blue vertical stripes. In February 1945, 3,400 members of the Jewish Brigade arrived in Italy to join the British Eighth Army fighting there.

The Jewish Brigade was in many respects a triumph for Zionist diplomacy during the war. The officers and the noncommissioned officers (NCOs) of the brigade were able for the first time to learn larger-unit tactics and organization. The lessons there would stand them, the Haganah, and Israel in good stead during the Israeli War of Independence (1948–1949).

SPENCER C. TUCKER

See also

Churchill, Sir Winston; Eden, Robert Anthony; Haganah; Holocaust; Weizmann, Chaim; World War II, Impact of

References

Laqueur, Walter. *A History of Zionism: From the French Revolution to the Establishment of the State of Israel.* Reprint ed. New York: Schocken, 2003.
Reinharz, Jehuda. *Chaim Weizmann: The Making of a Statesman.* New York: Oxford University Press, 1993.
Sachar, Howard M. *A History of Israel: From the Rise of Zionism to Our Time.* 3rd ed. New York: Knopf, 2007.
Weizmann, Chaim. *Trial and Error: The Autobiography of Chaim Weizmann.* New York: Harper, 1949.

Jewish Defense League

Militant Jewish group founded in the United States in 1968. Rabbi Meir David Kahane, responding to rising anti-Semitism in America's inner cities, created the Jewish Defense League (JDL) to protect Jews and property. The JDL came to be accused of harassment, stalkings, intimidation, murder, and bombings under Kahane's leadership. In 1971 he was convicted of a felony for manufacturing firebombs and received a probated sentence conditional on his avoidance of anything having to do with bombs, dynamite, weapons, or the encouragement of violence. He continued to lead the JDL from Israel, where he entered politics and held a seat in the Knesset for a brief time. But when he wrote letters urging the assassination of Soviet and Arab diplomats, he was convicted in May 1974 in the United States of violating the terms of his probation. He led the JDL until he was assassinated at a Zionist Emergency Evacuation Rescue Organization (ZEERO) conference in New York City on November 5, 1990.

The JDL considered itself an activist organization dedicated to protecting and defending with whatever means necessary Diasporic Jews against any individual or organization that threatened Jewish individuals or institutions. However, the Southern Poverty

A member of the Jewish Defense League firing at a rifle range near Los Angeles, California, January 1981. (David H. Wells/Corbis)

Law Center classified the JDL as a hate group, and the U.S. Federal Bureau of Investigation (FBI) considered it to be a violent extremist group. Two major organizations committed to the active protection of American Jewry, the Anti-Defamation League and B'nai B'rith, also denounced the JDL.

Although no acts of direct terrorism were attributed to the JDL after 1992, the FBI and the U.S. Central Intelligence Agency (CIA) attribute 35 to 50 such acts to the JDL. These include the bombings of San Francisco's branch of the Iranian bank Melli (1981), the United Nations (UN) Iraq mission (1982), and the Los Angeles offices of the American Arab Anti-Discrimination Committee (1985). The JDL is also believed to be responsible for the assassination in 1985 of former Waffen-SS member Tsherim Soobzokov. The JDL leadership denied organizational responsibility for all acts of terror.

Canadian-born Irv Rubin served as the JDL international chairman during 1985–2002. Rubin and JDL member Earl Krugel were both charged on December 12, 2001, with conspiracy to commit acts of terrorism for allegedly planning to bomb the offices of California's Arab American congressman Darrell Issa and the King Fahd Mosque in Culver City, California. The two were charged when Krugel took receipt of explosives in an undercover sting operation. Rubin died (some say he was murdered) at the Federal Metropolitan Detention Center in Los Angeles on November 4, 2002, after

allegedly jumping 18 feet to a concrete floor from a jail balcony. In February 2003, Krugel pled guilty to conspiracy to violate the civil rights of worshipers at the mosque and to conspiracy to bomb Issa's federal office. In September 2003, Krugel was sentenced to 20 years imprisonment as a part of a plea bargain that required him to name the JDL members who perpetrated the 1985 bombing of the Los Angeles offices of the American Arab Anti-Discrimination Committee. Krugel was murdered by a fellow inmate at the Federal Correction Institution in Phoenix, Arizona, on November 4, 2005.

Rubin's death and the continued antiterror scrutiny ultimately transformed the JDL into a propaganda and advocacy group. The JDL split into two factions in October 2004. One faction retained the name Jewish Defense League and is led by Shelley Rubin, the widow of Irv Rubin. The other is now known as the New Jewish Defense League and has been led by Ian Sigel since July 1, 2005. Sigel is a former contractor who joined the JDL's Chicago chapter in 1999. The new JDL claims to reject violence.

RICHARD M. EDWARDS

See also

Kahane, Meir David; Terrorism

References

Anderson, Sean Kendall, and Stephen Sloan. *Terrorism: Assassins to Zealots.* Lanham, MD: Scarecrow, 2003.

Anti-Defamation League. *Extremism in the Name of Religion: The Violent Record of the Kahane Movement and Its Offshoots.* New York: Anti-Defamation League, 1995.

Friedman, Robert I. *The False Prophet: Rabbi Meir Kahane, from FBI Informant to Knesset Member.* Westport, CT: Lawrence Hill, 1990.

Jewish Legion

Formation of Jewish volunteers raised by Great Britain, also known as the Jewish Battalions, who fought in World War I. Expelled by the Ottoman Empire, Palestinian Jews who retained citizenship with Entente countries gathered in Egypt in December 1914. Many of them, led by Vladimir Jabotinsky and Joseph Trumpeldor, petitioned to join the British Army. London initially rejected their offer but later formed the 650-man Zion Mule Corps under Colonel John H. Patterson with Trumpeldor as his second-in-command. The Mule Corps served with distinction in the Gallipoli Campaign carrying supplies to the front lines until disbanded at the campaign's conclusion.

Jabotinsky and others continued to lobby for the creation of Jewish combat units, believing that these would further the Zionist cause. In August 1917, shortly after issuance of the Balfour Declaration, British prime minister David Lloyd George and Foreign Secretary Arthur Balfour approved the formation of a Jewish regiment. Patterson, assisted by Jabotinksy, who became his aide-de-camp, recruited a battalion from Jewish refugees and Mule Corps veterans. This battalion, the 38th Royal Fusiliers (City of London Regiment), completed training in February 1918 and arrived in Alexandria, Egypt, in March. In April Britain formed the 39th Battalion, primarily from U.S. and Canadian Jewish volunteers, and in June recruited the 40th Battalion from Jews who had remained in Palestine. Grouped together and attached to the Australian and New Zealand Mounted Division, the Jewish battalions forced a crossing of the Jordan River, paving the way for Lieutenant General Sir Edmund Allenby's successful autumn offensive and the capture of Damascus.

Britain also formed the 41st and 42nd Reserve Battalions from Jewish volunteers. These remained in Britain and supplied replacements for the three combat battalions. In all, some 6,500 Jews served in these five battalions, including David Ben-Gurion, Israel's future first prime minister. Most of these veterans settled in Palestine after the war.

STEPHEN K. STEIN

See also

Allenby, Sir Edmund Henry Hynman, 1st Viscount; Balfour, Arthur James; Balfour Declaration; Ben-Gurion, David; Jabotinsky, Vladimir Yevgenyevich; Trumpeldor, Joseph; Zionism

References

Jabotinsky, Vladimir. *The Story of the Jewish Legion.* New York: Bernard Akerman, 1945.

Patterson, John Henry. *With the Judeans in the Palestine Campaign.* New York: Macmillan, 1922.

———. *With the Zionists in Gallipoli.* New York: George H. Doran, 1916.

Sachar, Howard M. *A History of Israel: From the Rise of Zionism to Our Time.* 3rd ed. New York: Knopf, 2007.

Jewish National Fund

Zionist organization founded in 1901 at the Fifth Zionist Congress in Basel. Mathematics professor Zvi Hermann Schapira had urged the establishment of such a fund at the Fourth Zionist Conference four years earlier. The Jewish National Fund (JNF) came into being at the Fifth Congress, thanks in large part to the strong support of Zionist leader Theodor Herzl. The JNF was established for the purpose of buying land for Jewish settlement in Palestine. Today it is a major landowner and is active in water projects, afforestation, and land reclamation projects within the State of Israel.

Yona Krementzky was the first head of the JNF. He initiated the Golden Book that honored paid inscriptions. He also began publishing JNF stamps, the proceeds from the sale of which went to the organization. The stamps were affixed to official Zionist documents or to letters, and many people collected them. The first, issued in 1902, had the Star of David and the word "Zion." Initially capitalized with the sum of £200,000, the JNF drew its funds from a variety of donors, many of them wealthy. Most of the money, however, came from perhaps 1 million little Blue Boxes in Jewish homes

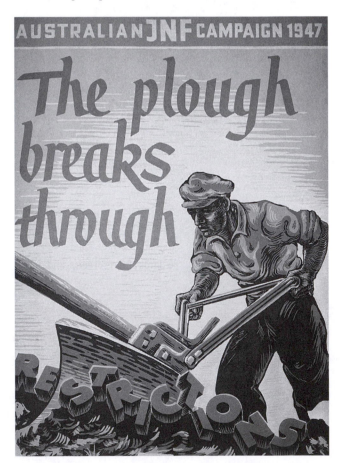

Australian poster promoting the Jewish National Fund, 1947. (Israeli Government Press Office)

worldwide. The idea had been suggested in a letter to the Zionist newspaper *Die Welt* by Galician bank clerk Haim Kleinman, and Krementzky adopted it.

The first JNF land purchase in Palestine was a 50-acre parcel purchased with a gift from Isaac Goldberg. Beginning in 1904, the JNF purchased many plots of land south of the Sea of Galilee and at Ben Shemen in central Palestine. Early on, the JNF embarked on afforestation in central Palestine at Hulda. There the JNF oversaw the planting of olive groves to honor the memory of Herzl. The JNF went on to become the leading environmental organization of Israel. The organization was also actively involved in establishing the city of Tel Aviv and in establishing secondary schools.

JNF landholdings grew steadily, from 25,000 acres in 1921 to 50,000 acres in 1927. By 1935, the JNF had planted 1.7 million trees on 1,750 acres. By the end of 1936, the JNF had secured 89,500 acres of land that made possible the establishment of 108 Jewish settlements. Most of the land was purchased from Arab landowners. In 1939, 10 percent of the Jewish population in Palestine lived on JNF land. From the inception, the JNF planned to lease the land long-term rather than sell it. In the summer of 1939, when the British prohibited the establishment of additional Jewish communities in new areas, the JNF defied the law. In Operation TOWER AND STOCKADE, it continued to purchase land and secretly establish new settlements.

In 1953 the JNF was reorganized as an Israeli company but essentially without any change. In 1960 there was a major change, however, when administration of JNF land, apart from forested areas, was transferred to the Israel Lands Administration, an Israeli government agency that manages 93 percent of Israeli land. In 2005 the JNF agreed to transfer its urban landholdings to the state in return for an equal area of rural land. At present the JNF owns about 14 percent of the land of Israel. It is today especially active in the Negev Desert area. In the 1990s it undertook the Hula Valley Redevelopment Project, the largest environmental undertaking in the Middle East. The project is designed to prevent pollutants from reaching the Sea of Galilee, to restore fertility in agricultural lands, and to enhance the general economy of the region. In its first century of existence, the JNF has planted more than 240 million trees in JNF forests, built more than 180 dams and reservoirs, and developed more than a quarter million acres of land.

JNF policy forbids leasing land to non-Jews, but this policy has been held to violate Israeli antidiscrimination laws and has been circumvented in practice, especially through short-term leases.

SPENCER C. TUCKER

See also

Herzl, Theodor; Zionism; Zionist Conference

References

Bar-Gal, Yoram. *Propaganda and Zionist Education: The Jewish National Fund, 1924–1947.* London: Boydell and Brewer, 2003.

Hirschmann, Ira. *The Awakening: The Story of the Jewish National Fund.* New York: Shengold, 1980.

Lehn, Walter. *The Jewish National Fund.* London: Kegan Paul, 1988.

Sachar, Howard M. *A History of Israel: From the Rise of Zionism to Our Time.* New York: Knopf, 1976.

Shilonv, Zvi. *Ideology and Settlement: The Jewish National Fund, 1897–1914.* Jerusalem: Magnes Press and Hebrew University, 1998.

Jiddi Pass

See Giddi Pass

Jihad

The term "jihad" (*jehad*) is often translated as "holy war." It means "striving," or "to exert the utmost effort," and refers both to a religious duty to spread and defend Islam by waging war (lesser jihad) and an inward spiritual struggle to attain perfect faith (greater jihad). The distinction between lesser and greater is not accepted by all Muslims in all circumstances. Many distinguish between jihad as an individual versus a collective duty, as when Muslims face invasion or cannot practice their faith, or in its defensive or offensive forms. In general, the broad spectrum of modern Islam emphasizes the inner spiritual jihad.

A Hamas poster declares "Jihad is our way," February 1993. (Israeli Government Press Office)

Pakistani demonstrator with a placard reading "Jihad is Not Terrorism, Jihad is our Life," October 15, 2001. (Pascal Le Segretain/Corbis Sygma)

Within the spectrum of Islamic belief, definitions of jihad have also rested on historical circumstances. Indian reformer Sayyid Ahmad Khan argued for a more limited interpretation of jihad whereby believers could perform charitable acts in place of armed struggle, which was only incumbent if Muslims could not practice their faith. The reform movement of Muhammad ibn abd al-Wahhab in 18th-century Arabia, in contrast, reasserted the incumbency of jihad as armed struggle for all believers. As the Koran contains verses that promote mercy and urge peacemaking but also verses (referred to as the Sword Verses) that more ardently require jihad of believers, there is a scriptural basis for both sides of this argument.

Koranic thought on the nature of jihad began to evolve when Muhammad moved from Mecca to Medina in 622 and created an Islamic state. The initial Koranic jihadic sanction (22:39) was for fighting in self-defense only, "those who stay at home," that could be taken as condemnation of those who abstained from an early key battle of the Muslims against the Meccan forces. Many Muslim scholars held that the admonition to pursue an aggressive jihad "with their wealth and their persons" (Koran 4:95) overrode verses revealed earlier on. Fighting and warfare (*qital*) are, however, differentiated from jihad, which is always accompanied by the phrase "*'ala sabil Allah*" (on the path of God) in the same way that just war is differentiated from other forms of conflict.

Some scholars differentiate the fulfilling of jihad by the heart, the tongue, or the sword as a means of discouraging Muslims from seeing armed struggle as a commandment, but such teachings have by and large been contradicted by the revival of activist jihad, first in response to colonialism and then again in the 20th century.

The broad spectrum of Islam considers foreign military intervention, foreign occupation, economic oppression, non-Islamic cultural realignment, colonialism, and the oppression of a domestic government, either secular or Islamic, of an Islamic people or country to be a sufficient reason, if not a Koranic mandate, to participate in a defensive jihad. The more militant and fundamental end of the Islamic spectrum asserts that a social, economic, and military defensive jihad is justifiable and necessary. However, a widespread discussion of jihad is ongoing in the Muslim world today in response to the rise of militancy, and there is a concerted effort to separate the concepts of jihad and martyrdom from each other when they are the rallying call of irresponsible extremists such as Osama bin Laden and his ilk.

Notable defensive jihads in the more recent history of Islam include the resistance of the Afghan (1979) and Chechnya mujahideen against their respective Soviet and Russian occupations and the Algerian War of Independence against France. Some Islamic religious scholars, such as Dr. Abdullah Yusuf Azzam, a former teacher of bin Laden, argued for jihad against the West. Numerous clerics and scholars have held, along with the views of their communities, that the Palestinian struggle against Israel is a defensive jihad because of the infringements on life and liberty, the use of collective punishment, and the seizure by Israel of waqf (endowment) lands.

Offensive jihad was essentially adopted by the early Muslim community, as no defensive action would have sufficed to protect them against the allied tribal forces determined to exterminate them. In such a jihad, the Peoples of the Book (*dhimma*), meaning other monotheistic traditions including Judaism and Christianity, must be treated differently than enemies who are unbelievers (*kuffar*). However, the Peoples of the Book must submit to Islamic rule, including the paying of poll and land taxes. Rules of engagement, truces, and treatment of prisoners and non-Muslims were all specified in medieval texts concerned with *siyar,* or Islamic international law.

Classical Islamic law and tradition asserts that a jihad that is a collective duty (simplified in Western texts as an offensive jihad) can only be declared by the caliph, the successor to the Prophet Muhammad and the lawful temporal and spiritual authority for the entire Islamic community. On the other hand, no authority other than conscience or the awareness of an oppression targeting Islam or Islamic peoples is necessary to participate in an individually incumbent jihad.

When the Mongols attacked Baghdad in 1258, the caliphate, long since a divided patchwork of sultanates and emirates, ceased to exist. It was the only legal, governmental, and clerical structure recognized by the classical interpretation of Islamic doctrine as being capable of declaring jihad. That did not prevent the Ottoman sultans from declaring themselves caliphs and calling for jihad, but the Muslim world did not recognize them as such. Other jihads were declared in the early modern period, for instance by the Mahdiyya of the Sudan, the Wahhabi movement in Arabia, and the Sanusiyya in today's Libya.

Leaders of such movements, like contemporary jihadists, have sometimes proclaimed jihads by issuing a fatwa or statement. Although a fatwa is supposed to be a legal response issued by a qualified jurist, self-proclaimed leaders and clerics sometimes say that the traditional ulama, crushed by modern state governments, have failed in their duty and therefore claim the right to speak in their stead.

Although many Muslims recognize their respective governments and political leaders as worthy of defining and declaring defensive jihads, there are many others who perceive their governments as illegitimate Islamic states or illegitimate Islamic political leaders. Turkey, Egypt, and Pakistan, for example, are quasi-democratic states that grant secular political parties and politicians the same rights as Islamic political parties and politicians. Islamic militant groups in all three countries see these governments and their leaders as heretical and illegitimate under Islamic law (Sharia). In a similar vein, some Muslims, most notably the takfirists, declare jihad against Muslim governments perceived as oppressive, anti-Islamic, or corrupt (being non-Muslim in their eyes). Additionally, many of the Islamic theocratic monarchies (Saudi Arabia, for example) are deemed illegitimate by fundamentalist Muslims. This perception is due in part to the willingness of some of these monarchies and democracies to cooperate and form alliances with non-Islamic nations or with nations that wage economic, cultural, or military war against Islam and Muslims. Additionally, some of these monarchies and democracies limit the power of the clerics within their countries.

Various Islamic movements, most notably Al Qaeda, have stepped into the void created by the disappearance of the caliphate and the resultant fractured Islamic political and religious world. These groups have interpreted Islam as they wish and declare jihad as they desire, although often with the assistance and support of some clerics and of leaders with a degree of religious knowledge. Because early Muslims killed in jihad were considered martyrs, there is an extensive tradition that exalts martyrdom. This adds to the modern jihadists' appeal, particularly to younger or more desperate followers. Defensive jihad, inclusive of martyrdom, is deemed appropriate in order to end Israel's occupation of the perceived Islamic territories of the West Bank, East Jerusalem, and Gaza, if not all of Palestine.

A martyr secures a place in paradise and may intercede for other Muslims. Antiterrorist campaigns in the Muslim world have argued, against the weight of literature and popular belief, that modern jihadists are not martyrs if they set out to martyr themselves because suicide is not allowed in Islam. Noncombatant Muslims who perish in a jihad are also considered martyrs. Jihadists thus excuse the deaths of innocents caught in their crossfire with targets or authorities. They explain the deaths of non-Muslim civilians as being deserved for their failure to submit to Islam or for their open oppression of Islam or Islamic peoples. In the case of Israeli civilians, the fact that all provide military service to their country means that they are not really considered civilians by the jihadists.

The term "jihad" is incorporated into the organizational names of numerous militant groups, including the Egyptian Islamic Jihad, the Egyptian Tawhid wa-l-Jihad, and the Palestinian Islamic Jihad.

The struggle in contemporary Islam to redefine jihad and detach its meaning from adventurism, martyrdom, and attacks on Muslim governments as well as Westerners is one of the most significant challenges at this time in history.

RICHARD EDWARDS AND SHERIFA ZUHUR

See also

Fatwa; Hamas; Islamic Jihad, Palestinian

References

Bostrom, Andrew G., ed. *The Legacy of Jihad: Islamic Holy War and the Fate of Non-Muslims.* Amherst, NY: Prometheus, 2005.

Delong-Bas, Natana. *Wahhabi Islam: From Revival and Reform to Global Jihad.* Oxford: Oxford University Press, 2004.

Esposito, John L. *Unholy War: Terror in the Name of Islam.* New York: Oxford University Press, 2002.

Fregosi, Paul. *Jihad in the West: Muslim Conquests from the 7th to the 21st Centuries*. Amherst, NY: Prometheus, 1998.

Kepel, Gilles. *Jihad: The Trail of Political Islam*. Cambridge, MA: Belknap, 2003.

John Paul II, Pope
Born: May 18, 1920
Died: April 2, 2005

Roman Catholic prelate and pope (1978–2005). Born in Wadowice, Poland, on May 18, 1920, Karol Jósef Wojtyła grew up in humble circumstances and knew hardship as a youth. His mother died when he was just nine years old, and three years later his only sibling, a brother, died. An engaging young man who was an exemplary student, Wojtyła enrolled in the faculty of philosophy at Jagellonian University in Krakow in 1938. To avoid imprisonment under the German occupation after September 1939, he was forced to work first in a stone quarry and then in a chemical plant. In 1942 he clandestinely entered an underground seminary in Krakow and enrolled in the faculty of theology at Jagellonian University.

Wojtyła transferred to the archbishop of Krakow's residence in August 1944, where he remained until Poland was liberated in 1945. In 1946 he completed his fourth year of studies, was ordained a priest, and left for Rome for postgraduate studies. In 1947 he earned his licentiate in theology. The following year he earned a master's degree and doctorate in sacred theology from Jagellonian University. In the late 1940s and into the mid-1950s he served in a variety of pastoral positions in Poland, began to publish, and ultimately became the chair of ethics at Poland's Catholic University in Lublin in 1956. Wojtyła was named auxiliary bishop in the archbishopric of Krakow in 1958, becoming its archbishop in 1964. All the while, he labored under the considerable restrictions of communist-controlled Poland, which was openly hostile toward the Catholic Church.

Wojtyła became a cardinal in 1967. During the early to mid-1970s he continued to publish prolifically on a wide range of scholarly and theological topics. He also traveled extensively.

On October 16, 1978, following the sudden death of Pope John Paul I, Wojtyła was elected pope on the eighth balloting, astounding many pundits. In honor of his immediate predecessor, he took the name John Paul II and became the first non-Italian pope in 455 years. At 58 years old, he was also an unusually youthful pontiff who was an avid skier, swimmer, and hiker.

From the very beginning of his pontificate, John Paul II, who spoke eight languages, eschewed many of the trappings of his office. Instead, he became known as a master communicator who relished personal contacts, often wading into huge crowds. Just eight months

John Paul II, who served as pope during 1978–2005, waves to a U.S. audience in 1979. (Library of Congress)

into his pontificate, he paid an emotional nine-day visit to his native Poland, the first pope to visit the nation. His sojourn caused great consternation among communist officials who feared that the pope's strong anticommunist sentiments would result in popular unrest. Although this did not immediately happen, communist officials had much to worry about. By the early 1980s, John Paul II had tacitly aligned himself with Poland's Solidarity movement and, by the early 1990s, was credited with being a key force behind the events of 1989 that swept away communist rule in Eastern Europe and hastened the end of the Cold War.

The pope's attitude toward the Middle East was in many ways a radical departure from that of his predecessors. He was a tireless proponent of peace in the region, and he championed both Muslim and Jewish causes. Although he decried the violence of radical Palestinians, he was nonetheless supportive of Palestinian statehood. Instead of highlighting the differences between Christianity and Islam, he viewed them as complementary religions, ones that shared many of the same tenets and historical figures. This was a far different path than the ones of his predecessors, who saw Islam in an antipathetic light. Indeed, the pope helped narrow the chasm between the Muslim and Christian worlds. At the same time, he was a supporter of Israel and tried to bridge the considerable and centuries-long gap between Jews and the Catholic Church.

Throughout his long papacy, the pope sought to build bridges with both the Jewish and Muslim communities. His explicit admissions of wrongdoing toward both groups by the Catholic Church of the past earned him a good number of supporters in each camp. Clearly, he was unable to heal the rift between Israelis and Palestinians or between Jews and Muslims. What he did do, however, was to identify with the injustices of all.

In 2001 John Paul II became the first pontiff in the 2,000-year history of the Catholic Church to officially visit a mosque. The dramatic gesture, which took place in an ancient mosque in Damascus, Syria, was heightened when the pope urged Christians and Muslims to forgive one another and work toward common goals of peace and justice.

In 1979 John Paul II visited the Auschwitz concentration camp, and in 2001 he visited Israel and prayed for forgiveness at Yad Vashem, which deeply moved many Jews. In 1986 he became the first pope to officially visit a synagogue, another hugely important act of symbolism. His approaches to the Jewish and Arab worlds were not without their detractors. Some hard-line Muslims savaged him for his attempts to heal the rift with the Jews. Many Israelis, on the other hand, criticized his failure to support the Iraq War (2003–). John Paul II was also critical of the U.S. war in Afghanistan and signaled only tepid acceptance of the Persian Gulf War of 1991.

Pope John Paul II was the most visible and well-traveled pontiff in history. During his reign he completed 104 foreign pastoral visits. He was also the first pontiff to visit a predominantly Orthodox nation (Romania in 1999). It is hard to overstate the impact that John Paul II had on world politics, as he reached out in an unprece-dented way to the world's Jews as well as Muslims and non-Catholic Christians.

In affairs of social justice, faith, and Church governance, John Paul II was at once liberal and conservative. On most social issues he was considered liberal and was a vocal critic of both communism and the excesses of capitalism. He frequently decried the gap between rich and poor nations and was a champion of the world's impoverished and downtrodden. He had little use for political oppression of any stripe and was also an ardent foe of the death penalty and abortion. These stances made him popular with both liberals and conservatives around the world. Yet in terms of Catholic doctrine, the pope was conservative if not orthodox. He steadfastly refused to consider the ordination of women, the abandonment of celibacy for Catholic clergy, or the lifting of the Church's ban on contraception.

John Paul II died in Rome on April 2, 2005, after battling a series of debilitating ailments, some of which were the result of a near-mortal gunshot wound he received at the hands of a Turkish extremist during a May 1981 assassination attempt in St. Peter's Square.

PAUL G. PIERPAOLI JR. AND LUC STENGER

See also
Pius XII, Pope

References
Ascherson, Neal. *The Struggles for Poland.* London: M. Joseph, 1987.

John Paul II, Pope. *In My Own Words.* New York: Gramercy, 2002.

McBrien, Richard P. *Lives of the Popes. The Pontiffs from St. Peter to John Paul II.* San Francisco: Harper San Francisco, 1997.

Szulc, Tad. *Pope John Paul II: The Biography.* New York: Scribner, 1995.

Weigel, George. *Witness to Hope: The Biography of John Paul II.* New York: HarperCollins, 1999.

Johnson, Lyndon Baines
Born: August 27, 1908
Died: January 22, 1973

U.S. politician and president of the United States (1963–1969). Lyndon Johnson was born in Stonewall near Austin, Texas, on August 27, 1908. He graduated from Southwest Texas State Teachers College in San Marcos in 1930 and became a high school teacher. In 1932 he went to Washington, D.C., as a congressional aide. He won the patronage of Franklin D. Roosevelt, the president who became Johnson's role model and appointed him Texas administrator of the National Youth Administration in 1935. Johnson was elected to the U.S. House of Representatives in 1936.

For six months after the Japanese attack on Pearl Harbor in December 1941, Johnson interrupted his congressional service to become a lieutenant commander in the U.S. Navy, visiting the Pacific theater on a fact-finding mission. Returning to Congress, he voted reliably for the internationalist policies of Roosevelt and President Harry S. Truman. In 1949 Johnson won election to the U.S. Senate as a representative from Texas. In the Senate he earned a towering political reputation because of his political shrewdness

Lyndon B. Johnson, president of the United States (1963–1969). (U.S. Department of Defense)

and uncanny persuasive abilities, most apparent when he was Senate majority leader, a position he held from 1955 to 1960. As such, he used his quick wit, imposing physical stature, and carrot-and-stick threats to persuade often balky senators and congressional representatives to reach consensus on sometimes controversial legislation. Liberal and populist in his instincts despite the need to conciliate the Democratic Party's conservative Southern wing to which he belonged, he was largely responsible for the passage of the 1957 Civil Rights Bill. He concentrated primarily on domestic policy, showing little interest in international affairs beyond the conventional Cold War opposition to communism and support for expansive U.S. policies overseas, including aid to developing countries. He also worked well with the administration of President Dwight D. Eisenhower.

Selected by Democratic presidential candidate John F. Kennedy as his running mate in the 1960 elections, Johnson became vice president in January 1961. As vice president he had little input on policy matters. He greatly resented Kennedy's failure to employ his superlative legislative skills to win passage of his domestic measures and his exclusion from Kennedy's inner circle. After Kennedy's assassination in November 1963 made Johnson president, he announced an ambitious range of civil rights and social welfare initiatives—his Great Society program—a sweeping attempt to eradicate poverty and social injustice in the United States that was his first priority. The 1964 Voting Rights Act and 1965 Civil Rights

Act were the most far-reaching legislation of the kind ever passed in the United States. In 1964 Johnson won reelection by a landslide against conservative Republican senator Barry Goldwater of Arizona, whose seeming readiness to contemplate using nuclear weapons alarmed many Americans.

Despite Johnson's stated preference for domestic policy, foreign affairs, especially the war in Vietnam, came to dominate his presidency. Although he feared that an expanded war in Vietnam might compromise his domestic reform programs, he nevertheless remembered well the political damage that attacks regarding the so-called loss of China had visited on President Truman. Thus, Johnson refused to consider abandoning South Vietnam to communism. Gradually he escalated the war, believing that there was some point at which North Vietnam would give up the struggle. Ultimately he dispatched U.S. ground forces, and by January 1969 there were half a million Americans in Vietnam. Meanwhile, domestic opposition to the war steadily escalated, his Great Society stalled, and the economy began to suffer from free-wheeling spending on war and welfare. Fearing that he could not win reelection, Johnson withdrew from the 1968 presidential campaign. The war continued under his successor, Republican Richard M. Nixon.

A tragic president, Johnson watched the impact of U.S. involvement in Vietnam leave his substantial domestic achievements vitiated, compromised, and underrated. The fiscal and economic problems that the war generated through the failure to increase taxes to pay for it denied his programs further funding and created long-term difficulties for the United States. Not until his presidency did Johnson show any sustained interest in the Middle East, although he generally took a pro-Israeli stance, as during the 1967 Six-Day War. As Senate majority leader during the 1956 Suez Crisis he sought to maintain the bipartisan consensus, and he loyally supported Eisenhower administration policies.

In the aftermath of assertive Soviet pronouncements on Suez, in early 1957 the Eisenhower administration promulgated the Eisenhower Doctrine, stating that the United States possessed vital interests in the Middle East and must use whatever means necessary to resist the extension of Soviet influence in the region and seeking congressional approval for economic assistance and potential military intervention. Johnson secured changes in the document's wording, giving Congress greater discretionary powers over economic and military assistance. He publicly opposed the administration's support for United Nations (UN) economic sanctions against Israel until it withdrew from the Egyptian Gaza Strip and part of the Sinai Peninsula, an issue that became moot once Israel did so in March 1957.

As president, Johnson assigned relatively low priority to the Middle East. Concern over Soviet arms sales to Egypt and Syria and Iraq's and Egypt's military buildup did lead him to approve increased U.S. arms sales to Israel and conservative Arab states, especially Jordan. The Johnson administration denounced as illegal Egypt's May 1967 closing of the Strait of Tiran to Israeli vessels. During the Six-Day War, when Israeli forces responded to escalating Arab military pressure by launching preemptive strikes against Egypt, Syria, Jordan, and Iraq, the Johnson administration remained neutral but deployed the U.S. Sixth Fleet near the Syrian coast to prevent potential Soviet military intervention. Even when Israeli airplanes attacked the U.S. intelligence ship USS *Liberty* off Sinai, killing 10 crewmen and wounding another 100, U.S. policies remained pro-Israeli, in part because the Soviet Union supported the Arab states. U.S.-supplied armaments were at least partly responsible for the Israeli victory. In the war's aftermath Arthur Goldberg, U.S. ambassador to the UN, was instrumental in the November 1967 passage of UN Resolution 242, calling for Israeli withdrawal from all occupied territories and the conflict's peaceful resolution, the basis of all subsequent U.S. policies toward the Arab-Israeli dispute.

In retirement, Johnson set about writing his memoirs. Four years after his presidency, he died at his Texas ranch on January 22, 1973.

PRISCILLA MARY ROBERTS

See also

Acheson, Dean; Eisenhower, Dwight David; Gaza Strip; Hussein, King of Jordan; Israel; Kennedy, John Fitzgerald; Roosevelt, Franklin Delano; Suez Crisis; Truman, Harry S.; United Nations Security Council Resolution 242; United States, Middle East Policy

References

Brands, H. W., ed. *The Foreign Policies of Lyndon Johnson: Beyond Vietnam.* College Station: Texas A&M University Press, 1999.
———. *The Wages of Globalism: Lyndon Johnson and the Limits of American Power.* New York: Oxford University Press, 1995.
Cohen, Warren I., and Nancy Bernkopf Tucker, eds. *Lyndon Johnson Confronts the World: American Foreign Policy, 1963–1968.* New York: Oxford University Press, 1994.
Dallek, Robert. *Flawed Giant: Lyndon Johnson and His Times, 1961–1973.* New York: Oxford University Press, 1998.
Gardner, Lloyd C. *Pay Any Price: Lyndon Johnson and the Wars for Vietnam.* Chicago: I. R. Dee, 1995.

Jordan

Middle Eastern nation covering 35,637 square miles, about the size of the U.S. state of Indiana. Jordan, officially known as the Hashemite Kingdom of Jordan, borders Israel and the West Bank to the west, Syria and the Golan Heights to the north, Iraq to the east, and Saudi Arabia to the east and south. From 1516 to 1919, Jordan was part of the Ottoman Empire. With the end of World War I and the collapse of the Ottoman Empire, Transjordan (as it was then known) became part of Britain's League of Nations mandate over Palestine in 1920. In 1921, Abdullah ibn Hussein, a member of the Hashemite dynasty, became the de facto king of Transjordan. Transjordan became a constitutional monarchy under Abdullah I, who was formally placed on the throne by the British in 1928. Nevertheless, Transjordan was still considered part of the British Mandate. That changed in May 1946 when Transjordan secured its independence.

Paramilitary units march through the streets of Amman on May 24, 1947, during Jordan's first Independence Day celebration. (Hans Pinn/Israeli Government Press Office)

Because Transjordan was a member of the Arab League when the State of Israel was created in May 1948, Abdullah was obliged to fight alongside his Arab neighbors against the Israelis. As with most Arabs, he flatly rejected Zionist ambitions. He gained control of the West Bank in 1949 as a result of the Israeli War of Independence (1948–1949) and officially changed his country's name to Jordan to reflect the new territories west of the Jordan River. Months later, he moved to permanently annex the West Bank, which deeply troubled Arab leaders. Many believed that the territory should have been reserved for the displaced Palestinians.

A large number of these displaced Palestinians, about 70,000 by 1949, fled to Jordan, and 280,000 Palestinians were already residing in or fled to the West Bank. The Palestinian population outnumbered the Jordanian population, and although these received citizenship, their identity and aspirations were a point of tension within Jordan. In 1951 a Palestinian assassinated Abdullah in Jerusalem, and the following year he was succeeded by his grandson, King Hussein I. Hussein ruled Jordan for the next 47 years.

A series of anti-Western uprisings in Jordan, combined with the 1956 Suez Crisis, compelled Hussein to sever military ties to Britain. The British government had taken part in the covert British-French-Israeli scheme to topple Egyptian president Gamal Abdel Nasser and wrest back control of the Suez Canal from the Egyptians.

In February 1958 Hussein formed the Arab Federation with Iraq. The king viewed this as a needed countermeasure to the newly formed United Arab Republic (UAR), formed between Egypt and Syria and dominated by Egypt's Pan-Arab nationalist President Nasser. The Arab Federation fell apart by autumn 1958, however, after the Iraqi king was overthrown in a coup. Later that same year,

The city of Amman, capital of Jordan, shown in 1996. (Moshe Milner/Israeli Government Press Office)

leaders of the UAR called for the overthrow of governments in Beirut and Amman. Hussein fought back by requesting help from the British, who dispatched troops to Jordan to quell antigovernment protests. The Americans had simultaneously sent troops to Lebanon to bolster its besieged Christian-led government.

Jordan's relations with the UAR remained tense. Indeed, in 1963 when a rival Jordanian government-in-exile was set up in Damascus, Syria, King Hussein declared a state of emergency. The crisis subsided when the United States and Britain publicly endorsed Hussein's rule. For good measure, the United States placed its Sixth Fleet on alert in the Mediterranean.

After the mid-1960s and more than a decade of crises and regional conflicts, Hussein turned his attention to domestic issues. He was devoted to improving the welfare of his people and launched major programs to improve literacy rates (which were very low), increase educational opportunities, bolster public health initiatives, and lower infant mortality rates. In these endeavors he was quite successful. By the late 1980s literacy rates approached 100 percent, and infant deaths were down dramatically. Jordan's economy also began to expand as the nation engaged in more trade with the outside world and as its relations with Egypt improved. Hussein also began to erect a modern and reliable transportation system and moved to modernize the country's infrastructure. Notable in all of

this was that he accomplished much without resorting to overly repressive tactics. Indeed, throughout the Cold War most Jordanians enjoyed a level of freedom virtually unrivaled in the Middle East. However, the government undertook sharp responses to antiregime elements and tensions with the Palestinian population.

By the late 1960s another Arab-Israeli conflict was in the making. After Egypt blockaded Israeli shipping in the Gulf of Aqaba in 1967, King Hussein signed a mutual defense pact with Egypt, setting aside his former differences with Nasser's government. Normally a moderating force in volatile Middle East politics, Hussein reluctantly entered the war on the side of Egypt, even as Tel Aviv was imploring him through diplomatic channels not to do so. When the June 1967 Six-Day War ended, Israel took from Jordan the entire West Bank and all of Jerusalem.

As a result of the war, thousands of Palestinians fled to Jordan from the West Bank, now controlled by Israel. Indeed, it is estimated that as many as 300,000 Palestinians poured into Jordan after June 1967, swelling the Palestinian refugee population there to almost 1 million. This massive influx severely taxed Jordanian infrastructure as well as schools, health care, and other services and engendered considerable resentment among some Jordanians. The number of Palestinians in Jordan by 1968 meant that Palestinian groups—especially resistance groups such as the fedayeen—increased their power and clout considerably within Jordan. These groups were well armed (receiving significant assistance from Syria and Egypt) and posed a serious threat to Hussein's rule. By 1970 it appeared as if the Palestinian resistance fighters were in the process of creating a Palestinian state within a state, much as they would do in Lebanon. This situation greatly alarmed King Hussein.

In early 1970 Palestinian guerrilla groups and the Palestine Liberation Organization (PLO) were already skirmishing with Jordanian troops. Open warfare erupted in June. Heretofore, the Jordanian Army had been unsuccessful in its attempts to stop Palestinian attacks on Israel from taking place on Jordanian soil. Hussein also opposed the Palestinian aims of creating a Palestinian state in the West Bank, which he hoped to regain in the future.

In September 1970 after 10 days of bloody conflict, thousands of Palestinians, including the leadership of the PLO, fled Jordan for Syria and Lebanon. Hussein and his government were deeply troubled by this conflict, as were many of the Jordanians of Palestinian origin. From the Palestinian perspective the fighting and forced expulsion in September were seen as a great betrayal. Indeed, the Palestinians referred to the events of September 1970 as Black September.

The early 1970s saw continued unrest. In 1972 King Hussein tried to create a new Arab federation, which would have included the West Bank as Jordanian territory. Israel as well as most of the Arab states flatly rejected the idea. Then in December 1972 Hussein was nearly assassinated by a Palestinian.

During the Yom Kippur War (1973) Hussein played only a minor role, ordering a limited troop deployment (one brigade) to fight in Syria. In 1974 he finally agreed to recognize the Arab League's position that the PLO was the sole representative of the Palestinian people.

Hussein strengthened relations with neighboring Syria beginning in the late 1970s, and he vigorously opposed the 1979 Israeli-Egyptian peace treaty. Jordan backed Iraq in the Iran-Iraq War (1980–1988). The 1980s was a period of economic chaos for the Jordanian people. Job creation did not keep pace with the expanding population, resulting in high unemployment. Inflation became a problem, foreign investment fell off, and exports declined. In 1989, riots occurred in southern Jordan over the lack of jobs and a government-mandated increase in basic commodities including electricity and water. These severe economic dislocations led Hussein to seek U.S. financial aid in the late 1980s. As a result, the nation's foreign debt burden grew substantially.

When King Hussein refused to condemn Iraqi dictator Saddam Hussein in the 1991 Persian Gulf War, U.S. assistance and much general Western aid was curtailed. Saudi Arabia and later Kuwait also withheld financial assistance. Jordan's economy went from bad to worse. When some 700,000 Jordanians returned to Jordan because they were now unwelcome in Kuwait and Saudi Arabia, the economic situation became truly dire. Jordan's tourism declined precipitously after 1991, oil came at a very high premium, and exports suffered enormously. By 1995 unemployment stood at 14 percent (as stated by the government), although other measures estimated that it may have been twice that. Not until 2001 did the economy begin to regain its footing. Hussein's decision to back Iraq put Jordanian-U.S. relations in a holding pattern, and his relations with other major Western powers were little better.

By 1993–1994, however, Jordanian-U.S. relations were on an upswing. The Jordanians decided to become an active partner in the Arab-Israeli peace process, and King Hussein actively supported United Nations (UN) sanctions on the Iraqi regime. On July 25, 1994, Hussein signed a historic nonbelligerent agreement with the Israelis (the Washington Declaration), which was soon followed up by the October 26, 1994, signing of the Israel-Jordan Peace Treaty.

King Hussein died in February 1999 and was succeeded by his son, King Abdullah II. Following the outbreak of the Second (al-Aqsa) Intifada in 2000, Abdullah has tried to continue Jordan's role as the force of moderation in the Middle East. He has attempted to keep avenues of dialogue open between the Israelis and the Palestinians and continues to counsel both sides that discussions and agreements are far preferable to conflict and war. Nevertheless, in a show of Arab solidarity, Jordan recalled its ambassador from Israel. This lasted until 2005. Although Abdullah publicly criticized the Iraq War that began in March 2003, he quietly provided assistance to the United States and Britain and has partnered with the West in an attempt to bring a semblance of control to war-torn Iraq.

PAUL G. PIERPAOLI JR.

See also

Abdullah I, King of Jordan; Arab League; Black September; Fedayeen; Hussein, King of Jordan; Israel-Jordan Peace Treaty; Jordan, Armed Forces; Nasser, Gamal Abdel; Palestine Liberation Organization; Persian Gulf War; Six-Day War; Suez Crisis; United Arab Republic; West Bank; Yom Kippur War

References
Lunt, James D. *Hussein of Jordan: Searching for a Just and Lasting Peace.* New York: William Morrow, 1989.
Salibi, Kamal S. *The History of Modern Jordan.* New York: William Morrow, 1993.
Satloff, Robert B. *From Abdullah to Hussein: Jordan in Transition.* New York: Oxford University Press, 1993.

Jordan, Armed Forces

The Jordanian armed forces, and especially the Jordanian Arab Army, are highly professional organizations with a heritage dating to the formation of the Transjordan (which was officially changed to Jordan in 1949) Arab Legion, which was initially led by British officers. Organized in 1920, the Arab Legion was at first a small police force led by Captain (later Major General) Frederick Gerard Peake, known to Transjordanians as Peake Pasha. In 1930 Captain (later Lieutenant General) John Bagot Glubb became second-in-command of the Arab Legion and a close personal friend and trusted political adviser of Transjordan's King Abdullah. Glubb Pasha, as the Jordanians called him, organized a Bedouin desert patrol consisting of mobile detachments based at strategic desert

A Jordanian soldier stands guard in front of a C-141B Starlifter aircraft at King Faisal Air Base, September 1987. (U.S. Department of Defense)

forts and equipped with communications facilities. On Peake's retirement in 1939, Glubb took command of the Arab Legion and made it into the best-trained military force in the Arab world. The Arab Legion participated in the Iraqi and Syrian campaigns in 1941.

By Transjordan's independence in 1946, the Arab Legion numbered some 8,000 soldiers in 3 mechanized regiments along with 16 infantry companies and included a civil police force of about 2,000 men. The Jordanian ground force officially changed its name in 1956 from the Arab Legion to the Jordanian Arab Army, but the older name remained in popular usage for some time afterward. General Glubb was dismissed in March 1956, a consequence of King Hussein's desire to show political independence from the United Kingdom and to Arabize the Jordanian officer corps. By 1956 the Jordanian military had grown to around 25,000 troops, with well-trained Arab officers replacing the British. This expansion was, nonetheless, supported by the continuation of British aid.

Jordan's most significant actual and potential military adversary from 1948 to 1994 was Israel. Jordanian forces fought in the 1948–1949 Israeli War of Independence and were certainly the most effective of the Arab militaries in that war. Jordanian forces (with some Iraqi military help) managed to retain control of the territory subsequently known as the West Bank as well as East Jerusalem and the entire Old City and especially control of the Jerusalem–Tel Aviv Road at Latrun, thus winning the only significant Arab victories of the war.

During the 1948–1949 war the Jordanians had no tanks, although they did possess some light artillery, around 50 armored cars, and mortars to support the infantry. Jordan received its first tanks, which were British-manufactured, in 1953. Jordanian forces did not fight in the 1956 Sinai Campaign stemming from the Suez Crisis. Jordanian military forces occasionally became involved in border skirmishing with the Israelis throughout the 1950s and 1960s, and Israeli forces conducted several major reprisal raids into Jordan during this period in response to Palestinian terrorism.

By the early 1960s Jordan was receiving limited military assistance from the United States in addition to support from the United Kingdom. The relationship with the United States expanded dramatically in August 1964 when Washington agreed to supply M-48 Patton tanks and armored personnel carriers. Later, in February 1966, the United States added fighter aircraft in the form of Lockheed F-104 Starfighters, aging systems that were being phased out of the U.S. Air Force inventory. The United States agreed to this expanded military relationship with Jordan out of fear that Amman might seek and receive Soviet aid in the absence of continuing Western supplies of arms. By early 1967, the United States and the United Kingdom had become Jordan's primary arms suppliers.

In the June 1967 Six-Day War with Israel, Jordanian forces suffered a massive defeat along with the militaries of Egypt and Syria. On the eve of the war, Jordan had about 55,000 troops and 350 tanks as well as a fledgling air force. Some thought that because Jordan had been under political attack by the republican and Arab socialist regimes of Egypt and Syria, it might be reluctant to engage Israel. Indeed, the Israelis hoped that Jordan would remain neutral, but the Israel Defense Forces (IDF) also planned for a full-scale Jordanian offensive. King Hussein indeed supported Egypt and Syria and tried to defend Jordan and the West Bank. The Jordanians fought well, but the army's performance suffered as a result of Israeli air supremacy. As a result of the 1967 war, Jordan lost all of the Palestinian territory that it had previously secured in the 1948–1949 war. The Israelis destroyed Jordan's entire small air force of 21 subsonic British-made Hawker Hunters, and Jordan also lost 179 tanks and 700 troops with large numbers wounded, missing, or taken prisoner. The four F-104 Starfighters then in Jordanian possession had not been fully integrated into the air force and were sent to Turkey before the war to escape destruction. By 1968 Jordan's military strength was somewhat restored by the U.S. transfer of 100 M-48 tanks. Then in 1969 and 1970, the Americans released 36 additional F-104 aircraft for transfer to Jordan.

The Jordanian military fought effectively against the Israelis in the March 1968 Battle of Karameh, when a large Israeli force crossed into Jordan to destroy Palestinian guerrilla forces operating from the kingdom. The Jordanians also defeated Palestinian guerrillas in September 1970 and again in July 1971 when these forces attempted to create a state within a state in Jordan. Additionally, Amman sent the Jordanian 40th Armored Brigade as an expeditionary force to aid the Syrians and protect their withdrawal during the 1973 Yom Kippur War.

King Hussein chose not to open an additional front with Israel in 1973, mistakenly believing (or at least claiming) that the mere presence of his army on the Jordanian-Israeli border would tie down large numbers of Israeli troops. Jordan also sent a limited number of Special Forces troops to fight in support of royalist forces in Oman in the 1970s. During the 1980–1988 Iran-Iraq War, Jordan supported the Iraqis and sent a token military force of volunteers to support the war effort against Iran. They apparently did not see combat in that war.

During the 1970s and 1980s, Jordan supplemented its military assistance from Western countries with financial support for military modernization from Arab oil-producing states. Such support allowed Jordan to make a number of major purchases, including U.S.-made Northrop F-5 Freedom Fighter aircraft to replace the aging F-104s, U.S.-made M-60 tanks, and a Hawk missile defense system to protect Amman. Nevertheless, in an abrupt turnabout, military procurement was disrupted in the 1990s as a result of difficulties in relations with the United States, Saudi Arabia, and Kuwait following King Hussein's decision not to join the U.S.-led

coalition in the Persian Gulf War of 1991. These problems severely disrupted the flow of outside aid necessary for the Jordanian military to make key purchases and carry out military modernization.

The Israel-Jordan Peace Treaty of 1994 ended the state of war between Jordan and Israel and brought about a major reorientation of the Jordanian Army to deal with other regional threats. The Jordanian military officially ended conscription in 1994 as a response to the peace treaty, although young men had only been drafted sporadically before then in response to variations in manpower needs and financial resources. Some Western military aid programs were restored by the mid-1990s, and in November 1996 Jordan was designated as a major non–North Atlantic Treaty Organization (NATO) ally.

Currently, the Jordanian armed forces comprise about 100,000 active duty personnel and 30,000 reservists. The most important branch of the service is the army. The Jordanian Arab Army is a highly professional force with top-notch officers and noncommissioned officers. Its chief maneuver combat units are two armored divisions, two mechanized divisions, and two separate brigades. Its combat doctrine is almost entirely defensive, as Jordan does not have the resources to conduct large-scale offensive operations. Jordanian forces are organized into four regionally based commands with a strategic reserve and a Special Operations Command. In addition to their self-defense role, Jordanian troops are called upon to secure the Jordanian border with Israel and prevent terrorist infiltration from Jordanian soil.

The Jordanian ground forces are in the process of converting to a lighter force structure that has smaller combat formations and greater mobility. Such a force is expected to have fewer tank battalions and is both cheaper and better equipped to deal with internal security problems than are armor-heavy units. Nevertheless, Jordan retains more than 1,000 tanks in active service, all of which are of U.S. or British manufacture. Since 2004, Jordan has undertaken a major upgrade program for its U.S.-made M-60 tanks. Some of Jordan's British-made Challenger tanks have been subject to either British or domestic Jordanian updating and modification. Some older tanks, including the M-48s and Centurions, are not operational or are in storage. The Jordanian Army has approximately 400 self-propelled artillery pieces (a significant number for a force its size) as well as about 100 older towed artillery pieces. It also has large numbers of modern and effective antitank weapons, such as the U.S.-made Javelin and upgraded Dragon.

Jordan's Special Forces troops are among the best in the region and in recent years have emerged as an especially important component of the Jordanian force structure. The Special Operations Command was formerly led by Abdullah when he served as a brigadier general prior to becoming king in 1999. In the years just prior to the 2003 Iraq War, Jordanian Special Forces troops played a leading role in securing the Iraqi border, where almost nightly clashes took place between Jordanian forces and Iraqi smugglers. In April 2002 Jordan sent a Special Forces training unit to Yemen to assist American forces training the Yemeni military to fight terrorist groups.

The Royal Jordanian Air Force (RJAF) is led by King Abdullah's brother, Prince Faisal, and has about 15,000 personnel. It has approximately 100 fixed-wing combat aircraft with 85 fighter aircraft including U.S.-made General Dynamics F-16 Fighting Falcons and French Mirage F-1s. Jordan also retains some of its older F-5 aircraft, which are increasingly obsolete. The RJAF also has 14 transport aircraft, including 4 American-made C-130 Hercules aircraft. Jordan also has more than 40 attack helicopters that are included within the RJAF. About 22 of these helicopters are equipped with TOW antiarmor missiles. While the RJAF has excellent pilots and good levels of training, its modernization efforts have been significantly restricted by long-term Jordanian resource constraints.

Jordanian air defense forces have likewise suffered from a period of neglect following the 1991 Persian Gulf War as well as other episodes of budgetary shortfalls. Jordanian air defense systems, including its improved Hawk missile batteries, have a number of limitations, although some upgrading has been taking place. The Jordanian military also has three Patriot missile batteries that include a limited antimissile capability.

The Royal Jordanian Coast Guard (sometimes called the Royal Jordanian Navy) is extremely small and operates out of Jordan's only port, at Aqaba. The coast guard has a few small patrol boats in the Dead Sea. There are approximately 500 personnel assigned to the coast guard and fewer than 20 coastal defense craft and patrol vessels. This service is nevertheless scheduled to expand in the future with the planned development of a special organization within the coast guard for counterterrorism and to help support planned upgrades in coastal and port security.

Jordanian military personnel have served during recent years in a range of multinational peace support missions and regional military exercises. Jordanian units have supported peacekeeping operations in the Balkans and Africa through the provision of infantry units, field hospitals, international monitors, and military staff officers in international missions. The peacekeeping missions that were most extensively supported were in Croatia in the 1990s (3,200 Jordanian troops deployed) and in Sierra Leone (where Jordan had a peak of about 1,800 troops in 2000). Jordan has also provided field hospitals to support the reconstruction of postwar Iraq and post-Taliban Afghanistan. The Jordanians also train Arab officers from friendly countries at their own facilities, including the Jordanian National Defense University. In coordination with the United States, Jordan has further supported an extensive effort to train army officers and police forces in postwar Iraq (after 2003).

The Jordanian military retains strong ties to the militaries of the United States and the United Kingdom. Leading male members of the royal family have a tradition of attending the United Kingdom's Royal Military Academy, Sandhurst. Jordanian officers and noncommissioned officers also participate in a variety of military education and training programs offered by the United States and other Western powers. A joint U.S.-Jordanian military commission has coordinated a number of important military concerns since 1974, and Jordanian cooperation with the West usually includes at least one major U.S.-Jordanian military exercise per year as well as Jordanian participation in multilateral exercises organized by the United States.

W. Andrew Terrill

See also

Abdullah I, King of Jordan; Arab Legion; Arms Sales, International; Glubb, Sir John Bagot; Hashemites; Hussein, King of Jordan; Israel-Jordan Peace Treaty; Israeli War of Independence, Israeli-Jordanian Front; Jordan; Latrun, Battles of; Persian Gulf War; Sinai Campaign; Six-Day War; Suez Crisis; West Bank; Yom Kippur War

References

Cordesman, Anthony H. *The Military Balance in the Middle East.* Westport, CT: Praeger, 2004.

El Edross, Syed Ali. *The Hashemite Arab Army, 1908–1979.* Amman, Jordan: Central Publishing House, 1986.

International Institute for Strategic Studies. *The Military Balance.* London: IISS, 2005.

Nevo, Joseph, and Illan Pappe, eds. *Jordan in the Middle East: The Making of a Pivotal State.* London: Frank Cass, 1994.

Jordan River

Key Middle East waterway that flows through the Great Rift Valley and empties into the Dead Sea. The Great Rift Valley, with its freshwater resources, was also important for the passage of early hominids from Africa into Asia and Europe between 1 million and 2 million years ago. The Jordan River provides much-needed water

The Jordan River Valley, as seen from space in 1997. The Mediterranean Sea is on the left. (NASA)

The Jordan River at Allenby Bridge, photographed circa 1910. (Library of Congress)

in a dry desert region. It has remained a contentious issue among Israel, Syria, Lebanon, Jordan, and the Palestinians.

The Jordan River rises in the western and southern Anti-Lebanon Mountains, where springs and snowmelt give rise to the Barayghit and Hasbani Rivers of Lebanon and the Laddan and Baniyas Rivers from Syria. These then coalesce. The river occupies the Jordan trough, part of the Great Rift Valley, and has a straight length of just 70 miles but a meandering length of about 200 miles. The river is about 60 feet at its widest and has a steep gradient, falling some 2,380 feet from its source at Mount Hermon to the Dead Sea. This is why it is called Jordan, a Hebrew term meaning "descender." At its source the Jordan River is 1,000 feet above sea level. At its end it is 1,300 feet below sea level, earning its status as the world's lowest river. The river is not navigable. It can be waded across in many locations and is not very wide at some points. The main crossing is at the Allenby Bridge on the road from Jerusalem to Damascus.

The Jordan may be divided into three constituent parts. The first is the section from its source to Lake Hula. The second is a roughly 10-mile stretch from Lake Hula to the Sea of Galilee (Lake Kinneret). The third part, about 65 miles in length, covers the area from the Sea of Galilee to its terminus in the Dead Sea. The latter section is also known as the Ghor, which in the north forms the border between Israel and Jordan and the border between Israel and the West Bank in the south. The Yarouk River, which is the Jordan's largest tributary, enters 5 miles south of the Sea of Galilee. The Jab-bok River also joins the Jordan River in this section. The Jordan Valley is home to rich fishing grounds and diverse bird populations.

The Jordan River is an important source of water for Syria, Israel, and Jordan. Together with the Sea of Galilee, it provides most of the water for agriculture, hydroelectric power, and domestic consumption. Water scarcity and the control of water resources are contentious issues in this arid region. The flow of water in the Jordan River has been reduced by as much as 90 percent because of draws for water supplies, and its diminished flow into the Dead Sea is responsible for the great contraction of the latter.

Israel's National Water Carrier Project focuses on the Sea of Galilee as a reservoir, while Jordan's East Ghor Project captures water from the Yarouk River for irrigation before it reaches the Jordan River. Similar projects in Syria and Lebanon also harness waters from the headstreams.

The Jordan River is an important feature in the Bible. This reflects its significance as a key source of water, a barrier, and a tribal or national boundary. There are numerous references to the Jordan River in both the Old and New Testaments, especially in relation to Jericho. According to the New Testament, John the Baptist baptized Jesus in the Jordan River, an act of great significance to Christians.

ANTOINETTE MANNION

See also

Dead Sea; Lake Kinneret

References

Allan, John A. *The Middle East Water Question: Hydropolitics and the Global Economy.* London: Tauris, 2002.

Lowi, Miriam R., et al., eds. *Water and Power: The Politics of a Scarce Resource in the Jordan River Basin.* Cambridge: Cambridge University Press, 1993.

Judaism

See Ashkenazic Judaism; Hasidic Judaism; Mizrahic Judaism; Reform Judaism and Zionism; Sephardic Judaism

K

Kadima Party

Israeli political party established on November 22, 2005, by Prime Minister Ariel Sharon. Kadima means "forward" or "in front" in Hebrew, and the name was chosen to demonstrate the party's desire to move ahead and become the most influential political party in Israel. By 2006 Kadima had accomplished exactly that. In the March 28, 2006, elections, the group garnered 29 seats in the Knesset (Israeli parliament), making it the largest party in terms of seats held.

In November 2005 Sharon, of the Likud Party, had grown frustrated with his inability to implement new settlement policies and bring about a peaceful resolution to the Israeli-Palestinian conflict. Indeed, he favored unilateral disengagement, which was to include settling on firm and mutually agreeable borders with the Palestinians and the dismantlement of Israeli settlements located on Palestinian lands. Unable to do this under the current coalition and encountering stiff resistance from those in his own party, he decided to form a new party that would, in his words, be a "centrist" and "inclusive" organization. When he bolted from the Likud Party, he took with him a sizable number of supporters, including cabinet ministers.

Among other things, Kadima's platform includes the eventual phasing in of a presidential-type election process in which voters would vote directly for the prime minister. It also advocates making territorial concessions to the Palestinian Authority (PA) with the caveat that Jerusalem and Jewish enclaves in the West Bank would remain under Israeli control. Finally, it is committed to following the so-called Road Map to Peace and the creation of a demilitarized, autonomous Palestinian nation.

As an allegedly centrist party, Kadima seeks to promote a secular government in Israel and thread a gap between the Labor Party's socialist economic prescriptions and Likud's absolute opposition to the creation of a Palestinian state. The Kadima Party in reality may be more of a center-rightist than truly centrist party, however, because it takes a hard-line conservative approach to issues relating to the political economy. Sharon was also an ardent advocate of the construction of an Israeli–West Bank wall (the so-called Israeli Security Fence), something that leftist politicians almost unanimously decried.

Sharon's move to create the Kadima Party resulted in a great shake-up in the Israeli political establishment. And its center-rightist message served to attract members from all parts of the political spectrum. Indeed, Kadima boasts members from Likud and Labor as well as from the Shinui, Noi, and Yisrael Beytenu parties. The incapacitation of Sharon by a massive stroke in January 2006 cast some uncertainty over the future and efficacy of the party. Nevertheless, Kadima thus far seems to be holding its own, and recent polls suggest that the party has gained some more ground among Israeli voters. Indeed, because Sharon is such a polarizing figure, Kadima may ironically benefit from his unfortunate circumstances.

By the same token, Sharon's replacement, Ehud Olmert, came under fire for his handling of the Israeli-Hezbollah War in the summer of 2006. There is some speculation that the rise of Kadima and the fact that a good number of Labor politicians have chosen to join it bode well for the party and the nation. With public support of the Kadima Party on the rise, there may also be growing support of Palestinian statehood among Israelis. This, in the end, might finally break the back of the Palestinian-Israeli struggle.

PAUL G. PIERPAOLI JR.

See also
Israeli Security Fence; Labor Party; Likud Party; Olmert, Ehud; Settlements, Israeli; Sharon, Ariel; West Bank

Kadima supporters celebrate the party's victory in the 17th Knesset elections on March 28, 2006, at party headquarters in Neve Ilan, Israel. (Amos Ben Gershom/Israeli Government Press Office)

References

Finkelstein, Norman H. *Ariel Sharon.* Minneapolis, MN: First Avenue Editions, 2005.

Hefez, Nir, and Gadi Bloom. *Ariel Sharon: A Life.* New York: Random House, 2006.

Kaffiyeh

A cloth headdress worn chiefly by Arab men. Sometimes, although rarely, the red-checkered kaffiyeh that is so identified with the Palestinian cause today was worn by women for special occasions. Both genders may use it as a neck scarf with casual wear. The kaffiyeh, or *hatta,* is usually fabricated from a square cloth and then folded and wrapped about the head. It may be held at the crown using a fabric or knotted cord called an *aqal.* Wearing it loose without a cord may symbolize religiosity, as with the salafis in Saudi Arabia. Wearing it tied in a particular way can also indicate the local origin of the wearer or Bedouin origin, again depending on the country and locale. In much of the Middle East, where extreme heat as well as blowing sand and dust are problematic, the kaffiyeh helps to protect the wearer's head from the sun and can be used as a makeshift filter over the nose and mouth.

The kaffiyeh may be made of white cloth, but others have a checkered pattern in black or red. In the Arabic countries of the Persian Gulf region, men's kaffiyehs are often white, with no pattern or adornment. In Jordan and among Palestinians, kaffiyehs of red and white patterns are quite common.

During the Arab Revolt of 1936–1939, the grand mufti of Jerusalem began urging all Palestinian Arabs to wear the kaffiyeh, instead of the fez, to protest against British policies and the Jews as well as the effendi, or white-collar class. Some sources attribute this decision to Damascus and not the mufti. In the 1960s, Palestine Liberation Organization (PLO) chairman Yasser Arafat made his white-and-black kaffiyeh his personal trademark and was almost never seen in public without it. The kaffiyeh then became somewhat of a political symbol among European young people and Americans, worn as a neck scarf variously symbolizing antiwar or pro-Palestinian sentiments. When new Palestinian parties have arisen,

A Palestinian man in East Jerusalem wearing the traditional black and white kaffiyeh. (Arkady Mazor/iStockPhoto.com)

they have also worn the kaffiyeh. The black-and-white version as worn by Arafat may signal loyalty to the PLO, and green-and-white kaffiyehs are often worn by followers of the Palestinian Islamic Jihad.

PAUL G. PIERPAOLI JR. AND SHERIFA ZUHUR

See also

Arafat, Yasser; Hamas; Islamic Jihad, Palestinian; Palestine Liberation Organization

References

El-Shamy, Hasan M. *Folk Traditions of the Arab World.* Bloomington: Indiana University Press, 1995.

Stillman, Yedida Kalfon. *Arab Dress: A Short History.* London: Brill, 2003.

Swedenburg, Ted. "The Role of the Palestinian Peasantry in the Great Revolt (1936–1939)." Pp. 129–168 in *The Israel/Palestine Question,* edited by Ilan Pappe. London: Routledge, 1999.

Kafr Qasim Massacre
Event Date: October 29, 1956

Massacre of Arab civilians by members of the Israeli Border Police and Israeli Army in the town of Kafr Qasim on October 29, 1956. The mass killings that claimed 49 lives (including 23 children and an unborn child) coincided with the opening of hostilities in the Suez Crisis, when Israeli forces invaded Egypt's Sinai Peninsula. Kafr Qasim was close to Tel Aviv and part of the Small Triangle area of villages populated by Arabs, located not too far from the Green Line, then the recognized border between Israel and Jordan. Believing that Jordan would enter the war on the side of Egypt, Israeli officials dispatched the Border Police under the command of Israel Defense Forces (IDF) brigadier general Issachar Shadmi to the area of Kafr Qasim. This was to ensure calm in the border area and to prevent Israeli Arabs from joining Jordanian forces. There were seven other Arab villages in this vicinity, and among the seven hamlets were some 40,000 Arab Israelis.

Shadmi's first action was to move back the curfew for Arabs from 10:00 p.m. to 5:00 p.m. He then is alleged to have issued shoot-on-sight orders for any Arab seen violating the new curfew. Major Shmuel Malinki, who headed the border patrol in Kafr Qasim, asked for clarification of the orders. Specifically, he was concerned about workers returning from the fields or jobs outside the village. If they had not known about the curfew, surely they could not be shot for violating it. Although Shadmi denies ever having had the discussion with Malinki, Malinki was given the impression that any persons found outside their homes after 5:00 p.m. were to be shot on sight. Malinki claims that Shadmi was emphatic that there would be no arrests.

At 4:30 p.m. on October 29, 1956, word went out concerning the new 5:00 p.m. curfew. Most villagers returned when they heard the news. Some did not, and it is hard to determine if they had indeed been warned. Slavishly following Shadmi's orders, a platoon commanded by Lieutenant Gabriel Dahan shot 49 Arabs between 5:00 and 6:30 p.m. as they tried to return home. Border patrol soldiers in the other nearby villages did not follow suit, as Shadmi's orders had been overridden by local unit commanders. The victims were hastily buried in a mass grave.

News of the massacre traveled quickly despite the Israeli government's attempts to conceal it. Amid much outrage, Prime Minister David Ben-Gurion lifted the press blackout in early January 1953, and the full details of the massacre were made known. Meanwhile, the government launched an investigation into the events, which was kept far from the prying eyes of the media. After international pressure and frequent street protests in Israel, 11 soldiers and border policemen were charged with murder. In October 1958, 8 were found guilty and sent to prison. Malinki and Dahan were given lengthy prison terms, but Shadmi was exonerated on murder charges and was given a token reprimand for having illegally changed the curfew. When Dahan complained that he had no choice but to follow orders, the judge retorted that none of the other platoons had followed the order, so he clearly had a choice. By 1959 all of the convicted parties were out of jail, the result of several postconviction appeals and commutations by Israeli military leaders and the Israeli president.

The Kafr Qasim case was instructive in that the Israeli court made it clear that while disobeying military orders on a purely subjective basis is prohibited, one has an obligation to disobey orders that are obviously illegal and morally reprehensible. Certainly, the killing of 49 innocent people for no apparent reason met both criteria. In 1957, the Israeli government tried to make amends for the tragedy by offering survivors of the massacre cash and land grants. The Kafr Qasim Massacre also led to significant reforms in the way Israel interacted with Arabs living within its borders.

PAUL G. PIERPAOLI JR.

See also

Ben-Gurion, David; Border War; Sinai Campaign; Suez Crisis

References

Lustick, Ian. *Arabs in the Jewish State: Israel's Control of a National Minority.* Austin: University of Texas Press, 1980.

Morris, Benny. *Righteous Victims: A History of the Zionist-Arab Conflict, 1881–2001.* New York: Vintage Books, 2001.

Robinson, Shira. "Local Struggle, National Struggle: Palestinian Responses to the Kafr Qasim Massacre and Its Aftermath." *International Journal of Middle East Studies* 35 (2003): 393–416.

Kahane, Meir David
Born: August 1, 1932
Died: November 5, 1990

Orthodox American rabbi and founder and leader of the Jewish Defense League (JDL) during 1968–1990. Meir David Kahane, also known as Michael King, David Sinai, and Hayim Yerushalmi, was born in Brooklyn, New York, on August 1, 1932, the son of an immigrant Orthodox Jewish rabbi, Charles Kahane. The friendship of Kahane's parents with Vladimir Jabotinsky, a leading Zionist and founder of the Jewish Legion during World War I who was a frequent guest in the Kahane home, inspired Kahane to join the youth wing of Revisionist Zionism known as Betar in 1946. Still in his midteens, he organized and led protests against British foreign secretary Ernest Bevin, who favored the formation of an Arab independent state rather than an independent State of Israel. Kahane was also active in the Free Soviet (Russian) Jewry movement that protested the Soviet Union's persecution of Zionists and the restraint of Soviet Jewish immigration to Israel (refuseniks).

Kahane earned a BA from Brooklyn College in 1954 and an LLB from New York Law School in 1956. In 1957 he received both an MA in international affairs from New York University and his ordination as an Orthodox rabbi (*smicha*) from Brooklyn's Mirrer Yeshiva. During the late 1950s and 1960s he worked as a teacher and a pulpit rabbi, edited the *Jewish Press,* and helped rally Jewish support for the Vietnam War. He responded to a rising anti-Semitism in America's inner cities in the mid-1960s by founding the JDL, a militant Jewish paramilitary group that had as its goals the protection of Jews and their property. The JDL under Kahane's leadership was soon accused of harassment, stalkings, intimidation, murder, and bombings, and in 1971 he was convicted on a felony charge of manufacturing firebombs. He received a probated sentence providing

Rabbi Meir David Kahane of the Jewish Defense League, shown in 1973. (Israeli Government Press Office)

---

that he had nothing further to do with bombs, dynamite, weapons, or encouraging violence.

Kahane and his family immigrated to Israel in 1971 and settled in Jerusalem. He founded the political party Kach soon after he arrived in the Jewish state, and the party ran its first candidates for the Knesset in 1973. He continued to lead the JDL from Israel. During this period, he wrote letters urging the assassination of Soviet and Arab diplomats. This led to his conviction in the United States in May 1974 for violating the terms of his probation.

Kahane moved to a Manhattan halfway house after eight months of imprisonment and remained there for the remainder of his sentence. He was also convicted in Israel for conspiracy to commit acts of violence in a foreign country. He later returned to Israel and attempted but failed to be elected to the Knesset in 1976 and again in 1980. In 1980 he was administratively detained for six months.

Kahane was finally elected to the Knesset in 1984. But the Labor Party and the Likud Party joined together to have the Central Elections Committee (CEC) ban both Kahane and his growing Kach Party from the 1988 elections because of alleged racism. Kahane appealed to the Israeli High Court, which ruled that the CEC was not authorized to ban Kahane or members of Kach from the elections. The Knesset responded by passing an amendment, known as the Anti-Racist Law of 1988, to section 7a of Basic Law barring candidates for election who incited racism. Kahane appealed the amendment to the Israeli High Court, which declared him unsuitable for election. This decision effectively banned Kahane and Kach from the Knesset and ended his political career in Israel.

On November 5, 1990, Kahane was shot to death at a Zionist Emergency Evacuation Rescue Organization (ZEERO) conference in New York City following a speech urging the mass aliya (immigration) of American Jewry to Israel. The alleged assassin, El-Sayyid Nosair, was acquitted because no one saw him fire the weapon, although he was convicted on gun possession charges. Nosair later received a sentence of life plus 15 years in prison as a member of the conspiracy that bombed New York's World Trade Center in 1993 and planned to bomb other New York landmarks as well as assassinate selected U.S. politicians.

Kahane asserted a distinctive set of beliefs known as Kahanism. He believed in the creation of a theocratic Greater Israel governed by the Jewish law (Halakha) codified in the Old Testament. He openly sought to ban mixed marriages between Jews and non-Jews, non-Jewish missionary efforts, and the sale of pork. He claimed that the idea of a Palestinian people as an ethnic group is a myth fabricated and perpetuated in the latter part of the 20th century (since 1948) by Arab states that did not and do not want to absorb the inhabitants who assumed residence in biblical Israel before the land was rightly regained by present-day Israel. Kahane based these assertions on his contention that no reference to Palestinian Arabs or a Palestinian people exists prior to the 20th century. It was this reasoning that caused him to propose evicting from Israel most Palestinian Arab Muslims, including Arabs with Israeli citizenship. Kahane's passionate belief in the return of Jews to Israel led him to be one of the first to advocate the rescue of Syrian and Ethiopian Jewry.

Two Kahanist factions emerged after Kahane's death. One faction kept the name Kach, and the second group, founded by Kahane's son Benjamin Ze'ev Kahane, was named Kahane chai (literally, "Kahane lives [on]"). Benjamin Kahane and his wife Talya were shot and killed on December 31, 2000, while driving with their children from Jerusalem to their home in the Israeli settlement of Kfar Tapuach.

RICHARD M. EDWARDS

See also

Jabotinsky, Vladimir Yevgenyevich; Jewish Defense League

References

Anderson, Sean Kendall, and Stephen Sloan. *Terrorism: Assassins to Zealots.* Lanham, MD: Scarecrow, 2003.

Anti-Defamation League. *Extremism in the Name of Religion: The Violent Record of the Kahane Movement and Its Offshoots.* New York: Anti-Defamation League, 1995.

Friedman, Robert I. *The False Prophet: Rabbi Meir Kahane, from FBI Informant to Knesset Member.* Westport, CT: Lawrence Hill, 1990.

Karameh, Battle of
Event Date: March 21, 1968

Military engagement involving Palestine Liberation Organization (PLO) fighters and Jordanian forces against Israel Defense Forces (IDF) on March 21, 1968. Karameh is a Jordanian village located near the Israeli border. At the time of the battle, the PLO, headed by Chairman Yasser Arafat, had its headquarters in Jordan. The town of Karameh served as the military and political control center of Fatah, the largest and most powerful of the PLO factions. It too was headed by Arafat.

After the June 1967 Six-Day War, PLO and Fatah forces began stepping up their guerrilla attacks against Israel from Jordanian territory. However, since late February 1968, IDF forces had been hitting back with ever-escalating retaliatory strikes. Determined to stop the attacks and destroy the PLO and Fatah leadership, Israeli officials began planning a major ground offensive into Jordan, focused on Karameh.

On March 21, 1968, IDF armored forces, whose numbers were estimated at some 15,000 men, stormed the makeshift Allenby Bridge (the original one had been destroyed in the Six-Day War) and moved against Palestinian guerrillas in and around Karameh. Although hopelessly outnumbered and outgunned by Israeli forces,

An Israeli soldier placing an explosive charge at an ammunition dump at Karameh, Jordan, March 21, 1968. (Bettmann/Corbis)

the Palestinians stood and fought valiantly. Jordan's King Hussein was highly ambivalent about sending his forces to reinforce the Palestinians. However, Jordanian Army tanks and artillery were finally sent in, and the combined Jordanian-Palestinian force inflicted considerable losses upon the IDF, which hastily retreated by day's end back into Israeli territory.

Several Israeli tanks were destroyed in the fighting, as were a number of other armored vehicles. When the day was done, the IDF had suffered 28 deaths and 90 more wounded, a stunning loss for the Israelis. The Palestinians suffered perhaps 10 times as many casualties, but for them the battle was a key turning point in that it served as a public relations bonanza for Fatah and the PLO. From a military vantage point, the Battle of Karameh was clearly an Israeli victory, but its relatively heavy casualties were a considerable surprise for the IDF.

Palestinian militants hailed the battle as a great victory and used it to garner support from within Jordan and the international community. Indeed, Karameh served to bolster the morale of both the Palestinian guerrilla fighters and the Palestinian Diaspora as a whole. PLO chairman Arafat said of the battle, "What we have done is to make the world . . . realize that the Palestinian is no longer refugee number so and so, but the member of a people who hold the reins of their own destiny." Within two days of the battle, Fatah claimed that 5,000 new recruits had signed up to join the struggle. Many claim that the Battle of Karameh served to enhance considerably the PLO's claims to its own autonomous state. The Soviet Union, for instance, began a major policy shift after 1968 by backing the PLO and Fatah, something that heretofore it had refused to do.

Yet there were also some negative repercussions for the Palestinians. The Battle of Karameh effectively ended Fatah's strategy of launching raids against Israel from border areas. After March 1968, Arafat and his forces were compelled to advance toward the Jordanian interior, making raids against their Israeli adversaries considerably more difficult. Karameh also set the PLO and Fatah on a collision course with King Hussein of Jordan. Emboldened by their success, the Palestinians continued to conduct raids on Israel, albeit from a greater distance. This placed them at odds with the Jordanian government, which did not wish to be drawn into another war with Israel over Palestinian tactics. Ultimately, the Jordanian-PLO clashes would result in Black September (1970), which saw Jordanian and Palestinian troops clash and the expulsion of the PLO from Jordan.

Realizing that it had to win over world opinion as much as enjoy military success, the PLO began to more actively cultivate such opinion after the Battle of Karameh. And within a decade the Palestinians had earned recognition from the United Nations (UN), which now stated that they had an inalienable right to statehood. Still, however, the lesson of Karameh was short-lived in the minds of some Palestinians. Before long, militant and radical Palestinian groups embarked on an orgy of international terrorism that included a spate of high-profile airline hijackings and bombings. This ulti-

mately reversed much of the public relations advantage gained at Karameh and tarnished the reputation of the Palestinian cause.

PAUL G. PIERPAOLI JR.

See also

Arafat, Yasser; Black September; Fatah; Hussein, King of Jordan; Jordan; Palestine Liberation Organization; Six-Day War

References

Dobson, Christopher. *Black September: Its Short, Violent History*. New York: Macmillan, 1974.

Golan, Galia. *The Soviet Union and the Palestine Liberation Organization: An Uneasy Alliance*. New York: Praeger, 1980.

Nassar, Jamal R. *The Palestine Liberation Organization: From Armed Struggle to the Declaration of Independence*. New York: Praeger, 1991.

Reische, Diana. *Arafat and the Palestine Liberation Organization*. New York: Franklin Watts, 1991.

Katsav, Moshe
Born: December 5, 1945

Israeli politician, Likud Party leader, and president of Israel (2000–2007). Born in Yazd, Iran, on December 5, 1945, Moshe Katsav immigrated with his family to Israel in 1951. He spent two years with his family in an immigrant tent encampment inland from the port city of Ashdod. Later the encampment became the development town of Kiryat Malachi ("City of Angels," so-named because it was built with donations from Los Angeles, California).

Katsav graduated from the Ben-Shemen Agricultural School and Beer Tuvia. Following service in the Communications Corps of the Israel Defense Forces (IDF), he studied at the Hebrew University of Jerusalem. There he was chairman of the Likud Party student council. He graduated in 1971 with a bachelor's degree in economics and history.

Katsav's first public office came in 1969 when he was elected mayor of his hometown of Kiryat Malachi. At age 24 he was Israel's youngest-ever mayor. Amid increasing Israeli nationalism during the late 1960s and early 1970s, the Likud Party came to power in 1977 as a result of resentment against the long-dominant Labor Party. Katsav first won election to the Knesset (Israeli parliament) that same year, representing the country's growing population of immigrants from Arab countries who felt discriminated against by the Labor government and were seeking greater services for their neglected towns. As a legislator, Katsav served on the Interior Affairs and Environment Committee as well as the Education and Culture Committee.

Katsav first joined the government in 1981 as a deputy in the Housing and Construction Ministry before becoming labor and social welfare minister in 1984, a post he held until 1988. He also served twice as transportation minister during 1988–1992. From 1992 to 1996 he served as chairperson of Likud in the Knesset before being named tourism minister and deputy prime minister in 1996. As a government minister, he acquired a reputation as a conservative

Israeli president Moshe Katsav, a member of the Likud Party. Elected in July 2000, he was forced to resign in July 2007. (Israeli Government Press Office)

hard-liner regarding Israel's relations with its Arab neighbors. In 1993, however, he was one of the first Likud ministers to accept the Israeli-PLO Agreement that had been negotiated by Prime Minister Yitzhak Rabin and his Labor Party government.

In July 2000 Katsav, an Observant Jew, was able to wrest the support of the right-wing Orthodox faction in the Knesset from former prime minister Shimon Peres, long a symbol of the Israeli establishment, who had been favored to cap off his decorated political career with a turn in the largely ceremonial post as head of state. Katsav won 63 votes in the 120-member Knesset, securing the presidency in a stunning upset. On August 1, 2000, he was sworn into office. He replaced Ezer Weizman, who had resigned the post just two years into his second five-year term amid corruption charges and threats of impeachment.

In July 2006 allegations surfaced that Katsav had sexually harassed and raped women in his offices. In August the police raided his home and seized computers and documents. Two months later, Israeli prosecutors drafted an indictment against Katsav on allegations that he sexually harassed and raped women in his employment.

Allegedly eight women came forward. Israeli prosecutors asked Katsav to resign or temporarily step down until a verdict was reached. He denied the allegations but announced through his lawyers that if indicted he would resign. On June 28, 2007, the Israeli government reached an agreement with Katsav in which he agreed to resign and to plead guilty to lesser charges of indecent acts and harassment and pay compensation to two women who accused him. Katsav resigned on July 1, 2007.

SPENCER C. TUCKER

See also

Likud Party; Peres, Shimon; Weizman, Ezer

References

Blumberg, Arnold. *The History of Israel.* Westport, CT: Greenwood, 1998.

Reich, Bernard. *A Brief History of Israel.* New York: Facts on File, 2005.

Shindler, Colin. *The Land beyond Promise: Likud and the Zionist Dream.* London: Tauris, 2002.

Katyusha Rocket

The Soviet Union's Katyusha multiple rocket launcher was developed by a design team headed by Gregory E. Langemak at the Leningrad Gas Dynamics Laboratory beginning in 1938 and was in direct response to German development in 1936 of the six-barrel Nebelwerfer rocket launcher. The Soviet rocket was at first intended for aircraft use and was approved on June 21, 1941, on the eve of the German invasion of the Soviet Union. It was first employed in combat in a truck-mounted mode by the Red Army against the Germans in July 1941. The rockets were unofficially named for the title of a popular Russian wartime song, with Katyusha a diminutive for Ekaterina (Catherine). The Germans knew the weapon for its distinctive sound as the Stalinorgel (Stalin Organ).

The unguided Katyusha rocket appeared in a variety of sizes. The first was the BM-8 (BM for *boyevaya mashina,* or combat vehicle) 82-mm, but by the end of the war the Soviets were using BM-13 132-mm rockets. The BM-13 was nearly 6 feet in length, weighed 92 pounds, and had a range of about three miles. Such rockets could be armed with high-explosive, incendiary, or chemical warheads. Although not an accurate weapon, the Katyusha could be extremely effective in saturation bombardment when large numbers of launch trucks were deployed side-by-side.

The launch system consisted of a series of parallel rails with a folding frame that was raised in order to bring the rockets into firing position. Katyushas were mounted on a variety of truck beds to fire forward over the cab. Each truck mounted between 14 and 48 launchers. Trucks included the Soviet ZiS-6 and the Lend-Lease–supplied and U.S.-manufactured Studebaker US6 2.5-ton. Katyushas were also mounted on T-40 and T-60 tanks and on aircraft for use against German tanks. They also appeared on ships and riverine vessels in a ground-support role. Artillerists were not fond of the multiple launch system because it took up to 50 minutes to load

A Katyusha rocket launcher, captured by Israeli forces in southern Lebanon during Operation PEACE FOR GALILEE, June 29, 1982. (Baruch Rimon/Israeli Government Press Office)

and fired only 24 rounds, whereas a conventional howitzer could fire four to six times as many rounds in a comparable time period.

Katyushas continued to undergo refinement. During the Cold War, Soviet forces were equipped with the BM-24 240-mm Katyusha, which had a range of about six miles. Each truck mounted 12 rockets. Two racks, one of top of the other, contained 6 rockets each. In 1963 the Soviets introduced the 122-mm BM-21. It was exported to more than 50 countries. Larger 220-mm and 300-mm Katyushas were developed.

The name "Katyusha" has, however, become a generic term applied to all small artillery rockets, even those developed by Israel and based on Katyushas captured during the 1967 Six-Day War. The Israeli Light Artillery Rocket (LAR) has a range of some 27 miles and can be loaded with a variety of different munitions. It was employed in the 1973 Yom Kippur War and in the 1982 invasion of Lebanon.

Katyushas have also been employed by Hezbollah and Islamic Jihad against Israel and by Iraqi insurgents. In March 2006, a BM-21 122-mm Katyusha was fired into Israel from the Gaza Strip, the first time a Katyusha had been sent into Israel from Palestinian-controlled territory. The 9-foot, 2-inch BM-21 has a range of nearly 13 miles and a warhead of nearly 35 pounds. Katyushas are much more a worry to Israel than the short-range, home-made Qassam rocket, fired by Hamas into Israel from the Gaza Strip. The United States developed the Tactical High Energy Laser (THEL) system specifically to defeat the Katyusha during flight.

SPENCER C. TUCKER

See also
Qassam Rocket

References

Bellamy, Chris. *Red God of War: Soviet Artillery and Rocket Forces.* Herdon, VA: Potomac Books, 1986.
O'Malley, T. J. *Artillery: Guns and Rocket Systems.* Mechanicsburg, PA: Stackpole, 1994.

Kaukji, Fawzi al-

See Qawuqji, Fawzi al-

Kennedy, John Fitzgerald
Born: May 29, 1917
Died: November 22, 1963

U.S. congressman (1946–1952), senator (1953–1961), and president of the United States (1961–1963). John F. Kennedy was born in

John F. Kennedy, president of the United States (1961–1963). (Hayward Cirker, ed., *Dictionary of American Portraits*, 1967)

Brookline, Massachusetts, on May 29, 1917, into a large and wealthy Irish Catholic family. He earned his bachelor's degree from Harvard University in 1940 and served four years in the navy during World War II. He was awarded the Navy and Marine Corps Medal and the Purple Heart for action as commander of *PT-109,* which was rammed and sunk by a Japanese destroyer in the South Pacific.

After the war, Kennedy worked for a brief time as a newspaper reporter before entering national politics at the age of 29, winning election as Democratic congressman from Massachusetts in 1946. In Congress, he backed social legislation that benefitted his largely working-class constituents and criticized what he considered to be President Harry S. Truman's weak stand against Communist China. Throughout his career, in fact, Kennedy was known for his vehement anticommunist sentiments.

Kennedy won election to the U.S. Senate in 1952, although he had a relatively undistinguished career in that body. Never a well man, he suffered from several serious health problems, including a back operation in 1955 that nearly killed him. Despite his fragile health and lackluster performance in the Senate, he won reelection in 1958. After losing a close contest for the vice presidential nomination at the 1956 Democratic National Convention, he now set his sights on the presidency. Four years later, he won the Democratic nomination for president on the first ballot.

Candidate Kennedy promised more aggressive defense policies, health care reform, and housing and civil rights programs. He also proposed his New Frontier agenda, designed to revitalize the flagging U.S. economy and to bring young people into government and humanitarian service. Winning election by the narrowest of margins, he became the nation's first Roman Catholic president. Only 42, he was also the youngest man ever to be elected to that office.

As president, Kennedy set out to fulfill his campaign pledges. Once in office, he was forced to respond to the increasingly urgent demands of civil rights advocates, although he did so rather reluctantly and tardily. By establishing both the Alliance for Progress and the Peace Corps, he delivered American idealism and goodwill to aid developing countries.

Despite Kennedy's idealism, no amount of enthusiasm could blunt the growing tensions in the U.S.-Soviet Cold War rivalry. One of Kennedy's first attempts to stanch the perceived communist threat was to authorize a band of U.S.-supported Cuban exiles to invade the communist island in an attempt to overthrow Fidel Castro in April 1961. The Bay of Pigs invasion, which turned into a disaster for the president, had been planned by the Central Intelligence Agency (CIA) under President Dwight D. Eisenhower. Although Kennedy harbored reservations about the operation, he nonetheless approved it. The failure further heightened Cold War tensions with the Soviets and ultimately set the stage for the Cuban Missile Crisis of 1962.

Cold War confrontation was not limited to Cuba. In the spring of 1961 the Soviet Union renewed its campaign to control West Berlin. Kennedy spent two days in Vienna in June 1961 discussing the hot-button issue with Soviet premier Nikita Khrushchev. In the months that followed, the crisis over Berlin was further intensified by the construction of the Berlin Wall, which prevented East Berliners from escaping to the West. Kennedy responded to the provocation by reinforcing U.S. troops in West Germany and increasing the nation's military strength. In the meantime, he had begun deploying what would be some 16,000 U.S. military personnel (so-called advisers) to prop up Ngo Dinh Diem's regime in South Vietnam. In so doing, Kennedy had put the United States on the slippery slope of full-scale military intervention in Vietnam.

With the focus now directed away from Europe, the Soviets began to clandestinely install nuclear missiles in Cuba. On October 14, 1962, U.S. spy planes photographed the construction of missile launching sites in Cuba. The placement of nuclear missiles only 90 miles from U.S. shores threatened to destabilize the Western Hemisphere and undermine the uneasy Cold War nuclear deterrent. Kennedy imposed a naval quarantine on Cuba that was designed to interdict any offensive weapons bound for the island. The world held its collective breath as the two Cold War superpowers appeared perched on the abyss of thermonuclear war. But after 13 harrowing days, the Soviet Union agreed to remove the missiles. In return the United States pledged not to preemptively invade Cuba and to secretly remove its obsolete nuclear missiles from Turkey.

Both Kennedy and Khrushchev had been sobered by the Cuban Missile Crisis, realizing that the world had come as close as it ever had to a full-scale nuclear war. Cold War tensions were diminished when the Soviet Union, Britain, and the United States signed the Limited Nuclear Test-Ban Treaty on August 5, 1963, forbidding atmospheric testing of nuclear weapons. To avoid potential misunderstandings and miscalculations in a future crisis, a hot line was installed that directly linked the Oval Office with the Kremlin.

As a congressman in 1951, Kennedy had visited the Middle East. Even then he voiced his opposition to colonialism in the region, urging that Middle Eastern nations should govern their own affairs. He specifically called upon the French to give independence to Algeria. Despite these early remonstrations, he nevertheless became the first U.S. president to agree to a major weapons sale to the Israelis, which gave the impression that his administration was pro-Israeli and, by definition, anti-Arab.

Such was not the case. While the Kennedy administration did support Israel, it was not because it was anti-Arab. The president approved the sale of U.S.-made Hawk air defense missiles to Israel chiefly because the Soviets, French, and even the British had supplied arms to Arab states. Kennedy hoped to readjust the balance of power in the Middle East by bolstering Israeli defenses. The administration made numerous commitments to and statements of support for Arab nations in the Middle East and exhibited compassion toward the Palestinian refugee issue.

In the end, President Kennedy refused to enter into a binding military alliance with the Israelis and was reluctant to sell large caches of armaments and weapons to them. To do so, he believed, would have placed the United States in a vulnerable position in a future Middle East crisis. He did not want a new world war to erupt in the Middle East, which was not out of the realm of possibility given the tense state of superpower relations. He did, however, accede to regularly scheduled consultations between Israeli and American military officials. The Kennedy administration's Middle East policies were guided more by pragmatism than ideology.

At the same time Kennedy agreed to send antiaircraft missiles to Israel, he was also engaging in quiet diplomacy with Egyptian president Gamal Abdel Nasser. Recognizing Nasser's importance and popularity in the Middle East, Kennedy sought rapprochement with Egypt. Indeed, he and Nasser exchanged personal letters many times. But Nasser's decision to intervene in the civil war in Yemen soured the growing relationship between the two leaders. Kennedy dispatched U.S. fighter aircraft to Saudi Arabia to protect it and to serve as a warning to the Egyptians not to increase their role in Yemen. Although Kennedy did not have to contend with any major crises in the Middle East, he nonetheless engaged in a delicate game of diplomatic chess by which he sought to aid the Israelis, engage the Arabs, limit Soviet influence, and keep the region's rich oil supplies flowing.

Following the nerve-wracking Cuban Missile Crisis, Kennedy looked toward 1963 with considerable enthusiasm. He was also buoyed by his successful efforts to reduce Cold War tensions. In an effort to mediate between warring conservative and liberal Democratic Party factions in Texas, a state that was vital to his reelection,

in November 1963 Kennedy embarked on a whirlwind tour there with his wife and vice president in tow. While riding in an open car in Dallas, Texas, on November 22, 1963, Kennedy was assassinated. In a great national outpouring of grief, the slain president was laid to rest in Arlington National Cemetery on November 25, 1963.

LACIE A. BALLINGER

See also
Arms Sales, International; Johnson, Lyndon Baines; Khrushchev, Nikita; Nasser, Gamal Abdel; Soviet Union and Russia, Middle East Policy; United States, Middle East Policy

References
Bass, Warren. *Support Any Friend: Kennedy's Middle East and the Making of the U.S.-Israel Alliance.* New York: Oxford University Press, 2003.
Dallek, Robert. *An Unfinished Life: John F. Kennedy, 1917–1963.* Boston: Little, Brown, 2003.
Druks, Herbert M. *John F. Kennedy and Israel.* New York: Greenwood, 2006.
Schlesinger, Arthur M. *A Thousand Days: John F. Kennedy in the White House.* New York: Houghton Mifflin, 1965.

Khalaf, Salah
Born: August 31, 1933
Died: January 14, 1991

Palestinian nationalist leader and one of the founders of the Fatah organization. Born Salah Khalaf in Jaffa, Palestine, in 1933, he was known as Abu Iyad within the Fatah organization. He fled with his family to Gaza in 1948 during the Israeli War of Independence when Jewish militias occupied Jaffa. As a student at Cairo University, he met and became a close friend of Yasser Arafat. There in 1952 Khalaf helped Arafat found the Association of Palestinian Students. In 1956 Khalaf was in Kuwait, where he taught high school for a time. One of the founders of Fatah in the 1950s, he was the chief of Palestine Liberation Organization (PLO) security.

Following the Six-Day War in 1967, Khalaf moved to Syria. Fatah now sought to expand its low-intensity guerrilla raids into Israeli territory as part of what became known as the War of Attrition (1967–1970). In this effort, on March 21, 1968, Khalaf and Arafat were nearly killed in a large-scale Israeli reprisal raid on the Palestinian refugee camp near Karameh in Jordan. Subsequently, Khalaf warned Arafat of impending problems between the PLO and Jordan. When fighting broke out between the Jordanian Army and militant Palestinians in September 1970 (Black September), Khalaf was arrested in Jordan, tried, and sentenced to death. This sentence was not carried out because of pressure from Arab governments, especially that of Egypt, and the Arab League on Jordan.

More opposed than ever to Israel, the air force of which had forced the Syrians to forsake military intervention on behalf of the PLO in Jordan, and also to the Jordanian government of King Hussein, Khalaf helped to found the even more militant Black September organization. Under his leadership Black September was responsible for the assassination of Jordanian prime minister Wasfi al-Tall in Cairo on November 28, 1971. It was also responsible for the destruction of an oil storage facility in Italy; the infamous 1972 Munich Olympics Massacre in which Israeli athletes were killed; the seizure of the Israeli embassy in Bangkok, Thailand; and the taking of the U.S. embassy in Khartoum, Sudan, in which three diplomats (two Americans and a Belgian) were slain. In this last action, the terrorists left behind documents that identified Khalaf as having authorized it.

By 1974 Khalaf, reportedly the number three man in the Fatah hierarchy after only Arafat and Khalil al-Wazir, was charged by Arafat with preventing the further splintering of Fatah. One of the organizations that sought to leave Fatah was the Fatah Revolutionary Council, headed by Abu Nidal (Sabri Khalil al-Banna), who had founded Black September. Strong enmity developed between the two former friends, Khalaf and Abu Nidal.

It has been charged, but not proven, that Khalaf ordered the assassination of four members of the Maronite Phalange militia in Lebanon in December 1975 on what became known as Black Sunday. Following the Israeli invasion of Lebanon in 1982, he relocated to Tunis with the rest of the PLO leadership. Khalaf was assassinated in Tunis on January 14, 1991, by an operative of Abu Nidal.

SPENCER C. TUCKER

See also

Abu Nidal; Arafat, Yasser; Attrition, War of; Black September; Black September Organization; Fatah; Hussein, King of Jordan; Munich Olympic Games; Palestine Liberation Organization

References

Musallam, Sami. *The Palestine Liberation Organization: Its Organization and Structure.* London: Amana, 1990.
Nassar, Jamal R. *The Palestine Liberation Organization: From Armed Struggle to the Declaration of Independence.* New York: Praeger, 1991.
Seale, Patrick. *Abu Nidal, a Gun for Hire: The Secret Life of the World's Most Notorious Arab Terrorist.* New York: Random House, 1992.
Tibi, Bassam. *Arab Nationalism: Between Islam and the Nation-State.* New York: St. Martin's, 1997.

Khaled, Leila
Born: April 9, 1944

Palestinian militant and terrorist. Born into a relative well-to-do Palestinian Arab family in Haifa in the British Mandate for Palestine on April 9, 1944, Leila Khaled (Layla Khalid) fled with most of her family to Lebanon in 1948 during the Israeli War of Independence (1948–1949). Her father remained behind to fight on the Arab side. In Lebanon, Khaled reportedly joined at age 15 the organization founded by George Habash that became the Popular Front for the Liberation of Palestine (PFLP). In 1962 she began studies at the American University of Beirut.

Following training in Amman, Jordan, Khaled was one of the first Palestinian women to take part in a terrorist attack, joining in the successful August 29, 1969, hijacking of Trans World Airlines

(TWA) Flight 840 from Rome to Athens. The terrorists diverted the Boeing 707 to Damascus and there blew up the aircraft, although no one was injured. Khaled then underwent several plastic surgeries designed to hide her identity.

On September 6, 1970, Khaled and Nicaraguan Patrick Arguello attempted to hijack El Al Flight 219 from Amsterdam to New York, planned as one of a series of semisimultaneous PFLP aircraft hijackings. The plan was foiled because of the presence on the aircraft of armed security personnel who shot and killed Arguello and overpowered Khaled, who was carrying two hand grenades on her person.

The plane was diverted to Heathrow Airport in London. On October 1, 1970, the British government released Khaled as part of a prisoner exchange. She then went to Syria, where she became a member of the Central Committee of the PFLP and secretary-general of the General Union of Palestinian Women. She returned to the autonomous area of Palestine in April 1996 to attend a meeting scheduled to amend the Palestinian charter. She has said that she no longer believes airline hijackings to be a legitimate means of protest. She chronicled her earlier experiences in her memoir, *My People Shall Live: The Autobiography of a Revolutionary* (1973). Reportedly she currently resides in Amman, Jordan, with her second husband (a physician) and two sons.

SPENCER C. TUCKER

See also

Habash, George; Popular Front for the Liberation of Palestine

References

Hasso, Frances S. "Modernity and Gender in Arab Accounts of the 1948 and 1967 Defeats." *International Journal of Middle East Studies* 32(4) (November 2000): 491–510.
Khalid, Layla. *My People Shall Live: The Autobiography of a Revolutionary.* Edited by George Hajjar. New York: Bantam, 1974.
Nald, Eileen. *Shoot the Women First.* London: Arrow, 1992.
Snow, Peter, and David Phillips. *Leila's Hijack War: The True Story of 25 Days in September, 1970.* London: Pan Books, 1970.

Khalid, Hasan
Born: 1928
Died: October 8, 1994

Palestinian Arab leader and cofounder of Fatah. Born in Haifa in the British Mandate for Palestine in 1928, Hasan Khalid (known popularly as Abu al-Said) finished his secondary education in Palestine before fleeing with his family to Lebanon during the Israeli War of Independence (1948–1949). He then moved to Syria, where he taught school and also attempted to organize Palestinian resistance cells against the Israelis.

One of the cofounders of Fatah in Kuwait in 1965, Khalid was a member of its Central Council. A close adviser to Yasser Arafat, Khalid also headed the Palestinian National Council's Committee for External Affairs and was a member of the Palestine Liberation Organization (PLO) Executive Committee during 1968–1974. He headed the political department of the PLO when Fatah took over its leadership in 1969.

Khalid took special interest in foreign affairs and headed up the PLO External Relations Committee, directing the organization's diplomatic efforts in Europe. Operating from Kuwait, he became a successful businessman there and established close ties with that country's leaders. Considered a moderate, Khalid's strong opposition to the PLO position of aligning with Iraqi dictator Saddam Hussein during the Persian Gulf War led him to remove himself from the PLO leadership and suspend all activities with the organization. Khalid also strongly disagreed with the Declaration of Principles and considered for a time forming his own organization that would demand the return of all 1948 refugees to Palestine.

A strong believer in democracy and the politics of the possible, Khalid was a moderate who opposed violence. He urged a Swiss-type confederacy of cantons with free movement for all its citizenry as a solution to the Arab-Israeli problem. A rotating executive would ensure Arab and Jewish representation. He advocated the 1948 Green Line as the border for Israel, with Jerusalem a separate canton and the capital of the confederacy. Khalid spent his last years living in Morocco and died of cancer in Rabat on October 8, 1994.

SPENCER C. TUCKER

See also

Arafat, Yasser; Fatah; Palestine Liberation Organization; Palestinian National Council

References

Nassar, Jamal R. *The Palestine Liberation Organization: From Armed Struggle to the Declaration of Independence.* New York: Praeger, 1991.

Rubin, Barry. *Revolution until Victory? The Politics and History of the PLO.* Reprint ed. Cambridge: Harvard University Press, 2003.

Khan Yunis

Palestinian town and refugee camp located in the southern Gaza Strip. The town is the site of two massacres, allegedly by Israelis, that took place during and immediately after the 1956 Sinai Campaign. The first took place on November 3, 1956, and the second one is thought to have occurred five weeks later on December 11.

The 1956 campaign began on October 28, 1956, with an Israeli attack of the Sinai. Israel claimed self-defense in its attack, reacting both to terrorist attacks mounted from Egypt and to the threat posed by the conclusion of a joint Egyptian-Syrian-Jordanian military command structure. The British and French governments were in collusion with Israel and soon attacked Egypt, supposedly to secure the Suez Canal. Soviet threats to intervene but primarily heavy pressure from the United States led Britain and then France and Israel to agree to withdraw.

Arab sources contend that following the Israeli withdrawal in early 1957, a mass grave was discovered at Khan Yunis. It contained the bodies of Palestinian Arabs who had been bound and killed by gunfire. There were at least 40 bodies in the grave, but some sources put the figure at more than 500. Each body had a bullet wound to the back of the head as if the person had been shot execution-style at close range. The dead might possibly have been killed by members of the Israeli 11th Infantry and 37th Armored Brigades, which had exercised control over the area. The killings were believed to have been in retaliation for attacks into Israel by the Egyptian-backed fedayeen.

As with many events in the region, the true nature of what happened at Khan Yunis is shrouded in mystery. Arab sources claim that the Israelis lined up women and children and executed them for no reason. Israeli military sources report that those killed and buried there were guerrillas who had engaged Israeli forces occupying the area. As irregular soldiers under international law, these fedayeen fighters were not entitled to the protection of The Hague or Geneva Conventions, and most armies accepted the execution of such combatants if caught.

The United Nations (UN) Special Report of November 1 to mid-December 1956 cites 275 civilians killed by gunfire at Khan Yunis on November 3, 1956. The report does not delve into what may have caused the killings but simply states that the Israeli authorities claimed that the dead were insurgents and fedayeen found in possession of arms. However, Arab refugees interviewed by the UN claimed that the killings were unprovoked and random. A later massacre allegedly took place at Khan Yunis on December 11, 1956, in which an additional 275 people were executed.

ROD VOSBURGH

See also

Al-Mawasi; Fedayeen; Sinai Campaign; Suez Crisis

References

Herzog, Chaim. *The Arab-Israeli Wars: War and Peace in the Middle East from the War of Independence to Lebanon.* Westminster, MD: Random House, 1984.

Turner, Barry. *Suez 1956.* London: Hoddle, Doyle, and Meadows, 2006.

United Nations. *Special Report of the Director of the United Nations Relief and Works Agency for Palestinian Refugees in the Near East: Covering the Period 1 November to Mid-December 1956.* New York: United Nations General Assembly, Eleventh Session, 1957.

Khartoum Resolution
Event Date: September 1, 1967

Joint resolution passed on September 1, 1967, in Khartoum, Sudan, by eight member states of the Arab League: Algeria, Egypt, Jordan, Syria, Lebanon, Iraq, Kuwait, and Sudan. Coming in the immediate wake of the stunning Israeli success of the June 1967 Six-Day War, the heads of eight Arab countries convened in Khartoum during August 29–September 1, 1967, with the express purpose of establishing a united front against Israel. As a result of the recent war, the Israelis had seized the Sinai Peninsula, the West Bank, the Gaza Strip, and the Golan Heights.

The Khartoum Resolution—actually a series of resolutions—not only established official Arab positions vis-à-vis Israel and the Arab-Israeli conflict but also acted as a vehicle by which Arab nations

Egyptian president Gamal Abdel Nasser (*left*) and Tunisian president for life Habib Bourguiba during the Arab League summit of 1967 in Khartoum, Sudan. Participants sought to establish a united front against Israel. (Corbis)

drew closer together and helped them put aside their differences. Perhaps most notable in this regard was Egyptian president Gamal Abdel Nasser's pledge to cease and desist from his ongoing attempts to destabilize the Middle East and topple Arab monarchies in the Persian Gulf. In return, Egypt was promised economic incentives, which were sorely needed at the time. The idea of supranational Arab unity, then, took a backseat to national and regional stability.

The Khartoum Resolution stressed seven principles. First, warfare against Israel would continue. Second, the oil boycott enacted against the West during the Six-Day War was to end. Third, the Yemeni Civil War should be ended. Fourth, economic aid packages for Egypt and Jordan would commence as soon as was practical. Resolutions five through seven, soon to be known as the "three nos," stated unequivocally that there would be no peace with Israel, no recognition of Israel, and no negotiations with the Israelis.

Clearly, the Khartoum Resolution seemed to have closed the door to any potential peace effort between Arabs and Israelis and lent credence to hard-liners in the Israeli government who argued that peace initiatives with the Arabs were pointless. Over the subsequent years, several of the countries involved in the Khartoum Resolution backed away from its positions, beginning with Egypt after the 1973 Yom Kippur War.

PAUL G. PIERPAOLI JR.

See also

Arab League; Nasser, Gamal Abdel; Six-Day War

References

Bickerton, Ian J., and Carla L. Klausner. *A Concise History of the Arab-Israeli Conflict.* 4th ed. Upper Saddle River, NJ: Prentice Hall, 2004.

Parker, Richard B., ed. *The Six-Day War: A Retrospective.* Gainesville: University Press of Florida, 1996.

Schulze, Kirsten E. *The Arab-Israeli Conflict.* New York: Longman, 1999.

Khatib, Anwar al-
Born: 1917
Died: February 7, 1993

Palestinian Arab and governor of Jerusalem. Born in Hebron, Palestine, to a landowning family in 1917 at the end of the long period of Ottoman rule, Anwar al-Khatib became a lawyer and served on the Palestine Higher Islamic Council. He served as mayor of East Jerusalem when it was under Jordanian control in the 1950s. In 1963 he was appointed Jordanian ambassador to Egypt. Later he joined the Arab Socialist Party. In 1991 he was an adviser to the Jordanian-Palestinian delegation to U.S.-sponsored peace talks. Al-Khatib died in East Jerusalem of a heart attack on February 7, 1993.

SPENCER C. TUCKER

See also
Jerusalem

References
Cheshin, Amir S., Bill Hutman, and Avi Melamed. *Separate and Unequal: The Inside Story of Israeli Rule in East Jerusalem.* Cambridge: Harvard University Press, 2001.
Idinopulos, Thomas A. *Jerusalem: A History of the Holiest City.* Chicago: Ivan R. Dee, 1994.
Morris, Benny. *The Road to Jerusalem: Glubb Pasha, Palestine, and the Jews.* London: Tauris, 2002.

Khatib, Rawhi al-

Born: 1914
Died: July 6, 1994

Arab politician and mayor of East Jerusalem. Born in Jerusalem in 1914 into a distinguished Muslim family that included officials at the al-Aqsa Mosque, Rawhi al-Khatib was educated at al-Rashidiyah High School and English College in Jerusalem. He taught for a time at the Islamic Orphanage School in Jerusalem. Beginning in 1931 he worked for the Department of Immigration in Palestine, and during 1943–1945 he was an official in the Department of Labor Affairs in Palestine. During 1946–1948, he headed the Arab Office of Information.

Following the Israeli War of Independence (1948–1949), al-Khatib organized the Arab Hotels Corporation, helping to establish the Arab-owned Zahra Hotel in Jerusalem. In 1951 he became a member of the first municipal council in Jerusalem. In 1956 he helped Palestinians organize the Jerusalem Electric Company. In 1957, King Hussein of Jordan appointed him mayor of East Jerusalem. The Israeli government deported al-Khatib to Jordan in 1968. He was permitted to return in October 1993 after the signing of the Declaration of Principles in Washington that September. Al-Khatib died on July 6, 1994.

SPENCER C. TUCKER

See also
Al-Aqsa Mosque; Hussein, King of Jordan; Jerusalem

References
Cheshin, Amir S., Bill Hutman, and Avi Melamed. *Separate and Unequal: The Inside Story of Israeli Rule in East Jerusalem.* Cambridge: Harvard University Press, 2001.
Morris, Benny. *The Road to Jerusalem: Glubb Pasha, Palestine, and the Jews.* London: Tauris, 2002.

Khomeini, Ruhollah

Born: May 17, 1900
Died: June 3, 1989

Shiite cleric, leader of the 1979 revolution that overthrew Muhammad Reza Shah Pahlavi, and religious and political head of the Islamic Republic of Iran (1979–1989). Born Ruhollah Mostafavi on May 17,

Iranians welcoming Ayatollah Ruhollah Khomeini on his return to Tehran, February 3, 1979. (Bettmann/Corbis)

1900, in Khomeyn (Khumayn), some 180 miles south of the capital of Tehran, he was the son and grandson of Shiite religious scholars and leaders (*fuqaha*). Mostafavi was taught the basics of Shia Islam and the Koran by his elder brother Ayatollah Pasandideh following the death of his mother. His father had been murdered when he was six months old. Mostafavi, who studied Islamic law at Arak and moved with his teacher in the 1920s to Qum, became a recognized Sharia (Islamic laws) scholar at the Faziye Seminary in Qum. He drew thousands of students to his viewpoint that blended the law, logic, mysticism, and philosophy. In the 1950s he was proclaimed an ayatollah (gift of God). At that time he changed his surname to that of his birthplace. By the early 1960s, Khomeini had become one of the supreme religious leaders, or grand ayatollahs, of Shia Islam.

Khomeini detested liberalizing foreign influences and governments that he believed were leading Iran away from true Islam. The primary Iranian force in this Westernizing and modernizing trend was the shah and his family. In 1921 the Russians had helped Pahlavi overthrow Iran's first constitutional government, and his son, Mohammad Reza Shah Pahlavi, rose to power in 1941 with the aid of Great Britain, France, and the United States. In 1953, aided by the U.S. Central Intelligence Agency (CIA), the shah led a coup that deposed Prime Minister Mohammad Mosaddeq. This event solidified the shah's hold on power. Khomeini, who publicly denounced the regime, was arrested and imprisoned for eight months. On his release, he was exiled from Iran to Turkey in November 1964 after challenging the emancipation of women and the shah's reduction of religious estates through his land reforms.

Seemingly a permanent exile, Khomeini eventually settled in the Shia holy city of Najaf in northern Iraq. It was there that he developed the doctrine that an Islamic state should be ruled by the clergy (*vilayet-e faqih,* or rule of the jurist). When Iraqi president Saddam Hussein forced Khomeini from Najaf, he and his followers moved to France in 1978 and from there urged the ouster of the shah and his U.S. allies. Khomeini also published numerous statements and books, among them *Islamic Government* (*Hukumat-e Islami*), a series of lectures delivered at al-Najaf in 1970. This laid out his principal beliefs in an Islamic state in which the leader should be a *faqih* (Islamic jurist and member of the clergy). With the Iranian revolution and the flight of the shah on January 16, 1979, Khomeini returned to the country. He arrived from France on February 1, acknowledged by millions of Iranians as the leader of the revolution.

On November 4, 1979, Khomeini's followers, most of them young, zealous Iranian students, stormed the U.S. embassy in Tehran and took 70 Americans hostage in blatant defiance of international law. Over the next 14 months, the U.S. government attempted without success to secure the release of the hostages through sanctions against Iran and the freezing of Iranian assets. The hostage takers were seemingly encouraged by Khomeini, who refused to intervene and bring an end to the standoff. President Jimmy Carter's failure to resolve the Iranian Hostage Crisis brought with it great frustration and embarrassment. A disastrous aborted hostage rescue attempt in April 1979 only added to American frustration over the situation. The hostage crisis was a major cause of Ronald Reagan's victory over Carter in the U.S. presidential election of November 1980. Only minutes after Reagan took the oath of office on January 20, 1981, the hostages were released.

In December 1980 Khomeini secured his goal of a new constitution in which Iran was officially declared an Islamic republic. Within several years hundreds of Khomeini's opponents had been executed. Although he believed that the clerics should govern the Islamic state, he asserted that the primary role of the clergy still resided in the study of the Koran, the propagation of Islam, and the proper application of Sharia to everyday life. To this end, women were forced to wear the *hejab* in addition to the traditional *chador,* punishments for the breaking of Sharia were prescribed by Islamic law, and alcohol along with Western music, attire, and culture were all banned. Khomeini's Iran remained rather insular on the international stage and became a vociferous opponent of Israel. Although Iran was not itself an active participant in fighting against Israel, it separated itself from the former shah's pro-Israeli positions and sent aid and training to organizations that fought Israel, including Hezbollah in Lebanon.

As Khomeini's revolution progressed, Iraq's Saddam Hussein attempted to take advantage of the turmoil of the revolution and the weakened state of the Iranian military by invading Iran on September 22, 1980. This sparked the devastating Iran-Iraq War, which lasted for eight long years (1980–1988) before both sides accepted a truce brokered by the United Nations (UN). Just as Khomeini had been headstrong about not bringing a quick end to the 1979–1981 hostage crisis, so too was he unwilling to end the war expeditiously. Only after Iran had suffered devastating human losses (some sources estimate more than a million dead) did Khomeini realize that nothing further could be gained by prolonging the war, which featured chemical and biological attacks by the Iraqis. As Khomeini's health declined and a clerical power struggle ensued, Khomeini attempted to preserve the revolution and the Islamic state by strengthening the authority of the presidency, the parliament, and other institutions. In so doing, he further entrenched the power of religious conservatives, who more often than not pursued counterproductive foreign policies that further isolated their country. The long war had also decimated the Iranian economy. Khomeini died on June 3, 1989, in Tehran. In the end, his legacy was a weakened economy, enmity with the United States, and a strong Islamic state as well as heightened state-sponsored terrorism.

RICHARD EDWARDS

See also

Carter, James Earl, Jr.; Hezbollah; Hussein, Saddam; Iran; Iran-Iraq War; Reza Pahlavi, Mohammad, Shah of Iran; Terrorism

References

Bill, James A. *The Shah, the Ayatollah, and the United States.* New York: Foreign Policy Association, 1988.

Heikal, Mohamed. *Iran, the Untold Story: An Insider's Account, from the Rise of the Shah to the Reign of the Ayatollah.* New York: Pantheon, 1982.

Hoveyda, Fereydoun. *The Shah and the Ayatollah: Iranian Mythology and Islamic Revolution.* Westport, CT: Praeger, 2003.

Khomeini, Imam. *Islam and Revolution.* Translated by Hamid Algar. Berkeley, CA: Mizan, 1981.

Marshcall, Christin. *Iran's Persian Gulf Policy: From Khomeni to Khatami.* Oxford: Routledge/Curzon, 2003.

Moin, Baquer. *Khomeini: Life of the Ayatollah.* New York: St. Martin's, 2000.

Khrushchev, Nikita

Born: April 17, 1894
Died: September 11, 1971

Leader of the Soviet Union (1953–1964). Nikita Sergeevich Khrushchev was born on April 17, 1894, to a peasant family in Kalinovka (Ukraine). At age 15 he began work as a pipe fitter, which exempted him from World War I military service.

In 1918 Khrushchev joined the Russian Communist Party, and the next year, as a political commissar, he accompanied Red Army forces fighting the Poles and Lithuanians. In 1922, following the end of the Russian Civil War, he returned to school and completed his education. In 1925 he became Communist Party secretary of

Nikita Khrushchev, leader of the Soviet Union (1953–1964). (Library of Congress)

the Petrovosko-Mariinsk District. Recognizing the importance of Russian Communist Party secretary Joseph Stalin, Khrushchev nurtured a friendship with Stalin associate and party secretary in Ukraine Lars Kaganovich, who helped him secure a post in the Moscow city party apparatus in 1931.

By 1935 Khrushchev was secretary-general of the Moscow branch of the Communist Party of the Soviet Union (CPSU), in effect mayor of the capital city. In 1938 he became a candidate (non-voting member of the Politburo), and in 1939 he was a full member. Khrushchev was one of few senior party officials to survive Stalin's Great Purges. After the German invasion of the Soviet Union in June 1941, Khrushchev was made a lieutenant general and was placed in charge of organizing resistance in Ukraine and relocating industry eastward.

Khrushchev took charge of Ukraine following its liberation by the Red Army. With the region suffering major food shortages in 1946, he focused on increasing agricultural production. Stalin wanted emphasis placed on heavy industry and demoted Khrushchev.

Back in favor by 1949, Khrushchev again headed the CPSU machinery in Moscow. As a consequence of the new party structure, which he helped organize in 1952, he became one of the powerful committee secretaries.

Following the death of Stalin in March 1953 there was no clear successor, and a collective leadership emerged. In what seemed an unlikely appointment at the time, Khrushchev became first secretary or head of the CPSU. During the Twentieth Party Congress of the CPSU in February 1956, he denounced the cult of personality associated with Stalin and condemned the many excesses of his regime, beginning the process known as de-Stalinization. Hungarians and Poles sought to use this thaw to change the systems within their countries. A revolution in Hungary in 1956 was crushed when Khrushchev sent Red Army tanks into Budapest.

Having survived an internal power struggle in June 1957, Khrushchev purged his opponents (who were not executed, as would have been the case under Stalin). Khrushchev then held unchallenged authority. He sought to carry out limited reform of the Soviet economy and agriculture, education, and weapons development programs. He also strongly backed the Soviet space effort, which achieved a number of impressive firsts. Khrushchev's pledge to improve overall Soviet economic performance and especially agricultural output proved to be unsustainable, however.

The last days of Stalin's reign had seen a marked rise in anti-Semitism in the Soviet Union, and during the Khrushchev era Moscow increasingly favored the Arab side against Israel. In the course of a speech in December 1955 Khrushchev sharply condemned the Jewish state, claiming that "from the first days of its existence" Israel had taken a "hostile, threatening position" toward its Arab neighbors. The shift in Soviet tactics made it hard for Israel to pursue a policy of neutrality, and Israel was inevitably drawn into a closer relationship with the United States.

In 1955 Egyptian president Gamal Abdel Nasser sought modern weapons from the West. When British and U.S. leaders rejected his request, he turned to the Soviet bloc and brokered an arms deal with Czechoslovakia, with full Kremlin backing. Indeed, despite frequent professions of neutralism and nonalignment, Nasser steadily improved Egyptian ties with the Soviet Union.

Determined to punish Egypt, the United States, followed by Britain, withdrew funding for the construction of the Aswan High Dam, Nasser's domestic agenda centerpiece. Nasser retaliated against the West by nationalizing the Suez Canal.

On October 29, 1956, during the resultant Suez Crisis, Israeli troops invaded the Sinai Peninsula and moved toward the canal. When British and French troops landed in Egypt to allegedly protect the canal but actually in collusion with Israel, both the Soviet Union and the United States voiced strong objection. Indeed, Khrushchev threatened to intervene militarily on Egypt's behalf, no doubt a hollow threat since the Soviet Union was at the time involved in crushing the Hungarian Revolution. Nonetheless, the Soviet Union and the United States stood together in condemning France, Britain, and Israel and calling on them to withdraw from Egyptian territory.

Following the crisis, Nasser not only received from the Soviet Union loans for construction of the Aswan Dam but also technical assistance, new weapons, and Soviet military advisers. Khrushchev visited Cairo and attended the ceremony for the first stage of the dam in May 1964. He also sought to use the enhanced Soviet prestige in the region following the Suez Crisis to improve Soviet ties with other Arab states.

Failures domestically, especially in agricultural production and in external affairs such as the Berlin Crises, the Cuban Missile Crisis, and the deterioration of bilateral relations with the People's Republic of China (PRC) led to Khrushchev's ouster from power in October 1964. He was subsequently placed under house arrest. Khrushchev wrote his memoirs, subsequently published in the West, and died in Moscow on September 11, 1971.

THOMAS J. WEILER AND SPENCER C. TUCKER

See also

Brezhnev, Leonid Ilyich; Egypt; Nasser, Gamal Abdel; Soviet Union and Russia, Middle East Policy; Suez Crisis

References

Donaldson, Robert H., and Joseph L. Nogee. *The Foreign Policy of Russia: Changing Systems, Enduring Interests.* Armonk, NY: M. E. Sharpe, 1998.

Khrushchev, Nikita S. *Khrushchev Remembers.* Edited and translated by Strobe Talbott. Boston: Little, Brown, 1970.

Taubman, William. *Khrushchev: The Man and His Era.* London: Free Press, 2004.

Ulam, Adam B. *Expansion and Coexistence: Soviet Foreign Policy, 1917–1973.* New York: Praeger, 1974.

Kibbutz Movement

Uniquely Israeli farming, industrial, or tourist community. The kibbutz ("communal settlement") movement began in 1909 as a means of settling Jews in Palestine. The land for the kibbutzim was purchased by the Jewish National Fund with coins deposited by Jews worldwide into special Blue Boxes. Kibbutzim combined Zionism and communism at a time when the harsh environment and dangers of Palestine made individual farming there impractical. Joseph Baratz founded the first kibbutz at the southern end of the Sea of Galilee. It was named Degania (Deganya) after the cereal grown by the collective.

Zionist pioneers (chalutzim) came to Ottoman Palestine not simply to make a living but also with the aim of reclaiming the ancient Jewish homeland. The kibbutzniks were generally inexperienced in farming. They also faced harsh conditions caused by a scarcity of water, a shortage of funds, a desolate and neglected environment, poor sanitation, and diseases such as malaria, typhus, and cholera.

Although many thought that the local Arab peasant population would be pleased with the economic benefits and agricultural innovations of these settlements, many Arabs lost their farming and grazing land to these kibbutzim. Moreover, the settlement policy was generally not to employ the Arabs as paid labor. Arabs therefore opposed the new settlements. As this enmity grew rather than dissipated and sometimes turned violent, the Jewish community in Palestine (Yishuv) began to prepare for self-defense. The kibbutzim played a foundational role in the founding of Haganah, the Jew-

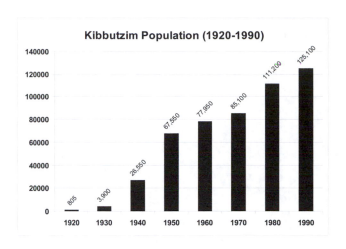

Kibbutzim Population (1920-1990)

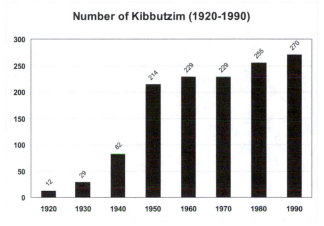

Number of Kibbutzim (1920-1990)

ish self-defense force that was the forerunner of the Israel Defense Forces (IDF).

In 1909 Hashomer (Guild of Watchman), a small group of Jewish immigrants, began guarding the Jewish settlements and kibbutzim for an annual fee. Hashomer was the predecessor of Haganah, which was organized after the Arab riots of 1920 and 1921. During 1920 to 1929 Haganah was composed of localized and poorly armed units composed primarily of Jewish farmers who took turns guarding one another's farms and kibbutzim. As Haganah grew, kibbutzim throughout Palestine served as defense and training centers. The establishment of the British mandatory government after the demise of the Ottoman Empire in World War I provided sufficient stability and security for the kibbutzim and the Yishuv to flourish.

As time passed, however, the diversity of the kibbutz movement became evident as nuanced differences arose. Some kibbutzim were religious, and others were not; some wanted to be small, and others wanted to be large; some wanted a binational state, and others sought a Jewish state carved from Palestine; some were simple farming communities, while others were strategically located military positions; and some wanted to combine all of the differences.

In 1927 Kibbutz Artzi formed as a countrywide consortium of kibbutzim, all of which had affiliations with European Zionist youth groups. The kibbutzniks of Kibbutz Artzi were committed to equality of the sexes, a left-wing socialist ideology, a binational state

Aerial view of Kibbutz Degania A and B, located in the Jordan Valley on the Sea of Galilee, December 30, 1938. (Zoltan Kluger/Israeli Government Press Office)

(Jewish-Palestinian) with free Jewish immigration, and secular, atheistic communities striving to be "monasteries without God." In 1936 Kibbutz Artzi organized its own political party, the Socialist League of Palestine, generally known as Hashomer Hatzair.

In 1928 the smaller kibbutzim formed Chever Hakvutzot, the Association of Kvutzot. These kibbutzim, such as Kibbutz Degania, wanted to limit their individual size to less than 200 members in order to facilitate an intimate collective life. United Kibbutz, or Kibbutz Hameuhad, emphasized growth, diversity, and expansion, with one member kibbutz, Givat Brenner, growing to more than 1,500 members. The more middle-of-the-road Kibbutz Hameuhad disparaged Artzi for its socialist elitism and Kvutzot for a lack of vision and growth.

The kibbutzim of Kibbutz Dati were overtly religious though collectivist. Their first kibbutz (Ein Tzurim) was located near Hebron (1946) but later moved to the Negev. Although most of the mainstream kibbutzim were not overtly religious, some characteristics, celebration days, and ceremonies of Judaism were incorporated into the life of some of the kibbutzim. Even in these more secular kibbutzim, Saturday labor was avoided when possible, Friday evening Shabbat was often celebrated, collective bar mitzvahs were organized, and Yom Kippur was remembered, although in some kibbutzim less as the religious Day of Atonement and more as a day of open discussion concerning the future of kibbutzim and Israel.

All kibbutzim played defense roles in the creation of Israel, but some were founded for the specific, strategic purpose of defining, expanding, and protecting the borders of the Jewish community in Palestine before and after the United Nations (UN) partition plan. Kibbutzim were established in the 1930s in anticipation of partition rather than the formation of a binational government. These kibbutzim were intended to expand the land area to be incorporated into Israel by establishing a Jewish presence well before the boundaries of partition were to be determined. Additionally, some kibbutzim, called Tower and Stockade kibbutzim, were established overnight in the years prior to partition for the specific purpose of enhancing land claims antecedent to partition. A dozen of these kibbutzim, for example, were erected overnight in the northern Negev in 1946, a project supported by David Ben-Gurion. This trend of setting up strategic kibbutzim for establishing, stabilizing, and enhancing the defensive perimeters continued through the 1960s under the IDF's Nahal group.

The role of the kibbutzim in the defense of Israel is illustrated by the causality figures from the 1967 Six-Day War. Israel lost 800 soldiers in the fighting. Even though kibbutzniks numbered less than 4 percent of the total Israeli population at the time, 200 of these deaths, or 25 percent of the total, were kibbutzniks.

In the kibbutzim, wealth and property are jointly owned by the members. They share equally and cooperatively in production and education as well as in the consumption of the fruits of their labors and the benefits of the community. Once the basic needs for food, clothing, shelter, health care, and future benefits have been met, the collective's profits are reinvested in the kibbutz.

Each kibbutz is governed by its members acting in a general assembly that formulates policy, elects officers, authorizes the budget, and approves new members but delegates the daily affairs to elected committees that oversee housing, finance, education, production planning, health, culture, and anything else deemed necessary by the assembly. The chairpersons of a select number of these committees along with the secretary (chief executive) constitute the executive committee that is the basic administrative structure of the kibbutz. The secretary, treasurer, and work coordinator are generally full-time positions.

Although most members work within the kibbutz, those who work outside its framework contribute their incomes to the kibbutz. Women have been equal participants in the labor and the governance from the beginning of the kibbutz movement. Older members contribute according to their ability to work. Although communal children's houses were common in the early years of the kibbutz movement, most children remain with their parents until high school, when they generally attend a regional high school that serves several kibbutzim. Although the family unit is growing in importance within the kibbutz community, special children's work assignments are emphasized. Approximately 40 percent of all kibbutz children return to settle on the kibbutz.

In the early 2000s there were approximately 270 kibbutzim throughout Israel with a total membership of approximately 130,000 people, or roughly 2.5 percent of Israel's total population, although their representation in the Knesset continues to be disproportionately higher than their actual population should warrant. The kibbutzim vary in size from 40 to 1,500 people, averaging 300–400 adults with an average total population of 500–600.

There is a good deal of debate about the kibbutzim because of the overall financial strains on Israel and the difficulties of sustaining profits in agriculture, even in a subsidized system with a high inflation. Some collectives have branched out to provide services, restaurants, and shops, with competing businesses complaining that they have no comparable subsidy.

RICHARD EDWARDS

See also

Balfour Declaration; Haganah; Irgun Tsvai Leumi; Israel Defense Forces; Zionism

References

Dreitzel, Hans Peter. *Family, Marriage, and the Struggle of the Sexes.* New York: Macmillan, 1972.

Gavron, Daniel. *The Kibbutz.* Lanham, MD: Rowman and Littlefield, 2000.

Leviatan, Uriel, Hugh Oliver, and Jack Quarter, eds. *Crisis in the Israeli Kibbutz.* Haverhill, MA: Praeger, 1998.

Near, Henry. *The Kibbutz Movement: A History.* 2 vols. London: Vallentine Mitchell, 1997.

Porat, Reuven, ed. *The History of the Kibbutz: Communal Education, 1904–1929.* Norwood, PA: Norwood, 1985.

Kinneret, Lake

See Lake Kinneret

Kisch, Frederick Hermann

Born: 1888
Died: April 7, 1943

British Army officer and Zionist. Born in Darjeeling, India, in 1888, Frederick Hermann Kisch was the son of a senior British official in the Indian civil service. His father instilled in young Frederick both Jewish tradition and history. Kisch entered the British Army in 1909 as an officer in the engineers. During World War I he fought on both the western front in France and in Mesopotamia.

In 1917 while he was serving on the General Staff, Kisch was introduced to British Zionist leader Chaim Weizmann. The meeting was a fateful one, for in 1922 when Kisch was attached to the British embassy in Paris, Weizmann approached him about joining the World Zionist Organization (WZO) Executive. Weizmann believed that Kisch would prove an effective negotiator with British government officials. Accepting Weizmann's invitation, Kisch arrived in Palestine in 1923 and became director of the Political Department of the Executive. From 1929 to 1931 he was the head of the Jewish Agency's Palestine Executive. In this position he worked to improve relations between the Jews and Arabs of Palestine and between Jewish leaders and British Mandate officials. In order to be more effective in his post, he learned both Hebrew and Arabic.

Kisch believed that in order for Zionism to be successful in Palestine, cooperation between the Jews and Arabs was essential. Toward that end, he proposed the creation of both mixed Arab-Jewish schools and a moderate daily Arab newspaper to counteract the extremists. In his opinion, and contrary to the view held by the British administration, the best way to achieve cooperation between the two groups was by means of direct talks between high-level Jewish and Arab officials. Kisch also called on the British to support Arab moderates rather than radicals such as Haj Amin al-Husseini, the mufti of Jerusalem. Kisch then enjoyed a friendly relationship with such moderate Arab leaders as King Hussein of the Hejaz and his son Abdullah. Kisch argued that the moderates had assured him that they were not opposed to Zionist activities in Palestine.

In 1931 when Weizmann failed to win reelection to the presidency of the WZO Executive, Kisch left Zionist public service. He decided to remain in Palestine, however. Settling in Haifa, he went into private business and became a strong supporter of Jewish cultural activities. He published his memoirs, *Palestine Diary,* in 1938.

When World War II began, Kisch rejoined the British Army as a lieutenant colonel of engineers. At the time of his death in Tunisia from a land mine on April 7, 1943, he was a brigadier and chief engineer of the British Eighth Army.

SPENCER C. TUCKER

See also

Abdullah I, King of Jordan; Hussein ibn Ali, Sharif of Mecca; Husseini, Haj Amin al-; Jewish Agency for Israel; Weizmann, Chaim; World Zionist Organization Executive

References

Shepherd, Naomi. *Ploughing Sand: British Rule in Palestine, 1917–1948.* New Brunswick, NJ: Rutgers University Press, 1999.

Sherman, A. J. *Mandate Days: British Lives in Palestine: 1918–1948.* Baltimore: John Hopkins University Press, 2001.

Kishinev Pogrom
Start Date: April 6, 1903
End Date: April 9, 1903

The Kishinev Pogrom of April 6–9, 1903, was an anti-Jewish riot that occurred in the city of Kishinev in Bessarabia, Russia. That city is now the capital of the Republic of Moldavia. The pogrom was fed by the anti-Jewish attitude of the Russian authorities, but the immediate cause of the rioting was the murder on February 6 of a Christian Russian boy, Michael Ribalenko, in the nearby town of Dubossary. Although it was soon established that the murderer of the boy was not a Jew but indeed a family member, the Russian-language, government-subsidized anti-Semitic newspaper *Bessarabetz* (Bessarabia) intimated that he had been killed by Jews. Another newspaper, *Svet* (Light), claimed that the boy had been slain by Jews so that his blood could be used in preparation of Passover unleavened bread (matzot). In early April a rumor spread that a Christian servant girl had also been murdered by Jews. Handbills then appeared announcing that the Russian authorities had given approval to inflict "bloody punishment" on the Jews during the three days of the Orthodox Christian Easter.

Indeed, a violent anti-Jewish riot in Kishinev began on schedule on Easter Day, April 6. When a group of Jews took up arms and tried to defend themselves, the police disarmed them. The rioting extended over three days. When the Jews appealed to the Russian governor, they were told that he could do nothing without direct instructions from St. Petersburg. Not until April 9 did such a telegram arrive from Minister of the Interior Vyacheslav von Plevhe, and troops were then sent into the streets to restore order. On the city's outskirts, however, the rioting continued until late in the evening.

In the course of the riots, 47 Jews were killed and another 92 severely injured. Another 500 Jews received minor injuries. In addition, more than 700 Jewish homes and businesses were looted, damaged, or destroyed. Synagogues were also desecrated.

The Kishinev Pogrom caused widespread indignation abroad, especially in Europe and the United States. The *New York Times* reported that the Jews had been "slaughtered like sheep." It also erroneously put the number of dead at 120 and injured at 500. Jewish organizations overseas rushed to send aid.

The Kishinev Pogrom had a pronounced impact on Russian Jewry, sharply increasing the number seeking to immigrate to Palestine. Among Jewish youths in Russia there were calls for militancy and the formation of self-defense organizations. The pogrom also had an effect on the Zionist movement. Zionist leader Theodor Herzl entered into negotiations with the Russian government, which was interested in facilitating Jewish emigration. Herzl called on the Russians to help in pressing the Ottoman Empire for a charter that would authorize the settlement of Jews in Palestine. Herzl also intensified his efforts to secure another location than Palestine as an immediate refuge for the Jews driven from their homes. The British government offered to the World Zionist Organization (WZO) territory in East Africa for this purpose. This so-called East Africa Scheme elicited much interest among the Zionist movement.

SPENCER C. TUCKER

See also

East Africa Scheme; Herzl, Theodor; Zionism

References

Adler, Cyrus, ed. *The Voice of America on Kishineff.* Philadelphia: Jewish Publication Society of America, 1904.

Doron, D. *Ghetto Kishinev: The Final Pogrom.* Jerusalem: Kiriat Sefer, 1977.

Judge, Edward H. *Easter in Kishinev: Anatomy of a Pogrom.* New York: New York University Press, 1995.

Kissinger, Henry Alfred
Born: May 27, 1923

U.S. national security adviser (1969–1975) and secretary of state (1973–1977) who, together with President Richard Milhous Nixon, devised and implemented a major reorientation of U.S. foreign policy. Of German Jewish extraction, Henry Kissinger was born on May 27, 1923, in Fürth, Germany. He left Adolf Hitler's Germany for New York in 1938 and became an American citizen five years later. After serving in the U.S. Army, Kissinger became a professor of government at Harvard University, publishing his doctoral dissertation, *A World Restored* (1955). It focused particularly on Austria's Prince Klemens Wenzel von Metternich, whom Kissinger admired and in some ways modeled himself upon. Kissinger also published a study of U.S. atomic policy for the prestigious Council on Foreign Relations.

Although his intellectual capabilities were highly respected, Kissinger's real ambitions lay in the practice, not the study, of international relations. He used his Harvard position to meet major political figures and served as an adviser to leading Republicans, including Gov. Nelson A. Rockefeller of New York and former vice

Henry Alfred Kissinger, U.S. national security adviser (1969–1975) and secretary of state (1973–1977). (Library of Congress)

president Nixon. Kissinger's efforts won him only minor assignments under President John F. Kennedy, but when Nixon became president he appointed Kissinger his national security adviser. Kissinger greatly overshadowed William P. Rogers, nominal secretary of state until August 1973 when Kissinger succeeded him, taking virtual control of U.S. foreign policy.

Kissinger's undoubted abilities included an immense capacity for hard work, a talent for grand designs and broad conceptualization, and the imagination to reformulate the international system to accommodate the relative weakness of the United States, de-emphasizing ideology in favor of a balance of power and the pursuit of closer relations with communist China and détente with the Soviet Union. This resulted in the 1972 Strategic Arms Limitation Treaty (SALT I) and the Anti-Ballistic Missile (ABM) Treaty, imposing limits on Soviet and American nuclear arsenals and delivery systems; the 1975 Helsinki Accords, normalizing relations between Eastern and Western Europe; the creation of the permanent Conference on Security and Cooperation in Europe (CSCE); and a rapprochement between communist China and the United States that Kissinger pioneered with a secret 1971 personal visit to Beijing.

Initially Nixon and Kissinger left Secretary of State William Rogers to handle Middle Eastern policy while they themselves concentrated on big-power diplomacy. Seeking to resolve outstanding issues from the 1967 Six-Day War, in 1969 Rogers and Joseph Sisco, assistant secretary of state for Near Eastern and South Asian affairs, developed a peace plan envisaging Israeli withdrawal from occupied territories in return for evenhanded Soviet and U.S. policies toward both Arabs and Israel in the Middle East and a brokered peace settlement guaranteed by both big powers. Kissinger privately informed Soviet ambassador Anatoly Dobrynin that the White House had no interest in this scheme, effectively sabotaging the Rogers Plan that the Soviet Union in any case rejected in October 1969.

U.S. Middle Eastern policy thereafter remained largely static until the October 1973 Yom Kippur War, when Egypt and Syria launched a surprise attack on Israel intended to regain the territories they had lost in the previous war. When the Israelis rallied and then counterattacked, threatening to wipe out the Egyptian Third Army, President Anwar Sadat of Egypt, who had tilted toward the United States the previous year in the hope that this would enable Egypt to regain the Sinai, appealed to the Soviet Union for aid. To prevent Soviet intervention, Nixon ordered military forces to a Def-Con 3 military alert, two levels below outright war, while successfully pressuring the Israelis not to destroy the Egyptian Third Army in return for shipments of U.S. arms to resupply Israel's depleted arsenals. Oil-producing Arab states reacted by imposing an oil embargo on the United States and other Western powers that had supported Israel while greatly enhancing the international clout of the Organization of Petroleum Exporting Countries (OPEC) by raising oil prices fourfold.

The Yom Kippur War and its aftermath diverted Kissinger from his previous preoccupation with triangular U.S.-Soviet-Chinese relations. The oil embargo marked the beginning of a decade of economic difficulties for all the Western powers. European powers quickly responded by adopting more pro-Arab policies, a shift that Nixon and Kissinger strongly resented and characterized as craven. Kissinger embarked on several months of high-profile shuttle diplomacy with Israel, Syria, and Egypt, showing himself an excellent negotiator and eventually brokering an armistice. Under both Nixon and President Gerald Ford, for the next two years Kissinger continued to mediate among the contending Middle Eastern powers, eventually negotiating the Sinai Accords of September 1975 whereby Israel returned part of the Sinai to Egypt, a settlement that probably contributed to the more extensive Camp David Accords that President Jimmy Carter negotiated in 1978.

Kissinger's weaknesses included a penchant for secrecy and intrigue, enormous vanity, and overweening personal ambition, all of which sometimes impelled him to decidedly unscrupulous behavior; an overriding concern to maintain international stability that often led him to endorse brutal right- or left-wing regimes; and a focus upon realism in foreign policy to the near-exclusion of all considerations of morality. The latter was apparent in his involvement in the secret bombing of Cambodia in the early 1970s, an operation that Congress halted when it became public in 1973, and the 1970–1971 invasion of that country despite Nixon's promise when he took office to end the Vietnam War as soon as possible; Kissinger's acquiescence in a 1973 military coup that brought the death of left-wing Chilean president Salvador Allende; Kissinger's endorsement of Indonesia's military takeover of Portuguese East Timor in December 1975 and the brutal suppression of indigenous resistance there; and his readiness to authorize wiretapping against American bureaucrats suspected of leaking official information to the press. These aspects of Kissinger, and his failure, constant negotiations notwithstanding, to end the Vietnam War—a conflict that his Cambodian policies effectively broadened—until 1973, made him the bête noire of many American liberals.

Conservative Republicans found equally opprobrious Kissinger's willingness to accommodate the communist Soviet Union and the People's Republic of China (PRC) and, if Sino-American rapprochement required, to jettison the Republic of China on Taiwan, a long-time U.S. ally. Under Ford, who became president in August 1974 when the Watergate Scandal forced Nixon's resignation, both the 1972 SALT I Treaty and the 1975 Helsinki Accords on Europe that Kissinger helped to negotiate with the Soviets became targets for attack by such conservatives as California governor and presidential hopeful Ronald W. Reagan, who assailed the Soviet human rights record. The fall of Vietnam to communist forces in April 1975, little more than two years after Kissinger had negotiated the Paris Peace Accords supposedly ending the war, also damaged his credibility. On November 3, 1975, Ford replaced Kissinger as national security adviser, although Kissinger remained secretary of state until Ford left office in January 1977.

Upon leaving government Kissinger established an influential business consultancy firm. He continued to provide unofficial advice to successive administrations, wrote and spoke extensively on international affairs, and published three weighty volumes of memoirs. He remains a perennially controversial figure. Liberals still denigrate his foreign policy accomplishments, and even decades later journalists including Seymour Hersh and, most notably, Christopher Hitchens argued that Kissinger's past behavior made him liable to trial and conviction for war crimes. Pointing out discrepancies between Kissinger's own account of his time in office and the increasingly available documentary record became almost an academic parlor game. Outside the United States, Kissinger was a less-polarizing figure, and as he began his ninth decade many in Europe and Asia still admire his achievements.

PRISCILLA ROBERTS

See also

Nixon, Richard Milhous; Reagan, Ronald Wilson; Rogers, William Pierce; Sadat, Anwar; Yom Kippur War

References

Hanhimäki, Jussi. *The Flawed Architect: Henry Kissinger and American Foreign Policy.* New York: Oxford University Press, 2004.

Hersh, Seymour. *The Price of Power: Kissinger in the Nixon White House.* New York: Simon and Schuster, 1983.

Isaacson, Walter. *Kissinger: A Biography.* New York: Simon and Schuster, 1992.

Kissinger, Henry A. *White House Years.* Boston: Little, Brown, 1979.

———. *Years of Renewal.* New York: Simon and Schuster, 1999.

———. *Years of Upheaval.* Boston: Little, Brown, 1982.

Schulzinger, Robert D. *Henry Kissinger: Doctor of Diplomacy.* New York: Columbia University Press, 1989.

Klausner, Amo

See Oz, Amos

Knesset

Israel's parliament, located in Jerusalem, and the supreme legislative body of the State of Israel. The Hebrew word *knesset* means "assembly." The first Knesset was elected on January 25, 1949, as a constituent assembly to draw up a constitution for the newly created Israeli state. On June 13, 1950, having disagreed on creating an entire constitution immediately, the Knesset adopted a resolution

Selected Political Parties of Israel

Party Name	Alignment	Date Founded	Still Active?	Notes
Agudat Israel	Orthodox	1949	yes	Umbrella party for Haredi Jews
General Zionists	Center	1949	no	Merged into Labor
Herut	Right	1949	no	Merged into Gahal
Mapai	Left	1949	no	Merged into Labor
National Religious Party	Center-Right	1956	yes	Created by merger of Mizrahi and Mizrahi Workers
Progress and Development	Arab interests	1959	no	Merged into United Arab List
Gahal	Right	1965	no	Merged into Likud
Labor	Center-Left	1968	yes	Merger of Mapai, Labour Unity, and Rafi
Likud	Center-Right	1973	yes	Merger of several political parties, including Gahal and National List
Ratz	Left	1973	no	Merged into Meretz
Shas	Orthodox	1984	yes	Created by Ovadia Yosef and Elazar Shach
Gesher	Center-Right	1996	no	Broke from and merged back into Likud
United Arab List	Arab interests	1996	yes	Merger of Arab Democratic Party and Islamic Movement
Israel Beytenu	Right	1999	yes	Created by Avigdor Lieberman
Kadima	Center	2005	yes	Created by Ariel Sharon

Israel's Knesset (parliament) building, dedicated in 1966, seen through the sculpted gates to the grounds beyond. (iStockPhoto.com)

that called for the gradual creation of a constitution, chapter by chapter, in the form of a series of basic laws.

The Knesset is a unicameral legislature comprised of 120 members who together form the plenum. Members of the Knesset are elected every four years according to the electoral system based on proportional representation. Thus, the number of seats that each party obtains in the Knesset is proportional to the number of votes it received of the total cast for all political parties. The only limitation is a 2 percent qualifying threshold, meaning that any party must receive at least 2 percent of the total votes to be seated. Potential candidates are selected within the framework of party lists, which are determined by the party leadership or, alternatively, may be selected in primaries by party members.

Given the difficulty of obtaining a clear majority, Israeli governments are formed through multiparty coalitions under the leadership of the prime minister. The prime minister is elected directly by the Israeli population through a two-ballot majority system.

The main task of the Knesset is to pass legislation, which can be initiated through government bills, by an individual member or group of members, or by a Knesset committee. The schedule and agenda of Knesset meetings is outlined by the Speaker in accordance with government proposals. One meeting per week is set aside for private bills. There are three readings of a proposed bill. A government bill is placed on the table of the Knesset 48 hours prior

to its first reading in the Knesset plenum. After the plenum debate regarding the proposed bill has taken place, the bill is voted on. If successful, the bill is sent to the relevant committee, which will discuss it in detail and propose amendments. If amendments have been proposed, the government is given the opportunity to consider the consequences of the changes adopted by the committee and is given the opportunity to withdraw the amended bill. If accepted with amendments, the bill goes to the plenum for a second reading. The bill becomes law after the third reading of the final bill, which is then signed by the prime minister, the president, the Speaker, and the minister responsible for the bill. A bill proposed by an member or group of members follows the same procedure. However, a preliminary reading of the proposed bill goes to the relevant committee before being presented to the Knesset plenum and committee second reading.

In addition to passing legislation, the Knesset elects the president of state and the state comptroller. It also has the power to revoke members' immunity from prosecution and may, with a majority of at least 61 members, remove the prime minister from government and bring about new elections. The Knesset, furthermore, has statutory authority over the nation's budget.

SERGIO CATIGNANI

See also
Israel

References

Arian, Asher. *Politics in Israel: The Second Generation.* Rev. ed. Chatham, NJ: Chatham House, 1989.

Hazan, Reuven Y. "Executive-Legislative Relations in an Era of Accelerated Reform: Reshaping Government in Israel." *Legislative Studies Quarterly* 22(3) (August 1997): 329–350.

Sharkansky, Ira. *Policy Making in Israel: Routines for Simple Problems and Coping with the Complex.* Pittsburgh: University of Pittsburgh Press, 1997.

Kollek, Theodor
Born: May 27, 1911
Died: January 2, 2007

Israeli politician and mayor of Jerusalem. Born to a Jewish family in Nagyvaszony near Budapest, Hungary, on May 27, 1911, Theodor "Teddy" Kollek was named for the Austrian journalist and Zionist leader Theodor Herzl. Kollek grew up in Vienna. In 1935 he immigrated with his family to the British Mandate for Palestine, and in 1937 he helped found Kibbutz Ein Gev near the Sea of Galilee.

In September 1938 Kollek went to England to work with the Habobim youth movement, training young people for kibbutz life in Palestine. Soon, however, he was involved in bringing Jewish youths to England from Germany, Austria, and Czechoslovakia. In the spring of 1939 he went to Czechoslovakia to ensure the safe transfer of funds for Jews immigrating to England. He then went on to Vienna, where he is credited with persuading Adolf Eichmann to allow the emigration of 3,000 Jews from Austria to Britain. Returning to Britain, Kollek began what evolved into a close friendship with David Ben-Gurion, later the first prime minister of Israel. Kollek also became friendly with British Army officer Orde Wingate.

Kollek returned to Palestine in the summer of 1942 and became increasingly involved in intelligence work and worked with the Jewish Agency movement in Istanbul to help secure the release of Jews in Europe and bring them to Palestine. He returned to Palestine in the summer of 1943 and then returned to work for the Jewish Agency in 1944 helping to secure arms and ammunition for Haganah from Jews serving in the British Army in Egypt. In 1945 after the end of the war in Europe, he traveled to London. He was there for a year and then returned to Palestine, where he worked to bring Holocaust survivors from the displaced persons camps of Europe to Palestine illegally.

In October 1947 Kollek traveled to New York at the behest of Ben-Gurion to represent Haganah and secure arms and ammunition. In early 1951 Kollek became deputy to Ambassador Abba Eban in Washington but, as a close personal friend and ally of Israeli prime minister Ben-Gurion, returned to Israel in the summer of 1952 and headed the prime minister's office until 1964.

Elected mayor of West Jerusalem in 1965, Kollek won six elections and held that position for 28 years. In June 1967 following the Six-Day War, he presided over the reunification of the city. Before

Theodor "Teddy" Kollek, mayor of Jerusalem from 1965 to 1993. (Jerusalem Municipality)

---

all else a Labor Zionist, he is generally credited with making Jerusalem into a modern city. This involved economic development but also attention to cultural activities, including the Jewish Theater. He was also the founder and director of the Israel Museum, a national museum complex. As mayor, he oversaw the rebuilding of the Jewish Quarter in the Old City and the restoration of historical landmarks. A highly successful fund-raiser, in 1991 he established the Jerusalem Foundation, which raised considerable sums to enhance the city both aesthetically and culturally. He also made an intense effort to bridge the gap between Jews, Arabs, and Christians. In 1988 he was awarded the Israel Prize, his nation's highest honor. He ran for mayor for a seventh time in 1993 but was defeated by Likud candidate Ehud Olmert. Kollek died in Jerusalem on January 2, 2007. Yitzhak Rabin called him the greatest builder of Jerusalem since Herod the Great.

SPENCER C. TUCKER

See also

Ben-Gurion, David; Eichmann, Karl Adolf; Jerusalem; Jerusalem, Old City of; Labor Zionism; Rabin, Yitzhak; Six-Day War; Wingate, Orde Charles

References

Kollek, Teddy. *For Jerusalem: A Life.* New York: Random House, 1978.

———. *Jerusalem, Sacred City of Mankind: A History of Forty Centuries.* London: Weidenfeld and Nicolson, 1968.

Kook, Abraham Isaac
Born: 1865
Died: September 1, 1935

First Ashkenazi chief rabbi in the British Mandate for Palestine and a Torah scholar. Born in Griva, Latvia, then part of Imperial Russia, in 1865, Abraham Isaac Kook underwent a traditional Jewish education and entered the Volozhim Yeshiva in 1884. Recognized as something of a prodigy, he secured his first rabbinical position at age 22 in 1887 in Zaumel, Lithuania, and in 1895 he became rabbi of Bausk (Bauskaa). During these years he wrote a number of important articles setting forth the tenets of a religious nationalism.

In 1904 Kook settled in Palestine, then part of the Ottoman Empire. He assumed the post as rabbi of Jaffa but also had responsibility for the nearby Zionist secular agricultural settlements. He was one of the few traditional Jews who took pleasure in the immigration to Palestine of large numbers of secular Zionists. This approach both shocked and angered traditional Jews.

Kook traveled frequently from Palestine to Europe to encourage traditional Jews to become Zionists. He was in Germany at the beginning of World War I and was unable to return to Palestine during the war. He moved first to Switzerland and in 1916 to London, where he accepted a post as a rabbi on the condition that he would leave when he was able to return to Palestine. While in London, he was involved in the talks with the British government that led to the Balfour Declaration of 1917.

Upon his return to Palestine after the war, Kook was appointed rabbi of Jerusalem. In 1921 he became the first Ashkenazi chief rabbi of the Yishuv (Jewish community in Palestine), and in 1924 he founded a yeshiva in Jerusalem. He worked to cement relationships between the very different communities of Jews in Palestine. Thus he continued to encourage secular Jews to become more religious but never rejected those who refused to do so. He was known for his broad world outlook. Although he welcomed the revival of Zionism and advances in science and technology, he was disappointed by the concomitant loss of religious commitment.

Kook was also a strong critic of the British administration in Palestine. Following the Arab riots of 1929, he charged that the British had not done enough to protect the Jewish community. He was a prolific writer on both Halakha and Jewish thought as well as of poetry, and a number of books were published, most of them posthumously. Kook died in Jerusalem on September 1, 1935.

SPENCER C. TUCKER

See also

Ashkenazic Judaism; Balfour Declaration; Palestine, British Mandate for

References

Elkins, Dov Peretz. *Shepherd of Jerusalem: A Biography of Rabbi Abraham Isaac Kook.* Lanham, MD: Jason Aronson, 1995.
Kaplan, Lawrence J., and David Shatz, eds. *Rabbi Abraham Isaac Kook and Jewish Spirituality.* New York: New York University Press, 1995.

Shepherd, Naomi. *Ploughing Sand: British Rule in Palestine, 1917–1948.* New Brunswick, NJ: Rutgers University Press, 1999.

Koran

The principal religious and sacred text of Islam. The Koran (Quran, al-Karim, or Noble Quran) to Muslims derives from the Arabic verb to declaim or recite. This text is so-named because the Koran is comprised of divine revelations dictated to the Prophet Muhammad by the angel Gabriel from about AD 610 until Muhammad's death in 632. Muslims hold that the Koran in the holy original Arabic is the literal word of Allah transmitted to the Prophet Muhammad (the Messenger) for humanity. Reading of the Koran is a duty for every Muslim. Specially trained reciters or readers (*qari'* or *muqri'*) present the Koran in a format called *tajwid*, a chanting in the musical modal system (*maqamat*) set to the natural rhythm of the Arabic words, with their longer or shorter syllables. The *tajwid*, which today may be enjoyed in audio recordings or over the radio, allow the listener to hear the voice of the text.

Epic poetry and other forms of oral literature were especially prized in pre-Islamic Arabian society. Hence, Koranic recitation provided Muslims a literary as well as a religious experience and an opportunity to reflect on the meaning of the text as well.

According to tradition, the Prophet Muhammad was illiterate, but like the other men of Mecca, he used to retreat to the hills beyond the city to spend time reflecting or meditating. At his retreat in a cave on Mount Hira, when he heard a voice commanding him to "read," Muhammad protested that he did not know how or what to read. The mysterious voice was that of the archangel Gabriel, and his words were the first of the Koran:

> Read [*Iqra'*]: In the name of thy Lord who created,
> Created a man from *Alaq* [a "clinging" clot, or small amount
>   of fetal material].
> Read: And thy Lord is the Most Generous,
> Who taught [the use of] the pen,
> Taught man that which he knew not.

This verse has been interpreted to mean that the omnipotent Allah (God) had the ability to bring and teach his Message even to an illiterate man. This passage, from the Surat al-'Alaq (96:1–5), was revealed to Muhammad in Mecca, and it is the first of thousands to be given to the Prophet over the next 23 years, signaling the beginning of the Divine revelation that was the Koran and the Message of Islam.

The Koran is not a story of the Prophet's life, but some understanding of his experience is helpful to the outsider seeking to comprehend the text. After 13 years, the ruling elite in Mecca, who were threatened by the growing crowds of followers and the messages of monotheism and strict moral codes that Muhammad was spreading, put pressure on the 53-year-old Prophet to leave. In 622, after

Palestinian girls study the Koran at the El Laksa Koranic school in East Jerusalem, March 18, 1991. (Sophie Elbaz/Sygma/Corbis)

the pressures were multiplied by the deaths of his wife, Khadija, and his uncle Abu Talib, Muhammad fled with his followers to the town of Yathrib, later renamed Madinat al-Nabi (City of the Prophet) on a journey now known as the Hijra. While the Muslims were living in Medina, the early and basic concepts and practices of the faith were defined, although some changed after Mecca was reconquered. Also, the Kaaba, or holy site where the Black Rock is located, was cleansed of its idols.

Early on, some of the Prophet's companions and his wives had partial collections of the Koran, and other collections were written down. These were different in the ordering of the surahs and the number of verses they contained. Many Koran reciters worked from memory and not written texts. There were different versions, including variant spellings and even more important differences. After a major battle when many Koranic reciters were killed, Omar asked the caliph Abu Bakr to assemble one written version of the Koran, which he then did. The caliph Uthman revised the Koran, creating a committee that met and approved one version based on their understanding of the text and the Qurayshi dialect. Uthman burned all the other versions of the Koran he could find and distributed this official version 23 years after the Prophet's death. The recension was controversial to different parties, especially the Shia Muslims. By the ninth century, Uthman's form, or codex, was vocalized, meaning that the normally unwritten Arabic vowels were in-

cluded to stabilize its meaning. Some suggest that because of an inability to destroy all variant versions, a tradition states that the Prophet Muhammad had approved seven valid readings of this text. More than seven exist, however.

The Koran is organized into the basic divisions of ayat, or verses; surahs, chapters with titles that concern particular themes; and juz, which is simply a section that is 1-30th of the entire Koran. Muslims use this 1-30th division to read the Koran over a one-month period, or they might divide it into 7 sections. There are 114 surahs in the Koran, each of a different length, from just 3 to 286 verses or ayat. Many of the shorter, more dramatic surat were revealed at Mecca, while the longer, more legalistic surat were revealed at Medina. The Koran is arranged so that the longest surat are at the beginning of the text.

Exegesis, or explanations of the Koran, are called *tafsir,* and these are a very important part of religious studies as well as a basis for Islamic law, or Sharia. The Koran is most important as the ultimate authority in Sharia. The Koran is used as liturgy—that is, in prayer—and devout Muslims recite a portion each night (or more often).

The Koran has also served as a basis for education. The goal of learning to read in Arabic is the completion of a Koran reading, often at a young age. The kuttab, or Koranic school, was found throughout the Muslim world. The Koran also serves various social purposes. It is read in funeral sittings and recited at public events or conferences. Contests in Koran reading are held. Calligraphy is based on the Koran.

The most basic aspect of the Koran is that it is proof of Allah's existence and gives information about His nature, which is at once powerful, tender, and mystical: "He is the First and the Last, the Outward and the Inward; and He is the Knower of every thing" (37:3). This is based on the notion of tawhid, or unicity or monotheism, that is demonstrated in a multiplicity of ways.

Theology as expressed in the Koran begins with monotheism. The unity of Allah, his attributes, and the descriptions of Heaven, Hell, and the angels are all supported by the Koran. Another basic message in the Koran concerns the nature of humankind, who have been warned through the revelations to follow the Straight Path, or Divine law, and must also overcome their tendencies toward insecurity, haste, and panic. If humans honor their pact with Allah, maintaining their trust in Him and living according to his rules, they will be rewarded. If not, they will be grievously punished.

During the seventh century, the Arabs at Mecca were polytheistic. Moreover, their society benefited the wealthy and the powerful. According to the Koran, however, the disenfranchised, orphans, and the poor are the responsibility of the Muslim community, for wealth comes from Allah and must be used for the good of his community. Another important message of the Koran has to do with living in accordance with Allah's will and avoiding sin, for the Day of Judgment and the Resurrection will come when all shall be reckoned with.

Islam means "submission," or "surrender to Allah," while Muslim means "one who submits." This does not, as in English, have any tinge of self-abasement. Rather, it implies one who trusts completely in God and thus in His Revelation, the Koran. The Koran describes the Muslim community, or ummah, in its covenant with Allah, as a "community in a state of surrender" (ummah muslimah) in which Muslims are accountable and responsible for their actions. The opposite of Islam is kufr, which means that one covers up, obscures, or denies Islam and all of its requirements.

The Koran is seen as the final of a series of revelations that began with the book of Genesis and the story of Adam and Eve as revealed to Moses and through the Gospels of Christ to the revelations given to Muhammad. The Koran continues to build its credibility by drawing a holy line of succession from Abraham to Muhammad (and thus all of Islam) as prophesied in Genesis 21:12. The Koran makes various references to prophets within and excluded from the Bible. The Koran refers to Jews and Christians (as well as Zoroastrians) as "Peoples of the Book," meaning that they and their scripture are to be respected and that they are not infidels or polytheists. However, in places the Koran also criticizes Christians and Jews for failing to follow the dictates of their own Holy Scriptures and not heeding the teachings of their prophets. The Koran also commands its followers to "struggle in the way of Allah," meaning to engage in jihad. This is interpreted to mean an armed struggle in battle as well as the struggle to fulfill all the elements of faith (iman) in Islam.

Muslims recite and learn the Koran in Arabic, as it is in that form that it is considered to be the literal word of Allah. Muslim clerics maintain that any translation of the words of the Koran is not divine speech. As the majority of Muslims are non-Arabic speakers, the requirement to learn and study the Koran in Arabic meant study of the Arabic language—even more so for scholars of the Koran—since many historic texts and commentaries that pertain to the Koran are also in Arabic. The book itself is treated with reverence. Translations typically were described as works of commentary, and there was resistance to the early 20th-century suggestion that Turkish be a language of worship. However, some popular translations, such as that by Abdullah Yusuf Ali in English, are very close to the original text, and these have helped to create and sustain Muslim scholarship and discussion about the Koran in other languages. Meanwhile, works of commentary on the Koran have led to discussions that are relevant to the political and social challenges facing Muslims today.

B. Keith Murphy and Sherifa Zuhur

See also
Bible; Genesis, Book of; Imam; Shia Islam; Sunni Islam

References
'Ali, Abdullah Yusuf. *The Meaning of the Holy Qur'an.* Beltsville, MD: Amana, 2001.
Ayoub, Mahmoud. *The Qur'an and Its Interpreters.* 2 vols. Albany, NY: SUNY Press, 1984, 1992.
Nelson, Kristina. *The Art of Reciting the Quran.* Austin: University of Texas Press, 1985.
Rahman, Fazlur. *Major Themes of the Qur'an.* Minneapolis, MN: Biblioteca Islamica, 1980.

Kosygin, Alexei
Born: February 21, 1904
Died: December 18, 1980

Soviet premier (1964–1980). Alexei Nikolayevich Kosygin was born in St. Petersburg on February 21, 1904. He graduated from the Leningrad Cooperative Technicum in 1924 and from the Leningrad Textile Institute in 1935 after having joined the Communist Party of the Soviet Union (CPSU) in 1927. Active in the Leningrad party apparatus, he began a rapid ascent in the CPSU, facilitated by the removal of many members during the Great Purges of the 1930s.

In 1939 Kosygin was named to head the Soviet textile industry and became a full member of the CPSU Central Committee. In 1940 he assumed the post of deputy chairman of the Council of People's Commissars (Council of Ministers after 1946), a post he held until 1953. He became a candidate member of the Politburo in 1946 and a full member in 1948. His ties to Andrei Zhdanov, who was purged in 1948, resulted in his demotion to candidate status in the Politburo (Presidium) in 1952.

Following Premier Joseph Stalin's death in March 1953, Kosygin's fortunes fluctuated wildly as Stalin's successors struggled for power. In the aftermath of Georgi Malenkov's failed bid to oust Nikita

Alexei Kosygin, Soviet premier (1964–1980). (Library of Congress)

Khrushchev from power in 1957, Kosygin was returned to candidacy status in the Presidium and was restored as deputy chairman of the Council of Ministers. In 1960 he was elected a full member of the Presidium.

Kosygin's disagreements with Khrushchev over economic policies led Kosygin to join the faction that pushed Khrushchev from power in October 1964. In the resulting reapportionment of power, Kosygin became chairman of the Council of Ministers (premier) in the new government. As premier, his most significant achievements were in domestic economic affairs. He sponsored the so-called Kosygin Reforms in 1965 that provided individual enterprises with increased autonomy from party control.

In 1967 Kosygin became actively involved in Soviet-Arab relations and in U.S.-Soviet relations in the Middle East. Although neither the United States nor the Soviet Union intended to modify their positions regarding the Middle East, both governments sought to promote peace in the region. To demonstrate his commitment to heading off conflict, on May 26, 1967, Kosygin sent a message to both Egyptian president Gamal Abdel Nasser and Israeli prime minister Levi Eshkol requesting them not to open hostilities. The request was ignored.

During the ensuing Six-Day War (June 5–10, 1967), Kosygin exchanged 20 hot-line messages with President Lyndon B. Johnson. Most of them asked the United States to pressure Israel into accepting a cease-fire. They also hinted that the Soviet Union would act more decisively to support its Arab allies if the Israelis did not adhere to a cease-fire.

On June 19, 1967, Kosygin delivered a speech before the General Assembly of the United Nations (UN). He proposed that the UN adopt a resolution calling on Israel to immediately remove its troops from Egypt, Jordan, and Syria. The proposal received little support at the time, although the UN would later adopt Resolution 242, which featured a similar goal of total Israeli withdrawal.

Kosygin and Johnson met in late June 1967 in Glassboro, New Jersey. These generally friendly discussions yielded no significant results in terms of the Arab-Israeli conflict. Johnson was primarily interested in issues involving Vietnam and the strategic arms race. Thus, no agreement related to the Middle East crisis was reached.

Kosygin's power was in decline by 1968. The 1968 Prague Spring crisis lessened Politburo interest in economic reform, and Leonid Brezhnev soon assumed control over foreign affairs. By the early 1970s, Kosygin was in a subordinate position to Brezhnev. Kosygin died in Moscow on December 18, 1980.

STEVEN W. GUERRIER AND IRINA MUKHINA

See also

Brezhnev, Leonid Ilyich; Eshkol, Levi; Johnson, Lyndon Baines; Khrushchev, Nikita; Nasser, Gamal Abdel; Six-Day War; Soviet Union and Russia, Middle East Policy; United Nations Security Council Resolution 242

References

Breslauer, George W. *Khrushchev and Brezhnev as Leaders: Building Authority in Soviet Politics.* London: Allen and Unwin, 1982.
Gelman, Harry. *The Brezhnev Politburo and the Decline of Detente.* Ithaca, NY: Cornell University Press, 1984.
Taubman, William. *Khrushchev: The Man and His Era.* London: Free Press, 2004.
Westwood, J. N. *The History of the Middle East Wars.* London: Bison, 1991.

Kreisky, Bruno
Born: January 22, 1911
Died: July 29, 1990

Austrian politician, diplomat, and chancellor (1970–1983). Bruno Kreisky was born in Vienna on January 22, 1911, the son of a Jewish clothing maker. He attended public schools in Vienna and joined the socialist youth movement at the age of 15. In 1935 he was arrested and imprisoned for being a member of the outlawed Social Democratic Party. After spending 18 months in jail, he was released and studied law at the University of Vienna. On the day after the Nazi Party took control of the Austrian government, he graduated from law school and then fled abroad, finding refuge in Sweden.

Kreisky returned home in 1946 and joined the Austrian Foreign Service. In 1953 he became undersecretary for foreign affairs. In that position he was a participant in the negotiations that led to the Austrian State Treaty, which restored Austria's full independence

Austrian chancellor Bruno Kreisky speaking during a press conference at Ben-Gurion Airport, Israel, March 13, 1974. (Israeli Government Press Office)

as a neutral power. In 1956 he was elected as a socialist to the Austrian parliament (Nationalrat). In the coalition government headed by Chancellor Julius Raab, Kreisky assumed the post of foreign minister in 1959. He held that post until 1966. He was elected socialist party leader in February 1967. In 1970, as leader of the Socialist Party, he became chancellor of a minority government. He was Austria's first Jewish chancellor. The Socialist Party became the majority in 1971 and went on to win large majorities in the elections of 1975 and 1979.

Kreisky did not support Zionism as a panacea for the problems faced by Jews around the world. He often sided with Arab nations in the Middle East, and his government enjoyed close relations with the governments of Egyptian president Anwar Sadat and Libyan strongman Muammar Qaddafi. Kreisky angered Israel and many Western nations when he received Yasser Arafat, leader of the Palestine Liberation Organization (PLO), on an official state visit to Austria in July 1979. Austria was the first Western government to receive Arafat. Kreisky's government established formal diplomatic relations with the PLO in 1980.

Kreisky attempted to use his position as the Jewish socialist leader of a neutral nation to broker peace talks between the Israelis

and their Arab neighbors. His efforts were largely in vain, however, because Israeli leaders viewed him as something of a traitor. Kreisky's relationship with Israeli prime minister Golda Meir was particularly acrimonious. In March 1982 Qaddafi visited Vienna, which once again raised the hackles of government leaders of other Western nations.

By 1983, Austrian voters had begun to tire of Kreisky's preoccupation with foreign affairs. After the Socialist Party lost its parliamentary majority in the April 1983 elections, Kreisky retired from public service. He died of heart disease in Vienna on July 29, 1990.

DAVE RAUSCH

See also

Arafat, Yasser; Meir, Golda; Palestine Liberation Organization; Qaddafi, Muammar; Sadat, Anwar

References

Bischof, Günter, and Anton Pelinka, eds. *The Kreisky Era in Austria.* New Brunswick, NJ: Transaction, 1994.

Bunzl, John. *Between Vienna and Jerusalem: Reflections and Polemics on Austria, Israel, and Palestine.* New York: Peter Lang, 1997.

Prittie, Terence. *Eshkol: The Man and the Nation.* New York: Pitman, 1969.

Kurds

People of Indo-European origin who inhabit the upcountry and mountainous areas chiefly in Iran, Iraq, Syria, and Turkey. Their primary area of concentration—in southern Turkey and northern parts of Iran and Iraq—is known as Kurdistan, although this is not an autonomous region. There are also small enclaves of Kurds in southwestern Armenia, Azerbaijan, and Lebanon. The total Kurdish population worldwide is estimated to be between 30 million and 35 million, and the Kurds represent one of the biggest ethnic groups in the world who do not enjoy their own autonomous nation. The Kurds, whose language is of Indo-European background, are not considered Arabs. However, numerous Kurds have intermarried with Arabs and have played an important role in Arab and Muslim history. Salah al-Din al-Ayyubi (Saladin, one of the greatest of Muslim leaders) was of Kurdish origin. There were numerous other Kurdish dynasties such as the Ziyarids, the Jastanids, and the Kakuyids.

The great majority of Kurds are Sunni Muslims, and their language is related to Persian (which is spoken chiefly in Iran, Afghanistan, and Tajikistan). There are numerous dialects of Kurdish divided into two primary dialect groups: Sorani and Kumanji. Just as they have their own language, the Kurds maintain their own unique culture and traditions.

Until the first few decades of the 20th century, most Kurds lived a pastoral, nomadic existence and divided themselves into tribes. For centuries, they led a somewhat isolated lifestyle that clung to tradition and was well ordered by tribal hierarchy and customs. The mountain Kurds' principal avocation was goat and sheep herding, which was migratory in nature. In this sense, they were not unlike

Kurdish children stand behind concertina wire observing U.S. marines building a tent city in northern Iraq, April 1991. (U.S. Department of Defense)

the Bedouin to the south. However, when the Ottoman Empire broke apart as a result of World War I, the Kurds found themselves circumscribed within newly created states, none of which was interested in allowing them to continue their centuries-old lifestyle and customs.

As new nations such as Iraq and Turkey—where the bulk of Kurds live—organized themselves into nationalistic nation-states, the Kurds came under great pressure to abandon their tribal ways and to assimilate into the majority culture. They were also greatly limited in their migratory patterns, which served only to further marginalize them. Soon after World War I, Kurds began to call for their own nation, Kurdistan. While the British gave some lip service to this idea, the Turks effectively quashed the idea, with Iraq and Iran agreeing that they would recognize no Kurdish state encompassing any part of their territory. While the Kurds were now subjected to discrimination and oppression in general, nowhere was the oppression worse than in Turkey. The Turkish government refused to recognize the Kurds as a distinct ethnic group (which continues today), forced them to abandon their language, banned their traditional garb, and lured them into urban areas to curtail their pastoral life. This, of course, only brought more discrimination and resulted in high unemployment and poverty rates for urbanized Kurds.

In Turkey the Kurds have periodically risen up in rebellions that have been promptly crushed by the Turkish government. However, an underground Kurdish guerrilla group, formed out of the Kurdish Workers' Party (PKK) in the 1980s, continues to pursue the dream of an independent Kurdish state and has engaged Turkish, Iranian, and Syrian troops in an ongoing military struggle. In the late 1940s and again in the late 1970s, Kurds attempted to form their own autonomous region in Iran. These efforts were both put down by the Iranians.

Most recently, and perhaps most infamously, Kurds have been subjected to brutal oppression by the Iraqi government. From 1960 to 1975, Iraqi Kurds under the leadership of Mustafa Barzani waged a guerrilla-style war with Iraqi regular forces. This brought significant casualties to the Iraqis and forced them in 1970 to enter into talks with the rebelling Kurds. That same year, the Iraqi government offered a peace deal to the Kurds that would have brought them their own autonomous region (but not sovereignty) by 1974. Meanwhile Barzani continued his campaign, and the peace offer never took hold. In 1975 the Iraqis began moving thousands of people into northern Iraq in an attempt to Arabize the region while simultaneously moving close to 200,000 Kurds out. The Iran-Iraq War (1980–1988) brought great misery and many fatalities to Iraqi Kurds. Saddam Hussein's government was brutal in its treatment of the minority, and in 1988 Hussein launched his so-called Anfal (Spoils of War) Campaign. Over a period of several months, Iraqi forces killed perhaps as many as 100,000 Kurds and destroyed some 2,000 villages, often employing chemical weapons. In 1991 Iraqi Kurds rebelled again, and they were once again crushed. After the 2003 Anglo-American invasion of Iraq and Hussein's overthrow, Kurds took control of Kirkuk and most of Mosul. Talks are currently under way to formalize an autonomous Kurdish region in northern Iraq.

PAUL G. PIERPAOLI JR.

See also

Hussein, Saddam; Iran; Iran-Iraq War; Iraq

References

Bulloch, John, and Harvey Morris. *No Friends but the Mountains: The Tragic History of the Kurds.* New York: Oxford University Press, 1993.

Ciment, James. *The Kurds: State and Minority in Turkey, Iraq, and Iran.* New York: Facts on File, 1996.

Izady, Mehrdad R. *The Kurds: A Concise Handbook.* Washington, DC: Crane Russak, Taylor and Francis, 1992.

McDowall, David. *Modern History of the Kurds.* London: Tauris, 1997.

Kuwait

Monarchy in the Middle East. Kuwait, with a 1945 population of some 100,000 people, occupies 6,880 square miles, including the Kuwaiti share of the Neutral Zone defined by agreement with Saudi Arabia in 1922 and partitioned by mutual agreement in 1966. Kuwait is thus about the size of the U.S. state of Hawaii. The current population is about 2.35 million people, of whom more than half are noncitizen workers attracted by job opportunities in this oil-rich Persian Gulf nation.

Kuwait is strategically located at the northern end of the Persian Gulf. It is bordered by Saudi Arabia to the south, Iraq to the west and north, and the Persian Gulf to the east. The topography is flat, low desert, and the climate is very hot and dry. More than 95 percent of the Kuwaiti people live in urban areas, mostly along the coast. The nation's major natural resources are oil and natural gas, comprising an estimated 10 percent of the world's known reserves. There is a minor fishing industry, but oil sales make up half of Kuwait's gross domestic product (GDP) and provide 80 percent of the government's yearly revenues. The large oil reserves have sustained a relatively high per capita GDP annually and allow for extensive social services for Kuwaiti citizens.

Oil and geographic location have made Kuwait a crucial strategic state far beyond what might be expected of a country its size and population. Kuwait has been a key to British imperial interests in the Middle East, a major player in regional affairs, a staunch Cold War ally of the United States, the focus of the 1990 Persian Gulf War, and an important staging area for subsequent American-led operations in Iraq.

In contrast to its current prominence, Kuwait was a remote part of the Ottoman Empire in the 18th century, largely left to manage

Liberation Tower in Kuwait City, named in commemoration of the expulsion of Iraqi forces in 1991. (iStockPhoto.com)

its own affairs. This earlier insignificance is manifest in the fact that the Utub tribes that settled in the area early in the 18th century called their central town Kuwait, the Arabic diminutive for *kut*, meaning a fortress built near water. By midcentury the Utub's al-Sabah tribe, whose descendants rule Kuwait to this day, had emerged as the most prominent in the area. The al-Sabah focused on developing the local pearl beds and taking advantage of location to promote regional trade.

Recognizing the fact that any increase in the wealth of Kuwait and the al-Sabah family would attract Ottoman attention and invite closer imperial control and higher taxation, Sheikh Mubarak al-Sabah sought the protection of Britain, the major European power in the region. The result was an 1899 agreement in which Kuwait ceded control over its foreign affairs and defense to the British. In return, Kuwait agreed to eschew alliances with other powers and promised not to cede any concessions—economic or military—to any other nation. Kuwait thus became a British protectorate. This situation remained fairly stable until Britain reduced its imperial commitments after World War II. Kuwait became fully independent in June 1961.

Kuwait then aligned itself with the West—the United States in particular—in regional and international affairs. The 1979 Iranian Revolution served to further strengthen this alliance, and Kuwait became a staunch supporter of Iraq during the Iran-Iraq War, which began in 1980. That support included nearly $35 billion in grants, loans, and other assistance to Iraq. After the war, which ended in 1988, Iraqi leader Saddam Hussein demanded that Kuwait forgive its loans, reasoning that Iraq had been the bulwark in the Arab world against Iran and was thus owed monetary concessions. Iraq also accused the Kuwaitis of slant-drilling for oil into Iraqi fields and then claimed that Kuwait was a lost Iraqi province, the administrative boundaries of which dated back to the defunct Ottoman Empire.

Angry with Kuwait's refusal to forgive the Iraqi debt and convinced that the kingdom was keeping oil prices artificially low by pumping too much oil, Hussein launched an invasion of Kuwait on August 2, 1990. The international response, which was divided into two stages, was strong and swift. The U.S.-led Operation DESERT SHIELD saw a large-scale military buildup in Saudi Arabia. Then in January 1991 when Hussein steadfastly refused to withdraw from Kuwait, Operation DESERT STORM began, during which the United States led an international military coalition, including other Arab nations, to drive Iraqi forces from Kuwait. The brief war ended on February 27, 1991, with Iraq compelled to recognize Kuwaiti independence.

Thereafter, Kuwait remained a firm ally of the United States and allowed its territory to be used as a staging area for the U.S.-led effort to oust Hussein from power in the spring of 2003. In return the United States has been restrained in any criticism of Kuwaiti internal affairs. In May 2005, however, Kuwait's parliament did grant full political rights to women. The United States maintains a significant military and naval presence in the region that protects the al-Sabah ruling family of Kuwait, which has had long experience in maintaining its position from the 19th century to the present.

Kuwait has not been a major player in the Arab-Israeli conflict. As Kuwait did not obtain independence from Britain until 1961, it did not participate in the 1948 and 1956 wars in and around Israel. After independence Kuwait aligned itself with the Arab side in the Arab-Israeli conflict, sending small numbers of troops to fight in the 1967 and 1973 wars. These were token forces, and Kuwait focused on internal development of its oil resources. The large proportion of Palestinians in the Kuwaiti workforce were taxed by Kuwait, and these funds were then used to support Palestinian causes. Yet there was a suspicion of Palestinians as a possible source of political dissidence, as had occurred in Jordan and Lebanon in the 1970s and 1980s. Palestine Liberation Organization (PLO) support for Iraq in the 1990 conflict with Iraq enraged Kuwaitis, who evicted the Palestinians after the conflict. Kuwait has an active Islamist opposition and is wary of Shia-dominated Iran. Kuwait has served as a primary forwarding point for U.S. troops deployed to Iraq.

DANIEL E. SPECTOR

See also

Hussein, Saddam; Iran-Iraq War; Iraq; Palestine Liberation Organization; Persian Gulf War; Saudi Arabia

References

Assiri, Abdul-Reda. *Kuwait's Foreign Policy: City-State in World Politics.* Boulder, CO: Westview, 1990.

Cordesman, Anthony J. *Kuwait: Recovery and Security after the Gulf War.* Boulder, CO: Westview, 1997.

Daniels, John. *Kuwait Journey.* Luton, UK: White Crescent, 1971.

United States Army. *Area Handbook Series: Persian Gulf States.* Washington, DC: U.S. Government Printing Office, 1984.

Kuwait, Armed Forces

In 1961, after 62 years as a British protectorate, Kuwait declared its independence. Immediately after the Kuwaiti declaration, Iraq claimed that Kuwait was actually an Iraqi province and threatened to invade its southern neighbor to enforce the claim. Despite Kuwait's independence, Britain flew troops into Kuwait to dissuade Iraq from invasion. Kuwait then gradually built a small military force that included an army, a navy, an air force, and a national guard.

During the Israeli War of Independence (1948–1949) Kuwait was not an official belligerent, although some Kuwaiti volunteers joined the Arab Liberation Army. Kuwait mobilized its armed forces prior to the June 1967 Six-Day War, and although Kuwait did not openly participate in the conflict, a contingent of the Kuwaiti Army took part in the fighting in the central sector. Kuwait also sent a token force to participate on the West Bank of the Jordan River during the Yom Kippur War of October 1973. In both wars, Kuwaiti participation was too small to have any significant impact. In the 1970s and 1980s, Kuwait gradually built a small but well-armed military force. The nation imported hardware from a wide variety of sources. The Kuwaiti Army relied on M-84 tanks (the Yugoslavian version of the Soviet T-72), French-built 155-mm howitzers, Soviet SA-7 and SA-8 surface-to-air missiles, and American anti-tank missiles. During the Iran-Iraq War (1980–1988) Kuwait sided with Iraq, providing loans for weapons procurement and allowing the Iraqi army to ship imported munitions across Kuwaiti territory.

On August 2, 1990, Iraq launched a massive invasion of Kuwait. The Kuwaiti military, tremendously outnumbered by the Iraqi Army, failed to prevent or even seriously hinder the invasion. Iraqi forces seized most of the heavy equipment of the Kuwaiti military and then used it against coalition forces that sought to expel the Iraqis. This included virtually the entire navy, which was subsequently sunk by invading coalition forces. The Kuwaiti tanks and armored personnel carriers that survived the Iraqi invasion were also destroyed during coalition air and ground attacks that led to the defeat of Iraqi forces and their expulsion from Kuwait in the Persian Gulf War (January 15–February 26, 1991). While the Iraqis were required under the terms of the cease-fire to return captured Kuwaiti military equipment, most of it was damaged beyond repair. Only the

Kuwaiti troops ready for review by King Fahd of Saudi Arabia as they take part in an assembly of coalition forces preceding the Persian Gulf War, March 8, 1991. (U.S. Department of Defense)

Kuwaiti Air Force escaped complete destruction, as most of its aircraft had escaped to Saudi Arabia during the initial assault.

In the post–Iraqi occupation era, Kuwait has sought to expand and modernize its armed forces. This has been accomplished with the assistance of a number of coalition members, most notably the United States, which views Kuwait as a vital strategic ally in the region. The current Kuwaiti government is committed to upgrading the Kuwaiti armed forces in the hopes that Kuwait can protect itself from its larger and more populous neighbors. The Iraqi threat has receded with the removal of Saddam Hussein from power by a coalition force that invaded Iraq in 2003. The Iraqi military, which was completely dismantled after the removal of Hussein, has been slowly retrained and rebuilt but is much smaller and more defensively oriented than previously. Currently, Kuwait spends almost 5 percent of its gross domestic product (GDP) on the military, for a total expense of more than $3 billion per year, making Kuwaiti per capita military spending one of the highest in the world.

Kuwait maintains an army, a navy, an air force, a national guard, and a coast guard. Its greatest weakness, however, is its small population. Of the 3 million permanent residents of Kuwait, less than 1 million are Kuwaiti citizens. At age 18, all Kuwaiti males are subject to compulsory military service, although no peacetime conscription is currently in place. Since 1999, females have been allowed to serve in Kuwaiti police and security forces, although they are not allowed in formal military service. It is estimated that there are perhaps 725,000 Kuwait males (ages 18–49) who are eligible and fit for military service. The large foreign population of Kuwait is of some concern to the Kuwaiti government. For example, prior to 1990, a substantial population of displaced Palestinians lived in Kuwait. However, after the Persian Gulf War, most were expelled because of Palestine Liberation Organization (PLO) leader Yasser Arafat's public support of Iraq in the war. Numerous foreign workers are employed in Kuwait, but in 1992 in an effort to increase internal security, Kuwait banned all noncitizens from military service.

Although small, the Kuwaiti forces are well trained and have top-quality U.S. equipment, including tanks, aircraft, and artillery. The total strength of the armed forces remains at about 14,000, of which 9,500 are in the army, 1,500 in the navy and coast guard, and 2,500 in the air force. Another 1,200 or so make up the General Staff. Kuwait's primary defensive tools remain economic and diplomatic, as it uses its oil reserves to maintain alliances with Western nations to hedge against Iraqi or Saudi Arabian aggression in the region. Kuwait maintains mutual-assistance agreements with the United States, Britain, and France and has allowed the U.S. military to preposition equipment on Kuwaiti soil.

PAUL J. SPRINGER

See also

Hussein, Saddam; Iraq, Armed Forces; Kuwait; Persian Gulf War; Six-Day War; Yom Kippur War

References

Crystal, Jill. *Kuwait: The Transformation of an Oil State.* Boulder, CO: Westview, 1992.

Finnie, David H. *Shifting Lines in the Sand: Kuwait's Elusive Frontier with Iraq.* Cambridge: Harvard University Press, 1992.

Herzog, Chaim. *The Arab-Israeli Wars: War and Peace in the Middle East from the War of Independence to Lebanon.* Westminster, MD: Random House, 1984.

Isiorho, S. A. *Kuwait.* Philadelphia: Chelsea House, 2002.

L

Labor Party

Israeli social-democratic political party formed in 1968 following the union of three political parties. While the Labor Party initially embraced many members who had hawkish outlooks, it has since become more centrist. The Labor Party was formed in 1968 by the joining of Mapai, formed in the 1930s as the most moderate of Israeli socialist parties; Ahdut Ha'avodah, a moderate leftist party that had split with the more extreme leftist Mapam party in 1954; and Rafi, a group that had split from Mapai only three years earlier.

During Israel's first three decades of existence, all Israeli prime ministers came either from the Labor Party or the parties that eventually formed it. David Ben-Gurion, who formed Rafi in 1951 and facilitated the split with Mapai, was the first prime minister of Israel, beginning in 1948. He favored rapid economic development and efforts to increase Israel's Jewish population, overseeing many projects such as Operation MAGIC CARPET to airlift Jews from Arab countries such as Yemen.

Ben-Gurion remained prime minister until 1963, when he resigned the post. When the Labor Party formed in 1968, Levi Eshkol, the Mapai leader, was Israeli prime minister. Golda Meir, the first and only female prime minister to date, succeeded Eshkol. Other major Labor Party leaders have included Yitzhak Rabin, who was assassinated in 1995 by a right-wing radical during a rally in support of the 1993 Oslo Accords; Shimon Peres, Rabin's successor; and Ehud Barak, who presided over the Israeli withdrawal from southern Lebanon in 2000.

Concerning the Arab-Israeli conflict, the Labor Party has supported a two-state solution. In contrast with the Likud Party, Labor proposed a qualified withdrawal from the West Bank and the Gaza Strip, arguing that incorporation of the territories into Israel was more of a threat to the Jewish state than an exchange of land for peace. Since Labor's movement to ally with the Kadima Party, formed in November 2005, and the post–Ariel Sharon restructuring of political parties, Labor leaders have expressed three differing approaches to a Palestinian policy. One group within the party supports peace negotiations with the Palestinians. This group, which includes former Labor Party leader Amram Mitzna, supported Sharon's 2005 plan that allowed for Israeli disengagement from the Gaza Strip. Another faction within the Labor Party supports negotiations conditional on the Palestinian renouncement of terrorism and replacement of the current Palestinian leadership with people who are committed to nonviolence. This faction also supported the Israeli withdrawal from occupied territories and includes former Labor Party leader Benjamin Ben-Eliezer. A third group deemphasizes withdrawal, is less compromising, and justifies Israeli targeting of terrorist leaders. The party's current leader, Amir Peretz, who took over in 2005, has given mixed signals. He announced that he favored peace negotiations while he also vowed to fight terrorism. The party has a history of supporting Israeli military actions against Palestinians and other Arabs, however.

In the past, Labor had been more proactive and hawkish on defense issues than it is today. While the party—or its predecessor parties—were in office, Israel attempted to capture the Suez Canal from Egypt in 1956 and reopen it to Israeli shipping. In 1967 when Levi Eshkol was prime minister, the Israel Defense Forces (IDF) launched a preemptive attack and won the Six-Day War, leading to the capture of the Gaza Strip and the Sinai Peninsula from Egypt, the West Bank from Jordan, and the Golan Heights from Syria. Following the 1967 war, Labor governments began establishing settlements in the occupied territories. The 1973 Yom Kippur War was

Mapai Party secretary Golda Meir opens the scroll-signing ceremony of the merger of the labor parties of Mapai, Ahdut Ha'avodah, Mapam, and Rafi on January 21, 1968. To Meir's left are Yitzhak Tabenkin and Shimon Peres (*far right*). (Moshe Milner/Israeli Government Press Office)

also waged during Labor's tenure, but more unhappily. The brush with defeat in this conflict led to the resignation of Labor prime minister Meir.

In November 2005 Peretz was elected chairman of the Labor Party, ousting Peres. In the party's 2006 election platform, Peretz sent mixed signals on foreign policy, vowing to "renew negotiations with the Palestinians while resolutely fighting terror and violence." Ephraim Sneh, chairman of the Labor faction in the Knesset (Israeli parliament), also stated that Israel could not negotiate with a Palestinian state that includes Hamas, with its history of violent action and lack of support for the Oslo Accords. Hamas is the Islamist Palestinian organization that won a majority of the seats in the Palestinian parliament in the January 2006 elections. Negotiations, according to the Labor Party 2006 platform, would be conducted on the principle of building two nations side-by-side, with the borders to be determined through further negotiations.

As part of any agreement, the Labor Party would, however, insist that Jerusalem be Israel's permanent capital with the sites holy to Judaism remaining under Israel's control. Peretz, in a speech at the 2006 Herzliya Conference, pointed to the agreements made between Israel and other Middle Eastern states such as Egypt and Jordan, which he believed proved that peace can work through diplomatic negotiations. Other important facets of the Labor Party's plan to make Israel more secure include support for completion of the controversial Israeli Security Fence and maintaining Israel's military advantage over its Arab neighbors.

During the March 2006 Israeli Knesset elections, Peretz emphasized economic and social issues, which few major Israeli political parties have done. Peretz called for an election when he decided that the Labor Party would leave the coalition that former Labor leader Peres had entered into with Israeli prime minister Sharon in November 2005.

The Labor Party declared that accelerating economic development while fairly dividing the profits from such development would be one of its main goals. In the 2006 elections, the party garnered 19 seats, which made it the second-largest Israeli party behind only the centrist Kadima Party, formed by Sharon in 2005. Nevertheless, the 2006 elections were a disappointment for Labor. Israel's other major political parties had placed much more emphasis on security, and the strategy that focused primarily on domestic issues backfired, as Labor lost two seats in the Knesset.

GREGORY MORGAN

See also
Hamas; Israeli Security Fence; Kadima Party; Likud Party; MAGIC CARPET, Operation; Palestinian Authority; Peres, Shimon; Settlements, Israeli; Sharon, Ariel

References
Ben-Gurion, David. *Israel: A Personal History*. Translated by Nechemia Meyers and Uzy Nystar. New York: Funk and Wagnalls, 1971.
Blumberg, Arnold. *The History of Israel*. Westport, CT: Greenwood, 1998.
Inbar, Efraim. *War and Peace in Israeli Politics*. Boulder, CO: Lynne Reinner, 1991.

Labor Zionism

Leftist, Zionist ideology that in very broad terms promoted a socialist Jewish state. Labor Zionism also sometimes refers to the social-democratic Mapai Party—which became Israel's top political party in the nation's first few decades—and groups affiliated with it, including the labor union Histadrut. As it evolved, Zionism manifested itself in two primary branches. One was political Zionism, propounded by Theodor Herzl and championed by Chaim Weizmann. Political Zionism was concerned chiefly with the creation of a sovereign Jewish state in Palestine. Thus, they viewed the Jewish dilemma as one of nationalism, to be resolved by the creation of a Jewish state with the help of the international community and the Jewish Diaspora. They were relatively unconcerned with how the goal of Zionism was to be achieved. Labor Zionism, on the other hand, viewed the Jewish problem in terms of a socialist dialectic. In other words, it held that because capitalism was a flawed system that was oppressing the Jewish people, the Zionist ideal would be realized once capitalism had been eclipsed by a socialist system, a society in which classes and inequities would not exist. Hence, Zionism could not be separated from the worldwide socialist movement, and any Jewish nation in Palestine had to be consonant with a classless, cooperative society constructed by Jewish labor. Labor Zionists in general took a dim view of bourgeois nations and Jews in the Diaspora funding the creation of a Jewish state.

The most important thinkers in labor Zionism were Moses Hess, Ber Borochov, Nahum Syrkin, and Aaron David Gordon. Attempts to wed socialism and Zionism were begun by the Po'ale Zion groups that arose first in Minsk, Russia, in 1900 and spread to other parts of the world in the years immediately after. In 1907 the Po'ale Zion groups formed a worldwide trade union that embraced the creation of a socialist-Jewish state in Palestine. By 1920 the union split, and one of the offshoots was the labor union Histadrut, which went on to become one of the most powerful Jewish organizations in the world and the most prominent one in Israel after 1948.

For Borochov, Zionism was interpreted entirely within a Marxist framework. In his eyes, the classic Marxian class struggle would be the vehicle by which the Jewish state would be created. Laborers—or the working class in Marxian language—would help construct the Jewish state and then use the power of that state to advance the socialist revolution around the world. Borochov and his adherents wanted no part of political Zionism and viewed agencies such as the World Zionist Organization (WZO) as front organizations for bourgeois Jews in the Diaspora.

Although Syrkin adhered to the basic Marxist theories, he believed that moral values—rather than class struggle and economics—were the sine qua nons of social change. In addition, Syrkin saw the free will of people as being more transformative than the Marxian historical dialectic. In the case of Zionism, he thus believed that Marxist prescriptions alone could not bring about a Jewish state. Because the Zionist ideal was not like that of a normal nation-state, Syrkin argued that other variables had to be involved in the resolution of the Jewish dilemma.

Gordon, who was not a socialist or Marxist in the classical sense, helped bridge the gap between classic political Zionism and socialism. Thus, he asserted that labor as an act of individual expression, as opposed to labor as merely a means of subsistence, was the true form that labor Zionism should embrace. For his part, Gordon rejected any formal ties between Zionism and the international socialist movement. This synergy among Borochov, Syrkin, and Gordon saw its conclusion in the kibbutz movement, which was a marriage of practicality and social experimentation that sought to attain perfect harmony among Jews in a communal society.

Not surprisingly, the fissures that divided world socialism manifested themselves in labor Zionism. As the divisions became more pronounced, the movement began to splinter. In 1930 a significant number of Jews wedded to leftist Zionism formed the Mapai Party, which became the most pronounced political movement in Palestine (and later Israel). More divisions occurred in the 1940s, and in 1944 a splinter group from Mapai formed Ahdut Ha'avodah, which grew to prominence because of its close ties to the kibbutzim and the Palmach. The power of Histadrut, Mapai, and, for a time, Ahdut Ha'avodah left deep and lasting imprints on the Israeli political landscape. Indeed, not until the rise of the rightist Likud Party in 1977 was the hegemony of the Left challenged with any seriousness.

By the mid-1980s, Labor Zionism's influence and prestige had peaked. Just as the size and scope of Histadrut began to drop off, so too did the strength of the traditional Left in Israel. To keep its agenda alive, Labor Zionism has to a considerable extent embraced liberal capitalism. Nonetheless, there is considerable debate in Israel over state funding and land use in order to make cooperatives more profitable. What also separates leftists and rightists in Israel are their orientations toward the Arab-Israeli peace process. In general, Labor Zionists and the leftists tend to support peace efforts, including the land-for-peace formula. The rightists are either opposed to or very cautious toward any accommodation with the Palestinians or neighboring Arab states.

PAUL G. PIERPAOLI JR.

See also
Herzl, Theodor; Hess, Moses; Histadrut; Kibbutz Movement; Weizmann, Chaim; Zionism

References

Avineri, Shlomo. *The Making of Modern Zionism: The Intellectual Origins of the Jewish State.* New York: Basic Books, 1981.

Bernstein, Deborah S. *Constructing Boundaries: Jewish and Arab Workers in Mandatory Palestine.* Albany, NY: SUNY Press, 2000.

Gorny, Yosef. *Converging Alternatives: The Bund and the Zionist Labor Movement, 1897–1985.* Albany, NY: SUNY Press, 2006.

Sachar, Howard M. *A History of Israel: From the Rise of Zionism to Our Time.* 3rd ed. New York: Knopf, 2007.

Lahoud, Émile Jamil
Born: January 12, 1936

Lebanese Army general and president of Lebanon since 1998. Émile (Imil) Jamil Lahoud (Lahud) was born on January 12, 1936, in Beirut, Lebanon. His father, General Jamil Lahoud, was a Maronite Christian and a founding officer of the Lebanese Army who later served as labor and social affairs minister in 1960 and as a member of the National Assembly in 1960 and 1964. Lahoud's mother was of Armenian descent and was born in Syria.

Continuing the family tradition, the younger Lahoud enrolled in the Lebanese military academy as a cadet in 1956 and was commissioned a sublieutenant in the Lebanese Navy in 1959. During 1958–1960 he studied naval engineering in Britain. He later earned a degree in maritime engineering in Britain and studied at the U.S. Naval War College at Newport, Rhode Island, during 1972–1973 and 1979–1980.

Lahoud rose steadily through the ranks of the Lebanese military throughout the 1970s and 1980s, serving in various military leadership positions and several senior posts at the Defense Ministry. He was promoted to rear admiral in 1985. In November 1989 he was advanced to vice admiral and assumed the post of commander of the Lebanese armed forces. Reportedly this appointment had the blessing of the Syrian government. As army commander, Lahoud established a reputation for efficiency and integrity. He worked to rebuild the fragmented forces, which had splintered into feuding Muslim and Christian militias during the country's 15-year civil war. Under Lahoud, nearly all of the militias were disarmed and dissolved, and order was restored to the military as the army was reunited and rebuilt.

In late 1998, with Syria largely controlling Lebanese affairs since 1989, Syrian president Hafez al-Assad negotiated with retiring president Elias Hrawi and gave his consent to Lahoud's candidacy for the presidency. With Syrian backing, Lahoud's election by the National Assembly was little more than a formality. Nonetheless, on October 15, 1998, Lahoud was voted in unanimously by all 118 deputies present. He was sworn in on November 24. His ascendancy to the presidency required a last-minute amendment to the Lebanese

President of Lebanon Émile Lahoud addressing the United Nations General Assembly in 2005. (Stephen Koh/United Nations)

constitution (1926), which had banned state officials from serving as president within three years of leaving their state posts.

Although the appointment of a military commander as president prompted criticism from those concerned about an increased military role in politics, many expressed expectations that the former armed forces chief would take on a new challenge to root out sectarianism as iterated in the Taif Agreement (1989) and corruption in the public sector. According to the Lebanese constitution, the president was limited to one six-year term. In 2004, again under Syrian pressure, the Lebanese parliament voted to extend Lahoud's term for an additional three years, to 2007. (The same situation had occurred with his predecessor, Hrawi.) Opposition leaders in Lebanon cried foul because this had been carried out in violation of the constitution and under foreign pressure. Critics included Maronite cardinal Nasrallah Sfeir and Druze leader Walid Jumblat (Junblat). Another outspoken opponent was Prime Minister Rafik Hariri, who resigned to protest the extension of Lahoud's term of office. Hariri was later assassinated, and the murder was suspected to have been instigated or arranged by Syria. Lahoud's tenure in office has seen continuing unrest in Lebanon, including the withdrawal of Syrian forces, the Israeli bombardment of Lebanon in July and August 2006, and the March 8th Alliance (Hezbollah and Michel Aoun's followers) protests against the government.

SPENCER C. TUCKER

See also

Assad, Hafez al-; Hariri, Rafik; Hrawi, Elias; Lebanon; Lebanon, Israeli Operations against

References

Fisk, Robert. *Pity the Nation: The Abduction of Lebanon.* 4th ed. New York: Nation Books, 2002.

Lake Kinneret

Lake Kinneret (the Sea of Galilee) is a freshwater lake in northeastern Israel. It is Israel's largest freshwater lake and the world's lowest lake. Lake Kinneret lies in the Dead Sea section of the Syrian-African Rift Valley, which was formed by the separation of the African and Arabian plates. This region is subject to earthquakes, and violent storms on the lake are common.

With a surface area of 64 square miles, Lake Kinneret is 15 miles long in a north-to-south direction and 10 miles wide in an east-to-west direction. The surface of the lake is almost 700 feet below sea level, and at its deepest the water is about 144 feet deep. Sediment eroded from the surrounding basalt hills gives the water a dark blue color. The lake is fed by the Jordan River bringing freshwater as well as by springs with saltwater within the basin and at its periphery. High evaporation rates due to a hot, dry climate increase Lake Kinneret's salinity and the outflow, via the Jordan River to the Dead Sea, is saltier than its inflow. The volume of water varies from year to year depending on the amount of rainfall received in its catchment, and persistent drought reduces water levels substantially. Politically,

Lake Kinneret is an issue of dispute between Syria and Israel because of the latter's 1967 annexation of the Golan Heights, which denies Syria access to an international boundary within the lake.

Israel's National Water Carrier Project uses Lake Kinneret as a reservoir from which water is transported through pumping stations, reservoirs, and tunnels to the south via the National Water Conduit to the Negev Desert for irrigation and to the west to recharge the overdrawn aquifers of the coastal plain. This highlights the value of the lake to Israel for water supply. Lake Kinneret contains about 700 million cubic meters of water and is described as the heart of Israel's water system. It is managed by the Lake Kinneret Authority, which was founded in 1969 to control pollution from sewage and agriculture and to regulate water use.

Fruit growing is important in the lake's catchment, and of the lake's 27 species of fish the most economically significant is the Galilee tilapia, also known as the Saint Peter fish. Fish farming occurs along the lake's margins and is a source of pollution by phosphates. Local and migratory birds, such as the stork and white heron, are abundant.

Recreation and tourism are also economic activities. The latter is encouraged by the interesting geology of the rift valley and the importance of the lake and its hinterland in human history. This includes its location on a likely route for early hominids to migrate from Africa into Asia and Europe. The earliest evidence, about 1.4 million years old, comes from the archaeological site of al-Ubaydiyya (once an Arab village), immediately south of Lake Kinneret, where stone tools, made by *Homo erectus,* occur as well as the fossils of large mammals. The lake was important in the Egyptian, Greek, and Roman eras when settlements on its shores were founded. Its association with the life of Jesus has made it an important site of pilgrimages for 2,000 years.

ANTOINETTE MANNION

See also

Geography of the Middle East; Golan Heights; Jordan River; Negev Desert; Syria; Water Rights and Resources

References

Beck, John A. *The Land of Milk and Honey: An Introduction to the Geography of Israel.* St. Louis: Concordia, 2006.

Orni, Ephraim. *Geography of Israel.* Philadelphia: Jewish Publication Society of America, 1977.

Tal, Y. *Pollution in a Promised Land: An Environmental History of Israel.* Berkeley: University of California Press, 2002.

Land Day
Event Date: March 30, 1976

Protest by Palestinian militants against confiscation of their land by the State of Israel. On March 30, 1976, 6 Arabs were killed and some 70 more wounded when Israeli soldiers opened fire on demonstrators hurling stones and firebombs in Nazareth. Palestinian and Israeli Arabs commemorate this event each year with Land Day, calling attention to Israeli land seizure and confiscation policies.

Israeli Arabs demonstrating in Galilee on Land Day, March 30, 1976. (David Rubinger/Corbis)

The incident was triggered by the Israeli government announcement on March 11, 1976, of plans to expropriate some 5,250 acres of land in Galilee. Reacting to the news, Arab militants called for a general strike on March 30. Rioting occurred the night before and on March 30. Land Day in 2006 saw demonstrations in the Israeli town of Lod, which is one-third Palestinian Arab, and Arab media in other countries included historical information about the dispossession of Palestinian lands and property.

SPENCER C. TUCKER

See also

Land Rights and Disputes

References

Farsoum, Samih K., and Naseer H. Aruri. *Palestine and the Palestinians: A Social and Political History.* 2nd ed. Jackson, TN: Westview, 2006.

La Guardia, Anton. *War without End: Palestinians and the Struggle for a Promised Land.* New York: Thomas Dunne, 2002.

Land Rights and Disputes

Disputes over land lie at the very heart of the conflict between Palestinians and Israelis. The Israeli War of Independence (1948–1949) forced out or caused much of the Arab population to flee the 10,000 square miles that was Palestine. This conflict arose because of the territorial conflict and followed years of land acquisition policies intended to expand areas of Jewish settlement. The resulting reappropriation of Arab-owned or Arab-tilled lands and property in the wake of the war continued through security measures and the application of military law and in new land policies that promoted continuing seizure of land owned or occupied by Arabs.

Jewish efforts to purchase land, especially property owned by absentee landlords, began early. Prior to 1920, however, most Arabs either did not understand the land acquisition policies or did not believe they would succeed in de-Arabizing Palestine. At the heart of Zionist land redemption policies was the maxim that once land was purchased or later seized from Palestinians or reclassified as land available for Jewish settlement, it could never be returned or resold to Arabs.

In the Ottoman period much land was held in tenancy, meaning that peasant villagers were never concerned about obtaining land to work on near the village. But these village lands were not necessarily registered in their names. The Ottomans had begun registering landowners for taxation purposes, but the collectively owned land later came under dispute. In addition, land that was not tilled, land with unpaid taxes, or land that had unclear heirs was considered miri, or state land.

As the flow of Jewish immigrants to Palestine continued and

accelerated, Arab concerns were heightened, especially when Jewish settlers' purchases of Arab lands became more widely known. In fact, an important dynamic in the 1930s was the large increase in landless peasants due to sales of common holdings to which they were not a party. Their resulting desperation led to the 1936–1939 Arab Revolt. The Holocaust, which took place during World War II and resulted in the deaths of some 6 million Jews, only aggravated the situation, as many of those Jews who had managed to survive were now determined to settle in Palestine.

The situation was further complicated by the 1947 United Nations (UN) partition plan of Palestine, which Arabs decried. The mutual distrust and hatred between Arabs and Jews deepened following the Jewish victory in the Israeli War of Independence. Arab anger mounted when Israel captured significant amounts of Arab land during the 1967 Six-Day War.

Conflict over landholdings and property took place all over the former British Mandate for Palestine. Under the military orders utilized after 1950, Palestinian property was constantly seized. Much of this was turned over to new occupants, most notoriously through use of Article 125 of the Emergency Regulations (dating back to 1945) that gave the military governor the authority to declare any area closed or forbidden. All Arab areas and villages were closed in the Triangle, the Galilee, and the Negev, meaning residents had to have a permit to enter and leave. Some were closed in the sense that residents were never permitted to return. An even more important method of expropriating land for the state was through the Absentee Property Law of 1950. The Israeli government used this law to claim the land of those who had fled or were driven out in 1948, including cultivated land, homes, and businesses and also those of so-called internal absentees, Palestinians who had fled to a different place within Israel. About 40 percent of their land was claimed in addition to all of the land abandoned by the external absentees.

From 1959, a new stage in land policy began with the aim of settling more Jewish Israelis in the Galilee. This idea may have originated with Joseph Nahmani, who aimed to break up large concentrations of Arab villages in that part of the country. Myriad schemes to balance areas of Arab population included the expropriation of 1,200 dunums of land northeast of Nazareth, confiscated from Arab owners under the 1943 Land Ordinance with the justification that it was needed for building government offices. The land was in fact used for Jewish housing, a chocolate factory, and textile factories to provide incomes to these new residents. The landholders protested this action to the Israeli Supreme Court to no avail. Projects in Maalot-Tarshiha and expropriation to build the town of Karmiel followed. The same process went on in the south and elsewhere, with at least 1 million dunums of land expropriated by about 1974.

Settlements increased inside Israel proper, and after the 1967 war Arabs landholdings and Arab freedom of movement decreased, especially in the area around East Jerusalem, the Gaza Strip, the West Bank, and the Golan Heights. Throughout, Israeli land policies turned the Palestinians into essentially resident aliens. Oddly, those inside of Israel are citizen resident aliens but not members of the nation. Those in the West Bank and Gaza were considered resident aliens who could never become Israeli citizens. As a result, the two-state solution became the only viable option for them.

Settlers were determined to establish bases even within the Muslim-defined area of the Old City in Jerusalem. They encountered and generated considerable hostility in order to extend greater Jewish control over East Jerusalem. This was by no means an effort solely led by settlers, however. By 2002 there were more than 200,000 Jews living in areas of Jerusalem annexed after 1967.

By 1967, a large number of Jewish settlements had been established. In the West Bank, 20 settlements were established in what is known as Greater Jerusalem. Eighteen settlements were established in West Samaria where the very large settlement of Ariel is located. Also, there were 12 settlements in West Benjamin, 44 in the Jordan Valley and the Judean Desert, 5 in the Reyhan-Dotan bloc by Wadi Ara, 4 in the Einav-Sali'it bloc, and 5 in the south closer to Beersheba and Arad in the Eshkolot-Smi'a bloc. Many organized Jewish groups have participated in these settlements, and each has needed safe transport, meaning road security and armored buses moving along bypass roads, which often were carved through Palestinian orchards, buildings, and fields. A great deal of official and unofficial settlement activity occurred since 1967. One category consists of official outposts (not contiguous with existing settlements). Seventy-four of these outposts were established after the Oslo Accords, and 27 new settlement outposts were built after the Wye Memorandum. Since March 2001, the government has approved some 15 new settlement outposts. In addition, unofficial settlements, or seized land, have been established, and the media was instructed not to report these as settlements but rather as Jewish neighborhoods. Two examples are Gilo and French Hill within Israel. This is in fact the main reason that Palestinians attacked Israeli civilians there.

The Israeli position is that the West Bank is not annexed and technically not occupied. Hence, the Geneva Convention does not apply to the West Bank. As with land expropriations inside the Green Line, the Absentee Property Law of 1950 was also applied to the West Bank. The Israeli withdrawal from Gaza in 2005 did also include a withdrawal from five small settlements in the West Bank.

Those groups that established settlements in Gaza created a security nightmare for the Israeli government and a burden on the residents of the Gaza Strip, whose mobility and livelihood were secondary to the security needs of the settlers. Following Israel's 2005 withdrawal of its settlements in Gaza, the Gaza Strip was handed over to the Palestinian Authority (PA), although Israel maintains control over maritime, airspace, and most other access to the Gaza Strip. In 2006, however, Israeli forces reentered the Gaza Strip following the kidnapping of an Israeli soldier and his removal to Gaza.

The Golan Heights has also witnessed the destruction of Arab villages and expropriation of land for Jewish settlements. But in addition, land is held in the Golan Heights for recreation, hiking, camping, historic sites such as Gamla, and access to the Jordan River.

One constantly transmitted message is that Israel is handling the resources of the region more responsibly than its former inhabitants. A general theme of land use that permeates public relations in Israel is the idea that Israel has created a garden in the dry and dusty land that Arabs had neglected. Certainly, the attachment to the land promoted by early Zionism (intended to appeal to the landlessness of the East European Jewry) has much to do with this theme, which also pervades popular culture, songs, and the like. Palestinians have also utilized metaphors of the land as a living being, a bride, to which they are attached.

Palestinian Arab refugees who were expelled or fled their homes during the 1948–1949 Israeli War of Independence claim that their land, now held by Israelis, should be returned to them or that some sort of compensation plan should be devised. This right of return has not been dealt with satisfactorily in any peace plan, with the possible exception of the unofficial Geneva Accords.

Legal scholars and world leaders still remain widely divided about most facets of the land dispute. Many previous attempts to settle this issue, including the 1936–1937 Peel Commission Plan, the 1947 UN partition plan, and the 1993 Oslo Accords, all failed to find an equitable answer to the question of who should control the disputed lands in Israel and Palestine.

GREGORY MORGAN AND SHERIFA ZUHUR

See also

Gaza Strip; Gaza Strip Disengagement; Jerusalem; Jerusalem, Old City of; Oslo Accords; Palestinian Authority; Peel Commission; United Nations, Role of; United Nations Palestine Partition Plan; West Bank

References

Jiryis, Sabri. *The Arabs in Israel.* Translated by Inea Bushnaq. New York: Monthly Review Press, 1976.

Pappe, Ilan. *A History of Modern Palestine: One Land, Two Peoples.* Cambridge: Cambridge University Press, 2003.

Smith, Charles D. *Palestine and the Arab-Israeli Conflict: A History with Documents.* 6th ed. New York: Bedford/St. Martin's, 2006.

Sheffer, Gabriel. *Moshe Sharett: Biography of a Political Moderate.* New York: Oxford University Press, 1996.

Takkenberg, Alex. *The Status of Palestinian Refugees in International Law.* New York and Oxford: Oxford University Press, 1998.

Tessler, Mark. *A History of the Israeli-Palestinian Conflict.* Bloomington: Indiana University Press, 1994.

Thomas, Baylis. *How Israel Was Won: A Concise History of the Arab-Israeli Conflict.* Lanham, MD: Lexington Books, 1999.

Laskov, Haim

Born: 1919
Died: 1982

Israeli general and chief of staff of the Israel Defense Forces (IDF) during 1958–1960. Haim Laskov was born in 1919 in Belorussia. In 1925 he immigrated to Palestine with his family. He lived in Haifa, and it was there that he joined the youth section of Haganah, the

Lieutenant General Haim Laskov, chief of staff of the Israel Defense Forces (1958–1960), pictured here in 1958. (Israeli Government Press Office)

secret Jewish self-defense military organization. In 1930 Laskov's father was killed by a group of Arabs.

During World War II, Laskov was commissioned in the British Army and served with it in North Africa. He then joined the Jewish Brigade and fought in Italy as a company commander with the rank of major. Returning to Palestine in 1947, he joined the staff of Haganah, which became the fledgling IDF. He received command of an armored car battalion.

In the 1948 campaigns during the Israeli War of Independence, Laskov first commanded the 79th Armored Battalion of the 7th Brigade in Operation NACHSHON. This was the first Israeli brigade-sized action and was devoted to opening the road to Jerusalem. The fighting centered around Latrun, and Laskov's forces were heavily engaged. Promoted to brigadier general, he took command of Operation DEKEL during which he commanded the 7th Brigade and elements of the Golani Brigade. During 10 days of fighting, his units took control of the entire area around Nazareth.

In 1951 Laskov became the commander of the Israeli Air Force, a position he held until 1953. The appointment of Laskov, who was not an airman, was undoubtedly an effort to continue the subordination of the air force to the army. Yet during his tenure, Laskov sought to establish the independence of the air force from the army. In 1953 he chose to study at Oxford University, but he was recalled in 1955 and became deputy chief of the General Staff. In 1956 he took command of the Armored Corps. During the Sinai Campaign that same year, he commanded a divisional-sized task force with the objective of capturing the key town of Rafa. In a well-coordinated attack through Egyptian minefields, Laskov's forces overcame a series of strong points and took Rafa.

In 1958 Laskov was appointed chief of staff of the IDF and advanced to lieutenant general. He served in that capacity until 1960. He retired from the military in 1961. He subsequently served as director-general of Israel's ports authority. In 1972 he was the ombudsman for the military. Laskov died in Tel Aviv in 1982.

RALPH MARTIN BAKER

See also

Israel Defense Forces; Latrun, Battles of; NACHSHON, Operation; Sinai Campaign; Suez Crisis

References

Golani, Moti. *Israel in Search of a War: The Sinai Campaign, 1955–1956.* East Sussex, UK: Sussex Academic, 1997.

Kurzman, Dan. *Genesis 1948: The First Arab-Israeli War.* New York: Da Capo, 1992.

Latakia, Battle of
Event Date: October 6, 1973

The Battle of Latakia (Ladhakiyya, Syria) occurred on the night of October 6, 1973, the first day of the Yom Kippur War. The naval engagement takes its name from Syria's chief seaport on the Mediterranean Sea. It was fought between Israeli and Syrian missile boats, the first battle between missile-firing ships in naval history.

The Egyptian and Syrian attack against Israel on October 6, 1973, caught Israeli forces by surprise. Israeli Navy missile boats put to sea that very evening to carry out a long-planned attack against units of the Syrian Navy. It would be the first combat test for the missile boats, on which the Israeli Navy had expended much energy over the previous decade. The task would not be an easy one, however. The Israeli Gabriel antiship missile used a joystick tracking system requiring that the operator keep it on target by radar. It had never been fired in actual combat. Meanwhile, the Soviet SS-N-2 Styx fire-and-forget (meaning that it does not require human tracing once fired) missile employed by the Syrians was combat-proven, with Egyptian missile boats having fired several of them to sink the Israeli destroyer *Eilat* in October 1967 and, in May 1968, sink the small wooden fishing vessel *Orit.* In addition, Israeli-developed electronic countermeasures (ECM) to defeat the Styx had never been tested in combat. Were these to fail, the Israeli missile boats would be easy prey for the radar-guided Styx missile, which had a range of some 27 miles, more than twice the 12-mile range of the Israeli Gabriel.

Nonetheless, with Israel's army and air force fighting desperately on land and in the air to contain the large Egyptian and Syrian offensives, the navy was determined to do its part and remove the possibility of a Syrian naval attack on the Israeli Mediterranean coast. The Israeli plan was to lure the Syrian missile boats out and engage them at the maximum range of their Styx missiles, which the Israelis hoped to defeat through chaff and electronic countermeasures (ECM). Once the Syrians had shot away their missiles, the Israelis planned to close and engage the Syrian boats at the effective range of their own missiles. Come what may, the Israelis were determined to engage the Syrians.

Commander Michael Barkai commanded the Israeli naval flotilla committed to the operation. It consisted of five missile boats (the Saar-class *Gaash, Hanit,* and *Miznak* and the Reshef-class *Mivtach* and *Reshef*). He took his flotilla wide to the west toward Cyprus to avoid Syrian coastal radar. Barkai planned to attack from the north, the direction the Syrians would least expect. The boats proceeded in two parallel columns: Barkai's own *Miznak* (flagship), *Gaash,* and *Hanit* to port and the *Mivtach* and *Reshef* to starboard and slightly behind, several miles closer to shore.

Some 35 miles southwest of Latakia, the *Miznak,* which was in the lead, picked up a radar contact four miles to the northwest moving east across the Israeli course and apparently making for Latakia at full speed. Lookouts on the *Miznak*'s bridge reported that the vessel in question had a low profile and was moving without lights. Fearful that the vessel in question might be a civilian ship, Barkai ordered the *Miznak* to fire warning 40-mm rounds. The unknown vessel then opened up with return machine-gun fire. A searchlight on one of the Saar boats enabled the Israelis to identify the vessel as a Syrian torpedo boat, undoubtedly a picket boat to warn against an attack. The three Saar-class missile boats in Barkai's column them opened fire on the torpedo boat but failed to hit it. The torpedo boat was too small a target to warrant a missile, and the *Reshef* in the right-hand column then opened fire with its 76-mm gun at extreme range of about 10 miles. Soon the wooden torpedo boat was dead in the water.

Syrian naval headquarters meanwhile had received a message from the picket boat of the attack, and it ordered a minesweeper, also on picket duty and some 10 miles from shore, to immediately seek the protection of Syrian coastal guns at full speed. Headquarters also informed three Syrian missile boats that had just headed from Latakia south of the Israeli presence at sea.

Barkai had to assume that the Syrian torpedo boat had reported the Israeli presence. He now abandoned the carefully rehearsed Israeli plan of an attack from the north and fighting at optimum distance in favor of an immediate descent on Latakia from the west. Barkai, however, detached the *Hanit* to sink the Syrian torpedo boat.

As the four remaining Israeli missile boats headed east, the *Reshef* picked up another radar contact some 15 miles to the east. It was the Syrian minesweeper heading at full speed to safety. Soon the *Goash* fired a Gabriel at the new target, but this was the extreme length of its range. The Syrian ship was able to increase the range in the two minutes it took the Gabriel to reach the area, and the missile fell short. The *Reshef* in the starboard column then fired another Gabriel at some 12 miles. This missile struck the 560-ton Syrian minesweeper dead on. The *Reshef* then fired a second Gabriel. It too hit home, although the minesweeper remained afloat. The detached *Hamit* subsequently finished it off from close range with another Gabriel and 76-mm cannon fire.

Even as it prepared to fire its second missile and the four Israeli missile boats were continuing their course for Latakia, the *Reshef* picked up three additional radar contacts. These were the Syrian missile boats, one Osa-class vessel and two Komar-class vessels, that had turned back to meet the attackers. As the Israeli missile boats continued on course, the Syrians fired their missiles at a range from which the Israelis could not reply. Their targets were the closest Israeli missile boats, the *Reshef* and *Mivtach*. As the Syrian missiles approached, the Israelis fired off chaff rockets and employed the jamming and deceptor systems to send out false radar signals to the incoming Styx missiles. Unlike the Gabriel, which was guided to its target by an operator on the mother ship, the Styx was a fire-and-forget missile, and those who fired it had no control over it once it was launched.

Israeli ECM systems functioned perfectly. The Syrian missiles either flew harmlessly overhead or fell short. The Israelis pressed their attack, now confident of success. Only one of the Syrian missile boats—the *Osa*—still had missiles left. It turned to face the Israeli flotilla as the two Komar-class missile boats fled for Latakia at high speed. The Israelis closed at full speed. At this critical juncture, a short circuit on the *Reshef* prevented a missile launch. The *Mivtach* was not equipped with missiles, and this left only the *Gaash* and *Miznak* capable of engaging the Syrians. They let loose a salvo of Gabriel missiles while at the same time defeating two more Styx missiles fired against them by the *Osa*. The 330-pound Gabriel warhead was more than sufficient to destroy the two Komar-class Syrian missile boats, which were about a third the size of the minesweeper and loaded with fuel.

The *Osa*, its missiles expended, raced for the shore, where its captain simply ran it up on the shore. Barkai was determined to destroy it with gunfire. He ordered the other three missile boats to keep out of range of the Syrian shore batteries, which had begun to fire, and took the *Miznak* in to a range of about half a mile, opening up with its three 40-mm cannon. Soon the beached *Osa* was ablaze and exploding. The battle was over. Shortly after midnight on October 7, the Israeli missile boats returned to base.

Following the Battle of Latakia, the Syrian Navy remained in port for the rest of the war. The battle also brought new prestige to the Israeli Navy, previously regarded by most observers as only a poor relation of Israel's highly regarded army and air force. Israeli ECM techniques employed in the battle set a new standard for subsequent naval engagements employing missiles.

SPENCER C. TUCKER

See also
Baltim, Battle of; Yom Kippur War

References
Erell, Shlomo. "Israeli Saar FPBs Pass Combat Test in the Yom Kippur War." *U.S. Naval Institute Proceedings* (September 1974): 115–118.
Rabinovich, Abraham. *The Boats of Cherbourg: The Secret Israeli Operation That Revolutionized Naval Warfare.* New York: Seaver, 1988.

Latrun, Battles of
Start Date: May 25, 1948
End Date: July 18, 1948

The first battle of Latrun was the single bloodiest defeat suffered by a modern Israeli Army. The town of Latrun, situated about 9 miles west of Jerusalem, sits on the first dominating piece of high ground rising from the coast. The Ayalon Valley just below Latrun is the site of the biblical battle in which Joshua defeated the Amorites. During the Crusades the Templars built a stronghold at Latrun, the gateway to the Judean hills. Following the Arab Revolt of 1936–1939, the British built a police fort, called a Taggert Fort, at Latrun in order to control the main road from Tel Aviv to Jerusalem.

When the British departed Palestine on May 14, 1948, two battalions of the 4th Brigade of the Transjordan Arab Legion occupied the fort at Latrun and the surrounding positions, including Hill 314. From there they were able to interdict Jewish supply columns into Jerusalem, effectively cutting off the Jewish population in the city. Israeli prime minister David Ben-Gurion was concerned that the Jews would lose all claims to Jerusalem if they could not break the siege before a cease-fire brokered by the United Nations (UN) went into effect on June 11. Over the objections of Yigal Yadin and other Haganah commanders, who argued that they simply did not have the military resources to accomplish the mission, Ben-Gurion ordered that the road had to be opened.

The first Israeli attack was launched in the early morning hours of May 25. Shlomo Shamir commanded a force of some 1,650 soldiers of the 7th Brigade and 450 soldiers of the 32nd Battalion, detached from the Alexandroni Brigade. Many of the Israeli soldiers were newly arrived immigrants, Holocaust survivors from Europe's displaced persons camps. Most had virtually no military training, spoke little Hebrew, and did not even know how to release the safeties on their rifles.

As an underground army, Haganah had conducted a number of successful operations against irregular Arab elements. As the new Jewish Army, however, it had never before fought a conventional battle against a regular force, and the Arab Legion was the best-trained and best-equipped army in the Middle East, with about two-thirds of its officers being British.

Moving forward in bright moonlight, Shamir's troops were easy targets for the Arab machine guns and modern 25-pounder field guns. The total Israeli artillery consisted of two 65-mm French-manufactured guns dating from 1906. Twelve hours after they started, the remnants of Haganah attackers staggered back to their lines of departure. Although the casualty figures for the battle have

Lieutenant Colonel Chaim Herzog (*center*) and Arab Legion representatives delineate the border at Latrun, July 1948. The battle at Latrun was a costly defeat for Israel. (David Eldan/Israeli Government Press Office)

been disputed for many years, the official total figure is 139 dead, almost all on the Jewish side.

After the failure of the first attack, Ben-Gurion appointed Colonel David Marcus, an American volunteer, as overall commander of the Jerusalem front with orders to lift the siege. The Israelis again attacked Latrun on May 30. This second attack was much better planned and executed and was supported by 22 locally fabricated armored cars and 13 half-tracks that Israeli agents had purchased in Antwerp. The battle was thus the first armored attack launched by an Israeli army. This force, however, was still not enough to overcome the Arab Legion.

Following failure of the second attack, Marcus concluded that the only solution was to go around the Arab Legion. Sending engineers and construction crews into the wild Judean hills south of Latrun, he oversaw the extension and improvement of a series of goat trails into a credible military road, which he wryly called the Burma Road. He meanwhile launched a number of holding attacks against Latrun to pin down the Arab Legion and prevent it from disrupting his road-building operation. Despite enormous obstacles, the new land bridge was completed on June 9, lifting the siege of Jerusalem. That same day, Marcus launched a third attack to take Latrun, this time from the rear. Again, the professional and well-armed Arab Legion could not be budged.

After the breakdown of the first cease-fire on July 9, the Israelis made a fourth attempt during July 14–18 to capture Latrun. They again failed. Even though they had managed to establish a thin land corridor into Jerusalem, Latrun remained a dagger pointed at the vital logistics artery. The Jordanian position was also only a few miles from Israeli's only international airport.

The IDF finally took Latrun during the 1967 Six-Day War. Today the Taggert Fort is the official headquarters of the IDF's Armored Corps and the home of its Armor Museum.

Latrun was one of the most formative experiences of future general and prime minister Ariel Sharon, who as a 20-year-old platoon leader in the 32nd Battalion was wounded seriously in the battle. In later years, Sharon noted that Latrun taught him the importance of properly training and equipping his men and of always holding the high ground.

DAVID T. ZABECKI

See also

Arab Legion; Arab Revolt of 1936–1939; Ben-Gurion, David; Haganah; Marcus, David; Sharon, Ariel; Six-Day War; Yadin, Yigal

References

Berkman, Ted. *Cast a Giant Shadow*. Garden City, NY: Doubleday, 1962.

Collins, Larry, and Dominique Lapierre. *O Jerusalem!* New York: Simon and Schuster, 1972.

Herzog, Chaim. *The Arab-Israeli Wars: War and Peace in the Middle East from the War of Independence to Lebanon.* Westminster, MD: Random House, 1984.

Lavon Affair
Start Date: July 1954
End Date: December 11, 1954

Part of a secret Israeli plan to have Egyptian Jewish citizens carry out acts of sabotage against American and British interests in Egypt with the aim of alienating the United States and Britain from the regime of Egyptian president Gamal Abdel Nasser. The Lavon Affair of 1954, known to the Israeli secret services as Operation SUZANNAH, involved Israel's military intelligence branch (Aman) organizing, training, and funding a group of Egyptian Jewish saboteurs. The operation was named the Lavon Affair after then-Israeli defense minister Pinhas Lavon, although he was not responsible for it. Rather, Colonel Benyamin Gibli, chief of Aman, initiated Operation SUZANNAH with the intended aim of possibly preventing Egypt from nationalizing the Suez Canal.

Aman had recruited members of a secret Egyptian ring prior to 1954, when Israeli intelligence officer Avram Dar went to Cairo posing as a British businessman named John Darling. There Dar trained a number of Egyptian Jews for covert operations. Aman also covertly brought the Egyptian Jews to Israel for training in the use of explosives. Aman activated the ring in the spring of 1954. In July of that year, the saboteurs bombed post offices, a railway terminal, two U.S. Information Agency libraries, and a British theater. Egyptian authorities arrested ringmember Robert Dassa, when his bomb prematurely ignited in his pocket. The authorities searched Dassa's home and found incriminating evidence and names of accomplices. On October 5, 1954, the Egyptians announced the arrest of a 13-person spy ring and put them on trial on December 11.

As a result of a public trial, two of the defendants were acquitted, five received sentences ranging from seven years to life imprisonment, and two were sentenced to death and hanged. Two had already committed suicide in prison. Because the Israeli government refused to acknowledge the operation during the trial, the Israeli public remained uninformed and the Jewish press characterized the trial as an outrageous, anti-Jewish frame-up.

The operation later caused a scandal in the Israeli government, and both Lavon and Gibli were forced to relinquish their positions. The Lavon Affair also damaged Israel's relations with the United States and Great Britain. Not surprisingly, the operation's tactics caused deep-seated suspicion of Israeli intelligence methods both in the Middle East and around the world.

PAUL J. MAGNARELLA

See also

Egypt; Israel; Nasser, Gamal Abdel; Suez Canal

References

Black, Ian, and Benny Morris. *Israel's Secret Wars: A History of Israel's Intelligence Services.* New York: Grove, 1994.

Golan, Aviezer. *Operation Susannah.* New York: Harper and Row, 1978.

Hirst, David. *The Gun and the Olive Branch: The Roots of Violence in the Middle East.* 2nd ed. New York: Nation Books, 2003.

Law of Return
Event Date: July 5, 1950

Law passed by the first Knesset (Israeli parliament) in July 1950 governing the return of Jews to Israel. The law stated that Israel was a homeland not only for Jews then residing there but also for Jews everywhere in the world. Prime Minister David Ben-Gurion announced regarding Israel, "This is not only a Jewish state, where the majority of the inhabitants are Jews, but a state for all Jews, wherever they are, and for every Jew that wants to be here. This right is inherent in being a Jew." The law was intended to encourage Jewish settlement in Eretz Israel (the Land of Israel). The law must be understood in the context of when it was passed. It occurred only five years after the end of World War II and the Holocaust that had seen the systematic slaughter of more than 6 million European Jews. Although Israel had emerged victorious over its Arab neighbors in its war for independence, Israelis worried both about their small numbers vis-à-vis their far more populous Arab neighbors and the possible return of Palestinians forced from their homes during the war.

The Law of Return was designed to fulfill Theodor Herzl's Zionist vision of a state that would protect all Jews. The law did not automatically grant Israeli citizenship, nor did it specifically exclude non-Jews. However, every immigrant must meet the requirements as stipulated in the Law of Entry to Israel and the Law of Citizenship of 1952. These requirements resemble the laws of most countries. For example, all immigrants must live in Israel for three years prior to submission of any application of citizenship. In addition, they must become legal residents in Israel and settle permanently there.

Interestingly, it is a requirement that before applying for Israeli citizenship, the potential immigrant must renounce all prior nationalities and citizenships or at least must legally prove that he or she will no longer be a foreign national upon becoming an Israeli citizen. While the law indicates who can be a citizen, it is also clear as to who may not become a citizen. Excluded are Jews who have converted to other religions as well as those who are an imminent danger to public health, state security, or the Jewish people as a whole. Terrorists, by any definition, are not entitled to return even if they are Jewish. The law permits the government to define "terrorist."

In 1970 the Knesset amended the Law of Return to allow for additional immigration, especially from the United States. It not only offered the right of immigration to Jews, defined as a person born of a Jewish mother or who had converted to Judaism, but also the right to the children and grandchildren of a Jew, to the non-Jewish spouses of Jews, to the non-Jewish spouses of children of Jews, and even the non-Jewish spouses of non-Jewish grandchildren of Jews.

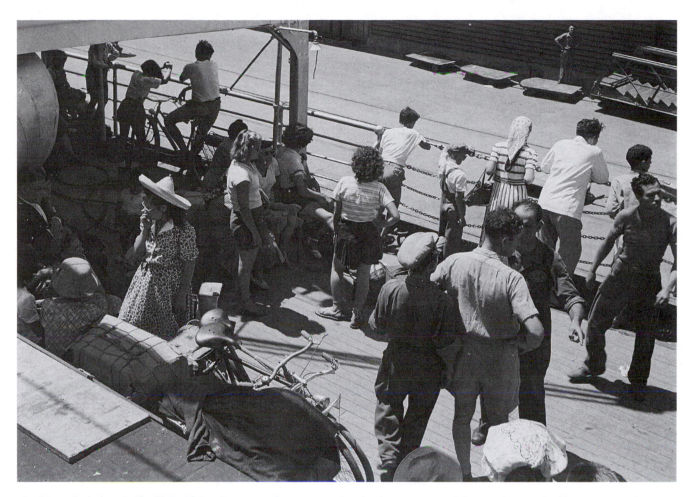

The ship *Negba* docks at Haifa with Jewish immigrants on July 6, 1950, one day after the Knesset passed the Law of Return. (Teddy Brauner/Israeli Government Press Office)

Since the mid-1980s, tensions in the Middle East and the influx of East European Jews into Israel have challenged the efficacy of the law. By December 1994, the large influx of Jews from the former Soviet Union placed an economic, social, and cultural strain on Israel. The Israeli government attempted to ease the crisis by creating temporary settlements in the West Bank, but this led to a military confrontation with the Palestinians.

One major issue has been that of who has authority over the validity of conversions to Judaism in order to immigrate to Israel and be eligible for citizenship. In a decision that angered Orthodox leaders, in March 2005 the Israeli Supreme Court ruled 7–4 that all conversions to Judaism conducted outside of Israel would be ruled as valid under the Law of Return. Interestingly, recent polls show that a scant majority of the Israeli public believes that there is no longer a need for Israel to accept additional immigrants.

JAIME RAMON OLIVARES AND SPENCER C. TUCKER

See also

Balfour Declaration; Herzl, Theodor; Zionism

References

Cohen, Michael J., ed. *The Rise of Israel, 1938–1945.* New York: Garland, 1987.

Friedman, Isaiah. *The Rise of Israel: From Precursors of Zionism to Herzl.* New York: Garland, 1987.

Harris, Ron. *The History of Law in a Multi-Cultural Society: Israel, 1917–1967.* Aldershot, UK: Ashgate, 2002.

Podeh, Elie. *The Arab-Israeli Conflict in Israeli History Textbooks, 1948–2000.* Westport, CT: Bergin and Garvey, 2002.

Sachar, Howard M. *A History of Israel: From the Rise of Zionism to Our Time.* 3rd ed. New York: Knopf, 2007.

Lawrence, Thomas Edward
Born: August 15, 1888
Died: May 19, 1935

British Army officer and partisan of the Arab cause. Born on August 15, 1888, at Tremadoc, Caernarvonshire, in Wales, Thomas E. Lawrence was the second of five illegitimate sons of Sir Thomas Chapman. He was about 10 years old when he learned of this, and some believe it had a permanent imprint on his personality. Educated at Jesus College, Oxford, he traveled to the Middle East in the five years prior to World War I to prepare material for his university thesis on the architecture of Crusader castles. An expedition he

T. E. Lawrence, British Army officer and partisan of the Arab cause during World War I. (Library of Congress)

accompanied to the Sinai in 1914, ostensibly to explore the area, was in reality designed to gain information for the War Office on military dispositions on the Turkish frontier east of Suez.

On the outbreak of World War I, Lawrence failed to meet the height requirement of 5'5" for the army and was posted to the Geographical Section of the War Office. Sent to Cairo, he was attached to the military intelligence staff as an intelligence officer concerned with Arab affairs. In October 1916 he accompanied a mission to the Hejaz, where Hussein ibn Ali, sharif of Mecca, had proclaimed a revolt against the Turks. The following month Lawrence, now a captain, was ordered to join as political and liaison officer Hussein's son, Faisal, commanding an Arab force southwest of Medina. Lawrence was instrumental in acquiring considerable material assistance from the British Army in Cairo for the Arab cause. Recognizing that the key to Turkish control lay in the Damascus-Medina railway, along which they could send reinforcements to crush the Arab Revolt, Lawrence accompanied Faisal and his army in a series of attacks on the railway, earning the name "Emir Dynamite" from the admiring Bedouin.

On July 6, 1917, Lawrence led a force of Huwaitat tribesman in the capture of the port of Aqaba at the northernmost tip of the Red Sea. It became a temporary base for Faisal's army. From there, Lawrence attempted to coordinate Arab movements with the campaign of General Sir Edmund Allenby, who was advancing from Jerusalem in southern Palestine.

In November 1917 Lawrence was captured at Dar'a by the Turks while conducting a reconnaissance of the area in Arab dress. He underwent a short period of humiliating torture but escaped and was present at the Battle of Tafila. For all his flamboyant poses and his adoption of Arab costume, he was never a leader of Arab forces. Command always remained firmly in the hands of Emir Faisal. Lawrence was, however, an inspirational force behind the Arab Revolt, a superb tactician, and a highly influential theoretician of guerrilla warfare. During the last two years of the war, his advice and influence combined with the Hashemites' own motivations to bind the Arabs to the Allied cause, thereby tying down about 25,000 Turkish troops who would otherwise have opposed the British Army. For his war service Lawrence was awarded the Distinguished Service Order and was promoted to lieutenant colonel. Subsequently he was present at the capture of Damascus on October 1, 1918, and returned the following month to England, where he was demobilized.

Unfortunately, despite all that he had done and endured, Lawrence witnessed the defeat of his aspirations for the Arabs when their hopes for a nation were dashed by the French claim to the mandates of Syria and Lebanon. Upon returning to England he lobbied vainly against the detachment of Syria and Lebanon from the rest of the Arab countries as a French mandate. He also worked on his war memoir. In 1921 he was wooed back to the Middle East as adviser on Arab affairs to Colonial Minister Winston Churchill. However, after the Cairo political settlements regarding the Middle East, he rejected offers of further positions and left the government in protest.

In August 1922, Lawrence enlisted (under the name John Hume Ross) in the Royal Air Force but was discharged six months later when his identity was disclosed by a London newspaper. He then enlisted as T. E. Shaw in the Royal Tank Corps and transferred to the Royal Air Force in 1925, remaining with that service until he was discharged in February 1935. He died at Bovington Camp Hospital on May 19, 1935, following a motorcycle accident.

Lawrence became an almost mythic figure in his own lifetime. His reputation was to an extent self-generated through his own literary accounts, including his war memoir *The Seven Pillars of Wisdom* (1922) and lecture tours, assisted by his postwar election to a research fellowship at Oxford University.

JAMES H. WILLBANKS

See also

Allenby, Sir Edmund Henry Hynman, 1st Viscount; Churchill, Sir Winston; Faisal I, King of Iraq; Hussein ibn Ali, Sharif of Mecca; World War I, Impact of

References

James, Lawrence. *The Golden Warrior: The Life and Legend of Lawrence of Arabia.* New York: Paragon House, 1993.

Lawrence, T. E. *Seven Pillars of Wisdom.* 1936. Reprint, New York: Anchor, 1991.

Wilson, Jeremy. *Lawrence of Arabia: The Authorized Biography of T. E. Lawrence.* New York: Collier, 1992.

League of Arab States

See Arab League

League of Nations Covenant, Article 22
Event Date: June 18, 1919

Provision in the covenant of the League of Nations, the predecessor agency to the United Nations, passed on June 18, 1919. The League of Nations was a supranational organization formed in the aftermath of the Paris Peace Conference held at the end of World War I. Article 22 of the League of Nations Covenant called for the creation of a mandate system that transferred the former colonies of Germany and the former territories of the Ottoman Empire to the custody of the League of Nations. Nations or regions falling under a mandate would be administered by a third-party nation upon the approval of the League of Nations. The principles of the mandate system have their legal precedent under the Roman principle of *mandatum,* which placed persons and property under the care of responsible parties. Newer precedents included the 1885 Berlin Conference, which established safeguards for the people of the Congo, and the 1892 Brussels Conference, which banned the import of alcohol and weapons to the Congo. At the convention of St. Germain in 1919, the signatories agreed to commit themselves to the protection and well-being of their colonies.

Under existing international law, colonies were considered to be wards under the responsibility of the colonial power. However, the question soon arose as to whom the colonial power was responsible. Through Article 22, the League of Nations was the authority that would oversee the conduct of the colonial powers in question. The former colonies and territories of Germany and the Ottoman Empire were distributed among the victorious Allied powers. Britain and France benefited the most by acquiring the majority of these territories as mandates. The British Dominions of Australia and New Zealand were given mandates as rewards for their service in the war. In the Middle East proper, Britain gained a mandate over Palestine, while the French administered mandates in Syria and Lebanon.

The mandates were classified as either A, B, or C according to the political and cultural development of the nations under mandate. The Middle Eastern mandates were classified as A Mandates because they were on the brink of independence and particularly because they had rebelled against the Turks during the war. The mandate powers in question were supposed to guide their mandates in the final steps toward statehood. The B Mandates, consisting of the former German colonies in Central Africa, were considered to be at a lower developmental stage than the A Mandates, and so it was the responsibility of the mandate powers to oversee their material needs and to prevent abuses such as slavery, exploitation of labor, and the importation of illicit liquor and drugs. They were also to allow access to other nations for trade purposes. The C Mandates were deemed to be at the lowest level of development, and independence for them was not considered in the short term. How the mandate system differed from old-fashioned colonialism was that the mandatory powers were required to make an annual report to the League of Nations. Ironically, Article 22 seemed to fly in the face of President Woodrow Wilson's call for self-determination, but the intellectual father of the League of Nations had been forced to compromise to get the organization up and running.

Not surprisingly, problems arose from the creation of the mandate system. The question of whether the League of Nations or the mandate power held the final authority continued to bedevil officials throughout the existence of the mandate system. In addition, international law did not have a mechanism for temporary sovereignty over a particular area. The League of Nations did not have enforcement powers within the mandates, and so mandate commission members could not visit a mandate to investigate problems. Issues of ascendant nationalism soon created tensions in Middle Eastern states, which ironically were supposed to be in the final stages of independence. Despite these problems, however, Article 22 helped change the face of colonialism and may have contributed to its ultimate demise after World War II. From the perspective of those people living in the mandates, however, especially in the Middle East, the situation seemed little different from the colonialism of the old order. In a sense, the League of Nations mandates in places such as the Middle East solved short-term difficulties but only amplified long-term problems.

Dino E. Buenviaje

See also

Arab Nationalism; Decolonization; Palestine, British Mandate for; United Nations, Role of

References

Nothedge, F. S. *The League of Nations: Its Life and Times 1920–1946.* Leicester, UK: Leicester University Press, 1986.

Ostrower, Gary B., and George Lankevich, eds. *League of Nations, 1919.* New York: Putnam, 1996.

Scott, George. *The Rise and Fall of the League of Nations.* New York: Macmillan, 1973.

Lebanon

Middle Eastern nation located on the eastern end of the Mediterranean Sea. Lebanon borders on Israel to the south and Syria to the east and north and covers 4,015 square miles (roughly twice the size of the U.S. state of Delaware). Lebanon's estimated 1948 population was approximately 1.5 million, but that was not based on an official government census. The only government census was conducted in 1932 when France held Lebanon as a League of Nations mandate and counted 861,399 people, which became the basis for the religious composition of the government. This gave a 6-to-5

Cedar forest at Bsharre in northern Lebanon. The Lebanon Cedar is the national symbol of Lebanon. (Edward Karaa/iStockphoto.com)

advantage to Lebanese Christians. The unwritten *mithaq al-watani* (national pact) formalized this arrangement as well as the allocation of leadership positions to specific confessional or religious sects, with, for example, the presidency allocated to the Maronites, once considered the largest sect; the office of the prime minister allocated to the Sunni Muslims; and the speaker of parliament allocated to the Shia. This continued after independence, with subsequent population figures being estimates based on demographic trends. A U.S. Central Intelligence Agency (CIA) population estimate in 2003 put the population at 3.72 million, split 70 to 30 percent between Muslims and Christians.

The Lebanese population is further split among the Sunni, Shia, and Druze sects of Islam and the Maronite, Greek Orthodox, Greek Catholic, Armenian Orthodox, and Syriac denominations of Christianity. The Shia community contained more poor workers and peasants, based on its concentration in the rural east and south. A belt of rural poverty also existed in the Sunni north. Certain Christian areas were also impoverished.

Lebanon's population suffered greatly during World War I, leading to high emigration in a pattern repeated during the lengthy civil war of 1975–1991. Remittances from Lebanese abroad were essential to the economy as were Beirut's services and banking. On the other hand, many areas of the country were dependent on agri-

culture and were farmed by peasants with small plots or who were landless and worked for large landholders. A neofeudal system remained even after independence whereby the larger landholders, traditional chieftains, counted on the political support of their dependents. Urban counterparts operated like political bosses.

Lebanon declared its independence from France in November 1941 and became a charter member of the United Nations (UN) in 1945, the same year it joined the Arab League. Although independence and international status were welcomed by the Lebanese, sectarian tensions have continually threatened internal peace. The country essentially developed different cultures tied to some degree to educational systems: the private and greatly superior French-language system as opposed to the national system, which in later years increasingly utilized Arabic.

The 1932 census awarded the Maronite Christians a privileged place in Lebanese government. Only a Maronite may become the president, only a Sunni may become the prime minister, and only a Shia may become the speaker of parliament. As demographic developments led to a Muslim majority by the 1960s, Maronite predominance came under increasing pressure from various Muslim groups. The fact that the Muslims were not a monolithic force further complicated matters. The Shia outnumbered the Sunnis, but many of the urban Sunni merchant families were far better off than the poverty-stricken Shia peasants or tobacco farmers. On top of this, the Arab cold war (or battle between conservative and military progressive states), the overall Cold War, and the ongoing Arab-Israeli conflict presented Lebanon with very serious challenges.

As a member of the Arab League, Lebanon sent troops to fight Israeli forces when the latter declared its independence in May 1948. Lebanese forces and Lebanese volunteers in the Arab Liberation Army fought alongside those from Syria in the north in the Israeli War of Independence (1948–1949) but were not successful. A series of battles ended with Israel in control of the Jordan River, the lakes of Galilee and Hulah, and a panhandle of territory jutting north and bordering on both Lebanon and Syria. Lebanon was not a major player in the 1956 Sinai Campaign or the 1967 Six-Day War between Israel and its Arab opponents because the Lebanese Army was so small.

This did not mean that Lebanon remained at peace, however, for sectarian troubles and the evolving Cold War between the United States and the Soviet Union brought their own set of challenges. Both sides sought to support local regimes that they believed would support them in the worldwide conflict. The Suez War boosted President Gamal Abdel Nasser's popularity, and his oratory that "the Arab nation is one nation" was greeted with considerable enthusiasm by Lebanese Muslims, especially the young. In 1958 the pro-Western monarchy in Iraq fell and was replaced by a government that tilted toward the Soviet bloc. Egypt had already rejected Western support in favor of Soviet aid and was pursuing union with Syria, which still had claims to Lebanon as part of the so-called Greater Syria. Lebanon's Christian Maronite-controlled government responded to these perceived threats by requesting American aid. President Dwight D. Eisenhower responded by sending U.S. marines to Beirut in the hopes of stabilizing the region. Almost simultaneously, the British sent troops to Jordan to prop up the monarchy there following an alleged coup attempt. The interventions actually heightened tensions and divisions in both nations. The extreme poverty of Lebanon's countryside was a contrast to its attraction for wealthy Arabs who came to vacation in the Switzerland of the Middle East. This mirage of Swiss neutrality belied the politics in Lebanon that simmered just under the surface. The relative degree of freedom of the press meant that political exiles of all types were present, but Lebanon was probably most important in this era as the banking and services capital of the region.

Gradually the Muslim population became the clear majority, and Lebanon could not avoid becoming involved in the Arab-Israeli conflict. After the Israeli victory in the 1948–1949 war, about 100,000 Palestinian refugees fled to Lebanon, where many Muslims supported them in carrying out hit-and-run actions against Israel. Lebanese Christians opposed these guerrilla operations, fearing that Israeli reprisals would threaten Lebanese independence.

The Six-Day War in 1967 and the Yom Kippur War in 1973 coupled with the expulsion of the Palestinians from Jordan in 1970 and 1971 (many relocating to Lebanon) increased the overall numbers of Muslims in the country. More important than tipping the

Smoke rises from a Beirut television tower during the July 2006 Israel-Hezbollah conflict. (U.S. Department of Defense)

sectarian balance, they fueled the conflict between Christian supporters of the political status quo and leftist and progressive and Muslim and Druze challengers to politics as usual. While the Lebanese military tried to maintain order and restrain the Palestinian guerrillas from using Lebanon as a base for attacks against Israel, the effort did not work. This led to clashes between Lebanese Christians and Muslims.

The result, ultimately, was a civil war that began in 1975, leading to the deaths of many Lebanese. In sectarian fighting between March 1975 and November 1976, 40,000 died and 100,000 more were wounded. The carnage continued. Lebanon was again brought into the larger Arab-Israeli conflict, with disastrous results. Repeated attacks by guerrillas operating in southern Lebanon brought the inevitable Israeli response. In June 1982 Israeli forces invaded Lebanon and even drove north to Beirut, which they occupied by August, leading to an agreement whereby the Palestine Liberation Organization (PLO) departed Beirut for Tunis. The conflict was temporarily ended by international agreements. But with the exodus of the Palestinian fighters and leadership, Lebanese Christian militias massacred scores of Palestinians in the Sabra and Shatila refugee camps in Beirut. Part of the truce agreement involved the United States sending U.S. marines into Beirut, and the French followed suit in 1983. Israel and Syria maintained significant forces in Lebanon and continued to do so for several years after the United States and French withdrew in response to suicide attacks on their forces in October 1983.

During the civil war, the Lebanese government was unable to carry out any of the normal functions of government, whether providing services or security, managing municipalities, or controlling the movement of goods or persons in or out of the country. Israel maintained forces and backed Lebanese allies in the south ostensibly to prevent raids and rocket attacks against Israeli territory.

The Syrian intervention in Lebanon came about in a piecemeal fashion, first with only 50 troops and then in a much larger force. This was eventually sanctioned by the Arab League as one component of the Araf Deterrent Force, supposedly under the command of the Lebanese president. Syria managed to influence the Lebanese political system as well as became a combatant in the civil war with alliances that shifted over time. In 1993 and in 1996, during the Israeli Operation GRAPES OF WRATH, hundreds of thousands of Lebanese fled their homes in the south to avoid Israeli attacks. Israel decided to withdraw from Lebanon in May 2000, hoping that this would lead to a stable border. Instead, the border became more dangerous for the Israelis, as Hezbollah controlled much of southern Lebanon. After 2000, Hezbollah militias were able to fortify their positions with Syrian help. Syria did withdraw its troops from Lebanon in mid-2005, and there was fleeting hope that Lebanon might enter a new era with foreign forces finally off its territory. However, those political and intelligence elements that had relied on Syria in the previous era began battling other new political forces on the scene.

Lebanon continued to be plagued by internal conflicts, including the continuing debate over the structure of its government and cabinet, which operate along outdated sectarian lines. Hezbollah had continued to arm its militia and participated in limited border hostilities with Israel during 2000–2006. In July 2006 war again erupted between Lebanon and Israel. Hezbollah by then effectively governed southern Lebanon and also had elected representatives in the national and local governments. The Lebanese refer to this 2006 conflict as the Fifth Arab-Israeli War.

On July 12, 2006, Hezbollah miscalculated the Israeli response to a raid on Israel. In addition to short-range Katyusha rocket attacks, Hezbollah raided Israeli territory and captured two Israeli soldiers. The reaction was massive and not anticipated by the Hezbollah leader, Hassan Nasrallah, who later admitted that the raid would not have been launched if he had known the likely Israeli response. The result was a month of war until a tenuous UN cease-fire was negotiated on August 14. Both sides suffered casualties and damage, although they were far more numerous on the Lebanese side. Hezbollah had about 1,000 fighters well dug into positions in southern Lebanon, backed by other militias and a civilian population that largely supported them, facing up to 30,000 Israel Defense Forces (IDF) troops.

Hezbollah fighters and militias supporting them sustained between 250 and 600 dead during the month-long war, while the Lebanese Army suffered 46 dead and about 100 wounded. Israel reported 119 dead, up to 450 wounded, and 2 captured. UN observer forces in the area also suffered 7 dead and 12 wounded. The worst toll, however, was among Lebanese civilians. About 1,187 Lebanese civilians died, while 4,080 more were injured. As many as 1 million Lebanese were displaced by the fighting. Some returned to their homes after Hezbollah issued a call for them to do so, leaving some 255,986 still displaced. Israel suffered 44 civilian deaths and more than 1,300 injured as a result of cross-border attacks.

Both sides used massive amounts of ordnance in the conflict. Israel had complete control of the skies and was able to fly 12,000 sorties over Lebanese territory. In addition to Israeli artillery, the Israeli Navy fired 2,500 shells against Lebanese targets. Lebanon suffered damage to its infrastructure that will require billions of dollars and many years to repair. The effective blockade imposed by Israel until September 2006 exacerbated the problems faced by Lebanon. The power of the Israeli military was not a surprise, but the robust defense put up by Hezbollah was. This militia had used its years of control over southern Lebanon to increase its stocks of weapons and prepare defensive positions. Hezbollah was able to fire 4,000 rockets into Israeli territory. These included not only the short-range Katyushas but also middle-range missiles capable of hitting Haifa and other points believed safe from the usual Hezbollah rockets. In southern Lebanon, Hezbollah was able to resist Israeli armored attacks, destroying 20 main battle tanks in two engagements. Launching what might have been a cruise missile against an Israeli warship was also a surprise.

The cease-fire called for a halt in the fighting, an end to the Israeli blockade, the deployment of UN forces to southern Lebanon to maintain peace, and the Lebanese Army to aid in that effort. Whether these measures would be successful was questionable. Hezbollah soon announced that it had already restocked its missiles.

The political fallout from the summer's war manifested itself in a struggle over the Lebanese cabinet's recommendation that a tribunal be established to hear evidence on the assassination of former prime minister Rafik Hariri. The issues at stake are the future of Syria's government and future influence in Lebanon, the willingness of Lebanese leaders to compromise, the role to be played by such groups as Hezbollah, Saad Hariri's Future Party and the pro- and anti-Syrian Christian elements, and the need to diminish sectarianism as spelled out in the Taif Agreements but not achieved since the end of the Lebanese Civil War. At the end of 2007, the Lebanese political scene remained very much in turmoil. Hezbollah had not disarmed, and sharp political divisions remained and were coupled with assassinations (alleged to be Syrian-sponsored) of leading political figures.

DANIEL E. SPECTOR AND SHERIFA ZUHUR

See also
Arab League; Arab Liberation Army; Black September; Expellees and Refugees, Palestinian; Hezbollah; Israeli War of Independence, Israeli-Lebanese Front; Katyusha Rocket; Lebanon, Armed Forces; Lebanon,

Civil War in; Lebanon, Israeli Invasion of; Nasrallah, Hassan; Palestine Liberation Organization

References

Gilsenan, Michael. *Lords of the Lebanese Marches: Violence and Narrative in an Arab Society*. London: Tauris, 1996.

Herzog, Chaim. *The Arab-Israeli Wars: War and Peace in the Middle East from the War of Independence to Lebanon*. Westminster, MD: Random House, 1984.

Hudson, Michael. *The Precarious Republic: Political Modernization in Lebanon*. Boulder, CO: Westview, 1985.

Rabil, Robert G. *Embattled Neighbors: Syria, Israel and Lebanon*. Boulder, CO: Lynne Rienner, 2003.

Lebanon, Armed Forces

During the French Mandate for Lebanon following World War I, the French authorities had recruited a special militia force known as the Troupes Spéciales du Levant that served all Syria, what is today both Syria and Lebanon, as well as a gendarmerie for internal security. This force was at first largely staffed with French officers, but the number of Arab officers increased over time. Recruitment was higher from rural areas and among the Druze, Circassians, Alawites, Christians, and Kurds. Special squadrons relied entirely on fighters of one sect or ethnicity, such as the Druze and Circassian cavalry squadrons.

Following the defeat of France by the Germans in June 1940, the Troupes Spéciales of Lebanon came under control of the Vichy French government. After the Allied invasion of Lebanon (Operation EXPORTER) in 1941, some Circassian squadrons led by Colonel Collet defected to the Allies, but most Lebanese units fought on the Vichy side. With the Allied victory, by June 1943 the reconstituted Troupes du Levant (the former Troupes Spéciales) operated under British forces in the Middle East. After Lebanon gained its independence in 1945, this 3,000-man force became the cadre of the Lebanese Army.

The Lebanese Army was a weak military force. This was a reflection of both the fragmented nature of Lebanese society and its small size. Some Christian Lebanese during the 1950s and 1960s feared that a strong army would only embroil Lebanon in the Arab-Israeli wars. Muslim political leaders also feared that a strong military force, commanded primarily by Christians, would be too easily used against Muslim interests, but, conversely, they also wanted the army to be strong enough to play a role in the Arab-Israeli conflict. Finally, all too many Lebanese political leaders, both Christians and Muslims, were also local warlords with their own militias who saw a strong national army as a direct threat to their own personal power.

Lebanon committed two battalions to the Israeli War of Independence, which began in earnest on May 15, 1948. The Lebanese also had small detachments of cavalry and a small number of armored cars and tanks. On May 15 Lebanese forces attempted to cross the Palestine border near Rosh HaNikra but were repelled by Israeli troops. When the Arab Liberation Army (ALA) found itself isolated from its Syrian bases, the Lebanese Army performed badly needed logistical services. After the ALA was defeated at the Battle of Sasra in late October 1948, ALA units withdrew to Lebanon for safety. When Israeli forces pursued them into Lebanon proper, Lebanese officials quickly negotiated an armistice, and the Israel Defense Forces (IDF) withdrew.

In 1958 when President Camille Chamoun unconstitutionally extended his presidency and met with political opposition, he requested U.S. military assistance to prevent what he described as a potential takeover by Nasserist elements. The 1958 events exposed the inherent weakness of Lebanese armed forces, which might have more effectively controlled the situation than did the Americans. However, by that time the army officer corps and leadership, who were predominantly Christian, also had loyalties to their respective political blocs. Lebanese officials made concerted efforts to augment the nation's military strength after 1958, at least to the point at which the Lebanese Army could maintain order and provide some measure of effective defenses.

By 1975, the year the Lebanese Civil War broke out, the Lebanese armed forces had expanded considerably. The Lebanese Air Force was equipped with 10 British Hawker Hunter and 9 French Dassault Mirage III aircraft. It also had a helicopter squadron with 16 aircraft, the majority of which were French Aerospatiale Alouette II/IIIs. The Lebanese Navy operated 6 patrol craft. The army had 17,000 combat-ready troops in 20 infantry battalions equipped with either the French Panhard armored personnel carriers or American M-113s. The army also operated 25 French AMX-13 tanks and 18 U.S. M-41 Walker Bulldog tanks. Artillery support consisted of 4 batteries of both 122-mm and 155-mm howitzers and 60 Charioteer self-propelled antitank guns. Missile systems included the ENTAC, SS-11, and TOW systems. Antiaircraft support was comprised of 15 M-42 Duster self-propelled 40-mm twin guns. In addition to the regular forces, the gendarmerie numbered about 5,000 men.

The civil war that began in 1975 effectively led to the dismemberment of the Lebanese Army. In January 1976, Sunni lieutenant Ahmed al-Khatib established the Lebanese Arab Army (LAA). Many of the Muslims who served in the lower ranks followed him, as the LAA joined ranks with the Lebanese National Movement. They mounted an attack on the presidential palace. Some of the recruits to the 140 independent Lebanese militias or small fighting forces that formed during the conflict came from the ranks of the regular army. The militias were able to acquire material that had been purchased during the civil war by the army from the United States and was worth several billion dollars. Further complicating the situation, Israel, France, Iraq, Syria, other Arab nations, and the Palestine Liberation Organization (PLO) equipped and supported the various competing militias. One of the largest of the predominantly Christian militias was the South Lebanon Army (SLA). The SLA was established after 1982 by Colonel Saad Haddad, who had formed a militia in 1978 while still serving in the Lebanese Army. The SLA was mainly Christian, but later it recruited Shia Muslims who would accept Israeli support in return for control of a sector of southern

Lebanon. The Israelis quickly allied themselves with this group, training and equipping many of its fighters. The Lebanese forces also received some funds, assistance, and other support from Israel. In addition, they profited from land speculation and levying of customs and taxes, through the port of Beirut, under the Sunduq al-Watani.

Druze militias on the opposing side numbered some 4,000 men. They drew closer to Syria until late in the war when Amal and the Druze came to blows. The Syrian Army also intervened early in the civil war and deployed more than 40,000 troops into the country, inevitably gaining control over many of the militia groups.

The regular Lebanese Army was re-formed in 1982. Toward the end of that year the Lebanese forces were reequipped by the United States with M-16 rifles, M-113 armored personnel carriers, and UH-1H helicopters. Under the reorganization program, Lebanese recruits received limited training from U.S. marines in the Beirut area prior to their withdrawal. The next phase of the civil war was particularly brutal, with the introduction of snipers paid simply to kill a set number of persons per day, numerous kidnappings and hostage takings, and reprisal actions by militias against not only leading individuals but also their entire families. Various re-alignments of the Christian political elements, the Syrians, and new groups such as Hezbollah occurred following the expulsion of the Palestinian leadership from Lebanon to Tunis.

By 1988 when the Lebanese Parliament failed to elect a new president, former president Amin Jumayyil (Gemayel) appointed a military government before leaving office. With two competing governments vying for power, the army was split between two different commands according to their location. The result was rapid military deterioration and polarization. In 1989 President Michel Aoun vowed to remove Syrian influence from Lebanon, and the following year the Lebanese Army was again unified. Syrian interference, however, subsequently forced Aoun from office.

In May 1991 after Syrian troops again battled Lebanese forces, most of the militias were dissolved, and the Lebanese Armed Forces began slowly to rebuild as Lebanon's only major nonsectarian institution. The military took little part in the 2006 war between Israel and Hezbollah guerrillas but was then deployed to southern Lebanon in advance and support of the United Nations Interim Force in Lebanon (UNIFIL). The military was also deployed to defuse tensions in the January 2007 public demonstrations in Beirut against the Fuad Siniura government but managed to do so without using force.

The present Lebanese Army consists of 11 mechanized brigades, 2 artillery regiments, 5 special forces regiments, 1 airborne regiment, 1 commando regiment, 1 Republican Guard brigade, and various support brigades. Total army troops number about 55,000. The primary weapons systems include some 100 U.S. M-48 tanks and 200 Soviet T54/55 tanks. With 725 of these, the U.S. M-113 APC is the most common armored fighting vehicle, but the Lebanese also have small numbers of French AMX-13s. Lebanese artillery consists of about 140 towed guns, an assortment of American 105-mm

and 155-mm guns, and Russian 122-mm and 130-mm guns. The Lebanese also have approximately 25 BM-21 multiple rocket launchers. The principal antitank weapons include the Milan and TOW.

The Lebanese Navy remains small and is limited to coast patrol activities and a naval commando regiment. During the civil war, the navy remained largely intact and was able to defend the Junieh naval base from the various militias. Militia forces captured the base in 1991, but the navy's patrol craft were able to escape. The Junieh base was rebuilt in 1991. The chief vessels are seven British-made Tracker- and Attacker-class patrol boats.

The Lebanese Air Force currently has no operational fixed-wing aircraft. The air fleet consists of 4 SA-342 helicopters and a variety of transport helicopters, of which the 30 UH-1Hs are the most common.

Current Lebanese military expenditures amount to $550 million, about 3.5 percent of Lebanon's gross domestic product (GDP).

RALPH MARTIN BAKER, DAVID T. ZABECKI, AND SHERIFA ZUHUR

See also

Israel; Israel Defense Forces; Lebanon; Lebanon, Civil War in; Lebanon, Israeli Invasion of; Palestine Liberation Organization; Syria; Syria, Armed Forces

References

Fisk, Robert. *Pity the Nation: The Abduction of Lebanon.* 4th ed. New York: Nation Books, 2002.
Gabriel, Richard. *Operation Peace for Galilee: The Israeli-PLO War in Lebanon.* New York: Farrar, Straus and Giroux, 1985.
Katz, Samuel, and Lee Russell. *Armies in Lebanon, 1982–84.* Oxford, UK: Osprey, 1985.
O'Ballance, Edgar. *Civil War in Lebanon, 1975–1992.* London: Palgrave Macmillan, 1998.
Salibi, Kamal. *A House of Many Mansions: The History of Lebanon Reconsidered.* Berkeley: University of California Press, 1990.

Lebanon, Civil War in
Start Date: April 13, 1975
End Date: August 1990

The Lebanese Civil War, which lasted from 1975 to 1990, had its origin in the conflicts and political compromises of Lebanon's colonial period. It was exacerbated by the nation's changing demographics, Christian and Muslim interreligious strife, and Lebanon's proximity to both Syria and Israel. Indeed, the Lebanese Civil War was part and parcel of the wider Arab-Israeli conflict and was emblematic of the inherent volatility and instability of the Middle East after World War II.

Lebanon in its present-day borders dates to 1920, when the French administered a mandate over the region. The French added several districts to the historic mustashafiyya, Mount Lebanon, a separate administrative district that had called for Western protection in the 19th century, eventually establishing Greater Lebanon. This meant the inclusion of areas whose populations had always been administered from Syria and did not necessarily support sep-

Teenage Christian girls, all members of the Phalangist Party, man a sandbagged barricade and point their rifles down a downtown Beirut street, November 2, 1975. (Bettmann/Corbis)

aration from that country. These heavily Sunni and Shia Muslim areas diluted the previous Maronite Christian and Druze majority of Mount Lebanon. When Lebanon won its independence from France in 1943, an unwritten power-sharing agreement was forged among the three major ethnic and religious groups. These included Maronite Christians (then in the majority), Sunni Muslims, and Shiite Muslims.

Lebanon's Muslim groups were discontented with the 1943 National Pact, which established a dominant political role for the Christians, especially the Maronites, in the central government. Druze, Muslims, and leftists joined forces as the National Movement in 1969. The Movement called for the taking of a new census, as none had been conducted since 1932, and the subsequent drafting of a new governmental structure that would reflect the census results.

Muslim and Maronite leaders were unable to reconcile their conflicts of interest and instead formed militias, undermining the authority of the central government. The government's ability to maintain order was also handicapped by the nature of the Lebanese Army. It was composed on a fixed ratio of religions, and as mem-

bers defected to militias of their own ethnicity, the army would eventually prove unable to check the power of the militias, the Palestine Liberation Organization (PLO), or other splinter groups.

Maronite militias armed by West Germany and Belgium drew supporters from the larger and poorer Christian population in the north. The most powerful of these was al-Kata'ib, also known as the Phalange, led by Bashir Jumayyil. Others included the Lebanese Forces, led by Samir Jaja (Geagea), and the Guardians of the Cedars.

Shiite militias, such as the Amal militia, fought the Maronites and later fought certain Palestinian groups and occasionally even other Shiite organizations. Some Sunni factions received support from Libya and Iraq. The Soviet Union encouraged Arab socialist movements that spawned leftist Palestinian organizations, such as the Popular Front for the Liberation of Palestine (PLFP) and the Democratic Front for the Liberation of Palestine. Prior to the civil war, the rise of Baathism in Syria and Iraq was paralleled by a surge of Lebanese Baathists. Within the civil war, these were also reflected in groups such as al-Saiqa, a Syrian-aligned and largely anti-Fatah Palestinian fighting force, and the Arab Liberation Front, an Iraqi-aligned Baathist movement.

Lebanese children play in the surf at Green Beach in Beirut, Lebanon, on February 26, 1984. In the background, U.S. marines prepare to load a 155-mm howitzer into a landing craft as part of the withdrawal of the multinational peacekeeping force. (U.S. Department of Defense)

In 1970 Jordan's King Hussein expelled the PLO from Jordan after the events of Black September. PLO chairman Yasser Arafat thus regrouped his organization in the Palestinian refugee areas of Beirut and South Lebanon, where other refugees had survived since 1948. The National Movement attracted support from the PLO Rejection Front faction, prominently including the PFLP, although Arafat and Fatah initially sought to remain neutral in the inter-Lebanese conflict. The National Movement supported the Palestinian resistance movement's struggle for national liberation and activities against Israel, and although Palestinians could not vote in Lebanon and, being outside of the political system, had no voice in its reformation, they nonetheless lent moral support to the movement's desire for political reformation. By the early 1970s, the Palestinian Resistance groups, although disunited, were a large fighting force. Maronites viewed the Resistance and the PLO as disruptive and a destabilizing ally of the Muslim factions.

On the morning of April 13, 1975, unidentified gunmen in a speeding car fired on a church in the Christian East Beirut suburb of Ayn ar Rummanah, killing 4 people, including 2 Maronite Phalangists. Later that day, Phalangists led by Jumayyil killed 27 Palestinians returning from a political rally on a bus in Ayn ar Rummanah. Four Christians were killed in East Beirut in December

1975, and in growing reprisals Phalangists and Muslim militias subsequently massacred at least 600 Muslims and Christians at checkpoints, igniting the 1975–1976 stage of the civil war.

The fighting eventually spread to most parts of the country, precipitating President Suleiman Franjieh's call for support from Syrian troops in June 1976, to which Syria responded by ending its prior affiliation with the Rejection Front and supporting the Maronites. This technically put Syria in the Israeli camp, as Israel had already begun to supply the Maronite forces with arms, tanks, and military advisers in May 1976. Meanwhile, Arafat's Fatah joined the war on the side of the National Movement.

Syrian troops subsequently entered Lebanon, occupying Tripoli and the Bekáa Valley, and imposed a cease-fire that ultimately failed to stop the conflict. After the arrival of Syrian troops, Christian forces massacred some 2,000 Palestinians in the Tal al-Za'atar camp in East Beirut. Anther massacre by Christian forces saw some 1,000 people killed at Muslim Qarantina.

Some reports charge al-Saiqa, the Syrian-backed Palestinian force, or a combination of al-Saiqa, Fatah, and the Palestine Liberation Army along with some Muslim forces with an attack on the Christian city of Damur, a stronghold of Camille Chamoun and his followers. When the city fell on January 20, the remaining inhabitants were subject to rape, mutilation, and brutal assassinations. The civilian dead numbered at least 300, with one estimate being as high as 582. Graves were desecrated, and a church was used as a garage. Also, former camp dwellers from Tal Za'tar were resettled in Damur and then evicted again after 1982. As a result of the massacre, other Christians came to see the Palestinian presence as a threat to their survival.

The nation was now informally divided, with southern Lebanon and the western half of Beirut becoming bases for the PLO and other Muslim militias and with the Christians in control of East Beirut and the Christian section of Mount Lebanon. The dividing thoroughfare in Beirut between its primarily western Muslim neighborhoods and eastern Christian neighborhoods was known as the Green Line.

In October 1976 an Arab League summit in Riyadh, Saudi Arabia, gave Syria a mandate to garrison 40,000 troops in Lebanon as the bulk of an Arab deterrent force charged with disentangling the combatants and restoring calm. However, in no part of the country had the war actually ended, nor was there a political solution offered by the government.

In the south, PLO combatants returned from central Lebanon under the terms of the Riyadh Accords. Then, on March 11, 1978, eight Fatah militants landed on a beach in northern Israel and proceeded to take control of a passenger bus and head toward Tel Aviv. In the ensuing confrontation with Israeli forces, 34 Israelis and 6 of the militants died. In retaliation, Israel invaded Lebanon four days later in Operation LITANI in which the Israel Defense Forces (IDF) occupied most of the area south of the Litani River, resulting in approximately 2,000 deaths and the evacuation of at least 100,000 Lebanese. The United Nations (UN) Security Council passed Resolution 425, calling for an immediate Israeli withdrawal. It also created the UN Interim Force in Lebanon, charged with maintaining peace. Under international pressure to do so, Israeli forces withdrew later in 1978.

However, Israel retained de facto control of the border region by turning over positions inside Lebanon to the group later known as the South Lebanon Army (SLA), led by Major Saad Haddad. Israel, meanwhile, had been supplying Haddad's forces. The SLA occupied Shia villages in the south, informally setting up a 12-mile-wide security zone that protected Israeli territory from cross-border attacks. Violent exchanges quickly resumed among the PLO, Israel, and the SLA, with the PLO attacking SLA positions and firing rockets into northern Israel. Israel conducted air raids against PLO positions, and the SLA continued its efforts to consolidate its power in the border region.

Syria, meanwhile, clashed with the Phalange. Phalange leader Jumayyil's increasingly aggressive actions (such as his April 1981 attempt to capture the strategic city of Zahla in central Lebanon) were designed to thwart the Syrian goal of brushing him aside and installing Franjieh as president. Consequently, the de facto alliance between Israel and Jumayyil strengthened considerably. In fighting in Zahla in April 1981, for example, Jumayyil called for Israeli assis-

tance, and Prime Minister Menachem Begin responded by sending Israeli fighter jets to the scene. These shot down two Syrian helicopters. This led Syrian president Hafez al-Assad to order surface-to-air missiles to the hilly perimeter of Zahla.

In July 1981 Israeli forces attacked Palestinian positions, provoking retaliatory shelling by the PLO. The Israeli response to this shelling culminated in the aerial bombardment of a West Beirut suburb where Fatah's headquarters were located, killing 200 people and wounding another 600, most of them civilians. The PLO rejoinder was a huge rocket attack on towns and villages in northern Israel, leaving 6 civilians dead and 59 wounded. These violent exchanges prompted diplomatic intervention by the United States. On July 24, 1981, U.S. special Middle East envoy Philip Habib brokered a cease-fire agreement with the PLO and Israel. The two sides now agreed to cease hostilities in Lebanon proper and along the Israeli border with Lebanon. The cease-fire was short-lived.

On June 3, 1982, the Abu Nidal organization attempted to assassinate Israeli ambassador Shlomo Argov in London. Although badly wounded, Argov survived. Israel retaliated with an aerial attack on PLO and PFLP targets in West Beirut that led to more than 100 casualties, a clear violation of the cease-fire. The PLO responded by launching a counterattack from Lebanon with rockets and artillery.

Then, on June 6, 1982, Israeli forces began Operation PEACE FOR GALILEE, an invasion of southern Lebanon to destroy PLO bases there. The Israeli plan was subsequently modified to move farther into Lebanon, and by June 15 Israeli units were entrenched outside Beirut. Israel laid siege to Beirut, which contained some 15,000 armed members of the PLO. Over a period of several weeks, the PLO and the IDF exchanged artillery fire. On a number of occasions, the Palestinians directed their fire into Christian East Beirut, causing an estimated 6,700 deaths of which 80 percent were civilians. On August 12, 1982, Habib again negotiated a truce that called for the withdrawal of both Israeli and PLO elements. Nearly 15,000 Palestinian militants had been evacuated to other countries by September 1. Within six months, Israel withdrew from most of Lebanon but maintained the security zone along the Israeli-Lebanese border.

Jumayyil was elected Lebanon's president on August 23, 1982, with acknowledged Israeli backing. But on September 14, 1982, he was assassinated. The next day, Israeli troops crossed into West Beirut to secure Muslim militia strongholds and stood back as Lebanese Christian militias massacred as many as 2,000 Palestinian civilians in the Sabra and Shatila refugee camps. This event was protested throughout the Arab world, especially because of the Israeli presence in Beirut.

With U.S. backing, the Lebanese parliament chose Amin Jumayyil to succeed his brother as president and focused anew on securing the withdrawal of Israeli and Syrian forces. On May 17, 1983, Lebanon, Israel, and the United States signed an agreement on Israeli withdrawal that was conditioned on the departure of Syrian troops. Syria opposed the agreement and declined to discuss the withdrawal of its troops. In August 1983, Israel withdrew from the Shuf (a district of Mount Lebanon to the southeast of Beirut), thus removing the buffer between the Druze and the Christian militias and triggering another round of brutal fighting.

By September the Druze had gained control over most of the Shuf, and Israeli forces had pulled out from all but the southern security zone. The collapse of the Lebanese Army in February 1984 following the defection of many Muslim and Druze units to militias was a major blow to the government. On March 5, 1984, the Lebanese government canceled the May 17 agreement.

This period of chaos had witnessed the beginning of retaliatory attacks launched against U.S. and Western interests, such as the April 18, 1983, suicide attack at the U.S. embassy in West Beirut that left 63 dead. Then, on October 23, 1983, a bombing in the Beirut barracks that hit the headquarters of U.S. military personnel left 241 U.S. marines dead. A total of 58 French servicemen also died in the attack. Months later, American University of Beirut president Malcolm Kerr was murdered inside the university on January 18, 1984. After U.S. forces withdrew in February 1984, anti-Western terrorism as well as that directed against Lebanese enemies continued, including a second bombing of the U.S. embassy annex in East Beirut on September 20, 1984, that left 9 Americans dead, including 2 U.S. servicemen.

Between 1985 and 1989, factional conflict worsened as various efforts at national reconciliation failed. The economy collapsed, and the militias that had participated in crime, car theft, hijackings, and kidnappings for ransom expanded their activities. The larger militias were also involved in profiteering, land investment, and sales, and they rather than the government also collected tariffs and customs.

Heavy fighting took place in the War of the Camps in 1985 and 1986 as the Shia Muslim Amal militia sought to rout the Palestinians from Lebanese strongholds. Many thousands of Palestinians died in the war. Sabra, Shatila, and Burj al-Barajnah were reduced to ashes. Combat returned to Beirut in 1987 with Palestinians, leftists, and Druze fighters allied against Amal, eventually drawing further Syrian intervention. Violent confrontation flared up again in Beirut in 1988 between Amal and Hezbollah.

Meanwhile, Lebanese prime minister Rashid Karameh, head of a government of national unity set up after the failed peace efforts of 1984, was assassinated on June 1, 1987. President Jumayyil's term of office expired in September 1988. Before stepping down, he appointed another Maronite Christian, Lebanese Armed Forces commanding general Michel Aoun, as acting prime minister, contravening the National Pact. Muslim groups rejected the violation of the National Pact and pledged support to Selim al-Hoss, a Sunni who had succeeded Karameh. Lebanon was thus divided between a Christian government in East Beirut and a Muslim government in West Beirut with two presidents.

In February 1989 Aoun attacked the rival Lebanese Forces militia. By March he turned his attention to other militias, launching what he termed a "War of Liberation" against the Syrians and their allied Lebanese militias. In the months that followed, Aoun rejected both the Taif Agreement that ultimately ended the civil war and

the election of another Christian leader as president. A Lebanese-Syrian military operation in October 1990 forced him to take cover in the French embassy in Beirut. He later went into exile in Paris.

The Taif Agreement of 1989 marked the beginning of the end of the fighting. In January 1989 a committee appointed by the Arab League, chaired by a representative from Kuwait and including Saudi Arabia, Algeria, and Morocco, had begun to formulate solutions to the conflict. This led to a meeting of Lebanese parliamentarians in Taif, Saudi Arabia. There in October they agreed to the national reconciliation accord. Returning to Lebanon, they ratified the agreement on November 4 and elected Rene Mouawad as president the following day.

Muawad was assassinated 18 days later on November 22 in a car bombing in Beirut as his motorcade returned from Lebanese Independence Day ceremonies. He was succeeded by Elias Hrawi, who remained in office until 1998. In August 1990 parliament and the new president agreed on constitutional amendments. The National Assembly expanded to 108 seats and was divided equally between Christians and Muslims. Because the Muslim sects together now outnumbered the Christians, this decision did not represent a one-vote–one-man solution but was nonetheless an improvement on the previous situation. In March 1991 parliament passed an amnesty law that pardoned all political crimes prior to its enactment. In May 1991 the militias were dissolved, and the Lebanese Armed Forces began to slowly rebuild as Lebanon's only major nonsectarian institution.

MOSHE TERDIMAN

See also

Arab League; Arafat, Yasser; Assad, Hafez al-; Begin, Menachem; Black September; Chamoun, Camille; Eitan, Rafael; France, Middle East Policy; Habib, Philip; Hezbollah; Hussein, King of Jordan; Hrawi, Elias; Israel; Israel Defense Forces; Lebanon; Lebanon, Armed Forces; Lebanon, Israeli Invasion of; LITANI, Operation; Palestine Liberation Organization; Popular Front for the Liberation of Palestine; Shia Islam; Suicide Bombings; Sunni Islam; Syria; Syria, Armed Forces; United Nations, Role of; United States, Middle East Policy

References

Barakat, Halim, ed. *Toward a Viable Lebanon*. London: Croom Helm, 1988.

Collings, Deirdre. *Peace for Lebanon? From War to Reconstruction*. Boulder, CO: Lynne Rienner, 1994.

El-Khazen, Farid. *The Breakdown of the State in Lebanon, 1967–1976*. Cambridge: Harvard University Press, 2000.

Fisk, Robert. *Pity the Nation: Lebanon at War*. Oxford: Oxford University Press, 2001.

Hanf, Theodor. *Coexistence in Wartime Lebanon: Decline of a State and Rise of a Nation*. London: Centre for Lebanese Studies and Tauris, 1993.

Petran, Tabitha. *The Struggle over Lebanon*. New York: Monthly Review Press, 1987.

Picard, Elizabeth. "The Political Economy of Civil War in Lebanon." Pp. 2292–322 in *War, Institutions, and Social Change in the Middle East*, edited by Steven Heydemann. Berkeley: University of California Press, 2000.

Rabinovich, Itamar. *The War for Lebanon, 1970–1985*. Rev. ed. Ithaca, NY: Cornell University Press, 1986.

Salibi, Kamal S. *Lebanon and the Middle Eastern Question.* Oxford, UK: Center for Lebanese Studies, 1988.

Lebanon, Israeli Invasion of
Start Date: June 6, 1982
End Date: September 1982

The Israeli invasion of Lebanon, code-named Operation PEACE FOR GALILEE, began on June 6, 1982, when Defense Minister Ariel Sharon, acting in full agreement with instructions from Prime Minister Menachem Begin, ordered Israel Defense Forces (IDF) troops into southern Lebanon to destroy the Palestine Liberation Organization (PLO) there.

In 1977 Begin had become the first Israeli prime minister from the right-wing Likud Party. He sought to maintain Israeli hold over the West Bank and Gaza but also had a deep commitment to Eretz Israel, the ancestral homeland of the Jews that embraced territory beyond Israel's borders into Lebanon and across the Jordan River.

Israeli defense minister Sharon, also a prominent member of the Likud Party, shared Begin's ideological commitment to Eretz Israel. Indeed, Sharon played an important role in expanding Jewish settlements in the West Bank and Gaza. He took a hard-line approach toward the Palestinians, endeavoring to undermine PLO influence in the West Bank and Gaza, and was also influential in the formation of Israeli foreign policy.

In June 1978, under heavy U.S. pressure, Begin withdrew Israeli forces that had been sent into southern Lebanon in the Litani River operation. United Nations Interim Force in Lebanon (UNIFIL) then took over in southern Lebanon. They were charged with confirming the Israeli withdrawal, restoring peace and security, and helping the Lebanese government reestablish its authority in the area. The Israeli failure to remove PLO bases in southern Lebanon was a major embarrassment for the Begin government.

UNIFIL proved incapable of preventing PLO forces from operating in southern Lebanon and striking Israel, which led to Israeli reprisals. Attacks back and forth across the Lebanese-Israeli border killed civilians on both sides as well as some UNIFIL troops. Israel, meanwhile, provided weapons to the force later known as the South Lebanon Army, a pro-Israeli Christian militia in southern Lebanon led by Major Saad Haddad, and the force used them against the PLO and local villagers.

In July 1981 U.S. president Ronald Reagan sent Lebanese-American diplomat Philip Habib to the area in an effort to broker a truce during the Lebanese Civil War. On July 24 Habib announced agreement on a cease-fire, but it was in name only. The PLO repeatedly violated the agreement, and major cross-border strikes resumed in April 1982 following the death of an Israeli officer from a land mine. While Israel conducted both air strikes and commando raids across the border, it was unable to prevent a growing number of PLO personnel from locating there. Their numbers increased to perhaps 6,000 men in a number of encampments, as PLO rocket and

An Israeli Air Force F-4 Phantom jet overflies Beirut, Lebanon, on August 21, 1982. (Israeli Government Press Office)

mortar attacks regularly forced thousands of Israeli civilians to flee their homes and fields in northern Galilee and seek protection in bomb shelters.

On June 3, 1982, three members of a Palestinian terrorist organization connected to Abu Nidal attempted to assassinate in London Israeli ambassador to Britain Shlomo Argov. Although Argov survived the attack, he remained paralyzed until his death in 2003. Abu Nidal's organization had been linked to Yasser Arafat's Fatah faction within the PLO in the past, and the Israelis used this as the excuse to bomb Palestinian targets in West Beirut and other targets in southern Lebanon during June 4–5, 1982. The PLO responded by attacking Israeli settlements in Galilee with rockets and mortars. It was this PLO shelling of the settlements rather than the attempted assassination of Argov that provoked the Israeli decision to invade Lebanon.

Operation PEACE FOR GALILEE began on June 6, 1982. It took its name from the Israeli intention to protect its vulnerable northern region of Israel from the PLO rocket and mortar attacks launched from southern Lebanon. Ultimately, Israel committed to the operation some 76,000 men, 800 tanks, 1,500 armored personnel carriers (APCs), and 364 aircraft. Syria committed perhaps 22,000 men, 352 tanks, 300 APCs, and 96 aircraft, while the PLO had about 15,000 men, 300 tanks, and 150 APCs.

The Israeli mission had three principal objectives. First, Israeli forces sought to destroy the PLO in southern Lebanon. Second, Israel wanted to evict the Syrian Army from Lebanon and bring about the removal of its missiles from the Bekáa Valley. Although

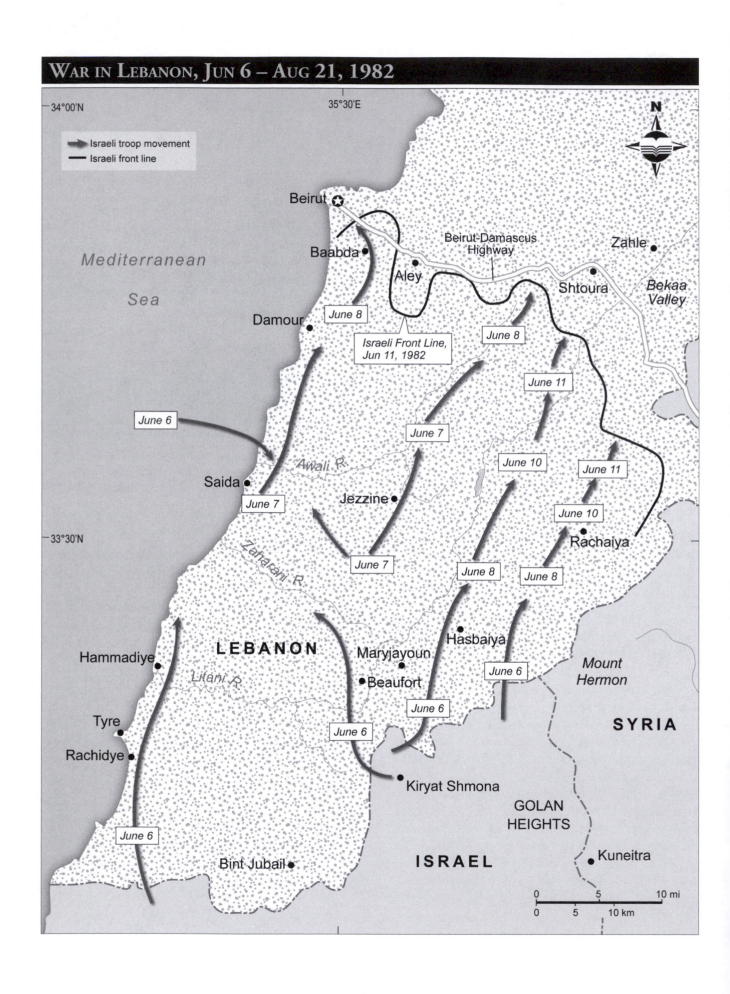

WAR IN LEBANON, JUN 6 – AUG 21, 1982

34°00'N   35°30'E

- →→ Israeli troop movement
- —— Israeli front line

Mediterranean

Sea

Beirut ✪

Baabda

Aley

Beirut-Damascus
Highway

Zahle

Shtoura

*Bekaa
Valley*

June 8

Damour

Israeli Front Line,
Jun 11, 1982

June 8

June 11

June 6

Awali R.

June 7

June 11

Saida

June 7

Jezzine

June 10

June 10

Rachaiya

33°30'N

Zaharani R.

June 7

June 8

June 8

LEBANON

Hammadiye

Litani R.

Maryjayoun

Hasbaiya

*Mount
Hermon*

June 6

Tyre

Beaufort

June 6

SYRIA

Rachidye

June 6

June 6

Kiryat Shmona

**GOLAN
HEIGHTS**

June 6

Kuneitra

Bint Jubail

ISRAEL

0		5		10 mi
0	5		10 km	

Israeli citizens demonstrating for the establishment of an official state inquiry into the massacre at the Sabra and Shatila refugee camps in Beirut, Lebanon, September 25, 1982. (Miki Shuvitz/Israeli Government Press Office)

Sharon perceived Syrian forces in Lebanon as a major security threat to Israel, he maintained that the IDF would not attack them unless it was first fired upon. Third, Israel hoped to influence Lebanese politics. Israel sought to ally itself with the Maronite Christians, led by Bashir Jumayyil (Gemayel), the leader of the Phalange (al-Kata'ib) and head of the unified command of the Lebanese Forces.

While the Phalange was mainly a political association, the Lebanese Forces was an umbrella military organization comprised of several Christian militias. Jumayyil had carried out a series of brutal operations to destroy the autonomy of the other Christian militias and had incorporated them into his Lebanese Forces. He was opposed to relinquishing the power held by the Maronites in traditionally Christian-dominated Lebanon to the Sunni and Shia Muslims of Lebanon. Many in the Phalange maintained that their heritage was Phoenician and not Arab, and they sought to maintain their historic linkages with France and the West. To this end, Jumayyil maintained a close relationship with Israel. As with the Israelis, he harbored intense opposition to a Syrian presence in Lebanon.

Palestinian militias were not only entrenched in the southern part of the country but were also well established in West Beirut. Understandably, the Israeli cabinet was loath to place its troops into an urban combat situation that was bound to bring heavy civilian

casualties and incur opposition from Washington and Western Europe. Begin and Sharon informed the cabinet that the goal was merely to break up PLO bases in southern Lebanon and push back PLO and Syrian forces some 25 miles, beyond rocket range of Galilee.

Once the operation began, however, Sharon quickly changed the original plan by expanding the mission to incorporate Beirut, which was well beyond the 25-mile mark. Many in the cabinet now believed that Begin and Sharon had deliberately misled them. The IDF advanced to the outskirts of Beirut within days. Tyre and Sidon, two cities within the 25-mile limit, were both heavily damaged in the Israeli advance. The entire population was rounded up, and most of the men were taken into custody. Rather than standing their ground and being overwhelmed by the better-equipped Israelis, the Palestinian fighters and PLO leadership withdrew back on West Beirut. Sharon now argued in favor of a broader operation that would force the PLO from Beirut, and for some 10 weeks Israeli guns shelled West Beirut, killing both PLO forces and civilians.

Fighting also occurred with Syrian forces in the Bekáa Valley. Unable to meet Israel on equal footing and bereft of allies, Syria did not engage in an all-out effort. Rather, much of the battle was waged in the air. By June 10, the Israeli Air Force had neutralized Syrian surface-to-air missiles and had shot down dozens of Syrian jets. (Some sources say the ultimate toll was as many as 80 Syrian jets.) The Israelis employed AH-1 Cobra helicopter gunships to attack and destroy dozens of Syrian armored vehicles, including Soviet-built T-72 tanks. The Israelis also trapped Syrian forces in the Bekáa Valley. Israel was on the verge of severing the Beirut-Damascus highway on June 11 when Moscow and Washington brokered a cease-fire.

In Beirut, meanwhile, Sharon hoped to join up with Jumayyil's Lebanese Forces. Sharon hoped that the Lebanese Forces might bear the brunt of the fighting in West Beirut, but Jumayyil was reluctant to do this, fearing that such a move would harm his chances to become the president of Lebanon.

Begin's cabinet was unwilling to approve an Israeli assault on West Beirut because of the probability of high casualties. Meanwhile, the United States had been conveying ambiguous signals regarding its position in the conflict. This only encouraged Arafat to entrench himself and the PLO in West Beirut.

Sharon disregarded cabinet opposition and placed the western (predominantly Muslim) part of the city under a siege from air, land, and sea. He hoped that this might convince the citizens to turn against the PLO. The bombing and shelling resulted in mostly civilian casualties, however, provoking denunciations of Israel in the international press. The PLO believed that it could hold out longer under siege than the Israelis could under international pressure, leading Israel to intensify its attack on Beirut in early August. Believing that there was an impending full-scale assault, the PLO then consented to a UN-brokered arrangement whereby American, French, and Italian peacekeeping forces, known as the Multinational Force in Lebanon, would escort the PLO fighters out of Lebanon by the end of the month. (The PLO relocated to Tunis.) Habib assured the PLO that the many refugees in camps in Lebanon would not be harmed.

On August 23, 1982, Jumayyil was elected president of Lebanon. He was dead within two weeks, the victim of assassination on September 14, 1982, by a member of the pro-Damascus National Syrian Socialist Party. Jumayyil had indeed paid for his connection to the Israelis. While the National Syrian Socialist Party took responsibility for the murder of Jumayyil, some suspected an Israeli conspiracy to kill him owing to his more recent attempts to disassociate himself from Israel.

Following the assassination of Jumayyil, Israeli forces occupied West Beirut. This was in direct violation of the UN agreement calling for the evacuation of the PLO and protection of the Palestinian refugees who remained behind. With the PLO removed, the refugees had virtually no defense against the Israelis or their Christian allies. Once Israel had control of the Palestinian refugee camps, in September 1982 Sharon invited members of the Phalange to enter the camps at Sabra and Shatila to "clean out the terrorists." The Phalange militia, led by Elie Hobeika, then slaughtered more than 1,000 refugees in what he claimed to be retaliation for Jumayyil's assassination. Estimates of casualties in the Israeli invasion and subse-

quent occupation vary widely, although the numbers may have been as high as 17,826 Lebanese killed and approximately 675 Israelis.

Israel had achieved a number of goals. It had accomplished its immediate aim of expelling the PLO from Lebanon and temporarily destroying its infrastructure. It had also weakened the Syrian military, especially as far as air assets were concerned. The Israelis had also strengthened the South Lebanon Army, which would help control a buffer, or security zone, in the south.

However, the invasion had negative repercussions as well. Much of Beirut lay in ruins, with damage estimated as high as $2 billion, and the tourist industry was a long time in recovering. Operation PEACE FOR GALILEE also became an occupation. In May 1983, with assistance from the United States and France, Israel and Lebanon reached an agreement calling for the staged withdrawal of Israeli forces, although the instruments of this agreement were never officially exchanged. In March 1984 under Syrian pressure, the Lebanese government repudiated it. In January 1985, Israel began a unilateral withdrawal to a security zone in southern Lebanon, which was completed in June 1985. Not until June 2000 did Israel finally withdraw all its forces from southern Lebanon.

Rather than producing a stable, pro-Israeli government in Beirut, the occupation led to contentious new resistance groups that kept Lebanon in perpetual turmoil. There was also considerable unrest in Israel. A protest demonstration in Tel Aviv that followed the Sabra and Shatila massacre drew a reported 300,000 people. Responding to the furor within Israel over the war, the Israeli government appointed the Kahan Commission to investigate the massacres at Sabra and Shatila. The commission found that Israeli officials were indirectly responsible, and Sharon was forced to resign as minister of defense. Begin's political career also suffered greatly. Disillusioned by the invasion and the high Israeli casualties, he resigned as prime minister in 1983, withdrawing entirely from public life.

BRIAN PARKINSON AND SPENCER C. TUCKER

See also

Begin, Menachem; Habib, Philip; Lebanon, Israeli Invasion of; LITANI, Operation; Palestine Liberation Organization; Sharon, Ariel

References

Friedman, Thomas. *From Beirut to Jerusalem.* New York: Anchor Books, 1995.

Rabil, Robert G. *Embattled Neighbors: Syria, Israel and Lebanon.* Boulder, CO: Lynne Rienner, 2003.

Rabinovich, Itamar. *The War for Lebanon, 1970–1985.* Rev. ed. Ithaca, NY: Cornell University Press, 1986.

Lebanon, Israeli Operations against

Start Date: July 13, 2006
End Date: August 14, 2006

Fighting between the Israeli military and Hezbollah fighters carried out over a 32-day period in southern Lebanon and northern Israel.

An Israeli tank fires into a Hezbollah camp in Lebanon during the 32-day Israel-Hezbollah conflict in 2006. (iStockPhoto.com)

Known to the Israeli military as Operation CHANGE OF DIRECTION, it began on July 13, 2006, and ended on August 14, 2006.

On July 12, 2006, Hezbollah fighters crossed the Israeli-Lebanese border into northern Israel and killed three Israel Defense Forces (IDF) soldiers and captured two others, evidently with the intent to use them for prisoner exchange purposes. This closely followed a similar operation mounted by Hamas in southern Israel in which one Israeli soldier was captured and two others were killed.

Holding the Lebanese government responsible for not enforcing security in the southern part of its country, Israel on July 13 began implementing an air, land, and sea blockade against Lebanon. The Beirut International Airport was also bombed. There were a number of Israeli objectives in CHANGE OF DIRECTION. The Israelis sought the return of the two kidnapped IDF soldiers but also wanted to remove the Hezbollah threat against Israeli territory by destroying its armaments and outposts and to establish long-term stability along the northern border. They also hoped to strengthen the anti-Syrian and anti-Hezbollah forces within Lebanon.

Israel's operation consisted chiefly of air and naval strikes on Lebanon's infrastructure, which destroyed a total of 42 bridges and damaged 38 roads. This effort also caused extensive damage to telecommunications, electricity distribution, ports, airports, and even private-sector facilities, including a milk factory and food warehouses. Roughly 70 percent of Lebanese civilians living in southern Lebanon fled north during the conflict. For its part, Hezbollah responded by launching an average of more than 100 Katyusha rockets per day into northern Israel, targeting such cities as Haifa and hitting hospitals, chemical factories, military outposts, and residential areas. Although the Israeli Air Force tried to strike at the launchers, they were virtually impossible to find, and many of the rockets were fired from residential areas, even near mosques.

Estimated Casualties during
Operation CHANGE OF DIRECTION (2006)

	Israel Defense Forces	Hezbollah	Lebanese Army	UN Personnel
KIA	119	80–400	46	7
WIA	400+	Unknown	100+	12
POW	2	13	0	0

Israeli air strikes against Lebanon and Hezbollah Katyusha rocket launches into Israel continued until July 21, 2006, when a new dimension was added to the conflict. Israel now began massing troops on the border and called up five battalions of army reservists (3,000 men) for a ground invasion. The ground offensive commenced on July 22, 2006, in the village of Marun al-Ras. IDF forces engaged Hezbollah fighters in Bint Jbayl, the largest Lebanese town near the border. One week later, Israel declared that it would occupy a strip inside southern Lebanon with ground troops. Meanwhile, four unarmed UN observers died when an errant Israeli air strike hit their observation post near the border.

U.S. secretary of state Condoleezza Rice visited the region during July 24–25 and again during July 29–31 in an effort to negotiate a cessation of hostilities. However, she opposed a cease-fire that would merely return the status quo. Meanwhile, discussions at the United Nations (UN) centered on how a negotiated solution to the conflict could prevent further violence and how an international— or Lebanese—force might control southern Lebanon and disarm Hezbollah. Talks were also undertaken in Rome among American, European, and Arab leaders in an attempt to reach a satisfactory end to the conflict, but to no avail.

On August 5, 2006, Lebanon rejected a draft UN resolution, proposed by the United States and France, that called for a full cessation of hostilities between Israel and Hezbollah. Lebanon claimed that the resolution did not adequately address Lebanese concerns. Nevertheless, the Lebanese government affirmed two days later that it would send 15,000 troops to the south as soon as Israeli troops withdrew from the area. Lebanon's prime minister, Fuad Siniura, repeatedly called for a quick and decisive cease-fire and for the immediate withdrawal of Israeli troops from southern Lebanon. His demands were echoed by thousands of demonstrators in cities around the world.

The IDF's ground offensive into Lebanon and its fierce clashes with Hezbollah fighters continued until August 11, 2006, when the UN Security Council unanimously approved UN Resolution 1701 in an effort to end hostilities. The resolution, which was approved by both the Lebanese and Israeli governments, also called for the disarming of Hezbollah, Israel's withdrawal from Lebanon, and for the deployment of the Lebanese Army and an enlarged UN Interim Force in Lebanon (UNIFIL) in southern Lebanon. Nevertheless, the 72 hours that preceded the effective date of the cease-fire on August 14, 2006, witnessed the fiercest fighting of the month-long conflict.

The Lebanese Army began deploying into southern Lebanon on August 17, 2006. However, Israel's air and sea blockade was not lifted until September 8, 2006. On October 1, 2006, the Israeli Army reported that it had completed its withdrawal from southern Lebanon, although UNIFIL denied these assertions.

The conflict killed an estimated 1,187 Lebanese civilians as well as 44 Israeli civilians, severely damaged Lebanese infrastructure, displaced some 1 million Lebanese and 300,000 Israelis, and disrupted life across all of Lebanon and northern Israel. By September, 60 percent of the towns and villages in the south had no water or electricity. Even after the cease-fire, 256,000 Lebanese remained internally displaced, and much of southern Lebanon remained uninhabitable because of more than 350,000 unexploded cluster bombs in some 250 locations south of the Litani River. Moreover, the Lebanese coasts witnessed a tragic oil spill that resulted from Israel's bombing of fuel tanks. About 40 percent of the coastline was affected. Both Hezbollah and Israel were accused of violating international humanitarian law during the conflict.

Hezbollah launched an estimated 3,970 rockets into Israel during the conflict, and the Israeli Air Force carried out about 15,500 sorties, striking more than 7,000 targets in Lebanon. Between 250 and 600 Hezbollah fighters were killed. Thirteen Hezbollah fighters were captured by the IDF during the conflict. The IDF reported 119 Israeli soldiers killed, more than 400 wounded, and 2 taken prisoner. The Lebanese Army suffered casualties as well: 46 killed and more than 100 injured. Finally, 7 UN personnel were killed, and 12 others were injured.

The parties to the conflict were in fact tangled in asymmetric warfare. On one hand, Hezbollah's munitions included some 14,000 short- to medium-range missiles and rockets in calibers ranging from less than 100 mm up to 302 mm, some of the warheads of which were loaded with ball bearings to maximize their lethality. In addition, Hezbollah possessed four types of advanced ground-to-ground missiles: Fajr 4 and 5, Iran 130, and Shahin 335-mm rockets with ranges of 54 to 90 miles. Hezbollah also possessed Iranian-built Zilzal 2 and 3 launchers, wireless detonators, Ra'ad 1 liquid fuel missiles, radar-guided ship-to-shore missiles, and a large number of optical devices.

Israel, on the other hand, possessed an impressive diversity of munitions, including precision-guided munitions, made in Israel or imported from the United States. It also completely dominated the skies and, in addition to fixed-wing jet aircraft, employed AH-64 Apache and AH-1 Cobra attack helicopters inside Lebanon. At least two unmanned aerial vehicles (UAVs) provided 24-hour coverage over Lebanon, with the Israel Aircraft Industries' Searcher 2 and the Elbit Systems Hermes 450 transmitting real-time targeting data directly into F-15 and F-16 cockpits.

In addition, the Israelis used American GBU-28 bunker-buster bombs on Hezbollah's Beirut headquarters. Multiple Launch Rocket System (MLRS) platforms were heavily used, and phosphorous munitions, which are restricted under the third protocol of the Geneva Conventions, were used as well. Although Israel's operation at first focused mainly on aerial and naval offensives, ground incursions became increasingly necessary. This was because most of Hezbollah's forces were able to make use of an extensive network of underground tunnels. Israeli troops faced fierce resistance and an unexpectedly strong performance by Hezbollah fighters, who multiplied ambushes and surprise attacks. Indeed, Hezbollah fielded an impressively innovative military force well tailored to meet a specific foe on particular terrain. Israeli intelligence, on the other hand, proved inadequate in this operation. For example, during the war Israeli forces launched a commando raid on Baalbek, capturing the Imam Khomeini Hospital where they supposedly found Iranians and a Syrian. No Iranians had been there for years, but a number of civilians were kidnapped and not returned. One may have been the central target of this raid, a grocer named Hasan Dib Nasrallah, unfortunately not the leader of Hezbollah. In fact, none of the objectives that the IDF had set for Operation CHANGE OF DIRECTION were realized. In a significant sense, the conflict was the result of both sides having misjudged the other. Hezbollah has stated that it would not have kidnapped IDF soldiers had it known the severity of Israel's response. Israel, meanwhile, was taken aback by the effectiveness of the Hezbollah defenses. There was sufficient anger in Israel over the results of the operation that the government was forced to appoint an investigating committee. In January 2007 IDF chief of staff Dan Halutz resigned in the face of increasing criticism of the IDF's performance in the war.

RANA KOBEISSI

See also

Hezbollah; Israel; Israel Defense Forces; Katyusha Rocket; Lebanon; Lebanon, Armed Forces

References

Allen, Lori, Suheir Abu Oksa Daoud, Nubar Hovsepian, Shira Robinson, Rasha Salti, Samer Shehata, Joshua Stacher, and Michelle Woodward. "Life Under Siege." *Middle East Report* No. 240. Washington, DC, Fall 2006.

International Crisis Group. "Israel/Hizbullah/Lebanon: Avoiding Renewed Conflict." The International Crisis Group Middle East Report No. 59. Brussels, Belgium, November 2006.

Schiff, Ze'ev. "The Fallout From Lebanon." *Foreign Affairs Magazine* (November–December 2006): 13–41.

USG Humanitarian Situation Reports #30–#32, August 29–31, 2006.

Lebanon, Israeli Security Zone in

A strip of territory in southern Lebanon that by 2000 encompassed an area of 600 square miles. Israel first created a security zone after its 1978 invasion of Lebanon in Operation GRAPES OF WRATH. The Israelis began a collaboration with Major Saad Haddad who had broken away from the Lebanese Army in 1976 and had established a Free Lebanon Army. The Israelis intended for Haddad's army to aid them in curtailing Palestinian and Lebanese anti-Israeli attacks in the south. When Haddad announced control over the security zone, he was dismissed from the Lebanese Army, and his own force became the South Lebanon Army (SLA). The SLA fought against the Palestinian Resistance Movement until the much broader Israeli invasion of Lebanon in 1982 in Operation PEACE FOR GALILEE. The devastation of southern Lebanon in the 1982 invasion was accompanied by massive repression and arrests of civilians as well as fighters. After the Israelis retreated to the zone in 1985, the SLA assisted the Israelis and kidnapped and held numerous prisoners without charge for years in the infamous Khiam detention center or transferred them to Israel.

The area became for many years the site of reciprocal rocket and artillery attacks between Hezbollah guerrillas and Israeli forces.

Opposition to the maintenance of this zone grew in Israel, however. Six weeks ahead of a planned withdrawal, Israel officially abandoned the zone over a two-day period in May 2000, paving the way for Hezbollah fighters and former residents to reclaim the land, and freed the Khiam prisoners. Because of the SLA's brutal practices and collaboration with Israel, many SLA members and their families fled to Israel. A number subsequently returned to Lebanon. Some 2,700 faced legal charges. Most of those tried received light sentences in an effort to promote reconciliation.

SPENCER C. TUCKER AND SHERIFA ZUHUR

See also

Hezbollah; Israel; Lebanon; Lebanon, Civil War in; Palestine Liberation Organization

References

Amnesty International. *Israel's Forgotten Hostages and Lebanese Detainees in Israel and the Khiam Detention Centre.* Pamphlet. July 1997.

Ball, George W. *Error and Betrayal in Lebanon: An Analysis of Israel's Invasion of Lebanon and the Implications for U.S.-Israeli Relations.* Washington, DC: Foundation for Middle East Peace, 1984.

Hamizrachi, Beate. *The Emergence of the South Lebanon Security Belt: Major Saad Haddad and the Ties with Israel.* New York: Praeger, 1988.

O'Ballance, Edgar. *Civil War in Lebanon, 1975–1992.* London: Palgrave Macmillan, 1998.

Lebanon, U.S. Interventions in

The United States has intervened militarily in Lebanon twice since the end of World War II. The first came in 1958 during what was called the Lebanon Crisis. This crisis was prompted by a political dispute with Druze and other Christian and Muslim opponents of Lebanese president Camille Chamoun and by American fears that Muslim pro-Nasserists might sway a pro-Western government friendly to them. The second U.S. intervention occurred from 1982 to 1984 during Lebanon's civil war and Israel's occupation of part of the country.

Unlike most nations of the Middle East, even before its establishment as an independent nation in 1943 Lebanon was characterized by considerable diversity, particularly with respect to religion. The country consists of an uneasy patchwork of Christian and Muslim sects residing in close proximity to each other. The Lebanese government was initially designed to prevent any one sect from dominating the government and country by requiring, for example, per the 1943 National Pact that the president be a Christian, the prime minister a Sunni Muslim, and the speaker of the National Assembly a Shiite Muslim. The National Pact also affirmed—according to a 1932 census—that Christians were to dominate the National Assembly by a ratio of six Christian members for every five Muslims. These sectarian differences and political prescriptions made national unity and governmental stability tenuous at best.

By 1958 a confluence of domestic and international developments plunged Lebanon into crisis with the possibility of civil war looming large. During Chamoun's presidency (1952–1958), sectarian disputes were exacerbated because of his desire to amend the

U.S. marines land at Beirut, Lebanon, from the amphibious attack transport *Chilton* offshore, July 16, 1958. (U.S. Naval Historical Center)

constitution and set the stage for his reelection to a second term. Meanwhile, Muslims demanded a new census, believing that its results would show that they were now the largest religious community in the country, giving them the right to dominate the National Assembly. Many Lebanese also wanted to see new political leadership. Regional and international developments such as the ongoing Arab-Israeli conflict, the U.S.-Soviet Cold War rivalry in the Middle East, and the call of charismatic Egyptian president Gamal Abdel Nasser for Arab unity against Western influences all pulled Lebanon's sectarian society in different directions.

Lebanese Muslims, including Sunni Muslim prime minister Rashid Karami, objected to President Chamoun's decision not to break diplomatic relations with Britain and France during the 1956 Suez Crisis and strongly supported Nasser. Indeed, Karami wanted Lebanon to join the newly created United Arab Republic, consisting of Egypt and Syria.

In the early summer of 1958, Muslim opposition to Chamoun's leadership sparked a rebellion. In response to this defiance, Chamoun ordered the army to suppress the revolt and compel rebels to recognize his authority. But commander in chief of the Lebanese Armed

Forces General Fuad Shihab refused to permit the army to become embroiled in the political dispute and in so doing almost certainly spared Lebanon from full-scale civil war. However, a coup led by General Abdul Karim Qassem on July 14, 1958, in Iraq prompted the embattled Chamoun to appeal to the U.S. for military assistance. Indeed, he feared that the coup was part of a concerted effort by Lebanese Muslims and perhaps Nasser and Qassem to take advantage of Lebanon's disorder and turn the country into a solidly Arab-Muslim state with closer ties to Egypt and the Soviet Union. Determined to preserve a friendly regime in Lebanon, the day after the coup in Iraq, U.S. president Dwight D. Eisenhower deployed 15,000 troops—most of them U.S. marines—to Lebanon. The presence of U.S. troops along with the National Assembly's selection of General Shihab as Chamoun's successor in September averted a civil war and cooled sectarian tensions. U.S. troops began withdrawing on October 25, and President Shihab implemented a series of reforms to foster greater national unity.

The U.S. intervention during the 1980s was prompted by a very different set of circumstances. Israel invaded Lebanon on June 6, 1982, in response to continuing raids and attacks by Palestinian guerrillas from bases in southern Lebanon. Although publicly proclaiming that its goal was only to destroy Palestinian forces in southern Lebanon, the Israeli leaders expanded their objectives to evict the Palestine Liberation Organization (PLO) from all of Lebanon, and Israeli forces then besieged Beirut. Despite heavy Israeli bombardment, PLO forces refused to surrender. Mounting civilian casualties and growing international opposition to the Israeli invasion compelled the United States to intervene in Lebanon in August and September 1982. The U.S. government strongly supported President Ilyas Sarkis and was believed by many Lebanese to be supplying the Lebanese Forces, as was Israel. In the intervention, American troops were to supervise, along with British, French, and Italian troops as part of the Multinational Force in Lebanon, the evacuation from Beirut of PLO fighters and to guarantee the safety of Palestinian civilians.

The basic terms of the intervention and PLO evacuation were negotiated by American envoy Philip Habib. The Habib Agreement stipulated that Israel would end its siege of Beirut and not invade the city or harm Palestinian civilians if PLO fighters evacuated Beirut and left the country, which they indeed did under the protection of the Multinational Force. By September 1, 1982, U.S. troops were withdrawn. However, the assassination of the newly selected Lebanese president Bashir Jumayyil, leader of the dominant Christian Maronite faction and an Israeli ally, prompted Israel to invade West Beirut that same month. At the same time, Israeli forces allowed Jumayyil's Phalange militia to enter two Palestinian refugee camps, Sabra and Shatila, leading to the massacre of hundreds of Palestinian civilians. Some estimates claim that as many as 3,500 died in the attacks. Many Americans, including President Ronald Reagan, regretted that the U.S. troops had been withdrawn so quickly and called for another multinational force.

The September massacres at Sabra and Shatila prompted the redeployment of U.S. troops to Lebanon later that month to support and stabilize the Lebanese government. But they gradually came under attack from the various factions fighting in the Lebanese Civil War. They fought Druze fighters and also the Lebanese Armed Forces and militias in South Beirut and fired on targets with naval gunfire from ships of the Sixth Fleet. The April 1983 bombing of the American embassy in Beirut and increasing fighting between U.S. marines and Druze and other militias demonstrated growing opposition of the warring Lebanese factions to the multinational and especially American presence in Lebanon. On October 23, 1983, the U.S. marine barracks in Beirut was destroyed by a truck bomb, killing 241 marines. An attack on the French Army barracks that same day killed 58 French soldiers. Continued attacks on the U.S. marines, increasing engagements between American and Syrian forces, and resurgent fighting in Beirut led Reagan to withdraw American military personnel in February 1984.

STEFAN BROOKS

See also
Habib, Philip; Lebanon; Lebanon, Armed Forces; Lebanon, Civil War in; Lebanon, Israeli Invasion of

References
El-Khazen, Farid. *The Breakdown of the State in Lebanon, 1967–1976.* Cambridge: Harvard University Press, 2000.
Fisk, Robert. *Pity the Nation: Lebanon at War.* Oxford: Oxford University Press, 2001.
Olson, Steven P. *The Attack on U.S. Marines in Lebanon on October 23, 1983.* New York: Rosen, 2003.

Lehi
See Lohamei Herut Israel

Levy, David
Born: December 21, 1937

Israeli political leader and foreign minister (1990–1998, 1999–2000). David Levy was born to Sephardic Jewish parents in Rabat, Morocco, on December 21, 1937. He completed high school and immigrated to Israel in 1958 and worked as a ditch digger and a construction worker before entering politics as a member of the Herut

David Levy, Israeli politician and foreign minister (1990–1998 and 1999–2000). (Israeli Government Press Office)

Party. He was first elected to the Knesset (Israeli parliament) in 1969, and when Likud (a coalition of the Herut and Liberal parties) won the national elections in 1977, he was chosen as minister of immigration. He became housing minister in 1979 and held that post until 1990.

In politics and government, Levy championed the cause of his Sephardic supporters and showed disdain for the elitism of the predominantly Ashkenazi Labor Party. He also maintained relative independence within his own party, exemplified when he criticized Likud for the Israeli invasion of Lebanon in 1982.

When Prime Minister Yitzhak Shamir formed a new government in 1990, Levy became foreign minister. He became a moderate force in the right-wing government, welcoming the mediation of the United States in the Middle East and showing a relative willingness to talk with Arab governments. At the same time, he fought with other leaders in the party, namely Housing Minister Ariel Sharon and Defense Minister Moshe Arens. Levy threatened resignation when his faction began to lose influence in early 1992. The following June, Likud was voted out of office.

On June 18, 1995, after months of disagreement with Likud leader Benjamin Netanyahu over internal electoral procedures that Levy claimed put his supporters at a disadvantage, the maverick party figure left Likud with his New Way faction (later known as Gesher, or Bridge) and declared his candidacy in the 1996 prime minister election. A deciding force in Israel's intricate coalition politics, Levy joined his center-right faction to the Likud bloc prior to winning the May 29, 1996, general elections. His relations with Prime Minister Netanyahu, a longtime Likud rival, remained prickly despite or because of Levy's top cabinet post as minister of foreign affairs.

In January 1998 Levy resigned as minister of foreign affairs to protest the lack of progress in peace negotiations with the Palestinian Authority (PA) and a lack of funding in the annual budget for social programs he supported. Gesher, which had withdrawn its support of Netanyahu and the Likud bloc, joined with the Labor Party in early 1999 to form the One Israel Movement ahead of national elections in May 1999. Levy went on to serve as foreign minister in the new government of Prime Minister Ehud Barak, who defeated Netanyahu in the 1999 elections.

By mid-2000 Levy's alliance with Barak had begun to fray, with Levy refusing to accompany the prime minister to final-status peace negotiations at Camp David, Maryland, in July 2000. Upon Barak's return from the talks, which ended without resolution, Levy accused the premier of making too many concessions to the PA, including offering to divide Jerusalem. In August Levy again resigned as foreign minister in protest and joined the right-wing opposition in pressing for new elections.

Levy did not directly participate in the government of Sharon and the Likud bloc after their victory in March 2001 but was appointed minister without portfolio in April 2002. He resigned that post in July 2002 to protest the severity of the government's austerity budget that dismantled some of the welfare provisions of the

Israeli state. Levy continued to serve in the Knesset and was a member of the Foreign Affairs and Defense Committee. He failed to win reelection in 2006, however.

SPENCER C. TUCKER

See also
Arens, Moshe; Barak, Ehud; Lebanon, Israeli Invasion of; Likud Party; Netanyahu, Benjamin; Sephardic Judaism; Shamir, Yitzhak; Sharon, Ariel

References
Karsh, Efraim, ed. *From Rabin to Netanyahu: Israel's Troubled Agenda.* London: Frank Cass, 1997.

Sharkansky, Ira. *Ambiguity, Coping, and Governance: Israeli Experiences in Politics, Religion, and Policymaking.* Westport, CT: Praeger, 1999.

Shindler, Colin. *The Land beyond Promise: Israel, Likud, and the Zionist Dream.* London: Tauris, 2002.

Liberty Incident
Event Date: June 8, 1967

On June 8, 1967, the electronic intelligence gathering ship USS *Liberty* was attacked by Israeli Air Force and naval units while it was on patrol 13 nautical miles off El Arish on Egypt's Sinai Peninsula. The reasons for the attack and charges of a cover-up have been the topics of conspiracy theories, but numerous inquiries in both the United States and Israel have concluded that the attack resulted from mistaken identity.

The U.S. Navy acquired the 7,725-ton civilian cargo ship *Simmons Victory* and converted it into an auxiliary technical research ship (AGTR). The conversion was completed in 1965, and the ship was renamed the *Liberty* (AGTR-5). Initially it operated off the west coast of Africa. With the Six-Day War in June 1967, the *Liberty* was directed to collect electronic intelligence on Israeli and Arab military activities from the eastern Mediterranean. Commander William L. McGonagle had command.

The attack occurred on the fourth day of the war. On June 4, the day before the start of the war, the Israeli government had asked the United States if it had any ships in the area. Washington responded that it did not because the *Liberty* was only then entering the Mediterranean.

By June 8 the Israelis had routed Egyptian forces in the Sinai Desert and Jordanian forces on the West Bank and were preparing to move aggressively against Syria. The Israelis, aware that their coastlines were vulnerable to naval attack, had warned the United States to keep its ships at a safe distance.

The *Liberty* was off the coast monitoring communications. Responding to the Israeli warning, Washington had sent several warnings to the *Liberty* not to close within 100 miles of the coast, but these messages were rerouted because of an overloaded U.S. Navy communications system and did not reach the ship before the Israeli attack.

A series of explosions in El Arish, which had been recently captured by the Israelis, led the Israelis to conclude that the town was

The U.S. Navy intelligence-gathering ship *Liberty* (AGTR-5) riddled with holes after an attack by the Israeli Air Force and the Israeli Navy off the Sinai Peninsula, June 16, 1967. (Time & Life Pictures/Getty Images)

being shelled by an Egyptian ship. It was later determined that the explosions had occurred accidentally in an abandoned ammunition dump. Israeli aircraft patrolling off the coast nonetheless mistakenly identified the *Liberty* as an Egyptian vessel. There was no wind, and a large U.S. flag flying from the *Liberty* was drooping and not identifiable. Identification markings on the side and stern of the ship were apparently not visible to the Israeli pilots, who attacked the ship head-on.

The Israeli attack began at 1:57 p.m. local time on June 8. Two or three Israeli air force planes, probably Dassault Mirage IIIs, strafed the ship with 30-mm cannon fire. The first Israeli pilot to reach the ship was Yiftav Spector, one of Israel's leading aces. This attack was followed by a comparable number of Dessault Mystères, which dropped napalm. More than 800 bullet holes were later counted in the ship's hull. Some 20 minutes later, three Israeli torpedo boats arrived on the scene, and members of the *Liberty*'s crew opened fire on them with two .50-caliber machine guns in the mistaken belief that the ship was under Egyptian attack.

McGonagle could not signal the Israeli vessels, as all the ship's searchlights had been destroyed. The Israeli torpedo boats fired a

number of torpedoes at the *Liberty,* one of which struck the ship on its starboard side and opened a large hole. The torpedo boats then approached to closer range and opened up with machine-gun fire against the American sailors, some of whom were attempting to launch life rafts. The torpedo boats then left the area.

The Israelis claimed that they did not know the *Liberty* was a U.S. ship until a life raft with U.S. Navy markings was found drifting in the water. Three hours after the attack, the Israeli government informed the U.S. embassy in Tel Aviv of events. Although the *Liberty* had been badly damaged, its crew managed to keep the ship afloat. The *Liberty* was able to make its way to Malta under its own power, escorted by ships of the U.S. Sixth Fleet.

Thirty-four American personnel died in the attack, and another 172 were wounded, many seriously. For his heroism and leadership, Commander McGonagle, who was wounded early in the attack, was subsequently awarded the Medal of Honor. His ship received the Presidential Unit Citation. Following stopgap repairs, the *Liberty* returned to the United States and was decommissioned in 1968. It was scrapped in 1970.

The Israeli government later apologized and paid nearly $13 million in compensation. Those dissatisfied with the official inquiries in the United States and Israel have speculated that the Israelis knew that they were attacking a U.S. ship and did so because they feared that intercepts by the *Liberty* would reveal that Israel was about to attack Syria. But such a theory fails to explain why Israel would risk the anger of its only superpower sympathizer. Knowledge of the imminent Israeli attack on Syria was also widespread and hardly a secret by June 8.

PAUL WILLIAM DOERR AND SPENCER C. TUCKER

See also

Six-Day War; Spector, Yiftah

References

Bamford, James. *Body of Secrets*. New York: Doubleday, 2001.

Cristol, A. Jay. *The Liberty Incident: The 1967 Israeli Attack on the US Navy Spy Ship*. Washington, DC: Brassey's, 2002.

Ennis, James M., Jr. *Assault on the* Liberty: *The True Story of the Israeli Attack on an American Intelligence Ship*. New York: Random House, 1979.

Oren, Michael B. *Six Days of War: June 1967 and the Making of the Modern Middle East*. Novato, CA: Presidio, 2003.

Rabin, Yitzhak. *The Rabin Memoirs*. 1st English-language ed. Boston: Little, Brown, 1979.

Libya

Predominantly Muslim North African nation covering 679,358 square miles. Libya borders Niger, Chad, and Sudan to the south; Tunisia and the Mediterranean Sea to the north; Algeria to the west; and Egypt to the east. The Ottoman Empire ruled Libya for much of the 19th century, but in 1907 Italy began to assert itself in the region. After a brief war with the Turks during 1911–1912, Italy gained control of Libya. A 20-year Libyan insurgency resulted, and Italy did not pacify the colony until 1931.

Libya was the site of significant fighting in the North African campaigns of World War II until it was ultimately secured by British forces in 1943. At the end of the war, Libya's status was immersed in the larger question of the fate of European colonial possessions in the Middle East and Africa. Ultimately, in 1949 the United Nations (UN) passed a resolution in favor of an independent Libya. Negotiations among the varied regions in Libya proved delicate. Those in and around Tripoli supported a large degree of national unity, while the more established government of Cyrenaica preferred a federal system and insisted on choosing the monarch. The process resulted in a constitutional monarchy, an elected bicameral parliament, and a federal system of government. Emir Idris of Cyrenaica was named hereditary king of Libya, and final independence was declared on December 24, 1951.

The new Kingdom of Libya had strong links to the West. Both Britain and the United States maintained military bases on its soil and helped support the state financially. Libya also had a strong Arab identity and joined the Arab League in 1953.

Arab nationalist movements grew in response to the 1948 creation of Israel, and Libya had experienced de-Arabization and a conflict of identity during the oppressive years of Italian colonization. The emergence of Gamal Abdel Nasser's Pan-Arab nationalist regime in Egypt by 1954 encouraged the growth of similar political thought in Libya, and the 1956 Suez Crisis only increased this trend. The discovery of oil in the late 1950s transformed the country, endowing it with wealth and increased geopolitical significance. Oil exports reached $1 billion by 1968.

The June 1967 Six-Day War proved a turning point for Libyan politics. On June 5, 1967, the day hostilities began, anti-Jewish and anti-Western riots broke out in Tripoli. When Nasser claimed that the Arab defeat was because of American and British assistance to Israel, Libyan oil workers refused to load Western tankers. The Libyan prime minister was forced to resign, and the king appointed a new cabinet.

In the months after the war, the government was under continued pressure from Arab nationalists. It pledged financial aid to Egypt and Jordan and demanded the closing of all foreign bases on Libyan soil (although the demand was not pressed). On July 31, 1969, a group of junior army officers seized power while the king was out of the country. The Revolution Command Council, headed by Colonel Muammar Qaddafi, took control with little opposition.

Qaddafi, an adherent of Nasser's version of Arab nationalism, stressed Arab unity, opposition to Western imperialism, and socialist economic policies. Qaddafi maintained that this agenda could be reconciled with a strong emphasis on an Islamic way of life, and an Islamic political and economic system. He rejected the Western presence in the Middle East but also communism or socialism. After Nasser's death, Qaddafi actively sought leadership in the Muslim world in the 1970s, promoting his so-called Third International Theory, a middle way between the communism of the Soviet Union and the capitalism of the West. Although he succeeded in convincing more than 30 African countries to reject relations with Israel, he never gained the confidence of certain other Muslim nations, perhaps because of his repression of the Muslim Brotherhood and other Muslim figures in Libya or more likely because of his advancement of radical causes and interference in regional politics.

Always an enemy of Zionism, Qaddafi supported Yasser Arafat's Fatah faction of the Palestine Liberation Organization (PLO) and sponsored terrorist attacks against Israel and related Western targets. As the 1970s progressed, Qaddafi voiced his support for anticolonialist movements around the world, including the Irish Republican Army (IRA), and Libya played host to a number of insurgent groups. Qaddafi also sought to build up the Libyan military and pursued significant arms purchases from France and the Soviet Union after 1970.

Internally, Qaddafi sought to remake Libyan society, insisting that a mixture of socialism and Islam would ensure social justice. He created a welfare state based on oil revenues and reformed the legal system to include elements of Koranic law (Sharia). His *Green Book* (1976) laid out his political and economic philosophy. In it he rejected representative government in favor of direct democracy. Finally, he transformed Libya's oil industry by insisting on a larger share of profits from international oil companies, setting a pattern that would be imitated by other oil-rich states.

Despite Qaddafi's radical politics, Libya and the United States avoided direct confrontation for much of the 1970s because of their economic relationship. This changed, however, when Libya vehemently opposed the 1978 Camp David Accords. Qaddafi viewed any Arab rapprochement with Israel as a betrayal. In 1977 President Jimmy Carter's administration listed Libya, Cuba, and North Korea as states that supported terrorism. U.S.-Libyan relations continued to sour. On December 2, 1979, rioters targeted the U.S. embassy in Tripoli in imitation of the attack on the American embassy in Tehran earlier that year. As a result, in May 1980 the United States withdrew its diplomatic personnel from Libya.

With the election of President Ronald Reagan in 1980, relations chilled further. On May 6, 1981, the Reagan administration expelled Libyan diplomats from the United States. The administration also pursued a freedom of navigation policy and challenged Libya's 1973 claims of sovereignty over the Gulf of Sidra in the Mediterranean. On July 19, 1981, the *Nimitz* carrier battle group was patrolling near the gulf when two of the carrier's Grumman F-14 Tomcat fighters were approached and attacked by two Libyan Soviet-made Sukhoi Su-22 fighter jets. The American planes evaded the attack and shot down both Libyan aircraft.

Tensions increased further, and in March 1982 the United States banned the import of Libyan oil. The sanctions had limited effect, however, as European nations did not adopt U.S. policies. Qaddafi continued to support revolutionary and terrorist activity. On April 5, 1986, an explosion in a Berlin nightclub killed 3 and injured 200, including 63 U.S. servicemen. The United States claimed Libyan involvement and retaliated with great ferocity. On April 15, 1986, U.S. Air Force and Navy planes bombed five targets in Libya. One of the targets was Qaddafi's home. He escaped injury but lost an adopted daughter in the raid.

The Reagan administration maintained that the raid resulted in significant disruptions to Libyan-supported terrorism, and such activity did decline for a number of years. However, on December 21, 1988, Pan Am Flight 103 was destroyed over Lockerbie, Scotland, by a terrorist's bomb. More than 270 died, and subsequent investigations pointed to 2 Libyan men as primary suspects. When the Qaddafi regime refused to extradite the men for arrest and trial, the UN imposed sanctions on Libya in 1992. American confrontations with Libya continued, and a second incident over the Gulf of Sidra resulted in the destruction of two Libyan MiG-23 fighter planes in January 1989. At the end of the Cold War, the Qaddafi regime remained steadfast in its support of revolutionary movements and terrorist actions against Israel and the West.

In recent years Qaddafi has taken a more conciliatory tone with the West, including turning over the men responsible for the Pan Am bombing and paying restitution to victims' families. After the September 2001 terrorist attacks on the United States, Qaddafi issued a stinging denunciation of the acts and condemned Al Qaeda and other terrorist groups. In February 2004 Libya declared that it would renounce its weapons of mass destruction (WMD) program and comply with the Nuclear Non-Proliferation Treaty. This began a thaw in relations with the United States, which resumed diplomatic relations that June and lifted all remaining economic sanctions in September 2004.

ROBERT S. KIELY

See also

Arab League; Arab Nationalism; Nasser, Gamal Abdel; Palestine Liberation Organization; Pan-Arabism; Qaddafi, Muammar; Six-Day War; Suez Crisis; Terrorism

References

Cooley, John. *Libyan Sands: The Complete Account of Qaddafi's Revolution.* New York: Holt, Rinehart and Winston, 1982.

Simons, Geoff. *Libya and the West: From Independence to Lockerbie.* London: Tauris, 2004.

Wright, John. *Libya: A Modern History.* Baltimore: Johns Hopkins University Press, 1981.

Likud Party

Israeli conservative political party, formed as a coalition of the La'am, Herut, and Gahal parties prior to the 1973 elections. The term *likud* is the Hebrew word for "consolidation." The Likud Party has been either the ruling party or the leading opposition party since its creation and has become the major conservative political party in Israel. The party came into being in opposition to the Labor Party.

In its domestic program, Likud claims to support a free-market economy. In power it has supported reductions in corporate and personal income taxes and in the value added tax (VAT). It has done away with certain government monopolies and has supported free trade agreements with the European Union (EU) and the United States. Likud has also emphasized Zionism and Israeli nationalism.

Likud has taken a hard line toward Palestinian-related issues. Until the election of Ariel Sharon as prime minister in 2001, Likud opposed any Palestinian state (Sharon announced in 2003 that he could accept a Palestinian state that was disarmed and not a threat to Israeli security) and strongly supported Israeli settlements in the West Bank and the Gaza Strip. A majority of Likud deputies in the Knesset (Israeli parliament) opposed the withdrawal from the Gaza Strip carried out by Likud prime minister Sharon in 2005. The party's agenda specified that "Jerusalem is the eternal, united capital of the State of Israel." It rejected proposals to divide the city as well as proposals to end Jerusalem's status as the capital of Israel.

The first Likud Party leader was Menachem Begin, leader of its Herut faction, who brought together the coalition of conservative and right-wing factions into the Likud bloc. Begin became the first Likud prime minister in 1977 when the coalition defeated the ruling Labor Party. Despite his hard-line reputation, he negotiated a peace agreement with Egypt in 1979. Yitzhak Shamir became party leader and prime minister when Begin retired in 1983. Following the 1984 national elections, Shamir and the Labor Party leader Shimon Peres governed together in a national unity government. The leaders alternated serving as prime minister. Likud operated as a coalition of the smaller parties until 1988, when the factions were formally dissolved, and Likud then began to operate as a single party.

The national unity government was reelected in 1988, and Shamir and Peres governed in coalition until 1990, when the Labor Party left the coalition. Likud was defeated in 1992, and Shamir stepped down as Likud Party leader in 1993. Benjamin Netanyahu replaced Shamir as party leader. In 1996 Netanyahu became prime minister after the Labor Party was voted out of power.

A number of right-wing politicians, including Begin's son and former prime minister Shamir, left Likud because they felt that it had become too moderate by agreeing to the Wye River Agreement. These politicians created the new Herut Party. Labor Party leader Ehud Barak defeated Netanyahu in the election in 1999, and Netanyahu stepped down as Likud Party leader. Sharon then became Likud leader. In 2001 he defeated Barak to become prime minister. Likud won twice as many seats in the Israeli Knesset in the 2003 elections, securing 40 out of 120 seats compared with the 19 it had won in the previous election. In November 2005 Sharon announced that he would leave Likud and form his own new centrist party, Kadima, and called for new elections in 2006. In the 2006 elections, the split in Likud proved disastrous. It was able to win only 12 seats in the Knesset, falling to third place. Likud leader Netanyahu vowed that "better days" for the party were ahead.

JOHN DAVID RAUSCH

See also

Begin, Menachem; Labor Party; Netanyahu, Benjamin; Shamir, Yitzhak; Sharon, Ariel

References

Akzin, Benjamin. *The Likud in Israel at the Polls: The Knesset Elections of 1977.* Edited by Howard R. Penniman. Washington, DC: American Enterprise Institute for Public Policy Research, 1979.

Arian, Asher. *Politics in Israel: The Second Generation.* Rev. ed. Chatham, NJ: Chatham House, 1989.

Shindler, Colin. *Israel, Likud and the Zionist Dream: Power, Politics, and Ideology from Begin to Netanyahu.* New York: Tauris, 1995.

Lipsky, Louis

Born: November 30, 1876
Died: 1963

Journalist and Zionist leader in the United States. Louis Lipsky was born in Rochester, New York, in 1876. His parents had immigrated to the United States from Poland. At age 15, Lipsky went to work in a cigar factory. He then spent two years in a law office, and at age 21 he became a journalist and edited a Jewish weekly paper. Moving to New York City in 1899, he briefly attended Columbia University. Until 1914 he helped edit the *American Hebrew.* He also contributed reviews to and wrote articles for several New York newspapers.

An ardent Zionist, Lipsky was perhaps its foremost exponent and theoretician in the United States. In 1901 he became the editor of the *Maccabean,* the monthly publication of the Federation of American Zionists (FAZ). He then edited its successor publication, the weekly *New Palestine.* He continued to write articles on Zionism that were widely read and praised worldwide. In 1903 he became a member of the Executive Committee of the FAZ and in 1911 was selected its chairman. He devoted himself entirely to Zionist activities until 1930, when he became president of the Eastern Life Insurance Company.

In 1918 Lipsky became general secretary of the Zionist Organization of America (ZOA), and he served as its president during 1925–1930. Throughout his life he traveled frequently throughout the United States to promote Zionism and raise money for Jewish activities in Palestine. He was one of the founders of the American Jewish Conference and used this forum to create support for the partition of Palestine and for the United Nations (UN) partition plan. In 1954 he was chairman of the American Zionist Council, and in 1957 he helped found the American Jewish League for Israel. He wrote a number of books, one of which was *A Gallery of Zionist Profiles* (1956). Lipsky died in New York City in 1963.

SPENCER C. TUCKER

See also

American Jewish Conference; American Jewish Congress; Zionism; Zionist Organization of America

References

Cohen, Naomi W. *The Americanization of Zionism, 1897–1948.* Waltham, MA: Brandeis University Press, 2003.

Klieman, Aaron S. *From Many, One: The Zionist Organization of America.* London: Routledge, 1991.

Meyer, Isidore S. *Early History of Zionism in America.* New York: American Jewish Historical Society, 1958.

LITANI, Operation

Start Date: March 14, 1978
End Date: March 21, 1978

Official name given to the Israel Defense Forces (IDF) invasion of southern Lebanon up to the Litani River that lasted during March 14–21, 1978. On March 11, 1978, 9 Palestinian terrorists landed on an Israeli beach, murdered an American tourist, captured 2 buses, and headed for Tel Aviv where, in a firefight with Israeli security forces, they were killed along with 28 Israeli passengers. Seventy-eight other Israelis were wounded in the assault. This was the culmination of a long series of Palestinian attacks originating from southern Lebanon.

At the time of the March 11 attack, Israel's new Likud Party government had just recently ended three decades of Labor Party dominance. The new government was headed by Prime Minister Menachem Begin, who was anxious to appear tough on the issue of terrorist attacks. Begin thus decided on a swift response to the Palestinian attack.

On the night of March 14, some 7,000 Israeli troops, accompanied by armor, artillery, and close air support, entered southern Lebanon with the stated goal of pushing the Palestine Liberation Organization (PLO) away from the Israeli border. The Israelis also hoped to bolster a splinter group within Lebanon, the South Lebanon Army (SLA), an Israeli ally. The resulting operation lasted for seven days and was the largest military operation the IDF had undertaken since the 1973 Yom Kippur War. Eventually, some 25,000 IDF troops were involved in the operation, which indeed saw the IDF reach the Litani River. The operation was a success for the Israelis, as PLO fighters retreated north of the river line. Lebanese deaths and casualties were extraordinarily high, however. Estimates of Lebanese dead range from as low as 300 to as high as 2,000. Worse, the Israeli incursion created perhaps as many as 250,000 refugees. The IDF suffered 20 dead.

In response to the invasion, on March 19 the United Nations (UN) Security Council adopted Resolution 425 (by a vote of 12 to 0) calling for the withdrawal of Israeli forces from Lebanon. On March 20 the Security Council adopted Resolution 426, entrusting the UN Interim Force in Lebanon (UNIFIL) to enforce this mandate and monitor the activities of the PLO guerrillas. On March 21 the IDF ceased offensive operations. UNIFIL arrived in Lebanon on March 23, 1978. Not until June 1978 did Israel agree to pull its forces out of Lebanon, exempting its security zone. At the same time, it turned over positions inside Lebanon to the SLA. In the years that followed, the SLA and the PLO periodically harassed UNIFIL forces.

Ultimately, UNIFIL failed to bring the Lebanese government's authority to the southern part of the nation where, despite UNIFIL efforts, the PLO reestablished itself. Southern Lebanon as a result remained a highly volatile and unstable area, a characteristic that has endured to the present day. Incidents in which the PLO and the Israelis exchanged fire were numerous. For the Israelis, the success

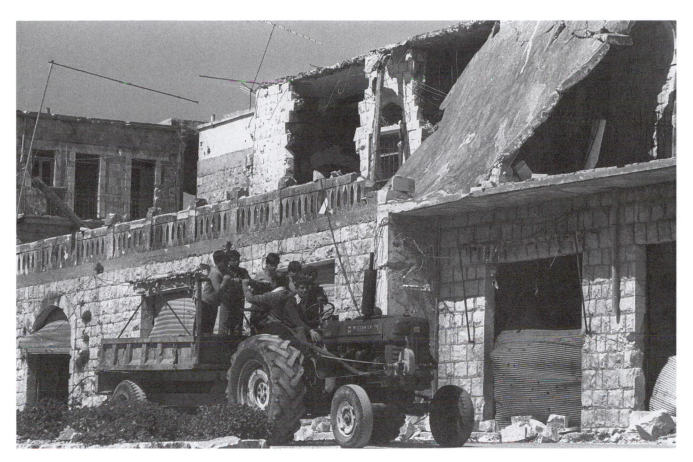

Boys on a tractor passing buildings damaged during Israel's Operation LITANI in Bent Gebail village in southern Lebanon, April 1978. (Moshe Milner/Israeli Government Press Office)

of Operation LITANI, particularly the fact that Israeli troops managed to operate without clashing with the Syrians, made the operation a dress rehearsal for the 1982 invasion of Lebanon, known as Operation PEACE FOR GALILEE. That operation, however, was considered only marginally successful. In 2000 the UN Security Council concluded that as of June 16, 2000, Israel had met the conditions of Resolution 425 by withdrawing all its forces from Lebanon. Southern Lebanon would once again become an issue in July and August 2006 when a short but bloody war occurred between Israeli forces and Hezbollah guerrillas located in southern Lebanon and Israel.

MICHAEL DOIDGE

See also

Hezbollah; Lebanon; Lebanon, Israeli Invasion of; Palestine Liberation Organization; United Nations, Role of

References

Bregman, Ahron. *Israel's Wars: A History since 1947.* 2nd ed. New York: Routledge, 2002.

Cobban, Helena. *The Palestinian Liberation Organization: People, Power and Politics.* New York: Cambridge University Press, 1984.

Fisk, Robert. *Pity the Nation: The Abduction of Lebanon.* 4th ed. New York: Nation Books, 2002.

Shlaim, Avi. *The Iron Wall: Israel and the Arab World.* New York: Norton, 2001.

Literary Club

Organization founded in Palestine in 1918 by Hasan Sidqi al-Dajani initially as a French-financed cultural association. The Literary Club (al-Muntada al-Adabi) dedicated itself to maintaining the distinctiveness of Arab Palestinians and agitating against British rule in Palestine. The club was based upon a similar organization created in Ottoman Turkey. It was associated with a leading Jerusalemite family, the Nashashibis. A similar organization, the Nadi al-Arabi, was associated with the competing family, the Husseinis, and headed by Haj Amin al-Husseini. The Literary Club, which actually had nothing to do with literature, brought Muslim and Christian Palestinians together and opposed British policies and Zionist activities.

Initially, the Literary Club served primarily as a social club and seemed unsure of its specific expectations. While its members resented British authorities, they despised the idea of Zionism and rejected calls for the establishment of a Jewish state in Palestine. By the 1930s, members of the club proclaimed the distinctiveness and national differences of Palestinian Arabs, arguing that Palestine should not be incorporated into a larger Arab nation.

Some underground organizations were created within the ranks of the Literary Club and took more direct actions to overthrow

British rule. In 1920 one such group, the Black Hand, attacked a British military outpost as a signal that a general Arab uprising should commence. The anticipated revolt did not occur, however, and the Black Hand disappeared as quickly as it had arisen. The first major Arab uprising in the region, the Arab Revolt of 1936–1939, was overtly supported by members of both of these Arab cultural clubs, ensuring that the British government would seek to destroy the organization after the revolt had been suppressed.

PAUL J. SPRINGER

See also

Arab Revolt of 1936–1939; Palestine, British Mandate for

References

Kimmerling, Baruch, and Joel S. Migdal. *Palestinians: The Making of a People*. New York: Free Press, 1993.

Tannous, Izzat. *The Palestinians: A Detailed Documented Eyewitness History of Palestine under British Mandate*. New York: I.G.T., 1988.

Literature of the Arab-Israeli Wars

Since the founding of Israel in 1948, the Arab-Israeli wars have left an indelible imprint not only on the history of global conflict but also on the fictional literature of the Western and Middle Eastern worlds. Israeli, Arabic, and Western writers have all given extensive treatment to the ongoing conflicts, targeting either a literary or a popular readership.

May 14, 1948, marked the beginning of what many Palestinians and other Arabs refer to as the Nakba (Catastrophe). At this time, the British Mandate for Palestine ended, and the State of Israel was proclaimed. Forces from states of the Arab League—Syria, Lebanon, Iraq, Egypt, and Jordan—joined Palestinian fighters to attack the new Jewish state. The Israeli victory in that war and the truce of January 24, 1949, led to the expulsion of at least 700,000 Palestinians from their homeland. Nakba marked a turning point in modern Arabic literature, inspiring a reorientation in literary form and content. It also vitalized a literature that chronicles the ongoing Arab-Israeli conflicts and the concomitant diasporas.

On the Palestinian side, the most prominent writer in the genre is Ghassan Kanafani. Born in Acre, Palestine, he became a refugee, moving among Lebanon, Syria, and Kuwait. The editor-in-chief of *Al-Hadaf,* the organ of the Popular Front for the Liberation of Palestine (PFLP), his life ended prematurely in an assassination by an Israeli car bomb on July 8, 1972.

Kanafani's first novella, *Men in the Sun* (1963), is the story of three Palestinians of varying social backgrounds who, in the wake of the 1956 Suez Crisis and Sinai War, try to escape to Kuwait in the tank of a water truck owned by Abu al-Khayzaran, a Palestinian who was rendered impotent during the 1948 war. For an exorbitant fee, Abu agrees to ferry the three men to safety, provided that they hide in the empty water tank at all security checkpoints. The journey takes place during the heat of daytime, and at the final stop the driver wastes time joking with guards about his sexuality. Consequently, the three men die from heat and suffocation. Thereafter,

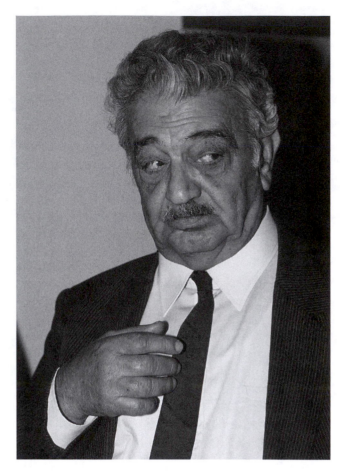

Imil Habibi, Israeli-Arab writer and politician, pictured here in 1994. (David Rubinger/Corbis)

Abu hurls the bodies on a trash heap, indignantly asking, "Why didn't you bang on the wall of the tank?" The story is a microcosm of the Palestinian Diaspora after 1948 and their disappointed hopes in garnering ongoing support from fellow Arabs.

The six additional stories in the *Men in the Sun* collection similarly reflect the post-1948 plight of the Palestinian people, as do Kanafani's subsequent novels, *All That's Left to You,* published in 1966; *Umm Sad* (Sad's Mother), published in 1969; and *Aid ila Hayfa* (Returnee to Haifa), published in 1970. *All That's Left to You* brings up the problem of collaboration with the enemy. Hamid's sister Maryam has been impregnated by an Israeli collaborator, whom she marries. Hamid decides to cross the desert from Israel to Jordan to save his sister's honor. The scene flashes between the agonized sister and her brother as both confront the past. Finally, Hamid meets an Israeli guard, killing him, at the same moment that Maryam murders her husband.

The next writer to rise to prominence was Imil Habibi, an Arab Israeli writer and politician who, as a communist leader, chose to remain in Israel and even served in the Knesset (Israeli parliament) from 1953 to 1972. After having written *Six Stories of the Six Day War* (1968), which probes the impacts of the 1967 conflict on Palestinians and sets into question official accounts of the war, he resigned from the Knesset to write his first novel, *The Secret Life of Saeed, the Pessimoptimist* (1974). This novel focuses on an antihero who, through his candor and foolishness, becomes first an informer to the Israeli state and later a supporter of the Palestinian resistance in a series of episodes reminiscent of both Voltaire's *Candide* (1759) and the Czech writer Jaroslav Hasek's *Good Soldier Schweik* (1932). The work met with acclaim both in Israel and abroad. The prominent Arab Israeli writer Anton Shammas translated it into Hebrew, and a stage version remained on the boards for a decade.

Other works, such as those of Jabra Ibrahim Jabra, take on nightmarish resonances. A portion of *Hunters in a Narrow Street* (1960) is set during the 1948–1949 Israeli War of Independence. Jameel Farran, digging in the rubble of a bombing, discovers the hand—complete with the engagement ring—of his fiancée. This serves as a symbol of what has happened to him personally and the fate that has overtaken Jerusalem.

Jabra's next novel, *The Ship* (1970), explores post-1948 feelings of alienation and yearning for the homeland coupled with the post-diaspora struggle for survival. Jabra's 1978 novel, *In Search of Walid Masoud,* focuses on the mysterious disappearance of Walid Masoud, a celebrated Palestinian intellectual and political activist living in Baghdad since the 1948–1949 war, and the attempts of his friends to probe his identity through monologues. Their attempts to reconstruct his essence point mainly to their own spiritual sterility. They have lost all sense of identity.

Among the female voices whose prominence is rapidly rising in Arab literature, Liana Badr has published novels, short stories, and children's books focusing on themes of women, war, and exile. Her best-known work, *Balcony over the Fakahani* (1983), is a collection of three novellas interweaving the stories of two women and one man during the successive uprootings of Palestinians from Palestine in 1948, Jordan in 1970, and Beirut between 1976 and 1982. Particularly stirring is her account of the 1976 Tel-al-Zaatar massacre by Lebanese right-wing Phalangists. In a flatly matter-of-fact tone that reflects her traumatized state, the first-person narrator, a young girl, recounts the day-to-day life of flight and camp existence, as when women wait 8 or 10 hours to fill jerry cans with water.

Another female novelist, Sahar Khalifeh, combines a feminist and a political mission in novels such as *Bab al Saha* (The Door of the Courtyard), published in 1990 and set during the First Intifada (1987–1990), and *Al Mirath* (The Inheritance), published in 1997 and focusing on worsening living conditions in the era following the 1993 Oslo Accords.

As in prose fiction, much Palestinian poetry focuses on the Nakba. Voices such as those of Fadwa Tuqan, Tawfiq Zayyad, and Samih al-Qasim joined in an effort to unite the experience of diasporic Palestinians with those who remained behind. Most prominent among this group is Mahmud Darwish who, after his village was razed during the 1948–1949 war, lived first as a refugee in Israel and, after 1970, in places so diverse as Lebanon, Moscow, Egypt, and Paris. In 1988 his militant poem "Passers By in Passing Words" met with acclaim in the Arab public but caused controversy among Israelis. His later poetry moved away from polemics and sought instead to construct a homeland in language.

With the Second (al-Aqsa) Intifada (2000–2004), however, which Darwish spent under siege in Ramallah, his poetry again took up themes of resistance in his widely acclaimed "Mohammad," "The Sacrifice," and "A State of Siege" (2001–2002). While the Israeli education minister suggested in March 2000 that some of Darwish's poems should be placed on the curriculum of Israeli schools, Prime

Literature about the Arab-Israeli Wars

Title	Author	Date Published
Good Soldier Schweik	Jaroslav Hasek	1932
Days of Ziklag	Yizhar Smilansky	1948
With His Own Hands: Alik's Story	Moshe Shamir	1951
Exodus	Leon Uris	1958
Hunters in a Narrow Street	Jabra Ibrahim Jabra	1960
The Open Door	Latifa Sayat	1960
The Death of the Old Man	A. B. Yehoshua	1962
Men in the Sun	Ghassan Kanafani	1963
Where the Jackals Howl	Amos Oz	1965
Levanter	Eric Ambler	1972
The Secret Life of Saeed, the Pessimoptimist	Emile Habiby	1974
Black Sunday	Thomas Harris	1975
Refuge	Sami Michael	1977
Gaza Intercept	E. Howard Hunt	1981
Balcony over the Fakahani	Liana Badr	1983
The Smile of the Lamb	David Grossman	1983
Operation Shylock	Philip Roth	1986
Des Enfants et des Chats (Of Kids and Cats)	Fawzia Assaad	1987
Bab al Saha (The Door of the Courtyard)	Sahar Khalifeh	1990
Hajar al Dahik (Stone of Laughter)	Huda Barakat	1990
Aunt Safiyya and the Monastery	Bahaa Taher	1996
If There Is a Heaven	Ron Leshem	2005

Author Yizhar Smilansky receives the Levy Eshkol Literature Award from Prime Minister Ariel Sharon at a ceremony held at the Israel Museum in Tel Aviv on December 16, 2001. (Moshe Milner/Israeli Government Press Office)

Minister Ehud Barak refused, claiming that Israel was not ready for such a move.

Non-Palestinian writers have also contributed a great amount of literature on the conflict. Egyptian writer Latifa Zayat began the tradition of women's war novels with *The Open Door* (1960). In this novel focusing on the 1956 Sinai Crisis, women discover their empowerment not only on the battlefield but also within their society and themselves. Other prominent novels from this tradition include Egyptian writer Bahaa Taher's *Aunt Safiyya and the Monastery* (1996), about Muslims during the 1967 Six-Day War who seek sanctuary in a Coptic monastery, and the Lebanese writer Huda Barakat's *Hajar al-Dahik* (Stone of Laughter), published in 1990, that probes the psychological effects of the Lebanon War on men and women alike. In *Des Enfants et des Chats* (Of Kids and Cats), published in 1987, Egyptian writer Fawzia Assaad represents the ongoing Arab-Israeli conflicts as the story of a war between twins whose souls have been transformed into those of cats.

The monumental work dealing with the Palestinian saga from 1948 onward has come from a Lebanese writer, Elias Khoury, who has written 11 novels and worked at the Palestine Research Centre in Beirut in the 1960s. He spent years gathering the refugees' tales that feed into his best-known book, *Gate of the Sun* (1998), an epic story of Palestinian life since the Nakba. The novel unfolds in a makeshift hospital in a refugee camp on the outskirts of Beirut where Yunis, an aging Palestinian freedom fighter, lies in a coma, and Dr. Khaleel tells him stories to keep him alive. Viewing the Palestinian plight as a mirror of Jewish experience, Dr. Khaleel asks Yunis, "In the faces of those people being driven to slaughter, didn't you see something resembling your own?" Other works by Khoury include *The Little Mountain* (1977), set during the Lebanese Civil War, and *The Journey of Little Gandhi* (1994), about a rural immigrant to Beirut who lives through the events of the civil war.

While the Nakba is a predominant theme in much Arabic writing of the post-1948 period, the picture in Israeli literature is more complex, with less exclusive focus on Arab-Israeli conflicts. Israeli writing combines themes such as coming to terms with the Holocaust and forging a nation from diverse immigrant groups with disparate origins. The question of Israeliness, or Jewish identity, is nevertheless profoundly marked by ongoing conflicts between viewing Israel as a Jewish state and viewing it as a multiethnic nation comprised of Jews and Palestinians alike. A general movement is visible as the focus of Israeli writing shifts from the initial euphoria of nation-building and conquest to a more critical stance that often raises controversy about political-military developments.

The first literary group of native-born writers has been dubbed the Palmach Generation, deriving its name from a military corps, or Dor Ba'aretz (Native Generation). Members of this group tended to idealize the *sabra,* or native-born Israeli, in the form of the youthful commander who sacrifices personal interests for the national ideal. Their approach is localized and fails to place the war in a larger historical context or to deal with the psychology of the fighters. Illustrative of this tendency are the trilogy of Shlomo Nitzan, *Between Him and Them, Togetherness,* and *Not Even a Tent Peg* (1953–1960), and Abba Kovner's two-volume novel *Face to Face* (1953–1955). Similarly, Moshe Shamir represents a Zionist ideal in his biographical novel *With His Own Hands: Alik's Story* (1951), about his brother killed in the 1948–1949 war, and in the historical novel *King of Flesh and Blood* (1954), where the deeds of Judean king Alexander Yanai and his heroic fighters reflect the ideals of the War of Independence. In a later novel, *That You Are Naked* (1959), Shamir questions the possibility of peaceful relations between Arabs and Jews, concluding that constant conflict is essential to the growth and prosperity of the Jewish state.

In contrast, the fiction of S. Yizhar (Yizhar Smilansky) reveals a change in attitude as the conflicts progress. His early novel *Days of Ziklag* (1948) follows seven days in the life of a platoon in September 1948 during the attack of Egyptian forces. Profoundly attached to the land, they are soldiers of conquest.

Yizhar's subsequent works are more critical of Israeli treatment of Palestinians and tend to undermine Zionist values, even though the conquered Arabs are represented as subhuman creatures who lack human dignity. For instance, his short stories "Hirbet Hizah" and "The Prisoner" (1949) depict the suffering caused by conquest, describing the devastation of Arab villages. Israeli soldiers are inwardly tortured by the sight of human misery but, in the face of the dehumanized victims, grow violent. In "Hirbet Hizah" the state of refugee villagers recalls to the soldiers the memory of Jews driven to slaughter, while in "The Prisoner" Israeli soldiers capture an Arab shepherd, steal his livestock, and beat him. Although the protagonist has qualms about the proceedings, he refuses a chance to release the prisoner. In short, both conquerors and vanquished are prisoners: the former psychologically and the latter physically.

A new generation of writers expressed disillusionment with Zionism, voiced outrage at the 1956 expulsion of refugees in the Gaza Strip, and condemned the Kafr Qasim Massacre on October 29, 1956. Foremost among the new literary voices was A. B. Yehoshua, a leading representative of what Israelis often call the generation of the state, or those writers who came of age after 1948. His controversial "Facing the Forests" (1963) is about a student employed in a summer job as a forest fire warden. At his workplace, he encounters his assistant, a mute old Arab whose tongue was cut out during the 1948 war. The student discovers that a village used to exist on the site and that the Arab's family was murdered. When, in the final development, the Arab sets the forest afire, the student does not try to stop him but watches with satisfaction: "the ruined village appears before his eyes; born anew."

Further reflecting post-Sinai disenchantment with militaristic conquest, Yehoshua's "last commander" in *The Death of the Old Man* (1962) depicts soldiers who want to sleep instead of fight. His first novel, *The Lover* (1977), reinforces this theme in the context of the 1973 Yom Kippur War, wherein a husband searches for his wife's lover, who disappears during the war. Told from multiple perspectives, the novel also features a 14-year-old Arab boy who loves his Jewish employer's daughter but eventually prefers to return to his village.

Another generation of the state writers addressed the ongoing Arab-Israeli conflicts obliquely and metaphorically in their fiction, as did Amos Oz, who since 1967 has written many articles and essays about the conflict and since 1977 has been a leading voice in the Peace-Now Movement aimed at a resolution of Israeli-Palestinian differences.

Oz's first volume of short stories, *Where the Jackals Howl* (1965), depicts characters in a kibbutz who hold neurotically distorted views of the Arab life surrounding them. Similarly, his first novel, *Elsewhere Perhaps* (1966), reflects on the ambiguous attitude of his fellow citizens toward the Arab population. *My Michael* (1968), set on the eve of the 1956 Sinai Campaign, metaphorically represents the Arab-Israeli conflict through the tortured marital relationship between a Jewish husband and his wife. In his *Touch the Water, Touch the Wind* (1973), set in 1967, he depicts two kibbutz members who, alongside an American hippie, decide to cross the boundary to the Palestinian territory and make peace with their neighbors. In *A Perfect Peace* (1982), published in the year of the Israeli invasion of Lebanon, Oz recounts a story from the Six-Day War that focuses on the shift of values from the founding fathers to contemporary Israelis, implying that yesterday's models have outlived themselves.

Other writers of the post-Sinai era also voice protest. Amos Kenan claims in *Shoah II* (1975) that occupation is synonymous with self-destruction. Amnon Dankner's collection of short stories published as *Berman Why Did You Do This to Me?* (1983) is, for the most part, a response to the war in Lebanon. In brutally explicit language, he portrays the conflict as a premeditated humiliation of other human beings. In one of the stories, "The Day the King Was Born," he depicts an Israeli military governor and his deputy extracting land from Arabs for private profit. An old Arab becomes suitably humble when the governor threatens to shoot his son. Sami Michael's *Refuge* (1977) concerns a communist Jewish couple who give refuge in their home to a Palestinian Marxist activist during the Yom Kippur War. Yet another novelist of the contemporary period, Shimon Ballas, is worthy of note as an Iraqi Jewish immigrant. Like the Arab Christian writer Anton Shammas (*Arabesques,* 1986), Ballas's native language was Arabic, and his first Hebrew novel appeared in 1964. Most of his fiction deals with the experiences of outsiders and addresses military conflict only obliquely. Nevertheless, *Clarification* (1972) deals with an Iraqi immigrant left out of the 1973 war.

The next major writer to emerge in Israeli literature was David Grossman with *The Smile of the Lamb* (1983), which, while not directly concerned with military conflicts, is an intimate depiction of life on the West Bank. Through a series of interior monologues, he represents the refugee condition of displacement and waiting. Like Oz, Grossman is also a prolific journalist and essayist, and his collection *Death as a Way of Life: Israel Ten Years after Oslo* appeared in 2003. More recently, Ron Leshem won Israel's prestigious Sapir Prize in Literature for *If There Is a Heaven* (2005), the story of a commander and his troop in the Lebanon war.

Among female Israeli writers, the experience of war often expresses itself in psychological terms and primarily through the medium of the short story. Jehudit Hendel's first collection, *They Are Different* (1951), deals with the insecurities of new immigrants against the backdrop of the Israeli War of Independence. Ronit Matalon's story "Photograph" (1992) is the first-person narrative of a woman who, with the help of a Palestinian friend, sneaks to the Gaza Strip to investigate the disappearance of other Palestinian friends. In a bizarre context, Orly Castel-Bloom's short story "The Woman Who Went Looking for a Walkie-Talkie" (1993) concerns an elderly woman who, to feel part of the current (unnamed) war, buys a walkie-talkie and begins talking incessantly at random frequencies. Through the power of her verbiage, she ends up commanding a number of absurd operations until the police confiscate her radio.

As in other fiction, early plays tended to glorify the *sabra,* as in Yigal Mossinzon's *In the Wastes of the Negev* (1949), which tells the story of a father who sends his son to certain death in a dangerous operation across enemy lines. Again, however, an increasingly critical tone emerges in later work. In a satirical cabaret titled *Queen of the Bath* (1970), for instance, Hanoch Levin attacked Israel's militaristic society and corruption in the army. The play was promptly censored. Similarly, Yitzhak Laor's 1989 play *Ephraim Returns to the Army* attacked militarism and, by drawing parallels between the interrogation and torture practices of Shin Bet (the Israeli security forces) and those of Nazi Germany, provoked controversy.

As with prose writers, Israeli poets also probed the complexity of postindependence Israel and the experience of repeated war, pressures voiced by prominent poets such as Natan Zach, Yehuda Amichai, and David Avidan. Esther Raizen's anthology of translations from major Hebrew poets, *No Rattling of Sabers: An Anthology of Israeli War Poetry* (1995), covering some 50 years and seven major wars, definitively illustrates the importance of the ongoing conflicts in contemporary Israeli poetry.

In contrast to Arab and Israeli fiction, Western work abounds with spy thrillers and adventure novels that frequently distort and even trivialize the Arab-Israeli conflicts. Among popular American novels, Leon Uris's immensely popular *Exodus* (1958) is by far the best known. Often attacked for its negative stereotyping of Arabs, it is the tale of an American nurse and an Israeli freedom fighter during the struggle to establish and defend the State of Israel. Uris's next novel set in the Middle East, *The Haj* (1984), depicts the lives of Palestinian Arabs from World War I to the Suez Crisis of 1956,

representing them as "gifted in matters of fantasy and magic." *Mitla Pass* (1988), a semiautobiographical novel, is set during the Sinai Campaign and features a young novelist who travels to Israel. Forsaking his new love, a Holocaust survivor, he joins the Israeli forces and is parachuted into the Mitla Pass, a dangerous location behind enemy lines.

In England, two pioneers of the sophisticated thriller—Eric Ambler and John Le Carré (David Cornwell)—produced tightly plotted novels centering on Arab-Israeli conflicts. Ambler's *Levanter* (1972) begins shortly after the Six-Day War. Businessman Michael Howell becomes unwittingly involved with the fictional Palestinian Action Force, a group analogous to the PFLP. Le Carré's *Little Drummer Girl* (1983) reveals an attempt to deal objectively with Arab-Israeli conflicts. Set in the early 1980s, shortly before the Lebanese War, a Palestinian group under the leadership of Khalil is conducting operations in Western Europe. Israeli secret agents plan a counteroperation whereby Charlie, a young British actress, is given a false identity and sent to Lebanon for military training. Returning to Europe, she eventually leads the Israeli team to Khalil, guided by Israeli agent Gadi Becker, who himself voices doubts about the legitimacy of Israeli policy.

Other popular novels, chiefly by American writers, offer suspenseful situations pasted against a vague backdrop of historical developments. In a similar vein as *The Haj,* D. W. Arathorn's *Kamal* (1982) follows Kamal Jibral through a terrorist career from South America to the Middle East. E. Howard Hunt's *Gaza Intercept* (1981) deals with a Palestinian plan to explode an atomic bomb over Tel Aviv, while another popular thriller, Ken Follett's *Triple* (1979), is about a Mossad agent delegated to beat the Arabs in an arms race by stealing 200 tons of uranium. *Shibumi* (1979) by Trevanian (Rodney Whitaker) traces the career of a superhero survivor of Hiroshima called upon to track down Palestinian terrorists who kill Israel athletes at the 1972 Olympics. Thomas Harris's *Black Sunday* (1975) moves the Arab-Israeli conflict to the American Super Bowl, where PLO terrorists have plotted to blow up 80,000 spectators, including the American president. Another thriller, Nelson De Mille's *By the Rivers of Babylon* (1978), follows United Nations (UN) delegates who, flying on a mission to bring peace to the Middle East, are forced to crash-land in a desert, where they are attacked by Palestinian commandos. Richard Chesnoff's *If Israel Lost the War* (1969) offers an alternative history of the 1967 war wherein the Arabs strike first on June 5, 1967.

More recently, Steven Hartov's thriller *The Heat of Ramadan* (1992) again takes up the 1972 Olympics, where an Israeli intelligence team mistakenly assassinates an innocent Palestinian, leaving the real terrorist alive to avenge himself. In his *Nylon Hand of God* (1996), Hartov deals with Israeli intelligence officers pitted against wily terrorists after a suicide bombing of the Israeli embassy in New York, while in *The Devil's Shepherd* (2000) the same agents hunt for a mole who has infiltrated Israel's nuclear missile defense system.

On the cusp between popular thrillers and serious fiction, Herman Wouk's two novels with a Middle Eastern setting, *The Hope* (1993) and *The Glory* (1994), span the period from 1948 to the bombing of Iraq's Osiraq nuclear reactor in 1981. In *The Hope*, which ends with the Six-Day War, Wouk combines a love story with the hero's military exploits and includes such historical figures as David Ben-Gurion, Moshe Dayan, and Golda Meir. Beginning with post-1967 fighting, *The Glory* follows some dozen military characters and their families through such developments as the Yom Kippur War, the 1976 Entebbe hostage rescue mission, and the attack on Iraq's nuclear installations in 1981.

On a more literary plane, Philip Roth's *Counterlife* (1986) and *Operation Shylock* (1993) voice a pluralist rather than Zionist stance. Not directly about the Arab-Israeli conflicts, *Counterlife* explores the fate of two brothers. Henry Zuckerman embraces the doctrine of Zionism, while Nathan finds that the belief "reverse[s] the very form of Jewish existence." Set in Jerusalem during the trial of suspected World War II war criminal John Demjanjuk, *Operation Shylock* deals both with a character named Philip Roth, a Jewish American novelist, and an impostor who takes on his identity. The imposter advocates diasporism, encouraging Israelis to return home to Eastern Europe, all the time that the real Roth attends the trial of a former Nazi and observes the harsh judgment that a West Bank military court metes out to young Palestinians. Apart from Roth's novels, English-language fiction offers a surprising dearth of serious treatments of the Arab-Israeli conflict.

Finally, mention should be made of James A. Michener's *The Source* (1965). A well-balanced historical novel, it traces the intertwining of the peoples who later became the Palestinians and the Jews. Michener made the point that they are basically the same people. The novel moves from 10,000 BC and the early history of the Jews through the impact of Christianity, the Crusades, the Ottoman Empire, and two world wars to the 1960s.

ANNA M. WITTMANN

See also

Darwish, Mahmoud; Film and the Arab-Israeli Conflict; Intifada, First; Intifada, Second; Israeli War of Independence, Overview; Kafr Qasim Massacre; Sinai Campaign; Six-Day War; Suez Crisis; Yom Kippur War

References

Glazer, Miriyam. *Dreaming the Actual: Contemporary Fiction and Poetry by Israeli Women Writers.* New York: SUNY Press, 2000.

Jayyusi, Salma Khadra, ed. *Anthology of Modern Palestinian Literature.* New York: Columbia University Press, 1992.

Oppenheimer, Yochai. "The Arab in the Mirror: The Image of the Arab in Israeli Fiction." *Prooftexts* 19 (1999): 205–234.

Orfalea, Gregory. "Literary Devolution: The Arab in the Post-World War II Novel in English." *Journal of Palestine Studies* 17(2) (1988): 109–128.

Perry, Menakhem. "The Israeli-Palestinian Conflict as a Metaphor in Recent Israeli Fiction." *Poetics Today* 7(4) (1986): 603–619.

Shaked, Gershon. *Modern Hebrew Fiction.* Translated by Yael Lotan. Bloomington: Indiana University Press, 2000.

Livni, Tzipi
Born: July 5, 1958

Israeli vice prime minister and minister of foreign affairs. Born in Tel Aviv on July 5, 1958, Tzipi Livni is the daughter of the former chief of operations for the Irgun Tsvai Leumi (National Military Organization), the right-wing Zionist underground in the British Mandate for Palestine. She earned a bachelor of laws degree at Bar-Ilan University and served as a lieutenant in the Israel Defense Forces (IDF) and later in the Mossad intelligence agency. She practiced law in a private firm from 1989 to 1999, specializing in commercial, constitutional, and real estate law. In 1996 she served as director-general of the Government Companies Authority. In this capacity, she oversaw the privatization of government corporations and monopolies.

Entering politics in 1999, Livni was elected to the Knesset (Israeli parliament) as a member of the opposition Likud Party. There she served on the Constitution, Justice, and Law Committee and on the Status of Women Committee. When Likud leader Ariel

Tzipi Livni, Israeli vice prime minister and minister of foreign affairs, shown here in February 2002. (Israeli Government Press Office)

Sharon became prime minister in July 2001, Livni became minister of regional cooperation and thereafter held a succession of cabinet posts including minister of agriculture and rural development, minister of immigrant absorption, and minister of housing and construction.

In October 2005 Livni was formally appointed minister of justice, having been acting minister for several months. She actively supported Sharon's disengagement policy and helped secure passage of his Gaza Strip withdrawal plan in the Knesset. In November 2005 she followed Sharon into the new Kadima Party.

Appointed minister of foreign affairs by acting prime minister Ehud Olmert in January 2006 as the successor to Silvan Shalom, who resigned, Livni continued to hold concurrently the post of justice minister until May 2006, when she gave up that post and retained only the foreign ministry position. Livni subsequently was designated acting vice prime minister in the government headed by Olmert. In May 2007 Livni called for Olmert to resign because of the publication of the Winograd Commission's interim report that was sharply critical of Israeli military operations in Lebanon in 2006. Livni offered herself as leader of the Kadima Party. In an unusual move, when Olmert declined to step down she continued in the cabinet as foreign minister. Livni is married and has two children.

A popular political figure in Israel, Livni is regarded by many Israelis as being both tough-minded and honest. She opposes any negotiations with terrorist organizations but was the first Israeli cabinet minister to separate attacks against Israeli military targets as nonterrorist acts of war from attacks against civilian targets as terrorist actions.

SPENCER C. TUCKER

See also

Irgun Tsvai Leumi; Kadima Party; Likud Party; Olmert, Ehud; Sharon, Ariel

References

Finkelstein, Norman H. *Ariel Sharon.* Minneapolis, MN: First Avenue Editions, 2005.

Yishai, Yael. *Between the Flag and the Banner: Women in Israeli Politics.* Albany, NY: SUNY Press, 1996.

Lloyd, John Selwyn
Born: July 28, 1904
Died: May 17, 1978

British Conservative Party politician and foreign secretary (1955–1960). John Selwyn Lloyd was born in West Kirby, Wirral, England, on July 28, 1904. He was educated at Fettes College, Edinburgh, and Magdalene College, Cambridge. He was called to the bar in 1930 and in the ensuing years built a successful law practice. During World War II he served in the European theater, rising to the rank of brigadier. In the 1945 general election, his strong war record helped him to victory as a member of Parliament for his native area of Wirral, a seat he held for 35 years. Although a poor public speaker

John Selwyn Lloyd, British Conservative Party politician and foreign secretary (1955–1960). (Corbis)

and somewhat introverted and shy, he won recognition as an expert on financial and economic questions and for his organizational skills.

In 1951 when the Conservatives regained power, Lloyd was appointed minister of state at the Foreign Office, where his duties included heading the British delegation at meetings of the United Nations (UN) General Assembly. He steadily advocated a firm line in resisting both Chinese and Soviet pressure in Asia and Europe. He also insisted that the United States must consult Britain over the conduct of the Korean War (1950–1953). During the Panmunjom truce talks, he devoted considerable energies to trying to resolve the impasse over the question of the repatriation of prisoners of war.

In 1954 Lloyd became minister of defense, and in December 1955 Prime Minister Anthony Eden, his former boss at the Foreign Office, made him foreign secretary. The most difficult question facing Lloyd was how to handle threats by Egyptian president Gamal Abdel Nasser to nationalize the Suez Canal, which Nasser eventually did in June 1956. Lloyd's preferred solution to the growing crisis was to persuade the UN to place the canal under international control, and only in mid-October 1956 was he informed of secret Franco-British plans to retake the canal by force of arms. Lloyd remained unaware that Israeli forces would simultaneously invade Egypt. During the 10-day Israeli invasion, which began on October 26 and was supplemented by British and French military operations beginning on November 1, Lloyd loyally supported his government's policies.

On November 6 Lloyd accepted the advice of Chancellor of the Exchequer Harold Macmillan that U.S. financial and economic pressure on Britain had become so damaging that the invasion must be called off. Lloyd later regretted endorsing such a humiliating decision, especially since the war ended on terms less favorable to Britain and France than those he had seemed likely to secure through negotiations.

Despite fevered speculation that he would resign and persistent verbal abuse and taunts from the opposition benches, Lloyd survived the Suez Crisis. The first priority for him and new prime minister Macmillan, who dominated the making of foreign policy, was to repair badly strained British-U.S. relations, which they did at the 1957 Bermuda Conference. Lloyd remained foreign secretary until 1960 when he became chancellor of the exchequer, a post he held until July 1962.

From October 1963 to September 1964, Lloyd was leader of the House of Commons. In 1971 he was elected Speaker of the House of Commons, a role in which he won general praise for his sedulous fairness to all parties and viewpoints. In 1976 he was created a life peer. Lloyd died at Preston Crowmarsh, Oxfordshire, on May 17, 1978.

PRISCILLA MARY ROBERTS

See also

Aswan High Dam Project; Eden, Robert Anthony; Egypt; Egypt, Armed Forces; Eisenhower, Dwight David; France, Middle East Policy; Israel; Israel Defense Forces; Macmillan, Maurice Harold; Nasser, Gamal Abdel; Suez Canal; Suez Crisis; United Kingdom, Middle East Policy

References

Kyle, Keith. *Suez: Britain's End of Empire in the Middle East*. London: Weidenfeld and Nicolson, 1991.

Lloyd, Selwyn. *Mr. Speaker, Sir*. London: Cape, 1976.

———. *Suez 1956: A Personal Account*. London: Cape, 1978.

Thorpe, D. R. *Selwyn Lloyd*. London: Cape, 1989.

Lloyd George, David
Born: January 17, 1863
Died: March 26, 1945

British political leader and prime minister (1916–1922). Born in Manchester on January 17, 1863, of Welsh parents, David Lloyd George grew up in Wales, where the family moved a year after his birth following the death of his father. Trained in the law, Lloyd George began practicing law in 1884. Six years later he entered politics and was elected to the House of Commons as a member of the Liberal Party. A member of the party's radical wing, he made his reputation as an articulate opponent of the South African War (Boer War) of 1899–1902 and as a strong advocate of progressive social reform.

A brilliant politician and gifted orator, Lloyd George rose quickly within the ranks of the Liberal Party. From 1905 to 1908 he

David Lloyd George, British political leader and prime minister (1916–1922). (Library of Congress)

served as president of the Board of Trade, and in 1908 he became chancellor of the exchequer, a position he held until 1915. In this post he promoted a progressive reform agenda. In 1909 he submitted the People's Budget, whereby he sought to balance the budget, pay for extensive naval construction, and carry out radical social reform through sharp increases in taxes on land and a supertax on the rich. The political struggle unleashed by the People's Budget resulted in the Parliament Act (1911) limiting the power of the House of Lords, which had attempted to block its passage.

Lloyd George initially hoped that Britain could stay out of a continental war, but he became an advocate of intervention following the German invasion of Belgium in August 1914. From the beginning of World War I, he sharply criticized the business as usual approach of Prime Minister Herbert Asquith toward the war effort. To deal with the shell crisis occasioned by a shortage of munitions, in May 1915 Asquith appointed Lloyd George minister of munitions. In that post he oversaw the reorganization of the economy to meet the demands of total war. In June 1916 he became minister of war. Increasingly dismayed by Britain's conduct of the war, he helped to bring down the Asquith government in December 1916, leading to his own appointment as prime minister.

As prime minister, Lloyd George created a five-member War Cabinet to oversee the war effort. Appalled by the horrifying losses on the western front, he advocated a peripheral strategy against Germany's allies, especially Turkey, to "knock out the props from under Germany." This brought him into conflict with Britain's military leadership.

Lloyd George was almost immediately confronted with a series of major strategic developments: Germany's resumption of unrestricted submarine warfare, revolution in Russia, the entrance of the United States into the war, and widespread mutinies in the French Army. The overall strategic situation in early 1917 coupled with the desire not to repeat the bloodletting of 1916 led Lloyd George to prefer a defensive stance on the western front and to await the formation of a large American army before launching further offensives in France. Nonetheless, he was persuaded to support another major offensive on the western front in 1917, resulting in the Third Battle of Ypres (Passchendaele), which cost Britain 400,000 casualties and horrified Lloyd George.

In November 1917 Lloyd George won a victory over his generals with the creation of the Supreme War Council to coordinate Allied strategy. He concurred with the reinforcement of the western front, even taking forces from the Middle East, in the desperate struggle that spring. The Allies went on the offensive that July, and the armistice followed in November 1918.

Victory in the war was followed by victory in the general election of December 1918 on a platform of "hanging the Kaiser" and "making the Germans pay." At the Paris Peace Conference of 1919, Lloyd George stood firmly with President Woodrow Wilson on most major issues and against French premier Georges Clemenceau's demand for a more punitive peace.

Among Lloyd George's most notable postwar achievements was the Government of Ireland Act of 1920, which ultimately paved the way for the creation of the Irish Free State in December 1921. Lloyd George resigned in October 1922. Although he never again held public office, he remained influential in the Liberal Party and in British politics.

Lloyd George's first involvement with the Zionist movement came in 1903 when his law firm provided advice on the so-called East Africa Scheme for the settlement of Jews in British East Africa. In November 1914 he expressed support for the proposal advanced by Herbert Samuel that called for the establishment in Palestine after the defeat of the Ottoman Empire of a national home for the Jewish people. Lloyd George championed Zionist Chaim Weizmann's views with Foreign Secretary Arthur James Balfour and enthusiastically supported the drafting of the Balfour Declaration of 1917 as a means of mobilizing Jewish support worldwide for the war effort. Lloyd George ensured the inclusion of that declaration in the peace treaty with Turkey and then strongly supported the British Mandate for Palestine, confirmed at the 1920 San Remo Conference. Lloyd George appointed Sir Herbert Samuel as the first high commissioner for Palestine.

Throughout the rest of his life, Lloyd George remained consistent in his pro-Zionist position. He opposed restrictions on Jewish immigration to Palestine and denounced in the House of Commons the British government's Passfield White Paper of 1930 as "a breach of national faith." He also condemned the report of the Peel Commission in 1937 and the White Paper of 1939, noting that the Jewish people had "honorably kept their part of the bargain."

In 1940 Lloyd George declined Winton Churchill's offer of a cabinet post. In January 1945 Lloyd George was elevated to the peerage as Earl Lloyd George of Dwyfor, Viscount Gwynedd of Dwyfor. He died in Ty Newydd, Wales, on March 26, 1945.

J. David Cameron and Spencer C. Tucker

See also

Balfour, Arthur James; Balfour Declaration; East Africa Scheme; Palestine, British Mandate for; Peel Commission; Samuel, Sir Herbert Louis; Weizmann, Chaim; White Paper (1930); White Paper (1939); Wilson, Thomas Woodrow

References

Constantine, Stephen. *Lloyd George*. New York: Routledge, 1992.

Gilbert, Bentley Brinckerhoff. *Lloyd George: A Political Life*. 2 vols. Columbus: Ohio State University Press, 1987–1992.

Grigg, John. *From Peace to War: Lloyd George, 1912–1916*. Los Angeles: University of California Press, 1985.

———. *Lloyd George: War Leader, 1916–1918*. New York: Penguin, 2003.

Rothwell, V. H. *British War Aims and Peace Diplomacy, 1914–1918*. Oxford: Oxford University Press, 1971.

Lobbies, Arab

A number of formally and informally organized groups lobby private U.S. organizations and the federal government in an effort to advance Arab interests in the United States and around the world. Unlike the Jewish lobby in the United States, which is large, well funded, and exceedingly well organized, the Arab lobby suffers from lack of organization and shortage of numbers. These disadvantages make it difficult for Arab interests to enjoy any significant clout with the U.S. government or private American groups.

In 1951 Saudi Arabia's King Saud bin Abdul Aziz helped found the first organized Arab lobby in the United States. He did so largely in reaction to the creation of the American Zionist Committee for Public Affairs, a large and influential Jewish lobby that today operates as the American Israel Public Affairs Committee (AIPAC). Today, AIPAC is thought to be the second most powerful political and special interest lobby in the United States. King Saud's efforts ultimately resulted in the formation of the National Association of Arab-Americans. As its name implies, this group is primarily focused on building a better image for Arabs and Arab Americans in the United States, encouraging them to participate in Democratic and Republican party processes. The group also organizes annual Model Arab League activities in universities and colleges.

The American-Arab Anti-Discrimination Committee, as its name suggests, acts as a watchdog organization for anti-Arab discrimination. It was organized by James Zogby. Other organized Arab interest groups, which may not necessarily lobby, include or have included the American Palestine Committee, Americans for Near East Refugee Aid, the Arab American Institute, and the Middle East Affairs Council.

Certainly one of the largest and most influential entities that lobby for better relationships with the United States are multinational oil companies. Saudi ARAMCO, formerly the Arabian American Oil Company, publishes a monthly magazine devoted to the Arab and Islamic world to better inform the English-reading public. The publication does not include political or policy topics but instead restricts itself to historical, geographical, social, and cultural subjects. The company is naturally concerned about public perceptions and policies impacting the Kingdom of Saudi Arabia.

Perhaps an unlikely source of lobbying may be found among certain Protestant Christian groups in the United States. Indeed, the National Council of Churches (NCC) has often been an outspoken opponent of Israeli policies. As early as 1980 it adopted a resolution calling for the immediate formation of a Palestinian state. While not lobbies, with the Internet numerous Arab organizations provide information or discussion on issues in the Middle East, including the Arab-Israeli conflict.

In numerous respects, the Arab lobby in the United States simply pales in comparison to the Jewish lobby. Its numbers are much smaller, its private donations are just a fraction of the Jewish groups', and its political donations are small. Part of the disparity lies in the sheer number of people in each group. While there are currently 6.155 million Jews residing in the United States, there are just 1.2 million Arabs, of which some 38 percent are Lebanese Christians. Whereas there is just one Jewish state, there are many Arab nations. Palestinian Americans have been very active politically, and as a result the Palestinian dilemma has tended to overshadow broader Arab causes in the United States. Another roadblock to Arab lobbying has been the consistently negative American public perception of Arabs and Arab states. Whether this antipathy has been earned or not is not the issue. The fact that Arab Americans have not been able to overcome these perceptions and stereotypes has prevented them from being more effective in promoting their causes. Terrorist attacks against the United States and the West have done nothing to reverse this trend.

PAUL G. PIERPAOLI JR.

See also

Bush, George Herbert Walker; Lobbies, Jewish; Organization of Petroleum Exporting Countries; Saudi Arabia

Reference

Terry, Janice. *U.S. Foreign Policy in the Middle East: The Role of Lobbies and Special Interest Groups.* London: Pluto, 2005.

Lobbies, Jewish

Formal and informal special interest groups dedicated primarily to affecting U.S. foreign policy toward Israel and the Middle East. It is no exaggeration to say that the American Jewish community has conducted one of the most successful lobbying efforts in modern American history.

By far the most influential of the Jewish lobbies is the American Israel Public Affairs Committee (AIPAC), founded in 1951. Its main mission has been to foster dialogue with U.S. congressional representatives, senators, and executive branch policymakers with an eye toward influencing legislation and official government policy. With a membership of more than 100,000 people, activity in all 50 states, an annual budget of $40 million, and more than 100 paid employees, AIPAC has been termed the second most influential lobby in the United States, ranking only behind the powerful American Association of Retired Persons (AARP).

Another large but somewhat more informal Jewish lobby at the national level is the Conference of Presidents of Major American Jewish Organizations, a conglomeration of some 55 leaders of different organizations who attempt to speak with one voice vis-à-vis issues important to Jews. This group concentrates its efforts on the executive branch. In addition, there are a number of pro-Jewish political action committees (PACs) that donate money directly to political candidates. However, such activity is fairly low.

"Jewish lobby" is a rather loose and fluid term, as there are many non-Jewish groups and individuals who also take up various Jewish causes. Indeed, one of the remarkable things about the Jewish lobby has been its ability to attract support from a wide variety of non-Jewish people and organizations and on both sides of the political spectrum. This support has included labor unions, clergymen, teachers, scholars, entertainers, and leaders of nearly every ilk. Indeed, fundamentalist Christians have, during the past 30 years, become one of the most vocal supporters of pro-Israel policies. They allegedly take this position more out of religious conviction than political expediency, however.

The Jewish lobby in the United States has an enviable record of affecting congressional legislation and U.S. government policy. The examples of this are far too numerous to list, but AIPAC has claimed responsibility for influencing at least 100 pieces of legislation per year in Congress. Of course, American Jews exercising their right to vote is another more informal way of advancing the pro-Israel agenda. As a whole, Jews have the largest voter turnouts of any ethnic group in the United States. Although Jews comprise just 2.3 percent of the population, almost 90 percent of them live in critical electoral college states, meaning that they can often influence the outcome of elections despite their small numbers.

During the last decade or so, the number of Jews elected to high offices in the United States has begun to rise. Currently, there are 13 Jewish American U.S. senators (or 13 percent of the entire Senate), while there are 30 Jewish members of the House of Representatives. There are, of course, many Jewish Americans in the executive branch of government as well.

U.S. public opinion has also been swayed by the powerful Jewish lobbies. Since 1967 when the first such polls were conducted, U.S. sympathy for Israel has ranged from a low of 32 percent to a high of 64 percent, with a statistical average of about 47 percent.

This stands in sharp contrast to public support for the Arab cause, which has averaged about 12 percent over roughly the same period of time. The Arab lobby, which is far less organized and numerically small, has been largely unable to reverse these numbers. Some Americans have claimed that the Jewish lobby exerts too much influence in Washington, although polls have consistently shown that such a perception is far from being the majority position. It is clear, however, that the success of groups such as AIPAC, which have carefully cultivated support for pro-Israel causes, has been a palpable factor in the relatively high level of support for Israel in the United States.

PAUL G. PIERPAOLI JR.

See also

American Israel Public Affairs Committee; Lobbies, Arab

References

Ben-Zvi, Abraham. *Alliance Politics and the Limits of Influence: The Case of the U.S. and Israel, 1975–1983.* Boulder CO: Westview, 1984.

Terry, Janice. *U.S. Foreign Policy in the Middle East: The Role of Lobbies and Special Interest Groups.* London: Pluto, 2005.

Tivnan, Edward. *The Lobby: Jewish Political Power and American Foreign Policy.* New York: Simon and Schuster, 1987.

Lod Airport Massacre
Event Date: May 30, 1972

Mass shooting on May 30, 1972, at Lod Airport in Tel Aviv, Israel. The Lod Airport attack was carried out by three Japanese men associated with the Japanese Red Army, an extreme left-wing militant group known for its terrorist activities. The Japanese Red Army had as its goals the overthrow of the Japanese government and the fomenting of a worldwide communist revolution. The group had historic ties to the Popular Front for the Liberation of Palestine (PFLP), having received both monetary funding and arms from the militant Palestinian organization. The three men responsible for the Lod Airport attack—Tsuyoshi Okudaira, Kozo Okamoto, and Yasuyuki Yasuda—had been sponsored and trained by the PFLP but were also acting at the behest of the Popular Front for the Liberation of Palestine–General Command (PFLP-GC). The PFLP-GC recruited the Japanese terrorists because they knew that airport security was vigilant of would-be Palestinian terrorists but not those of Japanese descent.

To aid their anonymity, the three terrorists inconspicuously boarded Air France flight 132 in Paris, bound for Tel Aviv. They showed no signs of trouble during the flight and were dressed in conservative business attire to further conceal themselves. They carried with them only long, thin cases that resembled an attaché case or draftsman's bag. They casually deplaned in Tel Aviv on May 30, produced assault guns from their cases, and began to fire randomly into the waiting room lounge, which was full of people. When their ammunition had run out, the men produced grenades and began throwing them into the panicked crowd, producing even more mayhem. Yasuda died from bullet wounds inflicted either by one of his compatriots or by airport security personnel, and Okudaira died

Japanese Red Army militant and Palestinian sympathizer Kozo Okamoto, the only terrorist to survive the suicide attack at Lod Airport, shown during his trial in Israel, May 30, 1972. (Richard Melloul/Sygma/Corbis)

when he threw himself on top of a grenade and detonated it. Only Okamoto survived the massacre. By the time airport security had gained control over the situation, 26 had died and another 78 had been wounded. Included among the dead were 16 Puerto Rican Americans on their way to a pilgrimage in the Holy Land. Okamoto, who was also badly hurt in the attack, was tried, convicted, and sentenced to life imprisonment in Israel.

In the immediate aftermath of the massacre, the PFLP-GC and PFLP claimed responsibility, stating that it was retribution for the 1948 Deir Yassin Massacre of Palestinians perpetrated by the Irgun Tsvai Leumi (National Military Organization). Okamoto left his Israeli prison cell in 1983 during a prisoner exchange between the Israeli government and the Palestinians. In 1997 he was again arrested in the occupied territories but was allowed to return to Lebanon, where he secured political refugee status.

PAUL G. PIERPAOLI JR.

See also

Deir Yassin Massacre; Irgun Tsvai Leumi; Popular Front for the Liberation of Palestine; Popular Front for the Liberation of Palestine–General Command; Terrorism

References

Hoffman, Bruce. *Inside Terrorism.* New York: Columbia University Press, 1999.

Shoham, Shlomo G., ed. *Terrorism and the International Community.* Oshawa, Ontario: De Sitter, 2005.

Lohamei Herut Israel

Radical armed Zionist organization active in Palestine during the 1940s. The last years of the British Mandate over Palestine were ones of great instability and even intense conflict. One organization, Lohamei Herut Israel (Fighters for the Freedom of Israel), also known as Lehi or the Stern Gang, contributed to the volatile situation by launching attacks against British authorities and the Arab population in Palestine.

Founded in September 1940 as a splinter group from the Irgun Tsvai Leumi (National Military Organization), Lehi was an intensely nationalist Jewish organization. It demanded an immediate end to British rule and rejected any notion of compromise or cooperation with the mandate government. The group, which never numbered more than a few hundred fighters, was disbanded by 1949.

Zionism and the Jewish drive for statehood in Palestine gave rise to a constellation of armed groups that struggled to speed the reestablishment of an independent Israel. Avraham Stern (also known as Yair), a radical Irgun member who denounced any plans to limit the borders of a Jewish Palestine, formed Lehi in response to a commitment by other Jewish militias to suspend attacks against the British after the outbreak of World War II. Stern failed to see that a defeat of Nazi Germany would necessarily strengthen Jewish interests and instead approved efforts in 1940 to approach Britain's foes and offer them an alliance.

Such ties never materialized, but Lehi's leadership was hardly dissuaded by the setback and initiated an independent terror campaign against the British. The first significant attack in this offensive was the December 1940 bombing of the immigration offices in Haifa, a symbolic strike against British-imposed restrictions on the flow of Jews into Palestine. In response, the British condemned Lehi and dismissed it as a criminal organization whose members had to be neutralized. However, even Stern's death at the hands of the British security forces failed to curtail the threat posed by the organization.

Under new leaders, the most prominent of whom was Yitzhak "Michael" Shamir, a future Israeli prime minister, Lehi continued its attacks, including the infamous killing of Lord Moyne, the British minister resident in Cairo, on November 6, 1944. The murder shocked the British and prompted the Jewish community in Palestine to crack down on the terrorists carrying out such attacks.

At the conclusion of World War II, a broad alliance and unified command emerged among Jewish armed groups in the mandate. Intent on driving out the British and speeding the establishment of an independent Israel, the militias, known collectively as the Hebrew Resistance Movement, renewed their joint operations against the security forces and Arab interests. Lehi fighters played a prominent role in the revived campaign, including participation in some of the most heinous terrorist acts committed during the last years of the mandate.

On January 4, 1948, Lehi operatives detonated a truck bomb outside the Arab National Committee offices at the city hall in Jaffa, killing 26 people and wounding scores more. Members of Lehi also joined the April 9, 1948, attack on the Arab village of Deir Yassin near Jerusalem. In a matter of hours, Jewish fighters massacred more than 100 civilians and underscored their determination to drive Arabs out of lands claimed for the State of Israel. Immediate and later efforts, be they Arab, British, or Jewish, to publicize the incident assured that it gained notoriety and became an action symbolic of the intense emotions that dominated the conflict over control of Palestine.

However, a terrorist attack of perhaps even greater significance was the assassination in Jerusalem of Count Folke Bernadotte, a Swedish nobleman and the United Nations (UN) mediator, on September 17, 1948. Carried out by fighters from Hazit HaMoledet (Homeland Front), a subgroup of Lehi, the killing revealed the level of radicalism that existed in the region, at least among a minority of activists, within the Zionist movement.

In the wake of the Bernadotte murder, the new Israeli government took steps to dismantle Lehi and imprison its leaders. Natan Yellin-Mor, one of the organization's most prominent figures, was soon convicted of involvement in the Bernadotte plot. However, within a year the authorities approved his early release and allowed him to occupy a seat in the Knesset (Israeli parliament). From armed outlaw activism to its establishment as a political party, Lehi assumed a position as a recognized and legitimate body within the ideological spectrum of Israel, and many of its former fighters found a home in the Israel Defense Forces (IDF).

JONAS KAUFFELDT AND SERGIO CATIGNANI

See also

Arab-Jewish Communal War; Bernadotte, Folke; Irgun Tsvai Leumi; Israel Defense Forces; Palestine, British Mandate for; Terrorism; World War II, Impact of

References

Bell, J. Bowyer. *Terror out of Zion: Irgun Zvai Leumi, Lehi and the Palestine Underground, 1929–1949*. New York: St. Martin's, 1979.

Goldberg, Giora. "Haganah, Irgun and 'Stern': Who Did What." *Jerusalem Quarterly* 25 (Fall 1982): 116–120.

Heller, Joseph. *The Stern Gang: Ideology, Politics, and Terror, 1940–1949*. London: Frank Cass, 1995.

Marton, Kati. *A Death in Jerusalem*. New York: Arcade, 1996.

Morris, Benny. *Righteous Victims: A History of the Zionist-Arab Conflict, 1881–2001*. New York: Vintage Books, 2001.

London Round Table Conference

Start Date: February 7, 1939
End Date: March 17, 1939

A British government policy statement that sought to mollify mounting Arab anger over increasing Jewish immigration into Palestine and plans for partition. Following the 1917 Balfour Declaration, the British government had issued position papers stating that the declaration was not an endorsement of a Jewish state in Palestine. In 1936, however, the Peel Commission had recommended partition of Palestine into Jewish and Arab states. In January 1938 the government established the Woodhead Commission to implement the Peel Commission by reporting back specific recommendations on

Chaim Weizmann and David Ben-Gurion (*foreground center*) at the Round Table Conference at St. James Palace in London, January 1949. (Israeli Government Press Office)

boundaries. The British government hoped that the Woodhead Report might mollify the Arabs.

The Woodhead Report, published on November 9, 1938, rejected the Peel Commission's findings. Its members were sharply divided and held that no partition plan would satisfy both Arabs and Jews. It recommended several possible alternatives, all of which involved a smaller Jewish state, restricted largely to the coastal plain.

The British government held that some sort of accommodation might yet be possible between Arab and Jew in Palestine, and in February 1939 it opened the London Round Table Conference (also known as the St. James Palace Conference) on Palestine. Already the British were seeking to restrict Jewish immigration. In December 1938 the mandatory government in Palestine had rejected Jewish calls for the rescue of 10,000 Jewish children from Eastern Europe.

Among attendees at the London talks were Emir Abdullah of Transjordan, Foreign Minister Nuri al-Said of Iraq, Prince Faisal of Saudi Arabia, and ranking officials from Egypt. The British also released Arab Higher Committee members interned in the Seychelles and accepted them as representatives of the Palestinian Arab delegation. The Jewish side was led by Chaim Weizmann, David Ben-Gurion, and Yitzhak Ben-Zvi. The Jewish delegation also included non-Palestinians such as Rabbi Stephen Wise, the leading spokesman of the Zionist cause in the United States, and Lord Reading, Britain's most distinguished Jew and a former viceroy of India.

The conference was held at St. James Palace in London during February 7–March 17, 1939. The Arab side refused to meet in the same room with the Jewish delegates, and as a result both delegations entered and left by separate entrances and met in different rooms. Thus, there were in reality two parallel conferences.

Weizmann sought to mollify Arab fears and implored the British not to cut off immigration in "this blackest hour of Jewish history." Jamil al-Husseini, the chief Arab spokesman, was uncompromising. He called for an immediate end to the mandate and to Jewish immigration in return for a treaty that would protect legitimate British interests in Palestine.

The Arabs also demanded that the British government make public the pledges it had made to Sharif Hussein during World War I. The Colonial Office reluctantly agreed, and on February 15 it released the letters between British high commissioner for Egypt Sir A. Henry McMahon and Hussein. The British, meanwhile, pressed the Jewish delegation to accept a ceiling on immigration for several years, after which immigration totals were to be based on Arab consent. When the Jewish side rejected this, chief British spokesman Colonial Secretary Malcolm MacDonald threatened them with the possibility of a British withdrawal from Palestine that would leave the Jews vulnerable to superior Arab power.

During the last two weeks of the conference, the British government proposed a number of possible solutions. These included a federation of cantons, a bicameral governmental structure with a lower house based on proportional representation and an upper house based on parity between Jews and Arabs, and other even more exotic formulations. None of these were acceptable to either side. On March 11, MacDonald bluntly told the Jewish delegation that Jewish immigration was at the heart of Arab anger and of a reviving anti-Semitism in Britain itself.

With no hope of agreement, on March 15 at the end of the conference MacDonald proposed that Jewish immigration be limited to 75,000 people over the next five years with immigration thereafter dependent on Arab agreement. He also stated the British government's desire to curtail land sales to Jews. His sole concession to the Jewish side was that the British government would not seek to impose an independent Palestinian state with a majority Arab government. This policy was in fact made official in the White Paper of March 17, 1939.

SPENCER C. TUCKER

See also

Abdullah I, King of Jordan; Balfour Declaration; Faisal, King of Saudi Arabia; McMahon-Hussein Correspondence; Peel Commission; Said, Nuri al-; White Paper (1939)

References

Bethell, Nicholas. *The Palestine Triangle: The Struggle for the Holy Land, 1935–48.* New York: Putnam, 1979.

Hurewitz, J. C. *The Struggle for Palestine.* New York: Schocken, 1976.

Sachar, Howard M. *A History of Israel: From the Rise of Zionism to Our Time.* 3rd ed. New York: Knopf, 2007.

Lovers of Zion

See Hoveve Zion

M

Machine Guns

Machine guns are relatively heavy rapid-firing, crew-served small arms that can provide continuous or frequent bursts of automatic fire. When Israel became a nation in 1948, access to Western weaponry and the creation of the Israel Defense Forces (IDF) allowed the Israelis to address the manpower imbalance with their Arab neighbors with an advantage in firepower. Machine guns have always been an integral part of Israeli infantry tactics.

In the late 1940s and the 1950s, the IDF was equipped with American-made M-1919A6 .30-caliber and M-2 HB .50-caliber Browning machine guns as well as the German 7.92-mm MG-34 and MG-42 and British .303-caliber Bren and Vickers machine guns. The requirement for high rates of fire have led the Israelis to enhance designs of others. The Uzi submachine gun and the Galil automatic rifle are two prime examples.

The recoil-operated, magazine-fed Dror machine gun, manufactured in 1947 and 1948, remains the only true machine gun actually developed and manufactured by the Israelis themselves, and even then only on a limited scale. The Dror closely resembled the U.S. Johnson M-1944 machine gun and was in fact manufactured using dies purchased from Johnson directly. Today, the IDF uses the Belgian-made Fabrique nationale (FN) 7.62×51-mm NATO MAG as its standard infantry machine gun. The Browning M-2 .50-caliber also plays a key role as the standard issue Israeli heavy machine gun. The FN MAG weighs 22.22 pounds unloaded and without bipod or butt and is capable of sustained rates of fire of between 700 and 1,000 rounds per minute. The M-2 heavy machine gun can fire 450 to 500 rounds per minute and weighs 84 pounds. Primarily a vehicle-mounted weapon, the M-2 in an infantry role required a 44-pound ground tripod.

The Arab states have fielded a large number of different types of weapons, and machine guns are no exception. In 1948 the various Arab forces were typically armed with the weapons most readily available from the colonial powers. For example, in Egypt the British Bren and Vickers gun predominated. Once Gamal Abdel Nasser came to power in 1952, the Egyptian military sought weapons that could produce a high volume of fire but at the same time were simple to operate and maintain and did not require extensive or complicated manufacturing and supply systems.

The Soviet-made RPD and RPK, with their interchangeable parts and ability to use the same 7.62×39-mm ammunition as the Kalashnikov AK-47 assault rifle, simplified both logistical and training requirements. In addition, the Kalashnikov family of weapons proved to be very dependable and well suited to the unique problems of desert and harsh-climate warfare. The RPK weighs 12.3 pounds unloaded and is thus lighter than the FN MAG. The standard AK ball round weighs 12.5 grams, and the NATO 7.62×51-mm round weighs 25.47 grams, which means that a common gunner can carry more rounds per pound than his Israeli counterpart. The RPK does, however, have certain drawbacks. It is not designed for long periods of sustained fire, and although its cyclic rate of fire is 600 to 650 rounds per minute, its sustained rate of fire is only about 150 rounds per minute. Still, so impressed were the Israelis that they borrowed liberally from the Kalashnikov design when producing and manufacturing their own Galil. The DShK 12.7-mm machine gun fires 550–600 rounds per minute, making it comparable to the M2 .50 caliber. The DShK weighs 78.5 pounds, and its mount, which is wheeled and has a seat for the gunner, weighs 259 pounds.

During the Cold War, the unflinching commitment of the United States to Israel led the Arab governments to be more receptive to Soviet offers of military aid. Soviet-made small arms, therefore,

Israel Defense Forces (IDF) chief of staff Lieutenant General Ehud Barak firing a Belgian-designed FN MAG machine gun at a firing range, 1992. (Israeli Government Press Office)

became widespread throughout the Arab world in the 1950s and continued through succeeding decades. Even Iran, which until 1979 had close ties with the United States and had used American .30-caliber and .50-caliber Browning machine guns as their standard machine guns for some time, in subsequent years largely replaced those weapons with the RPK and the 12.7-mm DShK heavy machine gun. Such was the case in large part because of supply and equipage issues associated with the Iran-Iraq War (1980–1988).

The machine gun has played an integral part in the development, execution, and sustenance of Arab-Israeli conflicts and engagements. The ability of both the Arabs and Israelis to produce high volumes of lethal fire with minimal training is in many ways out of proportion to the economic or demographic resources of either side in the conflict. Unlike most 20th-century conflicts in which machine-gun firepower is considered to be a force multiplier, in post–World War II Arab-Israeli conflicts the machine gun became by and large the force itself, demonstrating a very high ratio of lethality to needed support. In contrast to military aviation, armored forces, or artillery, all of which require a large logistical and maintenance infrastructure as well as hefty financial investment, machine guns are rea-

sonably inexpensive and easy to use and maintain, do not require a host of mechanics or technicians to operate, and allow a small number of minimally trained combatants to produce a high rate of lethal fire under almost any conditions. The machine gun has thus not only contributed to the outcomes of specific wars between the Arabs and Israelis but also to the inability of both sides to exhaust or fully overpower the other and thereby end the conflict.

EVERETT DAGUE

See also

Egypt, Armed Forces; Iran, Armed Forces; Iraq, Armed Forces; Israel Defense Forces; Jordan, Armed Forces; Lebanon, Armed Forces; Saudi Arabia, Armed Forces; Syria, Armed Forces

References

Dupuy, Trevor N. *Elusive Victory: The Arab-Israeli Wars, 1947–1974.* Garden City, NY: Military Book Club, 2002.

Hogg, Ian V. *Infantry Support Weapons: Mortars, Missiles, and Machine Guns.* London: Greenhill, 1995.

Smith, W. H. B., and Edward C. Ezell. *Small Arms of the World.* New York: Barnes and Noble, 1992.

Walter, John. *Modern Machine-Guns.* London: Greenhill/Lionel Leventhal, 2000.

MacMichael, Sir Harold

Born: 1882
Died: 1969

British career civil servant and high commissioner for the British Mandate for Palestine (1938–1944). Harold MacMichael was born in 1882. He graduated from Magdalene College, Cambridge, and after passing the civil service examination in 1904 was assigned to the Sudan. He had a lengthy tenure there and also served as British governor of Tanganyika.

In March 1938 MacMichael assumed the post of high commissioner for the British Mandate for Palestine, succeeding Sir Arthur Grenfell Wauchope. MacMichael's arrival in Palestine heralded a shift in British policy toward the mandate, occasioned by the Arab Revolt of 1936–1939. Wauchope had interpreted immigration policies liberally. With the Arab Revolt and the approach of World War II, however, British leaders greatly feared a possible Axis move against Egypt and Britain's imperial lifeline of the Suez Canal. London believed that Arab unrest might facilitate this and possibly even result in Britain's expulsion from the Middle East.

With the release of the British government White Paper in 1939, MacMichael retreated from the liberal policies of his predecessor regarding Jewish immigration, choosing instead to interpret regulations quite rigidly. This occurred in the midst of persecutions of Jews in Germany and in Poland, and it continued even with evidence of the Holocaust, the Nazi effort to exterminate the Jews in Europe. British authorities took into custody all Jews immigrating to Palestine illegally and sent them on to the Indian Ocean island of Mauritius. Land transfer regulations of 1940 sought to prohibit the further sale of Arab property to Jews.

In March 1943, MacMichael broadcast a message outlining the British government's plans for the postwar economic development program. Largely based on the 1939 White Paper, it created widespread Jewish anger. Mounting Jewish opposition to this and to the British immigration policy in the midst of the Holocaust led to the onset of Jewish terrorism, principally by the Irgun Tsvai Leumi (National Military Organization) and Lohamei Herut Israel (Lehi), against the British authorities in Palestine. Militant Zionists in Palestine held MacMichael responsible for much of British policy in Palestine. Indeed, MacMichael narrowly escaped an attempt on August 8, 1944, on his life that wounded his wife.

Sir Harold MacMichael, British career civil servant and high commissioner for Palestine (1938–1944), shown here circa 1937. (Library of Congress)

Upon leaving Palestine MacMichael was assigned to Malaya, where he wrote its constitution. He then served in Malta. MacMichael died in Folkstone, England, in 1969.

SPENCER C. TUCKER

See also

Arab Revolt of 1936–1939; Holocaust; Irgun Tsvai Leumi; Lohamei Herut Israel; Palestine, British Mandate for; Wauchope, Sir Arthur Grenfell; White Paper (1939)

References

Sachar, Howard M. *A History of Israel: From the Rise of Zionism to Our Time.* 3rd ed. New York: Knopf, 2007.

Shepherd, Naomi. *Ploughing Sand: British Rule in Palestine, 1917–1948.* New Brunswick, NJ: Rutgers University Press, 1999.

Macmillan, Maurice Harold
Born: February 10, 1894
Died: December 29, 1986

British Conservative Party politician, minister of housing (1951–1954), minister of defense (1954–1955), foreign secretary (1955), chancellor of the exchequer (1955–1957), and prime minister (1957–1963). Harold Macmillan, half-American by parentage, was born in London on February 10, 1894, into the prosperous Macmillan publishing family. Educated at Eton and Balliol College, Oxford, his service in World War I, with the rank of captain, prevented him from finishing his degree.

Following the war, Macmillan worked in the family firm until he was elected to Parliament in 1924. He held the northern industrial seat of Stockton until 1945 (except for the years 1929–1931), after which he represented the London suburban seat of Bromley. His Conservatism was of the progressive, mildly statist form, with a dash of the paternalist and the patrician. He was appointed a junior minister in 1940, and in 1942 Prime Minister Winston Churchill sent him to be resident minister at Allied Forces Headquarters in the Mediterranean, where he formed a friendship with U.S. general Dwight D. Eisenhower, which was to prove of uncertain value in the Suez crisis of 1956.

Following the Conservative victory of 1951, Macmillan served as minister of housing, moving to defense in 1954 and to the Foreign Office in April 1955. Prime Minister Anthony Eden (who had succeeded Churchill in 1955), shifted a disappointed Macmillan out of the Foreign Office and into the treasury in December 1955, a post he then held during the Suez Crisis of 1956.

Throughout this crisis, following Egyptian nationalization of the Suez Canal on July 26, Macmillan was at least as hawkish as Eden. In his diaries Macmillan describes Nasser as an "Asiatic Mussolini" and states that British policy should aim at bringing about his "humiliation" and "collapse." Macmillan strongly supported the use of force to take control of the canal, assuming that diplomacy would probably not succeed. Despite noting at the end of July that the United States would do all in its power to "restrain" the United

Harold Macmillan, British Conservative Party politician and prime minister (1957–1963). (Library of Congress)

Kingdom and despite receiving little support from Eisenhower when he visited Washington in September, Macmillan tragically managed to persuade himself and Eden that the United States would come around to supporting whatever action Britain might take or content itself with a formal protest. Macmillan thus encouraged Eden in his secret planning with the French and Israelis for a military attack on Egypt. Aware of the general nature of these plans, if not the details, Macmillan did not disapprove.

It came as a profound shock to the cabinet and to Macmillan personally when, following the British ultimatum to Nasser on October 30, the United States turned against the United Kingdom, exerting maximum pressure both in the United Nations (UN) and on British finances, to halt British and French military action. As chancellor, Macmillan was particularly angered by American pressure on the pound sterling and in general felt deeply let down by people he considered to be allies and friends. Perhaps unwilling to point the finger at Eisenhower, Macmillan later recalled that U.S. secretary of state John Foster Dulles had showed "a degree of hostility amounting almost to frenzy." Macmillan also expressed regret that he personally had contributed so much to the cabinet's profound miscalculation as to the likely reaction in Washington. His deep-seated feelings on this matter might be guessed from the title of the relevant chapter in his memoirs, "The Anglo-American Schism."

Under overwhelming U.S. pressure the British agreed to withdraw from Egypt. The humiliating failure of his plans and a recurrence of ill health led to Eden's resignation in January 1957. Macmillan then succeeded to the premiership, a development seen as an extraordinary outcome for one so deeply committed to the failed policy of his predecessor. As prime minister, Macmillan made it a priority to mend fences with the United States, traveling to meet President Eisenhower in Bermuda in March 1957.

Decolonization, particularly in Africa, was a major theme during Macmillan's prime ministership, and in 1960 he toured that continent, delivering his famous "Wind of Change" speech in South Africa, acknowledging African nationalism. He also developed a generally cordial relationship with new U.S. president John F. Kennedy. The two communicated closely during the 1962 Cuban Missile Crisis, yet at the December 1962 Nassau meeting with Kennedy, they engaged in robust diplomatic exchanges as Macmillan pressed the reluctant Kennedy to provide Polaris missiles to Britain. In the summer of 1963, along with the Americans and Soviets, Macmillan signed the Partial Nuclear Test-Ban Treaty.

In 1963 Macmillan's government was touched by scandal involving his defense minister, John Profumo. In the same year Macmillan was depressed by French president Charles de Gaulle's veto of Britain's belated application to join the European Common Market. The early 1960s also saw serious problems emerge in the British economy.

Macmillan fell ill in the summer of 1963 and resigned as prime minister in October. He retired from Parliament in 1964 and was made Earl of Stockton in 1984. During the Margaret Thatcher years he took great delight in criticizing her policies. Macmillan died on December 29, 1986, in Chelwood Gate, Sussex.

PAUL WINGROVE

See also

De Gaulle, Charles; Dulles, John Foster; Eden, Robert Anthony; Eisenhower, Dwight David; Kennedy, John Fitzgerald; Suez Crisis

References

Catterall, Peter, ed. *The Macmillan Diaries: Cabinet Years, 1950–1957*. London: Pan, 1957.

Horne, Alistair. *Macmillan, 1894–1957*. London: Macmillan, 1988.

———. *Macmillan, 1957–1986*. London: Macmillan, 1989.

Macmillan, H. *Riding the Storm, 1956–1959*. London: Macmillan, 1971.

Turner, John. *Macmillan*. London: Longman, 1984.

Madina

See Medina

Madrid Conference

Start Date: October 30, 1991
End Date: November 1, 1991

Conference held in Madrid, Spain, during October 30–November 1, 1991, that brought together for the first time Syrian, Lebanese, Jordanian, Palestinian, and Israeli officials with the aim of beginning the process of securing a comprehensive Middle East peace settlement. The United States and the Soviet Union cosponsored the meeting. Also in attendance were officials from Egypt, the European Union (EU), and the Gulf Cooperation Council. The Madrid Conference convened on October 30 and lasted three days. No formal declarations or accommodations resulted from the meeting, as it was designed principally to bring together the warring parties and serve as a springboard for future bilateral and multilateral conferences between Arabs and Israelis.

The Madrid Conference came in the immediate aftermath of the 1991 Persian Gulf War and the waning days of the Cold War. President George H. W. Bush's administration, in its attempt to construct a so-called new world order, set a goal of bringing lasting peace to the Middle East. In this it was aided—at least symbolically—by Soviet leader Mikhail Gorbachev. The Soviet Union would be officially dissolved only eight weeks after the Madrid Conference ended, but it was nonetheless important for Bush to engage the Soviets in the peace process because Russia and other post-Soviet successor states had vested interests in the Middle East. In addition, a number of Arab nations had enjoyed close ties to the Soviets.

It was understood by the parties attending the meeting that the resultant peace process should be guided by the land-for-peace formula first promulgated by the United Nations (UN) in November 1967 (UN Security Council Resolution 242) and later reiterated in UN Resolutions 338 and 425. The talks were designed to provide the proper dialogue between Israel and the Arab states of Lebanon, Syria, and Jordan so that bilateral peace treaties could soon be realized. In approaching the Palestinian-Israeli dilemma the congress was to begin a two-stage process, which included the establishment of interim self-government for the Palestinians followed by the creation of a permanent Palestinian government that would ultimately lead to an autonomous Palestinian state. These guidelines were also the basic framework for the Oslo peace process and Oslo Accords, which were finalized in August 1993. Indeed, the Oslo process began almost immediately after the Madrid Conference ended. The Oslo process was, however, opposed by a number of those involved in the Madrid Conference because of the purely bilateral nature of the accords as well as their design and substance.

Multilateral talks began in Moscow in January 1992 and focused on five major concerns: water allocation, environmental preservation, refugee issues, economic development, and regional arms control. Israel initially balked at discussing refugee and economic problems, and Syria and Jordan refused to join in multilateral talks because no real progress had been made in bilateral negotiations. In October 1994, however, Jordan and Israel signed a historic peace treaty. Several attempts were made to negotiate an Israeli-Syrian peace treaty, but last-minute complications torpedoed the effort. As a result of the Madrid Conference and the Oslo Accords that followed, the Palestinians were allowed to set up their own governing entity, the Palestinian Authority (PA).

Soviet leader Mikhail Gorbachev addresses the Madrid Conference, October 30, 1991. (Moshe Milner/Israeli Government Press Office)

The peace process stalled in the latter half of the 1990s as violence flared anew in the region and Israeli politics forced a retrenchment from wide-ranging peace initiatives. Formal bilateral talks would not resume until January 2000, and they made little headway thereafter. The dramatic September 13, 1993, signing of the Declaration of Principles between Israel and the Palestine Liberation Organization (PLO) on the White House lawn with a beaming President Bill Clinton looking on, was a direct result of the Madrid Conference. Indeed, the stipulations contained in them were the same basic guidelines as those propounded in Madrid. Perhaps the biggest winner in all of this was Israel, as the process that had begun in Madrid resulted in several key nations finally recognizing that state. These included India and the People's Republic of China (PRC) as well as Tunisia, Morocco, Qatar, and Oman. The Arab economic boycott of Israel also began to loosen.

PAUL G. PIERPAOLI JR.

See also

Oslo Accords; Palestine Liberation Organization; Palestinian Authority; United Nations Security Council Resolution 242; United Nations Security Council Resolution 338

References

Brown, Nathan J. *Palestinian Politics after the Oslo Accords: Resuming Arab Palestine.* Berkeley: University of California Press, 2003.

Freedman, Robert Owen, ed. *The Middle East and the Peace Process: The Impact of the Oslo Accords.* Gainesville: University Press of Florida, 1998.

Watson, Geoffrey R. *The Oslo Accords: International Law and the Israeli-Palestinian Peace Agreements.* New York: Oxford University Press, 2000.

Weinberger, Peter. *Co-opting the PLO: A Critical Reconstruction of the Oslo Accords, 1993–1995.* New York: Rowman and Littlefield, 2006.

Magen David

See Star of David

MAGIC CARPET, **Operation**

Start Date: June 1949
End Date: September 1950

Israeli government operation to airlift Jews from Yemen to Israel in 1949 and 1950. During Israel's first year of independence while fighting for its survival in the Israeli War of Independence (1948–1949) against its Arab neighbors, more than 250,000 Jews immigrated to Israel. One of the most dramatic mass migrations of people

Yemeni Jews wait at the airport in Aden, Yemen, to be flown to Israel, October 1949. (Zoltan Kluger/Israeli Government Press Office)

was the Jews of Yemen via Operation MAGIC CARPET. For hundreds of years, the Jewish community in Yemen had experienced persecutions. In May 1949 the imam of Yemen agreed to allow 45,000 of the 46,000 members of the Yemenite Jewish community to emigrate but insisted that they first sell their land and pay an exit tax. This initiated a response by the Israeli government to transport the Yemenites to Israel.

Since the destruction of the Second Temple in AD 70, Jews played a prominent role in Yemen's economy and politics. With the advent of Islam in the eighth century, however, Yemenite Jews were relegated to the lowest rung of the social ladder and to poverty. Until the Ottomans gained control of the area in 1872, Yemenite Jews were forbidden to leave the country. Since the late 19th century, Jews from Yemen had been escaping in small numbers to Palestine. By 1948 it was estimated that there were close to 28,000 Jews of Yemenite descent living in Israel.

In 1947 after the partitioning of Palestine, Yemeni Muslim rioters, joined by the local police force, killed 82 Jews and destroyed hundreds of Jewish homes. Jews in the Yemeni capital of Aden were economically paralyzed, as most of the Jewish stores and businesses were destroyed. Early in 1948, a false accusation against a Jew of the ritual murder of two girls led to more looting.

Fulfilling their desire to return to Zion (Israel) and escape further persecution in Yemen, Jews from all over Yemen picked up their few possessions and began to walk toward Aden. Along the way they were robbed and abused by the local Arab population. They reached Aden exhausted and on the verge of starvation. Once there, they waited for the promised airlift to Israel.

This complex Israeli evacuation, dubbed Operation MAGIC CARPET, took place from June 1949 to September 1950 with the support of British and American airlines. In all, some 380 flights transported the Jews of Yemen to Israel. Not until months after the completion of the operation was the news of the airlift made public. Once in Israel, the Yemenite Jews were settled in primitive camps called *ma'abarot* and slowly assimilated into modern Israeli society.

Although the operation was called MAGIC CARPET, it was far from luxurious for the Yemenites. The planes were overcrowded, and the refugee camps were at best Spartan. Most of the Jews from Yemen had never seen an airplane up close, let alone flown on one. But they were calmed by writings in the book of Isaiah that God had promised that his children would return to Zion with wings, as eagles.

Operation MAGIC CARPET is one of dozens of inspiring examples of rescue projects undertaken by Israel to provide refuge to distressed Jews. Today, the Jews of Yemen are just one of many cultures that make up the landscape and diversity of modern Israeli society. Afterward, a smaller continuous migration was allowed to continue until 1962, when civil war put an abrupt halt to any further Jewish exodus from Yemen.

MOSHE TERDIMAN

See also
Aircraft, Transport; Law of Return; Sephardic Judaism

References
Barer, Shlomo. *The MAGIC Carpet.* London: Secker and Warburg, 1952.
Lewis, Herbert S. *After the Eagles Landed: The Yemenites of Israel.* Boulder, CO: Westview, 1989.
Shulewitz, Malka Hilel. *The Forgotten Millions: The Modern Jewish Exodus from Arab Lands.* London: Cassell, 1999.

Magog
See Gog and Magog

Mahfouz, Naguib
Born: December 11, 1911
Died: August 30, 2006

Renowned Egyptian author and the only Arab writer ever awarded the Nobel Prize in Literature. Naguib (Najib) Mahfouz was born in Cairo on December 11, 1911, to a middle-class Muslim family and was the youngest of seven children. His family moved to the Abbasiyya quarter when he was 13 years old. He spurned his father's desire that he go into medicine in order to study philosophy. Mahfouz graduated with a philosophy degree from Cairo University in 1934 and worked for two more years on a master of arts degree, which he did not complete.

Mahfouz began writing at age 17, and it soon became clear that his talents were formidable. During his career, he would publish an astonishing 50 novels, several plays, more than 250 articles, and 13 collections of short stories. To help sustain himself financially, he entered the Egyptian civil service in 1939 and was employed as a civil servant in numerous capacities for the next 33 years. He served as the technical director for censorship and later as a consultant in the Ministry of Culture. After he left government service his creativity and output soared, and by the time he was awarded the Nobel Prize in Literature in 1988 at the age of 77 he had become a cultural icon in Egypt and much of the Middle East.

Mahfouz's works were not without their controversies, some of them quite significant. Indeed, his writing sometimes alluded to sacred subjects, and his belief in creative freedom caused problems for him. His most famous work may be his trilogy *Bayn al-Qasrayan, Qasr al-Shawq,* and *al-Sukkariyya* that shows life in Cairo through three generations. His 1959 novel *Children of Gabalawi* was banned by authorities in his native Egypt because of its allusions to all three monotheistic religions: Judaism, Christianity, and Islam. In this as in his other work, the characters, situated in a poor neigh-

Naguib Mahfouz, Egyptian author and Nobel Prize winner. (Nobel Foundation)

---

borhood, bore the names of early Muslims, as indeed many Egyptians do. In his work he explored the desperate circumstances of their lives. Many of his other works expressed Egyptian nationalism yet criticized the unforgiving bureaucracy and politics and the political correctness of Gamal Abdel Nasser's rule in the 1950s and 1960s. Mahfouz was a staunch supporter of President Anwar Sadat's rapprochement with Israel, leading to a boycott of his books in other Arab countries. Because of Mahfouz's support of writer Salman Rushdie and secularists, in 1994 a young radical attacked and nearly killed Mahfouz. The assailant said he had never read Mahfouz's work but had heard a sheikh condemning *Children of Gabalawi.*

Mahfouz's novels, many of which are set in his beloved Cairo, have been termed among the best written in the 20th century. Famed literary theorist and critic Edward Said has said that Mahfouz's work puts him in the pantheon of literary giants. Many of his writings became known for their realistic portrayals of modern Egyptian life, which had changed so dramatically during his long life. His prose was at the same time moving, unaffected, and lively. And as with all great literature, it had the ability to touch on the human condition, reaching far beyond the confines of Cairo or Egypt. Mahfouz died in Cairo on August 30, 2006.

PAUL G. PIERPAOLI JR.

See also
Literature of the Arab-Israeli Wars; Nasser, Gamal Abdel; Said, Edward

References
Beard, Michael, and Adnan Haydar, eds. *Naguib Mahfouz: From Regional Fame to Global Recognition.* Syracuse, NY: Syracuse University Press, 1992.

Rasheed, El-Enany. *Naguib Mahfouz.* London: Routledge, 1993.

Somekh, Sasson. *The Changing Rhythm: A Study of Najib Mahfuz's Novels.* Leiden: Brill, 1983.

Mahmud, Muhammad Sidqi
Born: 1923

Egyptian military officer and chief of the Egyptian Air Force (1953–1967). Muhammad Sidqi Mahmud was born in Egypt, probably in 1923. He attended the Egyptian Military Academy and then joined the air force. In the early 1950s he joined the Free Officers Movement that advocated land reform, modernization, and Arab nationalism. The Free Officers Movement seized control of Egypt in 1952, and Mahmud became commander of the Egyptian Air Force the next year. This appointment was part of a larger program of military appointments designed to give Gamal Abdel Nasser control of the armed forces in his power struggle with President Mohammad Naguib. Nasser ousted Naguib from power in October 1954.

Given the tensions between Nasser's Egypt and the West, the Egyptian Air Force relied heavily on the Soviet Union for training and matériel, and Mahmud presided over this process. Like many of the other Free Officers, he tended to take a parochial view of his service as a personal power base, which hindered the formation of a coordinated defense policy. In 1956 during the Sinai Campaign, French and British air forces wrought considerable destruction on Egyptian air assets on the ground. Nevertheless, Nasser chose not to fire Mahmud for this debacle.

In 1967 in the run-up to the Six-Day War, Mahmud warned the Egyptian leadership about the inability of his forces to undertake the air operations necessary to support a successful Egyptian ground offensive. Mahmud, now a lieutenant general, protested to Nasser that the Egyptian Air Force would sustain heavy losses in the event of an Israeli first strike. Both Nasser and Field Marshal Abdel Hakim Amer chastised Mahmud for this position. Perhaps because of this, Mahmud predicted that air force losses would be around 20 percent in the event of an Israeli preemptive strike.

On June 5, 1967, the first day of hostilities, the Israelis destroyed the majority of the Egyptian Air Force on the ground. The Israeli pilots were far better trained, but they were also familiar with the weaknesses of the Mikoyan Gurevich MiG-21 fighter, thanks to an Iraqi defector who had flown one to Israel in 1966. They also struck when the vast majority of the Egyptian crews were having breakfast and few planes were in the air, and Amer and Mahmud were in the air on their way to inspect troops in the Sinai. By the afternoon of June 5, Egypt had lost the entirety of its bombers and the vast major-ity of its fighters. This left the army at a serious disadvantage and ultimately resulted in a disorganized Egyptian ground retreat.

The Six-Day War was an abject failure for Egypt. Mahmud and others were blamed and imprisoned. Amer appears to have committed or was forced to commit suicide on September 14, 1967. Mahmud was tried before a military tribunal in February 1968 and was sentenced to 15 years in prison for dereliction of duty. Nasser had him retried, however, because of popular protests that erupted over what was perceived to be a lenient sentence. On August 29, 1968, Mahmud was again found guilty and sentenced to life imprisonment at hard labor. Pardoned on January 27, 1974, by Egyptian president Anwar Sadat, Mahmud has assiduously avoided politics since. While he must bear blame for the poor air force training before the Six-Day War, he cannot be blamed for the leadership's decision that Egypt could absorb an Israeli first strike, for he plainly warned of the likely consequences.

MICHAEL K. BEAUCHAMP

See also
Amer, Abdel Hakim; Egypt, Armed Forces; Nasser, Gamal Abdel; Six-Day War

References
Bowen, Jeremy. *Six Days: How the 1967 War Shaped the Middle East.* New York: Thomas Dunne, 2005.

Oren, Michael B. *Six Days of War: June 1967 and the Making of the Modern Middle East.* Novato, CA: Presidio, 2003.

Maki
See Communist Party of Israel

Makka
See Mecca

Makleff, Mordechai
Born: January 19, 1920
Died: 1978

Israel Defense Forces (IDF) general and its third chief of staff during 1952–1953. Mordechai "Moltke" Makleff was born in the British Mandate for Palestine in the village of Motza on January 19, 1920. His immediate family was killed by Arab villagers from neighboring Kolonia during the Arab Uprising of August 1929. Makleff survived by hiding under his bed and fleeing Motza with his sister Hana to a neighboring farm. He was reared by relatives in Jerusalem and Haifa, where he studied at the Hebrew Reali School. Makleff joined the Haganah as a teenager and in the 1930s served in the Palmach, counterattacking and proactively attacking Arab gangs and terrorists as a member of British Army officer Orde Wingate's Special Night Squads.

General Mordechai "Moltke" Makleff, Israel Defense Forces (IDF) chief of staff during 1952–1953. (Israeli Government Press Office)

Makleff fought in North Africa and northern Italy in World War II as part of the British Army's Jewish Brigade. At the end of the war he mustered out of the British Army as a 25-year-old major and remained in Europe facilitating illegal Jewish immigration to Palestine as well as weapons acquisitions for the Haganah.

As the senior operations officer and then brigade commander for the Carmeli Brigade in the Israeli War of Independence (May 1948–January 1949), Makleff fought near Haifa and Acre and participated in the capture of the Galilee (Operation HIRAM). As a lieutenant colonel he headed the Israeli delegation that negotiated the 1949 Israeli-Syrian and Israeli-Lebanon armistices and negotiated succeeding armistice-related concerns until he became the IDF chief of staff on December 7, 1952, after serving as Yigal Yadin's deputy chief of staff and IDF senior operations officer from November 1949.

The death of his family and his experience in the Special Night Squads shaped Makleff's response as chief of staff to Palestinian (fedayeen) attacks from the West Bank and the Gaza Strip on Israeli border settlements. He ordered Major Ariel Sharon to form and command a commando unit (Unit 101) specializing in reconnaissance,

intelligence gathering, and retaliatory raids designed to punish and deter the fedayeen. Sharon was criticized for targeting Arab noncombatants and condemned for killing more than 60 Jordanian civilians during the raid on the village of Qibya in the fall of 1953 while Makleff was the IDF chief of staff.

The 32-year-old Makleff had agreed to serve as the chief of staff for a single year and was succeeded by Moshe Dayan on December 7, 1953. Makleff then turned to business, and during 1955–1968 he led the expansion of Israel's phosphate industry and the construction of the Dead Sea dam, first as the general manager of the Dead Sea Works (now the Dead Sea Bromine Works, Ltd., or DSBW, whose headquarters building is named for him) and then as the director-general of its parent company, Israel Chemicals. DSBW's original process for the production of potassium chloride is known as the Makleff Cold Crystallization process. Makleff also served as the director-general of the Citrus Marketing Board of Israel (CMBI) that was responsible for the production and marketing of all of the citrus grown in Israel. Makleff died in 1978.

RICHARD EDWARDS

See also

Dayan, Moshe; Fedayeen; Haganah; Israel Defense Forces; Israeli War of Independence, Overview; Palmach; Sharon, Ariel

References

Bauer, Yehuda. *From Diplomacy to Resistance: A History of Jewish Palestine, 1930–1945.* Translated by Alton M. Winters. Philadelphia: Jewish Publication Society of America, 1970.

Farris, Karl. *Growth and Change in the Israeli Defense Forces through Six Wars.* Carlisle Barracks, PA: U.S. Army War College, 1987.

Goldstein, Yaacov N., and Dan Shomron. *From Fighters to Soldiers: How the Israeli Defense Forces Began.* Brighton, UK: Sussex Academic, 1998.

Van Creveld, Martin. *The Sword and the Olive: A Critical History of the Israeli Defense Force.* New York: PublicAffairs, 2002.

Mandler, Avraham Albert
Born: Unknown
Died: October 13, 1973

Israeli Army general. In the 1967 Six-Day War, Avraham Albert Mandler commanded Israel's 8th Mechanized Infantry Brigade. Operating in the Golan Heights against Syria, the brigade broke the Syrian defenses at Tel Fakher and moved eastward toward Kuneitra. As a major general, Mandler commanded the Sinai Defense Force during the Yom Kippur War (1973).

In October 1973 the Israel Defense Forces (IDF) was divided into three area commands (North, Center, and South). Defense of the Suez Canal and the Sinai Peninsula fell to Major General Shmuel Gonen's Southern Command. The command numbered some 18,000 men, but only 8,000 soldiers were properly positioned for what would prove to be a massive initial Egyptian attack. Mandler commanded this Sinai Defense Force of 2 infantry brigades, 1 armored division of 3 brigades, and 12 artillery batteries. Most of the force was in reserve in the eastern Sinai awaiting deployment in a preplanned mobilization (Operation SHOVACH YONIM) in support of the three tanks and 436 soldiers manning the Bar-Lev Line's 16 strong points.

Beginning at 2:00 p.m. on October 6, Egyptian aircraft launched a massive surprise attack against Israeli airfields, command headquarters, surface-to-air missile batteries, and other strategic locations in the Sinai. The attack occurred two hours before the Israeli reserve force was scheduled to be deployed (at 4:00 p.m.) after having received a noontime warning of an imminent Egyptian artillery attack. Fifteen minutes later, 8,000 Egyptian infantry and commando units equipped with heavy antitank weapons crossed the Suez Canal. These forces avoided the Israeli covering fire, bypassed the Israeli fortifications, and prepared ambushes for the anticipated reinforcing Israeli armor. By the time Gonen ordered the evacuation of Mandler's force at 9:30 a.m. on October 7, the Israeli infantry brigade at the Egyptian attack point had been decimated. Two-thirds of the 280 Israeli tanks were destroyed, and air support was limited to Israeli forces engaging the Syrians in the north. Mandler's southern sector force was then reinforced by two brigades, one in the northern sector of the Suez front under the command of Major General Avraham Adan and one in the center commanded by Sharon. These reinforcements stabilized the front by the evening of October 7.

Israeli forces then went over to offensive operations. Mandler was killed in the Suez Canal Zone on October 13, 1973, when his armored mobile command vehicle took a direct hit from Egyptian 122-mm rocket fire. The vehicle was targeted by means of what is believed by some in the IDF to have been an insecure radio conversation with Gonen.

RICHARD EDWARDS

See also

Bar-Lev Line; Gonen, Shmuel; Israel Defense Forces; Six-Day War; Yom Kippur War

References

Herzog, Chaim. *The War of Atonement: October, 1973*. Boston: Little, Brown, 1975.

Rabinovich, Abraham. *The Yom Kippur War: The Epic Encounter That Transformed the Middle East*. New York: Schocken, 2005.

Van Creveld, Martin. *The Sword and the Olive: A Critical History of the Israeli Defense Force*. New York: PublicAffairs, 2002.

Mapam Party

Leftist Israeli political party formed in January 1948 and incorporated and then dissolved to form the Meretz Party in 1992. Mapam, or the United Workers' Party, was a socialist-inspired organization that synthesized leftist Zionism, pure socialism, and accommodation and cooperation between Arabs and Jews in Palestine. For many years, the powerful labor federation Histadrut (General Federation of Labor) was a core component of the Mapam Party. The party played a key role in the World Zionist Organization (WZO) and since 1949 has maintained a permanent presence on the executive committee of the Jewish Agency.

Essentially a party of the working class, Mapam traced its philosophical and ideological origins to Ber Borochov, who pioneered the synthesis of pure socialism wedded to the Zionist ideal as a panacea for the Jewish dilemma. Like Borochov, then, the Mapam Party believed that Jews had to build a strong and numerous working-class base in Palestine out of which a socialist Jewish state could blossom. In this sense, Mapam's position lay at the very heart of Labor Zionism.

Its commitment to socialism and Zionism notwithstanding, the Mapam Party realized fully that Palestine's Arab population had to be treated with equity. Thus, the party tried at all times to include the Arabs in any deliberations or plans for the establishment of a Jewish state. Toward that end, the Mapam Party championed the curtailment of military administration over Arab regions in Israel and pushed for the inclusion of Arab workers in Histadrut, which was accomplished in 1959.

Mapam came about in 1948 by an alliance between the Hashomer Hatzair Workers' Party and Ahdut Ha'avodah-Po'ale Zion, another socialist political coalition in the tradition of Labor Zionism. With this merger and the creation of Mapam, the new party now became a key player in the kibbutz movement in Palestine. The groups and their predecessors that comprised the new Mapam Party had varying positions on Zionism and socialism. Some believed in a bi-state solution to Zionism, others sought to ally themselves with the worldwide socialist movement, and still others hoped to retain a pure socialist ideal within Zionism and the Yishuv (Jews living in Palestine).

By 1948 after a series of splits, fusions, and alliances, these groups had consolidated into the two major coalitions that formed Mapam. Thus, Mapam was initially quite an inclusive party. The catalyst for the fusion of the Left was the 1947 United Nations (UN) partition plan for Palestine, which made the Labor Zionist coalition in particular realize that it would have better success if it spoke with one voice.

By 1945 the many kibbutzim in Palestine comprised the core of the political and labor Left. They also became pivotal in the defense of Palestinian Jews and the fight against British authorities. In fact, many kibbutzim served as training bases for the Haganah and Palmach.

The 1948 coalition proved unsustainable, however. Arguments ensued over the place of Arabs within Zionism and how best to respond to Arab violence against Jews. Some favored self-restraint (or havlaga), while others wanted firm and swift retaliatory actions taken. In 1954 Mapam split, with a number of members moving toward the Mapai Party, a social-democratic alliance. During the 1950s and early 1960s, some critics of Mapam accused the group of harboring pro-Soviet sympathies. It did not, however, ally with the Soviet Union and decried the Soviets' enmity toward Zionism and its repressive policies toward Soviet Jews and other ethnic minorities within its borders.

In 1968 during its Fifth Party Congress, the Mapam Party sought to ally itself with the Labor Party in the forthcoming 1969 elections. The union was a success, and labor as a whole garnered 56 seats in the Knesset (Israeli parliament). Some members did not favor the alignment, arguing that the party had given up its autonomy. But the majority stayed with the alliance, and the Fifth Congress took pains to explain why such a fusion was then necessary. Among other things, it stated its opposition to the annexation of any more occupied territories, support for an increase in Jewish immigration to Israel, and the maintenance of an adequate standard of living for all Israelis, both Jewish and Arab. It also specifically condemned the Soviet Union's Middle East policies and urged the creation of a purely socialist state in Israel.

Mapam stayed in the labor alliance with Mapai and Rafi until 1984. The party then decided to leave the coalition because of Israeli prime minister Shimon Peres's decision to form a unity government with the rightist Likud Party. After this split, Mapam lost much of its influence and enjoyed only limited electoral success. In 1988 it won only three seats in the Knesset. Faced with dwindling power and support, Mapam joined with two other leftist labor parties in 1992 to form the Meretz Party, which became the fourth-largest political group in the Knesset after the 1992 elections. By 1997 Mapam was defunct and was absorbed into Meretz, which had become Meretz-Yachad by 2006.

PAUL G. PIERPAOLI JR.

See also

Havlaga; Histadrut; Kibbutz Movement; Labor Zionism; Likud Party; Meretz; Peres, Shimon

References

Avineri, Shlomo. *The Making of Modern Zionism: The Intellectual Origins of the Jewish State.* New York: Basic Books, 1981.

Sachar, Howard M. *A History of Israel: From the Rise of Zionism to Our Time.* 3rd ed. New York: Knopf, 2007.

Zochar, David M. *Political Parties in Israel: The Evolution of Israeli Democracy.* New York: Praeger, 1974.

Marcus, David

Born: February 22, 1902
Died: June 10, 1948

U.S. Army colonel and Israeli general. David Daniel Marcus, known his whole life as "Mickey," was born on New York's Lower East Side on February 22, 1902. The fifth child of Jewish immigrants from Romania, he graduated from the United States Military Academy, West Point, in 1924. While serving as a lieutenant of infantry at Governors Island, he attended law school at night in New York City. Leaving active duty after his initial assignment, he became an assistant U.S. attorney in New York and, working with Thomas E. Dewey, helped to shut down Lucky Luciano's crime ring. In 1934 Mayor Fiorello La Guardia appointed Marcus deputy commissioner and then later commissioner of corrections.

David Daniel "Mickey" Marcus, U.S. Army colonel and Israeli general, 1938. (Israeli Government Press Office)

With an Army Reserve commission in the Judge Advocate General's Corps, Marcus returned to active duty in 1940. Although a military lawyer, he established and commanded the first Army Ranger school in Hawaii. In 1943 he was posted to the Pentagon as the chief of planning for the War Department's Civil Affairs Division. He played a key role in the negotiation and drafting of the Italian surrender and the Instrument of Unconditional Surrender of Germany.

In 1944 Marcus was sent to Britain to initiate the planning for the occupation and control of postwar Germany. On June 6, 1944, he managed to wrangle his way onto one of the troop carriers of the 101st Airborne Division and made the combat jump into Normandy. He had never made a parachute jump before. Later in the war he personally witnessed the liberation of some of the Nazi concentration camps. He also served as a legal adviser to President Franklin D. Roosevelt at the Yalta Conference and to President Harry S. Truman at the Potsdam Conference. In 1946 Marcus headed the Pentagon's War Crimes Division, responsible for selecting judges and prosecutors for the war crimes trials in Germany and Japan.

Marcus left active duty in 1947, turning down a promotion to brigadier general, but later that year he accepted an invitation from the chairman of the Jewish Agency Executive, David Ben-Gurion, to come to the British Mandate for Palestine as his military adviser. As a reservist Marcus needed War Department permission to do that, which was granted with the proviso that he not use his American rank or real name. He arrived in Tel Aviv in January 1948 under the name of Michael Stone.

More of an organizer and a trainer than a tactical commander, Marcus helped establish a new command structure for the Jewish self-defense organization, Haganah, and wrote training manuals based on memory from similar U.S. manuals. When Israel declared independence on May 14, two Egyptian brigades attacked into the southern Negev within hours, exactly where Marcus had predicted the first attack would come.

As the fighting ground on, the center of gravity shifted to Jerusalem, which was cut off and surrounded by the Arab Legion. With a cease-fire brokered by the United Nations (UN) was scheduled to go into effect on June 11, the Israelis realized that they would lose all claim to the city unless they could establish a credible land bridge. After their May 25 attack at Latrun failed to break through, Ben-Gurion made the bold move of designating a single commander to control all combat operations to lift the siege. On May 28 Aluf (General) Michael Stone was appointed commander of the Jerusalem Front, with command over the Etzioni, Har-El, and 7th brigades. Marcus became the first Jewish soldier to hold the rank of general officer since Judas Maccabeus 2,100 years before.

Marcus launched another attack at Latrun on May 30. When that failed, he concluded that the only solution was to go around the Arab Legion. Sending engineers and construction crews into the wild Judean hills south of Latrun, he oversaw the extension and improvement of a series of goat trails into a credible military road, which he wryly called the Burma Road. Despite the enormous obstacles, the land bridge was completed on June 9, lifting the siege of Jerusalem.

On the night of June 10 Marcus was at his command post in the village of Abu Gosh, a few miles outside of Jerusalem. At 3:50 a.m. on June 11 he was accidentally shot dead by one of his own jittery sentries. The cease-fire went into effect at 10:00 a.m. Marcus was the last casualty of that phase of the war.

When Marcus's body was returned to New York, it was accompanied by Moshe Dayan and Yosef Hamburger, the captain of the blockade runner *Exodus*. Marcus was buried at the West Point post cemetery in July 1948. He is the only soldier buried there who died fighting under a foreign flag. In the 1960s movie *Cast a Giant Shadow*, Kirk Douglas played Marcus. Although the movie was a highly fictionalized account, Douglas vividly captured Marcus's fiery spirit.

DAVID T. ZABECKI

See also

Ben-Gurion, David; Dayan, Moshe; *Exodus* Incident; Haganah; Latrun, Battles of

References

Berkman, Ted. *Cast a Giant Shadow*. Garden City, NY: Doubleday, 1962.

Collins, Larry, and Dominique Lapierre. *O Jerusalem!* New York: Simon and Schuster, 1972.

Maritime Policies and Restrictions

The emergence of modern steam shipping in the 19th century transformed the eastern Mediterranean basin into a strategic zone that became of great interest to maritime powers. With the 1869 completion of the Suez Canal, which links Suez on the Red Sea to Port Said on the Mediterranean Sea, the Middle East became a key zone for the passage of international shipping. Although the 1888 Convention of Constantinople ensured, under British protection, the demilitarization of and free navigation within the canal to all navies, the canal nevertheless served as a powerful lever in international affairs. Control over the Suez Canal enabled Britain to influence maritime trade within the region. During World War I (1914–1918), France and Britain closed the canal to non-Allied shipping. Even after Egyptian independence in 1922, Britain had been allowed to maintain military forces in the Canal Zone. This right was bitterly defended by Britain during World War II (1939–1945).

If the Suez Canal had originally ensured an imperial link between Britain and its colonies, the growing reliance of European countries on oil after World War II made maritime policy in matters related to the Canal a growing concern. Indeed, the beginning of the Cold War and the creation of the State of Israel in 1948 introduced a maritime perspective to the budding Arab-Israeli conflict. As such, the control of maritime trade in the eastern Mediterranean basin in general and in the canal in particular served as a means of potentially influencing the outcome of the conflict.

In 1948, for example, Egyptian authorities introduced regulations prohibiting ships transiting from or through Israeli ports from entering the Suez Canal. The 1951 Egyptian denunciation of the 1936 Anglo-Egyptian Treaty, which guaranteed British control over the Canal, forced the pullout of British forces from the area. The nationalization of the canal by Egyptian president Gamal Abdel Nasser in July 1956 posed a significant danger to maritime policy in the area and threatened, in particular, the free flow of Middle Eastern oil to Europe. At the time, two-thirds of European oil passed through the canal. The ensuing Suez Crisis prompted interventions by Britain, France, and Israel to keep the Canal open. Upon U.S. and Soviet pressure, the three nations withdrew from the area, and a United Nations (UN) peacekeeping force maintained an uneasy peace, ensuring safe passage through the canal.

After blockading Israeli shipping in the Gulf of Tiran in 1967, which was a clear volition of international maritime law, Egypt closed the Suez Canal in the wake of the June 1967 Six-Day War. The canal would not reopen until June 1975. It was only in 1979 after the Israeli-Egyptian peace process that Israel gained unrestricted use of the canal. Israeli shipping was also blockaded in the Red Sea during the October 1973 Yom Kippur War, although shipping was not affected in the Mediterranean, as American seaborne supplies reached Israel unhindered.

In the post–Cold War period, protracted fighting in the Middle East and its threat to shipping and the maritime economy prompted the North Atlantic Treaty Organization (NATO) to introduce in 1994 the Mediterranean Dialogue. While attempting to ensure the stability of the Mediterranean basin in the face of growing terrorist threats and regional conflicts, NATO's objectives also sought to guarantee the stability of maritime trade in the context of the ongoing Arab-Israeli conflict. Although it constitutes only a peripheral aspect of the ongoing Arab-Israeli conflict, the control of maritime policy in the Middle East has also served, through its impact on navigation, to influence international support for the parties engaged in the conflict.

MARTIN LABERGE

See also
Port Said; Red Sea; Six-Day War; Strait of Tiran Crisis; Straits of Tiran; Suez Canal; Suez Crisis; Yom Kippur War

References
Gold, Edgar. *Maritime Transport: The Evolution of International Maritime Policy and Shipping Law.* Lexington, MA: Lexington Books, 1986.
Schonfield, Hugh Joseph. *The Suez Canal in Peace and War, 1869–1969.* Coral Gables, FL: University of Miami Press, 1969.

Marshall, George Catlett
Born: December 31, 1880
Died: October 16, 1959

U.S. Army general, chief of staff of the army (1939–1945), secretary of state (1947–1949), and secretary of defense (1950). Born on December 31, 1880, in Uniontown, Pennsylvania, George C. Marshall graduated in 1901 from the Virginia Military Institute, where he rose to be first captain. Commissioned a second lieutenant of infantry the following year, his first assignment was in Manila at the end of the Philippine-American War. Various postings within the continental United States followed, including four years (1906–1910) at the Infantry and Cavalry School at Fort Leavenworth, first as a student and then as instructor. He then served briefly as an instructor with the Pennsylvania National Guard, which gave him an early appreciation of the importance of effective civilian-military relations. During 1913–1916 he served again in the Philippines, making captain in 1916. From early in his career he won a reputation as a superlative staff officer with strengths in efficient management and problem-solving skills.

Following the U.S. declaration of war against Germany in April 1917, Marshall went to France as a training officer in the 1st Division. Promoted to lieutenant colonel in 1918, he became the chief of operations for the First Army, winning general admiration for his logistical skills in working out in a short span the movement of

General of the Army George Catlett Marshall, chief of staff of the U.S. Army (1939–1945), secretary of state (1947–1949), and secretary of defense (1950). (Library of Congress)

---

hundreds of thousands of troops across the battlefront. After working on occupation plans for Germany, in the spring of 1919 he became aide to General John J. Pershing, his wartime commander and now army chief of staff, a post that Marshall held until 1924. Pershing relied heavily on Marshall and became his mentor, patron, and close friend for the rest of Marshall's career.

Between the world wars Marshall spent three years in Tianjin (Tientsin), China, with the 15th Infantry Regiment and five years as assistant commandant in charge of instruction at the Infantry School, Fort Benning, Georgia, where he revised the curriculum and helped train numerous future American generals, among them Omar N. Bradley, Joseph W. Stilwell, Joseph Lawton Collins, Walter Bedell Smith, and Matthew B. Ridgway. Marshall won promotion to colonel in 1932, becoming commander of the 8th Infantry Regiment that year, serving as senior instructor to the Illinois National Guard from 1933 to 1936, and commanding the 5th Infantry Brigade as a brigadier general from 1936 to 1938. The U.S. Army's rapid interwar reduction in strength left Marshall convinced that to maintain strong military forces, greater civilian support and commitment were vital.

In 1938 Marshall became head of the War Plans Division in Washington, where he quickly became deputy chief of staff and then, on September 1, 1939, chief of staff of the U.S. Army. As war began in Europe and President Franklin D. Roosevelt leaned toward the Allied side, Marshall threw himself into enabling the American defense establishment to shake off its interwar somnolence. Increasingly assisted by pro-Allied civilian officials such as Secretary of War Henry L. Stimson, Marshall instituted and lobbied for programs to recruit and train new troops; expedite munitions production; assist Great Britain, China, and the Soviet Union to resist the Axis; and coordinate British and U.S. strategy. After the United States joined the war in December 1941, Marshall presided over an increase in U.S. Army strength from a mere 200,000 men to a wartime maximum of 8 million. His personal knowledge of American officers, many of whom he had trained, helped him select numerous commanders for both the European and Pacific theaters. Marshall was not only highly effective in supervising the massive U.S. war effort but also enjoyed excellent relationships with key senators and congressmen, who almost without exception admired and respected his professional abilities as well as his integrity.

Marshall was a strong supporter of opening as soon as possible a second front against Germany in Europe, a campaign ultimately deferred until June 1944. Between 1941 and 1945 he attended all the major wartime strategic conferences, including those at Placentia Bay, Washington, Quebec, Cairo, Tehran, Malta, Yalta, and Potsdam, and presidents Franklin D. Roosevelt and Harry S. Truman relied heavily on his advice. His greatest disappointment was perhaps that he did not get to command the Allied cross-Channel invasion force but remained chief of staff throughout the war. He was simply too valuable in Washington. In 1945 he also participated in discussions as to whether to drop the newly developed atomic bomb. Eager to end the war expeditiously, he supported its use.

Marshall retired from the army in November 1945, having received his fifth star as general of the army the previous December. He was the first U.S. Army officer to hold that rank. President Truman almost immediately sent him to China, where he spent all of 1946 unsuccessfully attempting to mediate the continuing civil war between the National and Communist sides. In January 1947 Marshall became secretary of state, facing the challenges with which the developing Cold War presented his country. In early 1947 he faced demands from financially strapped British leaders that the United States take over its military commitments to Greece and Turkey, pleas that resulted in the Truman Doctrine of March 1947 whereby Truman pledged the United States to resist communist incursions around the world. The most spectacular event during Marshall's time as secretary of state was the 11-month Berlin Blockade, when from June 1948 to May 1949 the Soviet Union attempted to starve the Western powers out of West Berlin, a move to which the United States and Britain responded by airlifting all needed supplies into Berlin. Marshall's most visible accomplishments as secretary of state were the Marshall Plan, or European Recovery Program, a coordinated $10 billion five-year scheme to rehabilitate the economies of Western Europe, and U.S. membership in the North Atlantic Treaty Organization (NATO), the first permanent security pact that the United States had ever entered.

One of the few issues over which Marshall differed significantly from Truman was the policy toward Palestine and the demands of Zionist Jewish nationalists for the creation of an independent state, pressures that brought the creation of Israel in May 1948. Conscious of the strategic value of Arab oil to the United States, Marshall and the State Department strongly opposed the establishment of a separate Jewish state, preferring that the United States should work to attain a solution of a unitary, multinational state, based on the 1939 British White Paper, that would be acceptable to Palestine's Arab as well as Jewish populations. Truman, by contrast, believed that the Jewish people deserved an autonomous state in recompense for their wartime sufferings during the Holocaust. A keen amateur historian, the president felt a somewhat romantic admiration for the Jewish people's lengthy past and their quest, despite almost two millennia in Diaspora, for a homeland. With a presidential election fast approaching, Truman's political advisers, especially the young Clark Clifford, also urged upon him the need to win the Jewish vote in such key states as New York and California.

Although Marshall thought that the U.S. decision to support the establishment of Israel and recognize the new state was a serious mistake, one he bluntly ascribed to political and electoral considerations, in public he loyally concealed his distaste and, rejecting suggestions that he resign in protest, supported the president's policy. Immediately after Israel's formal establishment on May 15, 1948, hostilities began as the Arab League states of Syria, Egypt, Iraq, and Transjordan all attacked Israel, while Palestinian Arabs within the new state also rebelled. When the Arab offensive flagged in the summer of 1948, United Nations (UN) mediator Count Folke Bernadotte of Wisborg sought to negotiate a truce, some of whose suggested territorial concessions, including relinquishing the strategically significant Negev Desert, the Israelis found unacceptable. In September, Jewish activists assassinated Bernadotte in Jerusalem. That same month Marshall publicly supported the Bernadotte Plan, an action that the Truman administration disavowed. Shortly after Truman's November 1948 reelection Marshall resigned, citing genuine health problems but almost certainly also driven by irritation over Truman's position.

Marshall left office in January 1949 and soon afterward agreed to head the American Red Cross. At the outbreak of the Korean War in June 1950, Truman persuaded Marshall to return to government service as secretary of defense, in which capacity Marshall once again built up American manpower and war production and pushed for selective service legislation. He also strongly supported Truman's dismissal of General Douglas MacArthur, commander of UN forces in Korea, for insubordination, a decision that later exposed Marshall to vehement and politically motivated accusations of procommunist sympathies from Sen. Joseph R. McCarthy and his followers.

Marshall left office in September 1951. In December 1953 his efforts for European recovery won him the Nobel Peace Prize. His final retirement was dogged by increasingly poor health, and he died at Walter Reed Army Medical Center on October 16, 1959.

PRISCILLA MARY ROBERTS

See also

Acheson, Dean; Bernadotte, Folke; Eisenhower, Dwight David; Holocaust; Israel; Israeli War of Independence, Overview; Roosevelt, Franklin Delano; Truman, Harry S.; White Paper (1939)

References

Cray, Ed. *General of the Army: George C. Marshall, Soldier and Statesman.* New York: Norton, 1990.

Marshall, George C. *The Papers of George Catlett Marshall.* Edited by Larry I. Bland. 5 vols. to date. Baltimore: Johns Hopkins University Press, 1981–.

Pogue, Forrest C. *George C. Marshall.* 4 vols. New York: Viking, 1963–1987.

Stoler, Mark A. *George C. Marshall: Soldier-Statesman of the American Century.* Boston: Twayne, 1989.

Masada

The term "masada" is a Latin transliteration of the Hebrew name Metzada, meaning "fortress." Masada refers to a rock mesa overlooking the Dead Sea in the eastern Judean Desert near Ein Gedi atop which Jewish Zealots stood against a Roman siege (AD 72–73) in the First Jewish-Roman War (66–73), also known as the Herodian Jewish Revolt or the Great Jewish Revolt.

Masada's eastern cliffs rise some 1,350 feet (150 feet above sea level) above the Dead Sea, with the more vertical western cliffs rising 300 feet above the floor of the Dead Sea Valley. The rhomboid-shaped flat plateau comprised an area some 1,200 feet by 900 feet. Access was limited to four very difficult and quite steep approaches: the Snake Path from the east, still used by some tourists today; the White Rock ascent from the west; and one approach each from the south and north. Three large cisterns hewn from the rock mesa collected rainwater. Numerous storehouses also dotted the site.

The Zealot defenders and their families were housed in barracks-like quarters and in the remains of a last century BC Herodian palace. The plateau was ringed by a watchtower-studded stone casement wall 4,200 feet long and 12 feet thick that incorporated the walls of the living quarters and storehouses.

King Herod the Great was a pro-Roman ruler and appointed Pompey as regent of Palestine in 47 BC. Herod first fled with his family to Masada in 40 BC when the Jews joined the Parthians in a rebellion against Rome. Herod then fled to Rome but was restored to his position in 37 BC after the Romans under Mark Antony crushed the rebellion. Fearing another Jewish rebellion and possible war with Cleopatra of Egypt, during 37–31 BC Herod fortified Masada to include an extensive and lavish palace.

Roman soldiers were garrisoned at Masada when in AD 66 it was captured at the beginning of the Great Jewish Revolt by Jewish Zealots led by Menahem ben Judah. Eleazar ben Ya'ir, nephew of Menahem, assumed command of Masada soon after rival Jews killed Menahem in Jerusalem that same year. Except for the Zealots at Masada, Jewish resistance ended when the Romans captured Jerusalem and destroyed its Temple in September AD 70.

The ruins of Herod's palace at Masada. (Joy Powers/iStockPhoto.com)

Lucius Flavius Silva, the Roman governor of Palestine, laid siege to Masada in AD 72 with a force of 10,000–15,000 men consisting of the Roman Tenth Legion, its support troops, and Jewish prisoners of war who were used as construction slaves. The Jewish defenders and family members numbered between 1,000 and 1,500 people.

After surrounding the fortress with eight military camps and a three-foot-high wall, the Romans oversaw in a nine-month period the construction by Jewish slave labor of an assault ramp to the top of Masada. It was during this time that the Jewish defenders reinforced the stone wall with an earthen and wooden wall.

The Romans first used a battering ram to breach the stone wall and then succeeded in burning the wooden wall. As the Romans prepared to exploit the breach the next day, Eleazar exhorted the Zealot defenders and their families to a final act of defiance. They burned their personal belongings and selected by lot 10 defenders to kill the general population. These 10 then killed each other in turn, leaving only a final defender to commit suicide. The contents of the storehouses were not burned so as to demonstrate to the Romans that the defenders and their families chose to die rather than suffer defeat by siege and assault. These details and the personal exhortation of Eleazar to his followers were related to the Romans by 2 women and 5 children who survived by hiding in one of the cisterns and were then recorded by the first-century Jewish historian Josephus.

Masada emerged as a symbol of Jewish and Zionist resolve and courage and became a widely visited pilgrimage site for many Zionist youth groups and the Haganah in the years prior to the formation in 1948 of the State of Israel. The Star of David flag of Israel was raised over Masada following the end of the Israeli War of Independence in 1949, and the site continues to be used by various units of the Israel Defense Forces (IDF) and contemporary youth movements for swearing-in ceremonies that conclude with the oath that "Masada shall never fall again." Masada is accessible today both by foot on the arduous Snake Path and by aerial tramway.

RICHARD M. EDWARDS

See also

Haganah; Young Israel

References

Ben-Yehuda, Nachman. *Sacrificing Truth: Archaeology and the Myth of Masada.* Amherst, NY: Humanity Books, 2002.

Miklowitz, Gloria D. *Masada: The Last Fortress.* Grand Rapids, MI: Eerdmans, 1999.

Yadin, Yigael. *Masada: Herod's Fortress and the Zealots' Last Stand.* New York: Welcome Rain, 1998.

Masada, Jewish Student Organization

Jewish student movement created in 1962 and aimed at U.S. youths. Masada, under the banner of the American Zionist Youth Foundation (AZYF) and then the Zionist Organization of America (ZOA), was the largest organizer of American Jewish youth trips to Israel from 1962 to 2004.

In 1897 the First Zionist Congress (FZC) created the World Zionist Organization (WZO). The FZC authorized the WZO to establish branches in all countries with considerable Jewish populations and determined Zionism's goal to be the creation of a Jewish homeland in Palestine. The WZO and its American campus subdivision, the AZYF, developed a nationwide strategy for creating a Jewish student movement by establishing Masada in 1962. Masada's goals were to mobilize students to support Israel, facilitate travel to Israel, and encourage immigration there.

The Zionist youth movements that blossomed in Eastern Europe in the early 20th century following the FZC provide the context for understanding the creation of Masada in the 1960s. The Zionist youth movements shared the WZO goal of a Jewish homeland and emphasized aliya, immigration to Israel, as the primary means of achieving that goal. These groups were integral to World War II Jewish resistance movements in the ghettos. They also led the exodus (Beriha) from Europe to the potential safe haven of Palestine and the soon-to-be State of Israel, a recognized Jewish state where the safety and freedom of Jews would be guaranteed. Israel came into being in 1948. Once its military was firmly established, its borders reasonably secured, the advantages and disadvantages of kibbutz life more thoroughly understood, and the threat of continuing wars and terrorism realized, Zionist youth movements in the United States began to wither. Although interest renewed somewhat before

and just after the 1967 Six-Day War, the zeal of American youths, both to support and settle in Israel, effectively disappeared.

The WZO and AZYF responded to this apathy by expanding Masada's campus affiliates using paid and specifically trained graduate students as itinerant organizers. Jewish students developed a renewed sense of community through small groups, Shabbat dinners, various campus events, supportive literature, and national conferences. Masada organized summer tours and more extended trips that emphasized work, study, and culture. This was all implemented within the context of the Jewish state and the challenges that faced Israel. Masada also began anew to emphasize aliya and especially garin aliya, or group immigration. Segev Bet, a moshav in Israel's western Galilee, was founded by Masada alumni and exemplified the evolution of aliya thought from kibbutz communalism to the greater freedom of moshav cooperatives.

The same factors that led to the formation of the AZYF and Masada caused them to cease operations in 1995. Although the AZYF and Masada were then the leading organizers of American Jewish youth trips to Israel, participation had so decreased that the WZO determined that a radical change was needed. Thus, a new consortium composed of the Council of Jewish Federations, the United Jewish Appeal, the Charles R. Bronfman Foundation, the Jewish Agency, and the WZO was formed to promote Zionism to American youths. Control of Masada then transferred to the ZOA.

The ZOA was founded in 1897 following the FZC and is the oldest Zionist pro-Israel organization in the United States. Masada targeted teenagers, young adults (single and married), and college students, but ZOA ended Masada in 2004 when it created the Campus Activism Network.

RICHARD EDWARDS

See also

Kibbutz Movement; World Zionist Organization; Young Israel; Zionism; Zionist Conference

References

Brenner, Michael. *Zionism: A Brief History.* Translated by Shelley Frisch. Princeton, NJ: Markus Wiener, 2003.

Ronsenberg, Shelley Kapnek. *History of the Jews in America: Civil War through the Rise of Zionism.* Springfield, NJ: Behrman House, 2005.

Masada2000.org

Extreme pro-Israel, anti-Palestinian Web site based in Sacramento, California, and run by Rockwell Lazareth for the Masada2000 organization. Masada2000.org claims members in the United States, Israel, Brazil, Switzerland, and Australia. The Web site espouses views in agreement with and frequently quotes Meir David Kahane. Kahane was the American Orthodox rabbi, right-wing militant Zionist, and former member of the Knesset (Israeli parliament) who was assassinated in 1990. Lazareth denies that the Web site and organization are Kahanist.

Masada2000.org is infamous for its alphabetized "Self-Hating and/or Israel-Threatening List" of nearly 7,000 Jews. The organization asserts that they "have a sick need to conspire with the enemies of Israel."

Jews on the list are called "Judenrats," a reference to the Jewish councils created by the German government during the World War II Holocaust to govern the Jews, provide Jewish slave labor, and expedite the deportation of Jews to the extermination camps. The list compiled by Masada2000.org includes such American Jewish notables as Thomas Friedman of the *New York Times,* Rabbi Michael Lerner of the liberal Zionist *Tikkun* magazine, Adam Shapiro of the pro-Palestinian International Solidarity Movement, Noam Chomsky, Woody Allen, and Gloria Steinem. Lerner is listed as one of "the five most dangerous Jewish enemies of the Jewish people."

The Masada2000.org Web site describes itself as "Israel 101: A Survival Kit for Dummies" and includes 36 topics, including "History of Palestine," "Palestinian Refugees," "Beware of Peace Treaties," "Arafat and the P.L.O.: So Much Blood, Cleverness and Filth All Together in One Man," and "The Cancer Within." The Web site includes many racist and graphic images, videos, parodies, and caricatures. A cartoon depicting Yasser Arafat wrapped in a full body suit of bacon is one of the least objectionable.

Masada2000.org asserts that the idea of a Palestinian people is a myth fabricated and perpetuated in the latter part of the 20th century by Arab states that did not want to absorb the inhabitants who had assumed residence in biblical Israel before the land was rightly regained by present-day Israel. Masada2000.org contends that the name "Palestine" was invented by a Roman procurator (AD 135) who sought to degrade Judaism and the Jewish people residing in the Land of Israel by renaming it "Palaistina," a distortion of "Philistia," the arch enemy of the Hebrew people. This renaming was also intended to delegitimize the Jewish claim to the land. Indeed, the Web site contends that the name has been used by the Arab states to label the Jews as occupiers and to legitimize the extermination of the Jews.

Masada2000.org makes several demands. It calls on Israel to revoke the citizenship of all non-Jews, expelling them to any of 24 Arab countries. Second, it calls for the creation of a Greater Israel encompassing the West Bank, Gaza, and the territory on the East Bank of the Jordan River. It also insists that Israel enforce a military solution to any intifada, execute all Arab terrorists, and destroy all Arab terrorist organizations.

RICHARD EDWARDS

See also
Jewish Defense League; Kahane, Meir David

References
Cohen-Almagor, Raphael. *The Boundaries of Liberty and Tolerance: The Struggle against Kahanism in Israel.* Gainesville: University Press of Florida, 1994.
Kahane, Meir. *Israel: Revolution or Referendum.* Secaucus, NJ: Barricade Books, 1990.

Masri, Munib al-
Born: 1936

Prominent Palestinian Arab businessman. Born into the powerful Masri family of Nablus in the British Mandate for Palestine in 1936, Munib al-Masri attended al-Najah High School in Nablus. He then went to Texas, where he earned both bachelor's and master's degrees in geology. He married in the United States and in 1956 moved with his wife to Jordan. In the 1960s he worked for the Phillips Petroleum Company in several Middle Eastern countries, rising to become first the head of its offices in Algeria and then the head of Phillips operations in the entire Middle East, with his offices in Beirut.

During 1970–1971 al-Masri accepted an invitation from the Jordanian government to become its minister of public works. There he helped mediate a resolution to the events of September 1970 (Black September) between Palestine Liberation Organization (PLO) leader Yasser Arafat and King Hussein of Jordan. The agreement ultimately led to the relocation of the PLO to Beirut.

In 1971 al-Masri formed the Development and Investment Company (PADICO), based in Nablus. In short order it became the largest and most influential company in the West Bank and the Gaza Strip. Reportedly it has invested some $500 million in the Palestinian territories. Its interests range from manufacturing and real estate to finance and power generation. Among al-Masri's business ventures in Nablus are a Palestinian stock exchange, a television assembly plant, and the headquarters building of Paltel, the Middle East's first privately owned telephone company. PADICO is also actively involved in promoting Palestinian tourism, including construction of a luxury hotel in Bethlehem, and it is the only private firm in a new Palestinian home mortgage corporation.

Al-Masri was widely praised for his economic development plans, bringing in offshore Palestinian capital for investment. Many of these projects were destroyed in the Israeli campaign in the spring of 2002 against West Bank cities and towns. Critics, however, charged that PADICO is rife with cronyism and nepotism and that it has benefited greatly from political connections and is in fact opposed to a free market system. This would not auger well for the future of business in a Palestinian state.

Al-Masri, a billionaire, serves on the board of directors of the Palestinian National Fund and the Arab Bank. He has also made substantial financial contributions to al-Quda University. A friend of long standing of Arafat, al-Masri served on the Central Council of the PLO. Reportedly, al-Masri refused Arafat's offer to become the first prime minister of the Palestinian Authority (PA).

SPENCER C. TUCKER

See also
Arafat, Yasser; Black September; Hussein, King of Jordan; Palestine Liberation Organization; Palestinian Authority

References

Aburish, Said K. *Arafat: From Defender to Dictator.* New York: Bloomsbury, 1998.

Hart, Alan. *Arafat: A Political Biography.* Rev. ed. London: Sidgwick and Jackson, 1994.

Mazen, Abu

See Abbas, Mahmoud

McGonagle, William Loren

Born: November 19, 1925
Died: March 3, 1999

U.S. Navy officer and commander of the electronic intelligence gathering ship USS *Liberty* when it came under Israeli attack during the Six-Day War. William McGonagle was born in Wichita, Kansas, on November 19, 1925. He attended secondary school in California and joined the Naval Reserve Officer Training Corps (NROTC) while a student at the University of Southern California. He was commissioned an ensign on graduation in June 1947.

During 1947–1950, McGongale served in the destroyer USS *Frank Knox* and the minesweeper USS *Partridge.* During the Korean War (1950–1953) he was assigned to the minesweeper USS *Kite* and took part in its extensive minesweeping operations. From 1951 to 1966 he served in various postings ashore and afloat, including command of the fleet tug *Mataco* and the salvage ship *Reclaimer.*

In April 1966, with the rank of commander, McGonagle assumed command of the *Liberty* (AGTR-5), taking the ship on intelligence-gathering missions off the west coast of Africa. Ordered to gather intelligence during the war between Israel and Egypt, Syria, and Lebanon, McGonagle took his ship into the Mediterranean. On June 8, 1967, the *Liberty* was located in international waters 13 miles off the Egyptian port of El Arish when it came under attack from Israeli aircraft and torpedo boats. Messages from Washington ordering McGonagle to move 100 miles from the coast were not received in time by the *Liberty.*

McGonagle was badly wounded early in the Israeli strike but remained at his station on the bridge for the next 17 hours. Only when his ship rendezvoused with a U.S. Sixth Fleet destroyer did he relinquish command. He also refused medical treatment until the most seriously wounded had been cared for. The attack on the *Liberty* claimed 34 dead and 172 wounded among its crew. The survivors were able to keep the ship afloat, however, and it steamed to Malta for stopgap repairs. For his heroism and leadership on that occasion, McGonagle was awarded the Medal of Honor. His ship received the Presidential Unit Citation.

Promoted to captain in October 1967, McGonagle commanded the new ammunition ship USS *Kilauea* and then led the NROTC Unit at the University of Oklahoma. He retired from active duty in 1974. McGonagle died at Palm Springs, California, on March 3, 1999.

SPENCER C. TUCKER

See also

Liberty Incident; Six-Day War; Spector, Yiftah

References

Bamford, James. *Body of Secrets.* New York: Doubleday, 2001.

Cristol, A. Jay. *The Liberty Incident: The 1967 Israeli Attack on the US Navy Spy Ship.* Washington, DC: Brassey's, 2002.

Ennis, James M., Jr. *Assault on the* Liberty: *The True Story of the Israeli Attack on an American Intelligence Ship.* New York: Random House, 1979.

McMahon-Hussein Correspondence

Correspondence in the form of 10 letters exchanged between British high commissioner for Egypt Sir A. Henry McMahon and Hussein ibn Ali, emir of the Arabian Hejaz and sharif of Mecca. Many Arabs have viewed the exchange as Britain's commitment to Arab autonomy and independence in the Middle East, including the entire area of Palestine. The exchange began with a letter from Hussein to McMahon, translated into English and read by McMahon on July 14, 1915. The last letter was one from McMahon to Hussein on March 10, 1916. The ambiguities in McMahon's proposals combined with subsequent British policies that flew in the face of the McMahon-Hussein correspondence have been a constant source of misunderstanding and frustration in the Middle East, and the issues the letters raised continue to present obstacles to this very day.

Hussein's initial letter to McMahon outlined the conditions of Arab participation in the British struggle against the Ottoman Turks during World War I. Essentially, Hussein pledged Arab support for the fight against the Turks in exchange for British concessions, most specifically those relating to Arab independence. In an October 24, 1915, letter McMahon assured Hussein that Great Britain would recognize and support independence for Arabs residing in areas outlined by Hussein. The territories affected included the Arabian Peninsula, greater Syria, Palestine, Lebanon, and Transjordan. Thus, areas east of Hama, Homa, Aleppo, and Damascus would therefore be eligible for Arab statehood, or the creation of a series of constituent Arab states. Quite naturally, many Arabs saw in this promise a British commitment to independence, either immediate or in the immediate wake of World War I (which would not end until November 1918).

At the same time, the British along with the French and Russians were drawing up the secret May 1916 Sykes-Picot Agreement, which would demonstrate that the British government had little intention of making good on the McMahon pledges. The Sykes-Picot Agreement was an arrangement whereby the powers would divide the Middle East into French, British, and Russian spheres of influence once the war was over. In 1917 Italy would also be added to that framework. These spheres incorporated much of the area that McMahon and Hussein had agreed would be subject to Arab autonomy. Not until December 1917 did Hussein learn the full details of the agreement, which had been leaked to him by the Turkish government in hopes that it would drive a wedge in the Anglo-Arab alliance.

As if the Sykes-Picot Agreement had not been enough to give Hussein pause over British intentions, the November 1917 Balfour Declaration clearly seemed to show British duplicity. In the declaration, the British government made known its intention to support the creation of a Jewish homeland in Palestine. This, in the eyes of Hussein and other Arab leaders, was a patent violation of the promises McMahon had made to Hussein in 1915 and 1916.

The British claimed that the McMahon correspondence did not apply to Palestine. Therefore, the Balfour Declaration could not possibly be contradictory to any earlier pledges made to the Arabs. Indeed, McMahon's letter of October 25, 1915, had not explicitly mentioned Palestine. Nonetheless, Palestine had always been included in historic Syria. From the Arab perspective, because these areas were not specifically excluded from the Arab sphere, they were by understanding to come under Arab control. Furthermore, McMahon and Hussein had agreed that land not purely Arab in makeup was to be excluded from the understanding. The British argued that because Palestine was neither completely Arab nor Muslim, it was not part of the agreement. The Arabs, however, saw things differently. They argued that Palestine was overwhelmingly Arab and should, therefore, be part of Arab-controlled areas.

Of course, events not soon after the McMahon-Hussein correspondence ceased would make many of these discrepancies moot. The Balfour Declaration certainly seemed to fly in the face of Hussein's understanding of McMahon's agreement, but even that declaration contains a phrase that implies protection of the rights of the existing Arab inhabitants of Palestine. British prime minister David Lloyd George's insistence at the 1919 Paris Peace Conference that Great Britain maintain control of Palestine (and Iraq) further demonstrated the British unwillingness to honor the agreements that McMahon had made. The final insult, in the eyes of the Arabs, was the League of Nations mandate that granted the British de facto control over Palestine. It is certainly easy to see how the McMahon-Hussein correspondence buoyed the spirits of Arab nationalists and how its aftermath sowed the seeds of a deep-seated distrust and enmity toward the West.

PAUL G. PIERPAOLI JR.

See also

Balfour Declaration; Sykes-Picot Agreement; United Kingdom, Middle East Policy; Zionism

References

Kent, Marian, ed. *The Great Powers and the End of the Ottoman Empire.* London: Routledge, 1996.

Smith, Charles D. *Palestine and the Arab-Israeli Conflict: A History with Documents.* 6th ed. New York: Bedford/St. Martin's, 2006.

Tauber, Eliezer. *The Arab Movements in World War I.* London: Frank Cass, 1993.

Mecca

Makka al-Mukarama (the Blessed), or Mecca, is a city in Saudi Arabia with a population of approximately 1.31 million people. It is home to the al-Masjid al-Haram (Sacred Mosque), the holiest Muslim place on Earth. Mecca is located in western Saudi Arabia about 50 miles east of the Red Sea. Presently, the king of Saudi Arabia is the official protector of Mecca (as well as Medina, also in Saudi Arabia). The king appoints the governor of Mecca. In years past, this role had been allocated to a sharif family in the region, namely the Hashemites.

The importance and centrality of Mecca to Islam is hard to overemphasize. When Muslim pray (five times per day), they are required to do so facing Mecca, regardless of what part of the world they inhabit. The direction of Mecca is known as the *qiblah* in Arabic. Also, all Muslims must journey to Mecca at least once in their lifetimes, assuming they have the physical and financial ability to do so. This is known as the hajj. The hajj and Saudi Arabia's historical significance as the cradle of Islam enhanced the country's importance in the Muslim world. The management of the hajj is a daunting logistical and sometimes politically delicate task. Many religious scholars and students have traveled to Mecca, remaining

Muslim pilgrims circle the Kaaba at the al-Masjid al-Haram (Sacred Mosque) in the holy city of Mecca before sundown prayer, January 3, 2006. (Ali Haider/Corbis)

there for periods of study and contributing to the cross-fertilization of ideas within the Muslim world.

The huge Sacred Mosque in Mecca surrounds a large building of granite known as the Kaaba (House of God), which Muslims believe was first constructed by Adam and then was destroyed in the Flood. Then Ibrahim (Abraham) and his son Ismail (Ishmael) reconstructed the Kaaba, which was also a place of worship in the polytheistic practices of pre-Islamic Arabs. At the eastern corner of the Kaaba is the black stone, of meteoric origin, that is covered by an embroidered cloth, the *kiswah*. The Kaaba has been revered since before the founding of Islam, when the Quraysh of Mecca were its custodians. When Muhammad was living in Mecca he received the Revelations of Allah (God) and accepted his role as the Prophet. In 630 the Prophet returned to Mecca in the Muslim conquest of that city, and the holy site at the Kaaba was reclaimed. Many Muslims choose to travel to Mecca during the Dhu al-Hijjah, or the final (twelfth) month in the Islamic calendar. At the peak of Dhu al-Hijjah, as many as 800,000 worshipers gather in the massive public worship spaces both inside and outside the mosque. It is estimated that approximately 3 million Muslims per year make the pilgrimage to Mecca. In the early 1980s, al-Masjid al-Haram underwent a major expansion and renovation, funded by the Saudi monarchy. Among the many improvements was the installation of elevators, escalators, and air conditioning.

Because of the sacredness of Mecca and its shrines, non-Muslims are barred entrance to the city. Rail lines and roads leading to the city are patrolled constantly to ensure that no one enters Mecca without sound reason. In 1979 the Sacred Mosque was taken over by a neo-Wahhabi rebel, Juhayman al-Utaybi, along with his brother-in-law and several hundred supporters. They failed to capture the king at prayers but took many hostages. The event shook Saudi Arabia, and foreign forces had to aid Saudi forces to eject the terrorists. More recently, Mecca was the site of a meeting designed to forge a truce between Hamas and Fatah fighters of the Palestinian Authority (PA).

PAUL G. PIERPAOLI JR.

See also
Saudi Arabia

References
Bianchi, Robert. *Guests of God: Pilgrimage and Politics in the Islamic World.* New York: Oxford University Press, 2004.
Peters, F. E. *The Hajj: The Muslim Pilgrimage to Mecca and the Holy Places.* Princeton, NJ: Princeton University Press, 1996.
———. *Mecca: A Literary History of the Muslim Holy Land.* Princeton, NJ: Princeton University Press, 1994.
Yamani, Mai. *Cradle of Islam: The Hijaz and the Quest for Arabian Identity.* London: Tauris, 2004.

Medina

City located in western Saudi Arabia and considered the second most holy site in Islam, after only Mecca. Situated north of Mecca and about 110 miles from the Red Sea in the Hejaz area of Saudi Arabia, Medina's current population is approximately 925,000 people. Medina is located on the site of an oasis that probably dates to antiquity. As such it was a natural gathering place, and today the area is known for its agricultural products, including dates, wheat, and fruit.

The city's name in the pre-Islamic period was Yathrib, and it was renamed Madinat al-Nabi (City of the Prophet) after the Prophet Muhammad brought the Muslim community from Mecca in the hijrah and developed that community religiously and politically. A document known as the Constitution of Medina formalized that community.

The Battle of Uhud was fought near Medina in 625 and is variously regarded as a temporary setback or a defeat for the Muslims who fought the Meccan forces in that battle. Medina is the location of the Prophet Muhammad's burial place. Later, Muslim rulers beautified the first mosque of the Muslims and the Prophet's tomb visited by Muslim pilgrims. The first four caliphs remained in Mecca, and then the Muslim capital shifted to Damascus in Syria.

Medina is surrounded by walls with periodic bastions and nine gates that allow access to and from the city. The Masjid al-Nabawi (Mosque of the Prophet) encloses Muhammad's tomb, which is known as the Qubbat al-Nabi (Prophet's Dome or Green Dome). The Mosque of the Prophet was erected next to Muhammad's home, and over the years expansions saw the large mosque encapsulate the home site. Medina also contains Masjid Quba, believed to be the first Islamic mosque ever built.

Like the Masjid al-Haram (Sacred Mosque) in Mecca, the Mosque of the Prophet is under the protectorate of the Saudi monarchy, and the Saudi king retains the title of custodian of the two holy mosques. This role had been traditionally left to high-ranking families who descended from the Prophet, the sharifs. Medina had become important to the Ottoman government as the terminus of the Hejaz railway, and Sharif Hussein ibn Ali fought the Ottoman troops stationed there in his reconquest of the Hejaz in the Arab Rebellion.

PAUL G. PIERPAOLI JR. AND SHERIFA ZUHUR

See also
Hashemites; Hussein ibn Ali, Sharif of Mecca; Mecca

References
Peters, F. E. *The Hajj: The Muslim Pilgrimage to Mecca and the Holy Places.* Princeton, NJ: Princeton University Press, 1996.
Yamani, Mai. *Cradle of Islam: The Hijaz and the Quest for Arabian Identity.* London: Tauris, 2004.

Meir, Golda
Born: May 3, 1898
Died: December 8, 1978

Prominent Israeli political leader and prime minister (1969–1974). Born in Kiev, then part of Russia, on May 3, 1898, Golda Mabovitch was one of eight children, five of whom died in childhood. Her father

Golda Meir, Israeli political leader and prime minister (1969–1974). (Library of Congress)

immigrated to the United States in 1903, and the remainder of the family joined him in Milwaukee in 1906. Intent on becoming a teacher, she enrolled at the Wisconsin State Normal School in 1916 but stayed there just one year, never finishing her degree. That same year she became an active member in the Zionist labor movement where she met Morris Meyerson, whom she married in 1917.

Golda Meyerson and her husband immigrated to Palestine in 1921. The Meyersons worked on a kibbutz, and Golda became active in the Histadrut, Israel's labor movement. She joined its executive community in 1934, became the head of its political department in 1940, and helped raise funds internationally for Jewish settlement in Palestine.

Shortly before the 1948–1949 Israeli War of Independence, Meyerson twice met secretly with Jordan's King Abdullah. While she was unsuccessful in averting a Jordanian invasion of the Jewish state, these secret contacts proved useful in limiting Jordanian participation in the war. Such secret meetings became the norm in Israeli-Jordanian relations. During the war Meyerson traveled to the United States, where she raised $50 million for Israel from private citizens. Following the war Israel's first prime minister, David Ben-Gurion, sent her to Moscow as Israel's ambassador. On his urging, she adopted the Hebrew surname Meir, which means "to burn brightly."

Elected to the Knesset (Israeli parliament) in 1949 as a member of Mapai (the Israel Workers Party), Meir was immediately appointed minister of labor by Ben-Gurion. Her greatest task was the resettlement of hundreds of thousands of Jewish refugees who immigrated to Israel during these years. The new arrivals, 685,000 of whom arrived in her first two years in office, lived in large tent cities, while Meir marshaled the new state's scant resources to construct housing for them, instruct them in Hebrew, and integrate them into Israeli society. Over the next six years, she gained a reputation as an aggressive politician, a powerful speaker, and a decisive manager.

Ben-Gurion, who once called Meir "the only man in my cabinet," forced moderate Moshe Sharett to resign as foreign minister on June 18, 1956, and appointed Meir in his place. She held that post until 1965, gaining international fame as one of the few women to hold a prominent position in international affairs. Ben-Gurion, who expected Sharett to oppose war, believed that Meir would support his decision to go to war with Egypt in collusion with France and Britain in 1956, and this proved correct. While uninvolved in planning the war, Meir supported Ben-Gurion's decision to take military action to break Egypt's blockade of Eilat, Israel's Red Sea port.

As foreign minister, Meir worked to strengthen Israel's relationship with the new nations of Africa, to which she dispatched a series of aid missions. This was possible only because Israel's victory in the 1956 Sinai Campaign had secured Israel's right of transit through the Red Sea. Meir hoped to build bridges between Israel and other developing nations and share Israel's practical experience in agriculture and land reclamation. As with many Israeli leaders, she believed that trade with Africa would prove vital to Israel and help offset the Arab economic embargo. She was also acutely conscious of Israel's desperate need for friendly nations that would support it in the United Nations (UN) and international affairs.

Meir also worked to improve U.S.-Israeli relations damaged by the Sinai Campaign, but she met a generally cold reception from President Dwight D. Eisenhower's administration. President John F. Kennedy's administration proved different, and Meir developed a particularly good relationship with Kennedy. In a conversation with Meir in December 1962, Kennedy first referred to a "special relationship" between Israel and the United States that resembled the relationship between the United States and Great Britain.

Along with Israeli ambassador Abba Eban, Meir convinced Kennedy to sell sophisticated Hawk antiaircraft missiles to Israel. This sale ended the U.S. embargo on arms sales to Israel and opened the door to further arms transfers. Presidents Lyndon B. Johnson and Richard M. Nixon both increased arms sales to Israel, and after the 1967 Six-Day War and a French embargo on arms to the Jewish state, the United States replaced France as Israel's primary arms supplier.

Due to worsening health, Meir resigned as foreign minister in 1965 but continued to serve in the Knesset, and the members of Mapai elected her the party's secretary-general. In that capacity she helped orchestrate the merger of Mapai with several smaller parties that created the new Labor Party, which dominated Israeli politics for the next decade as Mapai had for the previous two decades.

On February 26, 1969, the ruling Labor Party elected Meir prime minister following the death of Levi Eshkol. Meir, the fourth prime minister in Israel's brief history, faced daunting challenges, including Israeli national security imperatives and Middle Eastern instability. Her efforts to trade recently conquered land for peace with Egypt, Syria, and Jordan failed, and terrorist attacks and cross-border raids into Israel increased.

Skirmishing with Egypt escalated into the War of Attrition, which lasted through August 1970 and caused the deaths of 700 Israelis. Meir insisted on Israeli retaliation for any attacks and apparently hoped that increasingly successful Israeli commando raids and air strikes would force Egyptian president Gamal Abdel Nasser into either peace negotiations or resignation. Meir insisted that peace precede withdrawal. Nasser, who had arranged the Arab League's September 1967 resolution that stated there would be no peace, no recognition, and no territorial negotiations with Israel, remained intransigent and insisted on the return of all occupied territory as a prelude to any peace negotiations. A U.S.-brokered cease-fire ended the skirmishing in August 1970, but tensions hardly lessened, and Soviet arms shipments to Egypt increased. The following month, Syria invaded Jordan to support a Palestinian rebellion but withdrew its forces after Meir, encouraged by the United States, threatened an attack on Syria.

Meir increasingly coordinated Israel's foreign policy with the United States, and during her tenure as prime minister the special relationship between Israel and the United States blossomed. U.S. arms sales to Israel increased, while Israel shared important intelligence information with the United States and allowed U.S. technicians to examine sophisticated Soviet weapons systems captured by the Israeli Army during the War of Attrition. Meir developed a close relationship with President Nixon and Henry Kissinger, his key foreign policy adviser. Mired in Vietnam, Nixon and Kissinger both came to see Israel as a vital ally in the Cold War. Despite this increasingly close relationship with the United States, Meir managed to convince the Soviet Union to allow some Russian Jews to immigrate to Israel.

Anwar Sadat, who assumed power following Nasser's death on September 28, 1970, offered to reduce Egyptian troop strength west of the Suez Canal if Israel withdrew its forces 24 miles (40 km) from the canal. This came on the heels of the War of Attrition, and few of Meir's advisers trusted the Egyptian proposal, which would allow Egypt to reopen the canal but give nothing except promises to Israel. Despite protests led by opposition leader Menachem Begin, Meir indicated her interest in returning most of the territory occupied by Israel in the 1967 war in exchange for peace and limited the establishment of Israeli settlements in the occupied territories to a mere handful. The main stumbling block remained her refusal to withdraw from occupied territory as a prelude to negotiating a peace settlement, although other factors including the rivalry of Egypt's and Israel's superpower patrons also hindered the negotiations, which ended without result.

Tensions with Egypt and Syria increased steadily until the morning of October 6, 1973, when Israel's director of intelligence warned of an imminent attack. Concerned about Israel's international reputation, Meir rejected proposals to launch a preemptive attack, as Israel had done in 1967. That afternoon, as Meir met with her cabinet, Egyptian and Syrian forces invaded the Sinai and the Golan Heights, driving back the surprised and outnumbered Israeli Army units. While some leaders recommended deep retreats on both fronts, Meir overruled them. The Israeli Army held fast, retreating only when forced back by the furious Egyptian and Syrian assaults. The Soviet Union airlifted and shipped arms to sustain the Arab offensive, and the United States countered with an airlift that supplied vital equipment to Israel. Following a series of early defeats, Israeli counteroffensives finally contained both Arab forces and left Israel in possession of additional Arab territory on the Syrian front and in Egypt. Israeli forces crossed the canal and had almost cut off two Egyptian divisions east of the canal from their bases. Neither the Soviet Union nor the United States wished to see Egypt completely defeated, and under their pressure a cease-fire went into effect on October 24.

Although the war was won, the early setbacks, surprise of the invasion, heavy casualties, and rumors that Meir had considered using nuclear weapons during the first days of the war tarnished her administration. A special investigating committee, the Agranat Commission, cleared Meir of responsibility for the near disaster, blaming the head of military intelligence and the Israel Defense Forces (IDF) chief of staff, but she remained under constant attack from opposition politicians, particularly Likud leader Begin. Despite this, Meir led her party to another victory in the December 1973 elections and established a ruling coalition despite Labor's loss of six seats in the Knesset and the growing strength of the rival Likud Party.

In the following months, thanks to Kissinger's shuttle diplomacy, Meir negotiated cease-fire and disengagement agreements with Egypt and Syria. The complicated negotiations to extricate the trapped Egyptian Army paved the way for future negotiations that finally produced a lasting peace between Israel and Egypt. Meir resigned on June 3, 1974, and Yitzhak Rabin succeeded her as prime minister. Meir returned to private life and died of leukemia in Jerusalem on December 8, 1978.

Stephen K. Stein

See also

Abdullah I, King of Jordan; Attrition, War of; Begin, Menachem; Ben-Gurion, David; Eban, Abba Solomon; Israel; Kennedy, John Fitzgerald; Kissinger, Henry Alfred; Nasser, Gamal Abdel; Rabin, Yitzhak; Sadat, Anwar; United States, Middle East Policy; Yom Kippur War

References

Mann, Peggy. *Golda: The Life of Israel's Prime Minister.* New York: Coward, McCann and Geoghegan, 1971.

Martin, Ralph G. *Golda Meir: The Romantic Years.* New York: Scribner, 1988.

Meir, Golda. *My Life.* New York: Putnam, 1975.

Meretz

Israeli political coalition that arose in 1992 as an alignment of parties from the center-left. It brought together Shinui (Change), formed in 1974; Ratz (Citizens' Rights Movement), formed in 1973; and Mapam (United Workers' Party), formed in 1948. The party platform advocated a negotiated two-state solution to the Israeli-Palestinian conflict, the separation of religion and state, and an emphasis on human rights rooted in peace, pluralism, and democracy.

In 1997 Ratz, Mapam, and part of Shinui united as a formal party. In 2003 Meretz merged with Shahar, the ex-Labor faction of Yael Dayan and Yossi Beilin, taking the name Yahad, both an acronym for Social Democratic Israel and the Hebrew word for "together." Led since 2004 by Beilin (who succeeded Yossi Sarid and Shulamit Aloni), the Meretz party renamed itself Meretz-Yahad in 2005.

Meretz's principal ideological and institutional ancestor is the leftist-socialist Mapam, but it supports the kibbutz movement and a welfare state within the context of a socially responsible entrepreneurial economy. Meretz-Yahad is best known for its commitment to the peace process. Meretz politicians served in the Yitzhak Rabin, Shimon Peres, and Ehud Barak governments. In the wake of the failed 2000 Camp David and Taba negotiations and the Sec-

ond (al-Aqsa) Intifada, Beilin and Yasser Abed Rabo unveiled the Geneva Initiative in 2003, a model final-status agreement intended to show that there were partners for peace on both sides among politicians and the public alike.

Meretz-Yahad regarded the 2005 Gaza withdrawal as necessary but not sufficient. It urged prompt resumption of peace negotiations. When the latter prospect dimmed following the Palestinian Hamas electoral victory in 2006, the party proposed an international trusteeship for the West Bank.

JAMES WALD

See also

Arab Socialism; Barak, Ehud; Hamas; Intifada, Second; Labor Party; Rabin, Yitzhak; Sharon, Ariel; Zionist/Israeli Socialism

References

Beilin, Yossi. *The Path to Geneva: The Quest for a Permanent Agreement, 1996–2004*. New York: RDV Books, 2004.

Merhav, Peretz. *The Israeli Left: History, Problems, Documents*. San Diego and New York: A. S. Barnes, 1980.

Merkava Tank

The Merkava is the main battle tank (MBT) of the Israel Defense Forces (IDF) since its introduction in May 1979. Merkava means

A Meretz Party supporter, displaying the party's logo on his t-shirt, talks to a voter outside a polling station in Jerusalem, April 1999. (Amos Ben Gershom/Israeli Government Press Office)

An Israeli-built Merkava Mark III main battle tank. (iStockPhoto.com)

"chariot" in Hebrew. After the French embargoed sales of military hardware to Israel as a consequence of the 1967 Six-Day War, the IDF turned to Britain in search of armored vehicles. In 1969, however, the British bowed to Arab pressure and cancelled the development of the Chieftain tank, which was to serve as Israel's MBT. This left the Israelis short of critical armored vehicles during the Yom Kippur War (1973), which nearly saw the defeat of IDF forces. During that conflict, the Israelis had to deploy a number of different tanks, including those provided by the United States at the last moment.

As early as 1970, IDF officials had recognized the need for Israel to build its own MBTs in order not to be dependent on foreign suppliers for this critical weapons system, and they began preliminary development. The Yom Kippur War merely sped the process along. The design of the Merkava MBT was inspired by Major General Yisrael "Talik" Tal and took into consideration the unique features of Israeli warfare. It was also based on the lessons learned from past wars. The two primary concerns were firepower and crew protection.

There are four models of the basic design. The Mark I was introduced in 1978 and incorporated a number of innovative features. The main hull has a low sloping profile to decrease the chances of a successful impact by missiles and tank shells. The crew compartment and engine are located to the rear of the chassis. This design

increases the tank's ability to sustain and survive battle damage. There is a rear-mounted escape hatch to help ensure the survival of the crew in action. This compartment can be used to transport infantry or to carry extra ammunition.

The Merkava I mounted a 105-mm gun. It was also armed with three 7.62-mm machine guns. It had a crew of four, weighed about 59 tons, and had a road speed of about 29 miles per hour (mph). It had full nuclear-biological-chemical (NBC) protection, a digital fire-control system, and a laser rangefinder.

The Mark II entered service in 1983 and saw an upgrade in armor with additional composite armor on the front and sides, an improved fire-control system, and a more efficient transmission. The Mark III, introduced in 1989, was a major redesign to accommodate a larger 120-mm smoothbore main gun. It also mounts three machine guns. The Mark III has a longer hull, more powerful engine, new suspension system, new fire-control system, improved explosive-reactive armor, new vision equipment, and new NBC package. It weighs 61 tons and has a road speed of some 34 mph. The Mark IV Merkava is entirely made in Israel and incorporates an improved fire-control system and the capability to use the Lahat missile.

The IDF deployed the Merkava in its 1982 invasion of Lebanon, where it performed well against Soviet-built Syrian armor. Although

7 Merkavas were lost, 6 of these were because of mines. The Merkava has been used extensively in Israel's attempts to control the intifadas in the occupied territories and has demonstrated its ability to provide effective fire support with its integral mortar and machine guns. The Merkava's vaunted reputation, however, was seriously tarnished during Israel's 2006 incursion into southern Lebanon, where Hezbollah fighters reportedly damaged or destroyed 20 of the tanks.

RALPH MARTIN BAKER

See also

Israel, Defense Industry; Israel Defense Forces; Lebanon, Israeli Invasion of; Tank Warfare; Yom Kippur War

References

Gabriel, Richard. *Operation Peace for Galilee: The Israeli-PLO War in Lebanon.* New York: Farrar, Straus and Giroux, 1985.

Katz, Samuel M. *Merkava, Israel's Chariot of Fire.* Hong Kong: Concord, 1995.

———. *Merkava, Main Battle Tank, Mks I, II & III.* Oxford, UK: Osprey, 2001.

Middle East Policies

See China, People's Republic of, Middle East Policy; Czechoslovakia, Middle East Policy; France, Middle East Policy; Germany, Federal Republic of, Middle East Policy; Soviet Union and Russia, Middle East Policy; Turkey, Middle East Policy; United Kingdom, Middle East Policy; United States, Middle East Policy

Middle East Regional Defense Organizations

When the Clement Attlee government came to power in Britain in July 1945, British foreign minister Ernest Bevin moved to end British colonial rule in much of the Middle East. To that end he hoped to replace older British protectorate agreements with Iraq, Jordan, and Egypt with bilateral treaties that would reduce British commitments without giving up influence in the region. Talks for new agreements were frustrating, however. The Iraqis backed out at the last minute and did not sign the 1947 Portsmouth Agreement. The Egyptians were also unready to accept Britain's new terms and demanded the removal of British troops. While the Iraqi rejection did not pose any immediate difficulties for the British, Egypt's demand jeopardized Britain's main stronghold in the Middle East.

Britain's inability to reach a bilateral defense agreement with Egypt led the British and Americans to promulgate regional defense organizations instead. The latter included the Middle East Command (MEC), established in October 1951, and the 1953 Middle East Defense Organization (MEDO). It was believed that the organizations would commit Egypt to regional defense without subjecting it to British dominance. Nevertheless, the Egyptian monarchy and successive revolutionary regimes rejected any formal military link with the West.

Efforts to create a regional defense structure with Egypt at its core ended in May 1953 following a visit by U.S. secretary of state John Foster Dulles to the Middle East. Discussions with regional leaders—mainly with Egyptian officials—convinced Dulles that there was no chance of including Egypt in a regional defense organization. He suggested that a different country should be the linchpin of the organization, and Iraq seemed a viable alternative.

At the time, Turkey and Iraq were negotiating a mutual defense agreement. Cultural ties between Iraq and Turkey made such a pact a natural union. With tacit encouragement from Washington and with the understanding that the parties to a regional defense organization would be rewarded with military aid, the two governments agreed to expand the treaty and to use it as a platform from which to launch a regional defense organization that would include Turkey, Pakistan, and Iraq. Turkey and Pakistan had signed a defense agreement earlier, so the proposed regional defense organization was a logical extension.

In February 1955 Iraq signed a defense agreement with Turkey, the initial step toward the establishment of what became known as the 1955 Baghdad Pact that included Iraq, Turkey, Iran, Pakistan, and Great Britain. Washington thereupon announced that it would strengthen the Iraqi army, which stood on the front line against the Soviet Union.

Iraq took a leading role in the initiative, not simply from fear of the Soviets, and agreed to take part in a Western-oriented regional defense agreement so as to claim regional dominance over Egypt. At the time, Iraq was concerned about the new government in Egypt as well. Indeed, the Iraqis deeply resented the establishment of the Arab League under Cairo's auspices and saw an Iraqi-based defense organization, the headquarters of which was to be located in Baghdad, as an effective counterbalance to Egypt's push for regional hegemony.

Egyptian president Gamal Abdel Nasser did perceive the pact as a challenge to Egypt's position in the Arab world and was still reeling from criticism over the humiliating clause in the October 1954 Anglo-Egyptian agreement that would allow British troops access to Egyptian bases in case of war. Thus, the Egyptian leader fought back by suppressing opponents and adopting a strong Pan-Arab line. He devoted considerable energy to preventing any expansion of the Baghdad Pact. Waving the banner of Pan-Arab nationalism and resorting to manipulation and even violence, he spared no effort to ensure that other Arab states did not come under the Western sphere of influence.

Nasser's struggle against the Baghdad Pact stirred trouble for the pro-Western Jordanian and Lebanese regimes. His agitation reached its zenith in July 1958 when the Iraqi regime was toppled by anti-Western elements, and the Jordanian regime faced a similar danger. The United States and Britain were determined to prevent Jordan and Lebanon from falling under Nasser's influence, and American and British forces were sent to Beirut and Amman, respectively, in July 1958 to prop up the pro-Western governments. In March 1959 the new Iraqi republic withdrew from the Baghdad

Pact, which then became known as the Central Treaty Organization (CENTO). In the end, however, Nasser had his way, as the Baghdad Pact lost its main pillar, Iraq, and never expanded in the way the United States and Great Britain had envisioned.

DAVID TAL

See also
Arab Nationalism; Baghdad Pact; Iran; Iraq; Jordan; Lebanon; Nasser, Gamal Abdel; Turkey, Middle East Policy; United Kingdom, Middle East Policy; United States, Middle East Policy

References
Hahn, Peter L. *The United States, Great Britain and Egypt, 1945–1956: Strategy and Diplomacy in the Early Cold War.* Chapel Hill: University of North Carolina Press, 1991.

Podeh, Elie. *The Quest for Hegemony in the Arab World: The Struggle over the Baghdad Pact.* New York: Brill, 2003.

Middle East Treaty Organization
See Baghdad Pact

Mines and Mine Warfare, Land
Mines are used in land warfare for much the same reason they are used in naval warfare: to restrict or deter an enemy from using or moving through a given area. Land mines saw only limited use in the early Arab-Israeli fighting of 1948–1949, with Israeli units using them primarily as harassment weapons. But Arab armies used them increasingly as the Arab-Israeli conflict advanced. After the 1956 Suez Crisis, Egyptian strong points were protected by extensive minefields.

Before the 1973 Yom Kippur War, most Arab armies neglected the basic principle that the only effective minefields are those covered by fire. As a result, the Israelis were generally able to either avoid or quickly clear a path through most Arab minefields. After the Yom Kippur War, mines, primarily improvised mines, had become a favorite weapon of terrorist groups, used to harass Israeli forces operating outside of Israel. For example, Palestinian and Islamic militant groups in Lebanon regularly employed mines placed in locations frequented by Israeli forces simply to inflict casualties.

The Arab-Israeli wars were primarily wars of movement in which mechanized forces conducted most of the fighting. In consonance with that, most of the mines employed were antivehicle mines, intended to damage or destroy enemy armored vehicles. Antipersonnel mines were found primarily in the immediate vicinity of strong points or the entry points of areas where paratroopers or commandoes might be expected to land. Most of the mines were contact or pressure mines. That is, the target had to make contact with the detonating system (contact mine) or inflict sufficient

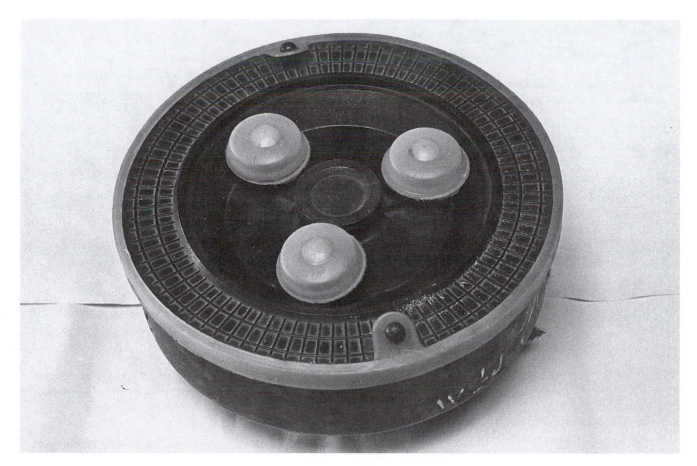

A plastic antivehicle mine of Egyptian manufacture, 1970. (Moshe Milner/Israeli Government Press Office)

Polish troops assigned to the United Nations Disengagement Observer Force sweep for mines in the Golan Heights, 1974. (Corel)

pressure on the earth above the mine to activate the detonation system. Pressure mines could be set to detonate only if a tank or loaded truck passed overhead. Many of the Soviet-supplied mines used by Egypt and Syria were constructed of wood or other nonmetallic materials to reduce their detectability by traditional mine-detection equipment. While a majority of the mines were of the surface blast type, some (such as the Soviet-supplied OZM-3 mines) launched into the air for an air burst to expand the burst and casualty radius.

The 1956 Arab-Israeli conflict saw little employment of mines and minefields. The Egyptian stronghold of Sharm al-Sheikh was protected by a ring of minefields employing World War II–era mines. Many had been recovered from World War II minefields, and others were acquired from redundant war surplus supplies. These had a high failure rate and were often improperly laid. The Syrians typically employed mines around fixed positions, but their expectation to be on the offensive limited their employment of mines. Moreover, few Western nations would sell mines to the countries of the Middle East. Most of Israel's land mines were derivatives of British mines of World War II. Some were ex-German mines acquired from East European countries. However, as with their Arab opponents, the Israeli emphasis on offensive action limited their employment of mines, although Israeli engineer troops were extremely proficient in mine-clearing operations.

The 1967 Six-Day War was also one of shock and movement. Only Jordan employed mines to any extent, primarily to protect key strong points west of Jerusalem. As in 1956, Egypt deployed minefields around Sharm al-Sheikh and the Mitla Pass, but neither Syria nor Israel deployed mines extensively. The stalemate that followed Israel's 1956 victory changed that situation. Syria deployed extensive minefields along its border with Israel, Egypt deployed significant minefields along the Suez Canal's west bank, and Israel deployed limited minefields around its strong points along the Suez Canal (the Bar-Lev Line). One of the indicators of the coming Egyptian assault in October 1973 that Israeli intelligence missed was the Egyptian engineers clearing paths through their own minefields to expand access to the canal's bank.

Mine warfare played only a minor role in the three conventional Arab-Israeli wars. Egypt, Israel, and Syria lost few personnel and a handful of tanks from entering minefields, in some cases their own, but in general mines and minefields achieved little purpose in those wars. This changed with Israel's 1982 invasion of Lebanon. That country's Islamic militant groups received extensive training as well as financial and material support from Iran's Islamic regime. Tehran provided land mines and ordnance expertise that its surrogates in Lebanon, primarily the Shia militant group Hezbollah, employed to great effect. Operating at night, these groups planted mines in roads and fields that the Israelis had previously cleared. They also employed remotely detonated mines against Israeli patrols. Although these tactics did not inflict significant casualties, particularly in comparison to the later suicide bombing attacks, they certainly added to the tensions and costs of the Israeli occupation. Hezbollah strong points remain heavily protected by minefields to deter Israeli commando raids, as does the Israeli-Lebanon border to prevent Hezbollah infiltration and attacks on Israel's northern settlements.

Mines remain an effective area denial weapon. However, they increasingly have become a terror weapon that afflicts more civilian than military casualties. Both sides of the Arab-Israeli conflict have escalated their employment of mines over the years as the stalemate that followed the 1967 and 1973 wars has continued. Outside conventional military forces, they have been supplanted by ad hoc weapons such as roadside bombs, improvised explosive devices (IEDs), and suicide bombers.

CARL OTIS SCHUSTER

See also
Bar-Lev Line; Hezbollah; Improvised Explosive Devices; Israeli War of Independence, Overview; Lebanon, Israeli Invasion of; Mines and Mine Warfare, Sea; Six-Day War; Suicide Bombings; Yom Kippur War

References
Asher, Jerry, and Eric Hammel. *Duel for the Golan: The 100-Hour Battle That Saved Israel.* Pacifica, CA: Pacifica Press, 1987.
Barler, A. J. *The Six Day War.* New York: Ballantine, 1974.

Dunstan, Simon. *The Yom Kippur War, 1973.* 2 vols. Westport, CT: Praeger, 2005.

Herzog, Chaim. *The Arab-Israeli Wars: War and Peace in the Middle East from the War of Independence to Lebanon.* Westminster, MD: Random House, 1984.

———. *The War of Atonement: October, 1973.* Boston: Little, Brown, 1975.

Isby, David C. *Weapons and Tactics of the Soviet Army.* London: Jane's, 1981.

Rabinovic, Itamar. *The War for Lebanon, 1970–1985.* Ithaca, NY: Cornell University Press, 1985.

Mines and Mine Warfare, Sea

Naval mines have been a common feature of warfare in the Middle East, particularly since the creation of modern naval establishments in many of the region's states from the early 1970s. From the onset of conflict between Israel and the Arab states, naval mines proved a cheap and effective method of disrupting the economic and military supply lines of an opponent.

Following World War II, Egypt was the region's major naval power. The new Israeli Navy was thus forced to operate defensively, limiting itself to keeping coastal waters free of surface threats and mine attacks. The navies of Egypt and Syria possessed considerable minelaying capability and used it to good effect, although it does not seem to have been used during the 1948–1949 Israeli War of Independence. Even by 1956, the Israeli Navy numbered only 13 ships with a limited minesweeping capability.

The Israeli Navy played only a limited role in the 1967 Six-Day War. The short duration of the war did not allow the Arab nations sufficient time to lay effective mine fields along the Israeli coast. Both sides nonetheless mined the Suez Canal. The bulk of the mines available were standard moored contact mines, which were moored to the bottom and could only be detonated by contact with the target. They were supplemented by moored magnetic mines, which are detonated by a ship's magnetic signature (the magnetic influence of its metal hull and machinery). Both Egypt and Israel also employed bottom-influence mines. The Egyptians had Soviet-supplied AMD (air-dropped) and KMD (surface ship–laid) mines. Most Egyptian bottom mines were either magnetic or acoustic. The latter was detonated by the ship's machinery noises. The Israelis reportedly employed bottom-pressure mines that were detonated by the water pressure generated below and ahead of a ship or submarine as it approached or passed over the mine.

The Yom Kippur War of 1973 saw much more extensive use of naval mines. In that war the Egyptians sought not to engage Israeli naval units but rather to disrupt Israel's lines of communication through mine warfare. Toward that end, before the war Egypt sent two destroyers with auxiliary support to Aden. Then, five days before the start of hostilities, these ships blockaded all shipping entering or leaving the Bab-El-Mandab Straits. Egyptian leaders intended that the squadron remain in place for more than six months, cutting off Israeli shipping from the port of Eilat. Auxiliary ships were to supply the squadron.

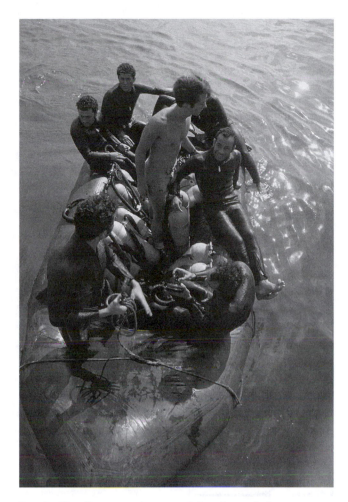

Egyptian Navy divers preparing to search for mines and other obstructions in the Suez Canal near Ismailiyya, Egypt, November 1974. (Jonathan Blair/Corbis)

The Egyptian destroyers were indeed able to lay a large number of mines off Eilat in the Gulf of Aqaba. In this operation the Egyptians relied on intelligence provided from Arab merchant ships, and despite the fact that they were observed by ships from the United States and the United Kingdom, they were able to operate freely. In the first few days of the war, Egyptian mines sank perhaps 48,000 tons of shipping bound for Eilat.

One of the chief Egyptian war aims was to disrupt Israeli oil imports. The Egyptians also attempted to blockade Israeli ports in the Mediterranean. Israeli warships equipped with Gabriel missiles were able to disrupt this process, however.

The Israeli Navy retaliated by instituting its own blockade of the Morgan oilfields in the Gulf of Suez. This forced Egypt to purchase oil abroad even though it was readily available on its own soil. Both sides laid many mines in the Suez Canal during the conflict.

As part of the peace agreement ending the war, an international task force was established to clear all the mines from the area. The United States was to lead the effort, but British, French, and Egyptian forces were also involved. The commander of Task Force 65, Rear Admiral Brian McCauley, who had overseen the sweeping of

A member of a multinational Explosive Ordnance Disposal team studies an Iraqi mine washed up on a beach in March 1991. The ordnance is one of many left in the wake of Operation DESERT STORM. (U.S. Department of Defense)

U.S. mines off the North Vietnamese port of Haiphong in 1973, commanded the operation to remove both mines and explosives that had been laid to damage the canal facilities. Most of the U.S. minesweeping in the canal was carried out by helicopters operating from two assault ships. Most of the mines were cleared within one month, and ultimately more than 9,000 pieces of ordnance were removed. The canal was reopened in December 1974.

The commercial sea lanes of the region were further disrupted with the outbreak of war between Iran and Iraq in 1980. With the land war degenerating into a stalemate that appeared to have more in common with the trench warfare of World War I, both sides turned to economic warfare and mounted attacks on oil tankers and port facilities, including those of neutral nations such as Kuwait. The United States responded by allowing Kuwaiti tankers to operate under the U.S. flag. Iran in particular replied with a widespread mining campaign in the Straits of Hormuz. Iranian revolutionary guards laid these moored contact mines using small outboard motor–powered vessels.

Initially, American forces did not react to this threat. By 1984, however, there were further problems in the region, for Libya had mined parts of the Red Sea's commercial shipping lanes. Nearly 20 vessels reported hitting mines, although none of the ships were sunk.

These incidents prompted the formation of a seven-nation mine-sweeping force led by the United States and the United Kingdom. The Egyptian government recognized the need to improve its navy's minesweeping capability and ordered its navy to participate. Helicopters played an important part in this operation and employed state-of-the-art sonar equipment. One squadron flew from an amphibious transport, the other from the port of Jiddah. However, very few mines were detected. Suspicions centered on a Libyan container ship as the minelayer.

In 1987 the U.S. government launched Operation EARNEST WILL, which lasted from 1987 to 1989. The U.S. Navy deployed an amphibious dock ship with four minesweepers and a number of small Navy SEAL craft. When it became apparent that Iran was targeting vessels flying under any flag, European nations joined the effort. This multinational effort managed to clear defined routes into major ports. At the same time, aircraft surveillance monitored Iranian activity. These operations culminated in U.S. tracking of the Iranian cargo ship *Iran Ajar,* which was actually laying mines. U.S. aircraft then attacked the ship, which was then boarded by Navy SEALs. Other mines were found on board. This success led to a significant reduction in minelaying by the Iranians. In April 1988, however, the American frigate USS *Samuel B. Roberts* struck a mine identified as a type used by the Iranians. The United States responded by launching Operation PRAYING MANTIS, which consisted of air strikes on two oil platforms from which it was believed the Iranians were mounting their mining operations. The conflict between Iran and Iraq ended in 1988, and the allied minesweeping operation ceased the next year.

Following its invasion and occupation of Kuwait in August 1990, Iraq laid mines in international waters along the Kuwaiti coast to prevent any coalition amphibious operation there. U.S. warships discovered and destroyed six mines during December. The U.S. Mine Countermeasures Group (USMCMG) was created with the objective of clearing the mines to make possible an amphibious assault as well as to permit surface ships to close on the coast in order to provide gunfire support. The U.S. Navy deployed three minesweepers, which were joined by minesweepers from Saudi Arabia, Kuwait, and the United Kingdom. USS *Tripoli,* which operated a number of minesweeping helicopters, served as the flagship for the operation.

The minesweeping operation commenced from a distance of 60 miles off the Kuwaiti coast and cleared a 15-mile-long path to a 35-square-mile box centered 8 nautical miles offshore designated as a battleship gunfire support area for USS *Wisconsin* and USS *Missouri.* It was situated just south of Faylaka Island. During this operation both the *Tripoli* and another U.S. ship struck mines, and both were withdrawn to Bahrain for repairs. During the successful ground campaign in February 1991, accurate maps captured from Iraqi naval sources showed the minefield in which the two U.S. ships had been hit. The field was one of six laid in a 150-mile arc from Faylaka Island to the Saudi-Kuwaiti border. Within the area encompassed by these minefields, more than 1,000 mines were laid during a five-month period. It took considerable time for the combined minesweeping force to ensure the safety of coalition vessels in the area.

During the 2003 Iraq War there were reports of naval mines in the approach to Basra. They were detected as minelike objects but were identified as abandoned ordnance and cleared by divers and ordnance personnel.

Naval mines continue to be a threat in the region. This threat is heightened by a proliferation of mine-producing and -exporting countries. Today, there are some 30 nations known to manufacture sea mines. Two-thirds of these export weapons to the Middle East. Egypt does not produce mines, and thus far neither Iran nor Israel has exported the mines they manufacture.

CARL OTIS SCHUSTER

See also

Eilat, Israel; Iran-Iraq War; Iraq War; Persian Gulf War; Suez Canal; Yom Kippur War

References

Herzog, Chaim. *The War of Atonement: October, 1973.* Boston: Little, Brown, 1975.

Levie, Howard. *Mine Warfare at Sea.* Boston: Brill/Martinus-Nijhoff, 1992.

Marolda, Edward, and Robert Schneller. *Shield and Sword: The United States Navy and the Persian Gulf War.* Annapolis, MD: Naval Institute Press, 2001.

Melia, Tamara. *Damn the Torpedoes: A Short History of U.S. Naval Mine Countermeasures, 1777–1991.* Washington, DC: Naval Historical Center, 1991.

Rabinovich, Abraham. *The Yom Kippur War: The Epic Encounter That Transformed the Middle East.* New York: Schocken, 2005.

Minsk Conference
Start Date: September 4, 1902
End Date: September 10, 1902

First official conference of Russian Zionists. Although an earlier conference of Russian Zionists had occurred in Warsaw in August 1898 prior to the Second Zionist Conference at Basle, Switzerland, that meeting did not have the sanction of Russian authorities. This time the Russian government formally agreed to a seven-day conference for 300 people.

As it worked out, more than 500 delegates representing 120 cities and other locations along with about 200 guests attended the conference, billed as the First All-Russia Conference of Zionists, at the Paris Hotel in Minsk during September 4–10. The delegates included some 50 Jewish writers and 40 rabbis. The chief issues at the conference were organizational and cultural, and debate over the latter was stormy. The delegates did resolve that the Jewish National Fund should purchase land as soon as possible rather than wait for the collection of larger sums of money, and it recommended cooperation with Hoveve Zion (Lovers of Zion) in matters related to settlement in Palestine.

The bright hopes raised among Russian Jews that the government permission for the conference signaled a shift in the position of the Russian government and people vis-à-vis the Jews and Zionism were shattered by the Kishinev Pogrom of April 1903. Then, two months later, the Russian government prohibited all Zionist activity on the claim that while Zionism had originally been dedicated to securing Jewish immigration to Palestine, it had now shifted to strengthening Jewish nationalism.

SPENCER C. TUCKER

See also

Hoveve Zion; Jewish National Fund; Kishinev Pogrom; Pale of Settlement

References

Brenner, Michael. *Zionism: A Brief History.* Translated by Shelley Frisch. Princeton, NJ: Markus Wiener, 2003.

Laqueur, Walter. *A History of Zionism: From the French Revolution to the Establishment of the State of Israel.* Reprint ed. New York: Schocken, 2003.

Missiles, Air-to-Air

Because air superiority had such a decisive impact on ground fighting during the Arab-Israeli wars, air-to-air missiles (AAMs) constituted one of the most important weapons. In that respect, the Israeli Air Force enjoyed a significant advantage over its Arab

A Shafrir air-to-air missile under the wing of an Israeli Mirage fighter, March 1973. (Moshe Milner/Israeli Government Press Office)

opponents. Israel's American-made AIM-9 Sidewinder and AIM-7 Sparrow and French-made Magic missiles were all superior to the Soviet-supplied AA-1 Alkali and AA-2 Atoll missiles used by the Arab air forces.

Israeli AAM superiority combined with superior pilot training and doctrine ensured Israeli air superiority in virtually every conflict with its Arab neighbors. In fact, the early days of the 1973 Yom Kippur War marked the only time Israel did not enjoy air supremacy, and that was because of extensive Egyptian employment of the SA-6 surface-to-air missile (SAM). Israel regained air supremacy once it defeated the SA-6 and has not been denied air superiority since.

The Sidewinder and Magic were infrared-guided missiles with exceptional reliability and maneuverability in a dogfight. Their infrared guidance systems tracked the target aircraft's exhaust heat and literally guided the missile into the target aircraft's engine. Their greater speed and agility provided a decisive edge in the close-in combat that characterized most Middle Eastern aerial engagements. The missiles' primary disadvantage was that prior to the 1990s, they could not be used in a head-on engagement but instead had to be launched from behind the target.

The Soviet-supplied AA-2 Atoll was a copy of an early Sidewinder and suffered its limitations. It had to be pointed directly into the target aircraft's exhaust plume, while the Israeli missiles only had to be pointed at the heat source. Also, Soviet missiles were more easily defeated by properly timed flare drops. More importantly, the Israeli-designed Python missiles that entered service in the late 1980s enabled the pilots to engage targets head-on and from wider pursuit angles, an advantage the Arab air forces did not enjoy.

The longer-ranged AIM-7 Sparrow's semiactive radar guidance system could be employed against an incoming target. However, its guidance system was not as reliable as the infrared system on the Sidewinder and Magic missiles. Semiactive radar-homing missiles require that the launch aircraft maintain radar contact with the target because the missile homes in on the radar signal reflected off the target aircraft. Nonetheless, it enabled Israeli pilots to initiate the engagement at a longer range, forcing their Arab opponents to turn away and exposing their exhaust plumes to the Israelis' infrared-guided missiles.

The Soviet AA-1 Alkali radar-beam riding missile offered no similar advantage. It had half the Sparrow's range of seven nautical miles and required that the aircraft pilot keep the plane's nose pointed at the target, something that is all but impossible to do in aerial combat. Moreover, the AA-1 was more susceptible to jamming and other electronic countermeasures than was the Sparrow.

Although the United States has now sold AAMs to Egypt, Jordan, Saudi Arabia, and the United Arab Emirates, it reserves its top-of-the-line AAMs for Israel. The resulting Israeli technological superiority has given Israeli pilots psychological as well as tactical and operational superiority over their Arab counterparts. The maintenance of technological superiority over its potential opponents is a key element in Israel Defense Forces (IDF) planning.

CARL OTIS SCHUSTER

See also

Aircraft, Fighters; Missiles, Surface-to-Air

References

Aker, Frank. *October 1973: The Arab-Israeli War.* Hamden, CT: Archon, 1985.

Aloni, Shlomo. *Arab-Israeli Air Wars, 1947–1982.* London: Osprey, 2001.

Church, Jimmy H. *The Battle for Air Superiority during the 1973 Arab-Israeli War.* Quantico, VA: Marine Corps Command and Staff College, 1983.

Hammel, Eric. *Six Days in June: How Israel Won the 1967 Arab-Israeli War.* New York: Scribner, 1992.

Nicholle, David, and Tom Cooper. *Arab MiG-19 & MiG-21 Units in Combat.* London: Osprey, 2004.

Shannon, Chris. *Air-to-Air Missile Directory.* London: Centurion, 2005.

Yonay, Ehud. *No Margin for Error: The Making of the Israeli Air Force.* New York: Pantheon, 1993.

Missiles, Air-to-Surface

Missiles launched from various aircraft (including fighters, bombers, and helicopters) and capable of hitting targets on both land and sea and containing their own propulsion systems. The growing lethality of air defenses has driven the world's air forces to develop guided air-to-surface missiles so that their pilots can avoid flying into the teeth of those defenses to deliver their attacks.

World War II saw the introduction of the first air-to-surface missiles, but those early systems were too large to be carried on the tactical fighter aircraft employed in the Arab-Israeli conflicts that immediately followed that war. However, it was the lessons learned from the Korean War (1950–1953) that drove the major powers to pursue developing lighter air-to-surface missiles. As a result, no such weapons were in service during the first three Arab-Israeli conflicts, but the French decision in 1967 to stop supplying Israel with arms forced Israel to shift its arms purchasing to the United States. That transition began in 1968, enabling Israel to enter the 1973 Yom Kippur War with a number of U.S.-supplied air-to-surface missile systems.

The United States developed the first modern tactical air-to-surface missile in 1959. Called the Bullpup and initially designated the ASM-N-7 by its sponsoring service the U.S. Navy, it became the AGM-12 under U.S. secretary of defense Robert McNamara's joint weapons designation system in 1962. Weighing in at just under 1,000 pounds, the Bullpup could be carried by the A-4 Douglas Skyhawks and McDonnell F-4 Phantoms that entered Israeli service in late 1969. Designed to enable the attacking aircraft to make a precision attack from outside antiaircraft artillery range, the early Bullpups had a 250-pound warhead and were powered by a small solid-fuel rocket engine. The A-4 pilot or the F-4 weapons operator visually guided the missile to the target via a joystick control, not unlike that used by the German Fritz X guided bomb of World War II.

As with the German weapon, the Bullpup had a burning tracer in the tail fin that enabled the operator to track the missile as it flew to the target. The Bullpup also came in a larger version with a 1,000-pound warhead and more powerful rocket engine to increase range and speed. Nonetheless, it lacked the range to enable a standoff attack from outside the reach of the SA-2 and SA-6 surface-to-air missile (SAM) systems then used by Egyptian and Syrian forces.

To deal with the SA-2 SAM threat, the United States had supplied the AGM-45 Shrike antiradiation missile. Essentially an AIM-7 Sparrow air-to-air missile with its seeker modified to home in on missile fire control and acquisition radars, the Shrike weighed less than 200 pounds and was carried by A-4 and F-4 aircraft. Although its range of 10–12 nautical miles placed the launch aircraft within the SA-2's maximum range, the Shrike's 44-pound warhead literally shredded the SAM's fire control radar. It also proved to be an easy system to modify in the face of newly emerging threats. For example, the United States developed and supplied an improved version capable of engaging the Soviet-supplied SA-6 within two weeks of reports that detailed SAM operations during the early days of the 1973 war. Arab radar operators often shut down their systems if they thought they were facing a Shrike attack, effectively ending the SAM threat to incoming Israeli aircraft without a mis-

sile being fired. Phased out in the early 1990s, the Shrike has been replaced by the Harpy Drone-based SAM suppression system.

Israel acquired the AGM-114 Hellfire missile from the United States in the early 1990s. Fired from the AH-64 Apache attack helicopter, the 100-pound missile has a maximum range of five miles and an 18-pound warhead. The Israelis have used the Hellfire primarily for precision strikes against Palestinian and Hezbollah leaders and strong points. Most often employed against Hamas and Palestinian Islamic Jihad leaders in the Gaza Strip, the Hellfire also saw extensive employment during Israel's 2006 conflict with Hezbollah in southern Lebanon.

Israel has also developed air-to-surface missiles (ASMs) of its own. The 3,000-pound Popeye I Have Nap missile first entered service in 1985. Propelled by a solid-fuel rocket engine, it has a range of more than 45 nautical miles. The early Popeye I used inertial guidance, but later variants employed either a new closed-loop imaging infrared and television guidance for the weapons officer to guide it into the target if necessary or other forms of terminal or precision guidance. The later and lighter Popeye II Have Lite missile incorporates those improvements and has a greater range (90 nautical miles). Both variants are carried by Israel's F-4 Phantom and McDonnell-Douglas F-15E Strike Fighter aircraft.

The only other major arms supplier to provide air-to-surface missiles to the Arab-Israeli conflict participants, the Soviet Union, was slower than the United States in developing them. Instead, the Soviets had focused on developing heavy, long-range strategic ASMs that largely were unsuitable to the conflicts of the Middle East. The Soviet Union did not introduce its first tactical ASM, the AS-7 Kerry, until 1968 and did not supply them to its Arab clients (Egypt, Libya, Iraq and Syria) until the mid-1980s. Carried on the Mikoyan-Gurevich MiG-23, the AS-7 was a beam-riding missile. That is, the missile's guidance system was designed to keep the missile within the guidance beam, which the pilot or weapon's operator kept centered on the target via a visual sighting system in the cockpit. The AS-7 had a range of 6.5 nautical miles and a 222-pound warhead. Although Iraq employed the missile against Iranian targets during the Iran-Iraq War (1980–1988), the AS-7 was never employed in any of the Arab-Israeli conflicts.

Carl Otis Schuster

See also

Arms Sales, International; Hamas; Hezbollah; Iran-Iraq War; Islamic Jihad, Palestinian; Lebanon, Israeli Operations against; Missiles, Air-to-Air; Missiles, Cruise; Missiles, Intermediate-Range Ballistic; Missiles, Surface-to-Air; Yom Kippur War

References

Aloni, Shlomo. *Arab-Israeli Air Wars, 1947–1982.* London: Osprey, 2001.
Church, Jimmy H. *The Battle for Air Superiority during the 1973 Arab-Israeli War.* Quantico, VA: Marine Corps Command and Staff College, 1983.
Cohen, Eliezer. *Israel's Best Defense: The First Full Story of the Israeli Air Force.* New York: Orion, 1993.
Cooper, Tom, and Bishop Paxxad. *Iran-Iraq War in the Air, 1980–88.* Cooperstown, PA: Schiffer, 1991.

Frieden, David R. *Principles of Naval Weapons Systems*. Annapolis, MD: Naval Institute Press, 1985.

Katz, Samuel. *The Shield of David: The Israeli Air Force into the 1990s*. Cape Girardeau: Concord, 2003.

Lambeth, Benjamin. *Moscow's Lessons from the 1982 Lebanon Air War*. Washington, DC: RAND, 1985.

Nicholle, David, and Tom Cooper. *Arab MiG-19 & MiG-21 Units in Combat*. London: Osprey, 2004.

Nordeen, Lon, and David Nicolle. *Phoenix over the Nile: A History of Egyptian Air Power, 1932–1994*. Washington, DC: Smithsonian Books, 1996.

Yonay, Ehud. *No Margin for Error: The Making of the Israeli Air Force*. New York: Pantheon, 1993.

Missiles, Cruise

One of the most dangerous weapons of modern warfare, cruise missiles essentially are unmanned aircraft that cruise at various altitudes until they dive or crash into their targets. Conceptually, all cruise missiles trace their roots to the German World War II V-1 buzz bomb. The only real differences between today's cruise missiles and the V-1 are the improved propulsion and guidance systems, range, accuracy, and warhead. The V-1's pulse jet engine and simple gyro-timing guidance system have given way to highly efficient turbofans and a variety of guidance systems tailored to the missile's specific mission or target. With those improvements have come a significant growth in price ($5,000 for a V-1, $500,000 for a modern U.S. Tomahawk) and capabilities. Today's cruise missiles can fly a terrain-hugging deceptive flight route to a target 1,000 miles distant and have a 70 percent probability of a direct hit (99 percent chance of hitting within 30 feet).

The United States and the Soviet Union both exploited the German V-1 in trying to develop their own cruise missiles after World War II. By 1950, both countries had working prototypes of turbojet-powered flying bombs under development. The best-known of the American models were the U.S. Navy's Regulus and the U.S. Air Force's Hound Dog cruise missiles. Like the V-1, these missiles were seen as area attack weapons, but the American missiles carried nuclear instead of conventional warheads. The Regulus had a range of 600 miles and was to be fired from submarines, while the similarly ranged Hound Dog was air-launched from Boeing B-47 Stratojet and Boeing B-52 Stratofortress bombers. Neither American missile was particularly accurate, and both left service by the mid-1960s.

With more accurate and powerful submarine-launched ballistic missiles entering service, the major Western naval powers dropped their cruise missile programs. Moreover, their possession of aircraft carriers obviated the need for their surface ships to have a long-range strike capability. However, the carrier-shy Soviet Union

A Soviet SS-N-2 Styx antiship missile on a transport dolly, photographed in October 1986. (U.S. Department of Defense)

The guided missile frigate USS *Stark* lists to port after being struck by an Iraqi-launched antiship Exocet missile on May 17, 1987, during the Iran-Iraq War. (U.S. Department of Defense)

lacked the resources and experience to build aircraft carriers and therefore pursued a different path, developing a cruise missile intended to attack ships, the SS-N-1, in 1958. It was followed two years later by the SS-N-2. These missiles differed from their American counterparts primarily in having a radar-based terminal guidance system that took them into the targeted ship. France was the only country to see any value in developing its own antiship missiles, but the program enjoyed only a low priority.

All this changed with Egypt's 1967 sinking of the Israeli destroyer *Eilat* with an SS-N-2 Styx ship-to-ship missile. Suddenly, all navies saw antiship cruise missiles (ASCMs) as the poor man's naval strike weapon. Moreover, they recognized the value of such weapons in situations where increasingly expensive aircraft carriers weren't available. That led the United States and other powers to initiate accelerated cruise missile programs. ASCMs, such as the French Exocet and the American Harpoon and Tomahawk, were the first to enter service, but their relative light weight and expense, compared to that of an aircraft carrier and its air wing, led some to examine their use in the land-attack role. Meanwhile, the Soviets developed their own family of long-range ASCMs: the SS-N-3, SS-N-12, SS-N-19 and SS-N-22.

The Yom Kippur War (1973) saw the first naval engagements fought entirely between ASCM-equipped patrol boats. Having been stung by these weapons in the 1967 Six-Day War, Israel had developed its own ASCM, the Gabriel Missile, and installed it on a new class of small patrol boats and corvettes. More importantly, Israel had developed tactics and electronic countermeasures to defeat the Soviet-built ASCMs supplied to Egypt and Syria. The October 7, 1973, Battle of Latakia saw six Israeli patrol boats sink five Syrian naval units. During October 12–13, the Israelis sank three Egyptian missile patrol boats in the Battle of Baltim. Superior electronic countermeasures and tactics enabled the Israelis to win those battles without suffering any losses or damage. The Syrian fleet and Egypt's Mediterranean-based fleets remained in port for the rest of the war. Unfortunately for Israel, it had not deployed missile patrol boats to its Red Sea port, Eilat, and Egypt's Red Sea blockade remained unbroken.

By the early 1980s, advances in microminiaturization, avionics, and navigation systems brought land-attack cruises back into vogue for both conventional and nuclear missions. The American Land-Attack Tomahawk initially had a Terrain Contour Matching guidance system that enabled it to navigate over land by matching its onboard radar's picture of the terrain below against a computer-developed map of its flight route to the target. By the late 1990s, this system was replaced by a module that guided the missile by using the Global Positioning System (GPS), making the missile accurate to within 1–2 meters. Finally, a Digital Scene Matching Area (DSMA) correlation feature was added to ensure that the missile would select the right target as it entered the target area by matching a digital image of the target scene (radar, optical, or infrared or a combination of them) against an onboard image data base. DSMA is particularly useful against mobile targets. By the end of the Cold War, treaties and other considerations had driven all of the nuclear cruise missiles out of service. Conventional cruise missiles were now so accurate that Western political and military leaders had come to see them as politically safe precision weapons that could be employed in an infinite variety of situations.

ASCMs figured prominently in the 1982 Falklands War, with Argentine naval air force units sinking two British warships and damaging four others with their French-supplied AM-39 Exocet missiles. Iraq employed the same weapon in larger numbers against Iranian shipping during the 1980–1988 Iran-Iraq War. Although the missiles failed to sink any tankers or merchant ships, they damaged more than 200, driving up insurance rates and forcing the United States to escort tankers through the Persian Gulf during the war's final year. More ominously, on March 17, 1987, the Iraqis hit the American frigate USS *Stark* (FFG-31) with two Exocets, killing 37 crewmen and injuring 21 (more than a third of the crew). The crew saved the ship, but it took more than 18 months to repair the damage and return it to service.

The 1991 Persian Gulf War saw the first major employment of land-attack cruise missiles. The anti-Iraq coalition opened Operation DESERT STORM by launching 122 of the U.S. Navy's Tomahawk land-attack missiles (TLAMs) against key Iraqi air defense posts, radar systems, and communications facilities. The TLAMs were employed almost entirely against targets considered too dangerous or risky for attack by aircraft. Typically, they preceded an air strike, taking out a key facility that was critical to the Iraqis' local or area air defense. The United States fired nearly 300 TLAMs during the war at a total cost of approximately $360 million. The TLAMs then became the weapon of choice for U.S. retaliation against terrorist attacks, striking Al Qaeda and related camps in Afghanistan in the 1990s. More than twice as many were fired during the later Operation IRAQI FREEDOM in 2003, and America's 2001 invasion of Afghanistan was also preceded by a series of TLAM strikes against Taliban-related targets.

Cruise missiles are a relatively inexpensive, expendable alternative to expensive aircraft and ballistic missiles. Unlike bomber aircraft, they do not put crewmen in harm's way. For nations not concerned with accuracy, cruise missiles remain a cheap solution to their long-range strike problem. However, for militaries seeking precision, for both antiship and land-attack missions, cruise missiles have become the complex weapons of choice for retaliatory strikes and the initial military operations conducted during a war. The newest have incorporated stealth technologies to make them more difficult to detect and engage. Others rely on supersonic dash speeds to defeat air defenses. In any case, cruise missiles are used to take out key enemy command centers, air defense sites, and air-

fields before manned aircraft are committed to the fight. In peacetime, cruise missiles are used for situations where a rapid and precise attack is required and the political-military leadership doesn't want to risk pilot losses.

China, France, India, Israel, Russia, Taiwan, and the United States produce ASCMs, but only two countries—the United States and Russia—manufacture land-attack cruise missiles. China, India, and Pakistan have their indigenous cruise missiles under development that are expected to enter operational service by 2010. Undoubtedly, the 21st century will see a proliferation of cruise missiles. In combination with unmanned aerial vehicles, they will become an increasingly prominent element of modern warfare.

CARL O. SCHUSTER

See also

Baltim, Battle of; *Eilat* Sinking; Latakia, Battle of

References

Finlan, Alastair. *The Gulf War, 1991.* Oxford, UK: Osprey, 2004.

Frieden, David R. *Principles of Naval Weapons Systems.* Annapolis, MD: Naval Institute Press, 1985.

Herzog, Chaim. *The Arab-Israeli Wars: War and Peace in the Middle East from the War of Independence to Lebanon.* Westminster, MD: Random House, 1984.

Hewson, Robert. *Jane's Air-Launched Weapons, 2001.* London: Jane's, 2002.

Hooten, Ted. *Jane's Naval Weapons Systems, 2001–2002.* London: Jane's, 2002.

Knight, Michael, ed. *Operation Iraqi Freedom and the New Iraq.* Washington, DC: Washington Institute for Near East Policy, 2004.

Tripp, Robert. *Lessons Learned from Operation Enduring Freedom.* Santa Monica, CA: RAND, 2004.

Missiles, Intermediate-Range Ballistic

Ballistic missiles with a range of 1,500–4,000 statute miles. The development of intermediate-range ballistic missiles (IRBMs) began in the early 1950s. They were derived from the successful German V-2 rockets of World War II. Both Cold War superpowers, the United States and the Soviet Union, initiated development of such missile systems in an effort to gain strategic advantage. For the Soviet Union, IRBMs offered a cheaper alternative to long-range bombers in order to attack America's forward-based strategic airpower. For the United States, IRBMs offered the ability to respond quickly to Soviet attack. Moreover, IRBMs were simpler and easier to develop than longer-ranged intercontinental ballistic missiles (ICBMs).

By 1956, both the United States and the Soviet Union had significant IRBM programs under way. The resulting missiles figured prominently in the Cuban Missile Crisis of 1962 and the nuclear disarmament talks of the late 1980s. More recently, IRBMs have figured prominently in the Middle East and South Asia, where several countries have developed or are developing nuclear-capable types.

In the United States, the U.S. Air Force had responsibility for the country's land-based IRBMs, while the U.S. Navy acquired control over sea-based missiles. The air force focused on liquid-fuel rockets because of the greater power they provided. The navy pursued solid-fueled missiles such as the Polaris and the Poseidon that could be stored safely on submarines. The air force IRBM programs, which were conducted in collaboration with Britain's Royal Air Force, were designated Jupiter and Thor. President Dwight D. Eisenhower accorded the program the same high priority as the Atlas and Titan ICBM programs. The first four U.S. Thor IRBM squadrons deployed to England in late 1957, followed by two more to Italy the next year. They were operational two years after deployment. By 1959, however, the Atlas ICBM program's steady progress made many question the value of the IRBM and call for their decommissioning as the Atlas squadrons came on line. Nevertheless, by 1960 Jupiter squadrons were being deployed to Turkey and the U.S. Air Force retained its IRBMs in service despite President John F. Kennedy's order to remove them shortly after he took office in January 1961.

In the Soviet Union, the Ministry of Armaments directed all strategic rocket research. As a result, all Soviet sea-based missiles were derived from land-based variants and were therefore liquid-fueled. As with their American counterparts, all Soviet ballistic missiles were derived from the initial work done by sequestered German engineers. The first Soviet IRBM to enter service, the R-12 (NATO designation SS-4) was based on the initial designs provided by the German engineers held on Gorodomlya Island during 1946–1950. Under development since 1953, the R-12 first entered testing in 1957. Unlike the American IRBMs, the R-12 and all later Soviet IRBMs were designed to be fired from mobile truck-drawn launchers. However, the R-12 was later modified for silo-based firing. The early model R-12s had a range of only 1,200 miles, and the first operational systems were deployed in late 1960. However, the R-12 is most famous for its September 1962 deployment in Cuba, which triggered the Cuban Missile Crisis. The withdrawal of the R-12s from Cuba, and the American agreement to pull its IRBMs from Turkey effectively ended the crisis.

France was the only other country to build IRBMs during the Cold War. Its program began in the late 1960s as the third leg of France's nuclear deterrent force, which President Charles de Gaulle had decided to develop in 1958, separately from the United States. The S-2 IRBM was first test-fired in 1968 and entered service in 1971. France built a longer-ranged S-3D that entered service in 1980. Both were silo-based missiles that carried a single 120 kiloton nuclear warhead, but the S-3D had a range of 1,800 miles versus only 1,200 for the S-2. France maintained a force of 18 silo-based IRBMs as the missile element of its nuclear deterrent force until 1996.

The escalating presence of IRBMs in Europe during the early 1980s led to the first international agreement that eliminated a nuclear weapons system, the Intermediate Nuclear Force (INF) Treaty of 1989. That treaty called for the destruction of all U.S. and Soviet IRBMs. Missiles covered by the agreement included the Soviet SS-4 and SS-20 and the U.S. Pershing IIa and ground-launched cruise missile (GLCM) systems. France subsequently decommissioned and destroyed its IRBM force in 1996.

Since that time, however, several nations have initiated IRBM programs, including the People's Republic of China (PRC), India, Iran, Israel, North Korea, and Pakistan. Israel's nuclear-capable Jericho II was the first to enter service in 1984. Iraq pursued IRBM development, but its defeat in the Persian Gulf War of 1991 prevented the program from reaching fruition. However, Iraq's successful use of modified Scud missiles as medium-range ballistic missiles led Iran to develop its own IRBMs. Nearby Pakistan and India had nuclear-capable IRBM programs well under way at the beginning of the 21st century. Iran's Shahab 3 and Pakistan's Gauri IRBM are based on North Korea's No Dong missile, while India's Agni-III is a totally indigenous missile design that traces its initial development back to 1979. These nuclear-capable systems are the easiest and cheapest long-range missiles to build and, when equipped with a nuclear, biological, or chemical warhead, enable a country to threaten any potential opponent within a range of 2,000–3,000 nautical miles. As such, these weapons are considered to be the most threatening weapons in existence today.

CARL O. SCHUSTER

See also
Nuclear Weapons

References

Davis, Jacquelyn, Charles M. Perry, and Jamal S. Al-Suwaidi, eds. *Air/Missile Defense Counter-Proliferation.* London: British Academic Press, 1999.
Owen, Wyn Q. *The Politics of Ballistic Missile Non-Proliferation.* Hampshire, UK: Palgrave, 2000.
Sioris, George M. *Missile Guidance and Control Systems.* New York: Springer Verlag, 2004.
Spencer, Jack. *Ballistic Missile Threat Handbook.* Washington, DC: Heritage Foundation, 2002.

Missiles, Patriot

See Patriot Missile System

Missiles, Surface-to-Air

Modern air defenses rely on a defense in-depth based on long-range detection and interception of incoming threats. Aircraft provide the distant reach, followed by surface-to-air missiles (SAMs) and, for close-in defense, antiaircraft artillery (AAA). SAMs are a relatively new development, first appearing in the final months of World War II. However, the advent of higher speed and more capable aircraft and aerial weapons drove the development of SAMs during the postwar period. Today, SAMs have supplanted AAA as the weapons of choice for all but point air defense operations.

SAMs fall into the three categories, based on their range and guidance system. Most short-range SAMs rely on infrared guidance, that is, they track the target's engine exhaust until intercept (e.g., U.S. Redeye, Stinger, and Chapparal and Soviet SA-7, SA-9, and SA-14). The one exception is the Swedish RBS series, which

An Egyptian SA-2 surface-to-air missile (SAM) deployed during a multinational joint service exercise, August 1985. (U.S. Department of Defense)

uses laser-beam guidance for its missiles. All short-range SAMs are launched against targets as they approach within 1–4 nautical miles (nm) of the SAM system. Medium (10–20 nm) and long-range (20–300 nm) SAMs rely on variations of radar guidance. Early radar-guided SAMs were beam-riding systems that flew or rode within the tracking beam of the fire-control radar that tracked the target (the Soviet SA-1 and U.S. Tatar and Terrier). However, these systems had range limitations and had difficulty engaging rapidly maneuvering targets.

Most Western SAMs that entered service between 1965 and 1980 (U.S. Hawk, I-Hawk, standard missiles, and the British Bloodhound) employ a variation on semiactive homing, while all post-1960 Soviet-based SAMs rely on what is called command guidance (the SA-2 through SA-6 and the SA-11). In the former, a fire-control radar tracks the target, and the missile guides on the radar signal reflected off the target. Command guidance involves one radar tracking the target while another tracks the missile and a computer provides guidance signals to the missile as it flies toward the target. Command guidance is more effective against long-range targets, while semiactive homing is better against a maneuvering target.

The U.S. ramjet-powered BOMARC SAM was the world's longest-ranged SAM, having a maximum range of more than 400 nm. The U.S. Navy's ramjet-powered TALOS conducted the world's longest-ranged SAM engagement, downing a North Vietnamese MiG at more than 90 nm in 1967. Both TALOS and BOMARC were retired in the 1970s.

Most 21st-century Western SAM systems, such as the American Aegis and Patriot SAMs, employ a combination of the two guidance systems. They use command guidance from launch until the terminal phase of the engagement, at which time they shift to semiactive or active homing. This system requires high-speed computers and very high-frequency and powerful radars, but it offers the ability to engage multiple targets simultaneously using a limited number of fire-control radars. It also provides a more accurate long-range engagement while retaining the ability to engage highly maneuverable targets. Finally, such guidance systems are far more effective in a heavy electronic-countermeasures environment.

SAMs are not an air defense panacea. They are exceptionally effective against aircrews who have not been trained or equipped to face them. Examples of that include the early engagements over Vietnam and during the first weeks of the Yom Kippur War. However, their effectiveness declines once aircraft and crews have been trained, equipped, and supported to deal with the SAM threat. Dealing with the SAM threat, however, obliges the attacking force to divert up to 60 percent of its combat power to countering the SAMs, and that contribution to a country's air defense cannot be ignored.

Today's SAMs are also being modified to engage ballistic missiles. SAMs will remain the backbone of most air defense systems until they are replaced by long-range energy weapons.

CARL OTIS SCHUSTER

See also
Artillery, Antiaircraft

References
Blake, Bernard, ed. *Jane's Weapons Systems, 1987–88*. New York: Random House, 1989.

Dunstan, Simon. *The Yom Kippur War, 1973*. 2 vols. Westport, CT: Praeger, 2005.

Frieden, David R. *Principles of Naval Weapons Systems*. Annapolis, MD: Naval Institute Press, 1985.

Isby, David. *Weapons and Tactics of the Soviet Army*. London: Jane's, 1981.

Pretty, Ronald T., ed. *Jane's Weapons Systems, 1972–73*. London: Jane's, 1973.

Mitla Pass

A strategic pass in the west-central Sinai Peninsula, located at a latitude of 30″02′ north and a longitude of 32″54′ east. The Mitla Pass lies approximately 20 miles east of the Suez Canal near the city of Suez. The Sinai Peninsula is Egyptian territory. It features very rugged terrain in the south and extensive sand dunes in the north. Better transportation routes are available in central Sinai, which is dominated by the Tih Plateau. Giddi Mountain (Jabal al-Jiddi), a limestone massif with peaks rising to 2,750 feet, separates the Tih Plateau from the sand dunes. Mitla Pass traverses Giddi Mountain and is a critical link in the ancient Darb al-Hajj (pilgrimage route), now Highway 33, that provides a direct route between Suez and Aqaba. Steep ridges on either side of the pass are only 150–300 feet apart in places. Its narrow confines, coupled with many caves, make it a natural fortification. Approximately 20 miles east of the pass, Highway 33 intersects with the road leading northeast to Bir al-Thamiada, one of the traditional Sinai invasion routes. Mitla Pass was an objective for Turkish and British forces during World War I and for Egyptian and Israeli forces in the 1956 Sinai Campaign, the 1967 Six-Day War, and the 1973 Yom Kippur War.

On October 29, 1956, a battalion of Major Ariel Sharon's 202nd Parachute Brigade landed 15 miles east of the Mitla Pass on the first day of hostilities during the Suez Crisis. The remainder of the brigade arrived by land the following evening. The next day, Sharon received permission to send a patrol into the pass but instead sent a battalion, which was ambushed. Although Israelis captured the pass, the unplanned battle cost the lives of 38 Israeli paratroopers. More than 200 Egyptians died defending it. Following a cease-fire,

Egyptian tanks and trucks destroyed by Israeli fighter-bombers at Mitla Pass during the Six-Day War, July 1967. (Ami Shamir/Israeli Government Press Office)

Israel withdrew its forces in a phased withdrawal completed in January 1957.

During the 1967 Six-Day War, the Israeli Air Force repeatedly strafed retreating Egyptian units in and around the Mitla Pass, turning it into a death trap. Israeli tanks arrived on June 7, 1967, and blocked the east side of the pass. The next day, Israeli forces secured the pass and trapped the remaining Egyptian soldiers in central Sinai. Thousands died from combat or the desert heat. Israel ultimately seized control of the entire Sinai Peninsula.

On October 6, 1973, Egyptian forces initiated the Yom Kippur War with a surprise crossing of the Suez Canal. Detailed planning and execution led to initial successes. On October 14, however, they launched a hastily planned assault on the Mitla and other passes. The poorly executed attacks failed and opened the door to effective Israeli counterattacks, which continued until a cease-fire was concluded on October 28.

Mitla Pass figured prominently in subsequent Egyptian-Israeli peace negotiations. The January 18, 1974, Sinai I Agreement involved the withdrawal of Israeli forces from the Suez Canal east to a defensive line that included the Mitla Pass. Israeli forces withdrew from the Mitla Pass as part of the September 4, 1975, Sinai II Agreement. That agreement included the stipulation that electronic sensors as well as human monitors would provide Israel with early warning of Egyptian military movements in the region. Successful international monitoring of the Mitla Pass contributed to the signing of the Israel-Egypt Peace Treaty on March 26, 1979, the result of the Camp David Accords of the previous year.

Chuck Fahrer

See also

Bar-Lev Line; Camp David Accords; Egypt, Armed Forces; Giddi Pass; Israel Defense Forces; Israel-Egypt Peace Treaty; Sharon, Ariel; Sinai; Sinai Campaign; Sinai I and Sinai II Agreements; Six-Day War; Yom Kippur War

References

Greenwood, Ned H. *The Sinai: A Physical Geography.* Austin: University of Texas Press, 1997.

Herzog, Chaim. *The Arab-Israeli Wars: War and Peace in the Middle East from the War of Independence to Lebanon.* Westminster, MD: Random House, 1984.

Marshall, S. L. A. *Sinai Victory.* New York: William Morrow, 1967.

Pollack, Kenneth M. *Arabs at War: Military Effectiveness, 1948–1991.* Lincoln: University of Nebraska Press, 2002.

Mizrahi Judaism

Jews descended from the Jewish communities of North Africa and the Middle East, also known as Mizrahi Jews and Mizrahim (Easterner). The term "Mizrahi Judaism" has an ethnic meaning, a religious meaning, and a meaning that merges the two. The term

Egyptian Mizrahi Jews arriving in Haifa are quizzed by Egyptian-born Israelis about family and friends during the period of the Suez Crisis, December 1956. (Israeli Government Press Office)

"Mizrahi Jew" is a 20th-century Israeli designation acting as a substitute for the terms "Arab Jew" or "Oriental Jew." Mizrahi Jewry is subdivided into ethnic subsets based on individual countries of origin and their indigenous traditions and practices. Some examples include Iraqi Jews, Tunisian Jews, Persian Jews, Ethiopian Jews, and Yemenite Jews, among many others.

Mizrahi Jews comprise more than half of Israel's current population. The Mizrahim began immigrating to Israel from their countries of origin following the formation of the State of Israel in 1948. The refugee immigration was due in great part to the fleeing of virtually entire populations of Mizrahi Jews from the growing animosity and persecution of indigenous Jewish populations in Arab and Muslim countries. This began just prior to the formation of the State of Israel, accelerated after the Israeli War of Independence (1948–1949), and continued into the 1990s. For example, 25,000 Mizrahi Jews were expelled from Egypt after the 1956 Suez Crisis, and most went to Israel. And the number of Ethiopian Jews who fled their country via Israel's Operation MOSES (1984) and Operation SOLOMON (1991) was so great that they now constitute approximately 1 percent of the contemporary Israeli population. More than 40,000 Mizrahim continue to reside in almost all of the Arab and Muslim states of North Africa and the Middle East, with large populations remaining in Uzbekistan, Iran, and Azerbaijan.

Although most Mizrahim arrived in Israel speaking the language of their countries of origin, all underwent intensive training in the Hebrew language. Most Mizrahim were craftsmen and merchants and remained so after immigration. Few had farming experience, and most either avoided settlement on moshavim (communal farms) or did not stay long once that option had been experienced. Mizrahi Judaism is not as doctrinally well developed or conservative in its understanding and regard of the Torah as Ashkenazic Judaism or even Sephardic Judaism. Mizrahi Judaism allows adherents wide latitude in the observance of the mitzvoth (commandments). The most conservative Mizrahim are regarded as observant, meaning that they closely follow or obey the commandments. The most liberal Mizrahim generally do not closely follow the commandments or consider obedience to them of prime concern. Many Mizrahim fall in between these extremes, but all Mizrahim regard mitzvoth observance as part of a progressive perfection. The observance of the mitzvoth for the Mizrahim is not a standard that one must meet or fail but rather a standard toward which one strives. In other words, total observance of the mitzvoth is the goal, but any observance is better than no observance and brings one closer to God.

RICHARD MILTON EDWARDS

See also

Ashkenazic Judaism; Hasidic Judaism; MOSES, Operation; Sephardic Judaism

References

Biale, David. *Cultures of the Jews: A New History.* New York: Schocken, 2002.

Dimont, Max. *Jews, God and History.* New York: Simon and Schuster, 1962.

Robinson, George. *Essential Judaism: A Complete Guide to Beliefs, Customs & Rituals.* New York: Pocket Books/Simon and Schuster, 2001.

Seltzer, Robert. *Jewish People, Jewish Thought.* New York: Macmillan, 1980.

Zohar, Zion, ed. *Sephardic and Mizrahi Jewry: From the Golden Age of Spain to Modern Times.* New York: New York University Press, 2005.

Mollet, Guy
Born: December 31, 1905
Died: October 3, 1975

French socialist politician, cabinet minister, and premier (1956–1957). Born on December 31, 1905, in Flers (Orne), Guy Mollet, the son of a textile worker, graduated from the University of Lille and then taught English at a Lycée in Arras. In 1921 he joined the French Socialist Party (SFIO), becoming its Pas-de-Calais regional secretary in 1928.

Mollet joined the French Army at the beginning of World War II and was wounded and captured by the Germans in 1940. Released in 1941, he returned to Arras and joined the French Resistance. Immediately after the war he was elected mayor of Arras, a position

Guy Mollet, French socialist politician, cabinet minister, and premier (1956–1957), shown here during a radio address in Algeria, February 27, 1956. (Bettmann/Corbis)

he held until his death. Mollet represented the Pas-de-Calais in both the 1945 and 1946 constituent assemblies.

In March 1946 Mollet was elected secretary-general of the SFIO, a position he would hold until 1969. He served as minister of state in Premier Léon Blum's government during 1946–1947. Mollet was appointed minister for European relations in René Pleven's cabinet during 1950–1951 and was vice premier in Henri Queuille's government in 1951. Mollet was also French representative to the Council of Europe and president of the Socialist Group. During 1951–1969 he served as vice president of the Socialist International.

In January 1956 Mollet became French premier. His domestic program included improved old-age pensions and annual paid vacations for workers. Although Mollet preferred to deal in domestic issues, foreign affairs dominated his tenure. Successes included closer relations with West Germany, fostered by the return of the Saar to Germany, and the inauguration of the Common Market. His government was undermined, however, by both the Suez Crisis and the Algerian War.

In July 1956 Egyptian president Gamal Abdel Nasser nationalized the Suez Canal. Nasser was a prominent supporter of the National Liberation Front that was fighting France to secure Algerian independence, and Mollet and many French government leaders believed falsely that Egyptian arms and money were keeping the revolt going. Mollet, an Anglophile, thus saw Nasser's action of nationalizing the canal as an opportunity to cooperate with the British government of Prime Minister Anthony Eden in seizing control of the canal and driving Nasser from power. Indeed, Mollet equated Nasser with Adolf Hitler.

Mollet and his foreign minister, Christian Pineau, initiated secret talks with British and Israeli leaders that resulted in extraordinary arms shipments to Israel and an agreement, dubbed the "Treaty of Sèvres," on October 23 that provided for an Israeli invasion of the Sinai and a threat to the canal that would be followed by French and British military operations against Egypt. Mollet made the mistake of believing that if worse came to worst, he could rely on U.S. support. As it turned out, the United States did not support the invasion. Heavy pressure from President Dwight D. Eisenhower's administration soon forced the British to withdraw, and Mollet was unwilling to continue without Britain. The French and the Israelis then also withdrew. Eden resigned in the aftermath of the Suez Crisis, but Mollet remained in power despite widespread opposition from within the SFIO to his decision to send troops to Egypt.

Mollet also prosecuted the Algerian War. Unable to convince the National Assembly to raise taxes in order to fund enhanced military operations in Algeria, Mollet resigned as premier in May 1957. The Fourth Republic collapsed a year later.

Mollet was among those French politicians who supported the return to power of General Charles de Gaulle in the crisis of May 1958 and backed de Gaulle's subsequent constitutional reforms creating a more powerful executive. During 1958–1959 Mollet served in the interim de Gaulle government as minister of state but broke with de Gaulle in 1962 in order to work to build a viable left-wing opposition movement. Mollet never fully embraced the demarche with the Communist Party that this would entail, however.

Mollet retired from politics in 1969 when the SFIO was absorbed into the Federation of the Democratic and Socialist Left. He died in Paris on October 3, 1975. Mollet acquired a posthumous reputation as a rightist machine politician who had betrayed socialism by fighting Algerian independence and supporting de Gaulle.

SPENCER C. TUCKER

See also

De Gaulle, Charles; Eden, Robert Anthony; Eisenhower, Dwight David; France, Middle East Policy; Pineau, Christian; Suez Crisis

References

Beaufre, André. *The Suez Expedition, 1956.* Translated by Richard Barry. New York: Praeger, 1969.

Codding, George, and William Safran. *Ideology and Politics: The Socialist Party of France.* Boulder, CO: Westview, 1979.

Lefebvre, Denis. *Guy Mollet: Le malaimé.* Paris: Plon, 1992.

Simmons, Harvey G. *French Socialists in Search of a Role, 1956–1967.* Ithaca, NY: Cornell University Press, 1970.

Thomas, Hugh. *Suez.* New York: Harper and Row, 1967.

Molotov Cocktail

The Molotov cocktail is an improvised gasoline bomb. The gasoline, sometimes with additives such as motor oil to make it stick to its target, is placed in a glass bottle, which is then stopped with a cork or other air-tight sealer. A wick or cloth rag is fixed securely to the neck of the bottle, soaked in gas, and lit before the bottle is thrown. The glass shatters on impact, and the gas immediately ignites. In war, the Molotov cocktail has been used against personnel and vehicles.

The Molotov cocktail was first used during the Spanish Civil War (1936–1939). It was widely used by the Finns against Soviet forces during the Finnish-Soviet War (1939–1940) and the so-called Continuation War between the same two states (1941–1944). The Soviets also employed it against German vehicles on the eastern front during World War II. The weapon is named for Vyacheslav Molotov, Soviet foreign minister from 1939 to 1949. The Finns gave it that name during the Finnish-Soviet War after Molotov claimed in a radio broadcast that the Soviets were not dropping bombs but rather delivering food to the starving Finns. The British also produced a hand grenade during World War II, known as a Sticky Bomb, that was in essence a Molotov cocktail.

Jewish forces used Molotov cocktails against the Germans during the Warsaw Ghetto Uprising in April and May 1943. Israeli forces employed Molotov cocktails against light Arab armor in the Israeli War of Independence (1948–1949). They have since been used against thin-skinned Israeli vehicles by Palestinian insurgents and rioters.

The Molotov cocktail's regular contemporary military counterpart is napalm. Other incendiaries include grenades, mortar rounds,

A Palestinian youth prepares to hurl a Molotov cocktail at an Israeli jeep during clashes at the Tulkarem refugee camp, West Bank, April 27, 2004. (Alaa Badarneh/epa/Corbis)

and artillery shells with white phosphorous fillers that ignite on contact with the air.

SPENCER C. TUCKER

See also
Antitank Weapons

Reference
Mountcastle, John W. *Flame On! U.S. Incendiary Weapons, 1918–1945.* Shippensburg, PA: White Mane, 1999.

Montefiore, Sir Moses
Born: October 24, 1784
Died: July 28, 1885

British Jewish financier, philanthropist, and supporter of Jewish projects in Palestine. Born in Livorno, Italy, on October 24, 1784, into an Italian Jewish family that had settled in England in the early 18th century, Moses Montefiore was an Orthodox Sephardic Jew. He began his business career as an apprentice to a firm of grocers and merchants and subsequently moved to London, where he amassed considerable wealth. In 1803 at only age 19 he became one of 12 Jewish brokers licensed by the City of London and secured a

seat on the London Stock Exchange. He married Judith Cohen, sister-in-law of Mayer Anschel Rothschild, with whom he worked closely. Montefiore's firm came to act as stockbrokers for the Rothschild family, and his wise investments included being one of the founders of the Imperial Continental Gas Association, which extended gas lighting to major European cities.

Montefiore's considerable personal wealth enabled him to retire at the age of 40 in 1824 and devote time to civic interests and philanthropy. A fellow of the Royal Society, his great popularity brought him election as sheriff of London (1837–1838). He was also president of the Board of Deputies of British Jews during 1835–1874. Montefiore was knighted by Queen Victoria in 1838 and made a baron in 1846.

Montefiore traveled to Palestine seven times. During his first trip there in 1827 he established a friendship with Egyptian sultan Muhammad Ali Pasha. Montefiore invested considerable financial resources in Palestine, helping to finance apartments, hospitals, synagogues, and agricultural settlements. His concern was not limited to Palestine, for he aided Jews who were being persecuted in Syria, Russia, Morocco, and Romania, intervening with the governments involved. In 1840 he was able to make use of this relationship to secure the release of 10 Syrian Jews in Damascus falsely

Sir Moses Montefiore, British Jewish financier, philanthropist, and supporter of Jewish projects in Palestine. (Library of Congress)

accused of blood libel (using Christian blood for religious rites). That same year he persuaded the Turkish government to extend to Jews the maximum privileges enjoyed by foreigners.

In 1855 during his fourth visit to Palestine, Montefiore bought 10 acres of land, where in 1860 he established the first Jewish residential quarter outside the walls of the Old City of Jerusalem. It was named Mishkenot Sha'ananim (Peaceful Habitation). The new neighborhood, which was financed from the estate of the Jewish philanthropist Judah Touro of New Orleans, was meant to house Ashkenazic and Sephardic Jews and had 16 apartments as well as both Ashkenazic and Sephardic synagogues. There was a windmill designed to produce flour (now a museum). This enterprise was part of Montefiore's wider effort to make the Jews of Palestine self-sufficient in the hopes of the eventual restoration of a Jewish state there.

A strictly observant Jew, Montefiore's strong opposition retarded the growth of Reform Judaism in Britain during his lifetime. Highly admired among Jews worldwide and the general British public, Montefiore died at Ramgate, England, at the age of 100 on July 28, 1885.

SPENCER C. TUCKER

See also
Palestine, Pre-1918 History of; Reform Judaism and Zionism

References
Goodman, Paul. *Moses Montefiore.* Philadelphia: Jewish Publication Society, 1925.
Posner, Raphael, ed. *Encyclopedia Judaica.* Jerusalem: Keter, 1982.

Morocco

Northwest African nation. The Kingdom of Morocco borders on the Mediterranean Sea to the north, the Atlantic Ocean to the west, Western Sahara to the south, and Algeria to the east. Morocco has an area of 172,414 square miles, slightly larger than the U.S. state of California. Morocco's 2006 population was approximately 33 million people.

Until the early 20th century, Morocco was relatively isolated from spheres of European, Middle Eastern, or sub-Sahara African influence. These circumstances resulted in a strong Berber and Arab Islamic national character. From 1912 to 1956, Morocco was both a French and Spanish protectorate. France granted independence to Morocco in 1956, although Spain continued to control the Western Sahara region until the mid-1970s and still retains the small enclaves of Cuenta and Melilla along the Mediterranean coast.

When the State of Israel was founded in May 1948, Morocco, like other countries in the Maghrib, was confronted with the considerable problem of Jewish emigration, which was to continue for the next several decades. From 1947 to 1960, approximately 50,000 Jews, or 25 percent of the Jewish population of Morocco, left the country, mostly to settle in Israel but some in Europe and the United States. Although most émigrés were poor or middle class, Jews were an important part of the country's economy. Neither the king, Mohammed V, nor the ruling Istiqlal party were anti-Jewish, and many members of the country's elite were Jewish including judges, government ministers, and university administrators. While Morocco attempted to limit emigration in opposition to the desires of the United Nations (UN) and the United States, this process nevertheless continued, frequently with the covert involvement of Israeli military forces. In 2006 the Jewish population in Morocco was estimated to be only 5,000 people.

In March 1961, Crown Prince Moulay Hassan succeeded his father, Mohammed V, as King Hassan II. He ruled for the next four decades until his death in July 1999. The king was both the nation's spiritual leader, as a direct descendent of the Prophet Muhammad, and its political head of government. Hassan, while lacking the charisma and unifying ability of his father, was nonetheless an effective leader, able to balance relations with the West, whose economic and political aid helped modernize his country, and the Middle East, whose Islamic heritage was his basis for power.

Unlike many other Arab nations, Morocco has maintained relatively amiable contacts with Israel since the early 1950s. At times these contacts have occurred directly between government representatives on matters of security and intelligence. Other times they have involved third parties such as Jewish organizations, intellectuals, journalists, and foreign diplomats seeking mutually

Prime Minister Yitzhak Rabin (*center*) and Knesset member Rafi Elul (*right*) meet with King Hassan II of Morocco in Casablanca on October 30, 1994, to establish semiofficial diplomatic relations between Morocco and Israel. (Ya'acov Sa'ar/Israeli Government Press Office)

beneficial political, economic, and cultural developments and information.

King Hassan II pursued a conciliatory foreign policy during his reign and sought to strengthen ties among Arabs and Jews, envisioning a powerful union of states that might bring the region prosperity similar to that of Western Europe and the United States. Morocco was essentially kept isolated from the June 1967 Six-Day War, although the relationship between Israel and Morocco was tested when Morocco provided military support to Syria during the October 1973 Yom Kippur War. In October 1976 Morocco hosted a meeting with Israeli prime minister Yitzhak Rabin. The following year Morocco hosted another meeting between Israeli foreign minister Moshe Dayan and Egyptian deputy prime minister Hasan Tuhami. Both meetings served to lay the groundwork for Egyptian president Anwar Sadat's groundbreaking visit to Israel and eventually Egypt's peace agreement with Israel in 1978.

To strengthen his position in the wake of political and military opponents of his centralized authority, Hassan embarked on an effort to secure the Western Sahara, which historically had been part of Morocco, after its abandonment by Spain in 1975. To allay widespread international criticism, Moroccan officials and a delegation of Moroccan Jews visited the United States in 1978 to win

support for the movement among allies of Israel in the U.S. Congress. Domestically, the social and economic disparity between urban and rural populations, education, health care, and communications all improved during Hassan's reign.

In the 1980s Hassan worked to secure Arab recognition of Israel and an end to the Arab-Israeli conflict. In November 1981 and again in September 1982 he hosted an Arab summit to address conflicts in the region through a Saudi-sponsored peace plan. The plan called for the Israeli withdrawal from all occupied territories and the establishment of a Palestinian state. In July 1986 he held two days of talks on continued Palestinian issues with Israeli prime minister Shimon Peres. Hassan also sought to improve relationships among other Arab states. In 1984 he organized the Islamic Congress of Casablanca and created the Arabic-African Union with Libya. During the 1991 Persian Gulf War, Morocco aligned itself squarely with the United States and sent troops to defend Saudi Arabia.

Morocco expressed agreement with the principles of the 1993 Oslo Accords and received Israeli prime minister Rabin and Foreign Minister Peres in Casablanca following the signing ceremony in Washington, D.C. On September 1, 1994, Morocco and Israel established semiofficial diplomatic relations with the opening of liaison offices in Jerusalem and Rabat. These offices served to promote tourism and trade between the two countries, an issue of great economic importance to Morocco. They remained open for eight years but closed following the Palestinian uprising in 2002.

The problems of rising Islamic fundamentalism posed difficult challenges for Morocco in the late 1980s and early 1990s and continue under the leadership of Hassan's son and successor, King Mohammed VI. On May 16, 2003, 12 suicide bombers of Salafiyya Jihadiyya, an offshoot of the Moroccan Islamic Combatant Group and believed to be affiliated with Al Qaeda, killed 45 people in Casablanca in five separate bombings. Although the attack on the Jewish Sabbath ultimately killed no Jews, the targets included a Jewish social club and restaurant, a Jewish cemetery, and a Jewish-owned Italian restaurant.

For the immediate future, it appears that domestic issues will continue to be the focus of the Moroccan monarchy rather than foreign policy. Other challenges facing the nation include continued fighting in Western Sahara, reducing constraints on private activity and foreign trade, increasing democracy, and achieving sustainable economic growth.

MARK SANDERS

See also

Israel-Egypt Peace Treaty; Oslo Accords

References

Entelis, John P. *Culture and Counterculture in Moroccan Politics.* Boulder, CO: Westview, 1989.

Laskier, Michael M. *Israel and the Maghreb: From Statehood to Oslo.* Tallahassee: Florida State University Press, 2004.

Pennell, C. R. *Morocco since 1830: A History.* New York: New York University Press, 2000.

Morrison-Grady Plan
Event Date: July 31, 1946

British proposal of July 1946 that called for a federal arrangement for Palestine under a British trusteeship. In the summer of 1946 both Jewish underground violence and the illegal immigration of Jews from Europe (Aliya Bet) began to impact British Palestinian policy. Arthur Creech-Jones, the somewhat pro-Zionist colonial secretary, succeeded in convincing Foreign Secretary Ernest Bevin that both the U.S. government and the Jews would insist on some restructuring of the British Mandate.

Following the British government's rejection of the Anglo-American Committee of Inquiry's report, U.S. president Harry S. Truman announced the appointment of a cabinet committee of the secretaries of state, war, and the treasury to advise him on Palestine policy and implementation of his proposal for the admission of 100,000 Jewish displaced persons (DPs) to Palestine. This committee in turn delegated a working body of three representatives headed by Assistant Secretary of State Dr. Henry F. Grady. This subcommittee then began discussions with a parallel British group

headed by Herbert Morrison, deputy prime minister and leader of the House of Commons. Their goal was to develop a joint Anglo-American plan for Palestine. In late June the American group flew to Britain, and during the next five weeks the two groups of experts met under the chairmanship of Morrison. There was considerable pressure on the conferees to come up with a solution, for violence in Palestine was on the upswing, capped by the Irgun Tsvai Leumi (National Military Organization) bombing of the King David Hotel on July 22, 1946, when 91 people died.

On July 31, 1946, the joint committee presented its findings to the British Parliament. The report, which basically adhered to the British position, began by expressing the hope that the governments of occupied Germany would create a situation favorable to the resettlement in Europe of a majority of those displaced by the war. Other nations were also encouraged to take numbers of refugees.

Regarding Palestine, the Morrison-Grady Plan (also known as the Cantonization Plan) proposed a federative solution whereby the mandate would be transformed into a trusteeship divided into four areas: an Arab province, a Jewish province, the Negev, and Jerusalem, with the latter two areas under continued British administration. Both the Arab and Jewish provinces would elect their own legislatures, and from these the high commissioner would select two separate executive branches. The high commissioner would retain full authority over defense, foreign relations, customs, the police, and the court system. He would also have veto power over all legislation for the first five years.

The proposal was most disadvantageous to the Jews, who would be left with only about 17 percent of the land area of Palestine, the smallest amount allocated to them under any partition plan to that point and less than 60 percent of that allocated to them under the Peel Commission partition plan. The Jewish province would include about two-thirds of the coastal plain, the Jezreel Valley, and much of eastern Galilee. The sole advantage for the Jews was the proposal to admit 100,000 refugees in the first year after the plan went into effect. Thereafter, the high commissioner would control additional immigration into Palestine on the basis of the ability of the land to sustain it. Implementation of the plan, however, rested on acceptance of it by both the Arabs and Jews.

The British government greeted the Morrison-Grady Plan with approval. The plan clearly suited British requirements, for with Egypt demanding a British departure, control of the Negev would permit Britain bases just to the north of the Suez Canal. London announced its intention to invite both Arab and Jewish representatives to a conference in London in September 1946 to settle the Palestinian issue. The Zionist Executive, meeting in Paris in July, rejected that invitation outright, stating that it would participate only if the Jews were promised an adequate share of the land of Palestine. Meanwhile, President Truman informed the British government that because of intense opposition to the Morrison-Grady Plan in the United States, the U.S. government would not endorse it.

The Palestinian Arabs also rejected participation in the conference as long as the mufti of Jerusalem was denied participation. Thus, when the conference opened in September 1946 it was limited to the British government and to Arab representatives from states beyond Palestine. The Arabs, however, were uncompromising. They insisted on a unitary state with its own popularly elected legislature but were prepared to guarantee freedom of religion. There would be 3 Jewish ministers out of 10, and Hebrew could be a second official language in districts where Jews were the absolute majority. But naturalization would be extended only to those people who had lived in Palestine for 10 years, thus excluding DPs.

In an early October 1946 letter to Prime Minister Clement Attlee, Truman expressed his opposition to the plan and his interest in the earliest possible admission of the 100,000 Jewish refugees to Palestine.

SPENCER C. TUCKER

See also

Aliya Bet; Anglo-American Committee of Inquiry; Bevin, Ernest; Irgun Tsvai Leumi; Peel Commission; World Zionist Organization Executive

References

Sachar, Howard M. *A History of Israel: From the Rise of Zionism to Our Time.* 3rd ed. New York: Knopf, 2007.

Shepherd, Naomi. *Ploughing Sand: British Rule in Palestine, 1917–1948.* New Brunswick, NJ: Rutgers University Press, 1999.

MOSES, Operation

Start Date: November 21, 1984
End Date: January 5, 1985

Covert operation undertaken by the Israel Defense Forces (IDF) working in conjunction with the United States and Sudan to evacuate Jews from Ethiopia during 1984–1985. Operation MOSES was named for the biblical Old Testament figure Moses, who led the Jews out of Egypt.

Since 1980, the Israeli government had supported the secret smuggling of Ethiopian Jews (known as Beta Israel) into Israel via Sudan to escape the repressive Marxist regime of dictator Mengistu Haile Mariam. Most of the refugees had walked out of Ethiopia into Sudan, and by 1982 approximately 2,500 had made it to safety. The Sudanese government tacitly agreed to grant the Ethiopian Jews access to their borders, as it opposed the Mengistu regime and hoped to garner aid from the United States. In 1983 the Israelis secretly airlifted hundreds of Beta Israel out of Sudan in Lockheed C-130 Hercules aircraft.

The situation in the Sudanese refugee camps, where the Jews were placed, became increasingly intolerable as more and more arrived. Hundreds died on the long treks to the camps, and many more

Immigrant children from Ethiopia take a morning stroll with their kindergarten teacher at the Kiryat Gat Absorption Center on January 4, 1985. The children fled Ethiopia as part of Operation MOSES. (Nati Harnik/Israeli Government Press Office)

perished in the squalid conditions while awaiting transport. Matters reached a crisis in late 1984 as famine gripped all of Sudan. Conditions in the refugee camps deteriorated all the more because the hard-pressed Sudanese government could not feed its own people, let alone the refugees. In an unprecedented show of mutual cooperation, the Israelis reached an agreement with the Sudanese government, brokered by the U.S. embassy in Khartoum, with the assistance of the Central Intelligence Agency (CIA) for a large-scale airlift of all Jewish refugees from Sudan. The mission was code-named Operation MOSES.

The operation began on November 21, 1984, as Hercules transports of the Israeli Air Force began flying into Sudan to begin the rescue of the 8,000 refugees. On the ground, IDF troops were met by Sudanese soldiers and mercenaries who assisted them with the operation. It is believed that at least 4,000 refugees had died on the trek from Ethiopia to Sudan, and many more would perish in the camps if they were not removed immediately. It was certainly unheralded for a Muslim government to assist the State of Israel, and when the media published the story, Arab governments applied pressure on Sudan to cease the operation. Sudan closed its airspace to Israel, and the last MOSES flight took place on January 5, 1985. In the end, some 8,000 Ethiopian Jews had been safely airlifted from Sudan. Approximately 1,000 Beta Israel were left behind in Sudanese camps but were later airlifted out by the U.S. Air Force through an agreement with Sudan in a mission dubbed Operation JOSHUA.

Operation MOSES was so successful that when the Mengistu regime fell in 1991 and civil war broke out in Ethiopia, the Israelis were able to fly directly to Addis Ababa and rescue the remaining 14,000 Beta Israel in Operation SOLOMON. Upon reaching Israel, the Ethiopian refugees had to undergo intensive education in training camps, some for as long as two years, in order to learn Hebrew and function in an industrialized society. Unfortunately, many Beta Israel were unable to assimilate into Israeli society and remain to this day a depressed, undereducated, and unemployed segment of society.

ROD VOSBURGH

See also
Israel; Israel Defense Forces

References

Naim, Asher. *Saving the Lost Tribe: The Rescue and Redemption of the Ethiopian Jews.* New York: Ballantine, 2003.

Parfitt, Tudor. *Operation Moses: The Untold Story of the Secret Exodus of the Falasha Jews from Ethiopia.* New York: Stein and Day, 1986.

Rapoport, Louis. *Redemption Song: The Story of Operation Moses.* Orlando: Harcourt, 1986.

Safran, Claire. *Secret Exodus: The Story of Operation Moses.* Louisville: Reader's Digest, 1987.

Semi, Emanuela Trevisan. *The Beta Israel in Ethiopia and Israel: Studies on Ethiopian Jews.* Oxford, UK: Routledge, 1998.

Moshavim

Cooperative agricultural settlements in Israel. Unlike a kibbutz, where all the land and resources are shared among all of the inhab-

A member of Moshav Talmei Yosef in the Pithat Shalom district of Israel in his flower greenhouse, July 1983. (Nati Harnik/Israeli Government Press Office)

itants, families who belong to a moshav actually own and control their own land. They engage in cooperative purchases and sales, however, in order to achieve greater economic efficiency and self-sufficiency. Like the kibbutzim, the moshavim originated among labor Zionists in the late part of the 19th century, when many Jews began to settle in Palestine (then controlled by the Ottoman Empire). In some ways, moshavim operate in similar fashion to the Grange movement and the farmers alliances of the latter half of the 19th century in the United States. These were attempts to form socially cohesive farmers' cooperatives by engaging in group purchasing and selling.

In most moshavim, the individual family land plots are of equal size and of similar land and soil type. Crops are raised using co-op labor resources, but profits go to the individual family farms and not into a common pool of capital.

There are two types of moshavim. The first are moshav ovdim, the most numerous, where families and workers labor under a cooperative arrangement but where families and individuals retain control over their own land and profits. In moshav shitufi, all work is done in collective fashion, and profits are shared equally (much as in a kibbutz). However, unlike the kibbutz, individuals and families retain autonomy over their own social affairs. For example, there are no attempts at collective child-rearing in the moshav shitufi, and there has been generally no insistence on gender equality. For this reason, moshavim have tended to attract a more socially conservative following than kibbutzim.

In 1921 the first moshav was developed in the Jezreel Valley. In the late 1980s, the last time a comprehensive survey was conducted, some 450 moshavim were operating in Israel, encompassing about 155,000 individuals. Of those 450 moshavim, slightly more than 400 were moshav ovdim. Unlike the kibbutz movement, which has attracted mostly Ashkenazic Jews, the moshavim have tended to attract a more eclectic—albeit more conservative—following. Moshavim have served well as vehicles by which new immigrants to Palestine and Israel have acculturated to life in a new land and, eventually, to life among the middle class.

Since the late 1960s, changing demographics and economic realities have conspired to alter the makeup of many moshavim. For example, as immigration to Israel began to trail off at the end of the 1960s and as the Arab population increased, moshavim have turned increasingly to outside labor. Many of these laborers are now Arab. The economic crises and dislocations of the 1970s and early 1980s also challenged the moshav. High inflation combined with falling prices for agricultural products forced a sizable number of Jews in moshavim to seek part-time (and even full-time) work outside their settlement. What's more, much of this work is not in agriculture. Indeed, many have secured jobs in the booming service sector. Because moshavim never enjoyed the vaunted status of kibbutzim in Israeli society, they have not experienced the precipitous decline in status, as the kubbutzim have, over the past 25 years.

PAUL G. PIERPAOLI JR.

See also

Ashkenazic Judaism; Hasidic Judaism; Israel; Kibbutz Movement; Mizrahic Judaism; Sephardic Judaism; Zionism

References

Schwartz, Moshe, Susan Leeds, and Gideon M. Kressel. *Rural Cooperatives in Socialist Utopia: Thirty Years of Moshav Development in Israel.* New York Praeger, 1995.

Weintraub, D., M. Lissak, and Y. Azmon. *Moshava, Kibbutz, and Moshav: Patterns of Jewish Rural Settlement and Development in Palestine.* Ithaca, NY: Cornell University Press, 1969.

Zussman, Pinchas. *Individual Behavior and Social Choice in a Cooperative Settlement: The Theory and Practice of the Israeli Moshav.* Jerusalem: Magnes Press, Hebrew University, 1988.

Mossad

Israeli organization responsible for intelligence and special operations outside the borders of Israel. The Central Institute for Intelligence and Special Missions, or Mossad (meaning "Institute"), was formed in April 1951 by Prime Minister David Ben-Gurion.

Telecom boxes bugged by Mossad operatives in an apartment building in Berne, Switzerland, February 27, 1998. Four of the five men arrested by Swiss police later disappeared; the fifth was convicted of spying in July 2000. (Stephane Ruet/Corbis Sygma)

The agency reports directly to the prime minister. Before Mossad's creation, the task of gathering foreign intelligence had been left to the Ministry of Foreign Affairs. Within two months of its inception, the Mossad had worked out an agreement with the U.S. Central Intelligence Agency (CIA) concerning the sharing of information between the two organizations.

The many operations the Mossad has carried out include securing a copy of Soviet leader Nikita Khrushchev's secret speech to the Twentieth Communist Party Congress on February 25, 1956, in which he denounced Joseph Stalin's policies. The Mossad passed a copy of the speech on to the CIA before that agency had obtained its own copy. The Mossad sponsored successful agents in Egypt (including Wolfgang Lotz from 1959 to 1964) and in Syria (Eliahu Cohen from 1962 to 1965). The agency also hunted down former Nazis who had been in hiding since the end of World War II. The most significant capture was that of Adolf Eichmann, living in Argentina in 1960. Eichmann was transported to Israel and later tried for war crimes, found guilty, and executed.

Major Members of the Israeli Intelligence Community

Branch	Primary Function	Still Active?
Aman	Responsible for military intelligence	Yes
Center for Political Research	Responsible for monitoring Middle Eastern political trends and attitudes	Yes
Lekem	Responsible for obtaining secret technology/weapons	No
Mossad	Responsible for gathering international intelligence, counterterrorism, and covert actions	Yes
Nativ	Responsible for covertly aiding Jewish immigration from the communist bloc	No
Shabak	Responsible for internal security and counterintelligence	Yes

Prior to the 1967 Six-Day War, the Mossad, along with the Israel Defense Forces (IDF) Directorate of Main Intelligence (Aman), collected information on neighboring Arab countries. This intelligence was an important factor in Israel's lightning victory. The Mossad was not successful, however, in warning the government prior to the 1973 Yom Kippur War. Mossad operatives were fairly certain that Egypt and Syria were planning an offensive against Israel sometime in late 1973. This time, however, Aman concluded that these Arab states were indeed not going to attack Israel and therefore dismissed the Mossad's information. The result was a stunning reversal for Israel in the early stages of the conflict.

In 1973 following the murders of the Israeli athletes at the 1972 Munich Olympics, the Mossad tracked down and assassinated 12 of the Palestinians involved in that operation. The Mossad also played a key role in helping to collect information in support of the successful Israeli raid in 1976 on the Entebbe Airport where hijackers had seized control of an Air France airliner and were holding as hostage its 97 passengers and crew.

The Mossad was also responsible for the destruction in April 1979 of two nuclear cores in France that were bound for the Iraqi nuclear power reactor Tammuz I. In June 1980 the Mossad engineered the assassination of an Egyptian nuclear physicist who was working with the Iraqis. Then in June 1981 Mossad agents, working with the military's intelligence agency, helped plan the Israeli air raid on Iraq's nuclear facility at Osiraq, near Baghdad. Israeli bombers completely destroyed the area.

The Mossad is widely suspected of being behind the March 1990 assassination in Brussels of Dr. Gerald Bull, the brilliant but erratic Canadian artillery designer. Bull at the time was working for Saddam Hussein on Project Babylon, a supergun that would give Iraq the capability of putting a 4,400-pound projectile into orbit. Bull was also helping Iraq upgrade the capabilities of its Scud missile arsenal. The Mossad has never denied its involvement in Bull's assassination.

Mossad agents continue to play a major role in Israeli security and intelligence-gathering operations. They have arranged covert meetings between members of the Israeli government and various Arab governments including those of Egypt, Jordan, and Lebanon. In early 1978 the Mossad facilitated meetings that ultimately led to the pathbreaking Camp David Accords of September 1978.

DALLACE UNGER

See also

Bull, Gerald Vincent; Camp David Accords; Eichmann, Karl Adolf; Entebbe Hostage Rescue; Munich Olympic Games; Osiraq Raid; Six-Day War; Tammuz I Reactor; Yom Kippur War

References

Black, Ian, and Benny Morris. *Israel's Secret Wars: A History of Israel's Intelligence Services.* New York: Grove, 1994.

Polmar, Norman, and Thomas B. Allen. *Spy Book: The Encyclopedia of Espionage.* New York: Random House, 1997.

Steven, Stewart. *The Spymasters of Israel.* New York: Macmillan, 1980.

Mount Scopus

High ground considered part of East Jerusalem and within the official city limits of Jerusalem, now under official Israeli control. Mount Scopus is 2,736 feet above sea level and is 1.24 square miles in area. It overlooks the Old City of Jerusalem to its immediate northeast. While considered a geographic extension of the Mount of Olives, its commanding height and location make the tiny hilltop enclave a strategic key to controlling and defending Jerusalem. The area, providing panoramic views of both Jerusalem and the Judean desert, takes its name from the Greek word *skopeo,* meaning "to look over." Mount Scopus was vital in the many battles fought for control of Jerusalem. In AD 70 the Roman Legions of Titus camped there, as did the Crusaders in 1099 and the British in 1917.

The area is dominated by cultural and humanitarian institutions. Unlike much of Jerusalem, there are no sites of religious significance. Two hospitals, Augusta Victoria and Hadassah, are located on Mount Scopus. A former Lutheran hospice, Augusta Victoria Hospital served as the headquarters of the British Mandate in its earliest years and was subsequently transformed into a United Nations (UN) Relief and Works Agency hospital. Hadassah Medical Center is an important hospital of medical research established in 1938 by the Zionist Women's Organization of the same name.

Mount Scopus is also the home of Hebrew University, a secular postsecondary institution opened in 1925, and the Jerusalem British Commonwealth War Graves Cemetery. The latest addition to the area, the Mormon Brigham Young University Jerusalem Center, opened amid religious opposition from some area Jews in 1989. It serves as a multidisciplinary study center for Mormons and also hosts regular music concerts for the area's inhabitants. Small Jew-

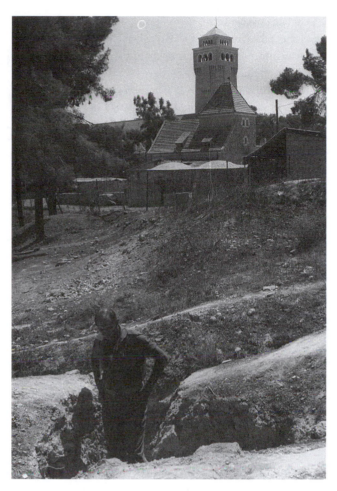

Arab Legion trenches at Augusta Victoria Hospital on Mount Scopus, Jerusalem, September 1967. (Ilan Bruner/Israeli Government Press Office)

ish neighborhoods and the Arab community known as Issawiya (with a population of some 8,000 people) are close by.

Mount Scopus has played an important role during Arab-Jewish clashes and in Israel's early conflicts. The most infamous event related to the area, the April 13, 1948, attack on a convoy traveling to Scopus through the Arab Sheikh Jarrah neighborhood, resulted in the deaths of 77 Jews. During the fighting that year, an Israeli garrison held out on Mount Scopus after Jordanian forces seized the Old City. Under the UN-monitored Mount Scopus Agreement of July 7, 1948, the area became demilitarized and was divided into Arab (Jordanian) and Jewish (Israeli) sections.

From 1948 to 1967, much of Mount Scopus, including Hadassah Medical Center and the Hebrew University, remained an Israeli enclave within Jordanian territory. Although the Israel-Jordan General Armistice Agreement of 1949 mentioned free access to the area, it was never permitted. For 19 years, regulated numbers of Israeli police and civilian workers reached the enclave and its closed buildings through an elaborate convoy system worked out with Jordan and the UN Truce Supervision Organization (UNTSO). Mount Sco-

pus was the site of many Israeli-Jordanian clashes during this time, most notably on May 26, 1958, when four Israeli police officers and an UNTSO peacekeeper were killed.

Israel captured the area early in the 1967 Six-Day War, helping make the subsequent seizure of the Old City possible. The institutions on Mount Scopus were reopened immediately following that conflict. The strategic and institutional significance of Mount Scopus makes the area both vital to Israel and a possible point of contention in future peace negotiations, particularly ones dealing with the status of Jerusalem.

ANDREW THEOBALD

See also

Arab-Jewish Communal War; Israeli War of Independence, Israeli-Jordanian Front; Jerusalem; Jordan; Six-Day War; United Nations Peacekeeping Missions

References

Golani, Motti. "Jerusalem's Hope Lies Only in Partition: Israeli Policy on the Jerusalem Question 1948–1967." *International Journal of Middle Eastern Studies* 31 (1999): 577–604.

Israeli, Raphael. *Jerusalem Divided: The Armistice Regime, 1947–1967.* London: Frank Cass, 2002.

Oren, Michael B. *Six Days of War: June 1967 and the Making of the Modern Middle East.* Novato, CA: Presidio, 2003.

Movement of Islamic Resistance

See Hamas

Mubarak, Hosni
Born: May 4, 1928

Egyptian Air Force air marshal and since 1981 president of Egypt. Muhammad Hosni Said Mubarak was born on May 4, 1928, in Kafr al-Musayliha, a town in the Nile River delta Egyptian governorate of al-Minufiyyah, where his father was an inspector in the Ministry of Justice. Mubarak graduated from the Egyptian Military Academy in 1949 and the Egyptian Air Force Academy at Bilbeis in 1950, from which he earned a degree in aviation sciences. He then took advanced flight training at the Soviet air base at Frunze Bishkek in what was then Soviet Kyrgyzstan. He completed his military training at the Soviet General Staff Academy in Moscow during 1964–1965.

Mubarak advanced steadily in the Egyptian Air Force from pilot to instructor, squadron leader, base commander (Western Air Force Base, Cairo West Airfield), head of the Egyptian Military Delegation to the Soviet Union (1964), commandant of the Egyptian Air Force Academy (1967–1969), chief of staff of the Egyptian Air Force (1969–1972) during the War of Attrition (1967–1970), and then deputy minister of war (1972–1975). The early success of the Egyptian Air Force in the October 1973 Yom Kippur War with Israel was

Egyptian president Hosni Mubarak at Andrews Air Force Base, Maryland, January 27, 1983. (U.S. Department of Defense)

in large part attributed to Mubarak's leadership and led to his promotion to air marshal in 1974.

In April 1975 President Anwar Sadat appointed Mubarak to the vice presidency. Three years later Mubarak was chosen to serve as the vice chairman of the ruling National Democratic Party (NDP). In October 1981 Sadat was assassinated by Muslim extremists. Mubarak was injured, although not seriously, in the attack. He then succeeded Sadat as president and became the chairman of the NDP.

Since the Sadat assassination, Mubarak has been elected to four additional six-year terms as Egyptian president (1987, 1993, 1999, and 2005). Only in the 2005 elections were any other candidates allowed to run for president, and these were severely hampered by election rules. As president, Mubarak has mediated the dispute among Morocco, Algeria, and Mauritania concerning the future of Western (Spanish) Sahara, and he has maintained sufficient neutrality in the Israeli-Palestinian conflict to mediate some of the elementary disputes of the Second (al-Aqsa) Intifada that began in 2000. He also played a role in the bilateral agreement between Israel and the Palestine Liberation Organization (PLO) in 1993 that emerged from the Oslo Accords.

Although Mubarak supports Egypt's 1979 peace treaty with Israel under the Camp David Accords, Egypt's relations with other Arab countries improved during his presidency. These ties had been badly strained by the 1979 peace accord. In 1989 Egypt was readmitted to the Arab League after being expelled for making peace with the Israelis. Its headquarters, originally in Cairo and then moved, were also relocated back to the Egyptian capital. A nongovernmental boycott of cultural, educational, and political relations with Israel continued during his presidency.

Mubarak also played a key role in the 1991 Persian Gulf War. In August 1990 Iraqi dictator Saddam Hussein sent his forces into Kuwait. The tiny nation was quickly overrun and occupied. After the 1990 United Nations (UN) sanctions against Iraq—supported by Mubarak—failed to dislodge Iraq from Kuwait, Mubarak organized the Arab League's opposition to the invasion of Kuwait. Based largely on the Saudis' decision to allow the U.S.-led international military coalition to use their nation as a staging area, Mubarak decided to contribute approximately 38,500 troops to the coalition. Indeed, Egyptian infantry soldiers were among the first of the coalition to enter Kuwait. Mubarak certainly had no use for Hussein, whom he viewed as a threat and a potential source of regional destabilization, but he was also attracted to the Kuwaiti cause by Western incentives to join the fight. The West—with the United States in the lead—promised many coalition nations, including Egypt, significant economic assistance and debt forgiveness in return for their support and involvement in the war.

But Mubarak dispatched no troops to the U.S.-led ouster of Hussein in the Iraq War of 2003. Indeed, Mubarak spoke out against the war, arguing that a war on Iraq would complicate the war on terror and that resolution of the Arab-Israeli conflict should take precedence over the unseating of Hussein. The United States continues to be Egypt's chief source of military equipment, also granting the country a smaller amount of economic aid. Since 2003 Egypt's relations with Russia have been strengthened, although Mubarak continues to forge a careful course of neutrality when dealing with the Americans and Russians.

Mubarak used the enormous power given to him under Egypt's 1971 constitution to continue the sweeping program of economic recovery instituted by Sadat and to implement privatization and rationalization policies pressed upon Egypt by the International Monetary Fund and the World Bank. But the large public sector is far from being dismantled. Mubarak's other major tasks have been to limit terrorism and control nonviolent opponents. In the late 1990s his government more directly confronted Islamic extremists, such as the Islamic Group and the Gamaat Islamiya. The latter was responsible for the killing of 60 foreign tourists at Luxor in 1997. The more moderate Islamist group, the Muslim Brotherhood, along with many small secular parties, also opposed Mubarak and the present Egyptian state. Mubarak was unharmed in an assassination attempt by five assailants in June 1995 in Addis Ababa, Ethiopia, and was slightly wounded in a second assassination attempt in Port Said on September 6, 1999.

Mubarak's government has encouraged joint ventures and is generally supportive of big business, so much so that workers and segments of the military have periodically rioted and demonstrated their displeasure. In the 1980s and 1990s the Egyptian economy suffered from debt, lack of savings, a trade imbalance, and blows to the tourist industry. The government could not abandon the subsidies it provides to its large population with a very low per capita income, and unemployment only increased. Nonetheless, the economy offered a favorable opportunity for investors, especially in the construction sector. During 2004–2006 terrorist attacks again threatened the tourist industry. Since December 2006, labor protests, sit-ins, and strikes have occurred around the country, including a strike of 10,000 workers in the textile industry. Unemployment persists at high levels.

Mubarak has twice served as chairman of the Organization of African Unity (OAU), during 1989–1990 and again during 1993–1994. Although he remains dedicated to Arab unity, the peaceful resolution of Middle East conflicts, positive neutrality, Egyptian economic growth, and a secular non-Islamic Egyptian state, opposition to his rule in Egypt appears to be growing. Much of the opposition stems from the almost complete power vested in the Egyptian presidency and the lack of a pluralistic political process. The Egyptian parliament is largely a pro forma body that merely rubber-stamps the wishes of the ruling party. Until 2005, presidential elections were seen as a sham. Vote rigging and election fraud have been endemic, and corruption in general seems on the increase. Until very recently, the media in Egypt has been one-dimensional and controlled by the state. This, of course, has only further entrenched the political system. Although the state still controls the major networks and newspapers, a few independent media outlets have surfaced and have offered mild criticism of the Mubarak government. Mubarak has been able to retain a tight grip on power thanks to a large and loyal military and security establishment, which has responded to repeated assassination attempts against him, foiled coups, and worked to counter the ever-present peril of Islamic extremists who have no use at all for the Egyptian government.

In the past several years, Mubarak has come under increasing international pressure to democratize Egypt. He has made small steps in that direction, but clearly his nation has a considerable way to travel in that regard.

RICHARD EDWARDS AND PAUL G. PIERPAOLI JR.

See also

Arab League; Attrition, War of; Camp David Accords; Egypt; Egypt, Armed Forces; Persian Gulf War; Sadat, Anwar; Six-Day War; Yom Kippur War

References

Cox, Viki. *Hosni Mubarak*. Philadelphia: Chelsea House, 2002.

Kassem, Maye. *Egyptian Politics: The Dynamics of Authoritarian Rule.* Boulder, CO: Lynne Rienner, 2004.

McDermott, Anthony. *Egypt from Nasser to Mubarak: A Flawed Revolution.* London: Routledge and Kegan Paul, 1998.

Tripp, Charles, and Roger Owen. *Egypt under Mubarak*. London: Routledge, 1990.

Muhammad, Prophet of Islam
Born: 569 or 570
Died: 632

Prophet of Islam who established the first community of Muslims in the Arabian Peninsula in the seventh century. Muhammad ibn Abdullah ibn Abd al-Mutallib, always referred to by Muslims as the Prophet Muhammad, was at once a military, political, and religious leader who effectively united the disparate tribes of the region into a single empire. As a prophet of Allah (God), he received a series of orally transmitted revelations, the Message, that were eventually transcribed as the Koran. The Prophet Muhammad is called the Seal of Prophecy, which means that he, following upon the earlier prophets of the Bible and Jesus, was the last and final prophet. Unlike Jesus the Prophet Muhammad is not considered to be a divine figure, but he is revered by Muslims as the Beautiful Model because his Sunna, or Way, provided the example for future generations of Muslims.

Muhammad was born in approximately 570, although some sources date his birth from 569. He was born into a branch of an important clan, the Banu Hashim of the Quraysh tribe, in Mecca, located on the western Arabian Peninsula area of the Hejaz. Prior to his birth, his father died. Thus Muhammad was, in the status of that era, an orphan. As an infant, he was sent as was the custom to a wet nurse, Halima, a tribal woman. While in her care there were signs and portents of his future greatness. Muhammad's mother died when he was six years old, and his grandfather, Abd al-Mutallib, died just two years later. Muhammad then passed under the guardianship of his uncle, Abu Talib, who was an influential merchant. Muhammad soon began accompanying his uncle on trading journeys during the pilgrimage season. On one journey to Bosra, Syria, he was greeted by a monk named Buhaira, who hailed Muhammad as a future prophet.

As an adult Muhammad entered the employ of Khadija (555–619), a wealthy 40-year-old widow, and managed her caravans, earning a reputation for honesty such that he was known as al-Amin (the faithful one). Khadija subsequently proposed to him. The two married in 595, and Muhammad remained devoted to her until her death in 619. The number of children born to the marriage remains in dispute. Some accounts argue that the pair had four daughters—Zaynab, Ruqayya, Umm Kulthum, and Fatima—and one or two sons who died. In any case, only Fatima was still living after her father's death. Muhammad married other women after Khadija's death, and he had a son by one of these wives who also died before the son was 2 years old. Of Muhammad's other wives, Aysha was said to be his favorite.

According to Muslim tradition, Muhammad received his first revelation in the year 610 while fasting in the cave of Hira, near Mecca. He heard the voice of the archangel Gabriel, who commanded him to recite verses of scripture, which Gabriel spoke to Muhammad. At first Muhammad did not know how to respond to

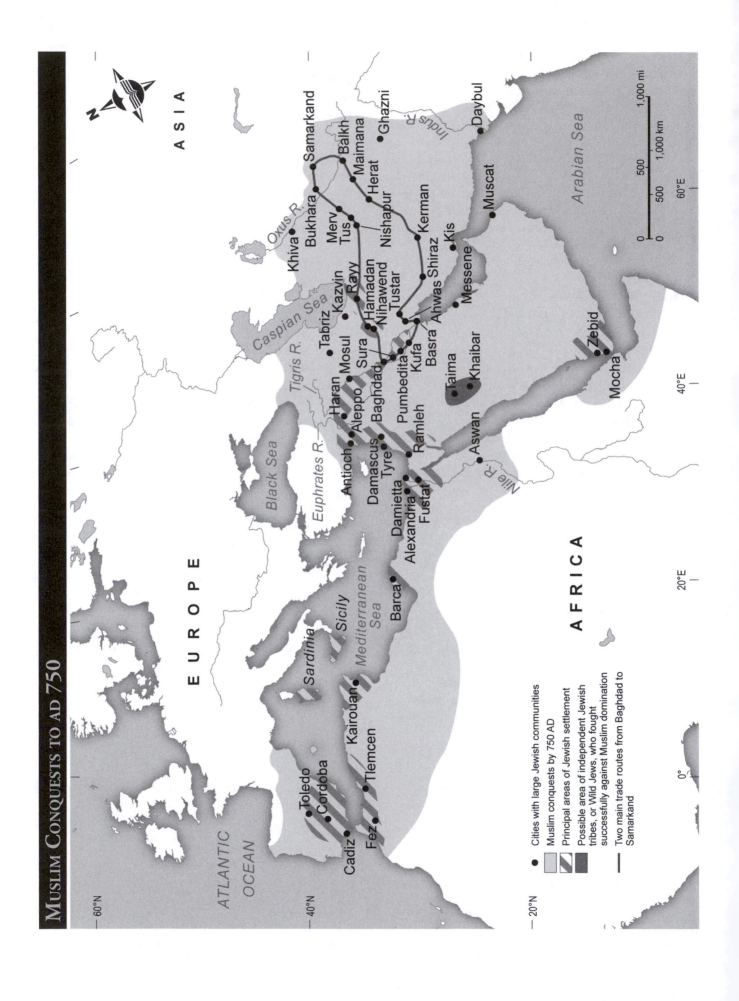

MUSLIM CONQUESTS TO AD 750

EUROPE

ASIA

AFRICA

ATLANTIC OCEAN

Black Sea

Caspian Sea

Mediterranean Sea

Arabian Sea

Tigris R.

Euphrates R.

Oxus R.

Indus R.

Nile R.

Sardinia

Sicily

Toledo
Cordoba
Cadiz
Fez
Tlemcen
Kairouan
Barca

Antioch
Haran
Mosul
Aleppo
Sura
Damascus
Baghdad
Tyre
Pumbedita
Kufa
Basra
Ramleh
Damietta
Alexandria
Fustat
Aswan
Taima
Khaibar
Messene
Ahwas Shiraz
Tustar
Nihawend
Hamadan
Rayy
Kazvin
Tabriz
Khiva
Bukhara
Merv
Tus
Nishapur
Kerman
Kis
Muscat
Zebid
Mocha
Samarkand
Balkh
Maimana
Herat
Ghazni
Daybul

N

Cities with large Jewish communities

Muslim conquests by 750 AD

Principal areas of Jewish settlement

Possible area of independent Jewish
tribes, or Wild Jews, who fought
successfully against Muslim domination

Two main trade routes from Baghdad to
Samarkand

60°N

40°N

20°N

0°

20°E

40°E

60°E

0 500 1,000 km
0 500 1,000 mi

his experience, but Khadija regarded his words as proof of a new revelation and thus became the first formal convert to Islam. For the remainder of his life, Muhammad continued to receive revelations. Within a few years of his initial revelations, he began to preach to any who would listen to his message about the One God, Creator and Judge of the World. As the Meccans then worshiped a pantheon of gods and goddesses, they were not very impressed with his message and later became increasingly hostile toward him.

As Muhammad's group of followers grew, they became perceived as a threat by the leadership of Mecca, including his own tribe. Some of the early converts to Islam came from the disaffected and disadvantaged segments of society. Most importantly, the Muslims' new set of beliefs implicitly challenged the Meccans' and the Quraysh tribe's guardianship over the Kaaba, the holy site dedicated to the gods and goddesses of the area that hosted an annual pilgrimage. The city's leading merchants attempted to persuade Muhammad to cease his preaching, but he refused. In response, the city leadership persecuted Muhammad's followers, and many fled the city. One group of his followers immigrated to Abyssinia. In 619 Muhammad endured the loss of both Khadija and Abu Talib, while the mistreatment of his followers increased.

The following year Muhammad undertook two miraculous journeys with the archangel Gabriel. The first, called the Isra, took Muhammad from Mecca to Jerusalem, where he ascended to the site of today's Dome of the Rock in the al-Aqsa Compound in Jerusalem. The second, called the Miraj, included a visit to heaven and hell. During the Miraj, Muhammad also spoke with earlier monotheistic prophets, including Abraham, Moses, and Jesus and saw Allah, "the Soul of Souls, the Face of Him who made the universe." Muhammad asked Allah for forgiveness for his ummah, the Muslim community, and Allah accepted his intercession (shafa). Allah assigned Muhammad with the task of 50 daily prayers for Muslims, and Moses advised Muhammad to return to Allah and request the number of prayers be reduced (to 5), which he did. The Isra and Miraj were accomplished in a single night. Scholars have presented the travels as both a spiritual vision and an actual physical experience.

In 622 Muhammad decided to leave the city of his birth at the invitation of groups residing in the city of Yathrib. Yathrib was located at a major oasis, and there Muhammad hoped to firmly establish a new community of Muslims free from the persecution of the Meccans. The immigration to Yathrib, called the Hijra, marks the beginning of the Muslim calendar. When Muhammad arrived in Yathrib he found a city divided by competing tribes, the Aws and the Khazraj. Both soon converted to Islam, uniting under Muhammad after a century of fighting. Yathrib later took the name of Madinat al-Nabi, or City of the Prophet. With the exception of a sizable Jewish community divided into three clans, the city of Medina was entirely under Muhammad's control by 624. At Medina, the rituals of Islam were established.

After Muhammad and most of his followers departed Mecca for Yathrib, the Meccans confiscated all Muslim property that had been left behind. In March 624 Muhammad led an abortive raid on a Meccan caravan. In retaliation, 1,000 Meccan warriors marched on Medina. Not content to await the attack, Muhammad led a force of approximately 300 warriors to meet the invading army. At Badr the armies collided, and Muhammad's followers achieved a decisive victory, inflicting more than 100 casualties at a cost of only 14 Muslims and driving off the Meccan army.

In 625 a Meccan army of 3,000 returned to menace Medina. Emboldened by the victory at Badr, Muhammad marched his army out of the city to face the enemy. At the Battle of Uhud the Muslims were defeated, but the Meccan leader, Abu Sufyan, chose to withdraw his army rather than raze Medina. Two years later Abu Sufyan again attacked Medina but failed to destroy Muhammad's army at the Battle of the Trench. In 628 Muhammad led a band of 1,400 followers to Mecca, ostensibly as a pilgrimage (hajj). They were refused entry to the city, although the differences between the Meccans and the Muslims were formally abolished in the Treaty of Hudhaybiyya. The truce lasted only two years. Renewed skirmishing led Muhammad to attack Mecca directly.

Eight years of converting other client tribes on the Arabian Peninsula provided Muhammad with an army of more than 10,000 followers, far too numerous for the Meccans to withstand. The polytheistic statuaries in Mecca were destroyed, and the majority of the populace converted to Islam. Following the conquest, Mecca became the heart of the Muslim empire, which rapidly unified the competing tribes of the region.

Muhammad did not live long after consolidating his power. In 632 he fell ill in Medina, and after several days of pain and weakness he died and was buried in a plot adjacent to his house. His followers quickly moved to expand his legacy, moving out of the Arabian Peninsula to challenge the Sassanians and the client tribes of the Eastern Roman (Byzantine) Empire. Eventually they conquered lands stretching from Central Asia to the Iberian Peninsula. However, political divisions coupled with external threats created competing dynasties rather than a united Muslim empire and also led to the growth of religious sects and varying intellectual trends within the religion and Muslim culture.

In nearly all these sects the Prophet Muhammad is honored to this day. His birthday is celebrated, and he has been a favorite subject of Muslim poets. The stories of his deeds and words, collected into the Hadith, remain an important source of religious law and history.

Modern Islam is one of the largest religions in the world, with approximately 1.3 billion adherents spanning across the globe.

PAUL J. SPRINGER AND SHERIFA ZUHUR

See also

Koran; Mecca; Medina; Shia Islam; Sunni Islam

References

Cook, M. A. *Muhammad*. New York: Oxford University Press, 1983.

Haykal, Muhammad Husayn. *The Life of Muhammad*. Translated by Isma'il R. al-Faruqi. Indianapolis: North American Trust Publications, 1976.

Schimmel, Annemarie. *And Muhammad Is His Messenger: The Veneration of the Prophet in Islamic Piety.* Chapel Hill: University of North Carolina Press, 1985.

Watt, W. Montgomery. *Muhammad at Mecca.* Oxford, UK: Clarendon, 1953.

———. *Muhammad at Medina.* Oxford, UK: Clarendon, 1962.

Weinberger, Eliot. *Muhammad.* New York: Verso, 2006.

Muhsin, Zuhayr

Born: 1936
Died: July 26, 1979

Secretary-general of the Palestinian militant organization al-Saiqa. Zuhayr Muhsin (later known as Issam al-Qadi) was born in Tulkarm on the West Bank in the British Mandate for Palestine in 1936. He fled with his family during the 1948–1949 Israeli War of Independence and moved to Amman, Jordan. Graduating from Amman Teachers' College with a degree in mathematics, he taught high school in Jordan for several years.

Following a number of confrontations with and several arrests by Jordanian authorities for political activism, Muhsin was expelled from that country in 1960. He then moved to Kuwait for eight years before settling in Damascus, Syria, in 1968. There he became closely affiliated with the Baath Party and also joined al-Saiqa, formed under the auspices of the Syrian government by Palestinians living in Syria.

In 1971 Muhsin became the secretary-general (head) of al-Saiqa. Founded in 1968, al-Saiqa is Arabic for "lightning" and is an acronym in Arabic for Vanguard of the Popular War of Liberation. Al-Saiqa withdrew from Palestine Liberation Organization (PLO) membership as part of the split that began over movement theory and leadership.

Muhsin was closely identified with the early fighting of the civil war in Lebanon. Some sources credit al-Saiqa or Muhsin with leading an assault on the Lebanese town of Damur in early 1976 that resulted in the deaths of a number of Lebanese Christian civilians. Muhsin also had a reputation for personal corruption. He was assassinated while leaving a casino in Nice, France, on July 26, 1979, a deed variously attributed to the Israelis and the Arab Liberation Front, a Palestinian group supported by Iraq's Baath Party.

SPENCER C. TUCKER

See also

Al-Saiqa; Arafat, Yasser; Palestine Liberation Organization

References

O'Neill, Bard E. *Armed Struggle in Palestine: A Political-Military Analysis.* Boulder, CO: Westview, 1978.

Quandt, William B., et al. *The Politics of Palestinian Nationalism.* Berkeley: University of California Press, 1973.

Rubin, Barry. *Revolution until Victory? The Politics and History of the PLO.* Reprint ed. Cambridge: Harvard University Press, 2003.

Mukhabarrat al-Amma

See General Intelligence Agency, Palestinian

Multinational Force and Observers in the Sinai

Independent military force drawn from many nations and involved in a peacekeeping mission in the Sinai Peninsula. The Multinational Force and Observers (MFO) was first conceptualized in 1979 as a result of the 1978 Camp David Accords and Israel-Egypt Peace Treaty of 1979. Following the conclusion of peace, the United States provided an interim monitoring force in its Sinai Field Mission while at the same time seeking to persuade the United Nations (UN) to establish a permanent force. When the United Nations refused, Egypt, Israel, and the United States began negotiations that led to a peacekeeping force apart from the UN. On August 3, 1981, a protocol to the peace treaty officially established the MFO. It first assumed its duties on April 26, 1982, the day that Israel turned over sovereignty of the Sinai to Egypt.

U.S. paratroopers board an El Al 747 jet bound for the Sinai for Multinational Force Observer duties, March 19, 1982. (U.S. Department of Defense)

MFO headquarters is located in Rome, Italy, and has representatives in both Cairo and Tel Aviv. Most of the observers operate in the Sinai Peninsula, with their logistical and support base, North Camp, located at al-Gurah about 15 miles from the Israeli border. The smaller South Camp is located at Sharm al-Sheikh on the southern tip of the Sinai Peninsula. Operating from these camps, the MFO maintains some 30 monitoring sites running the length of the peninsula. There is also one remote observation point on a small island that requires resupply by air. The MFO base at al-Gurah has been twice hit by Islamist militants. The first occurrence was on August 15, 2005, with a remote-controlled bomb that wounded two MFO members. The second was on April 26, 2006, just after deadly attacks at the nearby seaside resort of Dahab, when two suicide bombers targeted the base but killed no one but themselves.

A number of different nations have provided personnel for the MFO since its formation. Current participating nations are Australia, Canada, Colombia, Fiji, France, Hungary, Italy, New Zealand, the United States, and Uruguay. The United States provides the largest contingent, including a support unit and an infantry battalion on a rotational basis. Active army battalions were initially committed to the MFO mission but in recent years have been mobilized for duty with MFO. At any given point, the U.S. Army contingent averages 600 troops. Except for contributions from Germany and Japan, funding for the MFO is provided in three equal parts from Egypt, Israel, and the United States.

The basic mission of the MFO is to observe conditions in the Sinai and ensure that there are no violations of forces permitted to Egypt and Israel within certain zones. The MFO is also charged with ensuring freedom of navigation in the Strait of Tiran. To accomplish this mission, the MFO operates checkpoints and reconnaissance patrols along the international boundary between the two states.

SPENCER C. TUCKER

See also

Camp David Accords; Israel-Egypt Peace Treaty

References

Tabory, Mala. *The Multinational Force and Observers in the Sinai: Organization, Structure, and Function.* Westview Special Studies on the Middle East. Boulder, CO: Westview, 1986.

U.S. Congress, House Committee on Foreign Affairs. *Creation of the Multinational Force and Observers (MFO) for the Sinai.* Washington, DC: U.S. Government Printing Office, 1981.

Munich Olympic Games
Start Date: August 26, 1972
End Date: September 11, 1972

The games of the XX Olympiad, held in Munich during August 26–September 11, 1972, were the largest ever. The games set records in all categories, with 195 events and 7,123 athletes from 121 nations. But the games themselves were overshadowed and forever marred by a heinous act. These Olympic Games were the first to be held in Germany since 1936, and Germans hoped that they would help erase the racism that marked the 1936 Olympic Games in Berlin during the Nazi era. Yet the most memorable photograph to come out of the 1972 games was not American Mark Spitz receiving his seventh gold medal in swimming but rather the image of a masked Palestinian terrorist standing on a balcony and brandishing an automatic weapon.

Early on the morning of September 5, 1972, with 10 days of the games having gone by without incident and with but 6 days remaining, eight members of the Black September organization associated with Yasser Arafat's Fatah faction of the Palestine Liberation Organization (PLO), dressed as athletes, gained entrance to the Olympic Village, five of them by scaling a fence. Carrying their weapons in gym bags, they sought out the apartment building housing the Israeli athletes.

At about 5:00 a.m. there was a knock on the door of one of the Israeli rooms. Wrestling coach Moshe Weinberg opened it, saw the armed terrorists, and tried to close the door, shouting to other people in the room to flee. Weinberg died in a hail of bullets. An Israeli weightlifter in another room was also shot dead. The terrorists then took nine Israelis hostage.

As 300 German security police cordoned off the area, International Olympic Committee (IOC) president Avery Brundage met with his staff and decided that the games would continue. At about 9:30 a.m. the terrorists opened negotiations with German authorities, headed by Munich police chief Manfred Schreiber. The hostage-takers demanded that Israel free 234 Arab prisoners and that West Germany release 2 German terrorist leaders imprisoned in Frankfurt. The terrorists set a noon deadline and threatened to kill 2 of the hostages if their demands were not met.

Negotiations continued, and the deadline was repeatedly postponed. The terrorists rejected both a ransom payment and the proposal that Schreiber and two other high-ranking officials take the hostages' place. With Schreiber believing that the building could not be successfully stormed, that evening the two sides reached a deal providing for a plane that would take both the terrorists and their hostages to Cairo. Meanwhile, German sharpshooters took up position.

Security personnel set up a helicopter pad near the apartment complex, and at 8:40 p.m. the first of three helicopters landed. Fifteen miles away at the Fürstenfeldbruck military air base a Lufthansa 737 jet stood ready, with German sharpshooters also positioned there.

Shortly after 10:00 p.m. the bound-together and blindfolded hostages and their captors emerged from the apartment building and were herded onto a bus. The terrorists conducted this movement in such fashion that the police were unable to make any attempt to shoot them. Schreiber and two officials joined in the bus ride to the helicopters, which then ferried everyone to the airport.

Certain that the incident would end in the deaths of the hostages, German officials were determined to prevent the departure. At

Armed police drop into position on a terrace directly above the apartments in Munich where members of the Israeli Olympic team are being held hostage by Black September extremists, September 5, 1972. (Bettmann/Corbis)

3:00 a.m. on September 6, German sharpshooters opened fire on 2 terrorists who had just inspected the plane. In the bloody shootout that followed, a terrorist threw a grenade into one of the helicopters, killing all within. Other terrorists killed the remaining blindfolded hostages in another helicopter. In all, the incident claimed the lives of 11 Israelis, 5 terrorists, and 1 German policeman. Three of the terrorists were captured alive and imprisoned.

Less than two months later in response to the hijacking of a Lufthansa jet, the German government released the three imprisoned terrorists and allowed them to fly to Libya. Israeli prime minister Golda Meir and her cabinet, meanwhile, approved a top-secret operation by the Mossad (Israeli intelligence service) to track down and kill those responsible for the Munich atrocity. The Mossad's success in this operation and its moral implications are the subject of the 2005 film *Munich,* directed by Steven Spielberg.

SPENCER C. TUCKER

See also

Arafat, Yasser; Black September Organization; Fatah; Meir, Golda; Mossad; Palestine Liberation Organization

References

Espy, Richard. *The Politics of the Olympic Games.* Berkeley: University of California Press, 1979.

Hill, Christopher. *Olympic Politics.* 2nd ed. Manchester, UK: Manchester University Press, 1996.

Murphy, Robert Daniel
Born: October 28, 1894
Died: January 9, 1978

U.S. diplomat and State Department official. Born in Milwaukee, Wisconsin, on October 28, 1894, Robert Murphy attended Marquette and George Washington University, where he earned a law degree in 1917. He joined the foreign service that same year, and his first postings were as a consul in various European cities. Beginning in 1930 he served in various capacities in Paris, leaving there as chargé d'affaires in 1941.

Murphy's hitherto typical career took a dramatic turn when he was asked by President Franklin Roosevelt to be his representative to French North Africa, with the purpose of obtaining the defection of French forces from the collaborationist Vichy regime. Following this mission, Murphy was involved in the planning for the Allied invasion of North Africa in 1942. Following the German defeat of

May 1945, he became a political adviser in Germany and later director of the Office for German and Austrian Affairs.

During 1949–1952 Murphy served as U.S. ambassador to Belgium and then, in 1953, to Japan. He completed his government service as deputy undersecretary of state during 1954–1959. President Dwight Eisenhower called Murphy out of retirement in 1960 to assess the turbulent situation in the newly independent Congo, and during the Eisenhower era Murphy became a top diplomatic troubleshooter for the U.S. government. In 1953 Eisenhower sent Murphy to Seoul, South Korea, to convince Syngman Rhee to sign the armistice ending the Korean War. The following year Murphy traveled to Belgrade to encourage Marshal Josip Broz Tito to reach an agreement with Italy over Trieste. During the 1956 Suez Crisis Murphy was dispatched to London to evaluate the position of the British government.

Perhaps most significantly, during the American intervention in Lebanon in 1958 Murphy acted as a personal representative of the president. He established communications with all of the opposing factions in Lebanon, helped to ensure the safety of the 14,000 U.S. marines in Beirut, and promoted a peaceful handover of power from President Camille Chamoun to end the crisis. Before returning to the United States, Murphy visited Baghdad and Cairo in an effort to calm the tensions that had erupted in the Middle East during the tumultuous summer of 1958.

Following his retirement from government, Murphy served as the director of several companies, including Morgan Guaranty Trust Company and Corning Glass. He died in New York City on January 9, 1978.

BRENT M. GEARY

See also

Chamoun, Camille; Lebanon; Lebanon, U.S. Interventions in; United States, Middle East Policy

References

Brands, H. W. *Cold Warriors: Eisenhower's Generation and American Foreign Policy.* New York: Columbia University Press, 1988.

Murphy, Robert D. *Diplomat among Warriors.* New York: Doubleday, 1964.

Musa, Amr Mahmoud
Born: 1936

Secretary-general of the Arab League, formerly Egyptian minister of foreign affairs. Amr Mahmud Musa was born in Egypt in 1936. He graduated from Cairo University in 1957 with a degree in law and then worked as a lawyer.

In 1958 Musa joined the Egyptian Foreign Ministry and during 1958–1972 worked in several of its departments and also served in

Amr Musa, secretary-general of the Arab League and former Egyptian minister of foreign affairs, January 23, 2006. (European Commission/Berlaymont)

the Egyptian mission to the United Nations (UN). During 1974–1977 he was the assistant and adviser to the Egyptian minister of foreign affairs. During 1977–1981 and again during 1986–1990 he was director of the Department of International Organizations of the Egyptian Foreign Ministry. During 1981–1983 he served as alternate permanent representative of Egypt to the UN, and during 1983–1986 he was Egyptian ambassador to India. During 1990–1991 he was permanent chief representative of Egypt to the UN.

Musa became minister of foreign affairs in May 1991, and in October of that year he led Egypt's delegation to the Middle East Peace Conference in Madrid. He positioned his country as a staunch friend of the Palestinian people while maintaining a favorable relationship with Israel. He helped maneuver Egypt to the international forefront as a venue for subsequent peace talks between Israel and its Arab neighbors that culminated in the 1993 Israeli–Palestine Liberation Organization (PLO) Agreement and the 1994 Israeli-Jordanian Peace Accord.

Musa's outspoken, no-nonsense approach to foreign diplomacy at times ruffled feathers in the Western international community. In a February 1995 televised interview, he sharply criticized the Israeli government for failing to sign the Nuclear Non-Proliferation Treaty (1968). He announced to the UN two months later that Egypt could not support an extension of the treaty in light of Israel's refusal to join the pact. In June 1995 he was present during an assassination attempt on President Hosni Mubarak in Ethiopia during an African summit. Musa blamed the government of Sudan for planning the attack and initiated a freeze on relations with both Ethiopia and Sudan. His blunt talk endeared him to the Egyptian public and the broader Arab community. His popularity probably played a role in his being advanced by Mubarak from the office of foreign minister to that of secretary-general of the Arab League.

Musa tackled his new position with considerable energy, vowing to streamline the bureaucracy and reshape the Arab League into an effective voice for the Arabs in international affairs. While recognizing the need for change within the Arab world, he articulated a distinct, nuanced, and yet forceful point of view on matters concerning democratization, the Israeli-Palestinian conflict, and the Iraq War. Not surprisingly, under his leadership the Arab League, much like the UN, opposed the U.S.-led invasion of Iraq in March 2003. Musa remains a popular figure not only for his bluntness but also for his perceived integrity, sense of urgency, and efforts to involve other mediators in the 2006 crises in Lebanon and Gaza.

SPENCER C. TUCKER

See also
Arab League; Egypt; Madrid Conference; Mubarak, Hosni; Pan-Arabism

References
Kallen, Stuart A. *Egypt.* New York: Lucent, 1999.
Vatikiotis, P. J. *The History of Modern Egypt: From Muhammad Ali to Mubarak.* Baltimore: Johns Hopkins University Press, 1991.

Music

Music is a culturally defined phenomenon. In many Western societies, music may be defined as the art of sound organized within melodic, harmonic, metric, and rhythmic frameworks. Many other societies, however, do not have the same interpretation but closely classify the term within their own cultural context. This may include social, religious, and political connotations. This is the case when identifying music of the Middle East.

The position of the Middle East at the crossroads of Africa, Europe, and Asia contributed to its unique cultural and hence musical makeup. Its musical production can be divided into art music, produced for the royal courts and the elites such as classical Persian and Ottoman or Arabo-Ottoman music, some of which is still taught and performed today; folk or popular music; and modern musical forms that may combine indigenous and Western harmonies, instrumentation, or rhythms. Middle Eastern music has some overall unifying characteristics such as its instruments, which include the lute family, the *ud, saz, buzuq, nashat kar,* and *tar;* the lyre family, the *tanbura* and the *simsimiyya;* the horn and reed instruments, the *zurna, mijwiz, mizmar;* the reed flute, or *nay;* the zither family, including the *qanun* and *santur;* and the percussion family, clay and metal hand drums, larger drums (*tabl*) and tambourines with or without cymbals, finger cymbals, and spoons. Even the Arabic coffee grinder (a mortar and pestle) is used as an instrument in some folk music. These have been supplemented with Western instruments such as the violin, called *kamanja,* the same name as its Middle Eastern bowed predecessor; violas, cellos, and basses; the electronic keyboard or piano; concert flutes and brass; and the accordion. The most important and valued instrument is, however, the human voice. Other similarities are the avoidance of polyphony (one melodic line, no harmony); the use of microtones (usually quarter tones); melodic structures known as *maqam* (*maqamat*), which are modes rather than scales; the use of improvisation on the *maqamat,* which, when instrumental, is called *taqasim;* the use of ornamentation and call and response; the valuing of *tarab,* or emotional artistry rather than mere technique; and the dominance of percussion in many folk genres.

An early 20th-century ensemble performing classical or art music might have consisted of an *ud,* a *qanun,* a violin, a *nay* (reed flute), and the cymbaled tambourine (*riqq*) and was called a *takht* (meaning stage or platform). A pop musical group, or *firqa,* might consist of musicians playing the electronic keyboard, *tabla* or *darbakka* (the vase-shaped hand drum), and either violin, accordion, or possibly electrified bass. Musical performances are more interactive than in the West. If the music is considered excellent, the audience reacts emotionally and vocally.

Some religious music, such as the *samaiat* (a composition in a 10/8 rhythm) of the Sufi orders, may be close to art music or played in a simpler style. Other Sufi celebrations feature *inshad,* or Sufi

Palestinian antiglobalization activists perform music during the inauguration of the World Social Forum (WSF) in Karachi, Pakistan, on March 24, 2006. Employing music for political expression is a long-standing tradition in the Middle East. (AFP/Getty Images)

poetry sung with a full band playing a synthesis of Arab pop and folk melodies. Songs for the hajj and the *mulids* (days commemorating holy men and women) are also popular. The Coptic church, like the Syriac and other Arab churches, has its own liturgy and sung music. But religion does not dominate the music of the region.

The great popularity of music and the oral tradition in the region benefited from nationally subsidized radio from the 1930s to the 1950s when singers or instrumentalists such as Munira al-Mahdiyya, Umm Kulthum, Muhammad abd al-Wahhab, Asmahan, Farid al-Atrash, and others began their careers. Musical plays, such as the extravaganzas performed and recorded by the Rahbani Brothers of Lebanon with the singer Fayruz, and the recordings of these *masrahiyyat* spread a new popularized Lebanese folk sound.

Nearly all countries of the region established national folk ensembles to preserve their local musical and dance traditions. Cinema was also a very important vehicle for music, and many musical stars made films. In the 1960s few were as popular as the Egyptian singer Abdel Halim Hafiz. Television and most recently

music videos allowed audiences to experience established and newer performers as well as Western performance styles and musical content.

Egyptian artist Umm Kulthum (1904–1975), known as Kawkab al-Sharq (Star of the East) or by Egyptians as simply al-Sitt (the Lady), began her career as a child singing in religious celebrations and weddings. Family members performed with her, and she wore a male head-covering to indicate her modesty. After reinventing herself as a modern singer in Cairo and hiring modern composers and lyricists, she became the most celebrated singer of the Arab world. At the height of her career, she gave Thursday evening concerts that were broadcast throughout the Arab world, typically featuring one lengthy composition displaying her vocal power, improvisational skill, and emotional interpretation. Like other singers, she sang nationalist compositions such as the anti-British "University Song" and supported the Arab and Palestinian cause in 1948. After the Arab defeat in the 1967 Six-Day War, she staged a series of concerts and donated $2 million for reconstruction projects.

Other examples of political music might include male singer and udist Farid al-Atrash's song celebrating the union of Egypt and Syria in 1958, the concerts of Lebanese Marsal (Marcel) Khalifa, the Palestinian group Sabrin, the compositions of udist Iraqi Nasir al-Shamma, and single songs included in otherwise romantic and popular concert material such as by Iraqi singer Kadhim al-Sahir.

Popular music in Israel was largely state-controlled through media and cultural policies until the 1970s, when the Israel Defense Forces (IDF) entertainment ensembles (known as the *lehakot tsva*) performed songs that combined indigenous elements with international popular influences. After the 1970s, popular music became ethnic markers of different groups in Israel, such as the eastern Jewish communities emigrating from Arab countries. They consciously incorporated Arab and Yemenite musical characteristics, such as elongated melismatic embellishments or quarter tones, to signify their eastern Mediterranean style while voicing the political struggles of their particular group. A contemporary example of this is Ofra Haza and Dana International. Israeli and Palestinian songs allude frequently to the land itself and sometimes to various stages of their struggles with each other.

Palestinian musical performance suffered from the Nakba and Israeli censorship. The Israeli government created a radio orchestra for Arab music. However, the performers were from the Egyptian, Iraqi, and Syrian Jewish communities, and the orchestra's musical repertoire and apolitical content differed from the Palestinian music produced for private settings such as weddings. Traditional weddings featured a *zaffa*, a musical procession and songs accompanied by the *dabka*, a line dance also found in Lebanon, Syria and Jordan. Today, families might bring in DJs and recorded music instead of musical ensembles. The Islamist movement has also to some degree discouraged music at weddings in some Palestinian areas.

An exception to the commercial and individually based musicians was Hikmat Shahin. He taught the traditional repertoire at the Arab conservatory at Haifa and led the Arabic Music Ensemble of Tarshiha, which reorganized after his death as the Tarshiha Ensemble. There is also the Sabrin ensemble in the West Bank that blends more contemporary elements into its music.

Western classical music is also important in many countries of the Middle East. Some composers, including Israelis, Arabs, and Turks, have experimented with Middle Eastern themes or inspirations that either juxtapose Middle Eastern and Western music or combine the two. Examples are the Egyptian composers Abu Bakr Khayrat, founder of the Cairo Conservatory; Jamal (Gamal) abd al-Rahim; Aziz al-Shawan, composer of the first Egyptian opera; and Sharif Muhiddin.

Many Palestinians migrated into surrounding countries and to the West, but their performances of political music were constrained to some degree by their environment. Performers learned Lebanese, Gulf, Jordanian, Egyptian, and other songs to please their mixed audiences, but certain songs were composed and performed as a nationalist repertoire.

Fayruz (b. 1935) became known as the "Voice of Lebanon," although there were other singers such as Sabah who also popularized folk melodies. Fayruz produced an album, *Jerusalem in My Heart,* in 1966 that featured songs devoted to particular Palestinian sites along with vocals by Joseph Azar and a chorus.

In Iraq, a special type of small ensemble music now called *maqam* had developed early in the 20th century. This tradition began to fade away with the influx of popular music. Saddam Hussein's government sponsored traditional music to some degree, but this tradition is now mainly preserved in exile by such musicians as Farida Ali.

The unique music of the Arabian Gulf and of North Africa is found in two forms, a folk format and more polished and rearranged arrangements with less local influence. Saudi performer Muhammad Abduh's songs were learned by other Arab performers, and today many from the Levant and North Africa include one or two Gulf-style compositions in their recordings. In North Africa, a very specific classical tradition has been preserved. There is also lighter popular music. Rai music is a synthesis of Algerian folk tunes and irreverent, often counterculture, lyrics with Francified accordion and guitar settings. Some rai performers, such as Shab (Cheb) Khalid, became more widely known in Europe. Middle Eastern music has also synthesized in the Diaspora, where musicians of various national origins learn the tastes of their local audiences. Music remains a vital connection, shaping the cultural, societal, and national identity of members living abroad.

CAROLYN RAMZY AND SHERIFA ZUHUR

See also

Fayruz

References

Cohen, Dalia, and Ruth Katz. *Palestinian Arab Music: A Maqam Tradition in Practice.* Chicago: University of Chicago Press, 2004.

Danielson, Virginia. *The Voice of Egypt: Umm Kulthum, Arabic Song, and Egyptian Society in the Twentieth Century.* Chicago: University of Chicago Press, 1997.

Massad, Joseph. "Liberating Songs: Palestine Put to Music." *Journal of Palestine Studies,* 127 (2003): 21–38.

Zuhur, Sherifa, ed. *Colors of Enchantment: Theater, Music, Dance, and Visual Arts of the Middle East.* Cairo: American University in Cairo Press, 2001.

———, ed. *Images of Enchantment: Visual and Performing Arts of the Middle East.* Cairo: American University in Cairo Press, 1998.

Muslim Brotherhood

Muslim fundamentalist (Islamist) organization founded in Egypt in 1928 that promotes the Islamic way of life and has been active in the political arena for many years. With separate and autonomous branches in many other countries, the Muslim Brotherhood (Jami'at al-Ikhwan al-Muslimin, or Society of Muslim Brothers) provides education, social services, and fellowship for religiously active Muslims. The secret military wing of the organization was involved in assassinations or attempted assassinations after being outlawed by

A Muslim Brotherhood banner in the Maadi district of Cairo on November 2, 2005. The banner displays the organization's slogan, "Islam is the Solution." (Mona Sharaf/Reuters/Corbis)

the Egyptian government in the late 1940s and was also involved in an alleged assassination attempt on President Gamal Abdel Nasser in 1954. The Muslim Brotherhood opposed the formation of Israel and the Israeli seizure of Palestinian lands. It is impossible to speak of the Muslim Brotherhood as a unified body because its policies have necessarily varied in its various locations.

The Muslim Brotherhood was founded in March 1928 in Ismailiyya, Egypt, by Hasan al-Banna, a 22-year-old elementary school Arabic teacher and former leader of the Society for Moral Behavior and secretary to the Hasafiyya Sufi order. Al-Banna was deeply troubled by the British presence in the Suez Canal Zone and the gap between the Egyptian wealthy and the poor. He adopted some of the ideas of Egyptian-Syrian salafism, which called for a reform of Islamic society through education. He also believed that communities and youths needed an Islamic organization. Soon he had established branches in Port Said and Suez City and contacts elsewhere in Egypt. The organization's motto was "Islam is the solution." Al-Banna and his brother established the first Ikhwan branch in Cairo in 1932, and the organization expanded significantly in size over the next two decades, at least in part because of its nationalist stance because the Wafd Party was somewhat discredited by its enforced cooperation with the British.

The Ikhwan established its own companies, schools, and hospitals and also set up a secret military apparatus in the 1940s. It also carried out actions against British and Jewish interests in Egypt in the late 1940s.

Some members of the Muslim Brotherhood traveled to Syria in the 1930s, and Sudanese, Syrian, and Palestinian individuals either met with the Ikhwan in Egypt or became familiar with al-Banna's ideas. These individuals then formed their own associations. One example is Mustafa al-Siba'i, the Syrian Ikhwan's first general guide. A women's organization was established under Zaynab al-Ghazali and promoted political and charitable work as well as the wearing of the hijab, or Islamic dress. The Muslim Brotherhood, then as now, promoted dawa (its mission) and reform and later emphasized a shift to Islamic law.

On December 28, 1948, a member of the Muslim Brotherhood assassinated Egyptian prime minister Mahmud Fahmi al-Nuqrashi. Al-Banna was assassinated in February 1949, most likely by the Egyptian security forces. The next leader of the organization, Hasan al-Hudhaybi, hoped for a better relationship with the new revolutionary government since the Muslim Brotherhood supported the Free Officers Revolution in 1952. Anwar Sadat had been a liaison between the Free Officers and the Ikhwan, followed by Abd al-Munim Abd al-Rauf, a Brother and a Free Officer. General Mohammad Naguib was also linked to the Ikhwans. When Gamal Abdel Nasser succeeded Naguib and reined in political dissent, matters worsened for the Ikhwan. On October 26, 1954, an Ikhwan member attempted to assassinate Nasser. Nasser responded by outlawing the Muslim Brotherhood, executing a few of its number, and imprisoning more than 4,000 of its members, some for as long as 17 years. Other members fled abroad. This confrontation led to the radicalism expressed by an Ikhwan member, Sayyid Qutb, and a bitterness on the part of the Ikhwan toward Nasser and his regime. Qutb had previously promoted societal change through education and reform, but he wrote of the necessity of jihad and martyrdom in his last book, *Malim fi Tariq*, that was banned and for which he was executed in prison.

The first Jordanian branch of the Ikhwan was founded in Salt in 1946. Other centers formed and were led by a cleric, Haj Abd al-Latif al-Qurah. The group received informal approval from King Abdullah to operate as a religious and not a political organization. The organization grew in the West Bank and Jordan. In 1957 King Hussein rescinded all political parties except for the Muslim Brotherhood. The group formed an Islamic Charitable Society by 1964. The Muslim Brotherhood supported the king to some degree against Palestinian guerrilla fighters. But in the 1980s, it openly criticized corruption and immorality in Jordan, and King Hussein moved against the organization. When in 1989 the first Jordanian elections in 22 years were held, the Muslim Brotherhood won 22 of 80 seats, and its other Islamist allies won 12 additional seats.

In Syria, a small society in Aleppo transferred to Damascus and became the Muslim Brotherhood in 1944. It soon grew in Syria's urban Sunni-dominated centers. Those in Hama and Aleppo opposed the Baathist Alawite regime of Hafez al-Assad, but the

Damascus wing supported it until a controversy over the secular character of the constitution occurred in 1973. The Muslim Brotherhood assassinated some Baath officials and attacked buildings associated with the Baath Party and the army. The organization killed 83 Alawi cadets in 1979 and mounted large-scale demonstrations in 1980, when the government outlawed the Muslim Brotherhood. It then joined the Syrian Islamic Front. In a showdown between the Syrian military and the Syrian Islamic Front in the city of Hama, somewhere between 10,000 and 30,000 inhabitants were killed. Some of the leadership went into exile, and others went underground. However, the Muslim Brotherhood has revived in Syria in recent years.

Contacts began with Sudan in the 1940s, and the Sudanese Muslim Brotherhood was formed in 1954. There the organization advocated independence from Egypt. In 1964 Hasan al-Turabi became a leader of the Muslim Brotherhood in the Islamic Charter Front and much later in the National Islamic Front, founded in 1985. The National Islamic Front was associated with the military coup of 1989, and the succeeding regime implemented stricter Islamization practices.

Sadat, who became president of Egypt in September 1970 following Nasser's sudden death, released members of the Muslim Brotherhood from prison but refused to allow the organization to operate as a political party. He also encouraged Islamic student organizations. The Muslim Brotherhood operated within the regime's rules and argued for gradual change, in contrast with other extremist groups that emerged in the 1970s whose ideas were more similar to the later, more extreme ideas of Qutb. The Muslim Brotherhood attempted to forge an alliance with several of the small opposition parties, with the Wafd Party, and then with Socialist Labor and the Liberal Party to promote itself in parliament. A younger segment of its leadership also split off from the Ikhwan to become the Wasit Party. Electoral rules and corruption prevented the Muslim Brotherhood from achieving larger political gains than it might have made, but the party is today larger and more popular than ever in Egypt.

The Muslim Brotherhood also had a following in Gaza, and Sheikh Ahmed Yassin ran a welfare and educational organization for Palestinian Muslims in the 1970s. He gave his approval when physician Abd al-Aziz Rantisi, Salah Shihada, and Yahya al-Sinuwwar formed Hamas (Harakat al-Muqawama al-Islamiyya) in 1987. Sheikh Omar Abdel-Rahman al-Khalifa of the Muslim Brotherhood of Jordan also gave his assent to the formation of the West Bank branch of Hamas the following year. The Muslim Brotherhood has additionally had a strong influence in Kuwait and has or had members in other countries, such as Iraq. This is in line with the Muslim Brotherhood's stance that it is a universal Islamic assembly and not a movement restricted to Arabs or to one country.

AMY HACKNEY BLACKWELL AND SHERIFA ZUHUR

See also

Assad, Hafez al-; Egypt; Hamas; Hussein, King of Jordan; Jihad; Jordan; Nasser, Gamal Abdel; Sadat, Anwar; Syria; Yassin, Ahmed Ismail

References

Ayubi, Nazih N. *Political Islam: Religion and Politics in the Arab World.* New York: Routledge, 1993.

Baker, Raymond William. *Islam without Fear: Egypt and the New Islamists.* Cambridge: Harvard University Press, 1993.

El-Ghobashy, Mona. "The Metamorphosis of the Egyptian Muslim Brothers." *International Journal of Middle East Studies* 37(3) (August 2005): 373–395.

Mitchell, Richard P. *The Society of Muslim Brothers.* Oxford: Oxford University Press, 1993.

Mwawi, Ahmad Ali al-
Born: 1897
Died: Unknown

Commander of the Egyptian Army that fought in Palestine during the 1948–1949 Israeli War of Independence. Ahmad Ali al-Mwawi (variously spelled Ahmed Ali el-Muawi, Ahmed Ah el-Mawawi, Ahmed Ali al-Muwawi, or Ahmed Ali al-Muaw) was born in 1897 in Egypt. Little is known about the circumstances of his birth, but he graduated from the Egyptian Military Academy in 1916. A career military officer, by the end of World War II he had risen to the rank of major. In 1945 he was promoted to brigadier general and appointed commander of Egypt's 4th Infantry Brigade.

On the evening of Tuesday, May 11, 1948, al-Mwawi attended a secret meeting of the Egyptian parliament. Before the parliamentary vote to declare war on Israel, he dismissed warnings that the Egyptian Army was unprepared, opining that there would be little real fighting. On May 12 al-Mwawi, as a major general, was appointed commander of the Egyptian forces in the Sinai.

The Arab battle plan was still unclear, and worse yet, Egyptian war aims were vague, making al-Mwawi uncertain of his objectives. On May 15 he led the Egyptian Expeditionary Forces into Palestine. The Egyptians numbered between 7,000 and 10,000 troops, divided into two brigades.

During May 16–24, the Egyptian Army attacked the Jewish settlements of Kibbutz Nirim and Kfar Darom but failed to capture them. Yad Mordechai was repeatedly attacked until its defenders departed on May 24. Before reaching Gaza, the Egyptian Army split into two forces. The regular army units continued to move northward along the coast, while the irregulars (Muslim Brotherhood) pushed eastward toward Beersheba.

On May 24 the Egyptians reached Majdal. With supply lines stretched thin, al-Mwawi attempted to clear the area in front of his position. On June 3 the Egyptian 9th Rifle Battalion took Kibbutz Nitsanim, employing four tanks in a dawn assault following a night-long artillery barrage.

On July 18 during the second truce, al-Mwawi sent a report to Cairo describing Egyptian shortages in armaments and matériel. He also reported that the Arab coalition was so divided by mistrust that Egypt must either face serious losses or find a political solution to the crisis. On October 20, King Farouk I relieved al-Mwawi of his command. It is unclear what happened to al-Mwawi thereafter or when he died.

ANDREW JACK WASKEY

See also

Egypt; Egypt, Armed Forces; Farouk I, King of Egypt; Israeli War of Independence, Israeli-Egyptian Front

References

Gelber, Yoav. *Palestine 1948: War, Escape and the Emergence of the Palestinian Refugee Problem.* Portland, OR: Sussex Academic, 2001.

Tal, David. *War in Palestine, 1948: Strategy and Diplomacy.* New York: Routledge, 2004.

N

Nabhani, Taqi al-Din al-
Born: 1909
Died: December 20, 1977

Palestinian jurist, scholar, writer, activist, and founder of the Islamic Liberation Party (Hizb al-Tahrir al-Islami). Sheikh Muhammad ibn Mustafa ibn Yusuf Taqi al-Din al-Nabhani was born in 1909 in the village of Izjim, near Haifa, to a prominent, well-educated family. Al-Nabhani was the grandson of Ismail ibn Yusuf Nasr al-Din Nabhani, a well-known Sufi scholar, poet, judge, and antisalafi, said to be an associate of Izz al-Din al-Qassam and of the mufti Haj Amin al-Husseini. Al-Nabhani received his earliest Islamic education from his grandfather and traveled to Egypt for advanced Islamic education. He enrolled at al-Azhar University and Dar al-Ulum simultaneously in 1928 and graduated with distinction in 1932. That same year he returned to Palestine.

Al-Nabhani eventually left teaching because of his dissatisfaction with the British-imposed curriculum. He then worked in the Palestinian judiciary until the 1948–1949 Israeli War of Independence, when he fled to Beirut, Lebanon. Later he returned to Jerusalem and the West Bank; became a judge in the Islamic court system, serving in several districts; and taught at the Islamic College in Amman, Jordan.

Al-Nabhani joined the Muslim Brotherhood early in his career but later parted company with the organization, alleging that its approaches would never lead to the emancipation of Muslims. In 1951 he formed the Hayat al-Tahrir al-Islami, later called the Hizb al-Tahrir al-Islami (Islamic Liberation Party), in East Jerusalem, a pan-Muslim political party that opposed foreign occupations, including that endured by Palestinians, and aimed to establish an Islamic state with an elected caliph. The party grew quickly and established cells or branches that are sometimes confused with other organizations in much of the Arab Middle East.

The party attracted followers in the West Bank but was banned by Jordanian authorities. It had some difficulty as well because of the rising popularity of Nasserism and other secular Arab nationalist groups. Al-Nabhani participated in the failed coup of Wasfi al-Tall in Jordan, and Jordanian government pursuit of al-Nabhani eventually forced him from public life altogether.

Al-Nabhani moved first to Damascus and then to Lebanon, relocating the party there. He had to withdraw completely from any public appearances due to Jordanian attempts on his life, however, and devoted his time to writing and scholarship. The Islamic Liberation Party soldiered on, and party branches were set up in Lebanon, Iraq, Kuwait, and Syria as well as in Jordan and the West Bank. The party twice attempted a coup d'état in Jordan and mounted other such attempts in Syria and Iraq. Later, cells of this party were established in Saudi Arabia, the United Arab Emirates, Tunisia, Sudan, Turkey, Pakistan, Malaysia, and elsewhere in the Muslim world, including the Central Asian states.

Al-Nabhani wrote 19 books in addition to 5 more published under other names. These include *The Salvation of Palestine* and *Ruling System in Islam*. In the latter he expounded on the philosophy of the Islamic Liberation Party and outlined a detailed constitution for his proposed Islamic state. This and the detailed attention to party formation make the Hizb al-Tahrir somewhat unique in having a more detailed blueprint for itself and a future Islamic state. The three-volume work *The Islamic Personality* concerned the evolution of thought, concepts, and psychology, while other works concerned areas of Islamic law.

Presently, the Islamic Liberation Party is perceived as a radical Islamic organization. Many Westerners have labeled it anti-Semitic and a terrorist group. Nevertheless, the party has had branches in Europe. It was banned in Germany in 2003 and in Britain in 2005 on suspicions that it is a terrorist organization.

Al-Nabhani died in Beirut, Lebanon, on December 20, 1977. He left behind a legacy of Muslim militant activism and a wealth of knowledge, as evidenced by his authorship of so many books on various Islamic subjects.

YUSHAU SODIQ AND SHERIFA ZUHUR

See also

Expellees and Refugees, Palestinian; Husseini, Haj Amin al-; Islamic Movement in Israel; Muslim Brotherhood; Qassam, Izz al-Din al-

References

Commins, David. "Taqiyyu al-Din, al-Nabhani and the Islamic Liberation Party." *Muslim World* 81(3–4) (1991): 194–211.

Nabhani, Taqi al-Din al-. *Nizam al-Hukm fil-Islam.* Beirut: Dar al-Ummah, 1990.

Taji-Farouki, Suha. "Hizb al-Tahrir al-Islami." Pp. 125–127 in *The Oxford Encyclopedia of the Modern Islamic World,* Vol. 2, edited by John L. Esposito. Oxford: Oxford University Press, 1995.

Nablus

Ancient biblical city known as Shechem, the first capital of the Israelites and now the largest city in the West Bank. Nablus is situated between Mount Ebal and Mount Gerizim, some 38 miles north of Jerusalem at the intersection of two ancient and strategic commercial roads. One road connects the Israeli coast to the Jordan Valley, and the other road connects Galilee (north) and the Negev (south). Another local name for Nablus is Jabal al-Nar (hill or mountain of fire).

Now under the control of the Palestinian Authority (PA), Nablus proper has a population of slightly more than 100,000 people. The city is known for its *suq* (market) and the Casbah as well as its Knafah Nabulsia (a square-cut pastry dessert). It is also known as the epicenter of Palestinian resistance to Israel, which was carried on by youths and children of the town during the First Intifada, even after many of the adult men were arrested. The Palestine Stock Exchange and al-Najah National University (the largest Palestinian university) are located in the city. Nablus is an agricultural, commercial, and manufacturing center for soap, furniture, textiles, olive oil, wine, tile, stone quarrying, leather tanning, and handicrafts.

Nablus and its environs contain the largest Palestinian population in the Middle East. The area is home to five refugee camps. These are Ain Bayt il-Ma, also identified as Camp Number 1; Balata, the largest refugee camp in the West Bank; Askar al-Qaadim; Askar al-Jadid, a new area of Askar al-Qaadim, which is not officially recognized; and Fara camp, which lies about 10 miles outside of Nablus. The camps were built for Palestinians who fled what is now Israel during and after the 1948–1949 Israeli War of Independence following the United Nations (UN) partition of Palestine. The dis-

Aerial view of Nablus, the largest city in the West Bank, November 14, 2002. (Avi Ohayon/Israeli Government Press Office)

trict also contains numerous Israeli settlements and is surrounded by Israel Defense Forces (IDF) checkpoints. The latter are intended to disrupt the flow of Palestinian militants and arms into and out of Nablus.

The Palestinians assert that these encircling checkpoints are chokepoints that strangle the city and contribute to its extremely high unemployment. Indeed, the unemployment rate soared from 14.2 percent in 1997 to 60 percent in 2004. The Israelis assert conversely that the economic conditions in Nablus are the direct consequence of the mismanagement and corruption of the Palestinian Authority (PA) that has governmental, economic, political, and social control over the city and the West Bank.

Hamas, Fatah, and other Palestinian organizations are headquartered or represented in Nablus. The city is also reportedly something of a center for the production of explosive charges, suicide explosive belts, and rockets used to attack Israeli targets. On December 21, 2005, for example, the IDF intercepted a teenage boy smuggling two pipe bombs through the Hawara checkpoint.

The IDF occasionally takes control of the city, sweeps it for militants, and launches targeted military operations. Thus, the March 2002 Israeli sweep of the older residential area, the Casbah, followed a Palestinian suicide bombing in Kibbutz Metzer. More than 400 Palestinians from Nablus were killed by the IDF during the Second (al-Aqsa) Intifada. Nablus was also plagued in 2005 by internecine fighting among Palestinian militias, paramilitary organizations, criminals, and established Palestinian groups. The latter include, among others, Hamas, Fatah, the al-Aqsa Martyrs Brigades, the Popular Front for the Liberation of Palestine (PFLP), and the Democratic Front for the Liberation of Palestine (DFLP).

The PA asserts that this lawlessness was caused by the continuing IDF incursions and the economic chaos wrought by Israel's virtual economic blockade of the city. The Israeli government has responded that the conditions in Nablus were brought about by the PA's unwillingness or inability to control the Palestinian militants.

RICHARD EDWARDS

See also

Expellees and Refugees, Palestinian; Intifada, Second; Palestinian Authority; Palestinian Refugee Camps; Samaritans

References

Pappe, Ilan. *A History of Modern Palestine: One Land, Two Peoples.* Cambridge: Cambridge University Press, 2003.

Rubin, Barry. *Revolution until Victory? The Politics and History of the PLO.* Reprint ed. Cambridge: Harvard University Press, 2003.

Shahin, Mariam. *Palestine: A Guide.* Northampton, MA: Interlink, 2005.

NACHSHON, **Operation**
Start Date: April 5, 1948
End Date: April 20, 1948

Israeli military operation undertaken in April 1948 during the Israeli War of Independence (1948–1949). By April 1948, Jerusalem was under siege by Arab forces and cut off from Tel Aviv as the Arabs attempted to prevent Jewish forces from taking the areas assigned to them before the departure of the British from their Palestine Mandate. Jerusalem was divided into areas of Jewish and Arab control, and the Jewish enclave there had been deprived of both food supplies and support by Mufti of Jerusalem Hasan Salamah's Army of Salvation. With supplies and medicine critically scarce, a link had to be established between the Jewish area of Jerusalem and the rest of the Jewish portions of Israel. Prime Minister David Ben-Gurion ordered a relief operation despite opposition from many members of his staff.

The Israelis conceived an operation, code-named Plan DALET, to capture those areas mandated to the Jewish state by the United Nations (UN) or, according to other sources, to capture as many Arab-occupied villages and areas as possible. The first stage of this plan was to be Operation NACHSHON (NAKHSHON), the relief of Jerusalem, that would be accomplished by opening the road between Tel Aviv and the besieged city. The operation was named for the biblical figure Nachshon ben Aminadav, heralded as the first Israelite to have entered the Red Sea during the exodus from Egypt.

For the operation, Haganah fielded a brigade of approximately 1,500 men, its largest tactical deployment to that point. The largest Haganah force in one operation had been a mere company. Not even a battalion operation had been attempted.

The force committed to NACHSHON was largely comprised of the Givati Brigade under the overall command of Shimon Avidan, later a brigadier general. The plan called for the opening of a corridor that would be six miles wide in the coastal plain and some two miles wide in the mountains. Fortunately for the Israelis, a clandestine arms shipment of 200 rifles and 40 machine guns arrived by air on April 1.

To lay the groundwork for NACHSHON, Haganah troops attacked and blew up the headquarters of the grand mufti's Army of Salvation in the town of Ramla. In the process many key staff members died, impeding the ability of the Army of Salvation to react to the Israeli moves. The Israelis also captured the village of Kastal, an Arab settlement to the west of Jerusalem, and this effectively blocked access to the city.

NACHSHON officially commenced on the evening of April 5. Two battalions were committed to the initial attack, with one held in reserve. Blocking units covered seven Arab villages, while larger units took and held the Arab villages of Hulda and Deir Mulheism. At the same time, Palmach forces attacked the Arab village of Bayt Machsir Mahsir near Bab al-Wad and cleared the mountain road to Jerusalem. This allowed 60 Palmach trucks carrying supplies to get through to the city.

As the operation moved into high gear, Haganah forces captured the strategic junction town of Latrun on the Jerusalem Road, driving Arab units from the Wadi al-Sarrar military camp and routing Arab forces at Deir Mulheism and Arab Hulda. Arab units reacted by counterattacking the Haganah forces on April 7 and 8 near the town of Motza and began efforts to retake Kastal, which after six days of near continuous fighting they indeed accomplished. At Kastal the situation was dramatically reversed, however, when one of the best Arab commanders, Abd al-Qadir al-Husseini (aka Abu Musa), was killed when approaching an area held by the Israelis that he thought had already been taken. Arab forces then fell back in disarray. On April 11, a Palmach unit found Kastal unoccupied, and supplies then began moving into Jerusalem.

A great deal of controversy surrounds the actions of the Irgun Tsvai Leumi (National Military Organization) detachment and the forces of the Lehi during NACHSHON. These two units attacked the Arab village of Deir Yassin on the Jerusalem Road. According to some reports, at approximately 5:00 a.m. on April 9 an Israeli truck with a loudspeaker entered Deir Yassin and warned the inhabitants (mostly women and children) to evacuate because a battle was about to take place. Hundreds heeded the warning and departed, but many more stayed and came under tremendous danger as a pitched battle ensued. The battle raged for hours as Arab forces in the town put up a spirited resistance. When combat ceased, there were a number of civilian casualties as a result of the fighting. Israeli authorities place this figure at approximately 110, whereas Arab sources claim 250 civilians dead. The Arabs as well as the International Red Cross leveled allegations of Israeli bayoneting of pregnant women and other atrocities, including rape and mutilation. Recent historical research suggests that the Irgun and Lehi did carry out executions by firing squad after the battle.

The results of the events at Deir Yassin, however, were profound. In retaliation for the attack, Arab forces massacred 70 injured and sick Israelis when they captured an evacuation convoy on the Mount Scopus Road outside Jerusalem on April 13. The subsequent broadcasting by Israeli officials of the atrocities also led to panic among many Palestinians and caused a large-scale flight into exile.

As part of NACHSHON on April 8, Haganah forces also attacked Palestinian militia in the town of Tiberias to relieve Jewish residents there under siege and to help secure a road link to Haganah forces in the northern part of the country. Fighting was intense, but Palmach forces moved in to assist the Haganah, and the Arab forces were split. The Arabs called for British aid and, with their help, evacuated Tiberias on April 18.

The relief of Jerusalem was short-lived. Five convoys and the Palmach Harel Brigade made it into the city through April 20, but the relief effort ended that day when only part of an additional convoy got through. Arab forces again sealed off the city.

Operation NACHSHON was important not only because it was the first large military operation undertaken by the Haganah, which would later become the nucleus of the Israel Defense Forces (IDF), but also because it was the first occasion in which the fractious and often hostile factions of the Irgun, Lehi, Palmach, and Haganah were able to effectively work together in a joint operation. Although the success was only temporary, the relief of Jerusalem in the face of superior odds also demonstrated the élan and fighting abilities of the Israeli forces.

Operation NACHSHON, with the reports of Deir Yassin and the capture of Tiberias, also served to unify the Arab nations surrounding Palestine into support for the Palestinian cause. Arab forces from Egypt, Jordan, and other Arab nations invaded Israel in May 1948, widening the scope of the war. These attacks were largely in direct response to the Israeli successes in NACHSHON and related operations.

ROD VOSBURGH

See also

Burma Road; Deir Yassin Massacre; Expellees and Refugees, Palestinian; Haganah; Irgun Tsvai Leumi; Israeli War of Independence, Overview; Jerusalem; Latrun, Battles of; Lohamei Herut Israel; Marcus, David; Palmach

References

Herzog, Chaim. *The Arab-Israeli Wars: War and Peace in the Middle East from the War of Independence to Lebanon.* Westminster, MD: Random House, 1984.

Karsh, Efraim. *The Palestine War, 1948.* London: Osprey, 2002.

Kurzman, Dan. *Genesis, 1948: The First Arab Israeli War.* New York: Da Capo, 1992.

Lorch, Netanel. *The Edge of the Sword: Israel's War of Independence, 1947–1949.* Norwalk, CT: Easton, 1991.

Milstein, Uri. *History of Israel's War of Independence.* 4 vols. Lanham, MD: University Press of America, 1996–1999.

Naguib, Mohammad
Born: February 20, 1901
Died: August 29, 1984

Egyptian Army general and first president of the Republic of Egypt (1953–1954). Born in Khartoum on February 20, 1901, Mohammad Naguib (Najib) grew up in Sudan, which was then under de facto British control. Naguib's father was an Egyptian Army officer, and his mother was Sudanese. Naguib was educated at Gordon College and the Military Academy, from which he was commissioned as an artillery officer in 1918. He studied English, French, Italian, and German as well as political science and economics and earned a law degree in 1927.

Naguib soon came under suspicion for his strong nationalistic and anti-British political views. In 1934 he was transferred to the Coast Guard and posted to Sudan, where he was involved in efforts to prevent smuggling. In 1942, embittered over King Farouk's refusal to stand up to the British, Naguib submitted his resignation, which was rejected. He had distinguished himself as a brigadier general and brigade commander in the 1948–1949 Israeli War of Independence and was considered one of the few Egyptian war heroes from that conflict. In 1950 he was promoted to major general. He again sought to resign in 1951 to protest Farouk's policies.

In 1949 Naguib joined the Free Officers Movement. Led by Egyptian nationalist colonel Gamal Abdel Nasser and composed of young, relatively junior Egyptian Army officers, the Free Officers Movement sought to oust Farouk and reform the military due to their belief that it had been mismanaged in Palestine. They wanted to install a truly Egyptian government to the country (the royal family being Turko-Circassians) and put an end to all British interference. Naguib instead of King Farouk's preferred candidate was

Mohammad Naguib, Egyptian Army general and first president of the Republic of Egypt (1953–1954). (Hulton Archive/Getty Images)

elected president of the Officer's Club, a signal that the king no longer enjoyed the army's loyalty.

Discontent against the government had been increasing, and on January 19, 1952, rioting broke out at Ismailiyya. British troops then occupied the town, killing 40 of the local police and wounding 70. When the events at Ismailiyya became known in Cairo on January 26, mobs took to the streets, burning hundreds of well-known British- or other foreign-owned establishments. The human toll was 26 dead and 552 wounded. The government was slow to act, and a power vacuum existed. King Farouk and his ministers suspected trouble in the army and were planning to move against the Free Officers, but the latter acted first and seized power on July 23, 1952.

On July 26 a Revolutionary Command Council (RCC) demanded that King Farouk renounce the throne and leave Egypt. He departed the same day, abdicating in favor of his infant son as King Ahmed Fuad II. Ali Mahir served as prime minister, but Naguib soon replaced him.

The RCC of 13 army officers now held power, although the monarchy continued for one year with a regency council for the infant king. On June 18, 1953, the military junta ended the monarchy altogether and declared Egypt a republic. Naguib then became the unelected president.

Prime Ministers of Egypt (1946–Present)

Name	Political Party	Term
Mahmoud an-Nukrashi Pasha	Saadist Institutional Party	December 1946–December 1948
Ibrahim Abdel Hadi Pasha	Saadist Institutional Party	December 1948–July 1949
Hussein Sirri Pasha	none	July 1949–January 1950
Mustafa an-Nahhas Pasha	al Wafdu al Misri	January 1950–January 1952
Ali Mahir Pasha	Ittiha Party	January–March 1952
Ahmad Naguib Hilali Pasha	none	March–July 1952
Hussein Sirri Pasha	none	July 1952
Ahmad Naguib Hilali Pasha	none	July 1952
Ali Mahir Pasha	Ittiha Party	July–September 1952
Muhammad Naguib	Liberation Rally	September 1952–February 1954
Gamal Abdel Nasser	Liberation Rally	February–March 1954
Mohammad Naguib	Liberation Rally	March–April 1954
Gamal Abdel Nasser	Liberation Rally/Arab Socialist Union	April 1954–September 1962
Ali Sabri	Arab Socialist Union	September 1962–October 1965
Zakaria Mohieddin	Arab Socialist Union	October 1965–September 1966
Muhammad Sedki Sulayman	Arab Socialist Union	September 1966–June 1967
Gamal Abdel Nasser	Arab Socialist Union	June 1967–September 1970
Mahmoud Fawzi	Arab Socialist Union	October 1970–January 1972
Aziz Sedki	Arab Socialist Union	January 1972–March 1973
Anwar Sadat	Arab Socialist Union	March 1973–September 1974
Abdelaziz Muhammad Hejazi	Arab Socialist Union	September 1974–April 1975
Mamdouh Muhammad Salem	Arab Socialist Union/Hizb al Dimuqratiyah al Wataniyah	April 1975–October 1978
Mustafa Khalil	Hizb al Dimuqratiyah al Wataniyah	October 1978–May 1980
Anwar Sadat	Hizb al Dimuqratiyah al Wataniyah	May 1980–October 1981
Hosni Mubarak	Hizb al Dimuqratiyah al Wataniyah	October 1981–January 1982
Ahmad Fuad Mohieddin	Hizb al Dimuqratiyah al Wataniyah	January 1982–June 1984
Kamal Hassan Ali	Hizb al Dimuqratiyah al Wataniyah	July 1984–September 1985
Ali Mahmoud Lutfi	Hizb al Dimuqratiyah al Wataniyah	September 1985–November 1986
Atef Muhammad Naguib Sedki	Hizb al Dimuqratiyah al Wataniyah	November 1986–January 1996
Kamal Ganzouri	Hizb al Dimuqratiyah al Wataniyah	January 1996–October 1999
Atef Ebeid	Hizb al Dimuqratiyah al Wataniyah	October 1999–July 2004
Ahmed Nazif	Hizb al Dimuqratiyah al Wataniyah	July 2004–Present

The RCC did not cancel the liberal parliamentary form of government, but when the various political parties failed to come to agreement, the RCC took over the country's administration. Naguib was the nominal leader. Rural poverty and violence against large landowners had encouraged proposals for land reform in the Egyptian parliament, and discussion of the issue continued in the RCC. In 1952 Naguib announced the first Agrarian Reform Law, which sparked many panicked land sales.

Although Naguib was the nominal Egyptian leader, real authority remained in the hands of the RCC, which was split into two factions, one urging a return to a parliamentary system and the other, under Nasser, that opposed handing over power to the existing political parties. The two factions had other differences as well, including policies regarding the Muslim Brotherhood and the fate of Sudan.

Nasser's faction of the RCC won the power struggle. On February 14, 1954, the RCC announced Naguib's resignation from his posts, saying that he had demanded absolute authority and that this was not acceptable. Following popular demonstrations in Sudan and then one in Cairo with the near mutiny of a cavalry corps, the RCC reversed itself and withdrew Naguib's resignation on February 26. On April 18, however, Nasser became the prime minister and RCC chairman, leaving Naguib as president only and in an increasingly isolated position. Finally, on November 14, 1954, Naguib was placed under house arrest. The RCC accused him of involvement in an assassination attempt on Nasser by the Muslim Brotherhood. A Sudanese delegation preempted Naguib from being tried for conspiracy but could not bring him back to power. The RCC offered the presidency to Ahmad Lutfi al-Sayyid, who turned it down, and Nasser then assumed that position as well. Naguib was released from confinement in 1982 by order of President Hosni Mubarak. Naguib died on August 29, 1984.

SPENCER C. TUCKER AND SHERIFA ZUHUR

See also

Farouk I, King of Egypt; Mubarak, Hosni; Nasser, Gamal Abdel

References

Abdel-Malek, Anouar. *Egypt: Military Society, the Army Regime, the Left, and Social Change under Nasser.* New York: Random House, 1968.

Al-Sayyid Marsot, Afaf Lutfi. *A Short History of Modern Egypt.* Cambridge: Cambridge University Press, 1985.

Waterbury, John. *The Egypt of Nasser and Sadat: Political Economy of Two Regimes.* Princeton, NJ: Princeton University Press, 1983.

Nahariya

Northernmost Israeli city located on the Mediterranean Coast in Western Galilee. Located just 10 miles from Akko (Acre) and only 6 miles south of the Lebanese border, Nahariya is a popular beach and resort town with a current population of about 35,000 people. Almost 98 percent of the population is Jewish. Not far from Nahariya is the Kibbutz Lohamei HeGhettaot, founded by Holocaust survivors in 1949. During the 1940s Nahariya was a popular spot for ships filled with immigrant Jews to dock and unload. Today, the town is

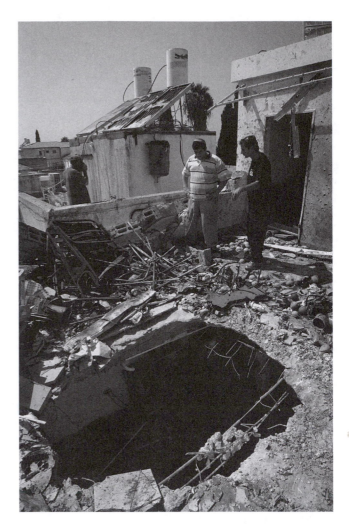

A resident of Nahariya returns to his home to inspect damage caused by a Hezbollah rocket in August 2006. (David Furst/AFP/Getty Images)

filled with quaint shops, restaurants, cafés, bars, and the like. Its beaches, which are all public, are considered among the best on the Israeli Mediterranean Coast. The town is also home to an acclaimed museum of fine arts and has several archeological sites that are open to public viewing.

Nahariya was founded in 1934 by German Jews of the Yishuv (Jews living in Palestine). The town's founders had initially envisioned the area as a center of agriculture, but they soon discovered that the climate and access to freshwater made that a questionable endeavor at best. Instead, they decided to use the town's beachside locale to establish a tourist industry, which has been quite successful. The town leaders also worked hard to attract industry, which too has enjoyed success. Several privately owned manufacturing firms are located in Nahariya, including the food conglomerate Strauss-Elite, an amalgam of the old Strauss Dairy Company, a high-tech metalworking and tool and die company, and a large meat-packing plant.

Because of its close proximity to southern Lebanon, Nahariya has seen several conflicts over the years. The town has witnessed cross-border raids from Lebanon as well as mortar and rocket attacks. This began in earnest in the early 1980s when Palestine Liberation Organization (PLO) fighters were launching attacks against Israel from Lebanon. During the Hezbollah-Israeli conflict of July and August 2006, Nahariya sustained hundreds of hits from Katyusha rockets launched by Hezbollah fighters in southern Lebanon. Besides suffering five fatalities and many more injuries, as many as 70 percent of Nahariya's citizens evacuated, which plunged the town's economy into a tailspin. Tourism, of course, was also nonexistent for much of the summer.

PAUL G. PIERPAOLI JR.

See also

Akko, Israel; Galilee; Hezbollah; Katyusha Rocket; Lebanon; Lebanon, Israeli Operations against

References

Payne, Robert. *The Splendor of the Holy Land: Egypt, Jordan, Israel, Lebanon.* New York: Harper and Row, 1976.

Sachar, Howard M. *A History of Israel: From the Rise of Zionism to Our Time.* 3rd ed. New York: Knopf, 2007.

Nahr al Bared Refugee Camp, Siege of
Start Date: May 20, 2007
End Date: September 2, 2007

Three-month siege by the Lebanese Army of militants in a refugee camp in northern Lebanon. The siege claimed more than 300 lives and captured the attention of all Lebanon. On May 20, 2007, Fatah al-Islam, a radical group of some 360 Sunni Muslims inspired by Al Qaeda, seized control of the Nahr al Bared refugee camp northeast of Tripoli near the Syrian border and carried out a series of attacks on nearby Lebanese Army checkpoints, killing 22 soldiers. Despite fears that fighting would spread to others of the 12 Palestinian refugee camps in Lebanon, the army responded by laying siege to and carrying out military operations against the camp. There was some fighting at Ain al Hilwe refugee camp at Sidon in southern Lebanon in early June, as members of Nahr al Bared there attacked an army checkpoint and demanded that the army halt its attacks on Nahr al Bared in the north. A cease-fire was soon secured at Ain al Hilwe, however.

Meanwhile, most of the estimated 30,000 inhabitants of Nahr al Bared fled as the army brought up artillery and helicopters and shelled and rocketed the camp. Palestinian refugee camps in Lebanon had long been considered off limits to the army, but on this occasion army forces entered the camp in order to rout out the insurgents.

At dawn on September 2, 2007, the remaining members of Nahr al Bared attempted to flee the camp. In the ensuing firefight with Lebanese forces, 31 of them were killed, including their leader Shakir al-Abassi. Another 32 were captured. Five Lebanese soldiers died. The army then took control of Nahr al Bared.

In all, the siege of Nahr al Bared claimed the lives of an estimated 120 militants, at least 42 civilians, and 157 soldiers. During the siege, the United States flew in substantial military aid to the Lebanese Army. During the siege, all major political factions in Lebanon, including Hezbollah, voiced strong support for the army, which was increasingly seen by the general population of a badly divided Lebanon as the one element in the country capable of holding it together. Events also greatly enhanced both the prestige and political clout of army commander General Michel Suleiman. Following the siege, Prime Minister Fuad Siniura pledged to rebuild the camp and secure the return of the refugees.

SPENCER C. TUCKER

See also

Lebanon; Lebanon, Armed Forces; Siniura, Fuad

References

Bakri, Nada. "Lebanese Troops Seize Refugee Camp." *New York Times,* September 3, 2007.

Fisk, Robert. *Pity the Nation: The Abduction of Lebanon.* New York: Simon and Schuster, 1991.

NAKHSHON, Operation
See NACHSHON, Operation

Narkiss, Uzi
Born: January 6, 1925
Died: December 17, 1997

Israeli military officer and commander of Israeli troops that unified the city of Jerusalem during the June 1967 Six-Day War. Uzi Narkiss was born on January 6, 1925, in Jerusalem to Polish immigrant parents. He was educated in the Rehavia Gymnasia. At age 16 he joined the Palmach, the Jewish paramilitary defense force. This marked the beginning of his 27-year military career.

In 1947 Narkiss became a leading commander during the Israeli struggle for independence. With the final departure of British forces from Palestine in 1947, he was put in charge of assisting the besieged Jewish Quarter of the Old City of Jerusalem. The Jewish Quarter was already under heavy attack from Jordanian forces. Although Narkiss's forces penetrated the Zion Gate and evacuated the wounded, he was forced to retreat when military reinforcements failed to arrive. The Old City thus fell to Jordanian troops and remained under Arab control after the State of Israel was declared in May 1948. Narkiss vowed to one day reunite the city under Israeli control.

In the mid-1950s Narkiss studied at the École de Guerre (French War College). In 1958 he was appointed the Israeli military attaché to Western Europe at the rank of brigadier general. During his several years' stay in France he was awarded the Légion d'Honneur. Upon his return to Israel he resumed his normal military career and in 1965 was appointed the first director of the Israel National Defense College at the rank of major general.

Israel Defense Forces (IDF) general Uzi Narkiss, March 1967. (Israeli Government Press Office)

The greatest military achievement for Narkiss, who was considered a master strategist, occurred during the June 1967 Six-Day War. With seven brigades under his command, he beat back a large-scale Jordanian offensive and quickly placed his troops in key sections of East Jerusalem. Although his plan did not call for the liberation of the Old City, he nevertheless decided to take control and reunify the entire city of Jerusalem. On June 7, 1967, Narkiss, along with Generals Moshe Dayan and Yitzhak Rabin, was photographed walking through the Lions' Gate. This event concluded the liberation campaign that Narkiss had begun 19 years earlier.

Narkiss left active duty in 1968 as a major general. He then served as the director of immigration in the Jewish Agency for Israel. In the 1970s and 1980s he also served as chairman of the information department of the World Zionist Organization (WZO) and headed the WZO's North American delegation. Considered the "Liberator of Jerusalem," Narkiss died in that city on December 17, 1997.

CHARLES F. HOWLETT

See also

Jerusalem; Jerusalem, Old City of; Six-Day War; World Zionist Organization

References

Dupuy, Trevor N. *Elusive Victory: The Arab-Israeli Wars, 1947–1974.* Garden City, NY: Military Book Club, 2002.
Hurewitz, J. C. *The Struggle for Palestine.* New York: Schocken, 1976.
Sacher, Howard. *A History of Israel.* New York: Knopf, 1979.

Nashashibi, Fakhri al-
Born: 1899
Died: November 9, 1941

Palestinian Arab nationalist. Fakhri al-Nashashibi was born in Jerusalem in 1899 into a prominent Arab family when Palestine was still part of the Ottoman Empire. In the 1920s he worked closely with the government of the British Mandate for Palestine and was one of the prominent opponents of the rival Husseini family. Al-Nashashibi was an official in such organizations as the Literary Club, the Palestinian Arab National Party, and the National Defense Party.

Al-Nashashibi participated in the Arab Revolt of 1936–1939, but he supported the British government's 1937 plan to partition Palestine. He was one of the organizers of the anti-Husseini Peace Gangs of 1938 and was the principal Arab target of the al-Husseini faction, which issued a death warrant against him, accusing him of collaboration with the Zionists. During World War II, al-Nashashibi helped recruit Palestinian Arabs into the British Army. He was shot to death in Baghdad by a member of the al-Husseini faction on November 9, 1941.

SPENCER C. TUCKER

See also

Arab Revolt of 1936–1939; Husseini, Haj Amin al-; Literary Club; Palestine, British Mandate for

References

Sachar, Howard M. *A History of Israel: From the Rise of Zionism to Our Time.* 3rd ed. New York: Knopf, 2007.
Sherman, A. J. *Mandate Days: British Lives in Palestine, 1918–1948.* Baltimore: Johns Hopkins University Press, 2001.

Nashashibi, Raghib
Born: 1881
Died: April 10, 1951

Palestinian political activist and mayor of Jerusalem (1920–1934). Born in Jerusalem in 1881, Raghib Nashashibi studied engineering at the University of Istanbul. He then returned to Palestine, where he became district engineer in Jerusalem. In 1914 he was elected as representative of Jerusalem in the Turkish parliament. He served in that post until 1918. In 1919 he headed the Ottoman Department of Public Works.

Returning to Palestine after the Allied victory in World War I and the establishment of a British mandate there, Nashashibi formed the Literary Club, an organization supporting plans for a greater

Syrian state. In 1919 he was a member of the All-Syrian Congress. He became mayor of Jerusalem in May 1920 and held that post until January 1935. In 1923 he headed the Palestine Arab National Party. In March 1930 he was one of the Arab representatives to the London Talks, and in December 1934 he became the leader of the National Defense Party and its representative to the Arab Higher Committee.

A moderate, Nashashibi recommended that the Arab leaders accept the British plans for the partition of Palestine and Jewish immigration. He maintained close ties with King Abdullah of Transjordan and supported the subsequent Jordanian annexation of the West Bank and East Jerusalem. This loyalty was rewarded by his appointment as minister of refugees and rehabilitation in August 1949 and, the next month, as governor-general of the Jordanian-annexed West Bank. In January 1950 he became custodian of the Holy Places of Jerusalem, a cabinet rank post. He subsequently held the posts of minister of agriculture and of transportation. Nashashibi died of cancer on April 10, 1951.

Spencer C. Tucker

See also
Arab Higher Committee

References
Khalaf, Ossa. *Politics in Palestine: Arab Factionalism and Social Disintegration, 1939–1948.* New York: SUNY Press, 1991.
Levenberg, Haim. *Military Preparations of the Arab Community in Palestine, 1945–1948.* London: Routledge, 1993.
Sayigh, Yezid. *Armed Struggle and the Search for State: The Palestine National Movement, 1949–1993.* New York: Oxford University Press, 2000.

Nasir, Jamal abd al-

See Nasser, Gamal Abdel

Nasrallah, Hassan
Born: August 31, 1960

Militant Lebanese Muslim politician and secretary-general of the Lebanese Hezbollah Party since 1992. Hassan Nasrallah, the oldest of nine children, was born in the Bourj Hammoud section of East Beirut on August 31, 1960, to a Shiite Muslim family. Interested in religious studies at a young age, he studied first at the al-Najah School and then at a public school located in Beirut.

When the Lebanese Civil War began in 1975, Nasrallah who was then 15 years old, moved with his family to his father's home village of Basuriyyah in southern Lebanon. There he attended secondary school and briefly joined the Amal movement, a new Shia party and militia that emerged from the Movement of the Dispossessed established by Imam Musa Sadr. Shortly thereafter, Nasrallah went to a Shiite seminary in Najaf, Iraq, for studies in Islamic law and the Koran. In 1979 after having completed the first part of his study reg-

Sheikh Hassan Nasrallah, militant Lebanese Muslim politician and secretary-general of the Lebanese Hezbollah Party since 1992, during a speech in Beirut, March 31, 2005. (epa/Corbis)

imen, he was forced to leave Iraq and returned to Lebanon when Saddam Hussein expelled many Shia.

The 1982 Israeli invasion of Lebanon devastated southern Lebanon. In response, Iran sent 1,000 Revolutionary Guards to mobilize the Shia of the Bekáa Valley area. Husayn al-Musawi, a teacher, accused the Amal movement of failing to resist the Israelis and, leading a new faction, Islamic Amal, went over to the Iranians. Within this resistance movement, various other groups, including that of Imam Fadlallah, began cooperating to mount attacks against the Israelis and provide help and protection to the southern villagers. Nasrallah, on his return, was associated with Islamic Amal's political office in the Bekáa Valley. Hezbollah (Party of God) began to operate in 1984, formally declaring itself and its platform in 1985 under Secretary-General Subhi al-Tufayli, and Nasrallah was associated with the group.

Still devoted to the pursuit of religious studies, in 1989 Nasrallah traveled to Qum, Iran, to immerse himself in Islamic law. In 1992 he became the leader of Hezbollah, following the assassination by Israeli operatives of his mentor Abbas al-Musawi, second Hezbollah secretary-general.

Determined to drive the Israelis out of Lebanon and to make their occupation of it untenable, Nasrallah reorganized and strengthened

Hezbollah's military wing, first formed in the context of the Resistance and the Lebanese Civil War. The party also provided services, including electricity and other aid, to residents of Beirut when fighting raged on there after the official ending of the civil war. This was in sharp contrast to the government, which did little for the residents of Beirut's poor areas. After 1992 or so, Hezbollah operations against the Israeli security zone claimed the lives of an average of some 25 Israeli soldiers per year. Both Hezbollah and Amal had ties with the Syrian government, although that government also supported various Lebanese Christian groups. Hezbollah became self-sufficient in terms of its community programs, but Iran provided help, including arms. Nearly all Lebanese were vehemently opposed to the Israeli presence in Lebanon. In 2000 when the Israelis pulled out of southern Lebanon earlier than they had planned after their 18-year occupation, Nasrallah was credited with having scored a significant victory in the ongoing Arab-Israeli conflict. He was also the driving force in the 2004 prisoner exchange between Hezbollah and Israel, another coup that was lauded throughout much of the Arab world. In spite of his popularity in Muslim and Arab circles, Nasrallah had been sharply criticized in the international community for essentially having thumbed his nose at repeated calls for the disarming of Lebanese militias. Hezbollah claimed that it needed to continue its resistance to Israeli occupation of the Shaba Farms area. However, disarmament was explicitly demanded by the September 2004 United Nations (UN) Security Council Resolution 1559.

Both Hezbollah and Nasrallah made news in the summer of 2006 after Hezbollah fighters took two Israeli soldiers captive in a daring cross-border raid. In retaliation, Israel unleashed a withering bombing campaign in southern Lebanon and imposed a naval and air blockade on all of Lebanon. By July 12, a state of war essentially existed between Israel and Hezbollah. Hezbollah had, in the past, fired Katyusha rockets into Israeli only if Lebanese civilians were attacked. As Hezbollah was targeted by the Israelis, the organization in turn began firing hundreds of rockets into civilian areas of northern Israel. Israel responded by stepping up its air campaign on virtually all areas of Lebanon and launching a ground offensive into southern Lebanon. Fighting ceased when a shaky cease-fire was brokered by the UN on August 14. On July 14 Israeli forces destroyed Nasrallah's offices and home, although the leader was unharmed in the attack. Nasrallah remains a powerful symbol of Islamist resistance to Israeli and Western policies in the Middle East. Hezbollah's 2006 war with Israel quite surprised both the Israelis and much of the world by the militia's ability to sustain operations and bring significant damage to Israel.

Nasrallah has made repeated public statements in which he seeks the return of all Lebanese and also Palestinian territory. He has stated that Hezbollah would not intervene in Palestinian-Israeli negotiations and that he would not interfere in a final settlement there. In interviews over the years, Nasrallah admits to being widely read and having studied Israeli prime minister Ariel Sharon and Benjamin Netanyahu's memoirs so that he can learn about the minds of his enemies.

PAUL G. PIERPAOLI JR. AND SHERIFA ZUHUR

See also

Hezbollah; Israel; Lebanon; Lebanon, Israeli Invasion of; United Nations Security Council Resolution 1559

References

Hamzeh, A. Nizar. "Lebanon's Hizbullah from Islamic Revolution to Parliamentary Accommodation." *Third World Quarterly* 14(2) (1993): 321–337.

Harik, Judith Palmer. *Hezbollah: The Changing Face of Terrorism.* London: Taurus, 2005.

Jaber, Hala. *Hezbollah: Born with a Vengeance.* New York: Columbia University Press, 1997.

Zuhur, Sherifa. "Hassan Nasrallah and the Strategy of 'Steadfastness.'" *Terrorism Monitor* 4(19) (October 5, 2006). http://www.jamestown .org/terrorism/news/article.php?articleid=2370155.

Nasser, Gamal Abdel
Born: January 16, 1918
Died: September 28, 1970

Egyptian nationalist leader, vice president (1953–1954), premier (1954–1956), and president (1956–1970). Born in Bani Mur, Egypt, on January 16, 1918, the son of a civil servant, Gamal Abdel Nasser at an early age developed great antipathy toward Britain's rule over Egypt, setting the stage for his later championing of Arab nationalism and unity. Settling on a military career, he graduated from the Egyptian Royal Military Academy in 1936 as a second lieutenant. While stationed in the Sudan, he met and became friends with future Egyptian president Anwar Sadat. Nasser fought in the 1948 war in Gaza and at the siege of Faluja. The Egyptian Army was poorly equipped, and it was rumored that the king's associates had purchased defective arms in Belgium. Following the war, scandal after scandal about King Farouk I rocked Egypt along with political infighting, strikes, and demonstrations.

In 1947 Nasser organized a secret nationalist and antigovernment association among fellow officers, known as the Free Officers Association. The members of the Free Officers Association were primarily of lower- and lower-middle-class backgrounds unlike most Egyptian politicians of the time, who were from the upper classes. The officers sought to end both British control and influence in Egypt and the reign of Farouk. The officers infiltrated and studied other political organizations, from the socialist groups to Misr Fatat (Young Egypt) to the Muslim Brotherhood.

After months of painstaking planning, the organization staged a bloodless coup against Farouk's government on July 23, 1952, seizing the radio and communications center and the main police station. Three days later, the king abdicated and was forced to go abroad. Meanwhile, a Revolutionary Command Council (RCC) of 13 Free Officers assumed authority over Egypt. Major General Mo-

Gamal Abdel Nasser, Egyptian vice president (1953–1954), premier (1954–1956), and president (1956–1970). (Bettmann/Corbis)

hammad Naguib, better known by the public, served as the spokesperson for the younger, junior, and more radical officers. He became commander of the Egyptian armed forces, while Ali Maher Pasha was made premier.

When the council declared Egypt a republic in June 1953, Naguib became its first president, and Nasser became vice president. Beginning in February 1954, a political power struggle ensued between Nasser and his faction of the RCC and Naguib's faction. By May, Nasser had taken de facto control as president of the RCC and premier of Egypt. Naguib was allowed to continue as president of Egypt, although this was in reality little more than a figurehead position.

Nasser and his faction consolidated their hold on power, and after an October 26, 1954, attempt on Nasser's life, in November Nasser ordered Naguib arrested and deprived of the presidency. Using the assassination attempt to solidify his power base, Nasser became premier of Egypt on February 25, 1955. Seven months later he also took the title of provisional president.

Nasser quickly moved to centralize his authority. The 1952 revolution was popular with the Egyptian public, but the power elite around Nasser contained opponents, first the labor movement and communists and then the Muslim Brotherhood. In June 1956 a national election occurred in which Nasser was the sole candidate for the presidency. Thus, he officially became Egypt's second president.

When the military junta came to power, it decreed a series of reforms, including the abolition of honorary and hereditary titles as a means of addressing the feudal power system in Egypt, where urban and rural *bashawat* (pashas) in effect controlled their poor subjects. Prior to the revolution, rural poverty and violence were rampant, with a small number of people owning much of the rural land. This situation had encouraged proposals for land reform in the Egyptian parliament and discussion of the issue continued in the RCC. In 1952 Naguib then announced the first Agrarian Reform Law, which sparked many panicked land sales. Under the terms of the legislation, individual rural landholdings could be no more than 200 feddans (about 208 acres).

President Nasser became even more popular when he nationalized the Suez Canal. He weathered the Suez War, which to Egyptians simply proved the enmity of the former colonial powers, Britain and France, along with Israel. In the wake of the Suez War, many minority groups left voluntarily or were forced out of Egypt.

The popular effort to join Egypt with Syria in the United Arab Republic (UAR) ended unsuccessfully in 1961. In its wake, Nasser put more effort into social and economic reform, including an additional land reform measure that was supposed to limit individual holdings to no more than 100 feddans (about 104 acres) and provide for the distribution of the surplus land to needy peasants. However, this measure was never fully implemented. While landless peasants in some areas did receive land, in other areas the old landowners actually returned.

The RCC government aimed to weaken the social class that had most benefited under the previous regime by both land reform and the sequestration of foreign-owned or large businesses and property. The term "foreign" applied to Egyptians who were holders of other passports. In addition, Nasser announced plans to increase agricultural production by the reclamation of lands in the delta area and construction of a new high dam on the Nile south of Aswan. To build the dam, he received promises of financial support from the United States as well as Great Britain.

Following an assassination attempt on him, Nasser outlawed the Muslim Brotherhood, arresting and imprisoning many of its members. He then banned the organization outright. The universities were purged of elements that supported the previous regime and those urging a return to parliamentary and constitutional life.

In foreign affairs, Nasser achieved several successes. On February 12, 1953, Egypt and Britain signed a treaty providing for the future of the Sudan. Over a three-year period the Sudan would develop self-governing institutions, after which the Anglo-Egyptian occupation would end and a Sudanese Constituent Assembly would choose its future course. Egyptian leaders agreed to this because by November 1952, they had acknowledged the right of Sudanese self-determination themselves. However, the RCC's delegate to the Sudan, Salah Salim, and others thought that if the Sudanese National Union Party dominated that country's assembly, it would choose union with Egypt. Nonetheless, the National Union Party decided that no referendum was necessary and announced the Sudan's independence in February 1955.

Egyptian nationalists had long worked for British withdrawal from the Suez Canal. On October 19, 1954, Nasser's government reached agreement with the British on the abrogation of the Anglo-Egyptian Treaty of 1936, the evacuation of all British troops from the Canal Zone within 20 months (the last troops departed in June 1956), maintenance of the canal base by British civilian technicians under the sovereign control of Egypt, and Britain's right to reenter Egyptian territory to protect the canal in the event of an attack "by an outside power on Egypt." The treaty also confirmed that the canal was "an integral part of Egypt" and provided for freedom of navigation in the canal.

Nasser stated early that he was basically inclined toward the West. Thus, he made it clear that communism was the only major threat to Egypt. At the same time, he warned the Western powers to postpone implementing any security pacts in the Middle East. Washington rejected this call, and by the end of 1954, relations between the Western powers and Egypt had badly deteriorated over the impending conclusion of the Baghdad Pact. Nasser strongly criticized the pro-British Iraqi prime minister over the new Egyptian radio station, Voice of the Arabs, in an effort to discourage other Arab signatories to the treaty.

Nasser was one of the leaders of the neutralist bloc at the Bandung Conference in April 1955, thereby angering John Foster Dulles, who viewed neutralism a cover for pro-Soviet attitudes. Nasser's increasing opposition to Western security arrangements led him to conclude in October 1955 military agreements with Saudi Arabia and Syria. The leaders of both states agreed to a joint command arrangement headed by Egyptian generals.

Following a strong Israeli military strike into Gaza in February 1955, Nasser increasingly devoted attention to Egyptian military preparedness because Egypt could not defend itself against Israeli attacks. To improve his armed forces, he approached the United States and Britain about purchasing arms, but after the failure of the Baghdad Pact, Washington refused. Nasser then turned to the communist bloc. In September 1955, with Soviet encouragement, he reached a barter arrangement with Czechoslovakia for substantial quantities of weapons, including jet aircraft and tanks, in return for Egyptian cotton.

The arms deal infuriated Dulles and directly impacted on the Aswan Dam construction project, which was the centerpiece of Nasser's plans to improve the quality of life for Egyptians. Its advocates claimed that the project would supply all of Egypt's electricity needs as well as increase the cultivated land of Egypt by some 30 percent. Nasser had sought Western financing, and in December 1955 Washington declared its willingness to lend $56 million for financing the Aswan Dam. Britain pledged $14 million, while the World Bank agreed to $200 million. The condition to the aid was that Egypt provide matching funds and that it not accept Soviet assistance.

Nasser was unhappy with the attached strings and in any case

expected a Soviet offer of assistance. The tightly controlled Egyptian press then launched an all-out propaganda offensive against the West, especially the United States. However, when no Soviet offer was forthcoming, Nasser finally accepted the Western aid package on July 17, 1956. Much to his chagrin, two days later Dulles announced that the offer had been withdrawn. The official U.S. reasons were that Egypt had failed to reach agreement with the Sudan over the dam (most of the vast lake created by the dam would be in Sudanese territory) and that Egyptian financing for the project had become uncertain. The real reasons were objections from some U.S. congressmen, especially Southerners fearful of competition from Egyptian cotton, and Dulles's desire to teach Nasser and other neutralists a lesson. Dulles was especially upset over Egypt's recent recognition of the People's Republic of China (PRC).

A furious Nasser took immediate action. On July 26 he nationalized the Suez Canal Company, claiming that this revenue would pay for the construction of the cherished dam project. Seeing an opportunity to gain additional influence with the Egyptians and the Arab world in general, Moscow quickly offered to help Nasser with the dam.

Nasser's action of nationalizing the canal and the failure of the United States and the United Nations (UN) to take a strong stand on the matter led to secret talks between the governments of France, Britain, and Israel. The leaders of these countries had the common aim of overthrowing Nasser. Their secret agreement culminated in the Suez Crisis (also known as the Tripartite War, or the Suez War in Egypt), one of the major events of the Cold War and the ongoing Arab-Israeli conflict.

On October 29, 1956, acting in accordance with a secret treaty with Britain and France, Israeli forces struck deep into Egyptian territory in the Sinai. The French and British governments then announced the existence of a threat to the security of the canal and demanded that both sides cease hostilities and withdraw from the canal area. When Egypt refused, French and British forces launched air attacks on Egypt on October 3. On November 5 French and British airborne forces landed in Egypt, and the next day they came ashore in an amphibious assault, the British at Port Said and the French at Port Fuad.

The United States, not privy to the secret discussions among France, Britain, and Israel, was taken by surprise and applied heavy pressure on the invaders, especially Britain. London caved under this pressure, and France and Israel were then forced to follow suit. The Soviet Union, distracted by the concurrent Hungarian Revolution, threatened intervention on the Egyptian side, but it was U.S. pressure that proved decisive in the outcome.

Far from being defeated, Nasser appeared vindicated by the Suez Crisis despite the fact that he had to surrender to Israel navigation in the Gulf of Aqaba. The event elicited great sympathy in the Arab world for Egypt, from the masses if not the leaders, and Nasser shrewdly used this so-called victory to further consolidate his rule at home and to promote Pan-Arabism throughout the Middle East. Photographs of him could be seen in every small storefront in the region. Indeed, the Suez Crisis turned Nasser into the chief spokesperson for the Pan-Arab movement.

Nasser relentlessly pursued his dream of Pan-Arabism on a variety of fronts, employing diplomacy, oratory, and subversion. In January 1958 Shukri al-Qawatli, a Syrian nationalist leader who hoped to forestall a communist victory in Syria, pressured Nasser to join Egypt into a formal union with that country. Nasser agreed to the creation of the UAR and became its president. In early March, Yemen joined Egypt and Syria in a federal union, forming the United Arab States that existed alongside the unitary state of the UAR. Nasser traveled by train through Syria and was hailed by large crowds as the hero of Arabism.

The UAR did not last. The struggle between Syrian factions that had predated the union intensified during this period. The Syrian middle class had not been subjected to authoritarian rule as had the Egyptians, and insufficient attention had been given to the structures needed to share power. Moreover, the head of Syrian military intelligence, who was loyal to Nasser, was very unpopular in Syria. The UAR fell apart when Syria withdrew on September 28, 1961. Nevertheless, Nasser continued to promote Arab nationalism and his vision of a Pan-Arab union, although the breakup of the UAR did cause him to place more emphasis on social class and property restructuring. These views and his attempts to topple the monarchies in the conservative Arab states, coupled with Western policies, brought about an Arab cold war.

Relations with the Soviet Union remained reasonably close, cemented by anti-imperialist rhetoric, Soviet support for the Arab position vis-à-vis Israel, and arms deals. The bulk of the Egyptian population disliked the presence of many Soviet advisers in the country. At the same time, however, Nasser was uncompromising in his repression of communism within Egypt. Under Nasser, relations with the United States fluctuated from good to poor.

Nationalizations that went beyond seizing properties belonging to the British and French went into effect after 1961 and included banks, insurance companies, and large enterprises. Businesses employing more than 4,000 people were taken over by the state, although some of these were later returned. These policies were not unpopular except for those directly affected. There were many economic problems, abetted by unrealistic state planning, poor management of industry, and the siphoning off of government revenues on defense spending. Nasser's government was state-capitalist in nature rather than socialist.

Nasser's nationalization program was unpopular in the West, but his attacks on the small rural and political elite that had run the country gained him the loyalty of the workers and peasants. Also, although the regime was quite repressive, it did produce a sense of pride in Egypt and things Egyptian that had not existed up to that time.

In September 1962 a military coup toppled the monarchy in Yemen. A civil war then ensued between supporters of the monarchy and the new republican government. The republican side sought help from Egypt, and Nasser eagerly responded, anxious to fulfill his commitment to Pan-Arab revolution. Egypt supplied equipment and increasing numbers of men. The Saudis, meanwhile, provided aid to the monarchist side. Yemen became a quagmire for Nasser who, by the mid-1960s, had committed some 80,000 men there. The war dragged on until 1967, and it might have continued far longer without Israel's defeat of Egypt that same year.

In 1966 Nasser signed a defense pact with Syria, and in early 1967 he began provoking the Israelis by a number of different actions, including insisting on the departure of UN peacekeepers from the Egyptian-Israeli border, where they had been in place since the 1956 Suez Crisis. He also ordered a blockade of the Gulf of Aqaba and moved Egyptian troops into the Sinai.

In retaliation for these actions, on June 5, 1967, the Israelis launched a surprise attack, first on Egypt, then on Syria, and, when it entered the war, on Jordan. In a matter of a few hours, the Israelis all but eliminated their opponents' air forces. The resulting Six-Day War proved to be a humiliating defeat for Nasser in which the Israelis conquered the entire Sinai Peninsula and entrenched themselves on the eastern bank of the Suez Canal. Nasser's belief that he could bluff his way through the crisis without fighting had cost 12,000 Egyptian dead and the loss of three-quarters of his air force. He took the blame himself and resigned, but mass public demonstrations in his support brought him back to power. He then blamed the army. His oldest friend, Abdel Hakim Amer resigned, calling for freedom of the press and more democracy. Two weeks later Amer committed suicide.

The cease-fire that halted the fighting steadily deteriorated into almost continuous firing across the canal and retaliatory Israeli air strikes deep into Egypt. Finally, in July 1970 Nasser agreed to a cease-fire arrangement put forward by U.S. secretary of state William Rogers, ending the so-called War of Attrition. Nasser's health may have deteriorated as a result of his efforts in 1970 to negotiate the crisis in Jordan between the Jordanian army and regime on the one hand and the Palestinian militants known as Black September on the other. By now in deteriorating health, Nasser died of a heart attack in Cairo on September 28, 1970. He was greatly beloved by ordinary Egyptians, and his funeral procession brought out more than 4 million people.

DALLACE W. UNGER, JR., SPENCER C. TUCKER,
AND SHERIFA ZUHUR

See also

Amer, Abdel Hakim; Aqaba, Gulf of; Attrition, War of; Dulles, John Foster; Egypt; Farouk I, King of Egypt; Israeli War of Independence, Overview; Muslim Brotherhood; Rogers, William Pierce; Sadat, Anwar; Six-Day War; Suez Crisis; Syria

References

Al-Sayyid Marsot, Afaf Lutfi. *A Short History of Modern Egypt.* Cambridge: Cambridge University Press, 1985.

DuBius, Shirley Graham. *Gamal Abdel Nasser, Son of the Nile.* New York: Third Press, 1972.

Kerr, Malcolm. *The Arab Cold War: Gamal Abd al-Nasir and His Rivals.* New York: Oxford University Press, 1971.

Lacouture, Jean. *Nasser: A Biography.* New York: Knopf, 1973.

National Democratic Party

Ruling Egyptian political party. The al-Hizb al-Watani al-Dimuqrati (NDP, National Democratic Party) is Egypt's governing party and has shaped the nation's political climate since 1984. The NDP was formed in 1978 by President Anwar Sadat as the nation's centrist governing party from the Arab Socialist Union first created by President Gamal Abdel Nasser. Following Sadat's assassination in 1981, President Hosni Mubarak, who had served as NDP deputy leader, was named to head the party at a 1982 congress. The NDP was at first, like the Arab Socialist Union, the only political party permitted in Egypt. Several extremely small opposition parties were then legalized, two to the political Right of the NDP and two to the Left. The NDP thus maintained near absolute control in all subsequent legislative elections until the introduction of limited reforms in 2005.

Under the leadership of Egyptian president Mubarak, the NDP has stood against any electoral reforms that would challenge its control of the legislature or presidency, and it has especially opposed the legalization of the Muslim Brotherhood as a political party. However, the Muslim Brotherhood formed alliances with several of the small opposition parties or ran as independents. The Muslim Brotherhood won approximately 20 percent of the parliamentary seats in the 2005 elections, despite widespread allegations of government oppression.

Spencer C. Tucker

See also

Egypt; Mubarak, Hosni; Nasser, Gamal Abdel; Sadat, Anwar

References

Israeli, Raphael. *Man of Defiance: A Political Biography of Anwar Sadat.* New York: Barnes and Noble Books, 1985.

Kassem, Maye. *Egyptian Politics: The Dynamics of Authoritarian Rule.* Boulder, CO: Lynne Rienner, 2004.

Solecki, John. *Hosni Mubarak.* New York: Chelsea House, 1991.

National Progressive Front

Syrian political alliance. Al-Jabha al-Wataniya al-Taqaddumiya (National Progressive Front, NPF) was formed in March 1972 by Syrian president Hafez al-Assad to provide for limited participation in the Syrian political process of other parties while at the same time preserving the primacy of the ruling Baath Party. (Article 8 of the Syrian Constitution states that the Baath Party "leads the state and society.") An alliance of five groups, the NPF is the nation's only legal political formation. Aside from 83 independents, the NPF holds all seats in the 250-member People's Assembly.

The NPF comprises the powerful socialist Baath Party (Hizb al-Ba'th al-'Arabi al-Ishtiraki), which has dominated Syrian politics since 1963 and is the leader of the coalition; the Syrian Communist Party (al-Hizb al-Ishtiraki al-Suriya), which has had cabinet representation since 1966; the Arab Socialist Union Party (al-Ittihad al-Ishtiraki al-Arabi); the Socialist Unionist Party (al-Haraka al-Tawhidiyya al-Ishtirakiyya); and the Arab Socialist Party (al-Hizb al-Ishtiraki al-Arabi). Although the NPF serves as the primary forum (along with the president) for determining matters of war and peace, the state budget, and politics, in reality the NPF as a whole exercises very little power, as the Baath Party tends to have the final say in most government matters. Therefore, despite the existence of five legal parties within the coalition, the smaller parties in the NPF adhere to Baathist policy and do not constitute a true multiparty system.

In early 1992 (and again in 2000) al-Assad indicated the possibility of liberalizing Syria's NPF-controlled political system, which is widely regarded as one of the most autocratic in the world. However, no new political parties have been allowed to form. In the 2003 legislative elections, the NPF secured 167 seats in the People's Assembly, with 135 NPF winners belonging to the Baath Party. Syrian president Bashar al-Assad, the son of Hafez al-Assad, heads the NPF.

Spencer C. Tucker

See also

Assad, Bashar al-; Assad, Hafez al-; Baath Party (Syria); Baathism; Syria

References

Lesch, David W. *The New Lion of Damascus: Bashar Al-Assad and Modern Syria.* New Haven, CT: Yale University Press, 2005.

Pipes, Daniel. *Greater Syria: The History of an Ambition.* New York: Oxford University Press, 1990.

Seale, Patrick. *Assad of Syria: The Struggle for the Middle East.* Berkeley: University of California Press, 1988.

Van Dam, Nikolaos. *The Struggle for Power in Syria: Politics and Society under Asad and the Ba'th Party.* London: Croom Helm, 1996.

National Security Forces, Palestinian

Al-Amin al-Watani (National Security Forces, NSF) is part of the Palestinian General Security Services (PGSS). After the 1993 Oslo Accords, signed by Israel and members of the Palestinian Authority (PA), the PGSS was established to oversee the disparate militia forces of the Palestine Liberation Organization (PLO). The PGSS incorporates three primary branches: the Interior, Intelligence, and National Security divisions. Within the National Security Branch are three organizations: the Air Guard, Coast Guard, and NSF. Of the three, the NSF is by far the largest, best financed, and most well equipped. The NSF essentially serves the function of a Palestinian national army. It patrols the borders of regions under the control of the PA and guards the checkpoints into Israeli territory. It works in cooperation with the Israel Defense Forces (IDF) to deter illegal immigration and reduce crimes along the border.

The NSF is composed of former members of the Palestine Liberation Army (PLA) as well as more recent recruits inducted from the Palestinian territories. The NSF includes roughly 15,000 members, armed with assault rifles, mortars, machine guns, and a smattering of antitank munitions. The commanders of the NSF were

Members of the Palestinian National Security Forces demonstrating their skills during a graduation ceremony on April 5, 2007, at Al-Nusairat, Gaza Strip. (Getty Images)

personally selected by PLO chairman Yasser Arafat, who maintained personal control over every PGSS organization. In the aftermath of Arafat's 2004 death, the loyalty of the NSF has been somewhat in question. The commanders report directly to PA president Mahmoud Abbas but are also subject to the influence of the National Council of the PA, dominated since the 2006 elections by Hamas. After assuming power, the leadership of Hamas announced that it would deploy members of its own security force in Gaza, leading to clashes between Hamas militia forces and the NSF.

Many of the NSF's responsibilities and activities are duplicated by other aspects of the PGSS. In particular, independent militias and intelligence organizations contribute to attempts to stabilize control of Palestinian areas. At times, these rival organizations have seemed to be at cross-purposes with the NSF.

The performance of the NSF since 1994 has been mixed. A particular problem is poor coordination with the IDF and an inability to curtail terrorist organizations. Both problems are exacerbated by the convoluted control system of the PGSS. The NSF's missions are complicated by the need to patrol the Gaza and West Bank areas

separately and by Israel's tendency to target the PA security apparatus during any disagreement with the PA.

The NSF, which remained beholden to Arafat for the first decade of its existence, remains under the control of handpicked Arafat loyalists. It has been repeatedly accused of corruption, especially facilitating criminal enterprises. These have included levying extralegal border crossing fees, demanding percentages of cross-border trade, and illegally taxing Palestinian residents at gunpoint. The NSF has unquestionably failed to prevent Palestinian attacks on Israeli settlements and facilities. Despite cooperating on joint patrols with the NSF, Israeli security officers maintain a poor opinion of Palestinian security forces, in part due to a lack of training that pervades much of the NSF. Abbas has promised to reform the NSF, including by allowing former members of Islamic militias to join the force if they forswear terrorism. However, the election of a Hamas-led government in January 2006 casts doubt on the president's ability to significantly improve the NSF.

PAUL J. SPRINGER

See also

Abbas, Mahmoud; Arafat, Yasser; Gaza Strip; Hamas; Oslo Accords; Palestine Liberation Army; Palestine Liberation Organization; Palestinian Authority; Palestinian General Security Services; West Bank

References

Giacaman, George, and Dag Jorund Lonning, eds. *After Oslo: New Realities, Old Problems.* Chicago: Pluto, 1998.

Hunter, Robert E., and Seth G. Jones. *Building a Successful Palestinian State: Security.* Santa Monica, CA: RAND, 2006.

Nazareth

Small city of Lower Galilee, where sites sacred to Christians are located. Nazareth is located some 15 miles west of the southern end of the Sea of Galilee on a plateau some 1,200 feet above sea level in the foothills that form the southern terminus of the Lebanon mountain range. In 2007 Nazareth had a population of some 70,000 people.

Archeological research indicates that the area was settled as early as 7000 BC. Nazareth remained exclusively a small Jewish village for several centuries following the Roman destruction of the Second Temple in AD 70. In fighting between the Byzantine Empire and the Persian Empire, Nazareth and most of Palestine supported Persia, and in consequence when the Byzantines took control they largely destroyed the town. The Muslims conquered Palestine in 637 and found Nazareth in ruins. The Christian Crusaders conquered Galilee in 1099 and largely rebuilt Nazareth, which became an ecclesiastical center. The Muslims retook the area in 1187. It reverted back to Christian control in 1229 in consequence of the Sixth Crusade, only to be taken by the Muslims in 1263. All Christian buildings were destroyed, and the Christian population was expelled until they were allowed to return in 1620. In the 18th century Nazareth was the administrative center of Lower Galilee.

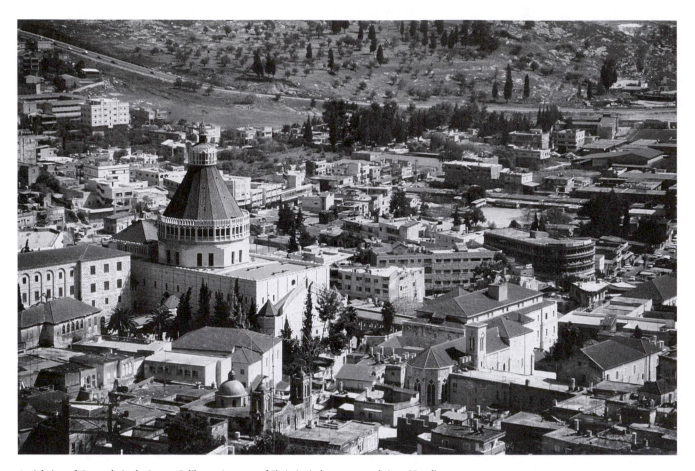

Aerial view of Nazareth, in the Lower Galilee region, one of Christianity's most sacred sites. (Corel)

During the Israeli War of Independence (1948–1949), Nazareth was occupied by forces of the Arab Liberation Army in June 1948 but was captured by the Israel Defense Forces (IDF) on July 16. Today the city has a mixed population. The majority of the inhabitants are Arab citizens of Israel, although Israeli settlements were established to provide a population balance. Muslims now outnumber the Christian Arab population, however.

Nazareth has been a major Christian pilgrimage site for centuries. Christians believe it to be the site of the Annunciation, where the archangel Gabriel informed Mary that she would give birth to Jesus, and the town where Jesus grew to manhood. The oldest archeological remains in the city are mosaics and columns of a church dating back to the time of Constantine the Great. Ruins also survive of the Crusader cathedral built there in the 12th century. Today the Church of the Annunciation in Nazareth is the largest Christian church in the Middle East. Other Christian churches are built on the presumed locations where Jesus preached, where his father had his carpentry shop, and where Jesus dined with his disciples following the Resurrection.

SPENCER C. TUCKER

See also
Galilee; Palestine, Pre-1918 History of

References
Murphy-O'Connor, Jerome. *The Holy Land: An Oxford Archeological Guide from Earliest Times to 1700.* New York: Oxford University Press, 1998.
Shahin, Mariam. *Palestine: A Guide.* Northampton, MA: Interlink, 2005.

Negev Desert

The Negev Desert is part of the Saharo-Arabian desert belt and comprises some 8,060 square miles. The triangular Negev makes up 60 percent of Israel's total land area. It is bounded in the north by the Judean Hills and in the east by Arabah, which separates it from Jordan. In the west it merges with the desert of the Sinai Peninsula of Egypt. Its southern point borders the Gulf of Aqaba, where its main settlement is Eilat.

Geologically, the dominant rock types are limestone, dolomite, and chalk, which comprise calcium carbonate deposited in the Tethys Ocean from the Middle Cretaceous to the Early Tertiary periods. Sandstone is also present. Tectonic activity has caused folding and faulting, and many of these strata are aquifers that contain important sources of water. They are overlain in places by sediments deposited by water during the Quaternary age (roughly the last 2 million years). Wind-blown deposits comprise a deep cover of loess often overlain with dune sands as in the area around Beersheba (population about 200,000 people), which is located near the northern edge of the Negev and is its chief settlement and gateway city. Near Eilat there are outcrops of Precambrian igneous rocks forming the varied relief of the Eilat Mountains, which rise to about 3,000 feet. The central Negev has three substantial craters: Makhtesh Ramon, the largest at 24 miles long, and Ha-Makhtesh ha-Gadol and Ha-Makhtesh ha-Katan, which are 1.2 to 6 miles wide. The Arava Rift Valley formed about 5 million years ago, and water erosion carved out the 1,600-foot-deep Ramon crater, which is part of the Ramon Nature Reserve. Weathering of calcareous rocks and movement of superficial deposits have produced distinct and varied desert land forms, including canyons and wadis.

The Negev climate is continental desert in a high-pressure zone. Rainfall varies from an average of as much as 12 inches a year to as little as 2 inches a year, depending on the particular region. It is also erratic, sometimes occurring in individual storms. The desert also has extremes of temperature. Diurnal temperatures range from 104 degrees Fahrenheit (40 degrees Centigrade) during the day to 14 degrees Fahrenheit (−10 degrees Centigrade) at night. There is an annual temperature range of about 60.8 degrees Fahrenheit (16 degrees Centigrade), with most months having an average temperature of more than 64.4 degrees Fahrenheit (18 degrees Centigrade).

Extreme conditions exert strong controls on flora and fauna. The vegetation cover is sparse and discontinuous. The fauna is also varied and includes ibex, many invertebrates adapted to aridity, and resident and migratory birds.

The Negev has a long history of human occupation. It lies on the route from Africa to Asia and Europe, which must have been traversed by early hominids about 2 million years ago. Its archaeological sites bear witness to the Nabatean culture of around 300 BC to AD 750, and today parts of the Negev have been developed for agriculture. The Negev Foundation actively promotes desert agricultural innovation.

The Israeli government and local leaders have supported settlement in the Negev. Israeli prime minister David Ben-Gurion was particularly devoted to the development of the Negev, and he is buried there at Sidi (Sde) Boker. A large Bedouin population still lives in the Negev, clashing in some cases with the newer arrivals, which include many Russian immigrants to Israel. The smaller revenues for the Negev in comparison to other parts of the country have led in past years to demonstrations and political dissension.

ANTOINETTE MANNION

See also
Bedouin; Eilat, Israel; Sinai

References
Beck, John A. *The Land of Milk and Honey: An Introduction to the Geography of Israel.* St. Louis: Concordia, 2006.
Chapman, Graham P., ed. *The Changing Geography of Africa and the Middle East.* London: Routledge, 1992.
Evenari, Michael, et al. *The Negev: The Challenge of a Desert.* 2nd ed. Cambridge: Harvard University Press, 1982.
Isralowitz, Richard, and Jonathan Friedlander, eds. *Transitions: Russians, Ethiopians, and Bedouins in Israel's Negev Desert.* Aldershot, UK: Ashgate, 1999.
Orni, Ephraim. *Geography of Israel.* Philadelphia: Jewish Publication Society of America, 1977.
Pulsipher, Lydia M., Alex Pulsipher, and Conrad M. Goodwin. *World Regional Geography: Global Patterns, Local Lives.* Gordonsville, VA: W. H. Freeman, 2002.
Tal, Duby, ed. *Earth Facing Sky: Skyline Negev.* Israel: Albatross Aeriel Photography, 2000.

Nehru, Jawaharlal
Born: November 14, 1889
Died: May 27, 1964

Indian prime minister (1947–1964). Jawaharlal Nehru was born into a Kashmiri Brahmin family on November 14, 1889, in Allahabad, India. After being educated in the best schools in India, he spent seven years in Britain, during which time he earned a law degree at Cambridge University in 1912. That same year he returned to India and was called to the bar. Nehru then practiced law for several years before entering politics.

Jawaharlal Nehru, Indian prime minister (1947–1964). (Library of Congress)

Following in his father's footsteps, Nehru rose to prominence in the Indian National Congress, a nationalist movement seeking to end British colonial rule in India. He eventually emerged as the protégé of the Indian nationalist icon Mohandas Gandhi. In 1942 during World War II, British colonial authorities imprisoned Nehru for 32 months because of his proindependence views.

Nehru became India's first prime minister when it became an independent nation on August 15, 1947. During his first years in office, he was forced to deal with the mass transfer of populations to and from India and Pakistan. During this movement there were considerable bloodshed and hundreds of thousands of deaths before agreement could be reached with Pakistan in the 1949 Delhi Pact. Although he remained a socialist, Nehru did not believe in the Soviet model of economic development. He fostered a system in which capitalism played a major role, albeit one overseen by a powerful and centralized state-control mechanism. At the same time, he actively sought capital investment from overseas to fuel India's economic development.

Nehru consistently sought a nonaligned foreign policy, and in the early 1950s he called on both the United States and the Soviet Union to end their nuclear tests. Yet only the Soviet Union provided significant funds for the development of heavy industry in India.

As a leader of the Non-Aligned Movement, Nehru attempted to maintain favorable relations with the Arab world and Egypt in particular. In order to counteract Pakistani influence in South Asia, secure access to Middle Eastern oil, and quell Muslim dissent at home, he took a pro-Arab stance in the ongoing Arab-Israeli dispute. Thus, in 1956 he met with Egyptian president Gamal Abdel Nasser and sharply condemned the invasion of Egyptian territory by Israel, France, and Britain. Relations with neighboring Pakistan frequently erupted into violence, which, notwithstanding Nehru's pro-Arab stance in the Arab-Israeli conflict, hurt India's relations with the Muslim nations of the Middle East.

In 1950 Nehru did not protest China's annexation of Tibet, but he did allow the Dalai Lama to set up a government-in-exile in India. Nevertheless, during the 1950s India and China maintained amicable relations. In 1962, however, China launched the Sino-Indian War over disputed territory along the border between Tibet and India. India's defeat in that conflict was a serious blow to Nehru's prestige. His critics argue that his condemnation of the 1956 invasion of Egypt flew in the face of his silence on China's land grab in Tibet and the Soviet crackdown during the 1956 Hungarian Revolution.

Nehru died of a sudden heart attack on May 27, 1964, in New Delhi. His only daughter, Indira Gandhi, became prime minister in 1966 after the death of Nehru's successor, Lal Bahadur Shastri. Gandhi was assassinated while still in office in 1984.

MICHAEL R. HALL

See also

Egypt; Nasser, Gamal Abdel; Suez Crisis

References

Brown, Judith. *Nehru: A Political Life*. New Haven, CT: Yale University Press, 2003.

Nehru, Jawaharlal. *Discovery of India*. Oxford: Oxford University Press, 1990.

Tharor, Shashi. *Nehru: A Biography*. New York: Arcade, 2003.

Netanyahu, Benjamin
Born: October 21, 1949

Israeli soldier, diplomat, and prime minister (1996–1999). Born in Tel Aviv, Israel, on October 21, 1949, Benjamin (Binyamin) "Bibi" Netanyahu moved with his family from Jerusalem to Philadelphia, where his father, Benzion Netanyahu, taught history at the University of Pennsylvania and where the younger Netanyahu attended high school. He returned to Israel in 1967 and entered the Israel Defense Forces (IDF) to serve as a soldier and officer in the antiterrorist Sayeret Matkal unit during 1967–1972. He participated in the IDF's Operation GIFT during December 28–29, 1968, at Beirut Airport and was wounded during the rescue, led by Ehud Barak, of hijacked Sabena Airlines hostages at Ben-Gurion Airport on May 8, 1972.

Netanyahu's studies for a degree in architecture from the Massachusetts Institute of Technology (MIT) were interrupted by his service as a captain in the Yom Kippur War of October 1973, but he returned to receive his bachelor's degree in 1974. He then earned a master's of science degree in management studies from MIT in 1976 and pursued studies in political science both at MIT and Harvard University. He joined the international business consulting firm of Boston Consulting Group in 1976, but in 1978 he accepted a position in senior management at Rim Industries in Jerusalem.

In Jerusalem Netanyahu created the Jonathan Institute, dedicated to the study of terrorism. The institute was named in memory of his brother, who was the only Israeli fatality of the successful raid to free the Jewish passengers and Air France crew held captive at the airport in Entebbe, Uganda, in 1976. The institute sponsored international conferences and seminars on terrorism.

As the deputy chief of missions at the Israeli embassy in Washington during 1982–1984, Netanyahu participated in initial discussions on strategic cooperation between the United States and Israel. As Israeli ambassador to the United Nations (UN) during 1984–1988, he was instrumental in opening the UN Nazi War Crimes Archives in 1987. A member of the conservative Likud Party, he won election in 1988 to the Knesset and served as deputy foreign minister during 1988–1991, as a coalition deputy minister to Prime Minister Yitzhak Rabin during 1991–1992, and as the Israeli spokesman during the Persian Gulf War (1991). Netanyahu also participated in the Madrid Peace Conference of October 1991 that saw the first direct negotiations among Israel, Syria, Lebanon, and a joint Jordanian-Palestinian delegation.

Following Likud's defeat in the 1992 elections, Yitzhak Shamir stepped down as party leader. Netanyahu won election as party leader in 1993, in part because of his opposition to the 1993 Israel–Palestine Liberation Organization (PLO) peace accords that led to Israeli withdrawals from the West Bank and the Gaza Strip.

Benjamin Netanyahu, Israeli politician, diplomat, and prime minister (1996–1999). (Israeli Government Press Office)

In the May 1996 national elections, for the first time Israelis elected their prime minister directly. Campaigning under the slogan "Netanyahu—making a safe Peace," Netanyahu hired an American campaign adviser and narrowly defeated Shimon Peres of the Labor Party, who had succeeded as prime minister after the assassination of Rabin. The election took place following a wave of Muslim suicide bombings that killed 32 Israeli citizens and that Peres seemed powerless to halt.

Netanyahu took office in June 1996. He was the youngest prime minister in Israeli history. He was also the first Israeli prime minister to be born after the establishment of Israel.

Netanyahu's tenure as prime minister was marked by worsening relations with Syria that led to the posting of Syrian troops in Lebanon who were not withdrawn until 2005. Relations with the Palestinians also deteriorated when he and Jerusalem mayor Ehud Olmert in September 1996 opened ancient tunnels under the Western (Wailing) Wall and the al-Aqsa Mosque complex. Netanyahu's position weakened within Likud when he ceased to oppose the Oslo Peace Accords of 1993 and withdrew troops from Hebron in the West Bank in 1997. His attempt to restore that support by increasing Israeli settlements in the West Bank, promoting Jewish hous-

ing in predominantly Arab East Jerusalem in March 1997, and decreasing the amount of land to be ceded to the Palestinians only served to provoke Palestinian violence and impede the peace process.

Netanyahu again angered the conservative wing of Likud when he agreed in the Wye River Agreement of 1998 to relinquish control of as much as 40 percent of the West Bank to the Palestinians. He again reversed himself and suspended the accords in December 1999. He resigned from the Knesset and the chairmanship of Likud after he was defeated by Barak in his bid for reelection in May 1999, stepping down as prime minister that July.

Netanyahu accepted the position of minister of foreign affairs in November 2002, and after the 2003 elections he became the finance minister under Prime Minister Ariel Sharon until August 2005. Netanyahu resigned to protest the Israeli pullout from the Gaza Strip. Following Sharon's departure from the Likud Party, Netanyahu was one of several candidates to replace him. In December 2005 he retook the leadership of Likud. He has written or edited a number of books. Among these are *International Terrorism: Challenge and Response* (1979), *Place among Nations: Israel and the World* (1992), *Fighting Terrorism: How Democracies Can Defeat Domestic and International Terrorists* (1995), and *A Durable Peace: Israel and Its Place among the Nations* (2000). Despite the fact that Netanyahu and his wife have been the subject of criminal investigations, in early 2007 many observers believed that Netanyahu was well positioned to become Israel's next prime minister. Public opinion polls showed his party with a wide lead over its opponents.

RICHARD EDWARDS

See also

Barak, Ehud; Gaza Strip; Hebron; Jerusalem; Jerusalem, Old City of; Likud Party; Madrid Conference; Netanyahu, Jonathan; Olmert, Ehud; Peres, Shimon; Rabin, Yitzhak; Sayeret Matkal; Sharon, Ariel; West Bank; Western Wall; Wye River Agreement

References

Caspit, Ben, and Ilan Kfir. *Netanyahu: The Road to Power*. Translated by Ora Cummings. New York: Birch Lane, 1998.

Lochery, Neill. *The Difficult Road to Peace: Netanyahu, Israel and the Middle East Peace Process*. Reading, UK: Ithaca Press, 1999.

Shindler, Colin. *Israel, Likud and the Zionist Dream: Power, Politics, and Ideology from Begin to Netanyahu*. New York: Tauris, 1995.

Netanyahu, Jonathan
Born: March 13, 1946
Died: July 3, 1976

Israeli military officer and commander of the daring 1976 raid on Entebbe. Jonathan (Yonatan, Yonathan) "Yoni" Netanyahu was born in New York City on March 13, 1946. His father, Benzion Netanyahu, was a historian who headed the U.S.-based New Zionist Organization and later held several professorships in the United States. Yoni's younger brother, Benjamin, served as Israel's prime minister (1996–1999).

Israel Defense Forces (IDF) lieutenant colonel Jonathan Netanyahu, commander of the daring 1976 Entebbe Raid. (Israeli Government Press Office)

In 1964 at age 18, Netanyahu joined the Israel Defense Forces (IDF). He fought in both the Sinai and the Golan Heights as a member of a paratrooper company during the 1967 Six-Day War. He then studied for a year at Harvard University before returning to duty during the War of Attrition (1967–1970). He studied for six months at Hebrew University of Jerusalem during late 1970–early 1971 before joining the Sayeret Matkal, the elite special operations unit of the IDF. Also known as General Staff Recon or The Unit, the Sayeret Matkal was modeled on the British Special Air Service (SAS). Both of Netanyahu's brothers followed him into the Sayeret Matkal.

In 1972 Netanyahu led an operation that captured senior Syrian military officers, who were then exchanged for Israeli pilots held captive by Syria. In 1973 he was part of the Sayeret Matkal contingent that, along with Shayetet 13 and the Mossad, assassinated members of the Black September organization responsible for the 1972 massacre of Israeli Olympic athletes in Munich.

During the 1973 Yom Kippur War, Netanyahu commanded a Sayeret Matkal force in the Golan Heights that blunted a Syrian commando raid. He also led the rescue mission that retrieved Lieu-tenant Colonel Yossi Ben-Hanan (Khannan) from behind enemy lines in the northern tip of the Golan Heights (Tal Shams). For his actions in the Yom Kippur War, Netanyahu was awarded Israel's Medal for Distinguished Service.

The heavy casualties sustained by Israeli tank crews in the Yom Kippur War severely depleted the Israeli Armored Corp's personnel. Consequently, in 1974 Netanyahu left the Sayeret Matkal and took command of the Barak Armored Brigade of the IDF Northern Command (Golan Heights) until the personnel crisis stabilized. He subsequently returned to the Sayeret Matkal in June 1975 as its commander with the rank of lieutenant colonel.

On June 27, 1976, a group of 4 terrorists (2 Palestinians and 2 Germans) boarded Air France Flight 139 in Athens. It was the stopover of a flight from Israel's Ben-Gurion Airport to Paris. The terrorists then hijacked the plane with its 246 passengers and 12 crew members. The plane was diverted to Benghazi, Libya, where a pregnant passenger was released before the plane flew on to Entebbe, Uganda. The plane landed at 3:15 a.m. Ugandan time on June 28. There the 145 non-Jewish and non-Israeli passengers were released. However, the 105 Jewish and Israeli passengers and the 12 crew members remained as hostages, to be held pending the demanded release of 40 Palestinians held in Israel and 13 detainees held in prisons in Kenya, France, Switzerland, and West Germany.

The Israeli government then directed Netanyahu to plan a rescue operation. He duly presented the plan to Brigadier General Dan Shomron who, as the commander of IDF's Infantry and Paratroopers Branch, assumed overall command of the operation. Shomron presented Netanyahu's plan to the IDF chief of staff Lieutenant General Mordechai "Mota" Gur and Israel Defense Minister Shimon Peres. Netanyahu became the assault force commander.

The rescue force landed at Entebbe at 11:01 p.m. local time on July 3. During the Sayeret Matkal raid, all of the hijackers were killed. Three hostages also died, at least two from Ugandan fire. One Israeli soldier was badly injured. Netanyahu was the only raider killed. While he was returning to the Old Terminal at Entebbe Airport, he was shot in the chest. As per his preaction casualty order prioritizing the safety of hostages over the treatment of wounded soldiers, he was not treated until all of the hostages were safe. By the time medical help arrived, he had died of his wounds. The flight crew, the hostages, the rescuers, and Netanyahu's body were airborne slightly before 1:00 a.m. on July 4, 1976, bound for Israel via Nairobi, Kenya. The raid on Entebbe was originally called Operation THUNDERBOLT (also Operation ENTEBBE). However, in honor of Netanyahu, it is now officially known as Operation YONATAN.

RICHARD EDWARDS

See also

Black September Organization; Entebbe Hostage Rescue; Israel Defense Forces; Munich Olympic Games; Sayeret Matkal

References

Netanyahu, Iddo. *Entebbe: A Defining Moment in the War on Terrorism; The Jonathan Netanyahu Story.* Toronto: Balfour, 2003.

Netanyahu, Iddo, and Yoram Hazony. *Yoni's Last Battle: The Rescue at Entebbe, 1976.* Jerusalem: Gefen, 2001.

Netanyahu, Jonathan. *The Letters of Jonathan Netanyahu: The Commander of the Entebbe Rescue Operation.* Jerusalem: Gefen, 2001.

Stevenson, William. *90 Minutes at Entebbe.* New York: Bantam, 1976.

New Wafd Party

One of Egypt's leading political opposition parties. The roots of the New Wafd Party (New Delegation Party, NWP), simply referred to as the Wafd, date back to the early 20th century, when the liberal Wafd Party was founded in 1919 to advocate against British rule. The Wafd Party was for decades the leading Egyptian political party. It was disbanded after Gamal Abdel Nasser and the Free Officers came to power in Egypt in a military coup in July 1952 and declared political parties illegal. When political parties were again legalized in 1978, a group with a similar philosophy to that of the Wafd Party formed as the New Wafd Party. It disbanded shortly thereafter but formed again in 1983.

The NWP is a liberal political force in Egypt, to the political Right of the government's National Democratic Party, advocating democracy, respect for human rights, an independent judiciary, increased foreign investment, a solution to the housing situation, enhanced ties with other Islamic nations, and a solution to the Palestinian problem. The party calls for an end to the emergency laws that have been in place ever since 1967 and that permit Egyptian president Hosni Mubarak to limit elections and freedom of the press. The party also advocates making Islamic Sharia law as the basis of Egyptian legislation, aligning itself on this issue with such groups as the Muslim Brotherhood. The Egyptian government's domination by Mubarak's National Democratic Party has made all opposition parties in the nation relatively weak. The NWP may be small, but its members are outspoken, and it has consistently won a handful of seats in the People's Assembly. In the 2005 presidential elections, the first in which multiple candidates were permitted to run, NWP candidate and party leader Numan Guma placed third behind Mubarak and Ghad Party candidate Ayman Nur (who was previously a Wafd leader). Although vote totals were hotly contested, Guma is estimated to have garnered between 5 and 7 percent of the vote.

JESSICA SEDGEWICK

See also

Egypt; Mubarak, Hosni; Muslim Brotherhood; Nasser, Gamal Abdel; National Democratic Party

References

Beattie, Kirk J. *Egypt during the Sadat Years.* New York: Palgrave, 2000.

Kassem, Maye. *Egyptian Politics: The Dynamics of Authoritarian Rule.* Boulder, CO: Lynne Rienner, 2004.

Nile River

The Nile River is located in northeastern Africa and flows through the countries of Sudan and Egypt. It has several sources, notably the

The Nile River winds north through Egypt to empty into the eastern Mediterranean Sea. The Sinai Peninsula and the Red Sea are on the right of this satellite photograph. (NASA)

White Nile that originates from Lake Victoria in Uganda and the Blue Nile that originates from Lake Tana in Ethiopia. These contribute approximately 28 percent and 58 percent, respectively, of the Nile's waters in Egypt. A further 14 percent comes from the Atbarah River, which originates in Ethiopia.

The Nile is the world's longest river and flows north for some 4,216 miles through 35 degrees of latitude ranging from the Sahara Desert to the Mediterranean Sea. It has a surface area of more than 1.86 million square miles and a discharge of about 829,000 gallons per second. Geographically, the Nile may be divided into three zones: the upstream region in which the tributaries coalesce (where the White and Blue Niles join) close to Khartoum in Sudan; the middle stretch between Cairo and Khartoum, which contains the Aswan Dam (Sadd al-Aali) and numerous waterfalls; and the delta region from north of Cairo where the river subdivides.

Abundant irrigation channels carry water beyond the fertile floodplain into the arid desert margins to create agricultural land, a major economic asset for Egypt, especially for cotton production. The delta region was once a wide estuary in which river-borne silt was deposited to produce a fan-shaped delta extending some 100 miles to the sea. The delta is about 150 miles wide and occupies some 13,600 square miles overall.

Historical documents indicate that the number of branches has changed in the last 2,000 years. Through natural silting and human engineering, seven branches have since been reduced to two, the Rosetta and Damietta Rivers. Numerous irrigation channels have also been constructed.

The Nile has always been important in the history of Sudan and Egypt. Its seasonal waters, dependent on rainfall in the headwater region, and fertile silt supported several great civilizations, including the Nubian and ancient Egyptian civilizations. So precious was the Nile floodplain that tombs and temples were constructed at the desert margins. Today, some 110 million people inhabit the Nile Valley, mostly in Egypt, and are mainly engaged in agriculture and tourism.

The construction of the Aswan High Dam, completed in 1971, altered the geography and economy of the Nile and its valley quite substantially. Not the least of these changes was the creation of the world's largest artificial lake, known as Lake Nasser. At the time of its construction, the Aswan High Dam was the world's largest dam. It has fulfilled its promise of regulated river flow and flood abatement as well as the provisioning of a large proportion of Egypt's electricity. Disadvantages include the loss of fertile silt deposition downstream and the consequent need for artificial fertilizers in agriculture as well as a decline in the fisheries industry in the eastern Mediterranean. Although the Aswan High Dam provided more water on a year-round basis instead of the annual flooding, a side effect of working in the fields irrigated by the river is infection by a small parasite, a blood fluke that spreads the debilitating bilharziasis (schistosomiasis) to large numbers of Egyptians, estimated to number in the 1960s at 40 percent of the entire population.

The Nile River and its discharge have been a constant source of political controversy between the Sudan and Egypt as well as the basis for numerous Nile political unity schemes. The Nile River and Aswan High Dam project in particular were at the center of the 1956 Suez Crisis during which Israel, France, and Britain invaded Egypt to take back control of the Suez Canal. Egyptian president Gamal Abdel Nasser had nationalized the canal earlier that year with the stated aim of raising funds for the construction of the Aswan High Dam. He did so when the United States and Great Britain reneged on an earlier offer to help fund the project after Nasser had purchased armaments from the communist bloc. Nasser's decision ultimately led to a British, French, and Israeli invasion of Egypt.

As with other freshwater supplies in the generally parched Middle East, the Nile River is also at the center of ever-increasing concerns over potable water supplies in the face of growing populations and increased industry and agriculture.

Antoinette Mannion

See also

Aswan High Dam Project; Egypt; Nasser, Gamal Abdel; Suez Crisis

References

Holmes, Martha, Gavin Maxwell, and Tim Scoones. *Nile: Unveiling the Secrets of the World's Greatest River*. London: BBC Books, 2004.

Said, Rushdi. *The River Nile: Geology, Hydrology and Utilization*. Amsterdam: Elsevier, 1993.

Tvedt, Terje. *The River Nile in the Age of the British: Political Ecology and the Quest for Economic Power*. London: Tauris, 2004.

Waterbury, John. *Hydropolitics of the Nile Valley*. Syracuse: Syracuse University Press, 1979.

1956 War

See Suez Crisis

1967 War

See Six-Day War

Nixon, Richard Milhous
Born: January 9, 1913
Died: April 22, 1994

American politician and president of the United States (1969–1974). Richard Nixon was born on January 9, 1913, in Yorba Linda, California, the son of a modest grocer. He graduated from Whittier College in 1934 and received his law degree in 1937 from Duke University Law School. That same year he passed the California bar exam, and he practiced law in Whittier until 1942. Following a brief stint in the Office of Price Administration, he spent four years in the U.S. Navy during World War II. In 1946 he was elected to Congress from California as a Republican, and in 1950 he won election to the Senate. Both races were notable for his use of anticommunist smear tactics.

In the 1952 presidential campaign, U.S. Army general Dwight D. Eisenhower, the Republican nominee, selected Nixon as his running mate. With an election victory that November, Nixon spent eight years as vice president, demonstrating particular interest in foreign affairs. In 1960 he narrowly lost a presidential race to John F. Kennedy, and in 1962 Nixon was defeated in the California gubernatorial race. In a bitter and close election race in 1968, however, he was elected president on the Republican ticket and won a second term with a landslide victory in 1972.

In 1968 the inability of the United States to achieve victory in the Vietnam War dominated the political agenda. Nixon had won the presidency in part by giving the impression that he had a secret plan to end the war expeditiously. Instead, he fell back on the policies of President Lyndon Johnson's administration while embracing Vietnamization, or the gradual withdrawal of American troops from Vietnam and their replacement by units of the South Vietnamese military. In August 1969 Henry Kissinger, Nixon's national security adviser, embarked on protracted negotiations with the North Vietnamese, which ultimately resulted in the accord signed in Paris in December 1972. After the South Vietnamese government balked at the terms and North Vietnam made them public, Nixon launched a renewed U.S. bombing campaign against North Vietnamese targets in December 1972, and the peace accords were finally signed in January 1973. The Vietnam War continued without the Americans, however, and in April 1975 North Vietnamese forces triumphed.

Richard Nixon, American politician and president of the United States (1969–1974). (National Archives and Records Administration)

American withdrawal from Vietnam was only part of the broader strategic realignment that Nixon and Kissinger (secretary of state from 1973) envisaged, terming it the Grand Design. The Nixon (Guam) Doctrine, announced in July 1969, called upon American allies to bear the primary burden of their own defense. Meanwhile, new worldwide economic realities and a deteriorating U.S. economy compelled Nixon in 1971 to remove the American dollar from the gold standard.

Conscious that growing economic difficulties mandated cuts in defense budgets, Nixon and Kissinger hoped to negotiate arms limitations agreements with the Soviet Union rather than unilaterally cutting U.S. military spending. To pressure the Soviets, Nixon began the process of reopening U.S. relations with the People's Republic of China (PRC). In 1972 he visited Beijing, where he had extended talks with Chinese officials. These tactics alarmed Soviet leaders, who facilitated a relaxation of Soviet-U.S. tensions, broadly termed détente, that led to the conclusion of a major nuclear arms control agreement.

Upon winning reelection in 1972, Nixon hoped to move toward full recognition of China and further arms control agreements. The outbreak of the Yom Kippur War in October 1973, however, diverted his administration's attention from these plans, as it precipitated an Arab oil embargo that contributed to fuel shortages, an international spiral of inflation, and high unemployment. From then on, the U.S. economy would bedevil three U.S. presidents: Nixon, Gerald Ford, and Jimmy Carter.

Initially, Nixon and Kissinger had let Secretary of State William P. Rogers handle Middle Eastern policy. Seeking to resolve outstanding issues from the 1967 Six-Day War, in 1969 Rogers and Joseph Sisco, assistant secretary of state for Near Eastern and South Asian affairs, developed an Arab-Israeli peace plan envisaging Israeli withdrawal from occupied territories in return for a brokered peace settlement guaranteed by both the superpowers. Kissinger privately informed the Soviets that the White House had no interest in this scheme, effectively sabotaging the Rogers Plan, which the Soviet Union rejected in October 1969.

U.S. Middle Eastern policy thereafter remained largely static until the October 1973 Yom Kippur War, when Egypt and Syria launched a surprise attack on Israel to regain the territories they had lost in the previous 1967 war. When the Israelis rallied and then counterattacked, threatening to wipe out the Egyptian Third Army, President Anwar Sadat of Egypt, who had tilted toward the United States the previous year in the hope that this would enable Egypt to regain the Sinai, appealed for aid to the Soviet Union. To prevent Soviet intervention, Nixon ordered military forces to a DEFCON 3 military alert, two levels below outright war, while successfully pressuring the Israelis not to destroy the Egyptian Third Army.

The oil-producing Arab states reacted to events by imposing an oil embargo on the United States and other Western powers that had supported Israel. This greatly enhanced the international clout of the Organization of the Petroleum Exporting Countries (OPEC) in a quadrupling of oil prices. The European powers quickly responded by adopting more pro-Arab policies, a shift that Nixon and Kissinger strongly resented. Kissinger embarked on several months of high-profile shuttle diplomacy with Israel, Syria, and Egypt, eventually brokering an armistice. Under both Nixon and President Ford, for the next two years Kissinger continued to mediate among the contending Middle Eastern powers, eventually negotiating the Sinai Accords of September 1975 whereby Israel returned part of the Sinai to Egypt, a settlement that probably contributed to the more extensive Camp David Accords that President Carter negotiated in 1978.

His superpower juggling apart, Nixon's record in foreign affairs was decidedly mixed. Relations with European nations were somewhat strained, as leading allies resented the secrecy and nonconsultation that characterized Nixon-Kissinger diplomacy. Japan particularly resented being left ignorant of U.S. intentions to reopen relations with China, an initiative that also horrified Chiang Kai-shek's Guomindang regime in Taiwan. In 1973, the Nixon administration also sanctioned Central Intelligence Agency (CIA) involvement in a military coup against left-wing Chilean president Salvador Allende, in the course of which Allende died. Critics charged that Nixon and Kissinger showed little understanding of or empathy toward developing nations and were overly eager to support authoritarian regimes. Critics also attacked U.S. diplomacy for its insensitivity to human rights.

The Watergate political scandal, which embroiled the president and his closest advisers in a web of lies and cover-ups, not only led to Nixon's resignation in disgrace in August 1974 but also finally aborted all his ambitions for further progress in overseas affairs. After his resignation, Nixon devoted his final two decades to writing his memoirs and numerous other publications on international affairs, part of a broader and ultimately successful attempt to engineer his personal rehabilitation and win respect from contemporaries, not to mention a place in history. Nixon died from complications of a massive stroke in New York City on April 22, 1994.

PRISCILLA MARY ROBERTS

See also

Arab Oil Embargo; Camp David Accords; Egypt; Israel; Kissinger, Henry Alfred; Organization of Petroleum Exporting Countries; Rogers, William Pierce; Rogers Plan; Sadat, Anwar; Sinai; Sinai I and Sinai II Agreements; Soviet Union and Russia, Middle East Policy; Syria; United States, Middle East Policy; Yom Kippur War

References

Ambrose, Stephen E. *Nixon.* 3 vols. New York: Simon and Schuster, 1986–1991.

Bundy, William. *A Tangled Web: The Making of Foreign Policy in the Nixon Presidency.* New York: Hill and Wang, 1998.

Greene, John Robert. *The Limits of Power: The Nixon and Ford Administrations.* Bloomington: Indiana University Press, 1992.

Hoff, Joan. *Nixon Reconsidered.* New York: Norton, 1994.

Nixon, Richard M. *RN: The Memoirs of Richard Nixon.* New York: Grosset and Dunlap, 1978.

Small, Melvin. *The Presidency of Richard Nixon.* Lawrence: University Press of Kansas, 1999.

Nordau, Max
Born: July 29, 1849
Died: January 23, 1923

Leading Zionist, author, and physician. Born Simon Maximilian Südfeld in Pest, Hungary, on July 29, 1849, his father, Gabriel Südfeld, was an Orthodox rabbi and teacher of Sephardic origin who was descended from a long line of Talmudic scholars. Young Südfeld received from his father a traditional Jewish education but in his late teens drifted away from observant Judaism without, however, entirely repudiating his heritage. He received his medical degree from the University of Pest in 1875. He had already begun a career in journalism in 1867, writing for the German-language newspaper *Pester Lloyd* under the pseudonym Max Nordau, and he adopted the pen name legally in 1873. Nordau first set up a medical practice in Pest, specializing in psychiatry, but in 1880 he moved to Paris and began working there as both a doctor and a correspondent for

Max Nordau, leading Zionist, author, and physician. (Library of Congress)

such prestigious newspapers as the *Pester Lloyd*, the Vienna *Neue Freie Presse*, and the *Frankfurter Zeitung*.

In 1883 Nordau gained international notoriety with the publication of his book *Die conventionellen Lügen der Kulturmenschheit* (The Conventional Lies of Our Civilization). In this work, he attacked prevailing social and political institutions. He criticized organized religion, monarchy, aristocracy, and hypocritical sexual attitudes and offered as an alternative a philosophy of solidaritarianism, a doctrine of radical freedom tempered by love and respect for fellow humans. The book was instantly successful but was banned in Austria and Russia, and it was also put on the index of forbidden books by the Catholic Church. Translated into more than a dozen languages, the book went through 73 editions. Nordau followed this work with *Paradoxes* in 1885, which expounded on many of the same themes.

Nordau published his most famous work, *Entartung* (Degeneration), in 1892. It was even more successful and controversial than his previous works and helped spawn a whole field of social criticism that would endure for more than half a century. Nordau used Italian criminologist Cesare Lombroso's concept of moral degeneracy to argue that modern industrial society was reversing the process of evolution and doing irreparable harm to humankind. Nordau found symptoms of degeneration in nearly every facet of modern life and believed that if this trend continued unabated, humanity faced certain doom.

Although social criticism remained central to his life, in 1892 Nordau encountered Theodor Herzl, the man who would introduce him to Zionism, which became the second abiding passion of Nordau's life. Herzl was a fellow Hungarian and Jew and was also in Paris as a correspondent for a German-language newspaper, so the two men had much in common. They were also witnesses of the rising tide of anti-Semitism in France, and both viewed the 1894 trial of Alfred Dreyfus with great alarm. In 1895 when Herzl told Nordau of his idea to establish a Jewish state in Palestine, Nordau became a convert. He remained a great supporter of Herzl's efforts to promote Zionism.

At the first Zionist World Congress at Basle, Switzerland, in 1897, Nordau was vice president and Herzl president. Together they helped draft the Basle Program, the founding manifesto of the movement. Nordau served as vice president of the first six congresses and president of four more after that. The highlight of the congresses was Nordau's inspired and eloquent speech on the plight of world Jewry. The texts of these orations became famous founding documents of the Zionist movement.

Although Nordau had private reservations and called the idea a "temporary solution," he supported the controversial East Africa Scheme to settle Jewish refugees in Uganda. In 1903 a young man ardently opposed to the plan attempted to assassinate Nordau. Remarkably, Nordau himself defended the young man's actions in court.

When Herzl died in 1904, expressing his wish that Nordau succeed him as president of the Zionist organization, Nordau refused to accept the position, preferring to remain outside the center of power. He also had fundamental disagreements with certain factions of the movement, especially the so-called cultural Zionism propounded by Ahad Ha-Am. Nordau sharply criticized this attempt to form Israel into a more or less exclusive center of Jewish spiritual life. He believed that this missed the point of agitating for a political homeland that would offer shelter to all Jews without regard to the depth of their religious commitment. He also criticized so-called practical Zionists such as Chaim Weizmann, who advocated the slow colonization of Israel through the establishment of agricultural communities. Nordau forcefully argued for the immediate creation of a viable political state in Israel as the only effective way to save millions of Jews living as persecuted minorities in other nations.

Nordau's differences with his fellow Zionists soon caused him to end his active involvement in the movement. At the Zionist Congress of 1911, he predicted that the 6 million Jews who lived in Russia and Eastern Europe, where anti-Semitism was endemic, faced death if a political refuge was not created in Israel to which they could escape. After 1911 when the Zionist movement was dominated by Weizmann's practical Zionism, Nordau ceased attending the congresses.

Nordau's Austro-Hungarian nationality led to his exile from France during World War I. He settled in Spain. In 1920 when the United Kingdom secured a mandate over Palestine, he produced a plan to transfer 600,000 Jews there from Russia and Ukraine. He also advocated resettling the rest of European Jewry there as soon as possible, but both the Zionist leadership and the British government rejected the plan as impracticable, and in 1921 Nordau retired from the Zionist movement for good.

Even while he was consumed with his work in the Zionist movement, Nordau continued to publish social criticism. He extended and elaborated on his philosophy of solidaritarianism in *Der Sinn der Geschichte* (The Interpretation of History), published in 1909; *Biology der Ethik* (Biology of Ethics), published in 1921; and *Der Sinn der Gesittung* (The Essence of Civilization), published in 1920. The central problem of modern society, he argued, was to combine true freedom with the needs of the community. This ambition could be achieved with compassion and intelligence, and he even espoused a kind of socialism that would limit private property without abolishing it altogether. He never advocated communism and called its Russian Bolshevik form "socialism gone mad."

Nordau died in Paris on January 23, 1923. He was buried there, but in accordance with his wishes his remains were moved to Israel and reinterred in Tel Aviv's Old Cemetery in 1926.

Spencer C. Tucker

See also

Anti-Semitism; Basle Program; Dreyfus Affair; East Africa Scheme; Herzl, Theodor; Weizmann, Chaim; Zionism; Zionist Conference

References

Bein, Alex. *Theodor Herzl: A Biography.* London: Jewish Publication Society of America, 1943.

Brenner, Michael. *Zionism: A Brief History.* Translated by Shelley Frisch. Princeton, NJ: Markus Wiener, 2003.

Laqueur, Walter. *A History of Zionism: From the French Revolution to the Establishment of the State of Israel.* Reprint ed. New York: Schocken, 2003.

Nouf, Abu, al-

See Hawatmeh, Nayef

Nuclear Weapons

Although no state—Middle Eastern or otherwise—has detonated a nuclear device in any of the Arab-Israeli wars, nuclear weapons have nevertheless played a role in regional politics, and the use of nuclear weapons has been implicitly threatened in crises. The four regional states engaged in significant nuclear activity since 1945 are Egypt, Iran, Iraq, and Israel. Since the late 1970s, efforts by these nations to acquire nuclear weapons and nuclear weapons technology have increased in size and scope. This has resulted in tense relations among Middle East nations and between Middle Eastern

View of the Israeli nuclear facility in the Negev Desert outside Dimona, August 6, 2000. Israel is widely believed to be in possession of nuclear weapons, probably manufactured with plutonium from this reactor. (Reuters/Corbis)

nations and those of the West. These developments also threaten to unravel nuclear nonproliferation arrangements in the early 21st century.

Egypt's interest in acquiring a nuclear weapon dates to the mid-1950s, when it acquired a research reactor from the Soviet Union. As evidence of Israel's nuclear reactor development became public, Egypt became more interested in acquiring or developing nuclear weapons. However, requests to both the Soviets and Chinese for a bona fide reactor were rejected. In 1968 Egypt signed the Nuclear Non-Proliferation Treaty (NPT) and apparently ended its nuclear weapons program. During the 1973 Yom Kippur War, the Soviet Union reportedly shipped missiles with nuclear warheads to Egypt. These were subsequently withdrawn. In the 1990s, however, Egypt became a vocal advocate for the creation of a nuclear weapons–free zone in the Middle East. More recently, Egypt's Jamal Mubarak, the son of President Hosni Mubarak and leader of the National Democratic Party, has suggested that Egypt should pursue a nuclear program.

Iraq's pursuit of nuclear weapons began in the 1970s. In 1975 the Iraqis reached an agreement with France for the construction of a nuclear reactor (at Osiraq), which was destroyed by an Israeli air strike in July 1981 just before completion. Although Iraq had signed the NPT, it covertly acquired nuclear technology from private Western firms in the 1980s. By 1990–1991, Iraq was probably only three years away from having the capability to produce nuclear weapons. After Iraq's defeat in the 1991 Persian Gulf War, Iraqi dictator Saddam Hussein shelved his effort to acquire nuclear weapons, although doubts about this persisted even though United Nations (UN) personnel were sent to Iraq to monitor this activity. The administration of U.S. president George W. Bush asserted that Iraq had not abandoned its efforts to acquire nuclear weapons and other weapons of mass destruction (WMDs), and the Bush administration used this as a principal justification for the invasion of Iraq in March 2003 (Operation IRAQI FREEDOM). Subsequent inspections confirmed that Iraq had indeed effectively ended its nuclear program after 1991, although some experts, documents, and perhaps even equipment were available to resume efforts in the future. No evidence of nuclear weapons or other WMDs was found after an extensive search by U.S. and coalition forces.

Iran sought to take advantage of President Dwight D. Eisenhower's Atoms for Peace program as early as the 1950s, although little came of it during the reign of pro-Western Mohammad Reza Shah Pahlavi. The revolutionary government that seized power in 1979 continued and intensified Iranian nuclear research, and Iran benefited from nuclear cooperation with Pakistan and the People's Republic of China (PRC) beginning in the 1980s and Russia in the 1990s. In 2002, Iranian resistance movements revealed the existence of a uranium separation facility at Natanz (based on Pakistani technology) and a heavy water production plant at Arak (both necessary for nuclear weapons production). In 2003 Iran admitted that it had carried out experiments in violation of its NPT commitments, and International Atomic Energy Agency inspections determined that Iran had successfully enriched uranium. Iranian president Mahmud Ahmadinejad's speeches during 2005 and 2006 included statements threatening to "wipe Israel off the map." It is hardly surprising, then, that Iran's nuclear capabilities remain a focus of international concern. And despite tortuous negotiations with the Iranians, no agreement has been reached on freezing or reversing their nuclear program, which they insist is for peaceful purposes only.

Israel's interest in nuclear energy and weapons had begun even before its creation in 1948. Under the leadership of Prime Minister David Ben-Gurion, the new state prioritized and pursued nuclear research at home and abroad, including the establishment of the Weizmann Institute of Science in 1949. In 1952 the government created the Israeli Atomic Energy Commission, and by 1953 Israeli scientists were engaged in research in France on nuclear reactor technology. From 1955 to 1960, several dozen Israeli scientists received training at U.S. nuclear research centers as part of the Atoms for Peace program, and the United States agreed to provide a small 5-megawatt research reactor to Israel, which was eventually built at Nahel Soreq.

In 1956 the Israeli government signed a major arms sale agreement with France and cooperated with Britain and France in military operations against Egypt during the Suez Crisis. As a result of negotiations between Shimon Peres, director-general of the Ministry of Defense, and French foreign minister Maurice Bourges-Maunoury, France secretly agreed to provide a nuclear reactor. In early 1957 the deal was revised to provide Israel with a larger 40-megawatt reactor and plutonium extraction facilities. In 1960 Israel reassured both France and the United States that the reactor was purely for peaceful purposes, and Israel allowed American teams to visit the facility on a number of occasions from 1962 to 1969. In a visit to the United States, Peres assured President John F. Kennedy that Israel would not be the first state to introduce nuclear weapons into the region. This statement became the foundation of Israel's public nuclear posture for more than four decades, a posture referred to as nuclear opacity in which Israel developed nuclear capabilities but declined to admit officially that they existed.

The Israelis began separating plutonium in 1966, and design work on Israel's first nuclear weapon was reportedly completed that year. In late May 1967 just prior to the June 1967 Six-Day War, Israel reportedly assembled two nuclear devices at Dimona. On July 12, 1969, U.S. scientists visited the Dimona complex for the final time, again finding no evidence of nuclear weapons production. Despite U.S. pressure, Israel refused to sign the NPT, and in July 1970 the U.S. Central Intelligence Agency (CIA) acknowledged that Israel had nuclear weapons. During October 8–9, 1973, in response to the successful Egyptian and Syrian conventional attacks that began the Yom Kippur War, Israel reportedly assembled at least a dozen nuclear devices. Reports of the shipment of Soviet nuclear warheads to Egypt on October 18, 1973, prompted another Israeli nuclear mobilization, and U.S. president Richard M. Nixon ordered U.S. forces—including the nuclear triad—to heightened readiness.

Israel's nuclear arsenal continued to expand in the 1970s. The power output of the Dimona reactor was reportedly increased from 40 megawatts to between 70 and 150 megawatts, significantly increasing the annual rate of plutonium production. An ex-technician at the Dimona complex, Mordechai Vanunu, reported in October 1986 that Israel possessed almost 200 nuclear weapons. He revealed that Israel produced both tritium and lithium deuteride, which are used to increase the explosive power of nuclear warheads. Vanunu was later kidnapped by Israeli agents, convicted of espionage, and sentenced to 18 years in prison. Israel is rumored to have cooperated with apartheid South Africa on nuclear weapons developments, including a possible nuclear test in the South Atlantic on September 22, 1979. Israel reportedly placed its nuclear forces on alert in January 1991 when Israel came under attack from Iraqi Scud missiles.

Reports in the 1990s suggested that Israel's nuclear stockpile might be more than 300 weapons, although most Western analysts put the number at between 60 and 200. These weapons can be deployed on Israeli Air Force strike aircraft and on mobile Jericho-1 and Jericho-2 missiles. Recent reports suggest that Israel has developed the capacity to launch nuclear-armed cruise missiles from submarines, and it is possible that the Israeli arsenal also includes smaller tactical nuclear weapons for battlefield use.

On February 3, 2000, the Knesset (Israeli parliament) held its first public debates on the nuclear program. The debates lasted just 52 minutes. The Israeli government's official position is that Israel will not be the first country to use nuclear weapons in the Middle East and that Israel supports preventing the spread of nuclear weapons and supports the creation of a region free of both nuclear weapons and ballistic missiles, provided this occurs after a sustained period of peace and diplomatic engagement.

TIMOTHY D. HOYT

See also

Dimona, Israel; Egypt; Iran; Iraq; Iraq War; Israel; Israel Defense Forces; Osiraq Raid; Six-Day War; Suez Crisis; Yom Kippur War

References

Cohen, Avner. *Israel and the Bomb.* New York: Columbia University Press, 1998.
Comprehensive Report of the Special Advisor to the DCI on Iraq's WMD. Washington, DC: Central Intelligence Agency, March 2005.
Feldman, Shai. *Nuclear Weapons and Arms Control in the Middle East.* Cambridge, MA: MIT Press, 1997.

October War

See Yom Kippur War

Oil as an Economic Weapon

The effectiveness of oil as a economic weapon in the Arab-Israeli confrontation has been a function of the unity of the Arab oil-producing states and of economic conditions in the industrialized oil-importing nations and the state of their dependence on imported oil. The threat of disruption of Middle Eastern oil supplies has been present since the founding of the Jewish state in 1948. The leadership of the oil-exporting Arab countries began discussing the use of oil as a weapon in the early 1950s. The rise of anti-Israel and anti-Western Pan-Arab nationalism led by Egyptian president Gamal Abdel Nasser heightened fears in the industrialized West that radical Arabs might overthrow moderate governments of the oil-producing states in the region and cut off oil to those states in the West that supported Israel. It was not until the October 1973 Yom Kippur War that the Arab petroleum-exporting states were able to effectively curtail the flow of oil to the United States and other Western nations. The embargo had a major impact on the Western industrial economies. Since the 1973–1974 embargo, Middle Eastern turmoil has often affected oil prices and production and has led to changes in U.S. foreign policy toward Israel and the region as a whole.

Prior to the 1973 war, the threat of an oil embargo by Arab nations to influence the pro-Israel stance of the United States and other Western states was limited by political and economic factors both in the region and internationally. Until the 1960s, the governments of the Arab oil-producing and -exporting countries had limited con-

trol of their own resources. The Americans and British dominated the major oil companies, which in turn controlled production, setting prices and production levels and keeping most of the resulting revenues for themselves. Moreover, until the close of the 1960s the United States still produced sufficient domestic oil and imported oil from Mexico, Venezuela, and other oil-exporting nations outside the Middle East to meet its own needs.

West European states were, however, highly dependent on Middle Eastern oil and hence more apprehensive about the impact of the Arab-Israeli conflict and instability in the Middle East, but not to the point of turning their backs on Israel. Arab resentment of the dominance of foreign oil companies over their economies, growing Arab nationalism, and the desire to gain greater control of production and a larger share of revenues caused the Arab states, led by Saudi Arabia, to take the lead in the formation of the Organization of Petroleum Exporting Countries (OPEC) in 1960. OPEC had little immediate impact on the oil industry, but its appearance was an early warning that Arab governments would not tolerate Western control of their oil resources indefinitely.

The potential of oil as an economic weapon in the event of war between Arab states and Israel had been apparent since the Suez Crisis, culminating in the Sinai War of 1956. The joint attack by Britain, France, and Israel on Egypt led to the closing of the Arabian pipeline and the Suez Canal, temporarily cutting off oil shipments to Western Europe and the United States. This in turn led to an economic crisis and a brief panic in Western commodities markets. The crisis quickly receded, however, when first Britain and France and then Israel were forced to withdraw from Egypt.

The crisis of May and June 1967 that culminated in the June Six-Day War marked the first attempt by the Arab states to use the threat of an oil embargo to induce the United States and its allies

A sign on a Texaco gas pump in Boston, Massachusetts, reflects the severe oil shortages in the United States during the OPEC oil embargo, February 1974. (Owen Franken/Corbis)

The Arab Oil Ministers Conference, then meeting in Baghdad, gave substance to the king's warning with two resolutions. The first declared that Arab oil would be denied to any country directly or indirectly committing aggression against an Arab state. The second explicitly promised that the oil companies based in any state supporting such aggression would have their holdings in Arab countries nationalized. The resolution also called on all Islamic and friendly oil-producing countries (particularly Iran) to cooperate in denying oil to Israel.

Attempts at an embargo materialized shortly after the outbreak of war on June 5, triggered by claims from Egypt and Syria that U.S. warplanes had participated in Israeli air attacks on their air bases. These accusations proved unfounded but were sufficient to precipitate action from Arab oil producers. Iraq, Saudi Arabia, Bahrain, Algeria, and Kuwait stopped oil shipments to Britain and the United States and closed the trans-Arabia pipeline but did not nationalize oil company assets.

OPEC was unable, however, to maintain a united front. Non-Arab members, such as Venezuela, resisted Arab pressure to join the embargo. In addition, the United States made up its shortfalls with imports from non-OPEC states such as Mexico. The quick Israeli victory also undermined the unity of the Arab states and the political position of the radical states (particularly Egypt) that had initiated the crisis that had led to war. As the crisis wound down and the Israelis consolidated their gains, the Arab oil-exporting states gradually resumed oil shipments to the United States and other Western nations. The embargo had failed due largely to the lack of unity among Arab producers and the reluctance of non-Arab OPEC countries to support an embargo. The ability of the United States to find alternative sources of fuel also led to the failure.

Although the 1967 crisis ended without serious damage to the oil companies or to U.S. interests, the embargo served as a warning that Middle Eastern oil was far from secure and that another Arab-Israeli war could have devastating economic and political consequences for the United States and its allies. In the six-year interim between the Six-Day War and the Yom Kippur War, several developments made the threat of an Arab oil embargo more compelling. First, the OPEC states had intensified their pressure on the major oil companies for more participation, or part ownership in, the companies' operations. Second, by 1973 the United States, Japan, and the other industrial nations had come to depend on Middle Eastern oil more and more as economic and population growth led to growing demand for oil. By the 1970s, the United States was importing more than one-third of its oil from the Middle East. In Japan and Western Europe, the percentage was far greater. At the same time, major producers such as Saudi Arabia, Kuwait, and the Gulf States were considering cutting back production both to control and conserve their oil resources.

Changing market conditions coincided with significant political developments in this interim period. Nasser's death in 1971 and the accession of Anwar Sadat as president of Egypt led to a rapproche-

not to support Israel. However, this initiative was as much a product of the rivalry between the moderate governments, led by Saudi Arabia and the Persian Gulf states on one hand, and the radical states, led by Nasser's Egypt as well as Syria and Iraq on the other, as it was a manifestation of anti-Western resentment. The first warnings came from Saudi Arabia. In May, with the crisis moving closer to war, the Saudis warned representatives of ARAMCO (the Arabian-American Company that was the consortium of major oil companies with holdings in Saudi Arabia and the Gulf States) and American diplomats in both Washington and Riyadh that if the United States openly supported Israel in the event of war, ARAMCO's holdings would be nationalized, and the United States would be finished as a power in the Middle East.

When war between Israel and the Arab states of Egypt, Syria, and Jordan began in June 1967, Saudi Arabia's King Faisal informed the head of ARAMCO in Saudi Arabia that the major Western powers must remain neutral. Without referring specifically to oil, Faisal asserted that any state supporting Israel would be subject to retaliation from the Arab states.

ment between Egypt and Saudi Arabia. Sadat's brand of Egyptian nationalism was viewed by the Saudi monarchy and the leaders of the other moderate Arab regimes as far less threatening than Nasser's radical Pan-Arab nationalism. Improved relations between the conservative Arab monarchies and the secular states of Egypt, Syria, and Iraq was a portent of improved unity in the Arabs' collective stance against Israel that was further strengthened by deepening anti-American and anti-Western resentment. This had grown from the West's support for Israel and the Israeli occupation of Sinai, Gaza, and the West Bank. Well before the onset of the Yom Kippur War, Arab pressure on oil company officials and President Richard M. Nixon's administration to reverse the pro-Israel orientation of U.S. foreign policy had intensified. Saudi Arabia in particular had warned American and British diplomats to move away from unconditional support for Israel.

There was nothing improvised about the Arab oil embargo of 1973–1974. The initiative to use the oil weapon came from Sadat. He was determined to force an Israeli withdrawal from Sinai and reopen the Suez Canal. In August 1973 he had traveled to Riyadh to inform King Faisal that Egypt and Syria were going to go to war with Israel and that it would begin with a surprise assault across the Suez Canal. Sadat asked the Saudi monarch for financial support and an oil embargo. Faisal pledged financial support and promised an oil embargo against any nation providing financial and material support to Israel.

The outbreak of war on October 6, 1973, caught both the United States and Israel by surprise. The early Egyptian and Syrian successes and the intensity of the fighting forced Israel to use its stocks of fuel and ammunition faster than they had anticipated. The massive and high-profile American airlift of supplies to Israel and Israel's rapid military recovery triggered the decision of the Arab oil-producing states to institute an embargo on October 16. The embargo against the United States and other Western states (including the Netherlands and Portugal) that supported Israel was total. Shipments to Japan and other West European states were severely curtailed and were accompanied by steep price increases in a short time span.

The embargo sent shock waves through the social and economic fabric of the industrialized nations. The impact in the United States was especially pronounced. Fuel shortages and a panic over the future availability of gasoline led to lengthening gas lines and partial rationing, the first time the nation had resorted to rationing since World War II. The embargo and the shortages it generated represented an abrupt break with America's past and severely undermined public confidence in the country's future. The ripple effect of high oil prices affected almost every industry and service. Inflation spiked while unemployment rose. The effects in Japan and Western Europe were even more dramatic, reawakening bitter memories of the deprivations and shortages of the immediate post–World War II years. The economic achievements of the 1950s and 1960s now seemed very precarious.

The embargo's impact on U.S. Middle Eastern policy was more limited but still profound. For all the economic dislocations caused by the embargo, U.S. material support for Israel continued unabated. Israel's rapid recovery and its eventual military successes over Egypt and Syria convinced Sadat and the rest of the Arab leadership that Israel's total destruction was no longer a viable goal. Arab oil-exporting states also faced economic reprisals from the West if the embargo became too severe. The ability of the United States to protect the moderate states in the region from Soviet-supported radical states (which still included Syria and Iraq) would be crippled without Arab oil. Chaos in the West and the threat of Soviet influence in the Middle East did not serve Saudi interests or those of the other oil-exporting states.

Led by the Saudis, oil exporters officially ended the embargo in March 1974 as the United States showed progress toward an Egyptian-Israeli disengagement and American officials committed themselves to pursuing a similar disengagement between Israel and Syria on the Golan Heights. On the other hand, the Israelis were forced to face the reality that their prospects for survival were tied to support from the United States and that the Arabs could use the oil weapon again if progress toward a general Middle Eastern peace settlement was not made. Under pressure from the Nixon administration to engineer a viable cease-fire, the Israelis reluctantly agreed to pull back from the Suez Canal, thus permitting its eventual reopening. The trends in U.S. diplomacy that began with the 1973 cease-fire led to a continued effort to induce Israel to trade land for peace.

The 1973 oil embargo also accelerated movements among Arab governments in the Middle East toward increasing nationalist controls on the production of oil. By the end of the 1970s, the old international order in the oil industry that had been dominated by a few British and American oil companies had been destroyed. The leverage this has given the Arab states since then has been a major factor in the U.S. diplomatic stance in the region.

Regional politics and the global energy market remain the governing factors in the viability of oil as a weapon for the Arab states in their dispute with Israel. The opening of the Alaska pipeline and the exploitation of North Sea oil as well as decreasing world demand linked to economic downturns in the West in the early 1980s and to Asian financial crises in the 1990s have cut into the dependence of the industrial world on Arab oil. With demand declining, oil was not a factor in the Israeli conflicts in Lebanon. The collapse of the Asian financial markets in 1997 and 1998 dragged the price of oil per barrel down as low as $12. Sharp curtailments by Arab producers, however, brought the per-barrel rate up to $30 by 2000.

The conditions resulting from the terrorist attacks on September 11, 2001, and the U.S. invasion of Iraq in 2003 have eclipsed Arab-Israeli tensions as sources of tension between the United States and Arab oil producers. The potential for trouble is still present, as the demand for oil in the industrial states has recently intensified with rapid economic growth in China and India. In the last several years, however, the government of Saudi Arabia has responded to U.S. concerns by bringing about an oil price decrease. The surge in oil prices that accompanied Israel's brief summer 2006 incursion into southern Lebanon against Hezbollah forces and the dramatic increase in the price of oil in 2007 nonetheless served as a reminder of how vulnerable the United States and the West are to any perceived threat to Middle Eastern oil.

WALTER F. BELL

See also

Arab Nationalism; Arab Oil Embargo; Egypt; France, Middle East Policy; Iran; Iraq; Israel; Kuwait; Nasser, Gamal Abdel; Organization of Petroleum Exporting Countries; Sadat, Anwar; Saudi Arabia; Six-Day War; Suez Crisis; Syria; United Kingdom, Middle East Policy; United States, Middle East Policy; Yom Kippur War

References

Bronson, Rachel. *Thicker than Oil: America's Uneasy Partnership with Saudi Arabia.* New York: Oxford University Press, 2006.

Quandt, William B. *Decade of Decision: American Policy toward the Arab-Israeli Conflict, 1967–1976.* Berkeley: University of California Press, 1977.

Randall, Stephen J. *The United States Foreign Oil Policy since World War I.* 2nd ed. Montreal: McGill-Queens University Press, 2005.

Old City of Jerusalem

See Jerusalem, Old City of

Oliphant, Laurence
Born: 1829
Died: December 23, 1888

British journalist, adventurer, mystic, and proto-Zionist. Laurence Oliphant was born in Capetown in the Cape Colony in 1829. His father was the attorney general of Cape Colony, but the family soon relocated to Ceylon, where the elder Olpihant became chief justice.

Oliphant's education was spotty, but he traveled widely. A prolific author, he published his first book, *A Journey to Katmandu,* in 1852. He settled in England for a time, where he halfheartedly pursued legal studies. He then traveled extensively. A trip to Russia resulted in another book, *The Russian Shores of the Black Sea* (1853). During 1853–1861 as secretary to Lord Elgin, Oliphant observed the Crimean War (1854–1856) and traveled to China and Japan. His adventures there are recounted in his two-volume work, *Narrative of the Earl of Elgin's Mission to China and Japan in the Years 1857, '58, '59* (1859).

Returning to England, Oliphant won election to Parliament in 1865 but resigned his seat in 1868, having fallen under the influence of spiritualist and mystic Thomas Lake Harris, whom Oliphant seems to have believed to have been a reincarnation of the Deity. Oliphant followed Harris to the United States and joined his Brotherhood of the New Life, a commune Harris established at Brocton on Lake Erie in New York State. There Olpihant worked as a laborer for three

Laurence Oliphant, British journalist, adventurer, mystic, and proto-Zionist. (Margaret W. Oliphant, *Memoir of the Life of Laurence Oliphant and of Alice Olipant, His Wife,* New York: Harper and Brothers, 1891)

---

years. In 1870 he published a well-received novel, *Picadilly.* He reported for the London *Times* during the Franco-Prussian War of 1870–1871 and then lived for a time in Paris, where he married. He then returned with his wife to Brocton, but this time he engaged in fund-raising activities for the group.

About this time, Oliphant became preoccupied with urging the return of Jews to Palestine, and in 1879 he traveled there to find a suitable location for such a settlement. He wrote to British prime minister Benjamin Disraeli and other British leaders urging the establishment of a company to facilitate such a step. Oliphant selected an area in northern Palestine east of the Jordan River near the Dead Sea and initiated negotiations with the Ottoman government for a lease of land there to establish a Jewish settlement, but his efforts were without result. In 1880 Oliphant published a book, *The Land of Gilead.* In 1881 he split definitively with Harris. In 1882 Oliphant returned to Palestine and settled in Haifa, assisting Jewish settlers in Palestine and publicizing their efforts there through his writing. He remained convinced that Jewish settlement in Palestine would be successful thanks to funds raised from Jews abroad.

His first wife having died in Palestine, Oliphant returned to the United States in 1888 and married the granddaughter of socialist Robert Owen. They then went on to England with the intention to leave for Palestine, but Oliphant became ill and died at Twickenham near London on December 23, 1888.

SPENCER C. TUCKER

See also
Bilu; Zionism

References

Henderson, Philip. *The Life of Laurence Oliphant: Traveler, Diplomat and Mystic.* London: Robert Hale, 1956.

Oliphant, Margaret. *Memoir of the Life of Laurence Oliphant and of Alice Oliphant His Wife.* New York: Arno, 1976.

Sachar, Howard M. *A History of Israel: From the Rise of Zionism to Our Time.* 3rd ed. New York: Knopf, 2007.

Olmert, Ehud
Born: September 30, 1945

Likud and Kadima Party politician, minister responsible for the Israel Lands Administration, mayor of Jerusalem (1993–2003), deputy prime minister of Israel (2003–2005), and Israeli prime minister (April 2006–). Born in Binyamina in the British Mandate for Palestine on September 30, 1945, Ehud Olmert graduated from the Hebrew University of Jerusalem in 1968 with a bachelor's degree in psychology and philosophy. In 1973 he earned a law degree. He began his mandatory military service with the Israel Defense Forces (IDF) in the Golani combat brigade. He completed his military service in 1971 as a military correspondent for the IDF journal *Bamachance.*

In 1973 Olmert took a seat in the Knesset (Israeli parliament), making him the youngest Knesset member at the time. From 1993 to 2003 as mayor of Jerusalem, he became a national figure as the first member of the Likud Party to hold the position. While in office, he spearheaded the development of the light rail system in Jerusalem, improved education, augmented infrastructure, and supported controversial housing developments reserved exclusively for Jews on the Mount of Olives and Ras al-Amud.

In January 2003 Olmert became a member of the 16th Knesset. Following the elections, he assumed the posts of deputy prime minister and minister of industry, trade, and labor. On August 7, 2005, he became acting finance minister, taking over for Benjamin Netanyahu who resigned in protest against Prime Minister Ariel Sharon's Gaza disengagement plan. Olmert had initially opposed withdrawing from land captured in the 1967 Six-Day War and had voted against the 1978 Camp David Accords. But he actively supported the Gaza pullout and championed Sharon's efforts to pave the way for a comprehensive settlement of the Palestinian problem.

As deputy prime minister in Sharon's second term, Olmert became his most important ally during the September 2005 unilateral

Ehud Olmert, Likud Party and Kadima Party politician and Israeli prime minister from April 2006. (European Commission)

disengagement plan, which met with howls of protest from many in the Likud Party. When Sharon bolted from Likud in November 2005 and formed a new party—the Kadima Party—Olmert became one of the first to join him.

On January 4, 2006, after Sharon suffered a catastrophic brain hemorrhage that permanently incapacitated him, Olmert became acting prime minister and acting chairman of Kadima. He continued many of Sharon's policies, including the construction of a highly controversial security fence to protect Israeli civilians from Palestinian bombers along the border of Israel and the West Bank. On January 24, 2006, Olmert formally announced at the Herzliya Conference that he backed the creation of a Palestinian state and asserted that Israel would have to relinquish parts of the West Bank to maintain its Jewish majority.

On April 14, 2006, Olmert became the prime minister of the 31st Israeli government. He continues to be challenged by the Palestinian land issue controversy and the erection of the security fence. In June 2006 he signaled his willingness to meet with Palestinian Authority (PA) president Mahmoud Abbas to fulfill the prescriptions of the so-called Road Map to Peace and create the way for the establishment of a Palestinian state. In the meantime, Olmert has said that Israel will continue to abide by the unilateral disengagement plan first introduced by his predecessor.

The brief but damaging Israeli-Hezbollah War in June and July 2006 resulted in a free fall of Olmert's approval ratings. He came under sharp criticism from both the Left and the Right because of his handling of the crisis. The Right accused him of not going far enough to break the back of the Hezbollah fighters, while the Left rebuked him for ordering attacks that devastated Lebanon's infrastructure and killed scores of innocent civilians. His administration was also roundly criticized in the international community for its actions during the brief conflict. At the end of the war his approval rating stood at just 22 percent, and the subsequent Winograd Commission interim report was sharply critical of his handling of the crisis. In September 2006 his chief of staff resigned, another signal that his support is eroding even among those in his own government. There were also investigations into alleged personal corruption. At the end of 2007, Olmert and Kadima stood in danger of losing the next national election to the resurgent rightist Likud Party, headed by Benjamin Netanyahu.

LaVonne J. Leslie and Paul G. Pierpaoli Jr.

See also
Abbas, Mahmoud; Camp David Accords; Gaza Strip Disengagement; Israeli Security Fence; Kadima Party; Likud Party; Netanyahu, Benjamin; Sharon, Ariel

References
Ben-Ami, Shlomo. *Scars of War, Wounds of Peace: The Israeli-Arab Tragedy.* New York: Oxford University Press, 2006.
Gorenberg, Gershom. *The Accidental Empire: Israel and the Birth of the Settlements, 1967–1977.* New York: Times Books, 2006.
Slater, Elinor, and Robert Slater. *Great Jewish Men.* Middle Village, NY: Jonathan David, 1996.

Olympics, Munich
See Munich Olympic Games

OPERA, Operation
See Osiraq Raid

Organization of Petroleum Exporting Countries

Oil cartel founded on September 14, 1960, during the Baghdad Conference to give oil-exporting countries leverage in negotiations with foreign oil companies that, at the time, controlled production and dictated prices and the share of profits going to producing nations. In the late 1960s and early 1970s, the Arab member nations of the Organization of Petroleum Exporting Countries (OPEC) enacted embargoes against supporters of Israel during the 1967 Six-Day War and the 1973 Yom Kippur War in an effort to influence Middle East policy. Since the 1980s, OPEC has acted largely apolitically, seeking to stabilize oil production and prices to maximize members' profits while guaranteeing a reliable oil supply to the world economy.

As early as 1945, oil-producing nations recognized that a unified stance on pricing and output would improve their effectiveness in bargaining with the major oil companies. In 1959 the U.S. government established a mandatory quota on all imported oil to the United States in an attempt to give preferential treatment to oil producers in Canada and Mexico. In so doing, the world's largest oil consumer had effectively imposed a partial boycott on Middle East oil. The net result was depressed prices for Persian Gulf crude. To make matters worse, the oil companies enacted a series of unilateral price cuts in 1959 and 1960 that caused oil prices to fall even lower.

The severe impact that these policies had on Middle East oil provided the impetus for the world's five largest oil exporters—Saudi Arabia, Iran, Iraq, Kuwait, and Venezuela—to band together with the express purpose of reversing these price cuts. Over its first two decades of operations, OPEC expanded its membership to include Qatar, Indonesia, Libya, United Arab Emirates, Algeria, Nigeria, Ecuador, and Gabon. During its first decade of operations, OPEC enjoyed little success. Prices continued to float lower well into 1971. In 1958 oil sold for $10.85 per barrel (in 1990 dollars). In 1971 it sold for just $7.46 per barrel. The cartel doggedly negotiated with oil companies but with little success in eroding the oil companies' power to set prices. Beginning in 1973, however, OPEC finally succeeded in wresting pricing power from the oil companies, which were increasingly vulnerable to political decisions made in the oil-producing states that housed their operations. On October 16, 1973,

Crude Oil Production in Selected Middle Eastern and North African Countries (in barrels per day, 1965–2005)

Country	Member of OPEC?	1965	1975	1985	1995	2005
Algeria	Yes	577,000	1,003,000	1,151,000	1,327,000	2,015,000
Bahrain	No	58,000	60,000	41,000	38,000	188,000
Egypt	No	126,000	228,000	882,000	924,000	696,000
Iran	Yes	1,908,000	5,387,000	2,205,000	3,744,000	4,049,000
Iraq	Yes	1,313,000	2,271,000	1,425,000	530,000	1,820,000
Israel	No	4,000	101,000	Negligible	Negligible	4,000
Kuwait	Yes	2,371,000	2,132,000	1,127,000	2,130,000	2,643,000
Libya	Yes	1,220,000	1,514,000	1,025,000	1,439,000	1,702,000
Oman	No	Unknown	341,000	502,000	858,000	780,000
Qatar	Yes	233,000	437,000	315,000	461,000	1,097,000
Saudi Arabia	Yes	2,219,000	7,216,000	3,601,000	9,127,000	11,035,000
Syria	No	Negligible	192,000	159,000	596,000	459,000
Tunisia	No	Negligible	97,000	114,000	90,000	74,000
United Arab Emirates	Yes	282,000	1,696,000	1,260,000	2,362,000	2,751,000

Negligible = less than 1,000 barrels a day

in reaction to the Yom Kippur War, OPEC cut production, which ultimately quadrupled the price of oil, beginning a series of price hikes that effectively ended the companies' control over all but the technical side of oil production.

As Arab nations' production made up an increasing share of the world oil market, they began to use their power politically, applying oil embargoes against Britain and France during the 1956 Suez Crisis and against the United States, Britain, and West Germany during the 1967 Six-Day War. These embargoes failed, however, in large part because of U.S. willingness to make up the oil shortfalls to its allies. Also, because oil is a worldwide commodity, limited embargoes have little effect, as nations targeted by an embargo will usually find other ways to purchase petroleum.

Arab oil producers' attempts to use the oil weapon to influence the Arab-Israeli conflict enjoyed great success in October 1973 during the Yom Kippur War, precipitated by Egypt and Syria's surprise attack on Israel. On October 17, one day after OPEC initiated its production cuts that spiked sharp price increases, the Organization of Arab Petroleum Exporting Countries (OAPEC) decreased overall oil production and initiated a five-month oil embargo against the United States and the Netherlands to protest their support for Israel. The oil price shock together with worldwide production cuts and the embargo caused severe economic disruptions in much of the world. The impact on the United States was particularly severe. The nation's economy, which was already groaning under inflation, relatively high unemployment, low growth, and budget deficits, tilted into a serious recession. Government efforts to cap prices and control supplies only worsened the situation, as shortages and even limited rationing of gasoline became widespread. From 1973 to 1974, the price of oil catapulted from about $8 per barrel to more than $27 (1990 dollars). The American economy remained in a virtual recession into the mid-1980s.

The Soviet Union, an oil exporter, had little to lose from the Arab states' use of oil as a weapon. As such, it encouraged the oil embargo because it weakened the West economically and resulted in increased oil revenues for itself. At the same time, the Soviets took advantage of decreased Arab production and higher prices, significantly increasing its oil exports to the United States during the embargo, a fact that neither nation publicized at the time.

The oil embargo caught Americans largely unprepared. As a result, the U.S. government instituted gasoline rationing that resulted in long lines at gasoline stations and national anxiety over energy supplies. In response to the price increases and embargo, the United States sought to establish a cartel of oil-consuming nations to confront OPEC directly, but the major importers' diverse oil needs and political positions on the Arab-Israeli conflict stymied this plan. In 1975 the U.S. Congress did pass legislation to establish a Strategic Petroleum Reserve (SPR) to protect against future supply disruptions. Since then, the government has stored millions of barrels of oil in massive underground salt caverns along the Gulf Coast. The SPR may exist more for psychological reasons than anything else, however. The reserve would run out very quickly in the event of a partial or complete oil supply shutdown, and there is not enough oil in the caverns to affect the worldwide price of oil.

Although the Arab states ended the oil embargo soon after hostilities ceased and without securing the desired Israeli withdrawal from territories occupied in 1967, this unprecedented assertion of Arab power transformed the position of oil-producing states, gave OPEC major clout, and fueled Arab nationalism. Since 1973, both the United States and the Soviet Union devoted increasing attention to the Middle East as a strategic battleground. The Arab world, meanwhile, endeavored to exercise political influence independent of the superpowers.

OPEC's achievement of higher oil prices in 1973 and 1974 ultimately damaged the oil producers' economies by the late 1970s, when the resulting worldwide recession produced inflation and falling demand for oil. Two major crises in the Middle East during 1979–1980 resulted in yet another oil price spike. As a result of the 1979

OPEC ministers meeting in Abu Dhabi to set a new price for oil, December 16, 1978. (Bettmann/Corbis)

Iranian Revolution, which saw the ousting of Mohammad Reza Shah Pahlavi, the imposition of an anti-Western Islamic fundamentalist government in his stead, and the taking of American embassy personnel by radical Iranian students, oil prices shot up from $24.46 per barrel (1990 dollars) to $49.52 by mid-1980. The effects on the world's economy were stunning. In the United States, inflation peaked at more than 13 percent, while interest rates approached 20 percent. The 1979–1980 oil shock was not part of OPEC's strategy, although it did benefit handsomely from it in the immediate term. Clearly, the markets were reacting to great regional instability in the Middle East, which began with the Iranian Revolution and was exacerbated by the start of the Iran-Iraq War (1980–1988).

Since the 1980s, OPEC has pursued a policy of relatively prudent price control, ensuring substantial profits without adversely affecting the world economy. Beginning in the mid-1980s, the price of oil dropped and continued to drop until the Iraqi invasion of Kuwait in August 1990 precipitated more jolting price hikes. After mid-1991, however, when an international coalition reversed the Iraqi invasion and soundly defeated Iraqi dictator Saddam Hussein's army, oil prices fell again. They would continue to drift downward, reaching new inflation-adjusted lows by the late 1990s. Since 2002, however, OPEC again began to reap record revenues, as war and unrest in the Middle East and simple greed drove oil prices to record

highs. Today, OPEC has 11 member states; Ecuador and Gabon left OPEC prior to the 1990s.

ELUN GABRIEL

See also

Arab Nationalism; Iran; Iraq; Kuwait; Persian Gulf War; Saudi Arabia; Six-Day War; Soviet Union and Russia, Middle East Policy; United States, Middle East Policy; Yom Kippur War

References

Ahrari, Mohammed E. *OPEC: The Failing Giant.* Lexington: University Press of Kentucky, 1986.

Al-Sowayegh, Abdulaziz. *Arab Petro-Politics.* New York: St. Martin's, 1984.

Klinghoffer, Arthur Jay. *The Soviet Union & International Oil Politics.* New York: Columbia University Press, 1977.

Rustow, Dankwart A. *Oil and Turmoil: America Faces OPEC and the Middle East.* New York: Norton, 1982.

Skeet, Ian. *OPEC: Twenty-Five Years of Prices and Politics.* Cambridge: Cambridge University Press, 1988.

Osiraq Raid
Event Date: June 7, 1981

Israeli air strike, also known as Operation OPERA, on Iraq's nuclear power facility on June 7, 1981. The slowly developing Iraqi nuclear program, begun in the 1960s, received French assistance in the late 1970s through a light water reactor at the al-Tuwaytha Nuclear Center, located some 11 miles southeast of Baghdad. The type of French reactor was known as Osiris, and it was named Osiraq (Osirak in French) for the reactor and Iraq. The Iraqis named it Tammuz I for the month in the Babylonian calendar when the Baath Party took power in Iraq in 1968.

Although the 40-megawatt light water nuclear reactor was ostensibly for peaceful purposes, there were widespread concerns that Iraqi dictator Saddam Hussein would instead use it as part of his plan to secure nuclear weapons. The International Atomic Energy Agency monitored the handling of fuel at the new facility, but there was general agreement that its oversight was not adequate.

On September 30, 1980, at the beginning of the Iran-Iraq War (1980–1988), two Iranian McDonnell-Douglas F-4 Phantom aircraft bombed the reactor as part of a larger strike on a nearby power facility. Damage was only minor, and the program was not seriously impeded.

Israel, meanwhile, greatly feared nuclear weapons in the hands of any Arab nation. Intelligence estimates about the Iraqi capability to develop an atomic bomb ranged from a few months to as long as 10 years. The government of Prime Minister Menachem Begin refused to accept Iraqi explanations that the Osiraq reactor was only for electricity generation. Nor was Begin prepared to wait to take action until after the Iraqis had actually built a nuclear bomb. But within Israeli political and even military circles, there was strong opposition to a preemptive strike against the facility. Some, such as Labor Party leader Shimon Peres, feared that such a raid would ostracize Israel within the international community or that the Arab-Israeli peace process would be derailed. Others fretted that a retaliatory Arab air strike would be launched against the Israeli nuclear facility at Dimona. Attempts on the part of Israeli foreign minister Yitzhak Shamir to enlist French and American assistance in halting Iraqi nuclear development failed. France was unwilling to end its assistance to Iraq. Iraq was a major purchaser of French arms, and the relationship assured France access to oil.

With Knesset elections looming in 1981, Begin feared that he might be voted out of office and that a new government might not have the resolve to stop Iraq's nuclear ambitions. By mid-1980, intelligence reports indicated that the French would soon deliver uranium fuel rods to the Iraqis. Once these were installed, any attack on the facility would lead to the dispersion of radiation. If a preemptive strike was to occur, it would have to be mounted soon.

In October 1980, convinced that the Osiraq nuclear reactor would soon allow Iraq to achieve nuclear status, Begin ordered Lieutenant General Rafael Eitan, chief of staff of the Israel Defense Forces (IDF), to begin planning for an Israeli Air Force (IAF) preemptive strike to destroy the plant no later than June 1981, when the reactor was expected to become operational. In the meantime, new Israeli foreign minister Moshe Dayan conducted talks with French, Italian, and U.S. officials, all without meaningful result.

Attacking the Iraqi nuclear facility presented the IAF with great challenges. Israeli planes would have to travel a greater distance than any other Israeli air sortie up to that time (a round trip of about 1,350 miles), and the flight would violate the air space of several Arab countries. Recently acquired American-made General Dynamics F-16 Fighting Falcon fighter-bombers gave the IAF the capability of flying that distance without refueling while carrying the necessary ordnance. Ironically, the F-16s that Israel purchased had originally been earmarked for sale to Iran, a deal that was cancelled after the overthrow of Mohammad Reza Shah Pahlavi in 1979.

In May 1981 Begin learned that enriched uranium was about to be shipped to the Osiraq facility. Israeli pilots had been carrying out practice attack sorties, and eight IAF pilots from the 116th and 117th Squadrons were then selected for the dangerous mission. Six McDonnell-Douglas F-15 Eagle fighter aircraft provided air escort for the eight attack F-16s, while an additional two F-15s provided communications support.

The strike, code-named Operation OPERA, was launched beginning at 3:05 p.m. on June 7, 1981, from Etzion Air Force Base in the Negev. Colonel Zeev Raz commanded the mission. Also flying on the mission were Yiftah Spector, Israel's second-highest scoring ace, and Ilan Ramon, who would become Israel's first astronaut and die in the Columbia space shuttle disaster of February 1, 2002. Each of the F-16s carried two 2,000-pound bombs fused for delayed detonation in order to ensure adequate penetration. In their flight to the Iraqi facility, Israeli aircraft violated the air space of both Jordan and Saudi Arabia.

Flying at extremely low altitudes to avoid detection by radar, the F-16s arrived in the vicinity of the facility at 5:35 p.m. local time. The F-16 pilots individually ascended to attack altitude and then dove toward the reactor. Iraqi antiaircraft and surface-to-air missile fire was poorly coordinated and had no effect on the outcome of the raid. The raid lasted less than two minutes. The raiders scored at least 10 direct hits, and the reactor lay in ruins. The attack was on a Sunday when the workers had the day off, and there were no civilian casualties. All IAF planes returned safely to base.

International condemnations of Israel immediately followed. Even the normally pro-Israeli United States voted in favor of the United Nations (UN) Security Council resolution formally condemning the attack. But there was also secret support for the successful mission. Other nations, notably Iran, had harbored fears of a Hussein-led nuclear-armed Iraq bullying its way to regional hegemony. Indeed, had Iraq achieved nuclear status, the regime there would have held the upper hand over Iran in the Iran-Iraq War.

After the attack, France at first agreed to rebuild Osiraq but then found excuses not to do so. Nevertheless, throughout the 1980s Iraq continued to seek nuclear weapons programs. During the 1991 Persian Gulf War air campaign, coalition raids decimated the Osiraq nuclear facility and ended the possibility of near-term success for Hussein's nuclear program.

THOMAS VEVE AND SPENCER C. TUCKER

See also

Begin, Menachem; Dimona, Israel; Eitan, Rafael; Hussein, Saddam; Iran-Iraq War; Nuclear Weapons; Peres, Shimon; Shamir, Yitzhak; Spector, Yiftah

References

Claire, Rodger W. *Raid on the Sun: Inside Israel's Secret Campaign That Denied Saddam the Bomb.* New York: Broadway, 2004.

Cohen, Eliezer. *Israel's Best Defense: The First Full Story of the Israeli Air Force.* New York: Orion, 1993.

Federation of American Scientists. *Israel's Strike against the Iraqi Nuclear Reactor, 7 June 1981.* Jerusalem: Menachem Begin Heritage Center, 2003.

Feldman, Shai. *The Raid on Osiraq: A Preliminary Assessment.* Tel Aviv: Center for Strategic Studies, 1981.

McCormack, Timothy L. H. *Self-Defense in International Law: The Israeli Raid on the Iraqi Nuclear Reactor.* New York: St. Martin's, 1996.

Perlmutter, Amos, Michael Handel, and Uri Bar-Joseph. *Two Minutes over Baghdad.* 2nd ed. London: Frank Cass, 2003.

Vandenbroucke, Lucien S. *The Israeli Strike against Osiraq: The Dynamics of Fear and Proliferation in the Middle East.* Washington, DC: U.S. Government Printing Office, 1984.

Oslo Accords
Event Date: September 13, 1993

The agreement commonly called the Oslo Accords and formally known as the Declaration of Principles on Interim Self-Government Arrangements was signed on September 13, 1993, in Washington, D.C., by Israeli prime minister Yitzhak Rabin, Palestine Liberation Organization (PLO) chairman Yasser Arafat, and U.S. president Bill Clinton. In the Oslo Accords, the PLO, the Palestinians' major representative party and de facto government-in-exile, formally recognized Israel's right to exist and Israel's sovereignty over 78 percent of historic Palestine and pledged to end military actions against Israel. Israel, while failing to recognize Palestinian statehood, did recognize Palestinian nationhood, including the right of self-determination, and the PLO's role as the Palestinians' legitimate representative body.

The document spelled out ways in which the Palestinians could achieve a degree of autonomy in parts of the West Bank and the Gaza Strip, which had been occupied by Israeli forces since the June 1967 Six-Day War. The hope was that by the PLO's demonstration of competent self-governance and control over anti-Israel violence, the Israelis would gain the confidence needed to make a phased withdrawal from the occupied territories and grant the Palestinians an independent state alongside Israel. Similarly, it was hoped that the removal of foreign occupation forces from certain areas, increasing levels of self-government, and the prospects of a viable independent state would give the Palestinian population the incentive to end the violence against Israelis. The interim peace period was to be completed by 1998, at which time a permanent peace agreement would be signed.

Although the U.S. government became the guarantor of the Oslo Accords, Washington had little to do with the agreement itself.

Soon after the election of a more moderate Israeli government in 1992, direct talks began in secret between representatives of Israel and the PLO. They were first facilitated by Norwegian nongovernmental organizations and later with the assistance of the foreign ministry. This apparently took place without the knowledge of American officials, who still took the position that the PLO should not be allowed to take part in the peace process, excluding it from the stalled peace talks then going on in Washington. As the secret negotiations in Norway progressed during the summer of 1993, the Clinton administration put forward what it called a compromise proposal for Palestinian autonomy. This compromise was actually less favorable to the Palestinians than what was then being put forward by the Israelis.

The U.S. role in the Oslo process began with a historic signing ceremony on the White House lawn on September 13, 1993. The agreement had been finalized in Oslo on August 20. Given the ambiguities in the agreement, both parties agreed that the United States should be its guarantor. Indeed, the Israelis saw the U.S. government as the entity most likely to support its positions on outstanding issues, and the Palestinians saw the U.S. government as the only entity capable of forcing Israel to live up to its commitments and able to move the occupying power to compromise.

Peace talks resumed in Washington in the fall of 1993 within the Oslo framework. Over the next seven years, the United States brokered a series of Israeli-Palestinian agreements that led to the withdrawal of Israeli forces from most of the Gaza Strip and parts of the West Bank. By the end of the decade, about 40 percent of the West Bank and the Gaza Strip, including most of its towns and cities, had been placed under the rule of the new Palestinian Authority (PA), headed by Arafat, and divided into dozens of noncontiguous zones wherein the Palestinians could for the first time exercise some limited autonomy within their sphere of control.

During this period, the Israeli government severely limited the mobility of Palestinians within and between the West Bank and the Gaza Strip, dramatically expanded its expropriation of land in the occupied territories for colonization by Jewish settlers, and refused to withdraw from as much territory as promised in the U.S.-brokered disengagement agreements. In addition, the United States tended to side with the Israelis on most issues during talks regarding the disengagement process, even after a right-wing coalition that had opposed the Oslo Accords came to power in Israel in 1996. This served to alienate many Palestinians who had been initially hopeful about the peace process and hardened anti-Israeli attitudes.

Meanwhile, much of the PA proved itself to be rather inept, corrupt, and autocratic in its governance of those parts of the occupied territories under its control. The corruption alienated much of the Palestinian population, and the PA's lack of control made it difficult to suppress the growth of radical Islamic groups. On more than two dozen occasions between 1994 and 2000, Islamic extremists from the occupied Palestinian territories engaged in terrorist attacks inside Israel, killing scores of Israeli civilians and thereby hardening anti-Palestinian attitudes.

U.S. president Bill Clinton watches as Israeli prime minister Yitzhak Rabin and Palestine Liberation Organization (PLO) leader Yasser Arafat shake hands at the ceremony for the signing of the historic Israeli-Palestinian Declaration of Principles (also known as the Oslo Accords) on September 13, 1993. (Avi Ohayon/Israeli Government Press Office)

The Palestinians had hoped that the United States would broker the negotiations based on international law that forbids the expansion of any country's territory by military force and prohibits occupying powers from transferring their civilian population into occupied land. The Palestinians also hoped that American officials would support a series of specific United Nations (UN) Security Council resolutions demanding that Israel honor these principles. From the Palestinians' perspective—as well as that of the UN, most U.S. allies, and most international legal experts—the onus of the burden was on Israel, as the occupying power, to make most of the compromises for peace. The Clinton administration, however, argued that the UN resolutions were no longer relevant and saw the West Bank and the Gaza Strip simply as disputed territories, thereby requiring both sides to compromise. This gave the Israelis a clear advantage in the peace process.

In signing the Oslo Accords, the Palestinians operated on the assumption that the agreement would result in concrete improvements in the lives of those in the occupied territories. They hoped that the interim period would be no more than five years and that the permanent settlement would be based on UN Security Council Resolutions 242 and 338, which called upon Israel to withdraw from the territories seized in the 1967 war. For their part, the Israelis had hoped that the Oslo Accords would lead to the emergence of a responsible Palestinian leadership and greater security. None of these wishes, however, came to pass.

STEPHEN ZUNES

See also

Arafat, Yasser; Clinton, William Jefferson; Palestine Liberation Organization; Palestinian Authority; Rabin, Yitzhak; United Nations Security Council Resolution 242; United Nations Security Council Resolution 338

References

Brown, Nathan J. *Palestinian Politics after the Oslo Accords: Resuming Arab Palestine.* Berkeley: University of California Press, 2003.

Freedman, Robert Owen, ed. *The Middle East and the Peace Process: The Impact of the Oslo Accords.* Gainesville: University Press of Florida, 1998.

Peres, Shimon. *The New Middle East.* New York: Henry Holt, 1993.

Weinberger, Peter. *Co-opting the PLO: A Critical Reconstruction of the Oslo Accords, 1993–1995.* New York: Rowman and Littlefield, 2006.

Ottoman Empire

The current situation in the Middle East, immediately arising from the Arab-Israeli conflict since 1948, is a product of the region's

Enver Pasha, one of the Turkish army officers who overthrew Ottoman sultan Abdulhamid in 1908, holding a *chibouk,* or traditional smoking pipe, circa 1910. (Roger Fenton/Corbis)

centuries of troubled history. That history witnessed the rise and fall of the Ottoman Empire and its partition by the Western powers in the post–World War I period. Until the beginning of the 20th century, the Ottoman Empire was the dominant political, economic, and military force in the Middle East. After centuries of expansion and conquest in the region, however, the Ottoman Empire began to lose ground to rival forces in Europe during the 18th and 19th centuries and thereby became vulnerable to external pressures from the West. The European powers, taking advantage of the endless wars in the empire's various provinces, found their way in through direct economic controls and military occupation of Ottoman territory at the end of the 19th and beginning of the 20th centuries. This culminated in the occupation of virtually every corner of the empire during World War I.

Following the collapse of the Ottoman Empire at the end of World War I, Britain, France, Italy, Greece, and other European nations colonized its territories and remained in control of its various provinces for several decades. The area stretching from the Persian Gulf to Palestine and Suez, down to the Arabian Peninsula, and across North Africa came under the jurisdiction primarily of Britain and France, who divided up these Ottoman territories to secure trade routes, raw materials, and new markets for the expanding European-controlled world economy. Local populations had begun to see the Ottomans as a form of foreign control and had not welcomed Western political control over their affairs. In some countries such as Iraq and Egypt, there were immediate efforts to oust the Europeans from their lands, and elsewhere there were protracted efforts to secure treaties granting European withdrawals. After long struggles for national liberation, some colonized regions of the empire gained political independence and set up a host of nation-states. Indeed, Egypt, Syria, Lebanon, Iraq, Jordan, Libya, Algeria, and others are largely a product of these struggles.

Following their invasion of the Byzantine Empire from northeastern Anatolia in the 11th century, the Turkmen Oguz nomads from Central Asia came to occupy Eastern and Central Anatolia a century later. The ancestors of Osman, the founder of the dynasty, were members of the Kayi tribe who entered Anatolia along with these nomads. One of the independent Turkic principalities established in Anatolia was that led by Osman. By 1300, Osman ruled an area stretching from Eskisehir to the plains of Iznik. And his successor Orhan, by capturing Uskudar in 1338, had brought the growing empire to the doorsteps of Constantinople, the Byzantine capital. From this point on, the Ottomans entered a long phase of territorial expansion in all directions.

Although it came into contact with numerous societies with different systems of production and exchange, the Ottoman Empire retained its dominant, despotic state for more than seven centuries. Interaction between Ottoman and Byzantine society developed after the conquest of Constantinople by Ottoman forces in 1453. This interaction as well as that with other European societies following Ottoman expansion into Europe in the 15th and 16th centuries and the state's land grant system (*timar*) led to the development of feudal forms in Ottoman agriculture and taxation (*iltizam,* or tax farming) whereby, over time, large-scale private property in land (*ciftlik*) acquired increasing importance, transferring a higher proportion of the land to a few owners. This system also consisted of the allocation of parcels of conquered lands to *sipahis* (rural cavalry with military and administrative functions in the provinces) and to the civilian sector of the *devsirmes* (top officials of the central bureaucracy) in the form of fiefs. The *sipahis* and civilian *devsirmes* were given these lands for the purpose of administering them in the name of the state. This system of land allocation was put into effect during the reign of Suleiman I. The *timar* system was in effect for quite some time. As the central state began to gradually lose its authority in the countryside, the *sipahis* and other fief holders increasingly evaded their obligations to the state and attempted to take the ownership of state lands. Realizing that the old rural military-administrative system had outlived its usefulness, the state moved against the *sipahis* and displaced them.

This transformation of the agrarian structure took place during the 17th and 18th centuries, and as a result a landed gentry (*ayan*) began to develop. They displaced the *sipahis* as intermediaries between the state and the producers. Later, at the end of the 18th and the beginning of the 19th centuries, the *ayans* became a fully developed feudal landowning class and began to challenge the authority of the central state by equipping their own armies. Although they never became powerful enough to overthrow the political supremacy of the central state, they nonetheless came close to it.

In 1839 Mehmet Ali Pasha (Muhammad Ali Pasha), governor of Egypt, defeated the Ottoman armies in Kutahya, near the Ottoman capital of Istanbul. Mehmet Ali's forces were soon driven back, however, by those of Britain and France, who intervened on behalf of the Ottoman state. Ali was only able to obtain recognition as hereditary ruler of Egypt. While the *ayans* were thus defeated in their bid for state power, they nevertheless continued to exercise economic control over vast areas of the empire.

While the position of landlords was strengthened as a result of the introduction of tax farming initiated by the state, interaction with Europe also facilitated the expansion of European commercial capital into the empire, leading to the development of a merchant class tied to European capital. However, the development of feudalism in agriculture and later capitalism in commerce and industry all took place within the confines of a society dominated by the despotic state, which permitted the coexistence of these diverse systems until the very end.

While private property in land and feudal relations of production began to develop in the Ottoman Empire in the 17th century and rapidly surpassed that owned by the state in many parts of the empire by the 18th century, the feudal lords were never able to overthrow the central state. Thus, they continued to coexist with the developing merchant class under the political rule of the Ottoman state. State power remained in the hands of the despotic rulers and the palace bureaucracy until the collapse of the empire.

To gain greater insight into the nature and transformation of Ottoman society in the late 19th and early 20th centuries, it is necessary to take into account the structure of social forces dominating the empire's economy and polity during the final phase of its development.

Political power in the empire rested in the throne of the central authority, the *padisah* (sultan) and his administrative deputy, called the *sadrazam* (grand vizier). Below this and under the direct control of the sultan there existed the large but carefully organized Ottoman palace bureaucracy. It was largely the corrupt practices of the sultan and the palace bureaucracy in the latter phase of the Ottomans' centuries-long imperial history that transformed the empire into a semicolony of the expanding European powers.

The dominant economic interests in the Ottoman Empire during this period were made up of powerful landowners (the *ayans, derebeys,* and *agas*) in the countryside and commercial capitalists of mainly minority ethnic origin in major urban centers. In 1913, the top 1 percent of farming families owned 39 percent of the arable land. The traditional landed gentry (the *ayans* and *derebeys*), together with the *agas,* comprising 5 percent of the farmer families, owned 65 percent of the arable land, while 87 percent of farming families, comprising broad segments of the peasantry, had access to just 35 percent of the arable land. As a result of their vast economic power in the countryside, the big landowners were able to monopolize local political power and, through links with the rural Islamic clergy, impose their social and cultural domination over the peasantry. The subjugation of the peasant masses by the landlord-clergy coalition

(the *esraf* or *ashraf*) thus served the double function of exploitation and legitimization.

Largely involved in import-export trade and domestic marketing tied to European imports, the minority commercial interests —comprised of Greek, Armenian, and Christian merchants and primarily concentrated in large urban centers—made up the basis of the empire's bourgeoisie, or urban middle class. The role of minority commercial interests was pivotal. Through their key position in the urban economy they were in effect the agency for external economic penetration and control, which contributed to the final demise of the empire's economy. Consequently, while their strategic role in accelerating contact with the West played a progressive role in the limited transformation of the despotic system in an earlier period, the continued existence of the minority commercial interests—as opposed to their transformation into industrial capitalists—perpetuated the backward and dependent structure of Ottoman industry. It also contributed to the further dependence of the Ottoman economy on European capital, which assisted the development of capitalism in Western Europe. It was the anti-developmental role of Greek, Armenian, and other non-Muslim agents of European capital that in good part gave rise to the nationalist movement of the Society of Union and Progress and to the Kemalist forces in the war of national liberation.

Closely linked with this minority commercial group and the palace bureaucracy was foreign finance capital. The penetration into Ottoman Turkey of foreign capital during this period was based on the empire's role as a raw materials–supplying semicolony of the expanding European economy. Concentrated largely in the raw materials sector, foreign capital was also engaged in the construction of a network of railways in western and central Anatolia, with the sole purpose of accelerating the process of raw materials extraction in Turkey. Hence, it was in this classic sense—as an exporter of raw materials and importer of finished goods—that the Ottoman Empire became, in essence, a dependent semicolony of Europe.

The dependent structure of the Ottoman economy during the 19th century coupled with its tributary position in the Mediterranean basin did not permit the development of large-scale local industry. However, smaller-scale industries, particularly in textiles, had developed in the Levant, Syria, Egypt, and Palestine. While a limited expansion did take place in small-scale manufacturing and processing industries, it was largely the minority urban bourgeoisie that, in addition to its traditional place in commerce, extended into the ownership and control of these industries. Although weak in numbers and economic strength, the political aspirations of Turkish industrialists coincided with and took expression in the leadership of the nationalist forces as their economic position began to deteriorate with the further expansion into industry of foreign and minority interests. It was this deterioration in the position of the Turkish national bourgeoisie that would drive its members on to the side of the nationalist leadership.

Nor surprisingly, the size of the working class was also small. Moreover, the ethnic composition of the working class was highly fragmented and did not allow for the development of working class unity. This fragmentation within the working-class reached its peak during the liberation struggles when non-Turkish workers joined the ranks of the forces of their own ethnic groups and fought against Turkish national liberation. Turkish workers were essentially cut off from Anatolia and could not contribute directly to or affect the outcome of the national liberation struggle.

In the countryside, the majority of the population consisted of peasants with small landholdings. Dispersed throughout the Anatolian interior and engaged in subsistence agriculture, the Ottoman peasantry was under the direct control of big landowners, who had connections to the rural Islamic clergy. Despite the enormous control exercised over them by the landlords and the clergy, the peasants rose up in arms in a number of mass peasant uprisings in Ottoman history.

Finally, in addition to the peasantry who had small landholdings, the rural areas of the empire also contained a class of small merchants and local artisans who, together with doctors, lawyers, teachers, and locally based government officials, made up the core of the Anatolian petit bourgeoisie. It was among this group that nationalist forces first found their crucial support. Dominated and controlled by imperialism and the minority urban bourgeoisie and oppressed under the *ayan, derebey,* and *esraf* rule in the countryside, the Ottoman petit bourgeoisie was fragmented, weak, and unorganized.

The centuries-old empire of the Ottomans began to face serious economic and political-military problems during the 18th and 19th centuries. The expanding power of local landowners and merchants along with peasant uprisings and wars of national liberation, losses of territory, the decline of industry and increasing dependence on the West, and expanding public debt were all major factors contributing to the disintegration of the Ottoman Empire.

The growth and expansion of tax farming and the development of Ottoman commerce that acquired an intermediary function between local landowners and European commercial capital contributed to two destructive trends. First, the authority of the central state vis-à-vis the new propertied and moneyed classes in the countryside declined. Second, the direct economic ties with European capital, which became the basis of the expansion of Western capitalism into the empire's economy, also weakened the centralized state apparatus.

The growing power of local landowners on the one hand and increasing repression by the central state on the other did not go unchallenged. The oppressed peasants and minority nationalities in various parts of the empire soon rose up in arms. The peasant uprisings of the 17th century continued in various forms during the 18th and 19th centuries. Although these revolts did not yield substantial results, they did nevertheless create an unstable situation for both the peasantry's local exploiters and the central state.

National minorities, especially in the Balkans, battled against the repressive Ottoman state to gain their independence. As a result of the prolonged wars with the European powers, which extended from the second siege of Vienna (1683) to the Treaty of Jassy (1792), the Ottoman state became more and more vulnerable, leading to massive territorial losses that included Hungary, Greece, Transylvania, Bukovina, Crimea, the northern coasts of the Black Sea, and other regions. This in turn encouraged more indigenous nationalist forces to rise up and put an end to Ottoman rule over their territories. By the 19th century, the Ottoman state faced serious challenges from every corner of the empire. By the end of the Balkan Wars (1912–1913), the Ottomans had lost almost all of their European possessions to Bulgaria, Serbia, Greece, Montenegro, and Albania. All in all, by mid-1913 the Ottomans had lost 83 percent of their territory and 69 percent of their population. The successful revolts of the colonized peoples reduced the area of plunder by the central state and the Ottoman lords. This contraction of the empire exacerbated the crises in the Ottoman economy and polity and further contributed to its decline.

While the Ottoman state was becoming rapidly weaker, Europe had completed its transition from feudalism to capitalism. Thus, by the late 18th century Europe's feudal economy had been transformed into an expanding capitalist economy. Growing trade between Western Europe and the Ottoman Empire during this period began to have adverse effects on local Ottoman industry. Faced with rising costs and operating under strict price regulations, the Ottoman guilds were unable to provide goods at prices low enough to compete with the cheap European-manufactured goods. Consequently, traditional Ottoman industry entered a period of rapid decline, and the empire became more and more dependent on European economies.

As European capital began to expand, there was no longer a need to depend on imports of manufactured goods from the East. In fact, the growing capitalist economy in Europe was in a position to bring about a complete reversal in international trade. Whereas Britain was previously an importer of textiles from the East, it now became an exporter of these. The process of European expansion into the Ottoman economy accelerated even more following the Anglo-Turkish Commercial Convention of 1838, for it extended extraterritorial privileges to all foreign traders and abolished the state's protective tariffs and monopolies. Consequently, whereas the Ottoman Empire had supplied almost all of Britain's cotton fabric imports in 1825, by 1855 this amount had fallen sharply to a point where it constituted only a fraction of these imports. British textile exports to Turkey continued to expand in the postconvention period. This reversal in the import-export pattern of the empire led to the destruction of the textile industry in Ottoman Turkey. While the dismantling of native Ottoman industry by the British had begun in the textiles sector, all other branches of Ottoman industry had become affected in a few short decades. Indeed, by the late 1800s the whole of Ottoman industry was on the verge of collapse.

These developments marked the end of industrialization through the manufacturing sector in Ottoman Turkey. Instead, the empire was relegated to increased raw materials production. Increases also occurred in agricultural exports such as raisins and dried figs, whose output nearly doubled from 1904 to 1913. Thus, the Ottoman

Empire, with its native industry destroyed, was transformed into an agrarian reserve of the expanding European economies.

This process coupled with continued territorial losses frustrated the state's efforts to raise revenue for the public treasury. And this greatly affected the empire's military power and placed its political and military strength in the region in great jeopardy. While increased taxation was seen as a short-term remedy to counteract these tendencies, the only long-term solution to the problem of revenue was seen to be foreign loans.

The first Ottoman foreign loan was in 1854, and by 1877 the nominal public debt was close to £191 million, or more than half the national revenue when interest was counted. Most of this debt was owed to two countries, with France accounting for 40 percent and England for 29 percent of the total in 1881. By 1877, the Ottoman state was no longer able to continue its loan repayments and, consequently, declared bankruptcy. A European-controlled organization, the Ottoman Public Debt Administration (OPDA), was set up in 1881 to collect payments on the loans. The OPDA subsequently acted as an intermediary with European countries seeking investment opportunities in Turkey and in this way was instrumental in facilitating the further penetration of European capital into the Ottoman economy.

By the 19th century, then, Ottoman Turkey had for all practical purposes become a semicolony of the expanding European powers. Widespread revolts throughout its conquered territories further weakened the rule of the sultanate and the palace bureaucracy and led to the emergence of nationalist forces destined to transform the collapsing Ottoman state.

In the early 1900s, a growing number of military students in Istanbul became discontented with the policies of the Ottoman state. Nationalist ideas were put forward by numerous intellectuals and journalists, the most prominent of whom was Namik Kemal. Abdulhamid II, the ruling sultan, tried to suppress the movement but without success. Secret societies were formed in army headquarters throughout the empire and in Paris, Geneva, and Cairo. The most effective of these were known as the Young Turks, which eventually became the Committee of Union and Progress.

Finally, in 1908, there was open discontent within the Third Army Corps in Macedonia. On July 4, 1908, the army, headed by Major Ahmed Niyazi, demanded from Salonika in Macedonia the restoration of the 1876 constitution and marched on Istanbul. The sultan's attempt to suppress the rising failed, and rebellion spread rapidly. Unable to rely on other troops, on July 23 Abdulhamid announced the restoration of the constitution. Elections were held, and a constitutional government was established. But in April 1909, Abdulhamid struck back with a counterrevolution, and the army moved up again from Macedonia to depose the sultan and install his brother, Mehmed V, as constitutional monarch.

The Committee of Union and Progress, which led the 1908 Young Turk Revolution, declared itself to be a political party—the Party of Union and Progress (PUP)—in April 1909 and took power through the elections of April 1912. The top leadership of the party was mainly composed of Turkish intellectuals who were to a great extent influenced by European progressive and nationalist thought. Their nationalist ideology brought them in line with their main class allies, namely the *esnaf* (artisans and self-employed) and the *tujjaar* (merchants and commercial interests) of the towns, the sectors out of which the PUP sought to forge a future Turkish national bourgeoisie. Hence, it was in this context—and after the massive territorial losses following the two Balkan Wars and the failure of the ruling PUP clique to safeguard Turkey from the onslaught of foreign occupation forces during World War I—that the stage was set for the final downfall of the Ottoman Empire.

BERCH BERBEROGLU

See also

France, Middle East Policy; United Kingdom, Middle East Policy; World War I, Impact of

References

Berberoglu, Berch. *Power and Stability in the Middle East.* London: Zed, 1989.

———. *Turkey in Crisis.* London: Zed, 1982.

———. *Turmoil in the Middle East.* Albany, NY: SUNY Press, 1999.

Berkes, Niyazi. *The Development of Secularism in Turkey.* Montreal: McGill University Press, 1964.

Blaisdell, D. C. *European Financial Control in the Ottoman Empire.* New York: Columbia University Press, 1929.

Earle, Edward Mead. *Turkey, the Great Powers, and the Bagdad Railway: A Study in Imperialism.* New York: Russell and Russell, 1966.

Ergil, Dogu. "From Empire to Dependence: The Evolution of Turkish Under-development." Unpublished PhD dissertation, State University of New York, 1975.

Gibb, H. A. R., and H. Bowen. *Islamic Society and the West,* Vol. 1. London: Oxford University Press, 1957.

Lewis, Bernard. *The Emergence of Modern Turkey.* 2nd ed. New York: Oxford University Press, 1969.

———. *What Went Wrong? The Clash between Islam and Modernity in the Middle East.* New York: Oxford University Press, 2002.

Oz, Amos
Born: May 4, 1939

Award-winning Israeli novelist and peace activist. Amos Oz was born Amos Klausner in Jerusalem on May 4, 1939. His father was a writer, and the family included many right-wing Revisionist Zionist scholars and teachers. Klausner's mother committed suicide when he was 12 years old, and three years later Klausner became a Labor Zionist and joined Kibbutz Hulda. It was while living in the kibbutz that he changed his surname to Oz (Hebrew for "strength"). During his life on Kibbutz Hulda, which was his primary residence from 1957 to 1986, he held various jobs as a tractor driver, a schoolteacher, and an agricultural worker in the cotton fields.

Oz attended Hebrew University in Jerusalem, earning a bachelor's degree in Hebrew literature and philosophy in 1965. He returned to Hebrew University as a writer-in-residence in 1975 and again in 1990. He has also been a visiting professor at several other

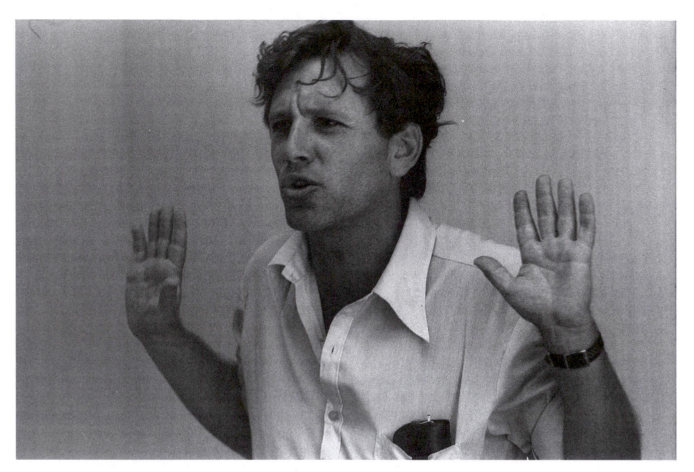

Amos Oz, award-winning Israeli novelist and peace activist, is the author of numerous works of fiction and nonfiction. (Herman Chanania/Israeli Government Press Office)

institutions, including St. Cross College in Oxford, England; the University of California at Berkeley; and Boston University in Massachusetts.

A sabra, or native-born Israeli, Oz served in the Israel Defense Forces (IDF) during both the 1967 Six-Day War and the 1973 Yom Kippur War. During the Six-Day War he saw combat with a tank unit in the Sinai, and in the Yom Kippur War he fought on the Golan Heights. He was one of the first influential Israeli figures to advocate a two-state solution to the Israeli-Palestinian conflict. He did so in an article in 1967.

The kibbutz experience furnished Oz with much of the inspiration for his writing. His first novel, *Makom acher* (Another Place), was published in 1966 and is considered by critics to be among the best fictional accounts of life on a kibbutz. Oz draws on kibbutz life for inspiration in much of his writing, viewing the collective community as a microcosm of Jewish life and a symbol of the Israeli Jewish family. *Michael sheli* (My Michael), published in 1968, is a disturbing account of the unraveling psyche of an Israeli homemaker. It became very popular in Israel despite the parallels Oz created between the isolation and fear of the protagonist and that of the country as a whole. *Michael sheli,* a best-seller in Israel, was the first among many Oz works to be published in English, becoming

My Michael in 1972. Later it was adopted into a successful Israeli-produced motion picture.

Written in Hebrew, Oz's books have been translated into 30 different languages, winning the author international recognition apart from his popularity at home. Another theme of Oz's writing is the conflict between Israeli Zionist ideals and the complex realities of a pluralistic society. As a leading proponent of an Arab-Israeli peace plan and a two-state solution, he has written numerous essays and articles about the ongoing conflict between Israel and the Palestinians and has been an active member of Israel's Peace Now Movement since 1977. In 1992 he was awarded a prestigious peace prize, the German Friedenspreis.

In addition to his early works of short fiction, Oz has written and published nonfiction, children's stories, novellas, and short story collections, including *Artzot ha'tan* (Where the Jackals Howl, and Other Stories), published in 1965; *Har he'etza ha'raah* (The Hill of Evil Counsel), published in 1976; and the children's book *Soumchi* (Youth), published in 1978.

Oz's novel *Black Box* set sales records in Israel immediately upon its release in 1987. His 1989 novel, *To Know a Woman,* represented a new direction in his art that provoked controversy. His most famous work of nonfiction is a collection of interviews he conducted with a cross-section of Israeli citizens titled *Po ve'sham b'eretz Yisra'el bistav* (1982). The compilation was published in English as *In the Land of Israel* in 1983 and won praise from critics, including one who compared Oz to George Orwell, calling him "a complex man obsessed with simple decency and determined above all to tell the truth, regardless of whom it offends."

For his many literary accomplishments, Oz has received international recognition in many forms. He was awarded the Holon Prize for Literature in 1965 and the Israel-American Cultural Foundation award in 1968. In 1973 he received the B'nai B'rith annual literary award, followed by the Brenner Prize in 1986 and France's Prix Femina Etranger (for best foreign novel) in 1988. Also in 1988 he received the prestigious Wingate Prize. Additionally, he has been appointed as an officer of arts and letters of France and was awarded the French cross of the Knight of the Légion d'Honneur by French president Jacques Chirac in 1997. Oz was also awarded the Israel Prize for Literature, Israel's most prestigious literary award, in 1998.

Having left kibbutz life in 1986, Oz resides in the southern town of Arad, where he continues to write, teach, and campaign for peace in Israel while holding the Agnon chair of Hebrew literature at Ben-Gurion University of the Negev in Beersheba, Israel. Oz is among the most influential intellectuals in Israel. For many years he was closely identified with the Labor Party, but in the 1990s he shifted from it to Meretz. He supported both the Oslo Accords and talks with the Palestine Liberation Organization (PLO), but he also supported the Israeli invasion of Lebanon in July 2006 as a necessary self-defense measure in light of Hezbollah attacks originating in southern Lebanon.

SPENCER C. TUCKER

See also

Kibbutz Movement; Lebanon, Israeli Operations against; Literature of the Arab-Israeli Wars; Oslo Accords; Palestine Liberation Organization; Zionism

References

Oz, Amos. *Black Box.* New York: Vintage Books, 1989.
———. *In the Land of Israel.* Orlando, FL: Harvest Books, 1993.
———. *Israel, Palestine and Peace: Essays.* Orlando, FL: Harvest Books, 1995.
———. *My Michael.* Orlando, FL: Harvest Books, 2005.

Categorical Index

Groups and Organizations

Index